PLANNING

FOR THE

FUTURE

PROVIDING A MEANINGFUL LIFE
FOR A CHILD WITH A DISABILITY
AFTER YOUR DEATH

L. MARK RUSSELL, ATTORNEY   ARNOLD E. GRANT, ATTORNEY

D1096730

Sixth Edition

Planning For The Future, Inc., Palatine, Illinois

Published by:
Planning For The Future, Inc.
86 W. King Henry Ct.
Palatine, IL 60067
www.specialneeedslegal.com

ISBN 0-912891-21-1

First Printing, 1993
Second Printing, 1994, revised
Third Printing, 1995, revised
Fourth Printing, 1996, revised
Fifth Printing, 2005, completely revised
Sixth Printing, 2006, revised

Design: Rivera Design & Communications, Evanston, IL

This publication is designed to provide accurate and authoritative information in regard to the subject matter covered. It is sold with the understanding that neither the author(s) nor the publisher is engaged in rendering legal, accounting, or other professional service. If legal advice or other expert assistance is required, the services of a competent professional should be sought.

PRINTED IN THE UNITED STATES OF AMERICA

Table of Contents

i

v

TABLE OF CONTENTS

Introduction

THE SINGLE MOST IMPORTANT ISSUE IN THE MINDS OF PARENTS who have a child with a disability, regardless of the age of the child, is what will happen to the child after the parents are gone. The parents know what they do for their child, and they need to be sure the child will be cared for in the future. Primary concerns include:

- Where will my child live?

- Who will look out for my child's interests?

- Will finances be adequate to take care of my child?

- Who will take my child to favorite activities? Expose my child to new activities?

- Will my child be healthy, happy and secure?

This book is intended to be a step-by-step guide to assuring a happy and secure life for a child with a disability after the parents are gone.

The book is a rewrite of a book that we first wrote more than ten years ago. In reality, however, it is a new book. Laws and practices relating to people with disabilities have changed substantially over the last ten years, and our experience in advising families has grown as well. This book answers every question that we have been asked over our collective thirty years of experience in advising families that have a child with a disability.

Planning to secure your child's future after your death is a daunting task, but it is achievable. We have helped many families over the years. Our book is designed to take you through the planning process in a simple, easy to understand, step-by-step way. Critical issues discussed include:

- What residential options are available for your child? What educational, employment and social programs are available, and how can they be used to allow your child to reach his or her maximum potential? Alternatives are discussed in detail; links to web sites are provided to permit you to access further information and find suitable programs near you.

- Who will look out for your child's interests after you are gone? Does your child need a legal guardian? What are the benefits and detriments to legal guardianship? What are the alternatives? You know a lot about your child, his or her needs, hopes and aspirations. How can you communicate this information to future caregivers so it is not lost when you are gone?

- The cost of lifetime care for a child with a disability can be prohibitively expensive. What types of government benefits are potentially available? How do you assure eligibility and maximize benefits?

- Many government benefit programs are not available to people who have assets above $2,000. What can you do if your child has excess assets, perhaps because your child has received a gift from well meaning relatives or a settlement as a result of an injury? There are steps you can take so your child retains access to these funds while still qualifying for government benefits.

- Government benefit programs provide *eats and sheets*, but little else. How can you provide funds for your child to enjoy the *extras* in life without impacting your child's eligibility for government benefits? Can you provide a pool of assets that will be available for your child if government benefits are reduced or prove to be inadequate? The answer is that you can, assuming applicable legal requirements are satisfied.

- Even if you think your child will not need government benefits, can you leave your child property in a manner that will permit proper management of the property and eligibility for government benefits if they become necessary in the future?

- How much must you leave for your child to protect his or her future? Tables and instructions for performing this calculation are provided. What types of investment strategies should you think about to protect your child?

- How do you reduce the cost of administering your estate? What can you do about estate tax? What income tax benefits are available to families that have a child with a disability?

Two real life situations demonstrate the unfortunate results of inadequate planning.

The first involved a client who came to us in near-panic to get her estate plan prepared. Apparently the woman's neighbor had died, leaving two children, a nine-year-old son with autism and a twenty-year-old college student who was away at school. The neighbor had done no estate planning, all her relatives lived out of town, and the younger child was left alone, with no where to go and no one to take care of him. All the details future caregivers needed to know—the child's medical history, his favorite foods, favorite activities—died with the parent. No financial planning had been done, and no one had any idea who was to look out for the child or provide for the child's future. Eventually the child was placed in an institution, but there had been no investigation of alternatives, no search for a proper placement.

The second situation involved one of our very first clients, a man whose mother had died without a will, owning more than $200,000 in property. Our client's sister, a forty-five-year-old woman with an intellectual disability, was residing in a state-funded residential facility. Under the probate laws in the state where the man's mother resided, his sister was entitled to one-half of her mother's estate. The state's Medicaid authorities seized the property for past cost-of-care liabilities. This left the woman with nothing.

There is much that both of these families could have done if only they had engaged in timely estate planning. With a proper estate plan, parents can avoid a drastic interruption in care and do everything that is possible to ensure that their child will have a comfortable and fulfilling life.

Estate planning for families with a member who has a disability is different from other types of estate planning, because there is so much more that has to be done. Our goal is to convince you that estate planning is *essential* for every family and not an activity for only the wealthy. Parents must plan their estates, regardless of size, to secure the continued care and well-being of their child. Future caregivers must be selected, living arrangements investigated, and alternatives discussed. Families with limited financial resources must learn to maximize government benefits so that their child's financial needs will be satisfied.

Although there are many alternatives that all parents with children who have disabilities should consider, there is no single magic formula for creating the appropriate estate plan. Every estate plan should be custom-fit to the family's circumstances and the needs of its members. The size of a family's estate affects the need for estate-tax planning and the importance of government benefits. The nature and degree of your child's disability will help determine the type of living arrangement that will be appropriate. The ages of your children–both those with disabilities and those without–affect your need for insurance. The size of your family might influence the distribution of property. The age and maturity of children without disabilities will determine whether you will need trusts for them, as well as for the child with a disability. In other words, estate planning is a process of weighing numerous alternatives and making decisions that you hope will improve and secure your child's life now and in the future.

A final warning. Our book is not intended to be a substitute for the services of attorneys and other advisors. Rather, it is intended to be a guide for parents in dealing with their advisors through the comprehensive estate-planning process, and an aid to help professionals understand all the planning issues faced by families that have a child with a disability.

Laws and requirements about estate-planning methods are changing constantly. Moreover, laws vary from state to state. It is therefore necessary to check all your plans closely with a knowledgeable attorney in your state before they become final. Once a plan is prepared, it should be periodically evaluated and revised to guarantee the maximum possible care for your child in light of changes in his or her life and changes in your financial situation.

Planning For The Future is an extremely comprehensive and vital new resource for parents who are concerned about their child's future well-being.

INTRODUCTION

The Life Plan

E STATE PLANNING FOR FAMILIES WITH CHILDREN WHO HAVE disabilities begins at the most basic level. How can you, as a parent, be assured that your son or daughter will lead as full and complete a life as possible after your death? What can you do to make sure your hopes and aspirations are realized?

In this chapter we take the first step toward answering those questions. We discuss the process of developing a *life plan*, which is simply a way of encouraging you, as a parent, to sit down and think about what you want for your son or daughter and, depending on the nature and extent of the disability involved, equally important, what your son or daughter wants for his or her self. This important information must be communicated to those who will have primary responsibility for your child's care after your death.

*D*eveloping a life plan *is an ongoing process. It involves articulating goals in the major areas of life and then developing a plan so that those goals will be achieved. This involves helping your child develop the skills needed to carry on after you are gone, and establishing a support system that will enable your child to live a happy and rewarding life.*

To aid you in the process, we discuss a number of options available to people who have disabilities, such as group living arrangements and supported employment opportunities. Many of the items discussed in this chapter will be of immediate interest to you. You may have a child living with you now who you believe is ready to *leave home* for another supervised environment, perhaps living with peers but having trained staff members available to help with everyday needs, and one or more of the alternatives discussed in this chapter may be what you are looking for.

Not all of the alternatives discussed in this chapter will be appropriate for everyone. Like everyone else, your child has likes and dislikes, abilities and disabilities, and it will be up to you, as a parent, in consultation with your child and other family members and advisors, to cull through the alternatives and develop a life plan for your child that is most appropriate given his or her abilities, desires, and aspirations.

Throughout this book we use the term child to refer to both minor children and adult children.

The Life Planning Process

Most parents never find time to really sit down and discuss what their future intentions are for their child. At best, Mom and Dad may talk about the matter while driving home from some family gathering and, in most cases, nothing will ever be resolved. The discussion will typically end with something like, "I'm sure Aunt Bessie will look out for Fred. She's responsible and she's certainly family oriented," or "Brother Bob loves him, and I'm sure he'll take care of him." No effort is ever made to inform Brother Bob or Aunt Bessie that they are expected to perform as future caregivers, or to tell them of Fred's needs and desires, or to investigate whether living with Bob or Bessie is the best alternative. The assumption is simply made that these relatives will gladly step into the parent's role and that they will know what to do as well as Mom and Dad do.

A comprehensive life plan leaves nothing to chance.

Issues are addressed openly and in depth, with active participation by family members and others who will be expected to carry on when you, the parents, are deceased. Often the person with the disability will be the most important participant, and we think it is right that this should be so. After all, it is your child's future that is under discussion. Depending on the type of disability involved, your child may have definite ideas that deserve respect and consideration.

This is not to say that you should frighten or intimidate your child by talking about your death in an open and direct way, or that you should base the life plan entirely on what your child says. It is often possible to get vital information from your child in nonthreatening ways. For example, Fred's parents could ask him where he would want to live if he couldn't live with them. Perhaps he would indicate that he wanted to live with his brother Bob, or maybe he has a friend who lives in a group home that he would like to try. Fred's parents may ask him about the types of social activity that he prefers, or the type of job he might like to try.

Even if Fred's answers do not initially appear realistic, it is often possible to cull useful information from them. For example, Fred may express a desire to become a doctor. While this may be unrealistic given Fred's disability, it may be possible for him to get a job as an orderly, or to work in a hospital in some other capacity.

Only you, as a parent, are the real expert on your child, and you must ask yourself what information you want to pass on to future caregivers. While professionals have come and gone, you have seen what has worked for your child, and what has not.

> *If you were to die today, what are the three priorities you would want for your child in terms of residential care?*

Would you want your child to live with Aunt Bessie, or with Brother Bob? Should your child live in a group home? If so, what size? Should your child have a private room or share a room with another? Where should the home be located?

William, the son of one of our clients, enjoys going to church on Sundays. It is something he looks forward to every week, and it is also the place where he is most integrated into the community. So it was important to find a place for William within walking distance of a church. His family didn't even know such a place existed. But William's father had indicated in his Letter of Intent (see Chapter Two) that he was looking for a six-bed group home within walking distance of a church where William could have his own room. The advance planning gave guidance to the entire family, and when William's father became aware of the existence of such a facility, the family was ready to act. William was put on the waiting list and when one of the residents moved out, William was ready to move into his new home.

Because the home was funded by private charities and the state in which William resided, the cost was negligible. As we discuss later in this chapter, many states and private corporations provide residential facilities for people who have disabilities and charge according to the residents' ability to pay. Because William has no assets in his name, the cost of the facility is borne entirely by private charities and the government. The federal government pays a percentage based on William's father's work history under the Social Security Disability Insurance Program (SSDI). The remainder of the cost is paid by private charities and the state government under Medicaid and other programs. SSDI, Medicaid, and other government programs are discussed in detail in Chapter Four. As we discuss in Chapter Six, it is possible to use trusts to supplement the income available to your child from government programs without reducing the benefits paid by those programs.

Thinking about your child's future social life is also important. Social activities are often the difference between a meaningful lifestyle and a neglected one.

For example, William's father has made it clear that he wants William to visit his relatives in New York once a year, go to rock concerts, go to religion camp every summer, and have money to buy CD players (William goes through about two a year).

Debbie, one of our clients, loves to bowl and also enjoys attending church. She was living with her mother and was showing signs that she wanted independence. Fortunately, Debbie's mother heard of a state-funded group home being constructed close by and was able to secure a place for Debbie. The home is near enough that she can drive Debbie to church and bowling. The facility even has a regular bowling league for its residents on Thursday nights.

Debbie's mother was also concerned about Debbie's diet. She was worried that Debbie might gain too much weight. Her Letter of Intent instructs future caregivers to give Debbie low-calorie foods such as fruit for dessert. She also listed a number of foods that Debbie relishes and recommended that Debbie's clothes be bought through an L.L. Bean catalogue. Debbie is quite hard on clothes, and her mother has found L.L. Bean clothing to be the most durable. She wanted money available to pay for Debbie to wear nice, age-appropriate, clothing.

Employment and education are other important categories.

We are still not far removed from the days when those with disabilities were simply warehoused in institutions with little in the way of programming or activity. As described in detail later in this chapter, there is an increasing array of job opportunities for people with disabilities.

For example, one of our clients who owns his own business has employed his daughter, who has schizophrenia, in a clerical position for many years. Our client was able to persuade the man who is to take over the business when our client retires to keep a job for his daughter. Another client has a son with an intellectual disability who works in a laboratory at a major university.

The following is a chart of priorities that we typically ask our clients to complete as a first step in the life planning process. You may wish to use the chart yourself. Keep one thing in mind, however: the life planning process is an ongoing job. As your child changes, and as you and other family members become aware of new and different opportunities, the plan will need to be revised.

In the next chapter we will describe how you can organize the life plan that you develop in the form of an instruction sheet called a *Letter of Intent*. This letter communicates your wishes to future caregivers. It is a good idea to review this letter on a periodic basis so that the letter remains accurate through all the changes in your child's life. One possibility may be to review the letter each year on your child's birthday, as well as whenever a life change dictates a change in planning.

RESIDENTIAL:
(If you die or go into a nursing home, where do you want your child to live?)

1.

2.

3.

4.

EDUCATION:
(You have a long perspective of your child's capabilities, share it!)

1.

2.

3.

4.

EMPLOYMENT:
(What has your child enjoyed? List his or her goals, aspirations, limitations, etc.)

1.

2.

3.

4.

SOCIAL/RECREATIONAL:
(What activities make life meaningful for your child? List sports, hobbies, etc.)

1.

2.

3.

4.

RELIGION:
(Is there a special church or synagogue for fellowship?)

    1.

    2.

    3.

    4.

MEDICAL CARE:
(What has and has not worked?)

    1.

    2.

    3.

    4.

BEHAVIOR MANAGEMENT:
(Does your child have special behavior problems? What behavior management techniques have been effective in the past?)

    1.

    2.

    3.

    4.

ADVOCATE/GUARDIAN:
(Who will look after your child, fight for your child, and be a friend?)

    1.

    2.

    3.

    4.

TRUSTEES:
(Who do you trust to manage your child's funds?)

1.

2.

3.

4.

OTHER AREAS OF CONCERN:

1.

2.

3.

4.

Obviously, developing an effective life plan requires a great deal of thought and consideration. In the remainder of this chapter we discuss a number of options relating to residence, education, employment, and social activities. Advocacy and guardianship are discussed in Chapter Three, and considerations relevant to the selection of a trustee are discussed in Chapter Six.

 TIP With the growth of the internet, the availability of valuable information has grown exponentially. In the course of this chapter, we will refer you to some excellent web sites where you can find more detailed information on topics of interest. We cannot stress enough the importance of using this extremely important resource. If you do not have a computer, take an afternoon, go to the library, and use theirs. The librarian will help you. *That is why you pay taxes.* There are many other equally valuable web sites that we do not mention due to space limitations. We have tried to focus on national sites that will have links to local sites. We encourage you to take the time to *surf the net,* and take advantage of what technology has to offer.

Residential Care Alternatives

There are several ways to obtain information about the types of residential alternatives available for persons who have disabilities. Obviously, finances are a major factor. One of our clients, who owns a large farm in the state of Wisconsin, indicated in her Letter of Intent that she wants her daughter to live on the farm and authorized the trustee of the trust she established for her daughter to hire full-time attendants to help her daughter with daily living needs. Her daughter has Down syndrome and very much enjoys riding horses that are boarded at the farm. Other clients have left homes in trust for their children, with the understanding that friends or relatives would also reside in the homes on a rent-free basis to help with living needs.

These options are not for everyone, both because of the cost involved and because they may not meet the particular needs of your son or daughter. First-rate living accommodations are available for persons who have disabilities, without regard to financial cost. However, these facilities are scarce, and parents should begin the search well in advance of the time they expect their child to move out of the house. We have already discussed group homes, many of which are paid for entirely by the government. Other options are also discussed in this section.

After completing this chapter, you will need to investigate the alternatives available in your area. Several sources of information are available. One of the best is word of mouth. Perhaps you know others who have family members with disabilities, and they may have ideas about living options. The web site for *Exceptional Parent Magazine* (www.eparent.com) contains a wonderful resource for connecting with other parents. Simply Click on the link for Resources and then Click Parent to Parent Programs directory.

Your local school district will also have useful information. All school districts are required to provide transition counselling, to help students with disabilities transition from school into the local community. The person responsible for transition counselling at your local school district will likely be able to help you. (For ease of reference, we refer to this person as the *transition counselor* even though this person may have other jobs as well.)

Parent advocacy groups are another very valuable resource. Exceptional Parent Magazine publishes an annual guide to national organizations and services for people with disabilities that is very helpful. Certain of these organizations are national in scope, with local chapters throughout the country that are very easy to locate. For example, the Arc of the United States is a nationwide organization that helps people with intellectual disabilities. Its web site is located at www.thearc.org. NAMI, which is a similar organization for people with mental illness, has a web site at www.nami.org. The Autism Society of America (www.autism-society.org) is another excellent resource.

It is also possible to obtain information from state and federal agencies. Most state and local governments have public agencies responsible for meeting the needs of persons with disabilities. You can obtain the names of the responsible agencies in your state through your local advocacy organization, at your local library, or by calling the general information number at your state capital.

On the federal level, information can be obtained from the National Dissemination Center for Children with Disabilities, a federally sponsored clearinghouse for information on planning for persons who have disabilities. The organization's web site, www.nichy.org, contains a great deal of very useful information. The Center provides referrals to local agencies as well as information packets that answer many questions relating to planning issues. Its web site includes links to resources for people with disabilities in all fifty states.

Two other extremely useful sources are the National Council on Disability (www.ncd.gov) and a relatively new site created by the government for people with disabilities (www.disabilityinfo.gov). These sites include information on housing, education, employment and social activity.

Family-Type Living Arrangements

Approximately one-half of our clients live with their children for their entire lives, and many of them prefer to keep their children in family-type situations after their deaths. Such clients generally feel that it will be less disruptive to continue family-type living, by having the child live with friends or other family members after they die.

Where this situation is possible, it can work quite well. Friends and relatives can be expected to know your child better than anyone else, and therefore may be in the best position to help your child in his or her daily life, particularly with the aid of information provided in the Letter of Intent. The critical factor is the choice of caregiver. Caregivers should not be selected without complete and open discussion with the person who is to be selected because, depending on the type of disability involved, the caregiver's responsibility can be quite extensive. As a parent, you know the level of responsibility required better than anyone, and it is important that the person you select as caregiver have as complete an understanding as possible.

Family-type living arrangements can be established in your home or in the home of the caregiver. If your son or daughter is to live in the caregiver's home, you can arrange for your son or daughter to pay rent, either with his or her own funds (perhaps through a trust which you may have established) or with funds provided by the government, such as Social Security Disability Insurance or Supplemental Security Income. These programs are discussed in detail in Chapter Four.

If the caregiver is to live with your child in your home, it is possible to permit the caregiver to live in your home on a rent-free basis. One of our clients selected a sister to act as caregiver, with the provision that the sister was to receive the home at the death of the person with the disability.

If the family-type living arrangement is selected, special attention should be paid to the employment, educational, and social categories. These activities may not be as readily achieved as they might if your child stays in a professionally managed residential setting and special attention will need to be paid to them.

People with more severe disabilities who reside in family-type situations often enroll in adult service programs during the day and then return home at night. These programs provide a continuum of services including sheltered work, socialization groups and custodial care. Adult service programs can be accessed through local advocacy groups and governmental agencies, which can be located through the web sites mentioned above.

If the caregiver is to live with your child in your home, you should make sure your child's resources are sufficient to pay real estate taxes, make required mortgage payments, and pay for general upkeep. As discussed in Chapter Six, payments would typically be made through a trust that you would establish for your son or daughter either while you are alive or at your death.

Adult Foster Care

Adult foster-care homes are similar to the family-type living arrangements discussed above. A person who has a disability lives with a caregiver in a small family-type environment. Unlike the family-type arrangement discussed above, however, the caregiver is typically not a friend or relative but is instead a concerned community member who has opened his or her home to others out of a desire to help. The caregiver usually receives expense reimbursements from the government.

Adult foster care has many of the strengths of the family-type living arrangements discussed above. The homes are generally small, and the living situation is generally family-like. In addition, adult foster care homes are regulated by governmental agencies.

However, there are risks involved in such living arrangements as well. A great deal depends upon the skill and character of the foster caregiver. It is the caregiver who will determine how well the home will meet your child's needs in terms of social, developmental, and educational programs. State supervision may not be adequate to ensure the quality of the home.

Moreover, there is always a risk that a foster caregiver will decide to stop providing care for your child. In such circumstances your child would be forced to find a new residence, which could be upsetting.

Thus, while many foster homes are very good, and while many adults with disabilities are undoubtedly very happy in them, great care should be taken in the investigatory process before such an approach is adopted.

 TIP If you select the adult foster alternative, you will be relying a great deal on the caregiver, and you will need to investigate the setting to assure yourself that the caregiver will do a quality job. This should include interviewing potential foster caregivers, requiring references, and interviewing those who give references.

The Group Home

Group home is a generic term that covers a wide variety of living arrangements. The distinguishing characteristic is that group homes tend to house several unrelated individuals who have disabilities.

Group homes can be owned by the state or by private corporations that may be operated on a for-profit or a not-for-profit basis. Some homes are even purchased by parents or groups of parents, sometimes with the aid of outside investors or charitable organizations. Parents then supply rooms for caregivers and other persons who have disabilities. Some parents may even leave their home to a child with a disability (typically in a trust) after their deaths and instruct the trustee to hire a qualified caregiver to live in the home and rent rooms to other persons with disabilities. Other parents will leave their home to a charity, with the understanding that the charity will run it as a group home.

As a consumer, you will probably be indifferent to the form of ownership of any group home that you may be considering unless, of course, you decide to purchase a group home yourself. For you, the critical issue will be the quality of the services provided and the cost of those services. So far as we are aware, there is no reason to believe that a home owned by the state will be any better or any worse than a home that is owned and operated by a private company, whether that company is operated for-profit or on a not-for-profit basis.

As for cost, residents of publicly owned facilities typically pay on an *ability to pay* basis. Assuming the resident has little in the way of income or assets, payment is usually limited to the resident's entitlements under the Social Security Disability Insurance or Supplemental Security Income programs. This is true of many privately run homes as well, whether run by for-profit or not-for-profit companies. Such homes tend to charge residents under the same financial needs formulas employed by public facilities, with the company operating the home receiving additional payments from the state under the Medicaid or other programs.

Some privately run group homes are quite expensive, however, and before deciding on a particular group home, you should make sure you have a clear understanding of the cost to you and your child and whether that cost will be met by government programs.

Many of our clients who do not choose a family-type living situation for their children select some type of group home alternative, and frequently the living arrangement is set in place long before our clients' deaths. In fact, in many cases the person with the disability has entered into a group living arrangement before the client contacts us.

TIP For people who select the group home alternative, it is generally advisable that the person with the disability enter the group home before the parents die. This is recommended for two reasons. First, obtaining a place in a particular group home can be very difficult, and parents will want to make sure the most appropriate home is selected. Second, having the living arrangement in place before the parents die will ease the transition when the parents actually do die. The death of a parent is traumatic enough, and the situation is only compounded if the person who has the disability also has to move to an unfamiliar environment.

Community Residential Settings. Within the group home continuum, a wide variety of choices is available. Many communities have homes located in residential neighborhoods that house people who have disabilities. These homes are generally referred to as *community care homes* or *community residences* and may be indistinguishable from other homes in the neighborhood.

Residents may have their own bedrooms, or they may share a room with someone else. The homes may have been converted from single family use, or they might be slightly larger, specifically constructed for group home living. It is possible that such homes already exist in or around your neighborhood and that you have no knowledge of them.

The level of care provided at such community residences generally depends upon the needs of the residents. Many such homes have live-in managers who are responsible for seeing to the needs of the house and the residents. Duties often include preparation of meals (frequently with the aid of the residents) and the development and implementation of training and social programs. Other homes employ rotating staff rather than house managers. Still others provide a combination of the two approaches, with house managers available for daily living needs and other staff members available for emergency situations and to provide the house managers with time off according to a regular schedule or on an *as needed* basis.

Where the disabilities of the residents are less severe, the level of supervision is reduced. In such circumstances there may be no staff member who lives in the home on a full-time basis or works a regularly scheduled shift. Instead, assistance may be provided on an *as needed* basis or for specified tasks such as meal preparation.

Community residences for people who require less supervision are often structured as apartment complexes, with staff members living in units in the complex. Residents tend to work in the community, or take vocational or other educational classes offered in the community, and are integrated into the community as completely and fully as is possible.

Intermediate-Care Facilities. Intermediate care facilities, or ICFs, are group living facilities for people with intellectual or other developmental disabilities. ICFs can be categorized in much the same way as community residences. There are large ICFs that typically consist of a complex of buildings designed to house many people, and smaller ICFs that look very much like community residences. Even in large ICFs with many buildings, each structure will typically house fewer than sixteen people. Residents may have their own bedrooms, or they may share a room with another.

As in a community residence, the level of care provided at an ICF depends on the needs of the residents. ICFs designed for residents who have moderate to severe disabilities provide for more supervision, frequently having live-in house managers, rotating staff, or a combination of the two, much like community residences for people with moderate to severe disabilities. Residents whose disabilities are less severe receive less supervision, generally receiving aid for specific tasks or on an *as needed* basis.

Many of the larger ICFs provide housing both for those needing a great deal of supervision and for those who are more independent. One benefit of this approach is that people who initially require a great deal of supervision can *graduate* to less supervised units as their living skills improve. Residents who have mild disabilities can graduate to an even more independent lifestyle, such as residence in a supervised apartment complex with one or more peers.

Depending on the degree of their disabilities, residents may work in sheltered workshops, take classes offered by the ICF, or take a bus to jobs in the community. Social activities are planned by staff members, with those whose disabilities are less severe doing the bulk of the planning for themselves.

Institutional Care

Institutional care tends to be more appropriate for people with very severe disabilities. Typically it involves large self-contained facilities that provide custodial supervision, evaluation, treatment and training. Institutions may be publicly owned, or they be owned by charities or private companies. Depending on the level of disability involved, there is great variety in the type of treatment and service available. Institutions differ from group homes in that the level of supervision tends to be greater, and residents tend to have greater needs. In some cases, institutional stays are temporary, with residents departing when they develop the skills required for less restrictive living alternatives.

Independent Supported Living

Independent supported living typically involves people living by themselves or with one or more roommates, in houses or apartments. The key characteristic of independent living is limited supervision. Individuals are helped to find a home or apartment. Family members, friends or professionals from adult service agencies visit on a regular basis to provide needed help and support.

Independent living is more common among those whose disabilities are less severe. For example, if your child has a job in the community and good living and social skills, yet needs assistance with certain tasks like money management, an independent living arrangement may be appropriate. Your child could live in an apartment, perhaps near a friend or family member who could help in those areas where assistance is required.

A recent trend in independent living is to have people with relatively mild disabilities live near one another for companionship and support. In addition, increasing numbers of those with mild intellectual disabilities and mental illness have been marrying, and independent living with informal supervision by friends, family, or agency officials has been found to be appropriate for many of them. Similarly, people with moderate to severe disabilities have done well living in apartments with roommates who do not have disabilities, although great care must be taken to select a roommate who is willing and able to help the person who has the disability with daily living needs.

In some cases families have even purchased duplexes—one side is rented to cover expenses while the other side is for the person with a disability. Local charities, friends, or relatives then provide regular visitation. There are also various government subsidy programs to help make independent living work, such as Section 8 Housing, in-home support programs, and even meals on wheels.

TIP A recent trend is for people with more moderate or severe disabilities to live independently with the help of adult service agencies. You can locate agencies that will help establish an independent living arrangement in your state at a web site sponsored by the Centers for Independent Living (www.virtualcil.net/cils). This web site can also be accessed through www.disabilityinfo.gov. Click on Community Life at the top and follow the link to Independent Living Centers on the right.

Deciding Among the Alternatives

The question of future living arrangements for your child is intensely personal, and the answer depends on the particular needs and desires of your child. What is important is that you consider the alternatives clearly and carefully and that you reach the best possible decision given the particular circumstances of your child and your family.

Ultimately, the decision is up to you and perhaps your child. It is simply a matter of where you believe your son or daughter will be happiest.

Depending on your child's desires and the degree of disability involved, an independent living arrangement, perhaps with a roommate or in an apartment complex near friends and family, may be appropriate. Bill, the son of one of our clients, lives in an apartment building next door to his brother. Bill has a mild intellectual disability and works at a job in the community. Given Bill's abilities, and his brother's willingness to help, the arrangement works ideally.

TIP If you decide on a supported independent living arrangement, make sure that the people you are relying on to help your child have a clear understanding of the type of help that will be needed, and that they are willing to provide this help. As described above, many adult service organizations help with independent living arrangements as well.

If your child has been living with you for his or her entire life, it may be desirable to continue a family-type living arrangement and have your child live with friends or relatives. This is probably the most common approach nationwide and is very common among our clients as well.

TIP If you decide on a family-type living arrangement, make sure that you have spoken with the people who you expect to provide a home for your child, and that these people are willing and able to help.

If your child is now living in a group home, or if you believe your child would benefit from the companionship or structure of group living, such an approach is probably the way to go. As we discussed above, there is a great deal of variation in approach among group homes, and it is important that you select the right home given your child's own particular needs and desires.

Some prefer community residences because of the smaller size and the greater degree of integration into community life. However, intermediate care facilities can be quite small, and the residents can be quite integrated into community life as well. Residents may travel to the community for jobs or for social or educational activities. Moreover, even in larger intermediate care facilities with several group homes, the homes themselves may be no larger than typical community residences. Finally, there are those who question the importance of integration into the community at large, preferring to focus on the quality of life of the residents at the particular facility.

The major benefits of group home living are twofold. First, the residents receive the benefit of professional supervision and organized social, employment, and educational assistance. Second, the residents receive social benefit from peer living arrangements. These benefits can be achieved at both community residences and intermediate care facilities. The critical factors are the quality of the programming and the concern and dedication of the people involved.

The best way to begin the investigation process is to make a list of the factors in a group home that you consider to be most important. Does the age of the other residents matter to you? How about the nature of their disabilities? The size of the home? Its location—for example, its proximity to you or the quality of the surrounding neighborhood? What is the cost? Are government benefits sufficient to cover expenses? Will your child have a private room? What types of recreational facilities are available? What type of food is served? What are the policies on visitors, telephone usage, or vacations? Will your child have access to a television or a stereo? What types of employment or educational opportunities are available? What types of behavior management techniques are used?

The list will help you narrow your search and provide a framework for questions when you actually begin visiting potential residences. However, you should be careful not to become too rigidly tied to your criteria. You will probably find that some factors you initially thought were important become less so as you observe actual procedures in the homes.

After making your list, you can visit the web sites and begin contacting the organizations mentioned in the beginning of this chapter to get a list of group living facilities in your area. You should then contact those facilities to receive whatever information is available regarding their operations. Talking to others who have family members with disabilities can also be helpful.

Homes that appear promising should be visited so you can gain an appreciation for what day-to-day life in the home is like. It is important that you schedule your visits when residents are present so you can see how the homes actually operate. It is also important that you take your child with you on as many visits as possible. After all, your child may be living in the home, and it is critical that he or she be comfortable there. You may even want to contact relatives of current residents in order to get their opinions.

In making your decision, you will probably find that it is your *feel* for the home that is most important. Do the other residents appear happy? How do they interact with the staff? With each other? What was your child's reaction? Was the staff enthusiastic? Did they appear to like what they were doing?

After all, the entire purpose of the life planning process is to make your child's life as happy and complete as possible, and your *feel* for the home is probably the best way to determine whether your child will be happy there.

TIP When you find a home you like, be patient because the waiting list almost certainly will be quite long. Almost every town in America has a severe shortage of housing for people with disabilities, and extremely long waiting lists are typical. If you think a group home will be appropriate for your child, find out what homes are available and get on the waiting list as soon as possible. It is advisable to consider applying to more than one home to increase the chance that a suitable arrangement will be found.

Educational Opportunities

Education is often crucial to help people with disabilities realize their maximum potential and is therefore a vital part of most life plans. Fortunately, special educational opportunities are available for people with disabilities, both children and adults.

Infancy Through Secondary School

Public education for people with disabilities is governed by the Individuals With Disabilities Education Act (IDEA). IDEA was initially enacted in 1990, was amended in 1997, and reauthorized at the end of 2004. The law is based on a philosophy of identifying people who need extra help as early as possible and then developing an individualized plan to provide that help.

Education for children with disabilities from birth to age three is based on an *individualized family service plan* (IFSP), which is to be developed and implemented by family members and service providers. The IFSP contains information about the services necessary to facilitate a child's development and enhance the family's capacity to facilitate the child's development. The IFSP addresses:

- the child's present levels of physical, cognitive, communicative, social and adaptive development;
- the family's ability to enhance the child's development;
- the major outcomes to be achieved;
- specific early intervention services necessary to meet the unique needs of the child and the family;
- the environments in which services will be provided (the law encourages providing services in the child's natural environment);
- the projected dates for initiation and completion of services;
- the name of the service provider who will be responsible for implementing the plan; and
- steps to support the child's transition to preschool or other appropriate services.

From ages three through five years of age, IDEA provides for a *preschool grants program*. Services provided to preschoolers with disabilities under the program generally include:

LEGAL

- special instruction
- development and implementation of IEPs (described below) or IFSPs
- assistive technology devices and services
- audiology
- counseling services
- early identification and assessment
- medical services for diagnosis or evaluation
- occupational therapy
- physical therapy
- speech-language therapy

 TIP If you think your child can benefit from an IFSP or services under the preschool grants program, contact the responsible officials in your area. The web site for the National Early Childhood Technical Assistance Center (www.nectac.org) includes contact information for program coordinators in all fifty states. Information can also be obtained from local schools, hospitals, your pediatrician, and local advocacy organizations.

When a child with a disability reaches school age, the school, together with the child's parents, prepares an individualized education plan (IEP). The IEP is reviewed and updated at least annually. By law, the IEP must include:

- An assessment of the child's current performance (known as the *present level of educational performance*).

- Annual goals that the child can reasonably accomplish in a year.

- A list of the special education and related services to be provided to the child.

- An explanation of the extent (if any) to which the child will not participate with children who do not have disabilities in the regular class and other school activities. Participation with children who do not have disabilities (or *mainstreaming*) is preferred.

- A statement of modifications required for the administration of achievement tests. If a test is not appropriate for the child, the IEP must state why the test is not appropriate and how the child will be tested instead.

- Beginning when the child is age 14 (or younger, if appropriate), a listing of the courses the child needs to take to reach his or her post-school goals. A statement of transition services needs must also be included in each of the child's subsequent IEPs.

- Beginning when the child is age 16 (or younger, if appropriate), a listing of transition services needed to help the child prepare for leaving school.

- Beginning at least one year before the child reaches the age of majority, a statement that the student has been told of any rights that will transfer to him or her at the age of majority. (This statement would be needed only in states that transfer rights at the age of majority.)

- A statement as to how the child's progress will be measured and how parents will be informed of that progress.

TIP There are several very good sources of detailed information relating to IDEA programs throughout the country. Sources of information include the National Information Center for Children and Youth with Disabilities (www.NICHY.org), ERIC clearinghouse on Disabilities and Gifted Education (www.ericec.org) and the Council for Exceptional Children (www.ideapractices.org). A more complete list of contacts can be found beginning at page 23 of the Department of Education's *Guide to the Individualized Education Program* (www.ed.gov/parents/needs/speced/iepguide/index.html).

Educational services are also available through private schools that are specifically designed to educate children with specified types of disabilities. You can obtain information regarding private schools from local advocacy organizations, or the Department of Education for your school district. The web site for the National Association of Private Special Education Centers (www.napsec.org) contains an excellent listing of private special education centers.

Public school education is typically free of cost. In fact, the law requires states that provide free education to children who do not have disabilities to provide free education to children with disabilities as well. The cost of private schools varies and usually is paid by families. However, if a state or local education system places a child in a private school because it lacks the facilities to educate children who have disabilities, the cost of the private school must be borne by the state or local educational system, although this is becoming rare since most public school districts now provide these services.

TIP IDEA provides that a person with a disability is entitled to special education services until the person reaches age 22. Because your child will have the legal right to make education decisions at the age of majority (in most states, age 18) you should consider asking your child to prepare a Power of Attorney for Education upon reaching the age of majority to give you the right to participate in educational decisions. Your attorney will be able to help you prepare such a document. In many areas, the Power of Attorney for Education is not necessary because the school district permits parental participation in education decisons for adult children even in the absence of a Power of Attorney for Education. A Power of Attorney for Education will not be valid unless your child has the capacity to understand the meaning of the document. Powers of attorney are discussed in Chapter Ten.

Post-Secondary Education

There has been a tremendous increase in educational opportunities for people with disabilities at all levels since the early 1990s. This change has come about as a result of changing attitudes, technological advances, and very helpful federal legislation such as the Rehabilitation Act of 1973, the Education for All Handicapped Children Act of 1975, the Individuals With Disabilities Education Act of 1990 and the Americans With Disabilities Act of 1990.

The Rehabilitation Act is designed to help integrate individuals with disabilities by helping them develop the skills and supports necessary to obtain and maintain employment. A person may be eligible for vocational rehabilitation services if the person has a disability, can benefit from rehabilitation services and requires such services to obtain or retain gainful employment.

Once enrolled, a client is assigned a rehabilitation counselor who meets with the client and helps the client develop an *Individual Written Rehabilitation Plan* (IRWP). The IRWP identifies employment and educational objectives and services to be provided. Services provided by state vocational rehabilitation agencies include career planning, vocational guidance and training, medical rehabilitation services, rehabilitation technology, mobility training for the blind, and on the job training. The vocational counselor also may provide referral services to service providers and may help with employment placement and post-employment follow-up.

*A*ll states now provide vocational rehabilitation services and offices can be found in most cities.

To locate the office nearest you, look in your local telephone book, ask at your local hospital, or ask the transition counselor at your local high school. You can also find contact information on the web site for the National Counsel on Disability (www.ncd.gov) by clicking on resources and following the link to State Vocational and Rehabilitation Agencies. Although fees are charged for most vocational rehabilitation services, financial assistance is available for people with limited resources.

Under the *Ticket To Work And Self-Sufficiency Program* (the Ticket Program), which is operated by the Social Security Administration, people who receive benefits under Social Security Disability Insurance (SSDI) or Supplemental Security Income (SSI) because of disability or blindness are eligible to receive employment services, vocational services or other services through *employment networks*, which are private organizations or government agencies that have agreed to work with Social Security in providing employment services to beneficiaries with disabilities. The program is strictly voluntary and offers greater choices in getting recipients services needed to go to work. The goal of the program is to help SSDI and SSI recipients earn enough money so they will not need Social Security cash benefits.

Information about the Ticket Program, can be obtained from Maximus, Inc. at 1-866-968-7842 toll-free (TTY 1-866-833-2967).

Maximus is a private company that is working with Social Security to help manage the program. Maximus can answer most questions about the Ticket Program, and can provide names, addresses, and telephone numbers of employment networks across the country. Additional information can be found at www.yourtickettowork.com and www.maximus.com.

Educational opportunities for people with disabilities have also increased on college campuses. In addition, many private agencies operate post secondary educational institutions specifically geared to people with disabilities. Transition counselors at local high schools and representatives at local advocacy groups will be able to point you to appropriate programs and services.

The National Clearinghouse on post secondary Education for Individuals with Disabilities, also known as the HEATH Resource Center (www.heath.gwu.edu), which is a part of George Washington University, is a wonderful resource describing post-secondary educational opportunities for people with disabilities.

The site contains a number of very useful listings of educational programs in various states that can be accessed by Clicking on *Publications* and then following the link to *Resource Papers*.

Adult Service Agencies

Most areas have private or quasi-private agencies known as adult service agencies devoted to providing aid to people who have disabilities. These agencies can be operated by for-profit or not-for-profit corporations, and many are partially supported by federal, state, or local governmental funds or by contributions from charitable organizations. The agencies may charge a fee for services, or their services may be offered free of cost.

The range of services offered by adult services agencies varies widely. Some are very much like the intermediate care facilities discussed previously, offering residential facilities and comprehensive programs in vocational rehabilitation, recreation, and employment services. In fact, such agencies may actually operate intermediate care facilities themselves.

Others are more limited in scope, perhaps providing employment training for specified types of businesses. Still others may limit themselves to clients with specified types of disabilities (for example, the hearing or visually impaired, or those with physical disabilities).

The process for locating and choosing among adult service agencies is very much like the process for locating and choosing among group homes. You can locate the agencies in your area by contacting your local advocacy organizations, state and local agencies responsible for programs involving people with disabilities, and your local high school's transition counselor.

It is also possible to obtain information from the vocational rehabilitation centers in your state. In fact, it will generally be advisable to contact an adult service agency only after you have dealt with the local vocational rehabilitation center. Because vocational rehabilitation centers typically have greater resources than private agencies, you will find the latter most useful if the local vocational rehabilitation center has been unable to help you (perhaps because it found your child to be unemployable).

Because adult service agencies offer such widely divergent services, care should be taken to select the agency that is most appropriate for your particular needs and circumstances. Accordingly, it is advisable to phone or write as many as you can and to visit those that appear most promising. Many of the factors you will want to consider will be similar to the factors to be considered in choosing among group homes, and you should review the section of this chapter relating to choosing residential settings for your child before visiting adult service agencies. In many parts of the country, choice is limited.

Special Educational Programs for People with Visual or Hearing Impairments

In addition to local school district programs, there are schools located throughout the country specifically for people who have visual or hearing impairments. These schools often accept children from infancy through 12th grade. Other special schools are available for college students and/or adults.

In addition to having a regular academic curriculum, schools for those with hearing impairments will often have special courses in speech therapy, lip reading, use of hearing aids, and sign language. Schools for those with visual impairments generally have a regular academic curriculum as well as special courses in braille, skills of daily living, orientation, and mobility. These schools often develop leaders for the hearing or visually impaired communities.

Many states also have special vocational rehabilitation units for the hearing and visually impaired. You can obtain information from your local vocational rehabilitation office as well as from the organizations listed in the previous paragraph.

Employment Options

Recent times have seen rapid increases in the amount and type of employment opportunities available for people with disabilities. Families and professionals tend to view employment in a positive light, focusing on the positive self-image that work frequently engenders and the increased opportunities for social relationships resulting from interaction with coworkers. In addition, people with relatively mild disabilities can sometimes earn relatively significant amounts of money.

Depending on the type of disability involved, employment may be an option for your child. You should not, however, feel pressured to seek employment for your child if you and your child do not think it appropriate. Remember, employment should be viewed as a means to a goal, as one of the elements in building a happy and fulfilling life for your child.

The following is a summary of some of the types of employment opportunities available for people with disabilities. Different alternatives will be appropriate for different people. As with the selection among possible residential alternatives, the proper choice will depend on the needs and desires of your son or daughter.

Sheltered Workshops

A sheltered workshop is a separate employment entity, all of whose workers have some type of disability. The workshop contracts with private businesses to perform certain tasks for the business at specified contractual rates. In most cases, the workshop will be involved in packaging, assembly, and shipping of products and will be paid based on the amount of work completed. For example, a workshop might contract with a doll-house manufacturer to pack various component parts supplied by the manufacturer into boxes for sale in stores.

Jobs are divided into small, simple tasks so they can be performed, in assembly-line fashion, by people with moderate to relatively severe disabilities. Workers are usually paid according to their productivity, rather than on an hourly basis.

For workers who lack the skills needed to participate in the performance of actual contracts, sheltered workshops often have educational programs known as prevocational training centers to aid in developing skills needed to perform in the workshop setting. For example, workers may practice tasks such as sorting, collating, and assembly and then move on to sheltered workshop employment if and when these skills are mastered.

Sheltered workshops have been criticized on several grounds. First, the workshops depend on contract work from private businesses, and such contracts can be difficult to find, particularly in hard economic times. As a result, many sheltered workshops may have significant periods when work is simply unavailable. While the better workshops seek to fill this downtime with educational and other activity programs, many workers frequently have too little to do. Second, the nature of the work received by sheltered workshops can limit opportunities to develop more advanced skills. In order to compete in the marketplace, workshops must bid on contracts that private industries are confident they can complete. These tend to be jobs requiring low-skill repetitive-type work. Third, workshops are, by their very nature, sheltered. As a result, opportunities for workers to interact with those who do not have disabilities are limited. Finally, workshops tend to be very low paying.

Despite these criticisms, however, sheltered workshops have a number of defenders. True, these defenders argue, it would be better if we could find higher-paying integrated employment for everyone. However, even with *job coaches* (discussed in the next section), integrated employment is not available or appropriate for everyone. The proper comparison, these people argue, is not always between workshops and community-based employment, but rather between sheltered workshops and unemployment.

Moreover, many workshops achieve the major goals of employment discussed above, strengthening the worker's sense of self-worth and fostering socialization with peers. Workers in sheltered workshops tend to work at a more relaxed pace than those in integrated employment situations, and many workers with disabilities find this to be beneficial. Finally, the better workshops utilize a variety of methods to combat isolation from the community. Some attempt to locate near other businesses to foster greater integration, and others provide integrated employment opportunities with job coaches for those whose disabilities are less severe.

As with group homes, sheltered employment workshops vary widely in quality. If you are interested in investigating sheltered employment options for your child, you should examine as many as you can and select the one that is most appropriate given your child's particular needs and abilities. In many parts of the country, choice is limited.

Community-Based Employment

Community-based employment refers to employment situations that are integrated into the community at large. That is, a person with a disability works alongside those who do not have disabilities. Several different types of community-based employment are available.

In one approach, known as *supported employment*, an individual is hired by a company and trained one-on-one by a *job coach*. The amount of training can be quite extensive. The job coach remains with the employee on a constant basis during the beginning of the training, making sure the work gets done and teaching the employee on a step-by-step basis. Employers favor this method because the presence of the job coach assures quality during the learning process. At the beginning of the training period, the job coach may actually do most of the work. As the employee learns what the job requires, the amount of *coaching* is reduced, with the coach fading entirely when the employee completely masters the job. Importantly, the job coach remains available if problems develop or if the employee requires additional training.

Job coaches may be provided by not-for-profit agencies, group homes, intermediate care facilities where the worker may reside, or even by a sheltered workshop from which the worker may have *graduated*. A recent trend is for the employer to select a trainer from among its workers, perhaps providing bonuses or extra pay in exchange for the added responsibility. This can work quite well, as it speeds the integration of the person with a disability into work life. Care must be taken by the private company to select a trainer who has a good heart and an adequate understanding of the needs of workers with disabilities.

In a second approach, known as *supervised employment*, or the *enclave*, a company will hire a group of individuals with disabilities to do specified tasks at a particular job site. The workers will interact with workers who do not have disabilities on a daily basis and will be supervised by a trained worker from an adult service agency who is responsible for their performance. In many cases, employment is temporary. The workers are hired for a specific job and are released when the job is completed, although permanent employment is sometimes possible.

Workers whose disabilities are relatively minor are able to work alongside those who do not have disabilities with minimal or no training. This is known as *competitive employment* and is very common in the cleaning and fast food industries.

Finding a Job for Your Son or Daughter

As already mentioned, a wide variety of methods are available for locating suitable employment for your son or daughter. The local vocational rehabilitation training center will have extensive information on employment and job opportunities in your area and will help with job training and placement. Similarly, many adult service agencies will have information on local job opportunities for adults with disabilities. The ticket-to-work program discussed under Post-Secondary Education above, presents wonderful opportunities as well.

If your son or daughter lives in a group home, the agency that operates the home will hopefully have information about local employment options and may have its own system for providing suitable employment. Even if your son or daughter does not live in a group home, local group homes would probably be willing to help you. Information on local employment options can also be obtained from local advocacy organizations, state and local agencies responsible for aiding those who have disabilities, and from the transition counselor at your local high school.

Finally, there are the time honored methods employed by those who do not have disabilities. Perhaps there is a suitable opening at a place where a friend or relative may work. Or maybe you can find something that appears promising in the want ads.

Obviously, you will want to make sure your son or daughter is happy with whatever job he or she ultimately selects.

This will require analysis of the type of work involved (Is it something your child will be happy doing?), the work environment (Is it safe and will coworkers be supportive?), the location (Can your child get to work easily?) and the benefit package (Is a mentor provided? Are wages fair? Are hours excessive? Is vacation time adequate and can it be scheduled at the proper times? Will insurance benefits be provided?)

In addition, you will need to assess how the wages received will affect your son or daughter's eligibility for government benefits. As discussed in Chapter Four, many of these governmental programs have strict income limitations, and your child could become ineligible for these programs if the limitations are exceeded. However, in most cases the self-esteem derived from work is more important than any loss in government benefits.

One final point to keep in mind. A vocational decision is not irrevocable. If your son or daughter is unhappy with a job, change is possible. A new workshop can be found. Additional vocational training can be taken to improve job skills. The vocational rehabilitation counselor can suggest other positions. If you are unhappy, you are entitled to ask for a change. As always, the goal is to increase the quality of life for your son or daughter. If a first effort to achieve that goal proves ineffective, there is nothing prohibiting you from changing your plan.

Social/Recreational Activities

As with any other person, your child's social and recreational desires are uniquely individual, and your goal in preparing a life plan and writing a Letter of Intent is to correctly identify those desires and make sure the life plan provides mechanisms that will enable your son or daughter to continue to enjoy the activities that provide pleasure in his or her life.

Identifying the things your son or daughter likes to do should not be difficult. You have raised or are raising your child and you, above anyone, know what your son or daughter enjoys doing and what he or she does not. You know which activities your child looks forward to eagerly, which activities are joined in without enthusiasm, and which activities your child must be dragged to, kicking and screaming.

Your job is to make sure your child's desires continue to be respected after your death.

For many, this will simply be a matter of communicating your child's desires to future caregivers in your Letter of Intent. You may have already selected another child to look out for the interests of a son or daughter with a disability, and you may have confidence that they will *do what needs doing.* (The Letter of Intent will still be important in case the child you select dies or moves out of state.)

For example, you will recall William, the son of one of our clients. He enjoys listening to music, socializing with friends, attending church, going to religion camp, and visiting relatives. William's father placed him in a group home near a church so William would have peers to interact with and a church to attend, and indicated in his Letter of Intent that every effort should be made to enable William to continue his favorite activities. William's two brothers, the people responsible for looking out for him after his father's death, are positioned to make sure William's desires will continue to be respected.

Similarly, Lisa, one of our clients, likes attending church and also likes to bowl. She lives in a group home that features many social programs: art, regular trips to movies and amusement parks, as well as a regular bowling league. Lisa has no relatives, other than her mother, living in the area, but her mother has several friends who have volunteered to make sure Lisa gets to church after she is gone.

If you are unsure what your son or daughter likes to do, or if you would like to offer your child new and different activities, perhaps to expand the range of his or her interests, several alternatives are available.

One of the great sources of pleasure in life is a simple get-together with friends, and many communities have loosely organized group get-togethers for people with disabilities. You can probably find out about them through local organizations that advocate for people with disabilities, or you may want to organize one yourself. It may also be possible to participate in recreational activities sponsored by local group homes even if your child is not presently a resident. Methods of contacting local group homes are discussed in a previous section of this chapter on residential alternatives.

Many organizations specializing in recreation, such as the YMCA and various special recreation associations, have programs specifically designed for people with disabilities. Activities include swimming, basketball, and informal get-togethers. Virtually all park districts have programs for people with disabilities.

Adult service agencies frequently sponsor *day activity programs* that combine social activities with educational programs designed to help those with disabilities improve their daily living skills. Such programs vary widely in content and quality and you should visit several before deciding on one. You can locate adult service agencies through local advocacy groups.

The Special Olympics programs for people with developmental disabilities also offer a first-rate forum for social enhancement. Participation is open to everyone regardless of ability, and the opportunity to participate with peers in sporting events, and perhaps to develop new and valued friendships, should not be overlooked. Perhaps the Special Olympics oath expresses the goals of the organization best: "Let me win, but if I cannot win, let me be brave in the attempt."

There is also some very good information about recreational programs for people with disabilities available on the internet. The federal government's new web site at www.disability.info contains a great deal of information. Click on Community Life at the top, then Click on Recreation on the left. There are links to a wide variety of programs. The National Sports Center for the Disabled in Colorado provides outdoor recreational opportunities for people with disabilities. Its web site is located at www.nscd.org.

The web site for Exceptional Parent Magazine (www.eparent.com) contains links to many summer camp programs for people with disabilities. Click on Camps on the left side. Even more extensive information about camp opportunities can be found at the web site for the American Camp Association (www.acacamps.org). Click on Find a Camp, then Special Needs/Special Clientele. On the right you can fill in the particular type of disability involved. For example, if you fill in *mental retardation* as the type of special need involved, you will find that the American Camp Association has 109 camps serving people with mental retardation in its data base.

Further information about recreational organizations for people with disabilities can be found in the Annual Resource Guide published by Exceptional Parent Magazine.

The importance of planning so that your child can continue to enjoy the activities that make life enjoyable cannot be overstated. Too many parents worry about the big things—residence, employment, and education—without paying sufficient attention to the little things, like recreation, that can be the difference between a rewarding life and a neglected one.

Mental Health Resources

A very important aspect of life planning for people with mental illness is controlling the symptoms of the disease. Two excellent sources of information are available: the National Mental Health Information Center (www.mentalhealth.org) and the National Mental Health Association (www.nmha.org). The web sites include information relating to all aspects of living with mental illness. The web site for the National Mental Health Association even includes information relating to finding qualified therapists.

Conclusion

Many parents who have a child with a disability do not prepare an estate plan because they feel uncomfortable with the traditional, legal document approach. They choose to do nothing in preference to doing the wrong thing.

For the minority of parents who prepare wills, there is a typical scenario. An attorney advises them to disinherit their child and leave some resources in trust for their child's benefit. (Trusts for beneficiaries with disabilities are described in Chapter Six.)

The attorney may spend an hour counseling the parents and then prepare typical estate planning documents. For the most part, any resources will be managed by a trustee, who may or may not know the parents' desires. The tragedy is that the parents leave the attorney's office thinking they have done everything—that their estate plan is finished. By the time they reach their car, though, they may stare at the pieces of paper in their hands and wonder just how their child really will be taken care of in the future. They don't feel they have covered all the bases.

One of the greatest illusions in the estate-planning field today is that the average family can guarantee a bright future for a person with a disability simply by preparing a will and a trust. The truth is that a will and a trust rarely carry out the wishes of the family unless the parents build a strong planning foundation by first developing a comprehensive and flexible life plan.

The life planning approach calls upon you to take the following steps:

- Decide what you want for your child in all of the major life areas: residential placement, education, employment, socialization, religion, medical care, final arrangements, and so on. Flexibility is important, so there should be many prioritized options listed under each heading. Your child may live another 50 to 60 years, and planning should try to cover the maximum life span.

- Put these hopes and desires in writing by using the nonlegal document known as a Letter of Intent. These letters are discussed in Chapter Two.

- Decide whether your child will need an advocate or a legal guardian. Advocates and guardians are discussed in Chapter Three.

- Decide on the combination of financial resources that will be needed to implement the life plan. The considerations relevant to making this decision are discussed in Chapters Four and Five.

There is a lot to consider, a lot of decisions to make. But plans must be made if you are to give your child the best possible chance to live a happy and rewarding life after your death.

Chapter 2

The Letter of Intent

NOW THAT YOU HAVE PREPARED A TENTATIVE LIFE PLAN FOR your son or daughter, you probably have a fair idea of what you would like his or her life to look like after your death. It is now time to communicate your ideas and knowledge to future caregivers.

In most cases, the future caregivers will be relatives. But even if these relatives are very close to your child, they may not be aware of important personal information. For instance, do the future caregivers know all the pertinent information about your child's medical history? Do they know the names, addresses, and phone numbers of all the professionals who serve your child? Do they know the names of professionals who you think should be avoided?

Moreover, if these relatives die or move away, successor caregivers will need explicit information.

Although not a legally binding document, a Letter of Intent is an ideal format. It allows you to communicate your desires to future caregivers and therefore will prove invaluable to them. The letter assumes even greater importance if these future caregivers are out of state and do not see your child frequently, or if the ultimate caregiver will be a trust officer at a bank.

To write a Letter of Intent, just follow the guide contained in this chapter, which covers vital details about what works well for your child in all of the major life areas: residential placement, education, employment, socialization, religion, medical care, final arrangements, and so on. Flexibility is important, so there should be several prioritized options listed under each heading. Possibly you will want to add some categories of your own to those listed in the guide, and you should feel free to make any adjustments necessary to meet the individual needs of your son or daughter.

Be sure to include enough information. For instance, if you write down a Social Security number, be sure to use the words "Social Security Number" so that someone reading the document after your death doesn't have to guess what those numbers represent. If you list your child's doctor, make sure to include his or her address and phone number. Also, using category headings similar to those in the guide may make it easier for anyone to find particular pieces of information.

If both parents are living, one of you may want to do the actual writing of the Letter of Intent while both of you will want to sign it. The letter can be typed or handwritten. It isn't an essay for school, and perfect grammar, spelling, or style are not the point. Your major concern is to make sure that your child will have a happy and meaningful life. Write clearly enough so that anyone who reads the letter in the future will understand exactly what you meant.

Some of the items we ask you to include in the Letter of Intent are discussed elsewhere in the book. For now, do your best, although you may want to make revisions after you have read the relevant discussions.

We also ask for a fair amount of information about your child's finances. Do the best you can for now, although the information in Chapters Four and Five may be of help for future planning.

We cannot stress too much the importance of reviewing the letter and making revisions as changes in your plans for your son or daughter arise.

Each year you should take out the letter and review it to make sure it remains current. Choose the same date each year, perhaps your child's birthday, so you won't forget. Occasionally there will be a significant change in your child's life, such as a new residential placement or a bad reaction to medication, and the letter should be revised immediately if any such change occurs. Many clients keep the letter on a word processor so changes can be made more easily.

The following material is only a guide to writing your Letter of Intent. It is a list of everything we could think of that parents might put in their Letter of Intent. Not every point will apply to your particular situation. Remember, the purpose of the Letter of Intent is to include personal information about caring for your child that you want to communicate to future caregivers.

Letter of Intent

Written by: _____Date: _____

_____

(Relationship to the person with the disability—mother, father or both)

To Whom It May Concern:

Information About _____
(Father's name)

General information: List the father's full name, Social Security number, complete address, phone numbers for home and work, county or township, date of birth, place of birth, city/town/country where raised, fluent languages, religion, race, blood type, number of sisters, and number of brothers. Indicate whether he is a U.S. citizen.

Marital status: Indicate the father's marital status. If he is currently married, list the date of that marriage, the place the marriage took place, and the number of children from that marriage. Also list the dates of any previous marriages, names of other wives, and names and birth dates of children from each marriage.

Family: List the complete names of the father's siblings and parents. For those still living, list their addresses and phone numbers, as well as pertinent biographical information.

Information About _____
(Mother's name)

General Information: List the mother's full name, Social Security number, complete address, phone numbers for home and work, county or township, date of birth, place of birth, city/town/country where raised, fluent languages, religion, race, blood type, number of sisters, and number of brothers. Indicate whether she is a U.S. Citizen.

Marital status: Indicate the mother's marital status. If she is currently married, list the date of that marriage, the place the marriage took place, and the number of children from that marriage. Also list the dates of any previous marriages, names of other husbands, and names and birth dates of children from each marriage.

Family: List the complete names of the mother's siblings and parents. For those still living, list addresses and phone numbers, as well as pertinent biographical information.

Information About _____

(Your son or daughter's name)

General Information

Name: List the full name of your son or daughter. Also list the name he or she likes to be called.

Numbers: List your child's Social Security number, complete address, county or township, telephone numbers for home and work, height, weight, shoe size, and clothing sizes.

More details: List your child's gender, race, fluent languages, and religion. Indicate whether your child is a U.S. citizen.

Birth: List your child's date and time of birth, as well as any complications. List your child's birth weight and place of birth, as well as the city/town/country where he or she was raised.

Siblings: List the complete names, addresses, and phone numbers of all sisters and brothers. Which ones are closest to the person with a disability—both geographically and emotionally?

Marital status: List the marital status of your son or daughter. If married, list the spouse's name, his or her date of birth, the names of any children, and their dates of birth. Also list any previous marriages, as well as the names, addresses, and phone numbers for the spouses and children from each marriage.

Other relationships: List special friends and relatives that your child knows and likes. Describe the relationships. These people can play an invaluable role, especially if the trustee resides out-of-state.

Guardians: Indicate whether your child has been declared incompetent and whether any guardians have been appointed. List the name, address, and phone number of each guardian and indicate whether that person is a guardian of the person or guardian of the estate, plenary or limited.

If successor guardians have been chosen, list their full names, addresses, and phone numbers. Even if your child has no guardian, it is often wise to state in the Letter of Intent your wishes about who you want to act as guardian if one is needed in the future. Make sure you have spoken with them.

Advocates: List the people, in order, who you foresee acting as advocates for your child after your death. Make sure you have spoken with them.

Trustee: Indicate whether you have set up a trust for your child and list the full names, addresses, and phone numbers of all the trustees.

Representative payee: Indicate whether your son or daughter has or needs a representative payee to manage public entitlements, such as Supplemental Security Income or Social Security.

Power of attorney: If anyone has power of attorney for your son or daughter, list the person's full name, address, and phone number. Indicate whether this is a durable power of attorney.

Final arrangements: Describe any arrangements that have been made for your child's funeral and burial. List the full names of companies or individuals, their addresses, and phone numbers. Also list all payments made and specify what is covered.

In the absence of specific arrangements, indicate your preferences for cremation or burial. Should there be a church service? If the preference is for burial, what is the best site? Should there be a monument? If cremation is the choice, what should be done with the remains?

Medical History and Care

Diagnoses: List the main diagnoses for your son or daughter's condition, such as autism, cerebral palsy, Down syndrome, epilepsy, impairment due to age, learning disorder, an intellectual disability, neurological disorder, physical disabilities, psychiatric disorder, or an undetermined problem.

Seizures: Indicate the seizure history of your son or daughter: no seizures; no seizures in the past two years; seizures under control; seizures in the past two years, but not in the past year; or seizures currently. Does anything act as a "trigger" for increased seizure activity?

Functioning: Indicate your child's intellectual functioning level (mild, moderate, severe, profound, undetermined, etc.).

Vision: Indicate the status of your child's vision: normal, normal with glasses, impaired, legally blind, without functional vision, etc. List the date of the last eye test and what was listed on any prescription for eyeglasses.

Hearing: Indicate the status of your child's hearing: normal, normal with a hearing aid, impaired, deaf, etc.

Speech: Indicate the status of your child's speech: normal; impaired, yet understandable; requires sign language; requires use of communication device; non-communicative, etc. If your child is non-verbal, specify the techniques you use for communication.

Mobility: Indicate the level of your child's mobility: normal; impaired, yet self-ambulatory; requires some use of wheelchair or other assistance; dependent on wheelchair or other assistance; without mobility, etc.

Blood: List your child's blood type and any special problems concerning blood.

Insurance: List the type, amount, and policy number for the medical insurance covering your son or daughter. What is included in this coverage now? Indicate how this would change upon the death of either parent. Make sure you include Medicare and Medicaid, if relevant.

Current physicians: List your child's current physicians, including specialists. Include their full names, types of practice, addresses, phone numbers, the average number of times your child visits them each year, the total charges from each doctor during the last year, and the amounts not covered by a third party, such as insurance (including Medicare or Medicaid).

Previous physicians: List their full names, addresses, phone numbers, the type of practice, and the most common reasons they saw your child. Describe any important findings or treatment. Explain why you no longer choose to consult them.

Dentist: List the name, address, and phone number of your child's dentist, as well as the frequency of exams. Indicate what special treatments or recommendations the dentist has made. Also list the best alternatives for dental care in case the current dentist is no longer available.

Nursing needs: Indicate your child's need for nursing care. List the reasons, procedures, nursing skill required, etc. Is this care usually provided at home, at a clinic, or in a doctor's office?

Mental health: If your child has visited a psychiatrist, psychologist, or mental health counselor, list the name of each professional, the frequency of visits, and the goals of the sessions. What types of therapy have been successful? What types have not worked?

Therapy: Does your son or daughter go to therapy (physical, speech, or occupational)? List the purpose of each type of therapy, as well as the name, address, and phone number of each therapist. What assistive devices have been helpful? Has an occupational therapist evaluated your home to assist you in making it more accessible for your child?

Diagnostic testing: List information about all diagnostic testing of your son or daughter in the past: the name of the individual and/or organization administering the test, address, phone number, testing dates, and summary of findings. How often do you recommend that diagnostic testing be done? Where?

Genetic testing: List the findings of all genetic testing of your child and relatives. Also list the name of the individual and/or organization performing the tests, address, phone number, and the testing dates.

Immunizations: List the type and dates of all immunizations.

Diseases: List all childhood diseases and the date of their occurrence. List any other infectious diseases your child has had in the past. List any infectious diseases your child currently has. Has your child been diagnosed as a carrier for any disease?

Allergies: List all allergies and current treatments. Describe past treatments and their effectiveness.

Other problems: Describe any special problems your child has, such as bad reactions to the sun or staph infections if he or she becomes too warm.

Procedures: Describe any helpful hygiene procedures such as cleaning wax out of ears periodically, trimming toenails, or cleaning teeth. Are these procedures currently done at home or by a doctor or other professional? What do you recommend for the future?

Operations: List all operations and the dates and places of their occurrence.

Hospitalization: List any other periods of hospitalization your child has had. List the people you recommend to monitor your child's voluntary or involuntary hospitalizations and to act as liaison with doctors.

Birth control: If your son or daughter uses any kind of birth control pill or device, list the type, dates used, and doctor prescribing it.

Devices: Does your son or daughter need any adaptive or prosthetic devices, such as glasses, braces, shoes, hearing aids, or artificial limbs?

Medication: List all prescription medication currently being taken, plus the dosage and purpose of each one. Describe your feelings about the medications. List any particular medications that have proved effective for particular problems that have occurred frequently in the past and the doctor prescribing the medicine. List medications that have not worked well in the past and the reasons. Include medications that have caused allergic reactions.

OTC: List any over-the-counter medications that have proved helpful, such as vitamins or dandruff shampoo. Describe the conditions helped by these medications and the frequency of use.

Monitoring: Indicate whether your child needs someone to monitor the taking of medications or to apply ointments, etc. If so, who currently does this? What special qualifications would this person need?

Procurement: Does your child need someone to procure medications?

Diet: If your child has a special diet of any kind, please describe it in detail and indicate the reasons for the diet. If there is no special diet, you might want to include tips about what works well for avoiding weight gain and for following the general guidelines of a balanced, healthy diet. You might also describe the foods your child likes best and where the recipes for these foods can be found.

What Works Well for _____

(Your son or daughter's name)

Housing

Present: Describe your son or daughter's current living situation and indicate its advantages and disadvantages.

Past: Describe past living situations. What worked? What didn't?

Future: Describe in detail any plans that have been made for your son or daughter's future living situation. Describe your idea of the best living arrangement for your child at various ages or stages. Prioritize your desires. For each age or stage, which of the following living arrangements would you prefer?

- A relative's home (Which relative?)
- Supported living in an apartment or house with _____ hours of supervision
- A group home with no more than ___ residents
- A state institution (Which one?)
- A private institution (Which one?)
- Foster care for a child
- Adult foster care
- Parent-owned housing with ___ hours of supervision

- Housing owned by your child with ____hours of supervision, etc.

Size: Indicate the minimum and maximum sizes of any residential option that you consider suitable.

Adaptation: Does the residence need to be adapted with ramps, grab bars, or other assistive devices?

Community: List the types of places that would need to be conveniently reached from your child's home. Include favorite restaurants, shopping areas, recreation areas, libraries, museums, banks, etc.

Daily Living Skills

IPP: Describe your child's current Individual Program Plan.

Current activities: Describe an average daily schedule. Also, describe activities usually done on "days off."

Monitoring: Discuss thoroughly whether your son or daughter needs someone to monitor or help with the following items:

- Self-care skills like personal hygiene or dressing.
- Domestic activities like housekeeping, cooking, shopping for clothes, doing laundry, or shopping for groceries and cleaning supplies.
- Transportation for daily commuting, recreational activities, and emergencies.
- Reinforcement of social and interpersonal activities with others to develop social skills.
- Other areas.

Caregivers' attitudes: Describe how you would like caregivers to treat matters like sanitation, social skills (including table manners, appearance, and relationships with the opposite sex). What values do you want caregivers to demonstrate?

Self-esteem: Describe how you best reinforce your son or daughter's self-esteem, discussing how you use praise and realistic goal setting.

Sleep habits: How much sleep does your son or daughter require? Does he or she have any special sleep habits or methods of waking up?

Personal finances: Indicate whether your son or daughter needs assistance with personal banking, bill payments, and budgeting. If so, how much help is needed?

Allowance: Indicate whether you recommend a personal allowance for your son or daughter. If so, how much? Also, list your recommendations about supervision of how the allowance is spent.

Education

Schools: List the schools your child has attended at various ages and the level of education completed in each program. Include early intervention, day care, and transition programs.

Current programs: List the specific programs, schools, and teachers your son or daughter has now. Include addresses and phone numbers.

Academics: Estimate the grade level of your son or daughter's academic skills in reading, writing, math, etc. List any special abilities.

Emphasis: Describe the type of educational emphasis (such as academic, vocational, or community-based) on which your son or daughter currently concentrates. What educational emphasis do you think would be best for the future?

Integration: Describe the extent that your child has been in regular classes or schools during his or her education. What are your desires for the future? What kinds of undesirable conditions would alter those desires?

Day Program or Work

Present: Describe your son or daughter's current day program and/or job.

Past: Describe past experiences. What worked? What didn't? Why?

Future: Discuss future objectives. Prioritize your desires.

Assistance: Indicate to what extent, if any, your son or daughter needs assistance in searching for a job, in being trained, in becoming motivated, and in receiving support or supervision on the job.

Leisure and Recreation

Structured recreation: Describe your son or daughter's structured recreational activities. List favorite activities and the favorite people involved in each activity.

Unstructured activities: What are your child's favorite means of self-expression, interests, and skills (going to movies, listening to music, dancing, collecting baseball cards, painting, bowling, riding a bicycle, roller skating, etc.)? List the favorite people involved in each activity.

Vacations: Describe your son or daughter's favorite vacations. Who organizes them? How often do they occur, and when are they usually scheduled?

Fitness: If your son or daughter participates in a fitness program, please describe the type of program, as well as details about where and when it takes place and who oversees it.

Religion

Faith: List the religion of your son or daughter, if any. Indicate any membership in a particular church or synagogue.

Clergy: List any ministers, priests, or rabbis familiar with your son or daughter. Include the names of the churches or synagogues involved and their addresses and phone numbers. Also indicate how often your child might like to be visited by these people.

Participation: Estimate how frequently your son or daughter would like to participate in services and other activities of the church or synagogue. Indicate how this might change over time. Also describe any major, valued events in the past.

Rights and Values

Please list the rights and values that should be accorded your son or daughter. Here are some examples of what you might list.

- To be free from harm, physical restraint, isolation, abuse, and excessive medication.
- To refuse behavior modification techniques that cause pain.
- To have age-appropriate clothing and appearance.
- To have staff, if any, demonstrate respect and caring and to refrain from using demeaning language.

Other

Give an overview of your child's life and your feelings and vision about the future. Describe anything else future caregivers and friends should know about your son or daughter.

Finances, Benefits, and Services for _____
(Your son or daughter's name)

Assets: List the total assets your child has as of this date. Indicate how those assets are likely to change—if at all—in the future.

Cash income: List the various sources of income your son or daughter had last year. Include wages, government cash benefits, pension funds, trust income, and other income. This might include

Social Security, Social Security Disability Insurance (SSDI), or Supplemental Security Income (SSI).

Services and benefits: List any other services or benefits your child receives. These might be services for children with physical impairments, developmental disability services, clinics sponsored by support groups, early periodic screening, diagnosis and treatment, employment assistance, food stamps, housing assistance, legal assistance, library services, maternal and child health services, Medicaid, Medicare, Project Head Start, special education, Title XX service programs, transportation assistance, or vocational rehabilitation services.

Gaps: Indicate whether any services or benefits are needed but are not being received by your son or daughter. Indicate whether plans exist to improve the current delivery of services or to obtain needed benefits.

Expenses: List all expenses paid directly by your child in various categories, such as housing, education, health care, recreation, vocational training, and personal spending. List all expenses paid directly by parents, guardians, or trustees in various categories. List estimates of all expenses paid by third parties, such as insurance companies paying doctors directly or Medicaid paying for residential services.

Changes: Indicate how your child's financial picture would change if one or both parents died. Be sure to list any additional cash benefits to which your child definitely would be entitled. Also list any cash benefits for which your child might be eligible.

Sample Letters

The following sample Letters of Intent may be useful when you write your own letter. All of them were written by clients of ours and have been reprinted with their permission. Names have been changed, and information regarding medications has been omitted. Otherwise, the letters are completely authentic.

Sam, the subject of the first, has cerebral palsy that was caused by brain trauma resulting from electrocution. James, the subject of the second, has an intellectual disability that was probably brought on by seizures that began at age 3. Lisa, the subject of the third, has schizophrenia that first appeared at age 21.

You may want to skim the letters or read them in their entirety. If your son or daughter has a physical disability, you should not assume that only the sample letter relating to physical disabilities will be of use to you. The same is true if your child has a mental illness or an intellectual disability. You may find any or all of the letters to be useful.

Sample Letter for Physical Disability

To Whom It May Concern:

I, Jane Doe, am writing this letter on behalf of my husband, Fred Doe, and myself to explain the intentions of our estate plan and to give future caregivers as much information as possible about our son, Sam Doe. It is our hope that this information will be used to provide the best possible care for Sam and is done with his knowledge and input.

Father: Fred Doe
Social Security Number: 000-00-0000
Residence: (Address & Phone number)
Business: (Name, Address & Phone number)
Blood Type: O+
Religion: Roman Catholic

Fred is a male Caucasian born (date) in (city, county & state). He was baptized and confirmed at (name, address of church). He graduated from (name of high school) and received a B.S. degree in Financial Management from (name of college). He served in the U.S. Army Reserve Corps from which he received an Honorable Discharge on (date).

Fred married Jane Deer on (date) at (name of church). They have a daughter, Sara Doe, born (date) and a son, Sam Doe, born (date).

Relatives: Frank Doe (father) is deceased.

Helen Doe (mother) is deceased.

Steve Doe (brother)

(Address & Phone number)

Steve is married to Jacqueline and they have 7 adult children, all living on the West Coast. He is retired but still does some work for his sons' businesses and also does some carpentry work. He moved to California in the early 1960's but comes back to Illinois for a visit every year or so.

Arnold Deer (father)

(Address & Phone number)

Arnold is a pediatrician with a practice in (name of city). He was born September 7, 1917 in (city & state) and raised there. He married his wife on (date) in (city & state) and moved to (city & state) in 1943 to do his residency at (name of medical center). He and his wife raised 4 children (list of their names). He has not had any major illnesses and is in excellent health. He is very involved in (name of church), especially their mission outreach program to Haiti. He also loves working in his yard and always has some household project going. Other hobbies include downhill skiing, fishing, and walking.

[The letter goes on to list and describe 9 other relatives.]

Sam Doe—General Information:

Social Security Number: 000-00-0000

Residence: (Street address & Phone number)

School: (School address & Phone number)

Blood Type: unknown

Religion: Episcopalian

Height: 5'7"

Weight: 85 lbs.

Shoe size: 7

Shirt size: boys 16-18 adult medium

Pants size: boys 16 waist size 27"

Hands: small

Sam is a male Caucasian born (date) at (hospital name) in (city, state & county) at 9:00 a.m. He weighed 6 lbs. 3 oz., and delivery was normal. He lived with his family first at (address) and since 1980 at (address). On (date) when Sam was 7 months old, he was electrocuted by a pole lamp with faulty wiring. The shock stopped his heart, which caused trauma to his brain resulting in cerebral palsy. He was hospitalized at (hospital name) for 26 days.

Sam was baptized at (name of church) on (date). He attended Sunday School there and at (name of church) from 1980 to 1988. Currently he attends church only 2 or 3 times a year.

Sam is a U.S. Citizen. Sam is not currently receiving any government benefits. Sam is an unemployed, full-time student being supported by his parents.

Relatives:

(Name & Address of grandparents)

Sam has a close relationship with his grandparents. They have often cared for Sam. He normally sees them a couple of times a year, both here and in (name of city). They are very comfortable with him and enjoy him tremendously, and Sam loves being spoiled by them. They understand Sam's wants and needs and are very supportive. Their home is well set up for Sam to stay with them, but physically both of them need to be available for any lifting or transferring.

(Name and Address of Aunt & Uncle)

Sam and his aunt have a special relationship and share a unique sense of humor. (name of aunt) has physically cared for Sam often. Sam has also become very fond of his uncle, who is very comfortable with him. His cousins (names) are also comfortable with Sam. They interact very naturally with him and enjoy his company. Sam spends a lot of time with this family when he is visiting in (name of city). They have also visited us a number of times.

[The letter goes on to describe Sam's relationships with 7 other relatives.]

Close family friends who know Sam well and with whom he has a good rapport:

Name, Address & Phone number

List of children & their current addresses

Sam has an extremely close relationship with the whole family. He has grown up knowing them, spending vacations and holidays together, etc. (Wife's name) has often cared for Sam and is very comfortable and inventive with him, although she is no longer able to lift him by herself. (Husband & Wife's names) understand Sam and also know our hopes and expectations for Sam. (Husband's name) owns and operates a rubber manufacturing plant in (city). (Wife's name) works for the (school district name) and is an aide in a special education classroom. She is currently taking classes at (name of college) and working towards a teaching certificate. The family is totally at ease with Sam and interacts very appropriately with him.

[The letter includes descriptions of 3 additional neighbors and friends.]

Peers:

Jenny Doe (Jerry & Jesse Doe, Parents)

(Address & Phone number)

Jenny is a friend of Sam's who also has cerebral palsy. They have been going to school and camp together since grade school. They have a unique relationship and can talk to each other about things they do not discuss with anyone else. They share many problems and frustrations, but mainly they enjoy making each other laugh.

Mary Doe

(Phone number)

Mary is a social worker in the (City name) school system. She has worked for North Suburban Special Recreation Association (NSSRA) in their summer camps, which is where Sam met her. She also volunteers time to NSSRA during the school year to help run programs for the orthopedically handicapped. A couple of times a year she will set up "dates" with Sam and Jenny to go to a movie or out for ice cream or pizza. She understands Sam and has helped him determine what is inappropriate or immature behavior with contemporaries.

Guardians: Not at this time

Trustees: (The letter lists 3 individuals and one bank official, with their addresses and phone numbers.)

Advocates: (3 individuals, their addresses, and phone numbers are listed.)

The above people have been consulted and are willing to act as advisors to the trustees for any decisions that have to be made regarding Sam and are willing to act in his behalf to aid the trustees with the execution of the trust. I expect the trust to reimburse them for the time they spend acting as Sam's advocates and for any travel expenses they incur in carrying out this function.

Power of attorney: Not at this time

Final Arrangements: We would choose to have a memorial service and have Sam buried at the (name of church), which adjoins our property in (city and state). We have a plot there and the certificate is in the strong box.

Medical History and Care

Sam has severe mixed spastic athetoid cerebral palsy with quadriplegic involvement, which resulted from a prolonged period of cerebral anoxia secondary to cardiorespiratory arrest due to accidental electrocution at age 7 months. His brain damage was mostly motor, so his disabilities are mainly physical although he has a lot of learning disabilities. He is totally dependent for all his physical needs. Sam does have some muscular control. His right side is less involved than his left, so he uses his right hand to drive his electric wheelchair, type, pick things up, etc. He can stabilize things with his left hand, but that is about all.

Seizures: Sam had some seizures when he was still in a coma after his accident, but has had none since.

Functioning: Sam is developmentally delayed but functions at a near normal level intellectually. He has severe learning disabilities.

Vision: With his glasses Sam has normal vision. His prescription is for far-sightedness but his glasses also aid in fixation. Sam is much less fatigued when doing school work or when working on the computer if he wears his glasses.

Hearing: Sam's hearing is normal.

Speech: Sam's speech is impaired but usually understandable. Sam is very patient and good at giving clues as to what he is talking about if he is not being understood. His speech therapist at (school name) is (therapist's name). She feels that Sam's articulation is the best that he is physically able to achieve, so she is concentrating on language skills. Sam has experimented with different communication devices, but so far speech is much more efficient for him, and more natural.

Mobility: Sam is nonambulatory and uses an electric wheelchair. Because of his poor postural control, he needs special supports built into the chair to be able to sit. When not in the chair he spends his time prone on the floor, lying over a special wedged support we had made. This wedge, or some similar object, is necessary as Sam needs to stretch out during the day to relieve muscle contractures, backaches, and cramping.

Sam's wheelchair is very heavy and not very portable, so we have a van with a lift to transport him. Sam cannot sit in his chair for extended periods of time, so the van also has a fold-out seat that he can lie on. We also have collapsible ramps (one for each wheel) for places that are not accessible. These work if the entrance is not too high.

Blood: (type not listed)

Insurance: Sam is covered on our health insurance policy, which we have through (name of firm). The coverage is very comprehensive. They pay 80 percent of all physician and therapist charges, except the pediatrician's routine physical; 100 percent of most tests and X-rays; 100 percent of almost all dental charges and then 80 percent; 80 percent of most devices that you can get a prescription written for; they do not cover eye exams and glasses. Basically I just submit everything.

[The letter then lists the name of the insurance company, with its address, phone number, and plan number.]

There are two different forms. The medical coverage is with (name and address of company). The dental coverage is with (name, address, and phone number of company).

As long as my husband is alive, Sam will be covered by our insurance. After his death, the insurance will remain in force for 6 months. It can then be renewed for only 2 years.

Physicians: see separate listing

Nursing Needs: None needed

Mental Health: Sam has never seen a professional except through the school system for psychological testing. He does participate in a program at (school name) called "Peer Group." This is a kind of confidential "rap session" conducted by the school psychologist in which the kids can discuss any subject they want. Sam participated in a similar program in grade school.

Therapy: Sam receives O.T., P.T., and speech therapy at (school name). The goals of these therapists are stated in Sam's I.E.P., which is attached to this letter. Older I.E.P. reports and other therapy evaluations would be found in the file cabinet in the basement.

Diagnostic testing: None done

Genetic testing: None done

Immunizations: Diphtheria, Pertussis, and Tetanus (list of dates shots given) Measles, Mumps, and Rubella (date shot given). TB skin test (date and result of test)

Diseases: Chicken pox (date)

Allergies: None

Other Problems: Sam has had a few ear infections from water that did not drain out of his ear. This happened during swimming and bathing. Sam is aware right away when this occurs and responds immediately to the drops prescribed by his pediatrician.

Sam wears adult diapers and sometimes gets a rash on the inside of his thigh from the plastic. We treat this with Desenex, or any other diaper rash medication, but it is sometimes hard to get rid of. This condition has improved drastically since Sam has become more conscientious about telling us when he needs to be changed.

Sam is sensitive to poison ivy. He got it twice when the dog rubbed against him after coming in contact with the plant. We used Cortaid and have an advantage because Sam simply isn't able to scratch.

A few times Sam has gotten burned or scraped himself badly. I feel this happened because he has lost some of his pain sensors as a result of his brain damage, but no professional will confirm this.

Procedures and General Care

All hygiene procedures have to be done for Sam by a caregiver and are done at home.

Toileting: Sam wears adult diapers. We started this about 4 years ago when positioning him on any kind of toilet became difficult. He was simply too uncomfortable to effectively use it. We use Depends in size regular, which can be purchased at most drug stores and some grocery stores. We have found the best prices at Castle Drug, and on sale at Osco or Walgreen's.

Bathing: We purchased a special shower wheelchair and had the seating adapted at the Rehabilitation Institute of Chicago. This chair can be wheeled into the walk-in-shower we had built. I use a hand held sprayer that can be hung on the wall. Sam does not like the water spraying on his head but tolerates it long enough to have his hair washed. After he is cleaned he likes to just sit in the shower for a while with the water aimed at the lower half of his body.

Teeth: Sam does not like having his teeth brushed, so he forgets to remind me to do it. He likes Aim gel toothpaste the best. I use an Interplak electric toothbrush on the lowest power.

Hair: I use Head & Shoulders shampoo because I only wash Sam's hair about every 3 days, but I'm not sure it makes any difference. I have Sam's hair cut about every 6 to 8 weeks. He enjoys going because he knows a lot of the beauticians and likes to visit (tease) with them. [The name of the beautician who cuts his hair is listed, as well as the name of the shop, the address, phone number, and cost of the hair cut.]

Shave: He just started. I am using a Remington Electric Razor. I started out doing it once a week, but I'm noticing that may not be enough.

Nails: Sam's finger and toenails need to be cut about once a month. He will let you know if a nail is bothering him. I use fingernail scissors.

Deodorant: I use Old Spice every morning when I dress Sam.

Nose: Sam needs to have someone wipe his nose for him. He wears a terry cloth wristband to wipe his chin and nose but is not very efficient with it. I try to keep a cloth (I have been using cloth diapers for this and for wiping his mouth during feeding) or Kleenex in the backpack of his wheelchair for this purpose.

Clothing: At this time almost all of Sam's clothing is ready-made, but I have purchased a few mail-order items especially made for people confined to a wheelchair from a company called Everest & Jennings Avenues, 3233 E. Mission Oaks Blvd., Camarillo, California 93012. I can foresee using this type of resource more in the future. I have a file folder with some information on this company and a few others in the file cabinet in the basement. Sam is most comfortable in casual clothing like T-shirts, sweatshirts and sweatpants, or elastic waist pants or shorts.

Shoes: Shoes are very hard to get on Sam because his toes curl and he has ankle contractures. He also has a startle reflex that causes him to stiffen. I buy shoes that are oversized and have purchased some specialty dress shoes from Avenues (see Clothing). He gets sores on his heel if the shoes are too stiff. He usually wears slippers or socks around the house.

Startle Reflex: Sam has a startle reflex when touched in a sensitive place that causes him to stiffen his body. This occurs most noticeably when putting on shoes, changing diapers, cutting his nails, etc. He can usually reduce this tension when told to relax.

Drooling: Sam has a real problem with this. He is working on it, but we constantly have to remind him and wipe his chin and mouth area. He wears a terry cloth wristband on his right hand so that he can wipe himself, but he is not always efficient with it.

Sneezing: Sam has a sneeze reflex when his nose is stimulated and when eating. He often sneezes several times first thing in the morning. When he does sneeze, he sneezes with his mouth open so it goes everywhere.

Snoring: Sam snores very loudly, which might be a problem if he shares a bedroom.

Feeding: I feed Sam most of his food. He can finger feed himself, but it takes him a long time. I will give him snacks to feed himself. We have a plastic dish with a nonskid bottom that I put food in, or I place it directly on his tray.

Sam has trouble chewing, so I have to cut up meat in very small bites. He does best with small bites of everything. He also has a hard time with liquid foods, like soup. I crush several saltine crackers in the soup and feed it to him that way. Sam does not like the taste of very spicy foods. They create a lot of saliva, making it harder for Sam to swallow.

Drinking: Sam drinks everything with a straw. I use flexible straws. He has a glass holder with handles for drinking by himself.

Operations: Sam had an adductor myotomy (release of the adductor muscle in the groin area) in October, 1978 at (name of hospital). The surgery was performed by (name of doctor). After the cast was removed, Sam spent a month in the hospital for intensive physical therapy.

Hospitalizations: The only other time Sam was hospitalized was when he was electrocuted and was in a coma. That was in October of 1973. If Sam ever does need to be hospitalized and needs someone to monitor his care and act as liaison with the doctor I would recommend (person's name) or (person's name). I would also want my parents consulted because of their medical background.

Devices or Special Equipment

Electric wheelchair: Sam is in a slim, narrow adult Rolls Arrow Power Drive wheelchair with a joystick control. The seating system was made by the Rehabilitation Institute of Chicago, Seating and Positioning Center.

Jay Cushion: This special seat is being used in Sam's wheelchair to alleviate pain in his buttock and back and cramping in his right leg. Extra gel packs have been inserted, plus a wedge on the left side.

Prone Wedge This was designed for Sam by the Rehab. Engineering Department at the Rehabilitation Institute of Chicago. It is a wedge he uses to lay on the floor with straps to prevent him from rolling off.

Shower/Commode Chair: Sam uses the Guardian chair from Sunrise Medical. The seating system was redone by the Rehabilitation Institute of Chicago to provide enough support for Sam.

Lift: We purchased a Braun semiautomatic wheelchair lift for our van so that we could transport Sam.

Phone: Sam has a GTE speaker phone in his bedroom. It has 12 programmable phone numbers.

Computer: Sam has an Apple Computer to do any homework or other writing. He can use the regular keyboard and a mouse with his right hand. We have the computer plugged into a power strip so that Sam can turn it on and off himself. Sam approaches the computer from his right side and uses only his right hand on a regular keyboard. If he is using the mouse we usually set it on his tray, and in that instance Sam sits facing the computer.

Bed: We purchased an extra high bed for Sam because this is where I change his clothes, diapers, etc., and it is much easier on me than bending over. It is also easier to transfer Sam to his wheelchair or shower chair or just pick him up from this raised position.

Medications: none

OTC Medications: Sam does not take liquid medications very well but has no difficulty swallowing a pill. I always buy coated ones, and he swallows them easily if you place them way back in his mouth. I give him a drink after he swallows.

[A list of OTC medications which Sam uses and the conditions for which they are needed is included here.]

Monitoring: Sam will always need to have someone give him any medication or apply ointments, etc.

Procurement: Sam will need someone to buy medications for him or take him to buy medications.

Diet: Sam does not require a special diet. He is so slender that I do not worry about him eating too much. He eats a very balanced diet because he is dependent for feeding and doesn't eat a lot of junk food. He is capable of telling you what he likes and wants, but being a typical teenager, he prefers McDonald's or pizza to home cooking.

Dairy: Sam is not fond of milk, but I give him a large glass of chocolate milk with dinner. He loves cheese, especially American or Velveeta. He likes cottage cheese and I often crush potato chips in it. He also likes yogurt but only the thick kind (like Yoplait, custard style) with fruit—strawberry or blueberry.

Bread & Cereal: Sam likes bread and crackers of any kind. Pretzels are a favorite snack. He loves garlic bread. Sam is not very fond of cereal and had trouble eating it because of the liquid. He will eat Rice Crispies with just a little milk and sugar. He also likes it when I mash some banana in it or some strawberries. He likes pancakes, waffles, and French toast. He doesn't like muffins but will eat banana bread or zucchini bread. Sam loves any kind of pasta, with or without sauce. If I fix a plain pasta, he likes butter and salt on it.

Fruits: Sam has difficulty eating most fruits because of their juiciness. It is easiest for him if they are cut up and spoon fed to him and, if they are tart, with some sugar on them. He likes bananas, strawberries, peaches, applesauce, blueberries, and grapes without seeds. He likes cherries, but I've always taken the pits out. He will tolerate pears and melons but no citrus fruit, juice, or pineapple.

Vegetables: Sam likes most vegetables but will not eat green beans, cabbage, or squash, although he will eat canned green beans. He cannot eat tossed salads or fresh tomatoes. In fact, he cannot eat any raw vegetable. He likes his vegetables with butter or cheese on them. Fresh corn has to be cut off the cob.

Meat & Fish: Sam likes meat. Again, it has to be cut up in small bites and the more tender it is, the easier it is for him. He does not like liver, sausages, or bacon but loves hot dogs. Sam likes fish and really loves shrimp and lobster.

Desserts: Sam likes dessert but usually prefers to have it later and doesn't eat it on a regular basis. He loves chocolate in any form. His favorite cookies are chocolate chip, sugar wafers, or Oreos.

Drinks: Sam prefers to drink Pepsi, lemonade, or Kool-aid (especially grape flavor). I do have him drink a glass of milk a day (chocolate).

Breakfast: Sam does not like to eat first thing in the morning. Since he starts school at 7:45 and I insist he eat something, we have come up with a breakfast of 2 tablespoons of peanut butter mixed with 2 tablespoons of strawberry or grape jam. He also drinks a

Pepsi. This was at the suggestion of one of the staff because he was having so much trouble staying awake during classes. It helped and is now a habit, like coffee.

Soup: Sam loves soups. His favorites are vegetable, Lipton's chicken noodle, split pea, tomato, navy bean and ham, and broccoli with cheese. I thicken the soup with several crushed saltine crackers; in some soups, like tomato or chili, he likes cheese.

Favorite Dishes: Cheeseburgers, hot dogs, spaghetti, pizza, lobster or shrimp dipped in butter, macaroni and cheese with ketchup on top, grilled cheese, grilled cheese and ham, broccoli with cheese, fried, grilled, or roasted chicken, turkey with gravy, pork roast, deep fried perch or walleye, fried shrimp dipped in ketchup, mashed potatoes and gravy or baked potatoes with sour cream, asparagus, corn, chocolate pudding, chocolate ice-cream or vanilla with chocolate sauce, strawberry shortcake, brownies.

I have been considering consulting a nutritionist about Sam's diet to see if any vitamins are recommended.

What Works Well for Sam

Housing: Sam currently lives with us in our home in (name of city). The first floor has a very open floor plan that is easily accessible to Sam. He has access to his bedroom, the bathroom, the living room where he keeps his computer, the family room, and the kitchen. Sam enters the house through the patio door in the back. The patio door is flush with a deck and the deck is ramped at the side of the house. The disadvantages are that there are no sidewalks in our immediate neighborhood so that when Sam goes out he is in the street. Fortunately the streets are very quiet. We are within "wheeling" distance of some shopping, but again there is a problem with sidewalks and some very busy streets.

For the immediate future we would like to see Sam finish the vocational program at (name of school), which will take 2 to 3 years, and then give a fair chance to the work program that they and the Department of Rehabilitation Services come up with for him. I would say a fair chance would be at least a year. In order to do that Sam would have to remain in the (name of area). The people I have listed as Advocates above have said they would be willing to help make arrangements for such a transition period. The most logical thing, it seems, would be to hire full-time help to live with Sam in our home in (name of city). Optimally Sam would qualify for the Illinois Supported Employment Program, which would place him in a public setting. At that time the Department of Rehabilitation Services or Access Living could aid in finding suitable living arrangements. Access Living specializes in setting up supported living in private settings or group home situations. Since this would be a large part of Sam's social life, we would suggest a group situation as best, but he would be able to make that determination. The group situations are never larger than 16 people so as not to lose SSI support. They are federally subsidized. The Ray Graham Association in Elmhurst and ELIM Christian School in Palos Heights, Illinois offer some similar arrangements and Miseracordia in Chicago has a project in the planning stages, but I have not investigated these programs thoroughly yet. These organizations also have programs for people on public aid.

If this type of program did not work out for Sam, and Sam's sister or another relative would want to house Sam, then we would want the trust to pay for any equipment, remodeling, or additions that would be needed to make the facility accessible to Sam and comfortable for the relative.

Another alternative would be for Sam to live on our property in (city and state named) with full supervision. Wisconsin also has state employment programs for the disabled. One program is run by The Opportunity Center in Madison, Wisconsin. I will investigate this more thoroughly in the next year. I want Sam to try every resource available to him because I feel some kind of employment would make his life more meaningful. If these resources do not work out we feel we have funded this trust to the extent that it would cover Sam's living expenses and full-time care for Sam in (city name). In such an instance, Sam's sister or one of the Advocates would need to supervise this situation on a regular basis. They could do that personally or hire someone from (city name) to do it; probably a combination of these two options would be best. The following people would be good sources of information about (city name) and are well acquainted with Sam. [A list of three couples, their addresses and phone numbers follows.]

Adaptations: Sam's living space does not have to be large, but it needs to be large enough and open enough to accommodate his wheelchair. He needs a private bedroom but not a private bath. He needs enough living space for a T.V. and a computer. His physical disabilities prevent him from using a kitchen, so that does not have to be accessible; in the bathroom, only the shower needs to be accessible. Someplace, bed or bathroom, needs a mirror so that he can see himself. The entrance to the living quarters needs to be wheelchair accessible.

Favorite Possessions: Sam's favorite possessions that he should be able to keep with him wherever he lives are: a remote control T.V.; his Apple computer, or whatever computer he has at the time; his Walk-man radio with preset stations; his speaker phone; his Wedge pillow; his shower chair; his Bulls hat; his books about space exploration and the solar system.

Sam is not very fussy about community. He likes to go to shopping centers and out to eat. He enjoys going to the movies and to the Bulls games, but other than the Bulls he is not very interested in sports. I would hope that any community in which Sam lives would have some type of recreational program available because that is an excellent source of social contact for him and because sometimes he needs motivation in this area.

Daily Living Skills

Current Activities: Sam is in school full-time and in the summer goes to day camp through North Shore Suburban Special Recreation Association (NSSRA). In his free time he likes to watch TV and play games on his computer. He is interested in anything about space. He likes to visit in the neighborhood and go to shopping malls. He loves the beach, but it is very hard to take him there now. He actively participates in recreation programs run by NSSRA. For example, this summer he is attending day camp; a Thursday night sports camp; Friday Night Comrades, which is a group outing in the community or just hanging out with friends; and a sailing field trip.

Monitoring: Sam needs help with all physical activities. He is totally dependent for self-care skills, all domestic activities, and transportation. Although he can maneuver his wheelchair himself, sometimes he likes help in tight situations. Socially he is very independent and self-confident.

Caregivers' Attitudes: We would want any caregiver to keep Sam reasonably clean and physically presentable. His relationships and social skills are appropriate, and we wouldn't expect a caregiver to have to be involved in these areas unless Sam asked for advice. We would expect any caregiver to be honest, compassionate, and amiable. A high energy level also would help!

Self-esteem: Sam has an outgoing personality and a good sense of humor. He is very adaptable and gets along in most situations. He is very self-confident and actually proud of being handicapped most of the time. He says he will fight for the rights of the handicapped.

Sleep Habits: Sam requires 8 to 9 hours of sleep a night. He prefers to stay up late and sleep late, so he gets to do that on the weekends. During the week I try to have him in bed by 10:30. He sometimes has trouble falling asleep, so I try not to give him any

Coke in the evening. He is very good about just lying in bed until he does fall asleep.

Sam sleeps on his stomach with a couple of cloth diapers folded under his face instead of a pillow. He likes to sleep with socks on because his feet get cold; he likes his feet tucked in. He likes his arms pulled up above his head. If he wakes up in the middle of the night, he usually needs a new diaper under his face because he has drooled too much, his feet covered, or his arm (right) pulled up.

Because Sam likes to sleep late, I don't get him up until the last minute. I usually get him up about 6:00 and change and dress him on the bed. Then I put him in his wheelchair and feed him right away, which only takes about 10 minutes. Then I brush his teeth and wash his face. The bus picks him up at 7:10. He "wakes up" during the half hour bus ride to school.

Personal Finances: Sam would need a lot of guidance with personal finances, as he has never had his own resources. He understands the basics of banking, credit, bill payments, etc. but has not had much practical experience in these matters. Also, Sam is not physically capable of signing his name by himself. I have always helped hold a pen in his hand and guided it with him.

Allowance: Sam is very capable of handling a personal allowance on his own. We would expect him to use this for personal entertainment and extras like going to a movie, out to eat, buying new computer games, books and magazines, candy, some special or novelty piece of clothing, gifts for relatives or friends on birthdays, Christmas, etc., special outings to a sports event or concert.

At this time these things are paid for by us. Sam is pretty active in special recreation programs. Excluding those programs, Sam spends about $50.00 a month on luxuries.

Education

Sam's school placement has been determined by NSSED (North Suburban Special Education District). This is a cooperative program that both (names of two nearby towns) belong to. We have had a very good relationship with it, and they have been responsive to us.

Schools Sam has Attended: [A list of six schools, their addresses, and the dates Sam attended them is included.]

Academics: Sam's academic skills are very poor. He functions at the 2nd to 3rd grade level in reading and math, but his verbal comprehension is much higher. He has a lot of learning difficulties and problems with memory retention. He is also somewhat immature and had taken a very casual attitude toward school, although he made great strides in these areas this year. He is especially interested in working with computers and works very hard on this subject. He is finally beginning to show some real pride in his work. His social maturity has also improved dramatically this year.

Emphasis: Sam has just started some vocational classes this year and will continue with that program for the next 2 years. He became a client of DORS this last semester, and they will try to assist with some vocational placement. The goal is to see if Sam could do some data processing; he is very motivated to do this.

Integration: All of Sam's basic academics have been in self-contained classes of the physically handicapped program. Some of these classes have also included kids identified as developmentally delayed and multiply handicapped. In the younger grades he was mainstreamed for classes like art, music, social studies, and science. He enjoyed these classes, and they helped tremendously with his social skills. Sam learns best in small groups or one-on-one situations. I would expect that (school name) will continue this type of program with Sam to finish up his academics and then concentrate on vocational skills.

Leisure and Recreation

Structured Recreation: Most of Sam's structured activities are programs conducted by the North Suburban Recreation Association. They run a summer day camp program that Sam has attended since he was 3 years old. During the winter they also run programs like teen clubs, bowling, swimming, special field trips. Sam enjoys participating in these programs because they allow him to spend time with his peers without parents around. The adults who run the programs are young enough to seem almost like peers to Sam, and Sam has always related well to them. Sam also enjoys spending time with and helping younger kids. He gets a chance to do this at summer camp.

Sam has also been a part of a Special Education Floor Hockey team and has attended dances, plays, and other programs at his school. He views these activities mainly as social. He loves to dance and has no inhibitions about it. He is also self-confident about going places on his own. Sam has also attended (camp name), a privately funded overnight camp for physically disabled kids. [The camp address is listed.]

Unstructured Activities: Sam's main form of entertainment is the TV and his computer. He likes games he plays on the computer but will also work at copying things into the computer just to improve his skills. Sam loves the Bulls and will watch wrestling or football on TV but doesn't have an interest in any other sports. Sam likes video games but it is hard for him to work most of them. He even enjoys watching someone else do it. Sam likes to go to movies. He likes action films and is fascinated by animation and special effects more than story. He also loves comedy. Sam likes to swim but is hard to get into a pool. He uses an oversized inner tube that he hangs onto; he needs someone to stay with him.

Religion

Faith: Sam was baptized at (name of church) in (name of city) on (date). He currently is a member of (name and address of church). He has attended Sunday School and services there in the past but currently goes very rarely.

Sam is acquainted with Rev. (name). His phone number at the church is (phone number). The Reverend has always been very receptive to Sam. Sam has been made to feel very welcome at church, but it is a very small facility and not easily accessible. Sam has resisted participating in church at this time but does have a background that may be a good source of social interaction and support for him in the future.

Rights and Values: Sam should be kept free from harm, physical restraint, isolation, abuse, and excessive medication.

With the guidance and advice of the trustees and advocates, Sam should be given the freedom to decide where he wants to live and work and under what circumstances. Sam should be encouraged to give input into decisions that are made about his lifestyle.

Sam should be provided with age-appropriate clothing, and his appearance should be well-groomed; clean, shaved, and hair cut. His surroundings should be pleasant and sanitary. Any caregiver should demonstrate respect and caring for Sam and refrain from using demeaning language. Sam should be allowed as much privacy as he wants and be given respect for his personal possessions.

General Comments

Once Sam has completed the vocational training program at (school name) and participated in a work program, both we and he will have a better idea of what kind of work program he will be capable of. Our hope is that he will be capable of placement in a public setting, but we realize that this would probably have to be some type of supported work program and that he would not be capable of a full-time position because of his physical limitations. Things like toileting, positioning, and eye strain will be a problem for him for extended periods of time. We do feel that some type of employment is important for Sam's sense of well-being and will also be important for him socially.

In Sam's work situation and private life we would wish for the least restrictive environment possible given his severe limitations. We are in the process of exploring alternate living arrangements now and will keep a file on this in Sam's file drawer. I will be updating this letter with specific suggestions as I discover appropriate options. Our plan is to continue to keep Sam at home until he finishes the vocational program and then to explore various living options. We feel that emotionally he would benefit from some form of independence and that socially a group situation might be best for him. His personality is such that he could easily fit into a variety of situations as long as his physical needs were taken care of.

It is our intention in setting up this trust that Sam be taken care of in the least restrictive environment that he can handle and that is emotionally and physically supportive to him. We want Sam to have input into decisions that are made concerning his living arrangements and how funds from the trust are spent. We have picked the trustees and advocates for their competence and their concern for Sam and his well-being. We have made his sister a joint trustee so that she can be as involved as she wants to be in helping make decisions. We have assigned advocates who are willing to give advice and, if needed, to help carry out the trust with visits to Sam, overseeing living arrangements, paying bills, etc.—whatever the trustees might like help with.

It is our intention that the trust funds be used to enhance Sam's life and give him as much financial assistance as he needs to live comfortably. If no other living arrangements are suitable to Sam and he has no other means of satisfying his financial requirements, it is our feeling that we have funded the trust so that Sam could be provided for in a private home in (town name) with live-in assistance. Should it become obvious that Sam will never use the property in (town name), then we would expect the trustee to make a decision as to whether to dispose of it or not, to the trust's benefit, according to the provisions stated in the (trust name). If (current trustee's name) is not then the acting trustee, he would be an excellent advisor on this subject.

If some other private situation should arise that Sam would prefer, such as living with a relative or his sister, we would want the trust to cover any expenses incurred in making the facility accessible for Sam and convenient for caregivers. Some examples would be: ramping; remodeling a bathroom to make it accessible; building a room addition to give Sam his own room; installing an intercom system that Sam could work; purchasing special furniture and equipment that works well for Sam or makes things convenient for the caregiver (examples would be Sam's high bed, a remote control TV, a remote control system for other electric appliances like lights, radio, etc.). If Sam is living with someone, we would expect him to pay rent and the caregiver to receive financial support and respite care.

Sam should have at his disposal a van with a lift so that he can be transported by the caregiver and visit friends or relatives; and so that anyone visiting Sam can take him out.

We would expect the trust to pay for special recreational activities for Sam. Some examples would be: tickets to a sporting event or concert; dining out with friends or relatives occasionally; participation in special recreation programs similar to those he currently joins now with NSSRA; going to a movie. We also would like the trust to pay for any vacation, within normal bounds, that Sam could take and the transportation and expenses of his traveling companion/caregiver. We would like to have Sam keep in contact with his relatives. If it would make more sense for them to visit him, and they are traveling with the express purpose of visiting Sam, then the trust may pay their traveling expenses. If there are any special devices that could be purchased to make an activity that Sam is interested in possible for him—such as a specialized life jacket, adaptive seating in a boat or sled, adaptive equipment like a fishing pole he could hold—and they are not covered by insurance, then we would want the trust to pay for them.

We expect the trust to pay the advocate and the trustee for their time involved in administering the trust and for any time they spend following up on what is being done—for instance, if they have to travel to check up on Sam or his caregivers, or research options for Sam, etc. It is also acceptable for the trust to pay the spouses of the trustee or advocate for any assistance they give in administering the trust or any visits they make to Sam.

Finances, Benefits, and Services

Assets: At this time Sam's only asset is his savings account (Account number and amount—name address and phone number of bank)

Cash Income: Sam has no income at this time, although we have recently applied for Supplemental Security Income.

Services or Benefits: Sam is in the special education program at (name of school).

Sam recently became a client of the Department of Rehabilitation Services. His representative is (name). Initially his contact with them will be through (school name).

Sam is currently part of the Audio Visual Service at the (name of local library), through which he receives Talking Books on cassette tapes.

Expenses: Currently most of Sam's expenses are paid by us. When he receives Supplemental Security Income, he will begin paying rent to us. His education and vocational training are covered in the public education program he is receiving at (school name). His health care is covered under my husband's insurance program. His clothing, food, and most recreational activities are paid by his parents.

The Paper Trail

Will: Sam does not have one at this time.

Safe-deposit Box: None for Sam. We have a safe-deposit box that we keep in the basement, on top of the file cabinet, in which are kept birth certificates, titles, school degrees, etc.

Life Insurance: None

Burial Papers: The cemetery certificates will be in our safe-deposit box. No other arrangements have been made at this time.

Health Insurance: [The name, address, phone number, plan number, and name of the company through which insurance is held is listed.]

There are two different forms. The medical coverage is with (name of company). The dental coverage is with (name of company). As long as my husband is alive, Sam will be covered by our insurance. After my husband's death, the insurance will remain in force for 6 months. It can then be renewed for only 2 years. Copies of these policies are in the file cabinet in our bedroom in the top drawer under the heading "Insurance."

There is a $300 yearly deductible ($500 for retired employees); then the medical plan pays 90 percent of the excess reasonable and customary medical expenses incurred for the year. After the insured has paid $2,000 of the excess, excluding the deductible, the policy pays 100 percent. This policy covers physical therapy, speech therapy, vision therapy, occupational therapy, chiropractic care, and ambulance service when the above are rendered by licensed or certified professionals or on outpatient basis. They do not cover routine eye care, physicals, private rooms in the hospital or TV, nonprescription drugs or preventative medicines, etc.. The insurer has been very good about covering devices, such as the wheelchair at 80 percent, as long as we have a doctor's prescription. The dental insurance covers all cleaning and most reasonable procedures at 80 percent.

Employee Savings Plans: None

Income Tax: None

Real Estate: Current real estate documents concerning our house and property in (name of state) are in our file cabinet in the bedroom. This would include real estate taxes, plat of survey, mortgage papers, etc. The deeds or certificates of title are in the safe-deposit box in the basement. We also have an appraised listing of some of our more valuable possessions in the file cabinet in the bedroom under "Valuables." Receipts for improvements and maintenances are in the file cabinet in the basement.

Advisors: [A list of the names, addresses, and phone numbers of the family's tax, financial, insurance, trust, and legal advisors is included.]

Other: All of Sam's current school, medical, recreational, and dental records are in the file cabinet in our bedroom in the top drawer under the corresponding headings. All past records are in the file cabinet in the basement in the top drawer under the corresponding headings. Also in that drawer are the manuals and warranties on any of Sam's equipment; information on housing and work programs; information I've collected on devices or equipment that have been used for Sam or might someday be useful; information on recreational programs; and any other resource materials I have saved. The second drawer of the file cabinet contains manuals and warranties for our property, receipts for home improvements, and other household information. The bottom two drawers contain copies of our income-tax records and related materials. All Sam's valuable papers such as birth certificate, baptismal records, social security papers, etc. are in the safe-deposit box kept on top of the file cabinet.

Sample Letter for Intellectual Disability

This Letter of Intent is written by William E. Smith and Wendy H. Smith, the parents of James A. Smith.

To Whom It May Concern:

Information about Father:
William E. Smith
(Social Security Number)

(Mr. Smith's current address, including county)

(Mr. Smith's current home and office phone numbers)

Date of birth (including county and state)

Raised in _____, _____

Roman Catholic religion

Caucasian Race

Blood type - A positive

One half-brother —(name)

U.S. citizen

Married to Wendy H. Smith on (date) in Chicago, Illinois

4 children (names listed)

Father: (name, address and phone number)

Mother: (name, address and phone number)

Stepmother: (name, address and phone number)

Half-brother: (name, address and phone number)

Information about Mother:

Wendy H. Smith

(Social Security Number)

Current address, including county

Current phone number including area code

Date of birth (including county and state)

Raised in _____, _____

Roman Catholic religion

Caucasian Race

Blood Type - unknown

No siblings

U.S. Citizen

Married to William E. Smith on (date) in Chicago, Illinois

4 children (names listed)

Father: (name, address and phone number listed)

Mother: (name, address and phone number listed)

Information about James A. Smith:

James is 5 ft. 10 inches tall, weighs 195 pounds, wears size 12 shoes, has a 36" waist, and wears large size shirts and coats. He is of the Caucasian race, has been baptized in the Roman Catholic Religion, has made his Communion, and has been Confirmed. James is a citizen of the United States. He was born on June 9, 1965, in _____, Illinois and was raised in _____, Illinois the first 19 years of his life. Since 1984, he has resided at the Somewhere, Illinois address.

Siblings: Marlene Smith (name address, phone number) Jeffrey E. Smith (name address and phone number)

Other Relationships: Walter Lock-Friend (name address and phone number)

Representative Payee: William E. Smith
                            Wendy H. Smith

Successor Payee: Jeffrey E. Smith

Power of Attorney: None, other than parents as guardians.

Final Arrangements: Burial in a Catholic cemetery. (Parents' intention is to purchase a family plot to include James.) There should be a Catholic church service. A monument should be erected. No cremation.

Medical History: Onset of petit mal seizures was at 3 years of age. Hospitalization and testing took place to try to find an appropriate drug and treatment program. Various drugs were tried over several years. They were not successful because James couldn't tolerate the particular drugs or their side effects. Grand mal seizures were first noticed at age 15. Tegretol was introduced at that time and is still being used as the drug of choice. Between the ages of 15 and the present time, attempts have been made to introduce additional anticonvulsants and/or behavior-modifying drugs. The additional attempts were not successful. In the years ____, ____, and ____, tests were administered to evaluate and review his current neurological, physiological, and behavioral status. The University of Chicago and Northwestern University administered EEG's (1 1/2 hour, full night's-sleep, and 6-hour-daytime-awake EEG) and an MRI test. Current drug program is to discontinue all other drugs except Tegretol and to raise its daily level to ____ mg/day. Tegretol is administered as follows:

[A chart showing James's medication schedule and dosages is included.]

James also is prescribed Maltsupex to counter a side effect of Tegretol. He receives __ tsp. dissolved in half a glass of water at bedtime. The Maltsupex relieves extreme constipation. James also receives the following liquid vitamins daily.

[A chart showing vitamins and dosage taken is included.]

The vitamins are needed to prevent a deficiency that causes severe cracking and bleeding at mouth corners due to long-term high dosage of Tegretol.

James has been tested for allergies since age 4. See attachment A for description of allergies and treatment on a monthly basis.

Functioning Level : Severely developmentally disabled; trainable level; I.Q. approximately 50-55.

Vision: Normal —does not use any eyeware.

Hearing: Normal

Speech: Verbal. Makes needs and wishes known. Uses words, phrases, and simple sentences. Uses a communication "break" card. Program was developed by a speech therapist. See attachment B. Program was recommended by Dr. _____,

Institute for Applied Behavior and Analysis, Los Angeles, California. Consideration is currently being given to the use of the facilitated communication program that uses the Cannon computer.

Mobility: Normal

Blood: Type not currently known - to be obtained at next blood test.

Insurance: See data provided. Upon death of father, all insurance coverage for James ceases. James would need insurance at that time. Plan to be developed by parents and/or others using the manual: "Health Care Financing for Severe Developmental Disabilities," by Arnold Birenbaum, Dorothy Guyot, and Herbert J. Cohen.

Regular Physicians: [A list of physicians, their addresses, and phone numbers as well as most recent fees is included.]

Previous Physicians: [The name, address, and phone number of James's pediatrician is provided.]
    Dr. _____ is deceased, but his records from birth to age 23 are kept at the offices of: _____.

Dental: [The name, address, and phone number of James's current dentist is provided.]
    James uses a removable partial-upper dental appliance. Expected life of appliance is 5 years. Molds of upper and lower teeth are located in fireproof cabinet containing James's binder. If Dr. _____ is unavailable, we suggest contacting one of the local university dental schools to obtain a reference to a dentist that serves the disabled.

Nursing Needs: James does not currently need nursing care.

Mental Health: James is currently not involved with any psychiatrist, psychologist, or mental health counselor.

Therapy: James has had an occupational evaluation performed by (name, address, and phone number).

It was their recommendation that he have periodic reviews and progress reports on an annual basis, or more often if the need is indicated, to be supportive of his other services or programs (vocational, recreational, residential, community, etc.)

Speech evaluation was performed but because the clinician was not going to be available, our intention is to pursue speech evaluation in Facilitated Communication or as part of the Continuance of Augmented Communication. Over the course of years, James has participated in speech and occupational evaluation and therapy programs. In the future, occupational and speech therapy evaluations, progress reviews, and/or therapy should be performed at the advice of a professional advisor or case manager. If certain devices or materials are suggested to assist James, they should be provided.

Diagnostic Testing: [A list followed of 14 individuals or testing organizations which performed diagnostic tests on James. Each one of these organizations' reports was bound in a binder as an appendix to this Letter of Intent.]

Genetic Testing: None

Immunizations: To be provided

Diseases: Chicken pox in 1969

Allergies: See attachment B

Other Problems: Skin irritation on either side of nose. Follow-up visit to skin specialist recommended. Condition less severe in summer months. At other times, an ointment such as (name of ointment) should be used.

Procedures:

- Check ears for wax buildup. Cleanse ears approximately every 3 months with peroxide. Can be done at home.
- Should be given a complete physical yearly. Remove wax at that time, if necessary.
- Toenails should be trimmed once a month.
- Can trim his own fingernails (with assistance) approximately twice a month.

Operations:

Tonsillectomy, 1970, _____Hospital
Myringectomy and tubes in ears, 1968, _____Hospital

Hospitalizations:

Tonsillectomy, 1970, _____Hospital
Drug testing and monitoring, 1969, _____Hospital

Birth Control: None

Devices: Uses a partial upper dental appliance (removable).

Medications:

1. Tegretol according to the following schedule:

   [Schedule shows times and dosages of this medication.]
2. Maltsupex: (Dosage listed) dissolved in a glass of water at bedtime.
3. Vitamins:

   [List of vitamins and dosages is included.]

OTC: The following are prescribed but are not paid for by public aid. Needed to prevent vitamin deficiency, which causes severe cracking and bleeding at mouth corners due to long-term high dosage of anticonvulsants. [The list is included.]

James needs to use a medicated shampoo (such as _____) to control a severe dandruff condition.

Monitoring: Medications listed above must be monitored.

Procurement: Someone must procure James's prescription, vitamins, and OTC medications for him.

Diet:

No caffeine products (chocolate, tea, coffee, or colas). Only clear soft drinks such as 7-Up, Sprite, etc. Food items should be low sugar, no preservatives or additives. Use cooked cereals, bran, oat, or whole wheat cereals and bread.

Except for items specifically mentioned above, a normal, well-balanced diet would be appropriate. Desserts should be fruit related. Muffins or donuts can be used as rewards after running exercise periods. Some exceptions can be made for "special" occasions or treats.

James enjoys almost all foods, but his favorites are cheeseburgers and fries, spaghetti, lasagna, pizza, fried chicken, roast beef, and blue cheese salad dressing. Strawberry cheesecake is a favorite dessert.

What Works Well for James
Housing

Present: James currently lives at home with his parents. He has his own room with the usual bedroom furniture plus an upholstered rocker. His room has calendars, program charts, and behavior management charts. He enjoys having stories read to him several times a week from his book collection in his room.

Past: James has always lived at home.

Future: Our choices for James's future housing are:
1. Supported living in an apartment or house with 24-hour coverage.
2. A group home with no more than 4 residents.
3. Housing owned by James's trust with 24-hour supervision.

James should live in an area that has established programs or provides access to reciprocal programs in other communities (such as SEASPAR, WEDSRA, a Place in the Sun, etc.).

Size: It is preferred that James live in one-half of a two-flat or duplex so that he has access to a yard. His unit should have 2 bedrooms that can be shared by James and up to 2 additional clients or staff. The building should be in close proximity to bus routes, work opportunities, and community resources. It should also be close to a running track James can use or a parklike area that has walking or running paths. This is necessary because James has been running 3 times per week, approximately 5 miles per time, since age 14.

Adaptation: The stove in the residence should have color-coded operating controls with electrical igniters that emit a "clicking" sound indicating flame ignition.

Favorites:
- An upholstered rocker
- T.V. set with a VCR to play video tapes
- An audio tape player
- Cross country skis and boots
- A large "bean bag" cushion with large support pillow and covers
- An AM-FM radio
- A storage cabinet or unit containing the following to be located in James's bedroom. This unit will be used to store: a library of picture books to look at and story books to have read to him, simple puzzles, coloring books and crayons, and arts and crafts materials
- Schwinn exercise bike kept in an accessible area and used on days when James doesn't run. Should be used in A.M.
- Schwinn conventional bicycle (no gears)
- A large inflated ball to be used to bounce as relaxation

- Softball and frisbee to be used to play catch with others

Community facilities that should be convenient:
- Family type restaurants
- Pizza restaurants
- Bakeries
- Fast-food restaurants
- Grocery stores—supermarkets and neighborhood markets
- Shopping areas and malls
- Drugstores
- Running track or park paths for running 3 times per week
- Facilities that provide programs and activities for people with mental disabilities
- Library
- Parks and/or recreation areas
- Barber shop
- Theaters and museums

Individual Program Plan:
- Behavior Management Program (DRO - use of penny holder and coins)—see binder for program.
- Behavior intervention procedures to be used when James is exhibiting irritability, agitation, and sensory or stress over-load. In a nonharsh manner, he should be told to go to his room and sit in his rocker. Using a timer, set an interval of time. When the time rings and he has regained control, he may leave his room and resume his activity.
- Behavioral charts to control outbursts of aggression. Use of coupons as incentive and reinforcement plan—see binder for program.
- Communication and/or break card—see binder for details.
- Vocational Competency Evaluation Report—to be added when completed.

• Facilitated Communication Evaluation and Report and device description will be added when available.

Current Activities: See summary and analysis of James's activities in binder.

Monitoring:

In order to help reduce James's hyperactivity, reduce levels of irritability, and to enhance the effect of his anticonvulsant medication, James engages in 3 early morning (before breakfast) runs per week. This activity was prescribed by one of James's previous neurologists. The runs should be conducted as follows on Sunday, Tuesday, and Thursday:

1. Run for a 10-minute-period
2. Take a 5-minute break, during which time he takes a drink of water or Gatorade
3. Run for a 10-minute period
4. Take a 5-minute break for another drink and to wipe off perspiration
5. Walk for 5 minutes to cool down

Because James is prone to seizures, he should use the following items:

1. Athletic supporter
2. Running shoes
3. Bicycle helmet
4. Visor (under the helmet)
5. Gortex running suit in winter months
6. Elbow pads

For self-help skill and domestic activity information, refer to the Summary and Analysis of James's activities in binder. James has had experience in using and paying for public transportation, but only in the company of his parents. James needs a program to reinforce his social and interpersonal skills when interacting with people across environments. James has utilized a chart that specifies self-help skills, striving for independence. Stars are used for a reinforcement on a daily basis.

Caregivers' Attitudes: We want caregivers to help James maintain set levels of expectation in his own personal cleanliness and grooming and the order and cleanliness of his environment. Caregivers should be kind and nonharsh, but they should expect James to comply with established behavioral requirements and see that he shares in chores and related activities. They should be firm but understanding. People that are easygoing and have a good sense of humor bring the most favorable responses from James.

Self-Esteem: The following statements can be used to keep him motivated, attentive, on target, and compliant:
"Good job."
"I like the way you're doing (or did) that."
"Much better, let's try that again."
"You worked very hard at that."
"Thank you for your help."
"Would you please do _____? Thank you."

When James has regained control of himself, say "Thank you, we can continue now."

Sleep Habits: James usually goes to bed at 10:00 p.m. and rises between 6:30 and 7:00 a.m. He usually sleeps all night except when he wakes to use the bathroom. Sometimes after a particularly exciting day, he may wake up during the night and talk to himself for a period of time and then fall back to sleep.

Personal Finances: James needs total supervision of his money management. He is able to sign his checks, fill out deposit and withdrawal slips, identify money denominations, and carry out money transactions—with direct supervision—during activities such as simple shopping. James should have a savings account in a bank. He should be supervised to make indicated withdrawals for his allowance approximately once a week. James has an envelope with materials and stencils to help him fill out his banking documents.

Allowance: James currently gets $17 in coins (1 roll of quarters, dimes, and nickels) every month. His behavioral reinforcement program usually results in $40 monthly dinner expenditures for James and a staff person ($20 for dinner for 2 twice a month). James usually spends $10 per month for a haircut. Nonprogrammed entertainment such as movies should take approximately $20. James should receive $6 per month to be used to "save" for more expensive items or entertainments at a later date. James needs total supervision in the expenditures stated in this section. Treats that are used as reinforcement in James's behavior-management program (items such as mixed nuts, peanuts, sesame sticks, yogurt covered raisins, California fruit and nut mix, and pretzels) should be purchased monthly for approximately $10 to $12 per month. These items are best purchased in bulk food stores. Approximately $20 should be used to purchase ice cream cones, potato chips, and 7-UP used as reinforcement at the special events James attends. These reinforcements of snacks or treats are part of the behavior management charts covering behavior at swimming, basketball, ice skating, etc. Sometimes french fries purchased at McDonald's can be substituted. James's current usage of vitamins is costing approximately $35 per month. See Medical History section for details.

Name Brands: When replacing James's personal items, or when buying new things for him, only brand name products should be considered because of quality, durability, and longevity. James's size and strength and the "wear and tear" pressure he puts on things require good quality. For instance, buy Schwinn for stationary and conventional bicycles, Zenith for electronics, London Fog and L.L. Bean for outer wear, and Levi for pants.

Education

Schools: [A list of the schools attended by James, and the dates of attendance, is included.] James started in a preschool program at the age of 2 1/2. He progressed through various special education programs until he graduated in _____.

Current Programs: James is not currently enrolled in any educational programs.

Academics: James is considered trainable and has tested out at the kindergarten level in some academic skills.

Emphasis: All of James's education was in the area of special education, with only one year of vocational training prior to graduation. We would like to see James participate in a functional skills program that would review previous skills and teach new skills necessary for maintenance and survival across varied environments such as residential, work, community, and recreational.

Integration: James was not in any mainstream classes, but he was located in a self-contained classroom in normalized settings.

Day Program or Work

Present: James is not in any current day program or work situation. At home, with parents' supervision, James does the following: cuts grass with power mower, sweeps sidewalk, helps wash cars, takes out garbage, wipes and puts away dishes, unloads dishwasher. While shopping, James selects items, bags items, and carries the bags to the car. See "A Summary and Analysis of James Smith" in binder for more details.

Past: In James's last year at _____ High School he: unloaded dishwasher in cafeteria, stacked chairs on tables, mopped floors, put chairs in place, vacuumed carpet in girls' gym, and picked up trash outdoors on school grounds.

Future: Our objective is to have James placed in a supported employment position in the community following a vocational competency evaluation.

Assistance: James's placement in a supported employment position will likely require a permanently assigned job coach.

Leisure and Recreation

Structure Recreation:

- A Place in the Sun Special Recreation Program provides open gym, organized games, camping activities, parties and dances, vacation trips, and participation in community-based activities and outings. Usually takes place on one evening a week (Tuesday) and some weekends.
- Ice Skating lessons at local ice arena on Wednesday evenings.
- Western DuPage Special Recreation Association Swim Team participation one evening a week (Thursday) and whenever meets are arranged. James also participates in basketball activities on Saturdays.
- Friday night Special Recreation Program that includes dinners out, dances, parties, and community-based activities and outings conducted by South East Special Parks and Recreation.
- Periodic special events and activities on weekends, conducted by the above mentioned organizations.

Unstructured Activities: James enjoys going to movies he can understand, bowling, dances, riding his bicycle, engaging in simple arts and crafts, and cross country skiing.

Vacations: James's vacations have been with his family or special recreation groups. James has gone to Florida's Disney World twice, California, Ohio, Indiana, Michigan, Wisconsin, and other places that have vacation attractions such as theme parks.

Fitness: James participates in a one-hour-per-week fitness program sponsored by A Place in the Sun that is conducted by a Chicago Health Club fitness instructor. Parents oversee James's running program. See Monitoring section above for details. On nonrunning days, James rides an exercise bike for approximately 45 minutes to an hour.

Religion

Faith: James is a member of the Roman Catholic Church.

Participation: James has been involved in a SPRED program for approximately 15 years. See "A Summary and Analysis of James Smith" in binder for details. He does not now regularly participate. He attends SPRED masses about 5 times per year. We would strongly recommend he participate in a similar program if available because he enjoys the activity. We would not be opposed to James participating in other denominational religious activities because he likes to sing, and enjoys music and "hospitality" activities. Weekly participation would be recommended.

Rights and Values

We believe James should be accorded the following rights and values:

- To be free from harm, physical restraint, isolation, abuse, and excessive medication.
- To refuse behavior modification techniques that cause pain.
- To have age-appropriate clothing and appearance.
- To have staff, if any, demonstrate respect and caring and to refrain from using demeaning language.

Other

In our experience with James, we have found that he wants to comply and please the people he interacts with, but because of his autistic attributes, he appears to withdraw and be aloof. With gentle intrusion and persuasion and nonpushy or nonharsh tactics, you can generally get James to go along with almost anything. He would rather be involved (even from the sidelines) than be left behind to sit and be inactive. James always shows enthusiasm for activities such as gift buying for birthdays and holidays, gatherings of people to celebrate events, and involvement in preparing food, etc.

In the event James should exhibit irritable or disruptive behavior, causative factors may be known or unknown. Some of the tactics we have found to be helpful in the home or out in public are:

- Indicate to James that we see he is angry or upset and remove him temporarily from the particular situation for a short period of time (perhaps 15 to 30 minutes). After attempts have been made to "give James some space" by sitting in a room alone, standing outside, taking a walk, or listening to some music, and it appears that James is getting himself under control, James should be asked if he has himself under control and if he is ready to come back and join the activity he left. If he is in control, he should be allowed to rejoin.

Measures we have used with James at home to soothe him during periods of irritability or extreme excitement with hyperactivity or loud vocalization:

- Have James sit in his room in his rocker for a specific period of time measured by a timer.
- Taking a warm soaking bath for 45 minutes.
- Ride his exercise bike and listen to soft music.
- Use a vibrator on his shoulders, scalp, temples, and palms of his hands.

The above practices have been useful in resuming the ongoing caring relationship with James.

Gifts for James

At each observance of James's birthday and at Christmas, a gift should be purchased for him. An appropriate card should be purchased to accompany the gift. The card should be signed "From

Mom and Dad." The gift should be approximately $50 to $75 in value.

Sample Letter for Mental Illness

Written by: Gary and Susan Jones, parents of Lisa Jones

To Whom It May Concern:

The goal of the Jones Family Special Needs Trust is to provide our daughter, Lisa Jones, the means to lead a full and comfortable life during her lifetime. This Letter of Intent is a nonlegal document intended to supply information about our daughter in order to aid the trustee and other caregivers to make appropriate decisions as needs arise.

Information About Father

General Information:

Name: Gary Jones

Social Security No.:

Address:

Telephone No.:

Born: (date and place)

Languages:

Religion: Methodist

Blood Type: unknown

Education: B.A. Chemistry, 1944 (name of school)

Ph.D. Biochemistry, 1950 (name of school)

Employment History: 1949 Univ. of _____

1950-57 _____ School of Medicine

1957-91 Univ. of ___ School of Medicine

Marital Status: Married to Susan Jones (date and place); two children

Family:

Father: (name) died at age 71 of stroke and heart failure

Mother: (name) died at age 33 from consumption

Stepmother: (name) current address

Brothers: One brother stillborn

(name) died at age 56 of homicide; had depressive disorder in middle age.

Sisters: (name) died at age 61 of pneumonia

(name) current address and phone number

(name) current address and phone number

Information About Mother

General Information:

Name: Susan Jones

Social Security Number:

Address:

Telephone No.:

Birth: (date and place)

Languages:

Religion: Methodist

Blood Type:

Education: B.A. Psychology, 1948, _____ University.

Employment: Editor (name of company), 20 years. Retired at age 60.

Marital Status: Married to Gary Jones (date and place); two children.

Family:

Father: (name) died at age 70 of accidental fall. No medical problems.

Mother: (name) died at age 87 from heart failure. Had diabetes.

Brothers: One stillborn.

One died in childhood from convulsions.

(name) Current address and phone number.

Sister: (name) Current address and phone number.

Information about Lisa Jones

General Information:

Name: Lisa Jones

Numbers: [Social Security Number, address, height, weight, and clothing size are included.]

More Details:

Gender: Female

Nationality: U.S.A.

Race: Caucasian

Language fluency: English

Religion: Methodist

Birth:

Date: June 10, 1956, 4:00 p.m.

Place: X Hospital, Chicago, IL

Weight: 7 lb. 10 oz.

Childhood years: (name of city)

Sibling: Cheryl Jones (sister)
(address, phone number)

Schools: Lisa attended local grammar and junior high schools, followed by four years at (name of high school). She was a gifted ceramicist in high school. She had a one-woman show at a college and was offered an art scholarship that she did not take. She was always good in art and music; and was a very fine bass guitarist in high school.

She attended one year at (name of school) and the (name of school) before leaving (city name) for (city name). Then, she went to (state) where she worked and attended many community colleges (list of colleges). She became ill, came home, and years later completed a B.A. degree at (name of school).

Marital Status: Single

Other Relationships: Good friends in or near (city name): (a list of friends names).

Guardians: None

Final Arrangements: None. Preference is cremation; church service; burial of ashes at (name of cemetery), which is where her uncle is buried; no monument, just a simple plaque.

Medical History and Care

Diagnoses: Diabetes mellitus, bipolar disorder

Seizures: None

Functioning: Mild

Vision: Normal with glasses. Date of last eye test (Date)

Prescription: myopia, astigmatism

Insurance: Medicaid

Regular Physicians: Dr. X at (name of clinic) is her current psychiatrist, whom Lisa has seen about once a month during the past year. Lisa is charged $5 a visit. She is presently seeking a psychiatrist at one of the university medical clinics because she feels she cannot afford to pay the $5 per visit. The clinic does not want her parents to pay. She has lately been attended to for other illnesses by various physicians at the clinics at (names of hospitals); these have accepted payment from Medicaid.

Previous Physicians: Drs. (names) are internists who have seen Lisa for general care and diabetes mellitus. (Drs. names, addresses and phone numbers listed).

Dentist: (name, address and phone numbers).

Mental Health: While working and living alone in (city) at age 21, Lisa first exhibited psychotic symptoms that led to a diagnosis of schizophrenia. She returned home to (city) to recuperate and was seen by (Dr.'s name). After a few months she felt well enough to consider going back to (city) and received permission from her psychiatrist to do so, as long as she continued to receive psychiatric attention. However, several months later, she experienced another psychotic episode and returned home again. During the following four years, she was hospitalized on three separate occasions for episodes related to her psychiatric condition, which was now diagnosed as a manic-depressive disorder. Each hospital visit was relatively short, none longer than three weeks. She was seen by (Dr.'s names) during this period.

Over the past five years, Lisa has slowly improved and has not required hospitalization. She has primarily remained at home and has looked for employment or tried to learn a new skill that she hoped would lead to a job. More recently, she spent a period of approximately one year and a half attending classes at (name of schools). She received a B.A. degree in Theater Arts from (name of school) in 1989. She was supported by her parents all during this time. She felt confident that she could find a permanent job after graduation and went to (name of city) once more in 1990 to pursue this goal. During the 11 months she spent in (name of state), she found a few jobs that did not pay very well. She did not seem to be functioning well. She was not eating and sleeping well and, at the advice of a psychiatrist, changed her dosage of calming medicines and became very hyper and "on edge." In December, 1990, she agreed with our suggestion that she return to (state) to recoup from her endeavors and to take a fresh view of her vocational pursuits.

Lisa does not outwardly appear to be seriously ill. However, following the development of her psychiatric illness approximately 12 years ago, she has not been able to find a part-time or full-time job that has lasted for more than a few months. She did work at a part-time clerical job at (name of college) for a longer stretch because she enjoyed her work and her boss and co-workers were easy to work with. Lisa has had problems working at most jobs because she feels the boss and others do not like her or her way of working. She is often paranoid about this, and if we (or the psychiatrist) try to convince her otherwise, Lisa will often get very angry to the point of shouting. She has become very sensitive to the fact that she has not been able to work, although she wants to very much. She becomes agitated and angry if she believes anyone is questioning her about going to work. She imagines that relatives and friends deride her because she doesn't work and that even strangers on public transportation know she doesn't work and are talking about her.

The subject of work has to be approached carefully. Lisa should be allowed to bring up the subject first. She has tried so often to find a job. She looks for help-wanted ads daily in major and local newspapers and often applies for work she is not suited to or capable of. It has been a heart-wrenching experience for her to endure and for her parents to watch.

A major obstacle to finding and keeping a job has been a side effect of the drug, lithium chloride, that increases urine output, which causes her to go to the lavatory frequently. As a consequence, she becomes extremely thirsty and drinks gallons of liquids. She is also a heavy smoker.

Therapy: Lisa has not seen a physical therapist at any time. She saw occupational therapists while hospitalized. Lisa had a minor speech problem in elementary school and saw a speech therapist for a time. She has no problem with speech at this time.

Diagnostic Testing: We are not aware that this procedure has been performed on Lisa.

Genetic Testing: We are not aware that this procedure has been performed on Lisa.

Immunizations: She has received all of the standard immunizations.

Diseases: Lisa had measles, mumps, and chicken pox during childhood.

Allergies: As a child, Lisa suffered from allergies but seems to have outgrown them. She has some mild hay fever during the autumn ragweed season. She also has a mild allergy (unknown cause) at other times.

Other problems: Lisa has gotten kidney stones that were painful on two separate occasions. She apparently passed these stones in the urine in each instance. She also noted their presence five other times when they obstructed flow but were not painful. She feels she ought to avoid dairy products, since she finds that after ingesting them she seems to form stones. At least, she suffers discomfort.

Operations: After a bout of measles when she was 6 years old, she had abdominal pain that was diagnosed as appendicitis. An appendectomy was performed, but the removed organ was normal.

Hospitalization: When Lisa was 14 months old, she was dehydrated after a bout of diarrhea and had to receive fluids at (name of hospital). As an adult, she was hospitalized for psychotic episodes at (name of hospital). These were relatively short stays (no longer than 3 weeks each time).

Devices: Lisa wears glasses for her myopia.

Medications: Lisa takes Lithonate (dosage) to stabilize her bipolar disorder and Trifluoperazine (dosage), an antidepressant. Klonopin (dosage) and valproic acid (dosage) have been tried as substitutes for Lithonate, but they did not appear to be suitable replacements. She takes (dosage) of insulin each morning. Since her fasting blood sugar levels were very low, she has been reducing her insulin intake.

OTC: Aspirin has been useful.

Monitoring: No assistance from another individual has been necessary for the taking of medications or the application of ointments.

Procurement: Lisa usually obtains her own medications with her green card at (pharmacy).

Diet: Lisa is a diabetic and should watch her food intake with respect to time, amount, and kind of food, but she is not conscientious. Her haphazard eating habits were developed over years of an irregular lifestyle. She has no obvious dislikes with regard to food.

What Works Well for Lisa Jones
Housing

Present: Lisa is currently living with her parents. The greatest advantage is that she gets free room and board. Living at home, she gets a lot of care and attention. The disadvantage is that she is not becoming accustomed to living independently, which she will need to do when her elderly parents are no longer living.

Past: She has previously lived alone, as well as in a cooperative arrangement. Living alone is unsatisfactory for her since she does not eat well and her housekeeping is slovenly. She tried living in a group situation in _____. This was better in that meals were provided, but there were certain disadvantages such as irregular meals, a shared bathroom among too many residents, and some residents who had problems that were disturbing to Lisa. This was not a healthy situation, and Lisa was right in leaving. We were hoping that she could find another room-and-board situation, but nothing was available.

Future: No definite plans have been made for Lisa's future living arrangements. The best plan may be for Lisa to live in an apartment managed by a group such as Thresholds. A communal eating arrangement may be the best for her. An apartment of her own does not seem to be an easy situation to find.

a. A relative's home might be a satisfactory solution, although no particular candidate comes immediately to mind. All of her relatives live in (name of state), and Lisa is not particularly close to any of them. Moreover, since it is difficult living with Lisa, it would probably not be a good idea to have her live in the same household with a relative.

b. A group home could be satisfactory, but we are not aware of the availability of a particular home at this time. We have a few leads which we will investigate.

Size: A studio apartment may be the minimum size that would meet Lisa's requirements, while an extra room may allow for more general comfort.

Adaptation: No devices that assist individuals with limited mobility are needed.

Favorite Recreation: C.D. player, radio, ethnic drums which she owns, writing poetry.

Community: Shopping areas, library, public transportation.

Daily Living Skills

Individual Program Plan: Lisa is devoted to either finding a job or to preparing herself to be eligible for a particular position. She seeks out help wanted ads and goes to interviews but almost always finds the position impossible, e.g., hours, location, etc., and fails to follow through. Her mother feels that she is actually afraid to go to work. Looking for a job is a way she fills her time. When she is at home, she engages her mother in constant conversation to the point where both feel it cannot continue. At times Lisa realizes that talking at her mother every waking moment is not a good thing, so she tries to leave the house to "get out of the way."

Current Activities: On a typical day, Lisa looks into want ads and makes phone calls. Sometimes, she goes to community colleges and the local library to look into requirements and courses for the jobs she has found in the paper. For a while, she thought of taking courses to become a teacher in English as a Second Language, which was suggested to her by a friend's wife. She was also interested in printing, but she learned that in printing she'd have to repair the machine. She says she doesn't want to do repair work, so she has checked that job off her list. She enrolled in a Spanish class recently but subsequently dropped out. She has asked the schools she attended to send transcripts and made some effort to enroll in graduate classes in order to teach.

Speech or English: She tries to convince herself that she should do these things but finally admits she doesn't want to study, read, or go to classes. One of her problems with work is that she doesn't want to do menial labor. She is too intelligent for such menial labor, but she doesn't have the emotional stability to do the things she thinks she'd like to do.

Monitoring: Lisa could use help with self-care skills such as hygiene and dressing and domestic activities such as housekeeping and cooking. Her mother keeps after her to pick up after herself, but she cannot seem to do so.

Caregivers' Attitudes: Caregivers could emphasize general standards of cleanliness, appearance, and social graces.

Self-esteem: We try to praise Lisa when she does do something well and to downplay apparent setbacks or feelings of inadequacy. She has a problem with self-esteem. We seem to have to treat her as a young adolescent in this regard rather than as the 35-year-old woman that she is.

Sleep Habits: Sleep habits are poor, since she goes to the bathroom often. When she has little to do, she often sleeps during the daytime. This undoubtedly disrupts her sleep pattern at night. When depressed she sleeps long hours, but this may also be due to poor management of her diabetes.

Personal Finances: She does not manage money well. She tends to spend without budgeting and therefore needs to borrow before the month is up and her check comes from Social Security. Certain habits, such as drinking soft drinks and smoking, use up a large portion of her funds. She does try to roll her own cigarettes in order to save money. We have suggested that she keep records of her spending and budget her money.

Allowance: Lisa needs an allowance to keep within certain limits of spending. Clothing and other expenses are currently special requests. At the present time, we are providing her with clothes, shoes, and glasses. Whenever Lisa sees a doctor who does not accept Medicaid, we have paid her fees. When she lived in (name of city), we bought an old used car for her and paid for insurance and other expenses. We often sent money to her because she didn't have enough, although she received more aid from welfare there than she did in our state.

Plans for Further Education

Current Programs: Lisa has spoken of taking courses in English as a Second Language and/or in Speech at (name of university), but she changes her mind constantly.

Academics: Lisa's attainments in reading and writing are about a B-C grade at the college level. Mathematics was at a D level. In certain courses she did get A grades, but her average grade point in college was about 3 on a 5 point scale.

Emphasis: Lisa has said at one time that she was hoping to be able to teach at a community college. However, she seems to have given this up after some thought. Her mother thinks that this was her father's understanding and believes that her father does not understand Lisa since he does not spend the hours with Lisa that her mother does. When she was at (name of college) and did some practice teaching, it was too stressful for her and she quit school. She then went to (name of college) and got her degree in theater arts. In other words, she transferred colleges and changed her major in order to complete her B.A. A highly academic course is something she doesn't seem to be able to handle. We encouraged her to get a degree primarily because it would keep her busy. We were surprised and pleased that she was able to get her degree: this indicated that she could complete her work. We were proud of her achievement but do not think she should tackle any rigorous graduate program. She does not enjoy reading and does not read books or newspapers. Her attention span is short: she is impatient and cannot seem to concentrate on anything other than her emotional and mental state. Mother, at least, does not think she is suited to a full graduate program. At present, Lisa says she does not want to go to classes but may change her mind later. Lisa dreams of a better life, earning respect as well as income. We hope her aspirations may be realized. But, unless she changes drastically, we realistically think she should only take one course at a time so as not to cause her stress.

Integration: Lisa has been in regular classes and schools during much of her education. She may have a chance at succeeding in her goal, but it is a very small one. She should consider other, less stressful options. She is presently hoping to learn silk screening from a friend, so that she can design and print T-shirts to sell. Perhaps, if she cannot sell her shirts, she can find a job using this new skill. Lisa is really better suited to a job that uses her artistic skills.

Day Program or Work

Present: She is actively seeking part-time or full-time employment.

Past: The side effect of lithium therapy involving great thirst, drinking, and frequent visits to the lavatory is a drawback in finding a suitable job. She has been easily discouraged. Her tendency to paranoid thoughts also complicates relationships with a boss and fellow workers. In other cases, she may not have been as quick in performing the work involved, compared with others. She can exhibit low self-esteem as well as temper and anger.

Future: Lisa should continue to be supported in her efforts to find some worthwhile occupation, since she appears to be motivated to do so. We are willing to send her to whatever classes/schools she wants to attend, but we feel she should take one class at a time.

Leisure and Recreation

Structured Activities: She had an important role in a play several years ago that was reviewed favorably by [name of newspaper]. She is no longer very involved in theater, though she has tried to find jobs as a theater tech. She likes to hear both popular and classical music and goes to free concerts alone. She has friends with whom she plays music, but she does this infrequently. Her parents have invited her to the theater, but she feels her frequent need to go to the bathroom makes it impossible for her to enjoy a play.

Unstructured Activities: She enjoys writing poetry and has recently gone to poetry readings. She was to read her poems one evening but left without participating or telling anyone. They were unhappy about this. She likes to listen to taped music and the radio. She took a class in folk dancing and enjoyed it, but she has not done this recently.

Vacations: She would probably enjoy vacations with her best friend, an old grammar-school friend, whom she visited in (city) for a week a few years ago. Another friend has invited her to visit, and she would perhaps like to.

Fitness: Lisa has not been involved regularly with a fitness program but she ordinarily walks a great deal. She thinks nothing of walking what others would consider a great distance, e.g., several miles each way to and from shopping malls and train stations.

Religion

Faith: Lisa was brought up in the Christian faith. She is nominally a member of the (church). She has expressed some interest in several other religions, but lately seems to be interested solely in Christian churches.

She believes that guardian angels guide and instruct her through her dreams. She has considered and has tried suicide, but in the last several years she has felt that God doesn't want her to do this. Her mother is partly responsible for this change with long talks against suicide.

Clergy: Reverend _____ of the (church) knows Lisa and is concerned about her. She has not been visited by ministers of any other religion, but she would probably enjoy engaging in conversation with them.

Participation: She would probably enjoy a church relationship if it did not involve extraordinary demands. At the (church) in (city) a member said something cruel and nasty to her and she quit attending.

Rights and Values

1. Lisa should be free from harm, physical restraint, isolation, abuse, and excessive medication.
2. Lisa should have the right to refuse behavior modification techniques that cause pain.
3. She should have the right to have age-appropriate clothing and appearance.
4. She should have health-promoting staff demonstrate respect and care. They should not use demeaning language.

Other

Lisa has had a difficult life. She has had no easy roads to travel. Learning to cope with diabetes at age 16 was a terrible adjustment and limited her activities. Since she did well in art and liked music, she did not study academic areas diligently. She did not want to go to a chiefly liberal arts college. Later in life, she found that job opportunities in fields associated with the arts were limited. She had one exciting job in (city) with a documentary film house. She helped make some films that were prize winners. Because of her diabetes, she could not join the Peace Corps, something that might have allowed her to have a structured existence for a while. As with many of her peers, she tried cocaine and other drugs and feels that she got a bad dose one day and became ill when this experience was "coupled with bipolar genes." This may be an overly simple explanation for the genesis of her illness. In any case, she has suffered long, and we hope to be able to smooth her way as much as possible in the future.

Finances, Benefits, and Services

Assets: She has essentially no assets except for a very few personal belongings. She has sold many possessions such as television set, cameras, film equipment, etc. She has also donated film equipment worth almost $3,000, music and film to various schools and organizations.

Cash Income: She spent most of last year in (city) looking for a job. During 8 months of this period, she received $5,000 from Social Security. Her parents supplemented this with $8,103. This included $2,700 for the purchase of a used car, $824 for car insurance, and $562 for two round-trip air fares. Her earnings were probably about $500.

Services: Medicaid pays for her medications.

Gaps: Lisa needs more money for transportation to get health care at (clinic) and other facilities. She will try to get a special pass so that she can find public transportation at a discount. She should get supplemental funds for room and board to pay her parents so they can put this money into her Special Needs Trust. At the present time, she is getting a bare minimum from Social Security.

Expenses: From her Social Security income, Lisa pays for cigarettes, soft drinks, some fast foods, bus fare, other transportation, and not much else. Her parents have been paying for the remainder of her expenses: housing, board, clothing, education, and health care not covered by Medicaid.

Changes: Lisa's financial picture would not change if one of her parents were to die. When both parents are dead, her trust will become effective.

The Paper Trail

Will: The new wills of Gary and Susan Jones are being drafted by (name of law firm). The principal beneficiaries are the Jones Family Special Needs Trust and Cheryl Jones. Cheryl and the (bank) are likely to be the initial co-trustees of the trust. A reminder to Cheryl is to name some successor trustees after she becomes a co-trustee to assure continuity with people who are close to Lisa.

Real estate: Lisa does not plan to live in her parents' home after both parents are deceased. After her father retires, the family home may be sold and other plans will need to be made.

Advisors: (names, addresses, and phone numbers)

Other: Papers, such as the most recently completed application form and award letter from the Social Security Administration, are located in Lisa's personal file folder, which may be found among her personal effects in her room in her parents' home.

Conclusion

The process of writing a Letter of Intent can be as difficult as it is important. We hope the sample letters provided in this chapter have been helpful to you, and we wish to thank those clients who gave permission to reprint them. There were many other letters we could have selected, and those of you who were not contacted should not feel slighted. Unfortunately, this book must be finite in length, and many caring and helpful letters had to be omitted.

Advocacy and Guardianship

T HE SINGLE BURNING ISSUE IN VIRTUALLY ALL OF OUR CLIENTS' minds is to make sure their child's interests will be protected in the future. They know everything they do for their child, and they know that whatever they put in their Letter of Intent, whatever they do in terms of residential care, their child will need someone who will look out for his or her interests after they themselves are gone.

Many assume that this means a guardian must be appointed. This is a very controversial issue and ultimately a very personal decision to be made by the family.

Some of our clients shy away from guardianship due to the expense, court involvement, and the need to have their child declared incompetent before a guardian can be appointed. These clients prefer having friends and relatives act as *informal* advocates to deal with personal issues and a combination of trusts and representative payees to handle financial concerns. Other clients prefer the formal, legally binding relationships created in guardianship proceedings.

In this chapter we discuss the factors you will need to consider in making your decision—what guardianship is, what alternatives to guardianship are available, and how you can decide which option is best for your child. Regardless of what decision you make, whether to pursue guardianship or to go with something less formal, far and away the most important thing you can do is to choose the right people to act on behalf of your child.

> *Neither guardianship nor advocacy will work if the wrong people are selected, and in most cases either option will work if the right people are in place.*

The Advocacy Function

No matter how effective a life plan you may develop, no matter how clear your Letter of Intent may be, in practice the plan will work only as well as the people selected to implement it.

This is almost too obvious for words if you expect your child to live with a friend or relative after your death. In such cases the future caregiver is required to step into your role—to cook and clean for your child, monitor school and work situations, drive your child to favorite recreational activities and outings with friends, watch over his or her medical condition and, in the best of all worlds, keep an eye open for new opportunities that will enable your child to lead a happy and rewarding life. In short, the future caregiver is required to do everything that you do currently and hopefully nearly as well.

If you plan on a group or independent living situation for your child, an effective advocate can be equally important. Too many people become intimidated by the structure of the social service system, by the programs, by the professionals who always seem to know what is best for the people in their care. While these professionals are almost always skilled and good-hearted, it is important that your child have an advocate, someone who has the personal knowledge, deep concern, and firm willingness to pursue your child's best interests.

Professionals may not know your child as a person, and their recommendations may be based on what's best for people who have disabilities generally, rather than on what's best for your child particularly. The person whom you select to act as advocate should know your child as an individual—his or her likes and dislikes, needs and capabilities—and should be able to act on that knowledge and communicate it to others.

In a supervised residential setting your child is likely to come across many professionals with different ideas about what is best. Also, many of the people who help your child—the house managers at a residential facility, the supervisors at a sheltered workshop—may not be professionals.

A 2002 report by the Pioneer Institute for Public Policy Research reveals some eye-popping facts about Massachusetts (which is typical of many other states).

- Low compensation levels (often as low as $9.50 per hour) and a dysfunctional service delivery apparatus, together with the difficulty of the work have driven turnover among direct care workers up to nearly 40 percent and some vacancy rates close to 30 percent.

- 38 percent of hirees into direct care positions left within the first year.

- Low wage levels mean that residential facilities compete with companies like McDonalds and Wal-Mart for workers.

According to reports by other organizations, many states recruit workers from the ranks of welfare recipients. This means that minimally trained staff, likely to stay on the job only a few months, care for people who have highly individualized, and often very complex, needs.

Obviously, then, selecting a person to look out for the interests of your child after your death can be of vital importance, even if your child lives in a supervised residential facility. The person you select may be the one constant in your child's life, the one person your child will be able to count on when the need arises.

What will this person be required to do? Asking questions is a good place to start. If decisions made by professionals appear questionable, your child's advocate will need to ask about them, understand why they were made. If, after speaking with the appropriate people, your child's advocate is not convinced a decision is right, the advocate must be able to push the point and get the decision reversed. A master's degree or Ph.D. in psychology is not required. What is required is basic common sense and a good heart.

To consider a real life example, one of our clients had a relative living in a group home situation. All of a sudden the boy's behavior dramatically changed. He stopped eating and became very quiet. The advocate made inquiries, but the staff said they had no idea what caused the change. Only after relentless investigation was it discovered that the boy was being verbally abused by one of the residential staff members. In short order, the staff member was fired.

Friendship is another important role an advocate must be able to fill. People who have disabilities often find themselves in insular environments, living alone in apartments or with others who have disabilities, isolated from the community at large. It is the advocate who must *break down the barriers*—taking your child to church, the library, the zoo; extending invitations to home-cooked dinners and family and holiday celebrations. A good advocate will work to involve your child in life outside the residential setting.

Finally, as we have continually stressed throughout this book, your Letter of Intent must be revised and updated periodically, because your son or daughter is a living, changing person. As needs and desires change, as new options and opportunities arise, the life plan must be revised as well. After your death, your child's advocate will be the person to make these revisions.

Selecting an Advocate

As you have read the beginning of this chapter, you have likely had a number of thoughts. First and foremost you will want someone who knows and cares for your child. There is no substitute for love and commitment, and the people you select should have plenty of both.

As a general rule, we ask our clients to select three or four people who care strongly for their child, regardless of their geographic location. That way, if the person with the disability outlives the initial advocate, there will be other people who are prepared to act. Sometimes our clients prefer to have two or three people acting at once, perhaps because the advocates have different strengths and weaknesses. Maybe one of the people you are considering is good with money, while another is more likely to foster your child's social relationships. In such a case, you may want both of them acting, each using their strengths to offset the weaknesses of the other. Other clients prefer the advocates to act in succession, perhaps an older sister acting first and a cousin taking over when the sister is no longer able.

 TIP You will probably want to select at least one advocate who lives relatively close to your child. This will better enable the advocate to monitor your child's needs.

The following are some of the factors to consider in selecting future advocates for your child:

- Will one or more of the advocates be able to visit your child frequently and be available in emergency situations?

- Are they free of conflicts of interest and able to act in your child's best interest?

- Can they serve as advocate for a long period of time? If not, can they be trusted to select appropriate successors?

- Do the advocates have good common sense?

- Do they have experience in dealing with everyday legal and financial problems—bill paying, investments, insurance, taxes, and so on? Can you trust them to seek the aid of professionals—doctors, lawyers, and financial advisors—when needed?

 TIP Whomever you select, be sure to discuss your decision with that person in an open and direct manner. That way you can be sure the prospective advocates will be willing to act, and the advocates can gain a clear appreciation of what is expected. You will probably want to let the advocates read a copy of your Letter of Intent.

If you are unable to think of anyone to act as advocate, you should be aware that many areas have public agencies or nonprofit organizations willing to provide such services. You can locate the applicable organizations in your area through the Department of Health for your state, as well as through many of the organizations that advocate for the rights of people with disabilities. Some of our clients who do not have friends or relatives living near their child select a trusted friend or relative who lives outside the local geographic area to act as advocate, with the understanding that the advocate will make use of local advocacy organizations.

Finally, a recent innovation in the mental health field is to teach self-advocacy skills to adults with disabilities. There are groups that teach such skills in many communities, and you may consider encouraging your child to join one. You might begin by calling a local group you are affiliated with and inquiring about self-advocacy programs. One of the authors was pleasantly surprised when he ran into his older brother (who has an intellectual disability) at a National Convention of the Arc of the United States. Unbeknownst to the author, his brother was representing a state self-advocacy group.

Often self-advocacy works best in conjunction with other types of advocacy arrangements. You could appoint a friend or relative as advocate to help a child who has developed self-advocacy skills.

In the remainder of this chapter we discuss the concept of guardianship and alternatives to guardianship. Thus far we have used the expression *advocate* in a generic sense, to refer to the person who will look out for your child's interests after you are gone. Mental health professionals generally view advocacy as an alternative to guardianship. A *guardian* is a person who is appointed by a court to look out for the interests of your child; an *advocate* acts without court appointment. In the remainder of this chapter we adopt the more formal usage.

Guardianship

The law presumes that individuals over the age of eighteen are competent; that is, that they are able to make their own decisions about what is best for them in their daily lives. This means that, as a legal matter, no matter how severe the disability may be, your child will have the right to make his or her own decisions about the future upon reaching the age of majority. If your child is now over eighteen and if a guardian has not been appointed, your child already has that right.

This presumption of competence can be overcome only in what has come to be known as a *guardianship proceeding*. The rules governing such proceedings vary by state. Typically, the proceeding begins with a petition filed in probate court by a *petitioner* (often a close friend or relative of a person with a disability) requesting a finding that the person with the disability is *incompetent* and the appointment of a *guardian*.

133

Guardianship is a court-approved legal relationship in which a competent adult (the guardian) has a defined degree of legal authority to act on behalf of a person who is found to be incompetent (the ward). In general, guardians can be classified into categories according to whether they make decisions regarding the personal care of the ward (guardian of the person), the financial care of the ward (guardian of the estate), or both (plenary guardians), or whether their authority is limited to very specific types of decisions (limited guardian).

Guardian of the Person

Subject to the specific court order, a guardian of the person is responsible for the personal welfare of the individual with a disability. The guardian's responsibilities may vary greatly. A guardian of the person may have to make decisions concerning the ward's residence, medical care, education, vocational development, food, clothing, leisure activities, need for professional services, and so forth. If the ward has children, the guardian of the person may be given custody over them as well.

Some states require the guardian of the person to submit a report at least once a year. The report varies from state to state. Normally, the report will briefly discuss the following:

- The current mental, physical, and social condition of the ward.
- The present living arrangement of the ward, and a description and address of every residence where the ward has lived during the period of guardianship and the length of stay at each place.
- The medical, educational, vocational, and other professional services given to the ward.
- A summary of the guardian's visits and activities on behalf of the ward.
- An indication whether or not there is a need for continued guardianship.

- Other relevant information.

Although a guardian of the person may have broad authority, there are some decisions that are too personal for a substitute decision maker to control. For instance, the guardian generally does not have the right to draft the ward's will. In many states a guardian cannot consent to or veto a ward's marriage, though the guardian may be able to bring a suit in court to have the marriage annulled if the guardian can establish that the ward lacked sufficient mental capacity to understand what he or she was doing.

In addition, most states will not allow a guardian (without court authority) to consent to extraordinary medical procedures such as sterilization, abortion, organ transplants from the ward to another person, or experimental treatment. Furthermore, most states provide safeguards against involuntary commitments to a mental facility. These states allow wards to commit themselves voluntarily to mental facilities, but prevent the person with a disability from being involuntarily committed without a hearing. Commitments in these states are treated as *involuntary* whenever the person with a disability protests the commitment. In addition, in some states the guardianship order must specifically grant the guardian of the person the authority to admit a ward into a residential facility.

Guardian of the Estate

Subject to the specific court order, a guardian of the estate is a person or organization appointed by the court to care for, manage, and invest the ward's property, with the duty to protect and preserve the property. The guardian of the estate must apply the principal and income of the estate for the ward's care, health, and comfort. It is the duty of the guardian of the estate to use the assets only for the benefit of the ward and not for the guardian's personal profit. Unlike a trustee, the guardian of the estate does not have legal title to the ward's property; rather, the guardian has a duty to manage the property. The guardian of the estate should not commingle or combine the ward's property or funds with his or her own property.

The legal system has established a standard of competence for the guardian of the estate. To meet this standard the estate guardian must use reasonable care and skill in managing the ward's financial affairs. This means the government must exercise the care and skill that a person of ordinary prudence would exercise with personally owned property. If the guardian of the estate does the best he or she can do but still performs below the standard of a reasonable person, the guardian has breached the duty of reasonable care.

There is a major qualification to the standard of care. The ordinary prudent person may take risks with a certain percentage of his or her own assets, but the guardian of the estate is not permitted to take undue risks with the ward's property. The estate guardian is a conservator of assets. For example, a guardian may invest a ward's assets in U.S. treasury securities in order to earn income safely but typically cannot invest the money in assets such as a real estate limited partnership. The estate guardian might even breach his or her duty by investing the money in higher-risk growth stocks.

In most states a guardian of the estate can invest a ward's assets without prior court approval. If there is any doubt about the advisability of an investment, however, the guardian should seek court approval. Similarly, most states permit a guardian of the estate to pay the ward's ordinary expenses without prior court approval. Typically this would permit the guardian to pay for routine items such as rent, food, clothing, medical needs and reasonable entertainment. The guardian should obtain court approval for *out of the ordinary* expenses.

In most states, a guardian of the estate is required to post a *performance* or *surety* bond which is a promise by the guardian to perform responsibly. The promise is backed up by an amount of money that must be forfeited if the guardian negligently mismanages the ward's estate or steals the ward's property.

Certain companies or individuals (bondsmen) specialize in guaranteeing payment of these bonds (for a fee) in case of mismanagement or dishonesty by the guardian. In some states, a judge has discretion to waive the bond requirement. In these states, the bond requirement is usually omitted when the assets of the ward are minimal or the guardian of the estate is a bank.

Finally, most states require a guardian of the estate to submit detailed reports (called *accounts* or *accountings*) to the court regarding management and expenditures of the ward's money. This means that the guardian must provide a written statement of earnings, investments and expenditures, and explain how and why these transactions have taken place. Normally the account is submitted to the court once a year, although each state's requirement differs. Furthermore, some courts require oral reports to supplement the written reports.

 TIP Accurate record keeping is very important for a guardian of the estate. Make sure that anyone you are relying on to perform this role has the requisite skills and disposition.

Plenary Guardian

A plenary guardian is both a guardian of the person and a guardian of the estate. A plenary guardian therefore has decision-making authority over both the personal and financial aspects of the ward's life. A plenary guardian is subject to court supervision in the same manner as a guardian of the person or a guardian of the estate.

Limited Guardian

Historically, according to most guardianship laws, judges could either declare a person with a disability totally incompetent and appoint a guardian or dismiss the case and leave the person without the protection of a guardian. Over the last several years, largely through the efforts of advocacy groups for people with disabilities, the law has begun to recognize that competence is not *an all or nothing* proposition. People with disabilities need varying levels of help. A person may need help in one area of life, but not in another, and guardianship should reflect this reality, offering help where needed but leaving the person with a disability to handle matters within his or her sphere of competence.

Virtually all states have now enacted laws permitting limited guardianship, which is designed to be a less intrusive form of guardianship.

In general, a limited guardianship provides a more realistic alternative to the *all or nothing* choice between a full guardian or no guardian at all. Limited guardianship restricts the guardian's decision-making to only those decisions that the person with a disability cannot make alone. Thus, the person with a disability will have responsibility over the decisions he or she is capable of making, while the guardian will be able to assist when necessary.

In most states, unlike full guardianship, a limited guardianship does not involve a finding that the person with a disability is legally incompetent. The following examples will illustrate how a limited guardianship might work.

Mary has an intellectual disability and is forty-two years of age. Although Mary is noticeably "slow," she is very independent and stable and has worked at the local library, shelving books, for years. Mary is overweight and has very high blood pressure. After her mother's death, Mary applied to a local community facility which is near the library where Mary works. The executive director of the facility insisted that Mary's sister become a limited guardian for Mary because of Mary's high blood pressure. Because of Mary's independence, Mary's sister needed only the authority to consent to medical treatment. The executive director told the family that there had been an increase in medical malpractice lawsuits at the local hospital, and most doctors were insisting that a guardian sign a consent-to-treatment form for persons with intellectual disabilities.

The doctors feared that such persons might lack the legal mental capacity to give "informed consent." Mary was admitted to the community facility after her sister became her limited guardian with the authority to consent to medical treatment. Mary retains control over the rest of the decisions in her life.

The second example illustrates a limited guardian of the estate rather than of the person:

Dick has an intellectual disability and is thirty-five years of age. Dick lives in a local group home and works in the mailing department of a local insurance company. When Dick's uncle died, Dick inherited $50,000. Dick's mother met with mental health professionals, and they decided Dick could competently manage his weekly salary but needed a limited guardian of the estate to manage and properly invest the $50,000 inheritance. Dick's brother, a CPA, petitioned the court to be appointed a limited guardian for this purpose. The court granted the petition, and Dick's brother will manage the $50,000 for the benefit of Dick. Dick can still take pride in managing his own weekly salary from the insurance company. If the state where Dick lives allowed only the appointment of a plenary guardian, Dick's life might have been different. A plenary guardian would have total control over the $50,000 and Dick's weekly salary. In losing control of his weekly salary, Dick might also have lost some of his self-esteem.

Unfortunately, in some areas of the country the availability of a limited guardianship may be more theoretical than real. Although virtually all states have enacted limited guardianship statues, some judges are reluctant to grant limited guardianship, feeling that the ward either needs a full guardian or no guardian at all. This allows the judge to avoid making a more refined assessment of the ward's functioning level.

Where limited guardianship is available, however, it can be very helpful. It can be flexibly drawn, to grant the limited guardian authority only over those areas where help is required. This avoids the necessity of declaring a ward incompetent and leaves the ward with authority over the areas that he or she can handle. The following list describes some areas in which the limited guardian might be given authority:

- To apply for and enroll the ward in public or private residential facilities, educational programs, or vocational rehabilitation programs.

- To consent to medical and psychological tests and treatment for the ward.

- To examine confidential records.

- To attend confidential professional staff meetings.

- To apply for governmental funds and services for the ward, including:

   Supplemental Security Income (SSI)
   Disability benefits under Social Security
   Title XX Services
   Vocational Rehabilitation Programs
   Medicaid
   Developmental Disability Services

- To contract and make purchases over $_____ for the ward.

- To cancel or negate contracts and purchases made by the ward over $_____. (Note: This provision has questionable legal validity. However, it may be useful in dealing with someone who has financially exploited the ward.)

- To manage the specific properties of the ward.

- To rent or buy real estate for the ward to live in.

- To file federal and state income tax returns for the ward.

- To file or defend a lawsuit on behalf of the ward.

 TIP The attitude of the law toward limited guardianship varies from state to state and often from judge to judge. If you are considering having a limited guardian appointed for your child, you will need to consult an attorney familiar with guardianship in your area. In establishing a limited guardianship, you should carefully consider your child's abilities to insure that your child retains as much responsibility as is appropriate.

Private Guardianship Agencies

In some states a private agency can be appointed as guardian of a person with a disability. The laws in most of these states require that the agency be a nonprofit organization.

Most of these nonprofit organizations have professional staffs that can act as guardians and also advise family guardians. It is wise to inquire about staff caseloads (the smaller the better), frequency of visits to wards, amount of time spent with the ward and the residential staff at each visit, size of budget, and resources. Interview the staff to insure that they are caring rather than bureaucratic. Often the staff can answer questions about the local mental-health network; about residential, vocational, and school placement; and about finding an attorney to draft an estate plan with your child who has a disability in mind.

If you are considering such a private agency as guardian or future guardian for your adult child, inquire about its budget and ask for an annual statement. You want an organization that will remain solvent during the entire lifetime of your child. Many of these organizations are suffering from a critical shortage of funds and some have gone out of business. Despite the expense, it is best if the organization charges for its services and is not totally reliant on government and charitable funds, which may disappear.

A private, nonprofit guardianship service can act quite effectively as a coguardian or as an advisor, providing professional services and support to the person with a disability and the other guardian. These organizations, if permitted by state law, can be named as coguardians or successor guardian after the parent's death.

Public Guardians

If a person with a disability needs a guardian but has no one to assume the responsibility, the court will appoint either a public official or a public agency, such as a state-administered guardianship service. Often public guardians are guardians *of last resort* and provide care when the person with a disability has no relatives or friends willing and able to serve as guardian. Most public guardianship agencies have professional staffs and do not charge for their services.

Alternatives to Guardianship

Before you decide whether your child needs some type of guardian, you should consider the alternatives to guardianship. These include trust funds, representative payees, and citizen advocates.

Trusts

Trusts are a highly recommended alternative to a guardian of the estate. Trusts accomplish the same objective as the guardian of the estate, management of the assets of a person with a disability. However, trusts offer several advantages as compared to guardians of the estate.

Chief among the advantages is a solution to the *resource problems* that might jeopardize the person's eligibility for governmental aid. As we discuss in Chapter Four, to be eligible for many governmental benefits, your child's total assets cannot exceed certain stated maximum amounts. As discussed in great detail in Chapter Six, amounts held for your child in *properly drafted* trusts do not count as your child's assets for these purposes, while amounts managed for your child by a guardian of the estate are considered assets of your child. Accordingly, if you think your child may require government benefits after your death, it is better to leave money in trust for your child than to have a guardian of the estate appointed and leave money to your child outright.

Trusts offer other advantages over guardians of the estate as well. In order to secure proper financial management, it is not necessary to declare the person who has a disability incompetent. There is no need for the constant, detailed reports that a guardian of the estate must submit to the court. It is not necessary to get approval from the court for expenditures on behalf of the person. The posting of a bond is not required. (However, with a professional trustee there will be management fees.) The trustee will also have greater flexibility in investing than a guardian of the estate, and parents can select a trustee without the approval of the court. The trust document containing the duties of the trustee can be written to include all the preferences of the parents.

While family objectives will vary, normally a trust is a better alternative than a guardian of the estate. Further details about trusts may be found in Chapter Six.

Representative Payee

A representative payee is a person or organization authorized to cash and manage public assistance checks such as Supplementary Security Income and Social Security for a person considered incapable of managing the money. The payee is appointed by the agency administering the funds. If the parents want a particular representative payee selected, they must notify the agency. If the representative payee is not a relative, service fees may be required. The representative payee must keep an accurate record of all expenditures made on behalf of the person with a disability. The representative payee can be an alternative to a guardian of the estate when the only money the person with a disability receives is from the government or from a trust.

Many clients mistakenly believe that guardianship is necessary to manage government benefits. Representative payees are a recognized alternative for this purpose.

Advocacy

An advocate is like a guardian of the person, but without court authority or oversight. The advocate looks out for the interests of a person with a disability and provides personal attention, guidance, and representation. An advocate can be either a friend or relative of the person with a disability or a staff professional of a mental health agency. Some mental health agencies advocate or lobby for laws that will benefit people with disabilities as a group, while other agencies lobby for individuals and their families. Agencies that advocate for the individual can be helpful in advising the person with a disability and the person's family concerning services in the local area. Increasingly, private, nonprofit agencies are being created to provide individual advocacy support.

The advocate can help the person with a disability on almost any matter. However, unlike a guardian, the advocate cannot legally make decisions for the person. For instance, the advocate would be unable to contract for the person with a disability, invest money without consent, or sign a medical consent-to-treatment form.

In substance, an advocate is like a guardian in terms of commitment and desire to act on behalf of a person with a disability, but the relationship lacks the formality of guardianship, and the advocate lacks the legal standing of a guardian. The advocate's ability to act on behalf of the person with a disability therefore depends on the cooperation of the person as well as the cooperation of service providers.

Power of Attorney

A power of attorney is a written document by which a person (the principal) authorizes another person (the agent) to act on the principal's behalf. The power of attorney is a simple document to draft and can be written for almost any situation in which the agent acts on behalf of the principal, such as buying and selling goods or contracting with third persons.

In limited circumstances, a power of attorney can be an appropriate method for acting on behalf of a person with a mild mental disability who does not need a guardian. For instance, many parents of a child with a disability hold a power of attorney to fill out and submit tax returns to the IRS. The powers of the agent are limited to those specified in the document. For the power of attorney to be effective, the person granting the power (your child) must understand its nature and purpose.

The Social Security Administration does not recognize a power of attorney for purposes of managing government benefit payments. A representative payee is therefore required.

Making the Choice: The Pros and Cons of Guardianship

We have already stated our views about guardianship for financial matters. In general, we prefer the use of trusts for several reasons:

- Assets held in properly drafted trusts will not be considered owned by your child and therefore will not imperil eligibility for government benefits or be seized for cost-of-care claims by the government.

- Trusts involve less expense than guardianships. There is a bonding requirement, no need for court appearances, and no need to file accountings.

- Trusts tend not to be as restrictive as guardianships in terms of investment decisions (although, if you prefer to restrict the trustee's investment options, a restrictive trust can be drafted).

- Trusts leave the person selected by the parents with final authority over spending decisions.

Financial guardianship can, however, be beneficial in certain circumstances. For example, some people who have disabilities have significant assets of their own (perhaps from earnings, gifts, or inheritance) and may lack either the mental capacity or the inclination to place those assets in trust. Problems can develop if the person with the disability lacks the skill to manage the assets. Some parents prefer guardianship in such circumstances, although it may not be necessary if the person with the disability listens to advice from friends or relatives who do not have disabilities or is willing to put the funds in trust. (As discussed in Chapter Seven, *payback trusts* are generally preferable in such circumstances if the person receives needs based government benefits such as Supplemental Security Income or Medicaid.)

Financial guardianship can also be beneficial for people who prefer court oversight of their child's funds. Although the degree of judicial attention varies by state, it is thought that the existence of court supervision will act as a deterrent to mismanagement or even theft.

It is, however, possible to build protection against mismanagement or theft into a trust document. Many such methods are discussed in Chapter Six. For example, in many cases we suggest that our clients name two people to act simultaneously as trustee of their child's trust. That way, assuming both trustees are vigilant, each can monitor the performance of the other. Where trusts are sufficiently large, we frequently advise a co-trustee arrangement between an individual and a bank. The bank holds the funds to protect against mismanagement and dishonesty, and the individual, who knows the child best, advises the bank about how to spend trust money.

By far, however, the majority of people who seek our advice about guardianship are not concerned about financial matters. Rather, they are worried about the personal issues that will arise after their death or, sometimes, about the personal issues that may arise while they are living. They want to know who will look out for their child, making sure that food, clothing, and shelter are provided, that exploitation is avoided, that service providers do what is best.

We have already discussed the concept of advocacy. Though it lacks the *official* court-recognized status of guardianship, some clients prefer advocacy for at least two reasons.

First, as we will discuss in the next section, establishing guardianship necessarily involves a court proceeding that can be expensive. Many clients prefer to avoid involvement with the legal system when possible, particularly if an advocacy arrangement is workable.

Second, the process of establishing guardianship involves a finding of legal *incompetence* and a stripping away of the ward's rights to make independent decisions. If your child's disability is sufficiently severe, you may not find this to be important. Your child's ability to participate in decision making may be almost nonexistent. In such a case, appointment of a guardian may actually provide added protection for your child's legal rights.

However, in cases where the disability is less severe, parents often prefer having their child participate with an advocate in the decision-making process. This can, of course, be accomplished through guardianship as well. There is nothing that prohibits a guardian from consulting the ward, and the best guardians do so. However, where there is no immediate need for guardianship, many parents rely on an advocacy arrangement, counting on friends and relatives to look out for their child while recognizing that they (or the advocate, if they are deceased) can commence a guardianship proceeding in the future if the need arises.

Families that decide in favor of guardianship do so for a variety of reasons. Some parents want to make absolutely sure that the person whom they select to act for their child after their death will indeed be able to perform that function. Sometimes they fear that service providers will not pay sufficient attention to the advocate or that a guardianship proceeding will commence after they die and someone other than the person they want will be appointed guardian.

Many states permit parents who are guardians of their adult children to appoint successor guardians by will (guardians appointed by will are called *testamentary guardians*). Parents sometimes commence guardianship proceedings so they can have themselves named as guardians and thereby control the successor designation.

148

Sometimes it is even possible to have successor guardians named in the original court order appointing the parents as guardian.

Often, however, these same objectives can be accomplished without guardianship proceedings. The parents of an adult with a disability who has not been the subject of a guardianship proceeding can make statements in their wills or Letter of Intent that a particular individual (the person the parents select as advocate) should be appointed if guardianship later becomes necessary. (For example, guardianship could be pursued if service providers ignore the advocate's wishes.) Although these recommendations are not binding, courts generally pay considerable attention to the wishes of the parents. The person who is selected can petition the court (using the parent's recommendation as evidence) if it is later determined that guardianship is needed.

Parents sometimes pursue guardianship to be prepared for possible medical emergencies. For example, parents may fear that their child might become injured and will be unable to obtain aid from medical professionals because doctors, fearing possible malpractice claims, will doubt the child's ability to give legally binding consent to medical treatment.

It is unclear how legitimate this concern really is. Doctors will generally provide treatment on an emergency basis without consent where the need is clear. We are unaware of any instances where a person with a disability was denied *emergency care* due to inability to give informed consent, although it is certainly possible that this has happened. You may want to speak with doctors and hospitals in your area to gain an understanding of the local practice in such situations.

Moreover, most states deal with this problem through a legal concept known as *temporary guardianship*. Temporary guardians are appointed for a temporary period of time (usually not more than 60 days) for persons with disabilities who do not have permanent guardians, in order to handle emergency situations. If needed, the temporary appointment is established quickly and simply, by having a judge sign a guardianship order either with a shortened court hearing or without a court hearing.

It is, of course, possible that an emergency could be so severe that there is not time to obtain even temporary guardianship. One would expect that a doctor would do what was needed in such circumstances, though there are no guarantees.

Guardianship is sometimes obtained in order to enable the person with a disability to receive services on a nonemergency basis. Typically, this is the case when the services are particularly invasive. For example, a doctor may require consent of a guardian before performing nonemergency surgery. If you pursue guardianship at the behest of a service provider, you should make sure it is for the benefit of your child, not merely for the convenience of the service provider.

Obviously, the question of obtaining guardianship for your child is difficult and will depend on your own particular facts and circumstances. In advising our clients, we tend to adhere to the following guidelines (though of course there are exceptions):

- If the person who has the disability is under eighteen years of age, the parents are already the natural guardians under law. Legal guardianship through a court proceeding is neither necessary nor typically available. The parents name guardians in their wills to act if they die before their child reaches age eighteen. If the parents die, the guardianship is effective until the child reaches age eighteen, at which time the guardians can petition the court if it is determined to be necessary to continue guardianship during adulthood.

- If the person with a disability has reached the age of majority and the parents have not yet seen a need to pursue guardianship, we tend to set up an advocacy arrangement. (That is, the parents name friends or relatives in their Letter of Intent to act as advocates for their child when they die.) The child's inheritance is managed by trustees, typically caring relatives. Parents also include a statement in their wills or Letter of Intent expressing the parents' wishes regarding guardians, should guardianship prove necessary after the parents have died. We discuss the pros and cons of guardianship so that parents can decide whether they wish to pursue guardianship during their lives.

- If the parents have already been named guardians, we have them name successor guardians by will.

Special Considerations for People with Mental Illness

Special considerations are relevant for families with a child who has mental illness. In many such cases, guardianship may be inappropriate, and may not even be obtainable, because the person's condition is episodic.

As you are undoubtedly aware, many types of mental illness can be treated with psychotropic drugs, which reduce the frequency of psychotic episodes. Unfortunately, however, psychotropic drugs can have serious side effects. The drugs can cause uncontrollable pacing, shaking, anxiety, intense apathy, blurring of vision, low blood pressure, difficulty with concentration, and uncontrollable facial ticks. As a result, patients often go off medication, and psychotic episodes increase in frequency.

The problem is that it can be hard to get a patient to go back on medication. Hospitalization becomes necessary, but families lack the legal authority to require it.

- If you have been appointed guardian, your authority likely will not extend to admitting your child to a hospital without your child's consent. Many states require guardians to obtain specific court approval to hospitalize a ward, or to make decisions with respect to needed treatment such as psychotropic drugs or electroconvulsive shock therapy.

- Even without guardianship, *involuntary commitment* may be possible. However, the legal requirements for involuntary commitment are difficult to satisfy. Although the law varies by state, typically you would need to establish that your child

151

is a danger to herself or himself or to others by reason of mental illness, and that institutionalization represents the least restrictive alternative.

- Another possibility is to try and convince your child to enter a hospital voluntarily. However, this can be difficult. Moreover, even if you are successful, your child can simply decide to leave. Some states allow discharge to be delayed for a few days, and in some cases it may be possible to convert the commitment into an involuntary commitment, but in most cases your child will have the ability to simply check out of the hospital.

Some states have dealt with this problem by permitting a person with mental illness to prepare a document appointing an agent to make treatment and commitment decisions if the person suffers an episode. The form is signed while the person is competent, and becomes effective if the person is unable to make rational decisions.

The Illinois statutory form is below. The form permits the agent to commit the person for up to 17 days. The person completes the form by filling in the blanks, signing in front of witnesses and initialing where appropriate.

 TIP If your child has mental illness and lives in a state that permits your child to prepare a Declaration For Mental Health Treatment, encourage your child to sign the document.

DECLARATION FOR MENTAL HEALTH TREATMENT

I, _____, being an adult of sound mind, willfully and voluntarily make this declaration for mental health treatment to be followed if it is determined by 2 physicians or the court that my ability to receive and evaluate information effectively or communicate decisions is impaired to such an extent that I lack the capacity to refuse or consent to mental health treatment. *Mental health treatment* means electroconvulsive treatment, treatment of mental illness with psychotropic medication, and admission to and retention in a health care facility for a period up to 17 days.

I understand that I may become incapable of giving or withholding informed consent for mental health treatment due to the symptoms of a diagnosed mental disorder. These symptoms may include: _____

PSYCHOTROPIC MEDICATIONS

If I become incapable of giving or withholding informed consent for mental health treatment, my wishes regarding psychotropic medications are as follows:

_____I consent to the administration of the following medications:

_____

_____I do not consent to the administration of the following medications:

_____

Conditions or limitations:

_____

ELECTROCONVULSIVE TREATMENT

If I become incapable of giving or withholding informed consent for mental health treatment, my wishes regarding electroconvulsive treatment are as follows:

_____I consent to the administration of electroconvulsive treatment.

_____I do not consent to the administration of electroconvulsive treatment.

Conditions or limitations:

_____

ADMISSION TO AND RETENTION IN FACILITY

If I become incapable of giving or withholding informed consent for mental health treatment, my wishes regarding admission to and retention in a health care facility for mental health treatment are as follows:

_____I consent to being admitted to a health care facility for mental health treatment.

_____I do not consent to being admitted to a health care facility for mental health treatment.

This directive cannot, by law, provide consent to retain me in a facility for more than 17 days.

Conditions or limitations:

_____

SELECTION OF PHYSICIAN (OPTIONAL)

If it becomes necessary to determine if I have become incapable of giving or withholding informed consent for mental health treatment, I choose Dr. _____ of _____ to be one of the 2 physicians who will determine whether I am incapable. If that physician is unavailable, that physician's designee shall determine whether I am incapable.

ADDITIONAL REFERENCES OR INSTRUCTIONS

_____

Conditions or limitations:

_____

ATTORNEY-IN-FACT
I hereby appoint:

NAME _____

ADDRESS _____

_____

TELEPHONE # _____

to act as my attorney-in-fact to make decisions regarding my mental health treatment if I become incapable of giving or withholding informed consent for that treatment.

If the person named above refuses or is unable to act on my behalf, or if I revoke that person's authority to act as my attorney-in-fact, I authorize the following person to act as my attorney-in-fact:

NAME _____

ADDRESS _____

TELEPHONE # _____

My attorney-in-fact is authorized to make decisions that are consistent with the wishes I have expressed in this declaration or, if not expressed, as are otherwise known to my attorney-in-fact. If my wishes are not expressed and are not otherwise known by my attorney-in-fact, my attorney-in-fact is to act in what he or she believes to be my best interest.

Date _____ Signed _____
(Signature of Principal)

AFFIRMATION OF WITNESSES

We affirm that the principal is personally known to us, that the principal signed or acknowledged the principal's signature on this declaration for mental health treatment in our presence, that the principal appears to be of sound mind and not under duress, fraud or undue influence, that neither of us is:

A person appointed as an attorney-in-fact by this document;

The principal's attending physician or mental health service provider or a relative of the physician or provider;

The owner, operator, or relative of an owner or operator of a facility in which the principal is a patient or resident; or

A person related to the principal by blood, marriage or adoption.

Witnessed By:

_____
(Signature of Witness/Date)   (Printed Name of Witness)

_____
(Signature of Witness/Date)   (Printed Name of Witness)

ACCEPTANCE OF APPOINTMENT AS ATTORNEY-IN-FACT

I accept this appointment and agree to serve as attorney-in-fact to make decisions about mental health treatment for the principal. I understand that I have a duty to act consistent with the desires of the principal as expressed in this appointment. I understand that this document gives me authority to make decisions about mental health treatment only while the principal is incapable as determined by a court or 2 physicians. I understand that the principal may revoke this declaration in whole or in part at any time and in any manner when the principal is not incapable.

_____
(Signature of Attorney-in-fact/Date)   (Printed Name)

NOTICE TO PERSON MAKING A DECLARATION FOR MENTAL HEALTH TREATMENT

This is an important legal document. It creates a declaration for mental health treatment. Before signing this document, you should know these important facts:

This document allows you to make decisions in advance about 3 types of mental health treatment: psychotropic medication, electroconvulsive therapy, and short-term (up to 17 days) admission to a treatment facility. The instructions that you include in this declaration will be followed only if 2 physicians or the court believes that you are incapable of making treatment decisions. Otherwise, you will be considered capable to give or withhold consent for the treatments.

You may also appoint a person as your attorney-in-fact to make these treatment decisions for you if you become incapable. The person you appoint has a duty to act consistent with your desires as stated in this document or, if your desires are not stated or otherwise made known to the attorney-in-fact, to act in a manner consistent with what the person in good faith believes to be in your best interest. For the appointment to be effective, the person you appoint must accept the appointment in writing. The person also has the right to withdraw from acting as your attorney-in-fact at any time.

This document will continue in effect for a period of 3 years unless you become incapable of participating in mental health treatment decisions. If this occurs, the directive will continue in effect until you are no longer incapable.

You have the right to revoke this document in whole or in part at any time you have been determined by a physician to be capable of giving or withholding informed consent for mental health treatment. A revocation is effective when it is communicated to your attending physician in writing and is signed by you and a physician. The revocation may be in a form similar to the following:

REVOCATION

I, _____, willfully and voluntarily revoke my declaration for mental health treatment as indicated

[_] I revoke my entire declaration

[_] I revoke the following portion of my declaration

Date _____Signed _____
(Signature of Physician)

I, Dr. _____, have evaluated the principal and determined that he or she is capable of giving or withholding informed consent for mental health treatment.

Date _____Signed _____
(Signature of Principal)

If there is anything in this document that you do not understand, you should ask a lawyer to explain it to you. This declaration will not be valid unless it is signed by 2 qualified witnesses who are personally known to you and who are present when you sign or acknowledge your signature.

Establishing Guardianship

If, after reading the information in this chapter, you decide you would like to pursue guardianship for your child, it will be necessary to begin a guardianship proceeding. The proceeding will determine the level of competence of your child, whether guardianship is needed, and if guardianship is needed, the type of guardian to be appointed and the amount of authority to be granted to the guardian.

Starting a Guardianship Proceeding

To initiate the proceeding, your lawyer will file a *Petition for Appointment of Guardian for a Disabled Person* with the court clerk (the title of the petition may vary slightly from state to state). Although each state provides a different petition form, the following information must be included by your lawyer in most petitions:

- The petitioner's relationship to and interest in the person with a disability. The petitioner is the person who asks the court to appoint a guardian for the person with a disability.
- The name, date of birth, and place of residence of the person with a disability.
- The reasons for requesting a guardianship.
- The name and address of the proposed guardian and, if an individual, his or her age and occupation.
- The approximate value of the personal property and real estate owned by the person with a disability.
- The approximate amount of the gross annual income and other receipts of the person with a disability.
- The names and addresses of the nearest relatives of the person with a disability.
- The type of guardianship requested.

Notice to the Person with a Disability

A formal notice or *summons* is given to the person with a disability to show that a guardianship petition has been filed. The summons indicates the time, date, and location of the court hearing. In most states, a summons and copy of the petition must be delivered or *served* on the alleged disabled person not less than 14 days before the hearing.

In some states, the sheriff delivers the summons to the person with a disability. If you believe a sheriff, who is a stranger, would frighten your child, ask your lawyer to motion the court for permission to use a *special process server*. The special process server is a person other than the sheriff who will deliver the summons to your child. With the approval of the court, the special process server in most states can be anyone over the age of eighteen who is not a party to the guardianship case. Therefore, with court permission you can select a friend of the family to deliver the summons.

Evidence of Incapacity

In most states, a report by a physician must be attached to the Petition for Guardianship. This physician (often a psychiatrist or an expert who has experience with the particular disability involved) must have examined the person with a disability, usually within 90 days of the hearing. The judge reads the physician's report as evidence of the mental capacity of the person in order to establish the need for guardianship and as an aid in determining the type and powers of the guardian. The physician must fill out a form that usually contains the following information:

- A description of the nature and type of disability.
- An evaluation of the person's mental and physical condition, including educational level, adaptive behavior, and social skills.
- An opinion as to whether a guardian is needed.
- An opinion, with reasons, about the type and scope of guardianship needed.

- A recommendation, with reasons, regarding the most suitable living arrangement and, where appropriate, treatment and rehabilitation plans.

- The signatures of all persons who performed the evaluations on which the report is based. At least one of these persons typically must be a licensed physician.

You should ask your lawyer for the physician's report form, have a doctor fill it out, then show it to your attorney. Your lawyer, after reading the report, will be able to determine how likely the judge will be to grant the guardianship. By determining the potential of the case prior to the court hearing, you can save considerable time and expense that might otherwise be wasted. It may even be advisable to discuss your child's condition with your lawyer before consulting a doctor. That way your attorney can tell you whether guardianship is possible before you incur any medical bills.

In order to justify the need for a guardian, the doctor's report must clearly and accurately demonstrate that the person's disability creates a need for guardianship. The doctor's report must not be vague. For instance, a physician's report stating only "This person is mentally ill and needs a guardian," will not be sufficient to justify the need for guardianship.

The same report written more specifically could probably justify the need for a guardian. Rather than simply stating "this person is mentally ill and needs a guardian," the doctor might write:

This person has had learning and emotional problems, probably related to unknown organic damage. He has had several schizo-affective psychotic episodes in which he was violent toward others. He will require psychiatric supervision, counseling, and psychotropic medication (currently proloxin and haladol). With proloxin and haladol he is free of psychotic symptoms, but he is incapable of independent living or of work because of an inability to make independent judgments in regard to personal care and ordinary social life.

He needs assistance in making personal, financial, and medical decisions. He is capable of making daily decisions of personal care within a stable, protected, nonchallenging environment. He will need guardianship authority to make decisions about residential placement through his lifetime. He also needs medication for heart problems and may need hospitalization in the future.

OR

Miss Doe has borderline intellectual disabilities with IQ scores in the 60 to 70 range. She is working at the Work Center, a sheltered workshop. Miss Doe is incapable of making personal and financial decisions.

 TIP If your child needs help in making decisions in regard to residential placement, it is wise to have the doctor comment on this. Most judges are understandably reluctant to give this authority to the guardian unless absolutely necessary.

Appointment of a Guardian Ad Litem

A guardian ad litem (GAL) is a person appointed by the court to act as attorney for a person who is alleged to be disabled in the guardianship petition. Your child, therefore, becomes the GAL's client.

The GAL examines the case and determines the rights of your child, defends him or her if necessary, and writes a report for the court indicating whether or not a guardian is needed and, if so, what type of guardian should be appointed. Acting as an investigator, the GAL visits your child in his or her normal living environment. If it is a residential facility, the GAL also meets with the staff and discusses the long-term prognosis for your child. The GAL must inform your child (often, orally and in writing) of the guardianship proceeding, the contents of the petition for guardianship, and the various procedural rights available.

In the report to the court the GAL will discuss your child's medical records, functional level, and long-term prognosis. The GAL will indicate to the court whether your child will need the help of a guardian in personal and/or financial matters. If, in the opinion of the GAL, a guardian is needed, the GAL will also recommend the type of guardian that would seem to be most appropriate. The GAL might communicate to the court your child's preference for a particular individual to be appointed guardian.

A GAL generally must be paid for his or her services. If you cannot afford a GAL, in some states the court will require the state to pay the GAL's fees. Moreover, in some states the judge may waive the requirement of a GAL and thus substantially reduce costs. If state laws permit such a waiver, the judge will most likely waive the requirement for a GAL when a close family member seeks guardianship and the medical report on the person with a disability appears conclusive and accurate. Sometimes the judge will agree to visit with the person with a disability in his or her chambers rather than appoint a GAL. To avoid the cost of a GAL, ask your lawyer whether the laws in your state and the circumstances of the case warrant a waiver of a GAL.

Hearing and Appointment

Usually, the actual guardianship hearing can be completed in about a half hour or less. It is the prehearing documentation that takes the time. The judge will examine the petition for guardianship, the physician's report, and any other documents. Your lawyer will explain the need for and type of guardian requested and answer any questions asked by the judge. The judge will talk with the person with a disability.

If the judge believes the evidence justifies the need to appoint a guardian, he or she will sign a court order appointing a guardian. Remember, the guardian's powers are restricted to those granted by the court. The guardianship order will specify the exact responsibilities and powers the guardian will assume.

Additionally, a case number will be on the guardianship order. The case number identifies the court case. If a question arises in the future, the guardian can give the case number to a court clerk, who can look up the case for clarification.

The formal document issued by the court indicating the appointment of a guardian is usually called the *Letters of Office*. The guardian can use this document to prove guardianship.

After the guardian has been appointed by the court, the guardian should notify the ward's contacts such as hospitals and relatives. These people and institutions should be informed who the ward's guardian is, so they can contact the guardian if they become aware of any problems. Also, this notification might protect the ward from someone's unscrupulous actions.

Modification or Discharge of Guardianship

By petitioning the court, the ward, the guardian, or any interested person can seek an alteration or termination of the guardianship. A hearing on the petition is required. If you want to change the guardian's authority, the petition must list the reasons for seeking the modification. Most modifications involve a change of guardian or an alteration in the guardian's authority—decreasing or increasing it.

Usually a guardian continues until granted permission to resign. A guardianship will terminate if a court determines the ward no longer needs a guardian, the guardian is no longer willing or able to continue as guardian, or the guardian does not do a competent job.

Rights of the Person with a Disability

Laws in all states entitle the person with a disability to rights at the guardianship hearing. These include the usual rights afforded to a defendant in a lawsuit: the right to an attorney, the right to a jury trial, the right to present evidence (including doctors' reports), and the right to confront and cross-examine witnesses.

The rights are granted to insure that a guardian is not appointed when a less-restrictive alternative would be sufficient, and to insure that, if guardianship is appropriate, the proper type of guardian is appointed. In most instances, these rights are not exercised because a parent or a concerned person is properly being appointed guardian. However, they can provide a safeguard against exploitation.

Checklist of Procedures for Your Lawyer
(Note: Each state will vary slightly in procedure.)

- Obtain evidence of incapacity of the person with a disability to be submitted at the guardianship hearing. The physician's report should be filled out in detail.

- Prepare a petition for guardianship and file it with the court clerk.

- Prepare a summons to be served on the person with a disability. Obtain hearing date and place from the court clerk. Give the summons to the sheriff for service, or prepare an order to use a special process server and an affidavit.

- Prepare a court order appointing a guardian ad litem (GAL), or prepare an order to waive the GAL.

- Prepare the mailing of notice to relatives and other persons named in the petition.

- If necessary, prepare a petition and order for a temporary guardian.

- Prepare a court order waiving the presence of the person with a disability or the physician if either cannot attend the hearing.

- Prepare a court order appointing a guardian of the person, guardian of the estate, plenary or limited guardian.

- If necessary, prepare a petition and order to deposit the ward's funds in an account.

- If necessary, prepare a petition and order for authority to make expenditures on behalf of the ward.

Conclusion

Whether you decide to pursue a guardianship or not, it will be important for you to name someone to look out for your child's personal and financial interests after you are gone. The key is to name the right people.

As a practical matter, parents trust a finite group of people to serve as their child's future caregiver. We generally ask our clients to rank these people in order of preference. Often these people act as advocates and trustees, and guardians if the client decides a guardianship is necessary. This is sensible because these are the people who are most likely to do a good job.

For instance, let's say Mom and Dad trust Bob (their son) first, then Carol (their daughter) second, then Uncle Don third, then niece Sandy fourth, to look out for the future interests of their son, Jon. Mom and Dad may name Bob and Carol to act as co-trustees to manage Jon's inheritance, with Don or Sally acting if something happens to Bob or Carol. These same people would act as Jon's advocates or as guardian if one was appointed.

Often a relative who acts as trustee to manage the child's inheritance lives out of state. In this case, we feel it is vital that parents recommend local advocates in their Letter of Intent, to serve as the *eyes and ears* of the out-of-state trustee. These local advocates might be friends of the family, neighbors, or professionals who know and care about the child. The out-of-state trustee can even pay the local advocate from trust funds to visit the child and report to the trustee about the child's needs.

Planning Your Child's Financial Future:

The Role of Government Benefits

FINANCIAL PLANNING FOR FAMILIES WITH MEMBERS WHO HAVE disabilities is fundamentally different from financial planning for other families. In the usual case, financial planning involves making sure resources are adequate to take care of children before they are old enough to *go it on their own*. Later, concern shifts to making sure the parents themselves have adequate resources. For example, in many cases young families will be concerned primarily with making sure their financial resources will be adequate to fund their childrens' educational requirements. As the parents grow older, they begin to think about retirement.

Except in the case of the very wealthy, planning for the requirements of adult children tends not to be a major factor. If money is left to pass on to children after the parents die, that is all well and good, but ensuring the financial future of adult children is not a primary planning goal. Children are usually expected to be able to take care of themselves, as the parents have.

Families with children who have disabilities require a different focus. In many cases, the children cannot be expected to earn enough to meet their financial needs. Therefore, as a parent, you will need to *take the bull by the horns* and develop a financial plan that will enable your son or daughter to meet his or her lifetime needs.

For most families, government benefits will play a very important role. The cost of lifetime care for a person with a disability can be quite high, particularly when the effects of inflation are considered. Few families have the resources to provide for children with disabilities through private means alone. We have *run the numbers* many times and, taking into account inflation, housing, the possible need for supervision, medical costs, and the huge assortment of other living expenses, the cost of providing for a child with a disability through private means alone can require a privately funded trust of more than a million dollars. This figure will be considerably lower if your child lives with friends or relatives on a cost-free basis, in your own home or the home of the friend or relative. The cost will also be lower if your child's disability is less severe, and less supervision is required. Cost is also heavily dependent on the age and life expectancy of the child.

Whatever the actual costs, you need to be very wealthy to rely exclusively on family dollars. That is why it is absolutely essential for most families to create an estate plan that will assure eligibility for government benefits. Even many of our wealthy clients, who expect to use private housing, leave money for children with disabilities in the types of trusts described in Chapter Six so that, if public housing or Medicaid should prove necessary in the future, government benefits will be available to them.

Government Benefit Programs for People with Disabilities

Many people who have disabilities are eligible for benefits under one or more of several government programs. These programs are designed to protect the person with the disability by making sure that the person's financial resources are sufficient to provide the basic necessities of life—food, clothing, shelter, and health care.

In general, the programs can be grouped into two categories. There are *needs based programs*, such as Supplemental Security Income (SSI) and Medicaid, that are available to individuals with disabilities who satisfy certain needs based requirements relating to income and assets. That is, to be eligible, your child cannot receive too much income or own too much property.

There are also programs classified as *social insurance programs*, such as Social Security and Medicare, that are potentially available regardless of how much income or property your child may have. Your child becomes entitled to benefits under these programs by virtue of the *premiums* that you or your child may have paid into the program. The premiums have been paid in the form of Social Security tax that has been withheld from your paycheck or, if you are self-employed, in the form of self-employment tax that you have been paying to the government on a quarterly basis.

Some of these programs are operated by the federal government, and others are run by the various states. Still others are jointly financed by state and federal governments and operated by the states in accordance with federally mandated guidelines.

Unfortunately, the rules relating to these programs are very complicated and you may have to read each section in this chapter several times before you understand it. It is not necessary that you understand everything, the basics are enough. The key points are these:

- If your child had a disability before reaching age 22, your child will likely be entitled to Social Security benefits when you or your spouse die, reach retirement age, or become disabled. If your child developed a disability after age 22, Social Security will be available *only* if your child had a significant employment history before becoming disabled.

- If your child has limited income and assets, he or she will likely be entitled to Supplemental Security Income benefits upon reaching age 18. It does not matter when your child first became disabled. For lower-income families, children under age 18 may also be eligible.

- If your child has limited income and assets, he or she will likely be eligible for a place in a government-funded residential setting (assuming space is available). Your child may be eligible for a place even if your child has significant assets, but the government will not pay.

- If your child resides in a residential setting that is funded by the state or federal government, Social Security or Supplemental Security Income benefits will be reduced substantially (to between $30 and $70 a month).

- If your child is eligible for Supplemental Security Income benefits, he or she will likely be eligible for Medicaid.

- If your child has been eligible for Social Security benefits for at least two years, he or she will likely be eligible for Medicare. It does not matter if your child actually received the benefits, just that the eligibility requirements were satisfied.

Establishing Disability

In order to qualify for government benefits as a person with a disability, your child will need to be considered to have a disability within the rules of the Social Security system. The Social Security regulations (20 CFR Section 404.1505) define disability as:

[T]he inability to do any *substantial gainful activity* by reason of any medically determinable physical or mental impairment which can be expected to result in death or which has lasted or can be expected to last for a continuous period of not less than 12 months.

Although substantial gainful activity is determined based on a variety of factors, the cornerstone of the analysis is a determination as to whether or not your child is capable of earning more than a threshold amount, which increases each year to account for inflation. For 2005, the critical issue is whether Social Security believes that your child is capable of earning $830 a month after deducting impairment related work expenses and employer subsidies (discussed below). If your child is visually impaired, the threshold for 2005 is $1,390 per month.

To make its determination, Social Security performs a five-step analysis:

First, Social Security will ask if your child is working. If your child is working and has average monthly earnings at the *substantial gainful activity* level (after deducting impairment related work expenses and employer subsidies), Social Security generally will not consider your child to be disabled.

Second, if your child's monthly earnings average less than the substantial gainful activity level, Social Security will seek to determine whether your child's medical condition is severe. This involves a determination as to whether your child's impairment significantly limits the child's ability to do basic work activities; for example, walking, sitting, seeing, and remembering. If the impairment does not limit your child's ability to perform such work activities, Social Security will not consider your child to be disabled.

Third, if your child's medical condition is considered severe, Social Security will seek to determine whether the impairment is on its list of disabling impairments. This list describes impairments for each major body system that are considered severe enough to prevent a person from doing any gainful activity. If your child has an impairment that meets or is medically equivalent to an impairment described on the list, Social Security will find that your child has a disability within the meaning of the Social Security rules. Social Security's list of impairments can be found in Appendix 1 to Subpart F of Volume 20 of the Code of Federal Regulations.

Fourth, if your child's medical condition is severe, but is not as severe as an impairment on the list, Social Security will look at your child's prior work history and seek to determine whether your child can do work previously done at the substantial gainful activity level.

Fifth, if your child cannot do past relevant work, Social Security will seek to determine whether your child will be able to do any other type of work at the substantial gainful activity level. In making this determination, Social Security will consider your child's age, education, past work experience, and transferable skills. If your child cannot do any other kind of work at the substantial gainful activity level, Social Security will find that your child has a disability within the meaning of the Social Security rules.

TIP The single most common reason for failing to qualify for benefits is a failure to submit information that is sufficient to permit Social Security to determine that a person has a disability within the meaning of its rules. As described in *Applying for and Maintaining Benefits* below, you will need to submit a physician's report with your child's benefit application. Although your child can qualify for benefits even if your child's disability is not described on Social Security's list of impairments, qualification is much easier if the impairment is listed. Your physician should review the definition describing your child's disability as set forth in Social Security's listing to make sure the report contains the language that Social Security requires.

For example, the listing of impairments for adults (Listing of Impairments, Part A, Section 12.05) describes mental retardation as follows:

Mental retardation refers to significantly subaverage general intellectual functioning with deficits in adaptive functioning initially manifested during the developmental period; i.e., the evidence demonstrates or supports onset of the impairment before age 22.

The required level of severity for this disorder is met when the requirements in A, B, C, or D are satisfied.

A. Mental incapacity evidenced by dependence upon others for personal needs (e.g., toileting, eating, dressing, or bathing) and inability to follow directions, such that the use of standardized measures of intellectual functioning is precluded;

OR

B. A valid verbal, performance, or full scale IQ of 59 or less;

OR

C. A valid verbal, performance, or full scale IQ of 60 through 70 and a physical or other mental impairment imposing an additional and significant work-related limitation of function;

OR

D. A valid verbal, performance, or full scale IQ of 60 through 70, resulting in at least two of the following:

1. Marked restriction of activities of daily living; or

2. Marked difficulties in maintaining social functioning; or

3. Marked difficulties in maintaining concentration, persistence, or pace; or

LEGAL

4. Repeated episodes of decompensation, each of extended duration.

A physician's report accompanying an application for benefits based on a diagnosis of mental retardation would need to include:

- Medical history;

- Clinical findings (such as the results of mental status examinations, including the results of any IQ tests);

- Laboratory findings (such as blood pressure, x-rays);

- Diagnosis;

- Treatment prescribed with response, and prognosis; and

- A statement describing in sufficient detail the physician's basis for concluding that your child has an impairment based on the definition set forth above. For example, the statement could list your child's IQ and describe an inability to understand, carry out and remember instructions, as well as an inability to respond appropriately to supervision, coworkers, and work pressures in a work setting.

Similarly, the Social Security listing describes schizophrenic, delusional (Paranoid), schizoaffective, and other psychotic disorders as follows:

LEGAL

Characterized by the onset of psychotic features with deterioration from a previous level of functioning.

The required level of severity for these disorders is met when the requirements in both A and B are satisfied, or when the requirements in C are satisfied.

A. Medically documented persistence, either continuous or intermittent, of one or more of the following:

1. Delusions or hallucinations; or

2. Catatonic or other grossly disorganized behavior; or

3. Incoherence, loosening of associations, illogical thinking, or poverty of content of speech if associated with one of the following:

    a. Blunt affect; or

    b. Flat affect; or

    c. Inappropriate affect;

OR

4. Emotional withdrawal and/or isolation;

AND

B. Resulting in at least two of the following:

1. Marked restriction of activities of daily living; or

2. Marked difficulties in maintaining social functioning; or

3. Marked difficulties in maintaining concentration, persistence, or pace; or

4. Repeated episodes of decompensation, each of extended duration;

OR

C. Medically documented history of a chronic schizophrenic, paranoid, or other psychotic disorder of at least 2 years' duration that has caused more than a minimal limitation of ability to do basic work activities, with symptoms or signs currently attenuated by medication or psychosocial support, and one of the following:

1. Repeated episodes of decompensation, each of extended duration; or

2. A residual disease process that has resulted in such marginal adjustment that even a minimal increase in mental demands or change in the environment would be predicted to cause the individual to decompensate; or

3. Current history of 1 or more years' inability to function outside a highly supportive living arrangement, with an indication of continued need for such an arrangement.

A psychiatrist's report accompanying an application for benefits based on diagnosis of schizophrenia would need to include:

• Medical history;

• Clinical findings (such as the results of mental status examinations);

• Laboratory findings (such as blood pressure, x-rays);

• Diagnosis;

• Treatment prescribed with response, and prognosis; and

• A statement describing in sufficient detail the psychiatrist's basis for concluding that your child has an impairment based on the definition set forth above.

The disability evaluation process generally takes several months. However, the law includes special provisions for people signing up for benefits under the supplemental security income program whose condition is so severe that they are presumed to be disabled. In these cases, assuming the other eligibility requirements discussed below are satisfied (see *Supplemental Security*

Income later in this chapter), SSI benefits are paid for up to six months while the formal disability decision is being made.

The following are the major disability categories for which Social Security will presume disability and make immediate SSI payments:

- HIV infection

- Total Blindness

- Total Deafness (in some cases)

- Cerebral palsy (in some cases)

- Down syndrome

- Muscular dystrophy (in some cases)

- Mental retardation

- Diabetes (with amputation of one foot)

- Amputation of two limbs

- Amputation of leg at the hip

If Social Security makes payments and later decides that the person's disability is not severe enough to qualify for SSI, the benefits do not have to be paid back.

Example One

Mary has Down syndrome. Mary does not work at the substantial gainful activity level.

- Assuming Mary's condition is sufficiently severe that Mary satisfies the requirements set out in Social Security's listing, Mary will be considered to have a disability for Social Security purposes.

- If Mary does not satisfy the listing requirements, Social Security will assess Mary's functioning level to determine if Mary has the capacity to perform substantial gainful activity. If Social Security determines that Mary does not have such capacity, Mary will be considered to have a disability for Social Security purposes. If Social Security determines that Mary has sufficient capacity to perform substantial gainful activity, Mary will not be considered to have a disability for Social Security purposes.

- If Mary is applying for SSI and meets the other eligibility requirements relating to income and resource level discussed below, Mary will be entitled to SSI benefits for up to six months while the formal disability decision is being made. If Social Security makes payments and later decides that Mary's disability is not severe enough to qualify for SSI, the benefits do not have to be paid back.

TIP Sometimes a family member who owns a business will employ a person with a disability and pay wages that exceed the substantial gainful activity level even though the person who has a disability may not be able to earn above that level on the open market. This can create difficulty if the person with a disability later applies for benefits, perhaps because the business is sold, because the person with a disability will have a record of earnings in excess of the substantial gainful activity level.

Social Security Disability Insurance

The Social Security Disability Insurance program, also known as SSDI, is one of the two primary cash benefit programs available for people with disabilities, the other being the Supplemental Security Income program (also known as SSI). People with disabilities can qualify for SSDI in either of two ways.

First, SSDI is generally available for workers who become disabled prior to attaining age 65, assuming the worker's work history satisfies Social Security's requirements. These requirements are relatively modest, and most people who have worked for more than a few years will qualify. The amount of the benefit is based on the worker's earning history.

Example Two

Fred becomes disabled before reaching age 65 after having worked for many years. Fred will be entitled to SSDI benefits based on his own earnings record.

Second, SSDI is also available to children (even adult children) of retired, disabled or deceased social security participants if the child has a disability that developed before the child reached 22 years of age. The benefit is based on the parent's work record. If the parent is retired or disabled, the benefit is one-half of the parent's benefit. If the parent is deceased, the benefit is three-fourths of the parent's benefit. Benefits may be reduced if more than one person receives benefits based on the parent's work record, and will cease if the child marries someone who is not entitled to social security benefits.

Example Three

John and Marlene have worked for many years and are contemplating retirement. They have one child, Mary, who has had an intellectual disability since birth.

- Because Mary had her disability before age 22, she will be entitled to SSDI dependents' benefits based on her parents' earnings records when the first of them reaches retirement age or becomes disabled. Mary will also be entitled to SSDI survivors' benefits when her mother or father dies. Her monthly check will be equal to approximately one-half of the larger of her parents' checks under the SSDI dependents' benefit program or three-fourths under the SSDI survivors' benefit program.

- If Mary lives in a government-funded residential facility, most of her SSDI check will likely be used to pay for room and board. Government-funded residential facilities are discussed below. In the typical case, Mary will be allowed to keep about $30 a month for her personal needs.

- If Mary's Social Security check is below the SSI minimum, Mary may be entitled to SSI as well. As with her SSDI benefits, most of Mary's SSI will be used to pay for room and board (assuming she stays in a government-funded residential facility). The SSI program is discussed below.

Example Four

John and Marlene have worked for many years and are contemplating retirement. They have one child, Fred, who has severe depression. Fred first showed signs of depression at age 22.

- Fred will not be entitled to SSDI dependents' or survivors' benefits based on his parents' earnings records because he did not have his disability until after his twenty-second birthday.

- Fred may be entitled to SSDI based on his own earnings' record if he has worked for a long enough period to qualify. Fred may also be entitled to SSI (discussed below).

One other aspect of the Social Security program bears mentioning because it is unique to families that have a child with a disability. The point relates to spousal benefits. In general, a worker's spouse is entitled to benefits when the worker retires, dies or becomes disabled if the spouse has reached a specified age or is caring for a child under age 16. Under a special rule, if the spouse is caring for a child with a disability, the spouse will automatically be eligible for benefits on the worker's retirement, death or disability regardless of age or other circumstances.

A person who is determined to be entitled to SSDI benefits generally must wait five months after the date of entitlement before SSDI payments begin. In certain instances, recipients may be entitled to retroactive benefits of up to 12 months.

Special SSDI Employment Supports

Many people with disabilities want to work. In the absence of special rules, however, an SSDI recipient who joined the work force would be at risk of losing SSDI benefits if such work rose to the level of *substantial gainful activity* (that is, based on 2005 figures, if the SSDI recipient demonstrated the ability to earn at least $830 a month). SSDI contains a number of rules, known as employment supports, that are designed to allow an SSDI recipient to work and still retain SSDI benefits for a period of time. The main SSDI employment supports are:

- Impairment-Related Work Expenses,

- Subsidy and Special Conditions,

- Unsuccessful Work Attempt,

- Trial Work Period,

- Extended Period of Eligibility,

- Continued Payment Under a Vocational Rehabilitation Program, also known as Section 301.

Impairment Related Work Expenses

An impairment related work expense, or IRWE, is an expense incurred by a person with a disability in order to work. These expenses are deductible for purposes of determining whether a person is engaged in substantial gainful activity (SGA). Social Security's Policy Operation Manual (POMs Section DI 10520.000) states:

> [T]he cost of certain items and services that a person with a disability needs in order to work can be deducted from earnings in determinations of SGA, even though such items and services are also needed for normal daily activities. The cost of certain attendant care services, medical devices, equipment, prostheses, and similar items and services may be deducted. The costs of routine drugs and routine medical services are not deductible unless the drugs or services are necessary to control the disabling condition to enable the person to work. Expenses that are not directly related to the impairment(s) cannot be deducted as IRWE.... The amount of impairment-related work expenses (IRWE) that may be deducted is subject to reasonable limits. Deductions for needed items and services will be made only if the cost is paid by the person.

Example Five

John has a Schizoaffective disorder. John is able to function in a work environment with medication. He earns $900 a month. However, his medication costs him $100 a month. John can claim the medication as an impairment related work expense, reducing his earnings to $800 a month, which is below the threshold for substantial gainful activity.

What types of expenses will potentially qualify as impairment related work expenses? The *Red Book of Employment Supports*, published annually by the Social Security Administration, provides the following summary:

1. Attendant Care Services	
DEDUCTIBLE	**NON DEDUCTIBLE**
Performed in the work setting.	Performed on non-workdays or helping with shopping or general homemaking, for example cleaning, and laundry.
Performed to help prepare for work, the trip to and from work, and after work, for example bathing, dressing, cooking, and eating.	Performed for someone else in the family, for example babysitting.
Services that incidentally also benefit the family, for example meals shared by the entire family.	Services performed by a family member for a cash fee where he/she suffers no economic loss. This includes services provided by a non-working spouse.
Services performed by a family member for a cash fee where he/she suffers an economic loss by reducing or ending his/her work in order to help.	Services performed by a family member for payment "in-kind," for example room and board (even if the family member suffers economic loss).

2. Transportation Costs	
DEDUCTIBLE	**NON DEDUCTIBLE**
The cost of structural or operational modifications to a vehicle needed in order to travel to work, even if the vehicle is also used for non-work purposes.	The cost of a vehicle whether modified or not.
The cost of driver assistance or taxicabs if public transportation is either unavailable or is inaccessible due to the disability.	The cost of modification to a vehicle not directly related to an impairment or critical to the operation of the vehicle, for example paint or pin striping.
Mileage expenses at an approved rate for limited to travel to and from employment if public transportation is either unavailable or is inaccessible due to the disability.	Travel expenses related to obtaining medical items or services.

3. Medical Devices

DEDUCTIBLE	NON DEDUCTIBLE
Wheelchairs, hemodialysis equipment, pacemakers, respirators, traction equipment, and braces.	Any device not used for a medical purpose.

4. Work-Related Equipment and Assistants

DEDUCTIBLE	NON DEDUCTIBLE
All impairment related work assistive devices, services, methods, or systems, including service animals.	If self-employed, any specific items that were deducted as a business expense.

5. Prosthesis

DEDUCTIBLE	NON DEDUCTIBLE
Artificial hip, artificial replacement of an arm, leg, or other parts of the body.	Any prosthetic device that is primarily for cosmetic purposes.

6. Residential Modifications

DEDUCTIBLE	NON DEDUCTIBLE
If employed outside of the home: Modifications to the exterior of the house that permit access to the street or to transportation, for example exterior ramps, railings, and pathways.	If employed outside of the home: Modifications to the house to help in the home, for example enlarge interior doorframes, lower kitchen appliances and bathroom facilities, and install interior railings or stairway chair lift.
If self-employed at home: Modifications made inside the home in order to create a workspace to accommodate the impairment. This includes enlarging doorway into an office or workroom, modifying office space to accommodate problems in dexterity.	If self-employed at home: Any modification expenses you previously deducted as a business expense in determining SGA.

7. Routine Drugs and Routine Medical Services

DEDUCTIBLE	NON DEDUCTIBLE
Regularly prescribed medical treatment or therapy that is necessary to control the disabling condition, even if control is not achieved. This includes: anti-convulsant drugs, blood level monitoring, radiation treatment, chemotherapy, corrective surgery for spinal disorders, and anti-depressant medication. Physician's fee relating to these services is deductible.	Drugs and/or medical services used for minor physical or mental problems, for example routine physical examinations, allergy treatment, dental examinations, and optician services.

8. Diagnostic Procedures

DEDUCTIBLE	NON DEDUCTIBLE
Any procedure related to the control, treatment, or evaluation of the disabling condition, for example brain scans, and electroencephalograms.	Procedures not related to the disabling condition, for example allergy testing.

9. Non-Medical Appliances and Devices

DEDUCTIBLE	NON DEDUCTIBLE
In unusual circumstances, devices or appliances are essential for the control of the disabling condition either at home or at work, for example an electric air cleaner to control a severe respiratory disease. A physician must verify this need.	Any device not used for a medical purpose.

10. Other Items and Services	
DEDUCTIBLE	**NON DEDUCTIBLE**
Expendable medical supplies, for example incontinence pads, elastic stockings, and catheters.	An exercise bicycle or other device used for physical fitness unless verified as necessary by a physician.
The cost of a helper animal including food, licenses, and veterinary services.	Health insurance premiums.

Note that an expense may not be deducted as an impairment related work expense if the expense is paid by others, such as through reimbursement by insurance or a vocational rehabilitation agency. Only expenses that your child incurs may be deducted as impairment related work expenses.

 TIP It is your responsibility to establish the existence of an impairment related work expense. If your child needs to deduct these expenses to stay below the substantial gainful activity threshold, make sure you (i) keep cancelled checks to verify that the expenses were actually incurred, (ii) obtain letters from a physician, employer, vocational counselor, or employment training specialist as appropriate to confirm that the expense is necessary for employment purposes, and (iii) report the expense to Social Security.

Subsidy and Special Work Conditions

Substantial gainful activity is determined based on the value of work performed. Although this determination is typically made based on wages received, in certain instances wages may not accurately portray work value. In such a case, a worker can claim that wages have been subsidized. Typically, the worker would submit a statement from the employer or a third party such as a job coach as to the real value of the work. Alternatively, Social Security may compute real value. Circumstances supporting a claim of subsidy might include:

- The worker receives more supervision than other workers doing the same or a similar job at the same pay;

- The worker has fewer or simpler tasks to complete than other workers doing the same or a similar job at the same pay;

- The worker has a job coach or mentor who helps perform some of the work.

If your child is earning less than the substantial gainful activity level (for 2005, $830 a month), there is no need to inform to inform Social Security that your child is receiving a subsidy or special work conditions. However, if your child is at or near the substantial gainful activity level, it is your responsibility to inform Social Security if you believe a subsidy is being received. Just call your local Social Security office and ask for a Work Activity Report (Form SSA-821-BK). You can also find the Form on the Social Security web site (socialsecurity.gov).

Example Six

John has a mild intellectual disability. He is able to work but requires the assistance of a job coach on a half-time basis. The cost of the job coach is covered by a local vocational rehabilitation agency. John earns $850 a month. John can claim a subsidy because he has a job coach who helps him perform some of his work. The value of the job coach is calculated by multiplying the number of hours of assistance by John's hourly wage. Since the job coach assists John on a half-time basis, John's countable income will be reduced by one-half for SSDI calculation purposes, and John therefore continues to satisfy the substantial gainful activity test. Note that John still receives $850 in wages even though he is treated as receiving less for SSDI benefit calculation purposes.

Unsuccessful Work Attempt

An unsuccessful work attempt is an effort to do substantial work that is stopped or reduced to below the substantial gainful activity level after a short time (6 months or less) because of:

- An impairment; or

- Removal of subsidies or special work conditions related to an impairment and essential to the further performance of your work.

Earnings during an unsuccessful work attempt are not considered for purposes of making a substantial gainful activity determination.

Example Seven

John suffers from depression. He finds a job, does well for his first month but loses the job in his third month due to excessive absence after going off medication. John's three month employment period will be considered an unsuccessful work attempt and will not be considered in determining whether John can engage in substantial gainful activity.

Trial Work Period

The trial work period allows an SSDI recipient to test work ability without loss of benefits even if earnings during the trial work period exceed the substantial gainful activity level. An SSDI recipient is generally permitted 9 months of trial work during any rolling sixty month period. A month counts against the trial work only if the beneficiary's earnings for the month exceed a specified amount (for 2005, $590). Impairment related work expenses and subsidies cannot be deducted for purposes of determining whether a month counts against the trial work period limit, though they will be considered at the end of the trial work period for purposes of determining whether the SSDI recipient can work at the substantial gainful activity level.

Example Eight

John has a Schizoaffective disorder and receives SSDI. He is able to work when on medication, but he goes off medication frequently, and works only intermittently. He begins work on January 1, 2005. He earns $500 a month through March, $750 a month in April, May and June and then loses his job. He gets a new job in October and earns $1,500 a month through the end of the year.

As of January 1, 2006, John will have used up 6 months of his trial work period (April-June and then October-December). John's work in January through March will not use up months in his trial work period since he earned less than $590 per month. John will therefore have 3 months of trial work period left.

If John loses his job in January, 2006 and does not work at pay above the $590 per month level (as increased for inflation) until August 1, 2010, his earnings for April-June 2005 will not count as part of the trial work period because they would fall outside the sixty month rolling period. As a result, John would have 6 months left in his trial work period.

Note that the trial work period can be used only after a person begins receiving SSDI. It cannot be used to create eligibility.

Example Nine

John has a Schizoaffective disorder. He is able to work when on medication, but he goes off medication frequently, and works only intermittently. He begins work on January 1, 2005. He earns $500 a month through March, $750 a month in April, May and June and then loses his job. He gets a new job in October and earns $1,500 a month through the end of the year. He applies for SSDI in January, 2006. In all likelihood, John will not receive SSDI because he has earned at the substantial gainful activity level, unless he can use impairment related work expenses or subsidy to reduce his earnings level.

After the trial work period is complete, Social Security performs a new analysis to determine whether the beneficiary can work at the substantial gainful activity level. If Social Security decides substantial gainful activity cannot be achieved, SSDI benefits continue. If Social Security decides the beneficiary can work at the substantial gainful activity level, SSDI benefits are paid for a three month *grace period* and are terminated thereafter.

Extended Period of Eligibility

After the expiration of the *trial work period*, SSDI beneficiaries are entitled to a 36 month *extended period of eligibility*. During this extended period of eligibility, the beneficiary is entitled to full benefits during any month in which income falls below the substantial gainful activity level (for 2005, $830 a month). The beneficiary is responsible for notifying the local Social Security of wages received during each month in the extended period of eligibility.

Example Ten

John has a mild intellectual disability. He started receiving SSDI benefits on June 1, 2002. His ninth month of earnings in excess of the minimum trial work period threshold occurred in May, 2004, and his trial work period therefore ended on May 31, 2004. He continued to receive *grace period* benefits during June, July and August. John's *extended period of eligibility* goes to May 31, 2007. If John earns at less than the substantial gainful activity level during any month within the *extended period of eligibility*, he is entitled to full benefits for that month. John can use *impairment related work expenses* and *subsidy* to reduce his earnings level during his extended period of eligibility. If John does not earn at the substantial gainful activity in May, 2007, his extended period of eligibility will continue until he demonstrates the ability to work at the substantial gainful activity level.

Continued Payment Under a Vocational Rehabilitation Program

Benefit payments generally stop once Social Security determines that a beneficiary no longer has a disabling impairment due to medical improvement. However, if the beneficiary participates in a vocational rehabilitation program, benefits may continue until the vocational rehabilitation program ends. To qualify:

- The beneficiary must have begun participating in an appropriate program of vocational rehabilitation services, employment services or other support services before the disability ended; and

- Social Security must review the situation and decide that continued participation in the program would increase the likelihood of permanent removal from the disability benefit rolls.

Benefits may continue until the beneficiary completes the program, ceases participation in the program, or Social Security decides that continued participation in the program will not increase the likelihood of permanent removal from the disability benefit rolls.

Supplemental Security Income

The Supplemental Security Income Program, known as SSI, is a *needs based* program designed to supplement the income of people who are elderly, blind, or disabled and lack sufficient resources to provide for their own needs. The program provides a monthly cash benefit, which is reset each year based on inflation. For 2005, the maximum monthly benefit was $579. In addition, many states pay benefits to some individuals to supplement their federal benefits. Some of these states have arranged with Social Security to combine their supplementary payment with the federal SSI payments into one monthly check. Other states manage their own programs and make their payments separately. The states that combine their supplementary payment with the federal SSI benefit are:

- California
- The District of Columbia
- Hawaii
- Massachusetts

- Nevada
- New Jersey
- New York
- Pennsylvania
- Rhode Island
- Vermont

Because SSI is needs based, strict income and resource limitations (discussed below) must be satisfied. Disability is defined in the same manner as for the SSDI program. A person is disabled if he or she is unable to engage in substantial gainful activity because of a mental or physical impairment that has lasted or can be expected to last for at least 12 consecutive months or is expected to result in the person's death. Unlike the requirement for SSDI when based on the parent's work records, there is no requirement that the disability occur before age 22.

The SSI Income Limitation

Under the rules of the SSI program, a person who has a disability is denied benefits for any month in which the person's income exceeds the allowable SSI limitation. The limitation is reset each year and is generally equal to the maximum federal benefit under the SSI program ($579 per month in 2005). Importantly, however, certain items of income are excluded from the calculation, including significant amounts of *earned income*. This exclusion is designed to encourage SSI recipients to enter the work force. (See Examples Twelve and Thirteen below.)

SSI defines income very broadly to include anything your child receives, in cash or otherwise, that can be used to provide food, clothing, or shelter. Thus, *income* for SSI purposes includes earned income such as salary, unearned income such as Social Security benefits, pensions, state disability and unemployment benefits, and *in kind* income such as free food, clothing, and shelter.

The following items are specifically excluded:

- The first $20 of unearned income received in a month.

- The first $65 of earnings received in a month, and one-half of earnings over $65.

- The value of food stamps.

- Income tax refunds.

- Food, clothing, or shelter based on need provided by private nonprofit agencies.

- Cash that is loaned and must be repaid.

- Money someone else spends to pay expenses for items other than food, clothing, or shelter. (For example, someone pays your child's telephone bills, airplane tickets, medical bills.)

- Medical care and services provided free of charge or paid for directly to the provider by a third party.

- Room and board received during a medical confinement.

- Gifts to pay tuition or education fees, including grants, scholarships and fellowships.

- Amounts excluded under the various work supports discussed below, including amounts paid as *impairment related work expenses*, amounts set aside under an approved *plan for achieving self-support*, and amounts excluded under the *student earned income exclusion*.

SSI Limitation Relating to Resources

To qualify for Supplemental Security Income benefits, your child must also satisfy a strict *resource* limitation. The limitation for a single person is $2,000 ($3,000 for couples). That is, SSI benefits are denied to anyone whose resources exceed $2,000 ($3,000 for couples).

SSI defines resources to include cash, liquid assets such as stocks and bonds, and any other items of property that the individual owns and can convert to cash to use for food, clothing, or shelter. The following items are specifically excluded:

- A home owned and occupied by the person with a disability.

- Household goods and personal effects with a total market value of less than $2,000 and equipment required because of a recipient's physical condition, regardless of value.

- A car up to $4,500 of its current market value. The entire value is excluded if the car is necessary for employment or medical treatment, or if it is modified for your child's use.

- Cash value of life insurance policies up to $1,500; and burial policies, burial plots, and term insurance policies, regardless of the death benefit.

Deeming of Income and Resources

In determining the resources and income of your child, a portion of your income and resources will generally be considered available to your child if your child lives with you and is under age 18. This process is called deeming and generally disqualifies children who live in families with income above the poverty line from receiving SSI benefits.

The Social Security Administration Policy Operation Manual (POMS Section SI 1330.200) states the rule with respect to deeming of resources as follows:

> In determining SSI eligibility of a child under 18 who lives with his parent(s) or with the spouse of a parent, the resources of the child include the value of the countable resources of the parent(s) or spouse of a parent.... The value of parental resources is subject to deeming whether or not those resources are available to the child.

The rule with respect to deeming of income (POMS Section SI 1320.500) is stated as follows:

> A child under age 18 who is applying for or receiving SSI and who lives in the same household with his/her parent(s) and/or the spouse of a parent is presumed to share in the parents' income. This presumption continues through the month the child attains age 18 and meets all other requirements of the definition of a child. Under this presumption, and subject to certain exclusions, the parents' income is deemed to be available income to the child.

Thus, in many cases, children with disabilities who themselves satisfy the income and resource requirements for SSI eligibility are denied benefits because their parents have too much income or too many assets. However, once the child reaches age 18, the parents' assets are no longer considered available to the child. The child then qualifies for benefits so long as he or she has less than $2,000 in resources and less than $579 in monthly income. Remember, these are 2005 figures and may be revised in future years. In addition, significant amounts of earned income are excluded from the calculation.

Calculating Your Child's SSI Benefit

SSI payments vary from state to state; the amount of your child's check will therefore depend on where you live. The basic federal SSI payment for 2005, which is the minimum the states can pay, was $579 a month. The payment is, however, subject to potential reduction by a variety of factors.

- Your child's SSI check for each month will be reduced by one dollar for every two dollars the child earns over $65 during the month.

- Your child's SSI benefit will also be reduced for every dollar of unearned income (such as Social Security) the child receives over $20 during any particular month. If your child does not have $20 of unearned income, he or she is allowed to keep an additional $20 of earned income.

- If your child lives in a private household (for example, your home) and does not pay a proportionate share of household expenses, the SSI payment is generally reduced by one-third. The theory is that the child needs less since free room and board are available. If your child pays fair rent and a proportionate share of household expenses, the one-third reduction rule generally does not apply. Some parents charge their children rent and a proportionate share of expenses in order to avoid a reduction in benefits. The portion of the payment attributable to rent could, however, be taxable income to the parents.

- If your child lives in a public or private institution where bills are paid from Medicaid funds, monthly SSI benefits will be *substantially* reduced (typically to around $30).

- If your child lives in a public institution that is not funded by Medicaid, SSI is generally available only if the home is designated as an educational or vocational school or a community residence for 16 or fewer individuals.

Example Eleven

Fred is 15 years old and has cerebral palsy with epilepsy. Fred is enrolled in special education classes at the local high school and lives at home with his parents. Fred's father earns a good living, and Fred's mother takes care of Fred and Fred's brothers and sisters.

- Fred is not entitled to SSDI benefits currently, but he will be entitled to such benefits based on his father's earnings record when his father dies, becomes disabled, or reaches retirement age, as discussed earlier in this chapter.

- Fred will not be entitled to SSI benefits because he will not satisfy the income and resource requirements. Remember, because Fred lives at home and is under 18, a portion of his parents' property is considered to be his under the deeming rules.

- Assuming Fred does not have substantial income or assets of his own, he will likely be entitled to SSI benefits when he reaches 18; the deeming rules will no longer apply.

- If Fred continues to live at home and fails to pay his share of household expenses, his SSI check will likely be reduced by one-third. If Fred lives in a public or private residential facility that is funded by Medicaid, his check will likely be substantially reduced (probably to around $30). If Fred lives in a public residential facility that is not funded by Medicaid, SSI will not be available unless the home is designated as an educational or vocational school or a community residence for 16 or fewer individuals.

Example Twelve

Fred is 25 years old and has a moderate cognitive impairment due to head trauma resulting from a motorcycle accident at age 23. Fred has earnings of $850 per month.

- Fred will not be entitled to SSDI based on the earning records of either of his parents because he did not have his disability before attaining the age of 22. Fred will be entitled to SSDI based on his own earnings record when he retires or becomes disabled.

- Fred likely will not be entitled to SSI because he probably will not be considered disabled since his monthly earnings exceed $830 a month. If Fred spends more than $20 per month on impairment-related work expenses (for example, medication to help him work), he will likely be entitled to benefits. Remember, impairment-related work expenses can be subtracted from Fred's earnings for purposes of determining whether Fred earns the $830 threshold amount. Similarly, amounts set aside under an approved plan for achieving self-support can also be subtracted from earnings for this purpose.

- If Fred earned just $720 per month, he would be entitled to benefits, though his earnings would result in a reduction in the benefit level. The first $85 of earnings would result in no reduction, and every dollar over $85 would result in a reduction of 50 cents. The reduction would equal $317.50 ($720 minus $85 divided by two). Based on 2005 numbers, Fred's federal SSI benefit, calculated without regard to any state supplement, would be $261.50 ($579 minus $317.50). Fred's benefit would not be reduced to the extent his earnings were used to pay for impairment-related work expenses or to fulfill an approved plan for self-support.

- If Fred lives in a private residence and fails to pay his share of household expenses, his Supplemental Security Income check will be reduced by one-third. If Fred lives in a public or private residential facility that is funded by Medicaid, his check will likely be substantially reduced (probably to around $30). If Fred lives in a public residential facility that is not funded by Medicaid, SSI will not be available unless the home is designated as an educational or vocational school or a community residence for 16 or fewer individuals.

Example Thirteen

Mary has schizophrenia and has been receiving Supplemental Security Income for many years. Mary is on medication and recently began working at a job that pays $850 per month after a long period of unemployment.

- Mary would not be entitled to receive benefits under the SSI program if she earned $850 at the time of her application. As illustrated in Example Twelve, she would not be considered disabled since her earnings would exceed $830 (the disability threshold). However, earnings of more than $830 after Mary has already been receiving benefits under the SSI program will not render her ineligible. Mary's earnings may trigger a *disability review*, which would be designed to determine whether Mary continues to meet the Social Security disability definition (that is, whether her medical condition has improved).

- Mary's wages will cause a reduction in her benefits of $382.50. The first $85 will result in no reduction, and the remaining $765 will result in a reduction of 50 cents for each excess dollar received. Based on 2005 numbers, Mary's federal SSI benefit, calculated without regard to any state supplement, will equal $196.50 ($579 less $382.50).

- Mary's wages will not result in any reduction to the extent they are used to pay for work-related expenses attributable to her disability or to fulfill an approved plan for self-support.

- If Mary lives in a private residence and fails to pay her share of household expenses, her Supplemental Security Income check will likely be reduced by one-third. If Mary lives in a public or private residential facility that is funded by Medicaid, her check will be substantially reduced (probably to around $30). If Mary lives in a public residential facility that is not funded by Medicaid, SSI will not be available unless the home is designated as an educational or vocational school or a community residence for 16 or fewer individuals.

Example Fourteen

Fred has Down syndrome and lives in his own apartment, near his brother. He earns $265 a month working as a bagger at the local grocery store. Fred also receives a Social Security check based on his father's work record of $150 a month.

- Fred's SSI check will be reduced by $130 as a result of his receiving Social Security. Remember, unearned income reduces SSI benefits for every dollar over $20. Because

Social Security benefits are considered unearned, the first $20 will have no effect on Fred's SSI benefits; the next $130 will cause a reduction.

- Fred's wages will cause a reduction of $100. The first $65 yields no reduction; the next $200 causes a reduction of $100. Remember, the first $65 of earned income causes no benefit reduction; every dollar over $65 results in a reduction of 50 cents.

- Based on 2005 numbers, Fred's basic federal SSI benefit (not including any state supplement) would therefore equal $349—the $579 basic benefit, less $130, less $100.

- Fred's wages will not result in any reduction to the extent they are used to pay for work-related expenses attributable to his disability or to fulfill an approved plan for self-support. Fred's Social Security check will not cause a reduction in SSI benefits to the extent it is used to fulfill an approved plan for self-support.

- You may have noticed that in Examples Eleven, Twelve, and Thirteen it was earnings in excess of $85 that resulted in a reduction in benefits, while in Example Fourteen it was earnings in excess of $65. The difference in this example is that $20 was used to offset the reduction due to receipt of Social Security benefits.

Special SSI Employment Supports

As was the case with SSDI, the SSI rules contain special employment supports. Several of these employment supports have already been discussed. First, for purposes of computing an SSI recipient's benefit, the *earned income exclusion* permits an SSI recipient to exclude the first $65 in earnings ($85 if the recipient does not have any unearned income) plus one-half of remaining earnings. The earned income exclusion cannot be used for purposes of initially qualifying for SSI. Operation of the rule is illustrated in Examples Twelve, Thirteen and Fourteen.

Second, the deduction for *impairment related work expenses* permits the deduction of expenses incurred by a person with a disability in order to work. Expenses can be deducted both for purposes of determining eligibility and for purposes of computing the SSI benefit level. The types of expense that can qualify are described under *Special SSDI Employment Supports—Impairment Related Work Expenses*.

Example Fifteen

John has a Schizoaffective disorder. John is able to function in a work environment with medication. He earns $1,000 a month when he applies for SSI benefits, which is above the threshold for substantial gainful activity (for 2005, $830 a month). However, his medication costs him $200 a month.

John can claim the medication as an impairment related work expense, reducing his earnings to $800 a month, which is below the threshold for substantial gainful activity. Accordingly, John qualifies for SSI benefits.

John computes his SSI benefit as follows.

$1,000.00	Gross earnings
- 200.00	IRWE
$800.00	
- 20.00	General income exclusion
$780.00	
- 65.00	Earned income exclusion
$715.00	
- 357.50	one-half remainder
$357.50	Countable income

....

$579.00	2005 Federal Benefit Rate
- 357.50	Countable Income
$221.50	SSI Payment

Third, the deduction for *subsidy and special work conditions* permits a deduction where a person can demonstrate that wages received exceed the value of work performed. The circumstances where this is possible are discussed in Special SSDI Employment Supports—Subsidy and Special Work Conditions. Subsidy and special work conditions can be claimed for purposes of determining SSI eligibility, but not for purposes of computing the amount of the SSI benefit.

Example Sixteen

John has a mild intellectual disability. He is able to work but requires the assistance of a job coach on a half-time basis. The cost of the job coach is covered by a local vocational rehabilitation agency. John earns $850 a month at the time that he applies for SSI benefits.

John can claim a subsidy because he has a job coach who helps him perform some of his work. The value of the job coach is calculated by multiplying the number of hours of assistance by John's hourly wage. Since the job coach assists John on a half-time basis, John's countable income will be reduced by one-half for purposes of determining John's eligibility for SSI benefits. John therefore satisfies the substantial gainful activity test.

John may not, however, reduce his countable income by reason of the subsidy for purposes of computing his SSI benefit. Accordingly, John computes his SSI benefit as follows.

$850.00	Earned income
- 20.00	General income exclusion
$830.00	
- 65.00	Earned income exclusion
$765.00	
- 387.50	one-half remainder
$387.50	Countable income

....

$579.00	2005 Federal Benefit Rate
- 387.50	Countable income
$191.50	SSI Payment

Fourth, as was the case with SSDI, an *unsuccessful work attempt* is not considered for purposes of determining whether an SSI applicant is capable of substantial gainful activity. Unsuccessful work attempts are discussed in *Special SSDI Employment Supports—Unsuccessful Work Attempt*.

Fifth, as was the case with SSDI, if an SSI beneficiary participates in a vocational rehabilitation program, SSI benefits may continue until the vocational rehabilitation program ends even if Social Security determines that a beneficiary no longer has a disabling impairment due to medical improvement. This rule is discussed in *Special SSDI Employment Supports—Continued Payment Under a Vocational Rehabilitation Program*.

Additional SSI employment supports are as follows:

Student Earned Income Exclusion

The student earned income exclusion permits unmarried students under age 22 who are regularly attending school to exclude up to $1,410 of earned income per month in figuring SSI benefits. The maximum yearly exclusion is $5,670. These amounts are for the year 2005; they are adjusted each year based on the cost-of-living. Other work supports—the earned income exclusion and the deduction for impairment related work expenses, can be deducted against income that is not excluded under the student earned income exclusion.

Regularly attending school means taking one or more courses of study and attending classes:

• In a college or university for at least 8 hours a week; or

• In grades 7-12 for at least 12 hours a week; or

- In a training course to prepare for employment for at least 12 hours a week (15 hours a week if the course involves shop practice); or

- For less time than indicated above for reasons beyond the student's control, for example illness.

If the student is home taught because of a disability, the student may be considered *regularly attending school* by:

- Studying a course or courses given by a school (grades 7-12), college, university or government agency; and

- Having a home visitor or tutor who directs the study.

Example Seventeen

This example is identical to an example provided by Social Security in POMS Section SI 00820.510, except that it is updated to use 2005 figures.

Jim Thayer, a student child, starts working in June, 2005 at a local hardware store. He had no prior earnings during the year, and he has no unearned income. Jim earns $1600 a month in June, July, and August. In September, when he returns to school, Jim continues working part-time. He earns $800 a month in September and October. Jim's countable income computation for June through October is as follows:

June, July, and August

$1600.00	Gross earnings
- 1410.00	Student child exclusion
$ 190.00	
- 20.00	General income exclusion
$ 170.00	
- 65.00	Earned income exclusion
$ 105.00	

- 52.50	One-half remainder
$ 52.50	Countable income

Jim has used up $4,230 of his $5,670 yearly student child earned income exclusion ($1,410 in each of the three months). His SSI benefit reduction is $52.50 as a result of earnings in each of June, July and August.

September

$ 800.00	Gross earnings
- 800.00	Student child exclusion
0.00	Countable income

Jim has now used up $5,030 of his $5,670 yearly student child earned income exclusion ($4,230 plus $800). There is no benefit reduction as a result of September earnings. Jim has $640 of his yearly student child earned income exclusion remaining ($5,670 minus $5,030).

October

$ 800.00	Gross earnings
- 640.00	Student child exclusion remaining
$ 160.00	
- 20.00	General income exclusion
$ 140.00	
- 65.00	Earned income exclusion
$ 75.00	
- 37.50	one-half remainder
$ 37.50	Countable income

Jim has exhausted his entire $5,670 yearly student child earned income exclusion. The exclusion cannot be applied to any additional earnings during the calendar year. SSI benefits are reduced by $37.50 as a result of October earnings.

Plan for Achieving Self-Support

A plan for achieving self-support (PASS) allows an SSI beneficiary to set aside income and/or resources for a specified time for a work goal, such as for education, vocational training, or starting a business. Income and resources set aside under a PASS is not counted in calculating the SSI payment amount or in determining initial and continuing eligibility for SSI. A PASS must:

- Be designed especially for the person with a disability;

- Be in writing, preferably on form SSA-545-BK (copies of form SSA-545-BK can be obtained from your local Social Security office, any PASS expert, or from the Social Security web site (www.socialsecurity.gov));

- Have a specific work goal which the person with a disability is capable of performing;

- Have a specific timeframe for the work goal;

- Show what money (other than SSI payments) and other resources will be used to achieve the work goal;

- Show how the money and resources will be used to reach the work goal; and

- Show how the money set aside will be kept identifiable from other funds.

Social Security will help you put together a PASS. You can get a PASS Expert's toll-free telephone number by calling 1-800-772-1213 or visiting the web site, www.socialsecurity.gov/work/ResourcesToolkit/pass.html. You can also get help from vocational counselors, social workers, or benefit specialists. PASS proposals must be approved by Social Security and are also periodically reviewed to assure that the plan is actually helping the beneficiary achieve progress.

If a PASS is stopped for *good reason*, the funds remaining in the PASS become a resource, and the Social Security beneficiary is given six months to spend the resources down below the $2,000 level. An SSI recipient who abandons a PASS without good cause is potentially subject to penalties.

 TIP Documenting a PASS is very important. Make sure that the savings and spending provisions in the PASS are followed. Savings should be recorded and receipts should be retained. Send a letter to the local Social Security office on a monthly basis to report income and PASS savings and expenses. Make sure to keep a copy of the letter and all receipts.

Example Eighteen

Lisa earns $850 a month. Assuming Lisa has no impairment related work expenses and cannot claim subsidy, her SSI reduction is $387.50 computed as follows:

$850.00	Earned income
- 20.00	General income exclusion
$830.00	
- 65.00	Earned income exclusion
$765.00	
- 387.50	one-half remainder
$387.50	Countable income

If Lisa places $200 in a PASS, the reduction is just $187.50 ($850 minus $85 divided by 2 minus $200). Of course Lisa must spend the $200 contributed to the PASS in accordance with the provisions of the PASS.

POMS Section SI 00870 lists the following examples of items and services for which expenses can be allowed under a PASS, provided that they satisfy the criteria set forth above:

- attendant care

- basic living skills training

- child care

- dues and subscription costs for publications for academic or professional purposes

- equipment, supplies, operating capital, and inventory required to establish and carry on a trade or business

- equipment and tools, including safety equipment, whether specific to the individual's condition or designed for use by a non-disabled person

- finance and service charges connected with obtaining any of the above, including finance and service charges related to a bank account that is set up solely for the purpose of keeping PASS funds separate and identifiable

- food and shelter while temporarily absent from one's permanent residence to attend educational, training, employment, trade, or business activities, if there is also a cost associated with maintaining the permanent residence

- job coaching/counseling services

- job search or relocation expenses

- meals consumed during work hours (including job-training and school)

- modifications to buildings, vehicles, etc., for operational or access purposes for persons with disabilities

- PASS preparation fees

- taxes and government-imposed user fees (e.g., permits and licenses) connected with obtaining any item on this list, except that income taxes or government-imposed penalties or fines are not allowable

- transportation—-hire of private or commercial carriers, or hire of person to drive the individual's vehicle

- transportation—-lease, rental, or purchase of a vehicle, plus associated costs for fuel, insurance, maintenance, registration, taxes, etc. transportation—-public transportation and common carriers

- tuition, books, supplies, and all fees and costs imposed by or in connection with an educational or occupational training facility, including fees for tutoring, testing, counseling, etc.

- uniforms, specialized clothing, safety equipment, and appropriate attire (e.g., suits, dresses) needed for job interviews or to begin working in an office or professional setting

Blind Work Expenses

SSI recipients with blindness are allowed to deduct the cost of *blind work expenses* both for purposes of determining eligibility for SSI and for computing the SSI benefit. A blind work expense is any reasonable expense that helps the beneficiary earn income. Some examples of blind work expenses are:

- Helper animal expenses,
- Transportation to and from work,
- Federal, State and local income taxes,
- Social Security taxes,

- Attendant care services,
- Visual and sensory aids,
- Translation of materials into Braille,
- Professional association fees, and
- Union dues.

Example Nineteen

John earns $405 in income. He incurs blind work expenses of $60. His SSI benefit calculated with and without deduction for the blind work expense, is as follows:

Without Blind Work Expense	With Blind Work Expense
$405.00 Earned income	$405.00 Earned income
20.00 General income exclusion	20.00 General income exclusion
$385.00	$385.00
- 65.00 Earned income exclusion	- 65.00 Earned income exclusion
$320.00	$320.00
- 160.00 one-half remaining earnings	- 160.00 one-half remaining earnings
$160.00 Countable income	$160.00 Countable income
	- 60.00 Blind work expenses
	$ 100.00 Countable income
$579.00 2005 Federal Benefit Rate	$579.00 2005 Federal Benefit Rate
- 160.00 Countable Income	- 100.00 Countable Income
$419.00 SSI Payment	$479.00 SSI Payment

Medicare

Medicare is a federal health insurance program run by the Social Security Administration. It is designed to pay the cost of health care for people over the age of 65 and for people with disabilities who are under the age of 65 and have been eligible to receive Social Security benefits for at least two years, or who need kidney dialysis treatments or a kidney transplant. It is not necessary that your child actually receive Social Security benefits for two years, only that the eligibility requirements were satisfied.

As with the Social Security programs discussed above, Medicare is non-needs based. Eligibility is based on premiums that the recipient (or a family member) has paid into the program in the form of payroll tax deductions and does not depend on financial need.

Substantial revisions to the program were adopted in the Medicare Modernization Act of 2003. Medicare recipients now have the ability to participate in the original Medicare program, or to choose expanded coverage through Medicare Advantage health plans. In addition, Medicare was expanded to provide prescription drug coverage.

The original medicare plan consists of two parts:

Part A (Hospital Insurance) provides hospital insurance benefits that help pay for care in hospitals and for related health-care services after leaving a hospital, including skilled nursing or rehabilitation care at facilities that have been certified by Medicare. No premiums are required. Benefits are available to eligible persons regardless of ability to pay. However, Medicare generally does not pay the entire cost of a hospital stay, and Medicare beneficiaries are generally required to finance a portion of each hospital bill from a non-Medicare source.

Part B (Supplemental Medical Insurance) helps cover the cost of medical services such as physician's services and outpatient hospital treatment. It also covers some other medical services that Part A does not cover, such as physical and occupational therapists, and some home health care. To be eligible for Part B, a person must be enrolled in Part A and pay monthly premiums. The government announces the premiums that apply for each year in September of the prior year. For 2005, the premium was $78.20 per month. Premium rates may be increased if program costs rise.

Under Supplemental Medical Insurance, Medicare generally pays 80 percent of the approved charges for doctors' services and the cost of certain other services that are not covered by Part A, after the insured pays a $110 deductible. Many individuals purchase Medigap policies from private insurance companies to fill gaps in the original Medicare plan. Medigap policies must follow federal and state laws.

The charts on the following two pages demonstrate which medical services are covered by the original Medicare plan and how the benefits are paid.

Table of Medicare Benefits
Effective after January 1, 2005

MEDICARE BASIC PLAN: HOSPITAL INSURANCE COVERED SERVICES PER BENEFIT PERIOD (1)			
Service	**Benefit**	**Medicare Pays**	**Person Pays****
HOSPITALIZATION Semi-private room & board, general nursing, & misc. hospital services & supplies. This includes inpatient care in critical access hospitals and mental health care.	First 60 days	All but $912	$912
	61st to 90th day	All but $228/day	$228/day
	91st to 150th day*	All but $456/day	$456/day
	Beyond 150 days	Nothing	All costs
POST-HOSPITAL SKILLED NURSING FACILITY CARE In a facility approved by Medicare. A person must have been in a hospital for at least 3 days and enter the facility within 30 days after hospital discharge. (2)	First 20 days	100% of approved amount	Nothing
	Additional 80 days	All but $114/day	$114/day
	Beyond 100 days	Nothing	All costs
HOME HEALTH CARE	Unlimited visits as medically necessary	Full cost of services, 80% of equipment	Nothing for services, 20% for equipment
HOSPICE CARE	Two 90 day periods, one 30-day period (and extensions as necessary)	All, but limit on cost for out-patient drugs & respite care	Limited cost for outpatient drugs & respite care
BLOOD	Blood	All but first 3 pints	For first 3 pints

*60 day Reserve days may be used only once; days used are not renewable.

(1) A Benefit Period begins on the first day a person receives service as an inpatient in a hospital and ends after he or she has been out of the hospital or skilled nursing facility for 60 days in a row.

(2) Medicare and private insurance will not pay for most nursing-home care.

MEDICARE SUPPLEMENT PLAN: MEDICAL INSURANCE COVERED SERVICES PER CALENDER YEAR			
Service	**Benefit**	**Medicare Pays**	**Person Pays**
MEDICAL EXPENSE Physician inpatient & outpatient medical visits, physical & speech therapy, supplies, ambulance, etc.	Medicare pays for medical services in or out of the hospital	80% of approved amount after $110 deductible	$110 deductible plus 20% of balance
HOME HEALTH CARE	Unlimited visits as medically necessary	100% of approved services, 80% of approved amount for durable medical equipment	Nothing for services, 20% for approved amount durable medical equipment
BLOOD	Blood	All but first 3 pints per calender year	For first 3 pints (or replace)

* Once a person has $110 of expense for covered services in 2005, the deductible does not apply to any further covered services for the rest of the year.

** A person pays for charges higher than the amount approved by Medicare unless the doctor or supplier agrees to accept Medicare's approved amount as the total charge for services rendered.

In addition to the copayments and deductibles discussed above, the original Medicare plan has several limitations. First, the original Medicare plan does not cover the cost of catastrophic health care (that is, the cost of hospitalization for periods outside the normal 90- or 150-day coverage periods). Second, the original Medicare plan provides less reimbursement for expenses incurred in treating mental illness than for other types of illnesses. Under the Basic Hospital Insurance Plan (Part A), benefits for psychiatric hospital care are subject to a lifetime limit of 190 days. Under the Supplementary Medical Insurance Plan (Part B), out-of-hospital psychiatric services are reimbursed at a 50 percent rate (as opposed to the 80 percent reimbursement rate applicable to other types of medical services). Finally, Medicare does not pay for the cost of nursing homes, other than for certain skilled nursing facilities.

Beginning in 2004, Medicare was expanded to permit Medicare recipients more choices among health plans. People who are enrolled under Medicare Parts A and B now have the ability to receive expanded coverage by enrolling in the Medicare Advantage Plan. Participants in Medicare Advantage Plans can generally choose between:

- Managed Care Plans, which generally restrict participants to doctors, specialists or hospitals on the plan's list, except in the case of emergencies. The list is referred to as the plan's network;

- Medicare Preferred Provider Plans, which permit visits to doctors, specialists and hospitals not on the plan's network, but at an added expense;

- Medicare Private Fee for Service Plans, which permit participants to go to any doctor or hospital that accepts the terms of the plan's payment; and

- Medicare Specialty Plans, that provide more focused health care for specific people.

Joining a Medicare Advantage Plan can often result in extra benefits. However, the participant will need to follow the special rules of the plan and may have to pay for the extra benefits.

Medicare has also added a new prescription drug benefit. In 2005, participants can obtain a Medicare-approved drug discount card. People with lower incomes can obtain a $600 credit for drug purchases. Beginning in 2006, the drug discount cards will begin to phase out, and Medicare recipients will have the ability to enroll in new Medicare prescription drug plans. In general, the premium will be $35 a month, participants will be required to pay the first $250 in yearly drug costs, 25% of yearly drug costs between $250 and $2,250, 100% of yearly drug costs between $2,251 and $3,600, and 5% of yearly drug costs in excess of $3,600. The Medicare prescription drug plan will pay the rest. People with lower incomes will receive extra help.

Most individuals with disabilities who lose SSDI benefits due to work continue to receive at least 93 consecutive months of hospital and supplementary medical insurance under Medicare. The period generally begins after the end of the trial work period. No premium is required for hospital insurance during this period. After premium-free Medicare coverage ends due to work, some individuals who have returned to work may buy continued Medicare coverage, as long as they remain medically disabled. Some individuals with low incomes and limited resources may be eligible for State assistance with the cost.

Medicaid

Medicaid is a federally sponsored program, administered by the states, to pay medical expenses of certain low-income individuals, principally those who are blind, disabled, elderly, or in families with dependent children. If your child is eligible for both Medicare and Medicaid, Medicaid can be used to supplement the coverage provided by Medicare. For example, Medicaid can be used to pay for expenses that are not covered by Medicare, such as nursing homes, catastrophic illnesses, and the copayments and deductibles required by Medicare.

In the vast majority of states, Medicaid is available to people who are eligible for SSI and for certain other people with limited resources. Certain states, known as Section 209(b) states, have made elections to apply more restrictive financial needs standards. There are currently thirteen Section 209(b) states: Connecticut, Hawaii, Illinois, Indiana, Minnesota, Missouri, Nebraska, New Hampshire, North Dakota, Ohio, Oklahoma, Utah, and Virginia. Even in Section 209(b) states, however, people with disabilities who are financially needy will generally qualify for Medicaid.

In addition, even if your child does not initially qualify for Medicaid because of the state's income or asset test (discussed in the section dealing with SSI eligibility), your child may qualify if medical expenses, when subtracted from personal income and assets, would bring the income and assets down to the state's eligibility level. This is known as the Medicaid *spend down* rule. If medical expenses cause your child to spend down income or resources, your child becomes eligible for the program. The spend-down rule has been adopted by most, but not all, of the states. In states that have not adopted the Medicaid spend down rule, it is sometimes possible for people with high medical expenses to qualify for Medicaid even if their income exceeds the state's limit if they transfer their income to trusts known as Miller trusts.

Finally, if your child receives SSI but loses eligibility because of an earnings increase, your child generally will retain eligibility for Medicaid until the government determines that he or she can afford private medical insurance. The required amount of earnings before losing Medicaid eligibility varies from state to state.

For 2005, the earnings threshold amounts are as follows:

State-By-State 2005 Thresholds for Individuals with Disabilities

STATE	THRESHOLD	STATE	THRESHOLD
Alabama	$20,553.00	Montana	$24,689.00
Alaska	$44,550.00	Nebraska	$30,801.00
Arizona	$24,489.00	Nevada	$26,738.00
Arkansas	$23,075.00	New Hampshire	$39,291.00
California	$30,754.00	New Jersey	$28,041.00
Colorado	$29,886.00	New Mexico	$27,339.00
Connecticut	$45,095.00	New York	$37,575.00
Delaware	$31,185.00	North Carolina	$26,403.00
Dist. of Columbia	$28,016.00	North Dakota	$31,353.00
Florida	$23,991.00	Ohio	$28,576.00
Georgia	$22,912.00	Oklahoma	$21,216.00
Hawaii	$23,450.00	Oregon	$24,655.00
Idaho	$34,527.00	Pennsylvania	$24,795.00
Illinois	$28,686.00	Rhode Island	$31,667.00
Indiana	$29,194.00	South Carolina	$24,593.00
Iowa	$24,212.00	South Dakota	$28,186.00
Kansas	$28,809.00	Tennessee	$19,091.00
Kentucky	$23,266.00	Texas	$26,014.00
Louisiana	$23,580.00	Utah	$26,326.00
Maine	$34,417.00	Vermont	$29,976.00
Maryland	$29,436.00	Virginia	$25,484.00
Massachusetts	$31,786.00	Washington	$22,630.00
Michigan	$21,365.00	West Virginia	$24,346.00
Minnesota	$39,531.00	Wisconsin	$29,921.00
Mississippi	$22,433.00	Wyoming	$22,988.00
Missouri	$26,668.00	N. Mariana Island	$14,916.00

Example Twenty

John is a resident of the state of Wisconsin. He has been on SSI and Medicaid for many years. He gets a job that pays him $1,245 a month and has no deductions for impairment related work expenses or other work incentives. John loses SSI eligibility. The calculation is as follows:

$1,245.00	Earned income
- 20.00	General income exclusion
$1,225.00	
- 65.00	Earned income exclusion
$1,160.00	
- 580.00	one-half remaining earnings
$ 580.00	Countable income

....

$579 00	2005 Federal Benefit Rate
- 580 00	Countable Income
$0.00	SSI Payment

Nevertheless, because John is a resident of the state of Wisconsin and his yearly earnings are less than $29,921, he retains Medicaid eligibility.

Many states have also enacted *Medicaid Buy-In Programs*, which are intended to permit certain people with disabilities to pay premiums to participate in the Medicaid program if such persons cannot qualify for Medicaid due to excess earnings. Although the rules vary by state, in most states that have the program, the program is generally available to a person whose income is less than 250% of the federal poverty level. For 2005, the federal poverty level is $9,570 per year, and 250% of this amount is $23,925 per year. As of the beginning of 2005, the following states offered this program: Alaska, Arizona, Arkansas, California, Connecticut, Florida, Illinois, Indiana, Iowa, Kansas, Maine, Minnesota,

Mississippi, Nebraska, New Hampshire, New Jersey, New Mexico, New York, Oregon, Pennsylvania, South Carolina, Utah, Vermont, Washington, Wisconsin and Wyoming.

By federal law, Medicaid is required to cover at least the following services:

- Necessary medical services provided by physicians.

- Hospital and skilled nursing-facility care.

- Home health-care services.

- Outpatient or clinical services.

- Independent laboratory and X-ray services.

Medicaid is the primary source of public funding of residential facilities for people with disabilities, including hospitals, nursing facilities, intermediate care facilities for persons with intellectual disabilities, home and community based services, prevocational, educational and supported employment, day treatment and other partial hospitalization services, psychosocial rehabilitation services and clinic services (whether or not furnished in a facility) for persons with mental illness.

Ticket to Work Program

The *Ticket to Work And Self-Sufficiency Program* (the Ticket Program) is for people who receive benefits under SSDI or SSI because of disability or blindness. The program is strictly voluntary and offers greater choices in getting recipients services needed to go to work. The goal of the program is to help SSDI and SSI recipients earn enough money so they will not need Social Security cash benefits.

Under the Ticket Program, SSDI or SSI recipients can receive employment services, vocational services or other services through employment networks, which are private organizations or government agencies that have agreed to work with Social Security in providing employment services to beneficiaries with disabilities.

Information about the Ticket Program, can be obtained from Maximus, Inc. at 1-866-968-7842 toll-free (TTY 1-866-833-2967). Maximus is a private company that is working with Social Security to help manage the program. Maximus can answer most questions about the Ticket Program, and can provide names, addresses, and telephone numbers of employment networks across the country.

Other Government Benefit Programs

State and federal governments also operate certain other programs that can be of help to people who have disabilities. Under the food stamp program, people who lack sufficient resources to provide for their own nutritional requirements are given stamps that can be exchanged for food at the local supermarket. In most cases, people who are eligible for SSI qualify for food stamps as well. Information about the food stamp program can be obtained from your local food stamp office or at any Social Security Office.

Your child can also qualify for housing assistance under various programs sponsored by the United States Department of Housing and Urban Development (HUD). One such program, known as Section 8, provides rental assistance for individuals with disabilities who satisfy certain needs based criteria. To qualify, your child must apply for benefits and live in a building that qualifies for Section 8 rental subsidies. This means that the landlord must agree to participate in the program, the building must pass an inspection by the local housing authority, and the landlord cannot charge more than is considered to be *fair* by the government. Rent is then subsidized. Your child pays what the government says he or she can afford, and the government pays the rest.

A second HUD-sponsored program, known as Section 811, provides loans directly to organizations that are interested in building residential facilities for people who have disabilities. The organizations must be operated on a not-for-profit basis and must satisfy the government that the loans will be repaid. Many group homes have been built with assistance under the Section 811 program.

Information about Section 8 and Section 811 can be obtained from the United States Department of Housing and Urban Development or from your local housing authority.

Applying for and Maintaining Benefits

We strongly encourage parents to apply for SSI for their child when the child turns 18. This is true for several reasons.

First, as discussed above, assuming the child satisfies Social Security's definition of disability, the child will generally become eligible for SSI upon reaching age 18 because the deeming rules no longer apply.

Second, in cases where it is unclear whether a child is disabled under Social Security's definitions, it tends to be easier to establish disability when the child is younger. As discussed above, a person is considered disabled under Social Security's definition if, by reason of a physical or mental impairment, the person is unable to engage in substantial gainful activity. A person is generally considered to be unable to engage in *substantial gainful activity* if, due to the impairment, the person cannot earn more than $830 per month. The $830 amount is based on 2005 figures and increases each year. In borderline cases, particularly in situations involving a mild intellectual disability, it is probably easier to establish disability when a child is very young and has no earning history.

Third, in most states a person who is eligible for SSI will also be eligible for Medicaid. Although your child may be covered by your health insurance policy, it is good to have Medicaid as a back-stop in case your child has medical needs that are not fully covered by private insurance. Also, Medicaid can be used to cover co-payments and deductibles.

Fourth, as discussed above, a child who is disabled before reaching age 22 will be eligible for SSDI benefits when the parents retire, die or become disabled. Although SSDI received will reduce the amount of your child's SSI benefit, SSDI benefits are general-ly substantially larger than SSI benefits. Moreover, once your child begins receiving SSDI, the child will automatically qualify for Medicare within two years. Applying for SSI when the child reach-es age 18 establishes that disability occurred before age 22 and therefore avoids possible future dispute with Social Security administrators regarding the date that disability occurred.

TIP Put it on your calendar. When your child turns 18, apply for SSI.

You can apply for SSDI or SSI benefits for your child by call-ing or visiting your local Social Security office. You should have your child's Social Security number, birth certificate, and informa-tion regarding your child's earnings available when you apply. If you are signing up your child for SSI and your child is under age 18, you also will need to provide records that show your income and your assets, as well as those of your child.

The medical evaluation specialists at Social Security will need detailed medical records to help them decide if your child is disabled. You can help by providing the child's medical records or helping Social Security get them. When you file, Social Security will ask you to provide names, addresses and telephone numbers of all doctors, hospitals, clinics and other specialists your child has visited. Be as specific and complete as possible.

TIP If there is any question about whether your child is disabled within the meaning of Social Security's rules, make sure your child's doctor is familiar with Social Security's listed impairments and, if possible, puts material in your child's medical records establishing that your child satisfies Social Security's rules. Listed impairments were discussed under *Establishing Disability* above.

You will need to be persistent and patient. If someone at the Social Security office tells you that your child is not eligible for a benefit that you think he or she is entitled to, proceed with the application in a formal, written fashion to get an official determination. Remember, while the people who work for Social Security can be helpful and knowledgeable, they can make mistakes like anyone else.

If your application is initially rejected, you have the right to request that Social Security reconsider your claim. Many people who are initially denied benefits are later granted benefits during the appeal process.

Generally, you have 60 days after you receive a notice of denial to file an appeal. If you miss the appeal deadline, file it anyway. Sometimes the Social Security Administration will waive the deadline if there is a compelling reason for the delay. The appeal must be submitted in writing, either by letter or on a special request form available from your local Social Security office. It is generally advisable to have an attorney who is familiar with the Social Security rules help you through the appeal process.

There are three stages of hearings:

- Administrative Hearing (review by the Social Security Administrative Law Judge).

- Appeals Council (review by the Social Security Appeals Council in Arlington, Virginia).

- Federal Court (review by an independent Federal District Judge).

If your child qualifies for benefits, your child will be subject to periodic reviews. The frequency of reviews depends on the nature and severity of your child's medical condition and whether it is expected to improve.

- If improvement is expected, your child's reviews generally will take place every six to 18 months.

- If improvement is possible, but cannot be predicted, the case will be reviewed about once every three years.

- If improvement is not expected, the case will be reviewed once every seven years.

At the review, Social Security will seek to determine whether your child's medical condition has improved. You will need to provide doctors' names, addresses and phone numbers and to bring patient record numbers for any hospitals and other medical sources that have treated your child since your last contact. If your child has worked since the last review, Social Security will also need information about work dates, pay received, and the kind of work that was done. Social Security generally does not conduct continuing disability reviews of participants enrolled in the ticket to work program.

If your child works, Social Security also requires your child to file monthly reports notifying Social Security of

- Enrollment in and completion of vocational rehabilitation programs

- Number of hours worked and hourly wage

- Monthly gross income accompanied by pay receipts

- Change in work status, such as separation from employment

- Any unearned income

It is also advisable to include in the report to Social Security information relating to any work supports that you are claiming, such as impairment related work expenses, subsidy, PASS, and the student earned income exclusion.

 TIP Always keep copies of everything you send to Social Security and carefully note the date of mailing. The Social Security Administration is very large, and papers get lost.

If your child's benefits stop due to excess earnings, your child has a restart period of five years during which your child will be able to start benefits immediately if your child is unable to continue working due to disability. Your child will not have to file a new disability application and will not have to wait for the end of the disability review process before benefits start.

Conclusion

As is apparent, the rules relating to government benefits are complex. If, after reading this chapter, you are unable to determine whether your child qualifies under a particular program, go ahead and apply. The worst that can happen is that you will be turned down. You can obtain answers to particular questions that you may have by contacting the Social Security Administration, your state's Public Welfare Department, or a social worker or attorney familiar with governmental benefits.

Calculating Your Child's Financial Needs

E
VEN ASSUMING YOUR CHILD MAKES MAXIMUM USE OF THE
government benefit programs described in the previous
chapter, in most cases government benefits will not be
enough to provide the kind of life you will want your child to have.
This is because government benefits pay for *eats and sheets* and
little else. That is, the government will provide your child with
room and board, but it will not provide funds for many of the activities that make life enjoyable and meaningful—vacations with
friends and relatives, a meal out, recreational programs at the local
YMCA, and all the other activities you listed when you prepared
your child's life plan way back in the first chapter of this book.

Moreover, some parents do not expect government programs
to be major contributors to their children's financial futures. While
these parents tend to keep open the possibility of using government
benefits in the future by leaving money to their children in the
types of trusts described in the next chapter, they require a realistic estimate of the cost of private care.

In this chapter we give you the tools you need to calculate
your child's lifetime financial requirements over and above government benefits, and how much must go into the trust to fund those
needs.

This is not to say that the amount you leave in trust should necessarily equal the amount you calculate to be required to meet your child's financial needs. None of us are omniscient. The calculations can be only estimates. It is possible that your child's financial needs will grow in the future or that government benefits will be reduced. Either circumstance would likely result in a substantial increase in your child's need for private funds.

Moreover, if you have other children, you will want to be fair to them as well. This is particularly true if your other children will be expected to act as their sibling's advocate in the future. You will not want to create a resentment that could affect a brother or sister's willingness to be helpful. In fact, when parents decide to leave a disproportionate share of their estate to a child with a disability, we frequently advise the parents to explain their reasoning to their other children in order to avoid resentment. Some parents leave an explanatory note in their Letter of Intent.

Calculating your child's financial requirements can, however, be quite instructive. It not only gives you a sense of what your child will need when you are gone, it also helps shape your decisions regarding the disposition of your estate and helps you to decide among various investment alternatives. For example, if you find that your estate will not be sufficient to meet your child's needs, you may decide to purchase additional life insurance.

One mistake to avoid. Some parents disinherit a child with a disability, leaving everything to other children with the informal understanding that the other children will look out for their sibling. This can be a disastrous choice.

The relative who receives the extra money to look after the person with a disability might enter a nursing home and be required by the government to spend the money on his or her own care. The person might go bankrupt and be required to give the money to creditors, or get a divorce and be required to split the money with his or her spouse, or die and will the money to others, or simply refuse to spend it on the person with a disability.

It is far better to leave money in trust as described in Chapter Six for the child who has the disability so that a separate fund of guaranteed money is available to the person who really needs it.

Financial Needs Analysis

The process is less mysterious than it sounds. Begin by simply calculating the amount you currently spend on your child over and above government benefits. If your child is very young, you will need to estimate what you will be spending when your child is older. You then have to build in a reserve to pay for things that you currently do for free, that your child may need to pay for after you have died.

The following are examples of some of the major items you will want to think about:

- **Advocacy and guardianship costs**. Will your child need the services of a professional advocate? If so, you will need to include the cost. If your child will rely on family members, will you want to reimburse them for their time? If not, how about their expenses? For example, a brother or sister may need to travel to visit a sibling. You may want them to be reimbursed for gas or airfare. Such payments may encourage a sibling to take the responsibility more seriously.

- **Emergency expenses for medical needs**. What kind of reserve will you need to provide for emergency medical and dental needs? Dental care can be a major expense. In some states, Medicaid does not pay the cost of dental care, and adults can incur substantial expenses for items such as root canals, crowns, or periodontal work.

- **Capital items**. Here we mean infrequent big-ticket items such as a television, VCR, a CD player, or some nice furniture.

- **Government benefits**. Obviously, your child's requirements will be significantly greater if your child does not receive government benefits such as social security, supplemental security income, medicaid, medicare, or state residential cost of care benefit programs. Even if your child relies on such programs, you may want a reserve in case these programs are reduced in the future. Many families compute the reserve by going through the calculation described in the following pages twice, once assuming government benefits continue at the current level and again assuming such benefits are reduced or eliminated. Although it is unusual for a family to be able to fund the trust assuming no government benefits, the calculation can be educational.

To complete your financial needs analysis, just complete the forms that follow. The first chart, which contains three parts, enables you to calculate your child's anticipated annual income requirements. Charts Three, Four and Five can then be used to calculate the amount required by the trust to fund those needs. Chart Two is a simple balance sheet. You can use it to calculate your net worth so you can see whether the amount you intend to leave for your child will be sufficient to meet his or her needs. If not, you can consider buying additional life insurance.

The calculations are not entirely exact, because we are necessarily required to make certain assumptions about inflation, interest rates and tax rates. The charts assume a 5 percent rate of return on money contributed to the trust, a 2.5 percent inflation rate, and a twenty percent tax on trust income. Although it is possible that the money you place in trust will earn more or less than 5 percent, or that our assumptions as to inflation will prove inaccurate, the assumptions seem reasonable.

The twenty percent tax rate also represents our judgment as to what is reasonable. In truth, the tax rate applicable to any trust that you create will depend on the amount of the trust's income and deductions. For example, if the trust pays substantial medical expenses for your child, it is possible that the trust will pay no tax at all because medical expenses are deductible for income tax purposes. The trust can also eliminate tax by investing in municipal bonds, though these tend to have a lower rate of return than taxable bonds. Moreover, it is possible that tax rates will change in the future.

The examples below illustrate how you can use the charts to calculate your child's financial needs. If you are interested in the results when we make different assumptions about tax rates and rates of return, you should refer to the charts and explanatory notes in Appendix Three. The information contained in Appendix Three is complicated and is probably unnecessary for most families. We include it only for the sake of completeness, and as a resource for financial professionals and others who are expert in financial matters.

It is advisable that you redo the calculations periodically, because your child's needs change over time. For example, if you do the calculations when your child is five, you will likely be interested in the amount required to meet your child's needs for 85 years, 90 years if your child is female. This is because the life expectancy of a 5 year old is 74 years if the child is male and 79 years if the child is female. However, by definition, 50 percent of the people outlive their life expectancy and it is therefore advisable for you to plan that your child will outlive his or her life expectancy by ten or more years. On the other hand, if you redo the calculations when your child is 20, your child's life expectancy will be reduced so fewer funds are required.

Example One

John and Mary complete parts one, two and three of Chart One and determine that their 39-year-old son, Sam, will need $250 per month to fund his needs over and above that which is provided by the government. This figure is multiplied by 12 to get Sam's annual needs—$3,000. John and Mary are not concerned about trust administration fees because they trust Sam's sister to handle his finances.

John and Mary then go to Chart Three and determine that as a 39-year-old male, Sam has a life expectancy of another 41 years. They add ten years to Sam's life expectancy *to be safe* and then go to the column on Chart Four for life expectancy of 51 years, read over to the second row, which assumes required annual expenses of $3,000, and determine that the trust must have an initial balance of $104,666 if it is to provide John with $3,000 per year for 51 years. (See chart, page 241.)

What if Sam needed $10,000 per year? As you can see from Chart Four, $348,887 would last 51 years. (See chart, page 244.)

If Sam needed $25,000 per year (perhaps because he did not receive government benefits), a little multiplication is necessary because the chart does not have a column for $25,000. Unfortunately, there was not enough paper for us to list every possibility.

John and Mary would go to the column for annual expenses of $1,000 and multiply by 25. Thus, if we continue to assume a life expectancy of 51 years, and if we also assume no administration fee, John and Mary would see from Chart Four that $34,889 must go into the trust if it is to provide Sam with $1,000 per year for his life. So to provide $25,000 per year, the trust would need $872,225 ($34,889 times 25).

Depending on the nature of Sam's disability, it would be possible that he would have a reduced life expectancy. John and Mary could likely find this out from Sam's doctor. In such a case, they could use the reduced life expectancy for the calculations, though it would still be advisable to assume that Sam would live several years beyond his life expectancy.

Example Two

The facts are the same as in example one, except John and Mary decide they need a professional trustee such as a bank to manage Sam's funds. John and Mary go through the same methodology as example one, except they use Chart Five instead of Chart Four. Chart Five makes the same assumptions relating to inflation, tax rates and interest rates, except it assumes a 1 percent trustee fee, which is a typical bank charge.

Thus, if we assume a life expectancy for Sam of 51 years, Sam would need $131,866 to provide $3,000 per year. If Sam needs $10,000 per year, the amount required is $439,554. (See chart, pages 250 and 253.)

PERSON WITH DISABILITY—MONTHLY INCOME

Source of Income	Monthly Amount
Employment	$ _____
Government Benefits	$ _____
SSI	$ _____
SSDI	$ _____
Survivors	$ _____
SSA Retirement	$ _____
State	$ _____
County	$ _____
Other	$ _____
Other Sources	
1. _____	$ _____
2. _____	$ _____
3. _____	$ _____
4. _____	$ _____
5. _____	$ _____
Total	$

$ _____Housing

_____Rent/Month

_____Utilities

_____Maintenance

_____Cleaning items

_____Laundry costs

_____Other

$ _____Care Assistance

_____Live-in

_____Respite

_____Custodial

_____Guardianship/Advocacy
(approx. $50-$75 per hr.)

_____Other

$ _____Food

_____Meals, snacks-home

_____Outside of home

_____Special foods/
gastric tube

_____Other

$ _____Clothing

$ _____Furniture

$ _____Medical/Dental Care

_____General medical/
Dental visits

_____Therapy

_____Nursing services

_____Meals of attendants

_____Evaluations

_____Transportation

_____Medications

_____Other

$ _____Insurance

_____Medical/Dental

_____Burial

_____Car

_____Housing/Rental

_____Other

$ _____Automobile

_____Payments

_____Gas, oil, maintenance

_____Other

$ _____Recreation

_____Sports

_____Special Olympics

_____Spectator sports

_____Vacations

_____TV/VCR

_____Summer camp

_____Transportation costs

_____Other

$ _____Education, Training, Etc.

_____Transportation

_____Fees

_____Books

_____Other

$ _____Employment

_____Transportation

_____Workshop fees

_____Attendant

_____Training

_____Other

$ _____**Personal Needs**

_____Haircuts, beauty shop

_____Telephone

_____Cigarettes

_____Church/Temple expenses

_____Hobbies

_____Books, magazines, etc.

_____Allowance

_____Other

$ _____**Special Equipment**

_____Environmental control

_____Elevator

_____Repair of equipment

_____Computer

_____Audio books

_____Ramp

_____Guide dog/other

_____Special animals

_____Technical instruction

_____Wheelchair

_____Other

$ _____**Total Monthly Expenses**

Monthly Expense Summary

1. Total Monthly Expenses (from page 228) _____

2. Total Monthly Income (from page 227) _____

3. Total Supplementary Funds Required (1 minus 2)_____

4. Reserve in case of Government Benefit Reduction _____

5. Total (3 plus 4) _____

FAMILY BALANCE SHEET

Assets	Joint	Father	Mother
Residence	$ _____	_____	_____
Other real estate	$ _____	_____	_____
Bank accounts	$ _____	_____	_____
Retirement accounts	$ _____	_____	_____
CD's	$ _____	_____	_____
Annuities	$ _____	_____	_____
Stocks, securities	$ _____	_____	_____
Business interests	$ _____	_____	_____
Other assets	$ _____	_____	_____

Liabilities

	Joint	Father	Mother
Mortgage debt	$ _____	_____	_____
Other debt	$ _____	_____	_____

Current Family Net Worth
(current assets less current liabilities) $ _____

Life Insurance	Joint	Father	Mother
Death benefit	$ _____	_____	_____
Premiums	$ _____	_____	_____
Cash value	$ _____	_____	_____
Potential Inheritances	$ _____	_____	_____

Future Expectancies (death benefits plus inheritances) $ _____

Total (current family net worth plus future expectancies) $ _____

CHART THREE
LIFE EXPECTANCY

Remaining Years of Expected Life			Remaining Years of Expected Life		
Current Age	**Male**	**Female**	**Current Age**	**Male**	**Female**
5	74	79	23	57	62
6	73	78	24	56	61
7	72	77	25	55	60
8	71	76	26	54	59
9	70	75	27	53	58
10	69	74	28	52	57
11	68	73	29	51	56
12	67	72	30	50	55
13	66	71	31	49	54
14	65	70	32	48	53
15	64	69	33	47	52
16	63	68	34	46	51
17	62	67	35	45	50
18	62	67	36	44	49
19	60	66	37	43	48
20	60	65	38	42	47
21	59	64	39	41	46
22	58	63	40	40	45

CHART THREE
LIFE EXPECTANCY *(CONTINUED)*

Remaining Years of Expected Life | Remaining Years Of Expected Life

Current Age	Male	Female	Current Age	Male	Female
41	39	44	59	22	27
42	38	43	60	23	26
43	37	42	61	22	25
44	36	41	62	21	25
45	36	40	63	20	24
46	35	39	64	19	23
47	34	38	65	19	22
48	33	37	66	18	21
49	32	36	67	17	20
50	31	35	68	16	19
51	30	35	69	16	19
52	29	34	70	15	18
53	29	33			
54	28	32			
55	27	31			
56	26	30			
57	25	29			
58	24	28			

CHART FOUR—STARTING PORTFOLIO NEEDED TO FUND VARIOUS ANNUAL EXPENSES ASSUMING NO TRUSTEE FEE

Life Expectancies	Annual Expenses $ 1,000	$ 2,000	$ 3,000	$ 4,000	$ 5,000	$ 6,000	$ 7,000	$ 8,000	$ 9,000
1	$ 962	$ 1,923	$ 2,885	$ 3,846	$ 4,808	$ 5,769	$ 6,731	$ 7,692	$ 8,654
2	$ 1,909	$ 3,818	$ 5,728	$ 7,637	$ 9,546	$ 11,455	$ 13,364	$ 15,274	$ 17,183
3	$ 2,843	$ 5,686	$ 8,530	$ 11,373	$ 14,216	$ 17,059	$ 19,902	$ 22,746	$ 25,589
4	$ 3,764	$ 7,527	$ 11,291	$ 15,055	$ 18,819	$ 22,582	$ 26,346	$ 30,110	$ 33,874
5	$ 4,671	$ 9,342	$ 14,013	$ 18,684	$ 23,355	$ 28,026	$ 32,697	$ 37,368	$ 42,039
6	$ 5,565	$ 11,130	$ 16,695	$ 22,261	$ 27,826	$ 33,391	$ 38,956	$ 44,521	$ 50,086
7	$ 6,446	$ 12,893	$ 19,339	$ 25,786	$ 32,232	$ 38,679	$ 45,125	$ 51,571	$ 58,018
8	$ 7,315	$ 14,630	$ 21,945	$ 29,260	$ 36,575	$ 43,890	$ 51,205	$ 58,520	$ 65,835
9	$ 8,171	$ 16,342	$ 24,513	$ 32,684	$ 40,855	$ 49,026	$ 57,197	$ 65,368	$ 73,539
10	$ 9,015	$ 18,029	$ 27,044	$ 36,059	$ 45,074	$ 54,088	$ 63,103	$ 72,118	$ 81,132
11	$ 9,846	$ 19,692	$ 29,539	$ 39,385	$ 49,231	$ 59,077	$ 68,924	$ 78,770	$ 88,616
12	$ 10,666	$ 21,332	$ 31,997	$ 42,663	$ 53,329	$ 63,995	$ 74,660	$ 85,326	$ 95,992
13	$ 11,473	$ 22,947	$ 34,420	$ 45,894	$ 57,367	$ 68,841	$ 80,314	$ 91,788	$ 103,261
14	$ 12,270	$ 24,539	$ 36,809	$ 49,078	$ 61,348	$ 73,617	$ 85,887	$ 98,156	$ 110,426
15	$ 13,054	$ 26,108	$ 39,162	$ 52,216	$ 65,270	$ 78,325	$ 91,379	$ 104,433	$ 117,487
16	$ 13,827	$ 27,655	$ 41,482	$ 55,309	$ 69,137	$ 82,964	$ 96,791	$ 110,619	$ 124,446
17	$ 14,589	$ 29,179	$ 43,768	$ 58,358	$ 72,947	$ 87,537	$ 102,126	$ 116,716	$ 131,305
18	$ 15,341	$ 30,681	$ 46,022	$ 61,362	$ 76,703	$ 92,043	$ 107,384	$ 122,725	$ 138,065
19	$ 16,081	$ 32,162	$ 48,243	$ 64,323	$ 80,404	$ 96,485	$ 112,566	$ 128,647	$ 144,728
20	$ 16,810	$ 33,621	$ 50,431	$ 67,242	$ 84,052	$ 100,863	$ 117,673	$ 134,484	$ 151,294
21	$ 17,530	$ 35,059	$ 52,589	$ 70,118	$ 87,648	$ 105,177	$ 122,707	$ 140,236	$ 157,766
22	$ 18,238	$ 36,476	$ 54,715	$ 72,953	$ 91,191	$ 109,429	$ 127,668	$ 145,906	$ 164,144
23	$ 18,937	$ 37,873	$ 56,810	$ 75,747	$ 94,684	$ 113,620	$ 132,557	$ 151,494	$ 170,431
24	$ 19,625	$ 39,250	$ 58,875	$ 78,501	$ 98,126	$ 117,751	$ 137,376	$ 157,001	$ 176,626
25	$ 20,304	$ 40,607	$ 60,911	$ 81,215	$ 101,518	$ 121,822	$ 142,125	$ 162,429	$ 182,733
26	$ 20,972	$ 41,945	$ 62,917	$ 83,889	$ 104,862	$ 125,834	$ 146,806	$ 167,779	$ 188,751
27	$ 21,631	$ 43,263	$ 64,894	$ 86,526	$ 108,157	$ 129,788	$ 151,420	$ 173,051	$ 194,682
28	$ 22,281	$ 44,562	$ 66,843	$ 89,124	$ 111,405	$ 133,686	$ 155,966	$ 178,247	$ 200,528
29	$ 22,921	$ 45,842	$ 68,763	$ 91,684	$ 114,606	$ 137,527	$ 160,448	$ 183,369	$ 206,290
30	$ 23,552	$ 47,104	$ 70,656	$ 94,208	$ 117,760	$ 141,312	$ 164,864	$ 188,416	$ 211,968

31	$ 24,174	$ 48,348	$ 72,522	$ 96,696	$ 120,869	$ 145,043	$ 169,217	$ 193,391	$ 217,565
32	$ 24,787	$ 49,574	$ 74,360	$ 99,147	$ 123,934	$ 148,721	$ 173,507	$ 198,294	$ 223,081
33	$ 25,391	$ 50,782	$ 76,172	$ 101,563	$ 126,954	$ 152,345	$ 177,736	$ 203,126	$ 228,517
34	$ 25,986	$ 51,972	$ 77,958	$ 103,945	$ 129,931	$ 155,917	$ 181,903	$ 207,889	$ 233,875
35	$ 26,573	$ 53,146	$ 79,719	$ 106,291	$ 132,864	$ 159,437	$ 186,010	$ 212,583	$ 239,156
36	$ 27,151	$ 54,302	$ 81,453	$ 108,605	$ 135,756	$ 162,907	$ 190,058	$ 217,209	$ 244,360
37	$ 27,721	$ 55,442	$ 83,163	$ 110,884	$ 138,605	$ 166,327	$ 194,048	$ 221,769	$ 249,490
38	$ 28,283	$ 56,566	$ 84,848	$ 113,131	$ 141,414	$ 169,697	$ 197,980	$ 226,262	$ 254,545
39	$ 28,836	$ 57,673	$ 86,509	$ 115,346	$ 144,182	$ 173,018	$ 201,855	$ 230,691	$ 259,528
40	$ 29,382	$ 58,764	$ 88,146	$ 117,528	$ 146,910	$ 176,292	$ 205,674	$ 235,056	$ 264,438
41	$ 29,920	$ 59,840	$ 89,759	$ 119,679	$ 149,599	$ 179,519	$ 209,439	$ 239,358	$ 269,278
42	$ 30,450	$ 60,900	$ 91,349	$ 121,799	$ 152,249	$ 182,699	$ 213,149	$ 243,598	$ 274,048
43	$ 30,972	$ 61,944	$ 92,916	$ 123,889	$ 154,861	$ 185,833	$ 216,805	$ 247,777	$ 278,749
44	$ 31,487	$ 62,974	$ 94,461	$ 125,948	$ 157,435	$ 188,922	$ 220,409	$ 251,896	$ 283,383
45	$ 31,994	$ 63,989	$ 95,983	$ 127,978	$ 159,972	$ 191,966	$ 223,961	$ 255,955	$ 287,949
46	$ 32,494	$ 64,989	$ 97,483	$ 129,978	$ 162,472	$ 194,967	$ 227,461	$ 259,956	$ 292,450
47	$ 32,987	$ 65,975	$ 98,962	$ 131,949	$ 164,937	$ 197,924	$ 230,911	$ 263,899	$ 296,886
48	$ 33,473	$ 66,946	$ 100,419	$ 133,892	$ 167,365	$ 200,839	$ 234,312	$ 267,785	$ 301,258
49	$ 33,952	$ 67,904	$ 101,856	$ 135,807	$ 169,759	$ 203,711	$ 237,663	$ 271,615	$ 305,567
50	$ 34,424	$ 68,847	$ 103,271	$ 137,695	$ 172,118	$ 206,542	$ 240,966	$ 275,390	$ 309,813
51	$ 34,889	$ 69,777	$ 104,666	$ 139,555	$ 174,444	$ 209,332	$ 244,221	$ 279,110	$ 313,999
52	$ 35,347	$ 70,694	$ 106,041	$ 141,388	$ 176,735	$ 212,082	$ 247,430	$ 282,777	$ 318,124
53	$ 35,799	$ 71,598	$ 107,396	$ 143,195	$ 178,994	$ 214,793	$ 250,592	$ 286,390	$ 322,189
54	$ 36,244	$ 72,488	$ 108,732	$ 144,976	$ 181,220	$ 217,464	$ 253,708	$ 289,952	$ 326,196
55	$ 36,683	$ 73,366	$ 110,048	$ 146,731	$ 183,414	$ 220,097	$ 256,780	$ 293,462	$ 330,145
56	$ 37,115	$ 74,231	$ 111,346	$ 148,461	$ 185,576	$ 222,692	$ 259,807	$ 296,922	$ 334,037
57	$ 37,541	$ 75,083	$ 112,624	$ 150,166	$ 187,707	$ 225,249	$ 262,790	$ 300,332	$ 337,873
58	$ 37,962	$ 75,923	$ 113,885	$ 151,846	$ 189,808	$ 227,769	$ 265,731	$ 303,692	$ 341,654
59	$ 38,376	$ 76,751	$ 115,127	$ 153,502	$ 191,878	$ 230,253	$ 268,629	$ 307,005	$ 345,380
60	$ 38,784	$ 77,567	$ 116,351	$ 155,134	$ 193,918	$ 232,702	$ 271,485	$ 310,269	$ 349,053

CHART FOUR—STARTING PORTFOLIO NEEDED TO FUND VARIOUS ANNUAL EXPENSES ASSUMING NO TRUSTEE FEE (CONTINUED)

Life Expectancies	Annual Expenses								
	$ 1,000	$ 2,000	$ 3,000	$ 4,000	$ 5,000	$ 6,000	$ 7,000	$ 8,000	$ 9,000
61	$ 39,186	$ 78,372	$ 117,557	$ 156,743	$ 195,929	$ 235,115	$ 274,300	$ 313,486	$ 352,672
62	$ 39,582	$ 79,164	$ 118,746	$ 158,329	$ 197,911	$ 237,493	$ 277,075	$ 316,657	$ 356,239
63	$ 39,973	$ 79,946	$ 119,918	$ 159,891	$ 199,864	$ 239,837	$ 279,809	$ 319,782	$ 359,755
64	$ 40,358	$ 80,716	$ 121,073	$ 161,431	$ 201,789	$ 242,147	$ 282,504	$ 322,862	$ 363,220
65	$ 40,737	$ 81,474	$ 122,212	$ 162,949	$ 203,686	$ 244,423	$ 285,161	$ 325,898	$ 366,635
66	$ 41,111	$ 82,222	$ 123,334	$ 164,445	$ 205,556	$ 246,667	$ 287,779	$ 328,890	$ 370,001
67	$ 41,480	$ 82,960	$ 124,439	$ 165,919	$ 207,399	$ 248,879	$ 290,359	$ 331,838	$ 373,318
68	$ 41,843	$ 83,686	$ 125,529	$ 167,372	$ 209,215	$ 251,058	$ 292,902	$ 334,745	$ 376,588
69	$ 42,201	$ 84,402	$ 126,603	$ 168,804	$ 211,006	$ 253,207	$ 295,408	$ 337,609	$ 379,810
70	$ 42,554	$ 85,108	$ 127,662	$ 170,216	$ 212,770	$ 255,324	$ 297,878	$ 340,432	$ 382,986
71	$ 42,902	$ 85,804	$ 128,705	$ 171,607	$ 214,509	$ 257,411	$ 300,312	$ 343,214	$ 386,116
72	$ 43,245	$ 86,489	$ 129,734	$ 172,978	$ 216,223	$ 259,467	$ 302,712	$ 345,956	$ 389,201
73	$ 43,582	$ 87,165	$ 130,747	$ 174,329	$ 217,912	$ 261,494	$ 305,076	$ 348,659	$ 392,241
74	$ 43,915	$ 87,831	$ 131,746	$ 175,661	$ 219,576	$ 263,492	$ 307,407	$ 351,322	$ 395,238
75	$ 44,243	$ 88,487	$ 132,730	$ 176,974	$ 221,217	$ 265,461	$ 309,704	$ 353,947	$ 398,191
76	$ 44,567	$ 89,134	$ 133,701	$ 178,267	$ 222,834	$ 267,401	$ 311,968	$ 356,535	$ 401,102
77	$ 44,886	$ 89,771	$ 134,657	$ 179,542	$ 224,428	$ 269,314	$ 314,199	$ 359,085	$ 403,970
78	$ 45,200	$ 90,399	$ 135,599	$ 180,799	$ 225,999	$ 271,198	$ 316,398	$ 361,598	$ 406,798
79	$ 45,509	$ 91,019	$ 136,528	$ 182,037	$ 227,547	$ 273,056	$ 318,566	$ 364,075	$ 409,584
80	$ 45,815	$ 91,629	$ 137,444	$ 183,258	$ 229,073	$ 274,887	$ 320,702	$ 366,516	$ 412,331
81	$ 46,115	$ 92,231	$ 138,346	$ 184,461	$ 230,576	$ 276,692	$ 322,807	$ 368,922	$ 415,037
82	$ 46,412	$ 92,823	$ 139,235	$ 185,647	$ 232,058	$ 278,470	$ 324,882	$ 371,293	$ 417,705
83	$ 46,704	$ 93,408	$ 140,111	$ 186,815	$ 233,519	$ 280,223	$ 326,927	$ 373,631	$ 420,334
84	$ 46,992	$ 93,983	$ 140,975	$ 187,967	$ 234,959	$ 281,950	$ 328,942	$ 375,934	$ 422,926
85	$ 47,276	$ 94,551	$ 141,827	$ 189,102	$ 236,378	$ 283,653	$ 330,929	$ 378,204	$ 425,480
86	$ 47,555	$ 95,110	$ 142,666	$ 190,221	$ 237,776	$ 285,331	$ 332,886	$ 380,442	$ 427,997
87	$ 47,831	$ 95,662	$ 143,493	$ 191,323	$ 239,154	$ 286,985	$ 334,816	$ 382,647	$ 430,478
88	$ 48,103	$ 96,205	$ 144,308	$ 192,410	$ 240,513	$ 288,615	$ 336,718	$ 384,820	$ 432,923
89	$ 48,370	$ 96,741	$ 145,111	$ 193,481	$ 241,851	$ 290,222	$ 338,592	$ 386,962	$ 435,332
90	$ 48,634	$ 97,268	$ 145,902	$ 194,537	$ 243,171	$ 291,805	$ 340,439	$ 389,073	$ 437,707

Annual Expenses

Life Expectancies	$ 10,000	$ 11,000	$ 12,000	$ 13,000	$ 14,000	$ 15,000	$ 16,000	$ 17,000	$ 18,000
1	$ 9,615	$ 10,577	$ 11,538	$ 12,500	$ 13,462	$ 14,423	$ 15,385	$ 16,346	$ 17,308
2	$ 19,092	$ 21,001	$ 22,911	$ 24,820	$ 26,729	$ 28,638	$ 30,547	$ 32,457	$ 34,366
3	$ 28,432	$ 31,275	$ 34,119	$ 36,962	$ 39,805	$ 42,648	$ 45,491	$ 48,335	$ 51,178
4	$ 37,637	$ 41,401	$ 45,165	$ 48,929	$ 52,692	$ 56,456	$ 60,220	$ 63,984	$ 67,747
5	$ 46,710	$ 51,381	$ 56,052	$ 60,723	$ 65,394	$ 70,065	$ 74,736	$ 79,407	$ 84,078
6	$ 55,652	$ 61,217	$ 66,782	$ 72,347	$ 77,912	$ 83,477	$ 89,043	$ 94,608	$ 100,173
7	$ 64,464	$ 70,911	$ 77,357	$ 83,804	$ 90,250	$ 96,697	$ 103,143	$ 109,589	$ 116,036
8	$ 73,150	$ 80,465	$ 87,780	$ 95,095	$ 102,410	$ 109,725	$ 117,040	$ 124,355	$ 131,670
9	$ 81,710	$ 89,881	$ 98,052	$ 106,223	$ 114,394	$ 122,565	$ 130,736	$ 138,908	$ 147,079
10	$ 90,147	$ 99,162	$ 108,177	$ 117,191	$ 126,206	$ 135,221	$ 144,235	$ 153,250	$ 162,265
11	$ 98,462	$ 108,309	$ 118,155	$ 128,001	$ 137,847	$ 147,694	$ 157,540	$ 167,386	$ 177,232
12	$ 106,658	$ 117,323	$ 127,989	$ 138,655	$ 149,321	$ 159,986	$ 170,652	$ 181,318	$ 191,984
13	$ 114,735	$ 126,208	$ 137,682	$ 149,155	$ 160,629	$ 172,102	$ 183,575	$ 195,049	$ 206,522
14	$ 122,695	$ 134,965	$ 147,234	$ 159,504	$ 171,773	$ 184,043	$ 196,312	$ 208,582	$ 220,851
15	$ 130,541	$ 143,595	$ 156,649	$ 169,703	$ 182,757	$ 195,811	$ 208,866	$ 221,920	$ 234,974
16	$ 138,274	$ 152,101	$ 165,928	$ 179,756	$ 193,583	$ 207,410	$ 221,238	$ 235,065	$ 248,892
17	$ 145,895	$ 160,484	$ 175,074	$ 189,663	$ 204,252	$ 218,842	$ 233,431	$ 248,021	$ 262,610
18	$ 153,406	$ 168,746	$ 184,087	$ 199,427	$ 214,768	$ 230,109	$ 245,449	$ 260,790	$ 276,130
19	$ 160,809	$ 176,889	$ 192,970	$ 209,051	$ 225,132	$ 241,213	$ 257,294	$ 273,375	$ 289,455
20	$ 168,105	$ 184,915	$ 201,725	$ 218,536	$ 235,346	$ 252,157	$ 268,967	$ 285,778	$ 302,588
21	$ 175,295	$ 192,825	$ 210,354	$ 227,884	$ 245,414	$ 262,943	$ 280,473	$ 298,002	$ 315,532
22	$ 182,382	$ 200,621	$ 218,859	$ 237,097	$ 255,335	$ 273,574	$ 291,812	$ 310,050	$ 328,288
23	$ 189,367	$ 208,304	$ 227,241	$ 246,178	$ 265,114	$ 284,051	$ 302,988	$ 321,924	$ 340,861
24	$ 196,251	$ 215,877	$ 235,502	$ 255,127	$ 274,752	$ 294,377	$ 314,002	$ 333,627	$ 353,253
25	$ 203,036	$ 223,340	$ 243,644	$ 263,947	$ 284,251	$ 304,554	$ 324,858	$ 345,162	$ 365,465
26	$ 209,723	$ 230,696	$ 251,668	$ 272,640	$ 293,613	$ 314,585	$ 335,557	$ 356,530	$ 377,502
27	$ 216,314	$ 237,945	$ 259,577	$ 281,208	$ 302,839	$ 324,471	$ 346,102	$ 367,733	$ 389,365
28	$ 222,809	$ 245,090	$ 267,371	$ 289,652	$ 311,933	$ 334,214	$ 356,495	$ 378,776	$ 401,057
29	$ 229,211	$ 252,132	$ 275,053	$ 297,974	$ 320,895	$ 343,817	$ 366,738	$ 389,659	$ 412,580
30	$ 235,521	$ 259,073	$ 282,625	$ 306,177	$ 329,729	$ 353,281	$ 376,833	$ 400,385	$ 423,937

CHART FOUR—STARTING PORTFOLIO NEEDED TO FUND VARIOUS ANNUAL EXPENSES ASSUMING NO TRUSTEE FEE (CONTINUED)

Annual Expenses

Life Expectancies	$ 10,000	$ 11,000	$ 12,000	$ 13,000	$ 14,000	$ 15,000	$ 16,000	$ 17,000	$ 18,000
31	$ 241,739	$ 265,913	$ 290,087	$ 314,261	$ 338,435	$ 362,608	$ 386,782	$ 410,956	$ 435,130
32	$ 247,868	$ 272,654	$ 297,441	$ 322,228	$ 347,015	$ 371,802	$ 396,588	$ 421,375	$ 446,162
33	$ 253,908	$ 279,299	$ 304,690	$ 330,081	$ 355,471	$ 380,862	$ 406,253	$ 431,644	$ 457,035
34	$ 259,861	$ 285,847	$ 311,834	$ 337,820	$ 363,806	$ 389,792	$ 415,778	$ 441,764	$ 467,750
35	$ 265,729	$ 292,302	$ 318,874	$ 345,447	$ 372,020	$ 398,593	$ 425,166	$ 451,739	$ 478,312
36	$ 271,511	$ 298,663	$ 325,814	$ 352,965	$ 380,116	$ 407,267	$ 434,418	$ 461,570	$ 488,721
37	$ 277,211	$ 304,932	$ 332,653	$ 360,374	$ 388,095	$ 415,816	$ 443,537	$ 471,258	$ 498,980
38	$ 282,828	$ 311,111	$ 339,394	$ 367,676	$ 395,959	$ 424,242	$ 452,525	$ 480,808	$ 509,090
39	$ 288,364	$ 317,201	$ 346,037	$ 374,873	$ 403,710	$ 432,546	$ 461,383	$ 490,219	$ 519,055
40	$ 293,820	$ 323,202	$ 352,584	$ 381,967	$ 411,349	$ 440,731	$ 470,113	$ 499,495	$ 528,877
41	$ 299,198	$ 329,118	$ 359,038	$ 388,957	$ 418,877	$ 448,797	$ 478,717	$ 508,637	$ 538,556
42	$ 304,498	$ 334,948	$ 365,398	$ 395,847	$ 426,297	$ 456,747	$ 487,197	$ 517,647	$ 548,096
43	$ 309,722	$ 340,694	$ 371,666	$ 402,638	$ 433,610	$ 464,582	$ 495,555	$ 526,527	$ 557,499
44	$ 314,870	$ 346,357	$ 377,844	$ 409,331	$ 440,818	$ 472,305	$ 503,792	$ 535,279	$ 566,766
45	$ 319,944	$ 351,938	$ 383,933	$ 415,927	$ 447,921	$ 479,916	$ 511,910	$ 543,905	$ 575,899
46	$ 324,945	$ 357,439	$ 389,934	$ 422,428	$ 454,923	$ 487,417	$ 519,911	$ 552,406	$ 584,900
47	$ 329,873	$ 362,861	$ 395,848	$ 428,835	$ 461,823	$ 494,810	$ 527,797	$ 560,785	$ 593,772
48	$ 334,731	$ 368,204	$ 401,677	$ 435,150	$ 468,623	$ 502,096	$ 535,570	$ 569,043	$ 602,516
49	$ 339,518	$ 373,470	$ 407,422	$ 441,374	$ 475,326	$ 509,278	$ 543,230	$ 577,181	$ 611,133
50	$ 344,237	$ 378,661	$ 413,084	$ 447,508	$ 481,932	$ 516,355	$ 550,779	$ 585,203	$ 619,627
51	$ 348,887	$ 383,776	$ 418,665	$ 453,554	$ 488,442	$ 523,331	$ 558,220	$ 593,109	$ 627,997
52	$ 353,471	$ 388,818	$ 424,165	$ 459,512	$ 494,859	$ 530,206	$ 565,553	$ 600,900	$ 636,247
53	$ 357,988	$ 393,787	$ 429,586	$ 465,384	$ 501,183	$ 536,982	$ 572,781	$ 608,580	$ 644,378
54	$ 362,440	$ 398,684	$ 434,928	$ 471,172	$ 507,416	$ 543,660	$ 579,904	$ 616,148	$ 652,392
55	$ 366,828	$ 403,511	$ 440,194	$ 476,876	$ 513,559	$ 550,242	$ 586,925	$ 623,608	$ 660,290
56	$ 371,153	$ 408,268	$ 445,383	$ 482,498	$ 519,614	$ 556,729	$ 593,844	$ 630,959	$ 668,075
57	$ 375,415	$ 412,956	$ 450,498	$ 488,039	$ 525,581	$ 563,122	$ 600,664	$ 638,205	$ 675,747
58	$ 379,616	$ 417,577	$ 455,539	$ 493,500	$ 531,462	$ 569,423	$ 607,385	$ 645,346	$ 683,308
59	$ 383,756	$ 422,131	$ 460,507	$ 498,882	$ 537,258	$ 575,634	$ 614,009	$ 652,385	$ 690,760
60	$ 387,836	$ 426,620	$ 465,403	$ 504,187	$ 542,971	$ 581,754	$ 620,538	$ 659,321	$ 698,105

61	$ 391,858	$ 431,044	$ 470,229	$ 509,415	$ 548,601	$ 587,787	$ 626,972	$ 666,158	$ 705,344
62	$ 395,821	$ 435,403	$ 474,986	$ 514,568	$ 554,150	$ 593,732	$ 633,314	$ 672,896	$ 712,478
63	$ 399,728	$ 439,701	$ 479,673	$ 519,646	$ 559,619	$ 599,592	$ 639,564	$ 679,537	$ 719,510
64	$ 403,578	$ 443,936	$ 484,293	$ 524,651	$ 565,009	$ 605,367	$ 645,725	$ 686,082	$ 726,440
65	$ 407,372	$ 448,110	$ 488,847	$ 529,584	$ 570,321	$ 611,059	$ 651,796	$ 692,533	$ 733,270
66	$ 411,112	$ 452,223	$ 493,335	$ 534,446	$ 575,557	$ 616,668	$ 657,780	$ 698,891	$ 740,002
67	$ 414,798	$ 456,278	$ 497,758	$ 539,238	$ 580,717	$ 622,197	$ 663,677	$ 705,157	$ 746,637
68	$ 418,431	$ 460,274	$ 502,117	$ 543,960	$ 585,803	$ 627,646	$ 669,489	$ 711,332	$ 753,175
69	$ 422,011	$ 464,212	$ 506,413	$ 548,614	$ 590,816	$ 633,017	$ 675,218	$ 717,419	$ 759,620
70	$ 425,540	$ 468,094	$ 510,648	$ 553,202	$ 595,756	$ 638,310	$ 680,864	$ 723,418	$ 765,972
71	$ 429,018	$ 471,919	$ 514,821	$ 557,723	$ 600,625	$ 643,526	$ 686,428	$ 729,330	$ 772,232
72	$ 432,445	$ 475,690	$ 518,934	$ 562,179	$ 605,423	$ 648,668	$ 691,912	$ 735,157	$ 778,401
73	$ 435,823	$ 479,406	$ 522,988	$ 566,570	$ 610,153	$ 653,735	$ 697,317	$ 740,900	$ 784,482
74	$ 439,153	$ 483,068	$ 526,983	$ 570,899	$ 614,814	$ 658,729	$ 702,645	$ 746,560	$ 790,475
75	$ 442,434	$ 486,678	$ 530,921	$ 575,165	$ 619,408	$ 663,652	$ 707,895	$ 752,138	$ 796,382
76	$ 445,668	$ 490,235	$ 534,802	$ 579,369	$ 623,936	$ 668,503	$ 713,070	$ 757,636	$ 802,203
77	$ 448,856	$ 493,742	$ 538,627	$ 583,513	$ 628,398	$ 673,284	$ 718,170	$ 763,055	$ 807,941
78	$ 451,997	$ 497,197	$ 542,397	$ 587,597	$ 632,796	$ 677,996	$ 723,196	$ 768,396	$ 813,595
79	$ 455,094	$ 500,603	$ 546,112	$ 591,622	$ 637,131	$ 682,640	$ 728,150	$ 773,659	$ 819,169
80	$ 458,145	$ 503,960	$ 549,774	$ 595,589	$ 641,403	$ 687,218	$ 733,032	$ 778,847	$ 824,661
81	$ 461,153	$ 507,268	$ 553,383	$ 599,499	$ 645,614	$ 691,729	$ 737,844	$ 783,960	$ 830,075
82	$ 464,117	$ 510,529	$ 556,940	$ 603,352	$ 649,764	$ 696,175	$ 742,587	$ 788,999	$ 835,410
83	$ 467,038	$ 513,742	$ 560,446	$ 607,150	$ 653,854	$ 700,557	$ 747,261	$ 793,965	$ 840,669
84	$ 469,917	$ 516,909	$ 563,901	$ 610,893	$ 657,884	$ 704,876	$ 751,868	$ 798,860	$ 845,851
85	$ 472,755	$ 520,031	$ 567,306	$ 614,582	$ 661,857	$ 709,133	$ 756,408	$ 803,684	$ 850,959
86	$ 475,552	$ 523,107	$ 570,662	$ 618,218	$ 665,773	$ 713,328	$ 760,883	$ 808,438	$ 855,994
87	$ 478,308	$ 526,139	$ 573,970	$ 621,801	$ 669,632	$ 717,463	$ 765,294	$ 813,124	$ 860,955
88	$ 481,025	$ 529,128	$ 577,230	$ 625,333	$ 673,435	$ 721,538	$ 769,640	$ 817,743	$ 865,845
89	$ 483,703	$ 532,073	$ 580,443	$ 628,814	$ 677,184	$ 725,554	$ 773,924	$ 822,295	$ 870,665
90	$ 486,342	$ 534,976	$ 583,610	$ 632,244	$ 680,878	$ 729,512	$ 778,147	$ 826,781	$ 875,415

CHART FOUR

STARTING PORTFOLIO NEEDED TO FUND VARIOUS ANNUAL EXPENSES ASSUMING NO TRUSTEE FEE (CONTINUED)

Annual Expenses

Life Expectancies	$ 20,000	$ 22,000	$ 24,000	$ 26,000	$ 28,000	$ 30,000	$ 32,000	$ 34,000	$ 36,000
1	$ 19,231	$ 21,154	$ 23,077	$ 25,000	$ 26,923	$ 28,846	$ 30,769	$ 32,692	$ 34,615
2	$ 38,184	$ 42,003	$ 45,821	$ 49,639	$ 53,458	$ 57,276	$ 61,095	$ 64,913	$ 68,732
3	$ 56,864	$ 62,551	$ 68,237	$ 73,923	$ 79,610	$ 85,296	$ 90,983	$ 96,669	$ 102,356
4	$ 75,275	$ 82,802	$ 90,330	$ 97,857	$ 105,385	$ 112,912	$ 120,440	$ 127,967	$ 135,495
5	$ 93,420	$ 102,762	$ 112,104	$ 121,446	$ 130,788	$ 140,130	$ 149,472	$ 158,814	$ 168,156
6	$ 111,303	$ 122,434	$ 133,564	$ 144,694	$ 155,825	$ 166,955	$ 178,085	$ 189,216	$ 200,346
7	$ 128,929	$ 141,822	$ 154,714	$ 167,607	$ 180,500	$ 193,393	$ 206,286	$ 219,179	$ 232,072
8	$ 146,300	$ 160,930	$ 175,560	$ 190,190	$ 204,820	$ 219,450	$ 234,080	$ 248,710	$ 263,340
9	$ 163,421	$ 179,763	$ 196,105	$ 212,447	$ 228,789	$ 245,131	$ 261,473	$ 277,815	$ 294,157
10	$ 180,294	$ 198,324	$ 216,353	$ 234,383	$ 252,412	$ 270,441	$ 288,471	$ 306,500	$ 324,530
11	$ 196,925	$ 216,617	$ 236,310	$ 256,002	$ 275,695	$ 295,387	$ 315,080	$ 334,772	$ 354,464
12	$ 213,315	$ 234,647	$ 255,978	$ 277,310	$ 298,641	$ 319,973	$ 341,304	$ 362,636	$ 383,967
13	$ 229,469	$ 252,416	$ 275,363	$ 298,310	$ 321,257	$ 344,204	$ 367,151	$ 390,098	$ 413,045
14	$ 245,390	$ 269,929	$ 294,469	$ 319,008	$ 343,547	$ 368,086	$ 392,625	$ 417,164	$ 441,703
15	$ 261,082	$ 287,190	$ 313,298	$ 339,406	$ 365,515	$ 391,623	$ 417,731	$ 443,839	$ 469,947
16	$ 276,547	$ 304,202	$ 331,856	$ 359,511	$ 387,166	$ 414,821	$ 442,475	$ 470,130	$ 497,785
17	$ 291,789	$ 320,968	$ 350,147	$ 379,326	$ 408,505	$ 437,684	$ 466,863	$ 496,042	$ 525,221
18	$ 306,811	$ 337,493	$ 368,174	$ 398,855	$ 429,536	$ 460,217	$ 490,898	$ 521,579	$ 552,261
19	$ 321,617	$ 353,779	$ 385,940	$ 418,102	$ 450,264	$ 482,426	$ 514,587	$ 546,749	$ 578,911
20	$ 336,209	$ 369,830	$ 403,451	$ 437,072	$ 470,693	$ 504,314	$ 537,935	$ 571,556	$ 605,176
21	$ 350,591	$ 385,650	$ 420,709	$ 455,768	$ 490,827	$ 525,886	$ 560,945	$ 596,004	$ 631,063
22	$ 364,765	$ 401,241	$ 437,718	$ 474,194	$ 510,671	$ 547,147	$ 583,624	$ 620,100	$ 656,577
23	$ 378,735	$ 416,608	$ 454,482	$ 492,355	$ 530,228	$ 568,102	$ 605,975	$ 643,849	$ 681,722
24	$ 392,503	$ 431,753	$ 471,003	$ 510,254	$ 549,504	$ 588,754	$ 628,005	$ 667,255	$ 706,505
25	$ 406,073	$ 446,680	$ 487,287	$ 527,894	$ 568,502	$ 609,109	$ 649,716	$ 690,323	$ 730,931
26	$ 419,447	$ 461,391	$ 503,336	$ 545,280	$ 587,225	$ 629,170	$ 671,114	$ 713,059	$ 755,004
27	$ 432,628	$ 475,890	$ 519,153	$ 562,416	$ 605,679	$ 648,941	$ 692,204	$ 735,467	$ 778,730
28	$ 445,619	$ 490,180	$ 534,742	$ 579,304	$ 623,866	$ 668,428	$ 712,990	$ 757,551	$ 802,113
29	$ 458,422	$ 504,264	$ 550,107	$ 595,949	$ 641,791	$ 687,633	$ 733,475	$ 779,318	$ 825,160
30	$ 471,041	$ 518,145	$ 565,249	$ 612,353	$ 659,457	$ 706,562	$ 753,666	$ 800,770	$ 847,874

31	$ 483,478	$ 531,826	$ 580,174	$ 628,521	$ 676,869	$ 725,217	$ 773,565	$ 821,912	$ 870,260
32	$ 495,735	$ 545,309	$ 594,883	$ 644,456	$ 694,030	$ 743,603	$ 793,177	$ 842,750	$ 892,324
33	$ 507,816	$ 558,598	$ 609,379	$ 660,161	$ 710,943	$ 761,724	$ 812,506	$ 863,288	$ 914,069
34	$ 519,723	$ 571,695	$ 623,667	$ 675,639	$ 727,612	$ 779,584	$ 831,556	$ 883,529	$ 935,501
35	$ 531,457	$ 584,603	$ 637,749	$ 690,895	$ 744,040	$ 797,186	$ 850,332	$ 903,478	$ 956,623
36	$ 543,023	$ 597,325	$ 651,628	$ 705,930	$ 760,232	$ 814,534	$ 868,837	$ 923,139	$ 977,441
37	$ 554,422	$ 609,864	$ 665,306	$ 720,748	$ 776,190	$ 831,633	$ 887,075	$ 942,517	$ 997,959
38	$ 565,656	$ 622,222	$ 678,787	$ 735,353	$ 791,918	$ 848,484	$ 905,050	$ 961,615	$ 1,018,181
39	$ 576,728	$ 634,401	$ 692,074	$ 749,747	$ 807,420	$ 865,092	$ 922,765	$ 980,438	$ 1,038,111
40	$ 587,641	$ 646,405	$ 705,169	$ 763,933	$ 822,697	$ 881,461	$ 940,225	$ 998,989	$ 1,057,753
41	$ 598,396	$ 658,236	$ 718,075	$ 777,915	$ 837,754	$ 897,594	$ 957,434	$ 1,017,273	$ 1,077,113
42	$ 608,996	$ 669,896	$ 730,795	$ 791,695	$ 852,594	$ 913,494	$ 974,394	$ 1,035,293	$ 1,096,193
43	$ 619,443	$ 681,388	$ 743,332	$ 805,276	$ 867,221	$ 929,165	$ 991,109	$ 1,053,053	$ 1,114,998
44	$ 629,740	$ 692,714	$ 755,688	$ 818,662	$ 881,636	$ 944,610	$ 1,007,584	$ 1,070,558	$ 1,133,532
45	$ 639,888	$ 703,876	$ 767,865	$ 831,854	$ 895,843	$ 959,832	$ 1,023,820	$ 1,087,809	$ 1,151,798
46	$ 649,889	$ 714,878	$ 779,867	$ 844,856	$ 909,845	$ 974,834	$ 1,039,823	$ 1,104,812	$ 1,169,801
47	$ 659,747	$ 725,721	$ 791,696	$ 857,671	$ 923,645	$ 989,620	$ 1,055,595	$ 1,121,569	$ 1,187,544
48	$ 669,462	$ 736,408	$ 803,354	$ 870,300	$ 937,247	$ 1,004,193	$ 1,071,139	$ 1,138,085	$ 1,205,031
49	$ 679,037	$ 746,941	$ 814,844	$ 882,748	$ 950,652	$ 1,018,555	$ 1,086,459	$ 1,154,363	$ 1,222,267
50	$ 688,474	$ 757,321	$ 826,169	$ 895,016	$ 963,863	$ 1,032,711	$ 1,101,558	$ 1,170,406	$ 1,239,253
51	$ 697,775	$ 767,552	$ 837,330	$ 907,107	$ 976,885	$ 1,046,662	$ 1,116,440	$ 1,186,217	$ 1,255,995
52	$ 706,941	$ 777,636	$ 848,330	$ 919,024	$ 989,718	$ 1,060,412	$ 1,131,106	$ 1,201,801	$ 1,272,495
53	$ 715,976	$ 787,574	$ 859,171	$ 930,769	$ 1,002,366	$ 1,073,964	$ 1,145,562	$ 1,217,159	$ 1,288,757
54	$ 724,880	$ 797,368	$ 869,856	$ 942,344	$ 1,014,832	$ 1,087,320	$ 1,159,808	$ 1,232,296	$ 1,304,784
55	$ 733,656	$ 807,022	$ 880,387	$ 953,753	$ 1,027,118	$ 1,100,484	$ 1,173,850	$ 1,247,215	$ 1,320,581
56	$ 742,305	$ 816,536	$ 890,766	$ 964,997	$ 1,039,227	$ 1,113,458	$ 1,187,688	$ 1,261,919	$ 1,336,149
57	$ 750,830	$ 825,913	$ 900,996	$ 976,078	$ 1,051,161	$ 1,126,244	$ 1,201,327	$ 1,276,410	$ 1,351,493
58	$ 759,231	$ 835,154	$ 911,077	$ 987,000	$ 1,062,924	$ 1,138,847	$ 1,214,770	$ 1,290,693	$ 1,366,616
59	$ 767,511	$ 844,263	$ 921,014	$ 997,765	$ 1,074,516	$ 1,151,267	$ 1,228,018	$ 1,304,769	$ 1,381,521
60	$ 775,672	$ 853,240	$ 930,807	$ 1,008,374	$ 1,085,941	$ 1,163,508	$ 1,241,076	$ 1,318,643	$ 1,396,210

CHART FOUR—STARTING PORTFOLIO NEEDED TO FUND VARIOUS ANNUAL EXPENSES ASSUMING NO TRUSTEE FEE (CONTINUED)

Annual Expenses

Life Expectancies	$ 20,000	$ 22,000	$ 24,000	$ 26,000	$ 28,000	$ 30,000	$ 32,000	$ 34,000	$ 36,000
61	$ 783,715	$ 862,087	$ 940,459	$ 1,018,830	$ 1,097,202	$ 1,175,573	$ 1,253,945	$ 1,332,316	$ 1,410,688
62	$ 791,643	$ 870,807	$ 949,971	$ 1,029,135	$ 1,108,300	$ 1,187,464	$ 1,266,628	$ 1,345,793	$ 1,424,957
63	$ 799,456	$ 879,401	$ 959,347	$ 1,039,292	$ 1,119,238	$ 1,199,183	$ 1,279,129	$ 1,359,074	$ 1,439,020
64	$ 807,156	$ 887,871	$ 968,587	$ 1,049,302	$ 1,130,018	$ 1,210,734	$ 1,291,449	$ 1,372,165	$ 1,452,880
65	$ 814,745	$ 896,219	$ 977,694	$ 1,059,168	$ 1,140,643	$ 1,222,117	$ 1,303,592	$ 1,385,066	$ 1,466,541
66	$ 822,224	$ 904,447	$ 986,669	$ 1,068,892	$ 1,151,114	$ 1,233,337	$ 1,315,559	$ 1,397,782	$ 1,480,004
67	$ 829,596	$ 912,556	$ 995,515	$ 1,078,475	$ 1,161,435	$ 1,244,394	$ 1,327,354	$ 1,410,314	$ 1,493,273
68	$ 836,862	$ 920,548	$ 1,004,234	$ 1,087,920	$ 1,171,606	$ 1,255,292	$ 1,338,979	$ 1,422,665	$ 1,506,351
69	$ 844,022	$ 928,424	$ 1,012,827	$ 1,097,229	$ 1,181,631	$ 1,266,033	$ 1,350,436	$ 1,434,838	$ 1,519,240
70	$ 851,080	$ 936,188	$ 1,021,296	$ 1,106,404	$ 1,191,511	$ 1,276,619	$ 1,361,727	$ 1,446,835	$ 1,531,943
71	$ 858,035	$ 943,839	$ 1,029,642	$ 1,115,446	$ 1,201,249	$ 1,287,053	$ 1,372,856	$ 1,458,660	$ 1,544,463
72	$ 864,890	$ 951,380	$ 1,037,869	$ 1,124,358	$ 1,210,847	$ 1,297,336	$ 1,383,825	$ 1,470,314	$ 1,556,803
73	$ 871,647	$ 958,812	$ 1,045,976	$ 1,133,141	$ 1,220,306	$ 1,307,470	$ 1,394,635	$ 1,481,800	$ 1,568,964
74	$ 878,306	$ 966,136	$ 1,053,967	$ 1,141,798	$ 1,229,628	$ 1,317,459	$ 1,405,289	$ 1,493,120	$ 1,580,950
75	$ 884,869	$ 973,356	$ 1,061,842	$ 1,150,329	$ 1,238,816	$ 1,327,303	$ 1,415,790	$ 1,504,277	$ 1,592,764
76	$ 891,337	$ 980,471	$ 1,069,604	$ 1,158,738	$ 1,247,872	$ 1,337,005	$ 1,426,139	$ 1,515,273	$ 1,604,407
77	$ 897,712	$ 987,483	$ 1,077,254	$ 1,167,025	$ 1,256,797	$ 1,346,568	$ 1,436,339	$ 1,526,110	$ 1,615,881
78	$ 903,995	$ 994,394	$ 1,084,794	$ 1,175,193	$ 1,265,593	$ 1,355,992	$ 1,446,392	$ 1,536,791	$ 1,627,191
79	$ 910,187	$ 1,001,206	$ 1,092,225	$ 1,183,243	$ 1,274,262	$ 1,365,281	$ 1,456,300	$ 1,547,318	$ 1,638,337
80	$ 916,290	$ 1,014,536	$ 1,099,548	$ 1,191,177	$ 1,282,806	$ 1,374,436	$ 1,466,065	$ 1,557,694	$ 1,649,323
81	$ 922,305	$ 1,021,057	$ 1,106,766	$ 1,198,997	$ 1,291,228	$ 1,383,458	$ 1,475,689	$ 1,567,919	$ 1,660,150
82	$ 928,234	$ 1,027,484	$ 1,113,880	$ 1,206,704	$ 1,299,527	$ 1,392,351	$ 1,485,174	$ 1,577,997	$ 1,670,821
83	$ 934,076	$ 1,033,818	$ 1,120,892	$ 1,214,299	$ 1,307,707	$ 1,401,115	$ 1,494,522	$ 1,587,930	$ 1,681,338
84	$ 939,835	$ 1,040,061	$ 1,127,802	$ 1,221,785	$ 1,315,769	$ 1,409,752	$ 1,503,736	$ 1,597,719	$ 1,691,703
85	$ 945,510	$ 1,046,214	$ 1,134,613	$ 1,229,164	$ 1,323,715	$ 1,418,266	$ 1,512,817	$ 1,607,368	$ 1,701,919
86	$ 951,104	$ 1,052,279	$ 1,141,325	$ 1,236,435	$ 1,331,546	$ 1,426,656	$ 1,521,766	$ 1,616,877	$ 1,711,987
87	$ 956,617	$ 1,058,255	$ 1,147,940	$ 1,243,602	$ 1,339,264	$ 1,434,925	$ 1,530,587	$ 1,626,249	$ 1,721,911
88	$ 962,050	$ 1,064,146	$ 1,154,460	$ 1,250,665	$ 1,346,871	$ 1,443,076	$ 1,539,281	$ 1,635,486	$ 1,731,691
89	$ 967,405	$ 1,064,146	$ 1,160,886	$ 1,257,627	$ 1,354,368	$ 1,451,108	$ 1,547,849	$ 1,644,589	$ 1,741,330
90	$ 972,683	$ 1,069,952	$ 1,167,220	$ 1,264,488	$ 1,361,756	$ 1,459,025	$ 1,556,293	$ 1,653,561	$ 1,750,830

CHART FIVE—STARTING PORTFOLIO NEEDED TO FUND VARIOUS ANNUAL EXPENSES ASSUMING A 1% TRUSTEE FEE

Life Expectancies	Annual Expenses								
	$ 1,000	$ 2,000	$ 3,000	$ 4,000	$ 5,000	$ 6,000	$ 7,000	$ 8,000	$ 9,000
1	$ 971	$ 1,942	$ 2,913	$ 3,883	$ 4,854	$ 5,825	$ 6,796	$ 7,767	$ 8,738
2	$ 1,937	$ 3,874	$ 5,811	$ 7,748	$ 9,685	$ 11,622	$ 13,559	$ 15,496	$ 17,433
3	$ 2,899	$ 5,797	$ 8,696	$ 11,594	$ 14,493	$ 17,391	$ 20,290	$ 23,188	$ 26,087
4	$ 3,855	$ 7,711	$ 11,566	$ 15,421	$ 19,277	$ 23,132	$ 26,987	$ 30,842	$ 34,698
5	$ 4,807	$ 9,615	$ 14,422	$ 19,230	$ 24,037	$ 28,845	$ 33,652	$ 38,460	$ 43,267
6	$ 5,755	$ 11,510	$ 17,265	$ 23,020	$ 28,775	$ 34,530	$ 40,285	$ 46,040	$ 51,795
7	$ 6,698	$ 13,396	$ 20,094	$ 26,792	$ 33,490	$ 40,188	$ 46,886	$ 53,584	$ 60,281
8	$ 7,636	$ 15,273	$ 22,909	$ 30,545	$ 38,182	$ 45,818	$ 53,454	$ 61,090	$ 68,727
9	$ 8,570	$ 17,140	$ 25,710	$ 34,280	$ 42,851	$ 51,421	$ 59,991	$ 68,561	$ 77,131
10	$ 9,499	$ 18,999	$ 28,498	$ 37,998	$ 47,497	$ 56,996	$ 66,496	$ 75,995	$ 85,494
11	$ 10,424	$ 20,848	$ 31,272	$ 41,697	$ 52,121	$ 62,545	$ 72,969	$ 83,393	$ 93,817
12	$ 11,344	$ 22,689	$ 34,033	$ 45,378	$ 56,722	$ 68,066	$ 79,411	$ 90,755	$ 102,100
13	$ 12,260	$ 24,520	$ 36,781	$ 49,041	$ 61,301	$ 73,561	$ 85,821	$ 98,082	$ 110,342
14	$ 13,172	$ 26,343	$ 39,515	$ 52,686	$ 65,858	$ 79,029	$ 92,201	$ 105,373	$ 118,544
15	$ 14,079	$ 28,157	$ 42,236	$ 56,314	$ 70,393	$ 84,471	$ 98,550	$ 112,628	$ 126,707
16	$ 14,981	$ 29,962	$ 44,943	$ 59,924	$ 74,905	$ 89,886	$ 104,867	$ 119,848	$ 134,829
17	$ 15,879	$ 31,758	$ 47,638	$ 63,517	$ 79,396	$ 95,275	$ 111,154	$ 127,033	$ 142,913
18	$ 16,773	$ 33,546	$ 50,319	$ 67,092	$ 83,865	$ 100,638	$ 117,411	$ 134,184	$ 150,957
19	$ 17,662	$ 35,325	$ 52,987	$ 70,650	$ 88,312	$ 105,975	$ 123,637	$ 141,299	$ 158,962
20	$ 18,548	$ 37,095	$ 55,643	$ 74,190	$ 92,738	$ 111,285	$ 129,833	$ 148,380	$ 166,928
21	$ 19,428	$ 38,857	$ 58,285	$ 77,714	$ 97,142	$ 116,570	$ 135,999	$ 155,427	$ 174,856
22	$ 20,305	$ 40,610	$ 60,915	$ 81,220	$ 101,525	$ 121,830	$ 142,135	$ 162,440	$ 182,745
23	$ 21,177	$ 42,355	$ 63,532	$ 84,709	$ 105,886	$ 127,064	$ 148,241	$ 169,418	$ 190,595
24	$ 22,045	$ 44,091	$ 66,136	$ 88,181	$ 110,227	$ 132,272	$ 154,317	$ 176,363	$ 198,408
25	$ 22,909	$ 45,818	$ 68,728	$ 91,637	$ 114,546	$ 137,455	$ 160,364	$ 183,274	$ 206,183
26	$ 23,769	$ 47,538	$ 71,307	$ 95,075	$ 118,844	$ 142,613	$ 166,382	$ 190,151	$ 213,920
27	$ 24,624	$ 49,249	$ 73,873	$ 98,497	$ 123,122	$ 147,746	$ 172,370	$ 196,995	$ 221,619
28	$ 25,476	$ 50,951	$ 76,427	$ 101,903	$ 127,378	$ 152,854	$ 178,330	$ 203,806	$ 229,281
29	$ 26,323	$ 52,646	$ 78,969	$ 105,292	$ 131,614	$ 157,937	$ 184,260	$ 210,583	$ 236,906
30	$ 27,166	$ 54,332	$ 81,498	$ 108,664	$ 135,830	$ 162,996	$ 190,162	$ 217,328	$ 244,494

CHART FIVE—STARTING PORTFOLIO NEEDED TO FUND VARIOUS ANNUAL EXPENSES ASSUMING A 1% TRUSTEE FEE (CONTINUED)

Life Expectancies	Annual Expenses								
	$ 1,000	$ 2,000	$ 3,000	$ 4,000	$ 5,000	$ 6,000	$ 7,000	$ 8,000	$ 9,000
31	$ 28,005	$ 56,010	$ 84,015	$ 112,020	$ 140,025	$ 168,030	$ 196,035	$ 224,040	$ 252,045
32	$ 28,840	$ 57,680	$ 86,520	$ 115,360	$ 144,200	$ 173,039	$ 201,879	$ 230,719	$ 259,559
33	$ 29,671	$ 59,342	$ 89,012	$ 118,683	$ 148,354	$ 178,025	$ 207,696	$ 237,366	$ 267,037
34	$ 30,498	$ 60,995	$ 91,493	$ 121,991	$ 152,488	$ 182,986	$ 213,483	$ 243,981	$ 274,479
35	$ 31,320	$ 62,641	$ 93,961	$ 125,282	$ 156,602	$ 187,923	$ 219,243	$ 250,564	$ 281,884
36	$ 32,139	$ 64,279	$ 96,418	$ 128,557	$ 160,696	$ 192,836	$ 224,975	$ 257,114	$ 289,254
37	$ 32,954	$ 65,908	$ 98,862	$ 131,817	$ 164,771	$ 197,725	$ 230,679	$ 263,633	$ 296,587
38	$ 33,765	$ 67,530	$ 101,295	$ 135,060	$ 168,825	$ 202,590	$ 236,355	$ 270,120	$ 303,885
39	$ 34,572	$ 69,144	$ 103,716	$ 138,288	$ 172,860	$ 207,432	$ 242,004	$ 276,576	$ 311,148
40	$ 35,375	$ 70,750	$ 106,125	$ 141,500	$ 176,875	$ 212,250	$ 247,625	$ 283,000	$ 318,376
41	$ 36,174	$ 72,348	$ 108,523	$ 144,697	$ 180,871	$ 217,045	$ 253,219	$ 289,394	$ 325,568
42	$ 36,969	$ 73,939	$ 110,908	$ 147,878	$ 184,847	$ 221,817	$ 258,786	$ 295,756	$ 332,725
43	$ 37,761	$ 75,522	$ 113,283	$ 151,044	$ 188,804	$ 226,565	$ 264,326	$ 302,087	$ 339,848
44	$ 38,548	$ 77,097	$ 115,645	$ 154,194	$ 192,742	$ 231,291	$ 269,839	$ 308,388	$ 346,936
45	$ 39,332	$ 78,664	$ 117,997	$ 157,329	$ 196,661	$ 235,993	$ 275,325	$ 314,658	$ 353,990
46	$ 40,112	$ 80,224	$ 120,336	$ 160,449	$ 200,561	$ 240,673	$ 280,785	$ 320,897	$ 361,009
47	$ 40,888	$ 81,777	$ 122,665	$ 163,553	$ 204,442	$ 245,330	$ 286,218	$ 327,106	$ 367,995
48	$ 41,661	$ 83,321	$ 124,982	$ 166,643	$ 208,303	$ 249,964	$ 291,625	$ 333,286	$ 374,946
49	$ 42,429	$ 84,859	$ 127,288	$ 169,717	$ 212,147	$ 254,576	$ 297,005	$ 339,435	$ 381,864
50	$ 43,194	$ 86,388	$ 129,583	$ 172,777	$ 215,971	$ 259,165	$ 302,360	$ 345,554	$ 388,748
51	$ 43,955	$ 87,911	$ 131,866	$ 175,822	$ 219,777	$ 263,733	$ 307,688	$ 351,643	$ 395,599
52	$ 44,713	$ 89,426	$ 134,139	$ 178,852	$ 223,565	$ 268,278	$ 312,990	$ 357,703	$ 402,416
53	$ 45,467	$ 90,933	$ 136,400	$ 181,867	$ 227,334	$ 272,800	$ 318,267	$ 363,734	$ 409,201
54	$ 46,217	$ 92,434	$ 138,651	$ 184,868	$ 231,085	$ 277,301	$ 323,518	$ 369,735	$ 415,952
55	$ 46,963	$ 93,927	$ 140,890	$ 187,854	$ 234,817	$ 281,781	$ 328,744	$ 375,707	$ 422,671
56	$ 47,706	$ 95,413	$ 143,119	$ 190,825	$ 238,532	$ 286,238	$ 333,944	$ 381,651	$ 429,357
57	$ 48,446	$ 96,891	$ 145,337	$ 193,782	$ 242,228	$ 290,674	$ 339,119	$ 387,565	$ 436,011
58	$ 49,181	$ 98,363	$ 147,544	$ 196,725	$ 245,907	$ 295,088	$ 344,269	$ 393,451	$ 442,632
59	$ 49,913	$ 99,827	$ 149,740	$ 199,654	$ 249,567	$ 299,481	$ 349,394	$ 399,308	$ 449,221
60	$ 50,642	$ 101,284	$ 151,926	$ 202,568	$ 253,210	$ 303,852	$ 354,494	$ 405,136	$ 455,778

61	$ 51,367	$ 102,734	$ 154,101	$ 205,468	$ 256,835	$ 308,202	$ 359,569	$ 410,936	$ 462,304
62	$ 52,089	$ 104,177	$ 156,266	$ 208,354	$ 260,443	$ 312,531	$ 364,620	$ 416,709	$ 468,797
63	$ 52,807	$ 105,613	$ 158,420	$ 211,226	$ 264,033	$ 316,840	$ 369,646	$ 422,453	$ 475,259
64	$ 53,521	$ 107,042	$ 160,563	$ 214,084	$ 267,606	$ 321,127	$ 374,648	$ 428,169	$ 481,690
65	$ 54,232	$ 108,464	$ 162,697	$ 216,929	$ 271,161	$ 325,393	$ 379,625	$ 433,857	$ 488,090
66	$ 54,940	$ 109,880	$ 164,819	$ 219,759	$ 274,699	$ 329,639	$ 384,579	$ 439,518	$ 494,458
67	$ 55,644	$ 111,288	$ 166,932	$ 222,576	$ 278,220	$ 333,864	$ 389,508	$ 445,152	$ 500,796
68	$ 56,345	$ 112,689	$ 169,034	$ 225,379	$ 281,724	$ 338,068	$ 394,413	$ 450,758	$ 507,103
69	$ 57,042	$ 114,084	$ 171,126	$ 228,168	$ 285,210	$ 342,253	$ 399,295	$ 456,337	$ 513,379
70	$ 57,736	$ 115,472	$ 173,208	$ 230,944	$ 288,680	$ 346,416	$ 404,152	$ 461,888	$ 519,625
71	$ 58,427	$ 116,853	$ 175,280	$ 233,707	$ 292,133	$ 350,560	$ 408,987	$ 467,413	$ 525,840
72	$ 59,114	$ 118,228	$ 177,342	$ 236,456	$ 295,570	$ 354,683	$ 413,797	$ 472,911	$ 532,025
73	$ 59,798	$ 119,596	$ 179,393	$ 239,191	$ 298,989	$ 358,787	$ 418,585	$ 478,383	$ 538,180
74	$ 60,478	$ 120,957	$ 181,435	$ 241,914	$ 302,392	$ 362,870	$ 423,349	$ 483,827	$ 544,306
75	$ 61,156	$ 122,311	$ 183,467	$ 244,623	$ 305,779	$ 366,934	$ 428,090	$ 489,246	$ 550,401
76	$ 61,830	$ 123,659	$ 185,489	$ 247,319	$ 309,149	$ 370,978	$ 432,808	$ 494,638	$ 556,467
77	$ 62,500	$ 125,001	$ 187,501	$ 250,002	$ 312,502	$ 375,003	$ 437,503	$ 500,003	$ 562,504
78	$ 63,168	$ 126,336	$ 189,504	$ 252,672	$ 315,840	$ 379,007	$ 442,175	$ 505,343	$ 568,511
79	$ 63,832	$ 127,664	$ 191,496	$ 255,329	$ 319,161	$ 382,993	$ 446,825	$ 510,657	$ 574,489
80	$ 64,493	$ 128,986	$ 193,479	$ 257,973	$ 322,466	$ 386,959	$ 451,452	$ 515,945	$ 580,438
81	$ 65,151	$ 130,302	$ 195,453	$ 260,604	$ 325,755	$ 390,906	$ 456,057	$ 521,208	$ 586,359
82	$ 65,806	$ 131,611	$ 197,417	$ 263,222	$ 329,028	$ 394,833	$ 460,639	$ 526,444	$ 592,250
83	$ 66,457	$ 132,914	$ 199,371	$ 265,828	$ 332,285	$ 398,742	$ 465,199	$ 531,656	$ 598,113
84	$ 67,105	$ 134,211	$ 201,316	$ 268,421	$ 335,526	$ 402,632	$ 469,737	$ 536,842	$ 603,947
85	$ 67,750	$ 135,501	$ 203,251	$ 271,001	$ 338,752	$ 406,502	$ 474,253	$ 542,003	$ 609,753
86	$ 68,392	$ 136,785	$ 205,177	$ 273,569	$ 341,962	$ 410,354	$ 478,747	$ 547,139	$ 615,531
87	$ 69,031	$ 138,062	$ 207,094	$ 276,125	$ 345,156	$ 414,187	$ 483,219	$ 552,250	$ 621,281
88	$ 69,667	$ 139,334	$ 209,001	$ 278,668	$ 348,335	$ 418,002	$ 487,669	$ 557,336	$ 627,003
89	$ 70,300	$ 140,599	$ 210,899	$ 281,199	$ 351,498	$ 421,798	$ 492,098	$ 562,398	$ 632,697
90	$ 70,929	$ 141,859	$ 212,788	$ 283,717	$ 354,647	$ 425,576	$ 496,505	$ 567,434	$ 638,364

CHART FIVE—STARTING PORTFOLIO NEEDED TO FUND VARIOUS ANNUAL EXPENSES ASSUMING A 1% TRUSTEE FEE (CONTINUED)

Annual Expenses

Life Expectancies	$ 10,000	$ 11,000	$ 12,000	$ 13,000	$ 14,000	$ 15,000	$ 16,000	$ 17,000	$ 18,000
1	$ 9,709	$ 10,680	$ 11,650	$ 12,621	$ 13,592	$ 14,563	$ 15,534	$ 16,505	$ 17,476
2	$ 19,370	$ 21,307	$ 23,244	$ 25,181	$ 27,118	$ 29,056	$ 30,993	$ 32,930	$ 34,867
3	$ 28,985	$ 31,884	$ 34,782	$ 37,681	$ 40,579	$ 43,478	$ 46,376	$ 49,275	$ 52,173
4	$ 38,553	$ 42,408	$ 46,264	$ 50,119	$ 53,974	$ 57,830	$ 61,685	$ 65,540	$ 69,396
5	$ 48,075	$ 52,882	$ 57,690	$ 62,497	$ 67,305	$ 72,112	$ 76,919	$ 81,727	$ 86,534
6	$ 57,550	$ 63,305	$ 69,060	$ 74,815	$ 80,570	$ 86,325	$ 92,080	$ 97,835	$ 103,590
7	$ 66,979	$ 73,677	$ 80,375	$ 87,073	$ 93,771	$ 100,469	$ 107,167	$ 113,865	$ 120,563
8	$ 76,363	$ 83,999	$ 91,636	$ 99,272	$ 106,908	$ 114,545	$ 122,181	$ 129,817	$ 137,453
9	$ 85,701	$ 94,271	$ 102,841	$ 111,411	$ 119,981	$ 128,552	$ 137,122	$ 145,692	$ 154,262
10	$ 94,994	$ 104,493	$ 113,993	$ 123,492	$ 132,991	$ 142,491	$ 151,990	$ 161,489	$ 170,989
11	$ 104,241	$ 114,665	$ 125,090	$ 135,514	$ 145,938	$ 156,362	$ 166,786	$ 177,210	$ 187,634
12	$ 113,444	$ 124,788	$ 136,133	$ 147,477	$ 158,822	$ 170,166	$ 181,511	$ 192,855	$ 204,199
13	$ 122,602	$ 134,862	$ 147,123	$ 159,383	$ 171,643	$ 183,903	$ 196,163	$ 208,424	$ 220,684
14	$ 131,716	$ 144,887	$ 158,059	$ 171,230	$ 184,402	$ 197,574	$ 210,745	$ 223,917	$ 237,088
15	$ 140,785	$ 154,864	$ 168,942	$ 183,021	$ 197,099	$ 211,178	$ 225,256	$ 239,335	$ 253,413
16	$ 149,810	$ 164,791	$ 179,772	$ 194,753	$ 209,734	$ 224,716	$ 239,697	$ 254,678	$ 269,659
17	$ 158,792	$ 174,671	$ 190,550	$ 206,429	$ 222,309	$ 238,188	$ 254,067	$ 269,946	$ 285,825
18	$ 167,730	$ 184,503	$ 201,276	$ 218,049	$ 234,822	$ 251,595	$ 268,368	$ 285,141	$ 301,914
19	$ 176,624	$ 194,287	$ 211,949	$ 229,612	$ 247,274	$ 264,936	$ 282,599	$ 300,261	$ 317,924
20	$ 185,476	$ 204,023	$ 222,571	$ 241,118	$ 259,666	$ 278,213	$ 296,761	$ 315,309	$ 333,856
21	$ 194,284	$ 213,712	$ 233,141	$ 252,569	$ 271,998	$ 291,426	$ 310,854	$ 330,283	$ 349,711
22	$ 203,050	$ 223,355	$ 243,660	$ 263,964	$ 284,269	$ 304,574	$ 324,879	$ 345,184	$ 365,489
23	$ 211,773	$ 232,950	$ 254,127	$ 275,304	$ 296,482	$ 317,659	$ 338,836	$ 360,014	$ 381,191
24	$ 220,453	$ 242,499	$ 264,544	$ 286,589	$ 308,635	$ 330,680	$ 352,725	$ 374,771	$ 396,816
25	$ 229,092	$ 252,001	$ 274,910	$ 297,820	$ 320,729	$ 343,638	$ 366,547	$ 389,456	$ 412,366
26	$ 237,689	$ 261,457	$ 285,226	$ 308,995	$ 332,764	$ 356,533	$ 380,302	$ 404,071	$ 427,839
27	$ 246,243	$ 270,868	$ 295,492	$ 320,117	$ 344,741	$ 369,365	$ 393,990	$ 418,614	$ 443,238
28	$ 254,757	$ 280,233	$ 305,708	$ 331,184	$ 356,660	$ 382,135	$ 407,611	$ 433,087	$ 458,562
29	$ 263,229	$ 289,552	$ 315,875	$ 342,198	$ 368,521	$ 394,843	$ 421,166	$ 447,489	$ 473,812
30	$ 271,660	$ 298,826	$ 325,992	$ 353,158	$ 380,324	$ 407,490	$ 434,656	$ 461,822	$ 488,988

31	$ 280,050	$ 308,055	$ 336,060	$ 364,065	$ 392,070	$ 420,075	$ 448,080	$ 476,085	$ 504,090
32	$ 288,399	$ 317,239	$ 346,079	$ 374,919	$ 403,759	$ 432,599	$ 461,439	$ 490,279	$ 519,118
33	$ 296,708	$ 326,379	$ 356,049	$ 385,720	$ 415,391	$ 445,062	$ 474,733	$ 504,403	$ 534,074
34	$ 304,976	$ 335,474	$ 365,972	$ 396,469	$ 426,967	$ 457,464	$ 487,962	$ 518,460	$ 548,957
35	$ 313,205	$ 344,525	$ 375,845	$ 407,166	$ 438,486	$ 469,807	$ 501,127	$ 532,448	$ 563,768
36	$ 321,393	$ 353,532	$ 385,671	$ 417,811	$ 449,950	$ 482,089	$ 514,229	$ 546,368	$ 578,507
37	$ 329,541	$ 362,496	$ 395,450	$ 428,404	$ 461,358	$ 494,312	$ 527,266	$ 560,220	$ 593,175
38	$ 337,650	$ 371,416	$ 405,181	$ 438,946	$ 472,711	$ 506,476	$ 540,241	$ 574,006	$ 607,771
39	$ 345,720	$ 380,292	$ 414,864	$ 449,436	$ 484,008	$ 518,580	$ 553,152	$ 587,724	$ 622,296
40	$ 353,751	$ 389,126	$ 424,501	$ 459,876	$ 495,251	$ 530,626	$ 566,001	$ 601,376	$ 636,751
41	$ 361,742	$ 397,916	$ 434,091	$ 470,265	$ 506,439	$ 542,613	$ 578,787	$ 614,962	$ 651,136
42	$ 369,695	$ 406,664	$ 443,634	$ 480,603	$ 517,573	$ 554,542	$ 591,512	$ 628,481	$ 665,451
43	$ 377,609	$ 415,370	$ 453,131	$ 490,892	$ 528,653	$ 566,413	$ 604,174	$ 641,935	$ 679,696
44	$ 385,485	$ 424,033	$ 462,582	$ 501,130	$ 539,678	$ 578,227	$ 616,775	$ 655,324	$ 693,872
45	$ 393,322	$ 432,654	$ 471,986	$ 511,319	$ 550,651	$ 589,983	$ 629,315	$ 668,648	$ 707,980
46	$ 401,121	$ 441,234	$ 481,346	$ 521,458	$ 561,570	$ 601,682	$ 641,794	$ 681,907	$ 722,019
47	$ 408,883	$ 449,771	$ 490,660	$ 531,548	$ 572,436	$ 613,325	$ 654,213	$ 695,101	$ 735,989
48	$ 416,607	$ 458,268	$ 499,928	$ 541,589	$ 583,250	$ 624,910	$ 666,571	$ 708,232	$ 749,892
49	$ 424,293	$ 466,723	$ 509,152	$ 551,581	$ 594,011	$ 636,440	$ 678,869	$ 721,299	$ 763,728
50	$ 431,942	$ 475,137	$ 518,331	$ 561,525	$ 604,719	$ 647,914	$ 691,108	$ 734,302	$ 777,496
51	$ 439,554	$ 483,510	$ 527,465	$ 571,421	$ 615,376	$ 659,331	$ 703,287	$ 747,242	$ 791,198
52	$ 447,129	$ 491,842	$ 536,555	$ 581,268	$ 625,981	$ 670,694	$ 715,407	$ 760,120	$ 804,833
53	$ 454,667	$ 500,134	$ 545,601	$ 591,068	$ 636,534	$ 682,001	$ 727,468	$ 772,935	$ 818,401
54	$ 462,169	$ 508,386	$ 554,603	$ 600,820	$ 647,037	$ 693,254	$ 739,471	$ 785,687	$ 831,904
55	$ 469,634	$ 516,598	$ 563,561	$ 610,525	$ 657,488	$ 704,451	$ 751,415	$ 798,378	$ 845,342
56	$ 477,063	$ 524,770	$ 572,476	$ 620,182	$ 667,889	$ 715,595	$ 763,301	$ 811,007	$ 858,714
57	$ 484,456	$ 532,902	$ 581,347	$ 629,793	$ 678,239	$ 726,684	$ 775,130	$ 823,575	$ 872,021
58	$ 491,813	$ 540,994	$ 590,176	$ 639,357	$ 688,538	$ 737,720	$ 786,901	$ 836,082	$ 885,264
59	$ 499,134	$ 549,048	$ 598,961	$ 648,875	$ 698,788	$ 748,702	$ 798,615	$ 848,529	$ 898,442
60	$ 506,420	$ 557,062	$ 607,704	$ 658,346	$ 708,988	$ 759,630	$ 810,272	$ 860,914	$ 911,556

CHART FIVE—STARTING PORTFOLIO NEEDED TO FUND VARIOUS ANNUAL EXPENSES ASSUMING A 1% TRUSTEE FEE (CONTINUED)

Annual Expenses

Life Expectancies	$ 10,000	$ 11,000	$ 12,000	$ 13,000	$ 14,000	$ 15,000	$ 16,000	$ 17,000	$ 18,000
61	$ 513,671	$ 565,038	$ 616,405	$ 667,772	$ 719,139	$ 770,506	$ 821,873	$ 873,240	$ 924,607
62	$ 520,886	$ 572,974	$ 625,063	$ 677,151	$ 729,240	$ 781,329	$ 833,417	$ 885,506	$ 937,594
63	$ 528,066	$ 580,873	$ 633,679	$ 686,486	$ 739,292	$ 792,099	$ 844,905	$ 897,712	$ 950,519
64	$ 535,211	$ 588,732	$ 642,253	$ 695,775	$ 749,296	$ 802,817	$ 856,338	$ 909,859	$ 963,380
65	$ 542,322	$ 596,554	$ 650,786	$ 705,018	$ 759,251	$ 813,483	$ 867,715	$ 921,947	$ 976,179
66	$ 549,398	$ 604,338	$ 659,278	$ 714,217	$ 769,157	$ 824,097	$ 879,037	$ 933,977	$ 988,916
67	$ 556,440	$ 612,084	$ 667,728	$ 723,372	$ 779,016	$ 834,660	$ 890,304	$ 945,948	$ 1,001,592
68	$ 563,447	$ 619,792	$ 676,137	$ 732,481	$ 788,826	$ 845,171	$ 901,516	$ 957,860	$ 1,014,205
69	$ 570,421	$ 627,463	$ 684,505	$ 741,547	$ 798,589	$ 855,631	$ 912,673	$ 969,715	$ 1,026,758
70	$ 577,361	$ 635,097	$ 692,833	$ 750,569	$ 808,305	$ 866,041	$ 923,777	$ 981,513	$ 1,039,249
71	$ 584,267	$ 642,693	$ 701,120	$ 759,547	$ 817,973	$ 876,400	$ 934,827	$ 993,253	$ 1,051,680
72	$ 591,139	$ 650,253	$ 709,367	$ 768,481	$ 827,595	$ 886,709	$ 945,823	$ 1,004,936	$ 1,064,050
73	$ 597,978	$ 657,776	$ 717,574	$ 777,372	$ 837,169	$ 896,967	$ 956,765	$ 1,016,563	$ 1,076,361
74	$ 604,784	$ 665,263	$ 725,741	$ 786,219	$ 846,698	$ 907,176	$ 967,655	$ 1,028,133	$ 1,088,611
75	$ 611,557	$ 672,713	$ 733,868	$ 795,024	$ 856,180	$ 917,336	$ 978,491	$ 1,039,647	$ 1,100,803
76	$ 618,297	$ 680,127	$ 741,956	$ 803,786	$ 865,616	$ 927,446	$ 989,275	$ 1,051,105	$ 1,112,935
77	$ 625,004	$ 687,505	$ 750,005	$ 812,506	$ 875,006	$ 937,507	$ 1,000,007	$ 1,062,507	$ 1,125,008
78	$ 631,679	$ 694,847	$ 758,015	$ 821,183	$ 884,351	$ 947,519	$ 1,010,687	$ 1,073,854	$ 1,137,022
79	$ 638,321	$ 702,154	$ 765,986	$ 829,818	$ 893,650	$ 957,482	$ 1,021,314	$ 1,085,146	$ 1,148,979
80	$ 644,931	$ 709,425	$ 773,918	$ 838,411	$ 902,904	$ 967,397	$ 1,031,890	$ 1,096,384	$ 1,160,877
81	$ 651,509	$ 716,660	$ 781,811	$ 846,962	$ 912,113	$ 977,264	$ 1,042,415	$ 1,107,566	$ 1,172,717
82	$ 658,056	$ 723,861	$ 789,667	$ 855,472	$ 921,278	$ 987,083	$ 1,052,889	$ 1,118,694	$ 1,184,500
83	$ 664,570	$ 731,027	$ 797,484	$ 863,941	$ 930,398	$ 996,855	$ 1,063,312	$ 1,129,769	$ 1,196,226
84	$ 671,053	$ 738,158	$ 805,263	$ 872,368	$ 939,474	$ 1,006,579	$ 1,073,684	$ 1,140,789	$ 1,207,895
85	$ 677,504	$ 745,254	$ 813,004	$ 880,755	$ 948,505	$ 1,016,256	$ 1,084,006	$ 1,151,756	$ 1,219,507
86	$ 683,924	$ 752,316	$ 820,708	$ 889,101	$ 957,493	$ 1,025,885	$ 1,094,278	$ 1,162,670	$ 1,231,063
87	$ 690,312	$ 759,344	$ 828,375	$ 897,406	$ 966,437	$ 1,035,469	$ 1,104,500	$ 1,173,531	$ 1,242,562
88	$ 696,670	$ 766,337	$ 836,004	$ 905,671	$ 975,338	$ 1,045,005	$ 1,114,672	$ 1,184,339	$ 1,254,006
89	$ 702,997	$ 773,297	$ 843,596	$ 913,896	$ 984,196	$ 1,054,495	$ 1,124,795	$ 1,195,095	$ 1,265,394
90	$ 709,293	$ 780,222	$ 851,152	$ 922,081	$ 993,010	$ 1,063,940	$ 1,134,869	$ 1,205,798	$ 1,276,727

Annual Expenses

Life Expectancies	$ 20,000	$ 22,000	$ 24,000	$ 26,000	$ 28,000	$ 30,000	$ 32,000	$ 34,000	$ 36,000
1	$ 19,417	$ 21,359	$ 23,301	$ 25,243	$ 27,184	$ 29,126	$ 31,068	$ 33,010	$ 34,951
2	$ 38,741	$ 42,615	$ 46,489	$ 50,363	$ 54,237	$ 58,111	$ 61,985	$ 65,859	$ 69,733
3	$ 57,970	$ 63,767	$ 69,564	$ 75,361	$ 81,158	$ 86,955	$ 92,752	$ 98,549	$ 104,346
4	$ 77,106	$ 84,817	$ 92,527	$ 100,238	$ 107,949	$ 115,659	$ 123,370	$ 131,080	$ 138,791
5	$ 96,149	$ 105,764	$ 115,379	$ 124,994	$ 134,609	$ 144,224	$ 153,839	$ 163,454	$ 173,069
6	$ 115,100	$ 126,610	$ 138,120	$ 149,630	$ 161,140	$ 172,650	$ 184,160	$ 195,670	$ 207,180
7	$ 133,959	$ 147,355	$ 160,751	$ 174,146	$ 187,542	$ 200,938	$ 214,334	$ 227,730	$ 241,126
8	$ 152,726	$ 167,999	$ 183,271	$ 198,544	$ 213,816	$ 229,089	$ 244,362	$ 259,634	$ 274,907
9	$ 171,402	$ 188,542	$ 205,683	$ 222,823	$ 239,963	$ 257,103	$ 274,243	$ 291,384	$ 308,524
10	$ 189,988	$ 208,986	$ 227,985	$ 246,984	$ 265,983	$ 284,981	$ 303,980	$ 322,979	$ 341,978
11	$ 208,483	$ 229,331	$ 250,179	$ 271,028	$ 291,876	$ 312,724	$ 333,572	$ 354,421	$ 375,269
12	$ 226,888	$ 249,577	$ 272,266	$ 294,955	$ 317,643	$ 340,332	$ 363,021	$ 385,710	$ 408,399
13	$ 245,204	$ 269,725	$ 294,245	$ 318,765	$ 343,286	$ 367,806	$ 392,327	$ 416,847	$ 441,368
14	$ 263,431	$ 289,775	$ 316,118	$ 342,461	$ 368,804	$ 395,147	$ 421,490	$ 447,833	$ 474,177
15	$ 281,570	$ 309,727	$ 337,884	$ 366,041	$ 394,198	$ 422,355	$ 450,512	$ 478,669	$ 506,826
16	$ 299,621	$ 329,583	$ 359,545	$ 389,507	$ 419,469	$ 449,431	$ 479,393	$ 509,355	$ 539,317
17	$ 317,584	$ 349,342	$ 381,100	$ 412,859	$ 444,617	$ 476,376	$ 508,134	$ 539,892	$ 571,651
18	$ 335,460	$ 369,005	$ 402,551	$ 436,097	$ 469,643	$ 503,189	$ 536,735	$ 570,281	$ 603,827
19	$ 353,249	$ 388,573	$ 423,898	$ 459,223	$ 494,548	$ 529,873	$ 565,198	$ 600,523	$ 635,847
20	$ 370,951	$ 408,046	$ 445,141	$ 482,237	$ 519,332	$ 556,427	$ 593,522	$ 630,617	$ 667,712
21	$ 388,568	$ 427,425	$ 466,282	$ 505,138	$ 543,995	$ 582,852	$ 621,709	$ 660,566	$ 699,422
22	$ 406,099	$ 446,709	$ 487,319	$ 527,929	$ 568,539	$ 609,149	$ 649,759	$ 690,369	$ 730,979
23	$ 423,545	$ 465,900	$ 508,254	$ 550,609	$ 592,963	$ 635,318	$ 677,672	$ 720,027	$ 762,382
24	$ 440,907	$ 484,997	$ 529,088	$ 573,179	$ 617,269	$ 661,360	$ 705,451	$ 749,541	$ 793,632
25	$ 458,184	$ 504,002	$ 549,821	$ 595,639	$ 641,457	$ 687,276	$ 733,094	$ 778,913	$ 824,731
26	$ 475,377	$ 522,915	$ 570,453	$ 617,990	$ 665,528	$ 713,066	$ 760,603	$ 808,141	$ 855,679
27	$ 492,487	$ 541,736	$ 590,984	$ 640,233	$ 689,482	$ 738,730	$ 787,979	$ 837,228	$ 886,477
28	$ 509,514	$ 560,465	$ 611,417	$ 662,368	$ 713,319	$ 764,271	$ 815,222	$ 866,173	$ 917,125
29	$ 526,458	$ 579,104	$ 631,749	$ 684,395	$ 737,041	$ 789,687	$ 842,333	$ 894,978	$ 947,624
30	$ 543,320	$ 597,652	$ 651,984	$ 706,316	$ 760,648	$ 814,980	$ 869,312	$ 923,644	$ 977,975

CHART FIVE—STARTING PORTFOLIO NEEDED TO FUND VARIOUS ANNUAL EXPENSES ASSUMING A 1% TRUSTEE FEE (CONTINUED)

Annual Expenses

Life Expectancies	$ 20,000	$ 22,000	$ 24,000	$ 26,000	$ 28,000	$ 30,000	$ 32,000	$ 34,000	$ 36,000
31	$ 560,100	$ 616,110	$ 672,120	$ 728,130	$ 784,140	$ 840,150	$ 896,160	$ 952,170	$ 1,008,180
32	$ 576,798	$ 634,478	$ 692,158	$ 749,838	$ 807,518	$ 865,197	$ 922,877	$ 980,557	$ 1,038,237
33	$ 593,416	$ 652,757	$ 712,099	$ 771,440	$ 830,782	$ 890,124	$ 949,465	$ 1,008,807	$ 1,068,148
34	$ 609,953	$ 670,948	$ 731,943	$ 792,938	$ 853,934	$ 914,929	$ 975,924	$ 1,036,919	$ 1,097,915
35	$ 626,409	$ 689,050	$ 751,691	$ 814,332	$ 876,973	$ 939,614	$ 1,002,255	$ 1,064,895	$ 1,127,536
36	$ 642,786	$ 707,064	$ 771,343	$ 835,621	$ 899,900	$ 964,179	$ 1,028,457	$ 1,092,736	$ 1,157,014
37	$ 659,083	$ 724,991	$ 790,900	$ 856,808	$ 922,716	$ 988,624	$ 1,054,533	$ 1,120,441	$ 1,186,349
38	$ 675,301	$ 742,831	$ 810,361	$ 877,891	$ 945,421	$ 1,012,951	$ 1,080,482	$ 1,148,012	$ 1,215,542
39	$ 691,440	$ 760,584	$ 829,728	$ 898,872	$ 968,016	$ 1,037,160	$ 1,106,304	$ 1,175,448	$ 1,244,593
40	$ 707,501	$ 778,251	$ 849,001	$ 919,752	$ 990,502	$ 1,061,252	$ 1,132,002	$ 1,202,752	$ 1,273,502
41	$ 723,484	$ 795,833	$ 868,181	$ 940,530	$ 1,012,878	$ 1,085,226	$ 1,157,575	$ 1,229,923	$ 1,302,272
42	$ 739,390	$ 813,329	$ 887,268	$ 961,207	$ 1,035,146	$ 1,109,085	$ 1,183,023	$ 1,256,962	$ 1,330,901
43	$ 755,218	$ 830,740	$ 906,261	$ 981,783	$ 1,057,305	$ 1,132,827	$ 1,208,349	$ 1,283,870	$ 1,359,392
44	$ 770,969	$ 848,066	$ 925,163	$ 1,002,260	$ 1,079,357	$ 1,156,454	$ 1,233,551	$ 1,310,648	$ 1,387,745
45	$ 786,644	$ 865,309	$ 943,973	$ 1,022,637	$ 1,101,302	$ 1,179,966	$ 1,258,631	$ 1,337,295	$ 1,415,959
46	$ 802,243	$ 882,467	$ 962,692	$ 1,042,916	$ 1,123,140	$ 1,203,364	$ 1,283,589	$ 1,363,813	$ 1,444,037
47	$ 817,766	$ 899,543	$ 981,319	$ 1,063,096	$ 1,144,872	$ 1,226,649	$ 1,308,426	$ 1,390,202	$ 1,471,979
48	$ 833,214	$ 916,535	$ 999,857	$ 1,083,178	$ 1,166,499	$ 1,249,821	$ 1,333,142	$ 1,416,463	$ 1,499,785
49	$ 848,587	$ 933,445	$ 1,018,304	$ 1,103,163	$ 1,188,021	$ 1,272,880	$ 1,357,738	$ 1,442,597	$ 1,527,456
50	$ 863,885	$ 950,273	$ 1,036,662	$ 1,123,050	$ 1,209,439	$ 1,295,827	$ 1,382,215	$ 1,468,604	$ 1,554,992
51	$ 879,109	$ 967,019	$ 1,054,930	$ 1,142,841	$ 1,230,752	$ 1,318,663	$ 1,406,574	$ 1,494,484	$ 1,582,395
52	$ 894,258	$ 983,684	$ 1,073,110	$ 1,162,536	$ 1,251,962	$ 1,341,388	$ 1,430,814	$ 1,520,239	$ 1,609,665
53	$ 909,335	$ 1,000,268	$ 1,091,202	$ 1,182,135	$ 1,273,069	$ 1,364,002	$ 1,454,936	$ 1,545,869	$ 1,636,803
54	$ 924,338	$ 1,016,772	$ 1,109,206	$ 1,201,640	$ 1,294,073	$ 1,386,507	$ 1,478,941	$ 1,571,375	$ 1,663,809
55	$ 939,269	$ 1,033,195	$ 1,127,122	$ 1,221,049	$ 1,314,976	$ 1,408,903	$ 1,502,830	$ 1,596,756	$ 1,690,683
56	$ 954,126	$ 1,049,539	$ 1,144,952	$ 1,240,364	$ 1,335,777	$ 1,431,190	$ 1,526,602	$ 1,622,015	$ 1,717,428
57	$ 968,912	$ 1,065,803	$ 1,162,695	$ 1,259,586	$ 1,356,477	$ 1,453,368	$ 1,550,260	$ 1,647,151	$ 1,744,042
58	$ 983,626	$ 1,081,989	$ 1,180,352	$ 1,278,714	$ 1,377,077	$ 1,475,439	$ 1,573,802	$ 1,672,165	$ 1,770,527
59	$ 998,269	$ 1,098,096	$ 1,197,923	$ 1,297,750	$ 1,397,576	$ 1,497,403	$ 1,597,230	$ 1,697,057	$ 1,796,884
60	$ 1,012,840	$ 1,114,124	$ 1,215,408	$ 1,316,692	$ 1,417,977	$ 1,519,261	$ 1,620,545	$ 1,721,829	$ 1,823,113

61	$ 1,027,341	$ 1,130,075	$ 1,232,809	$ 1,335,543	$ 1,438,278	$ 1,541,012	$ 1,643,746	$ 1,746,480	$ 1,849,214
62	$ 1,041,772	$ 1,145,949	$ 1,250,126	$ 1,354,303	$ 1,458,480	$ 1,562,657	$ 1,666,834	$ 1,771,012	$ 1,875,189
63	$ 1,056,132	$ 1,161,745	$ 1,267,358	$ 1,372,971	$ 1,478,585	$ 1,584,198	$ 1,689,811	$ 1,795,424	$ 1,901,037
64	$ 1,070,422	$ 1,177,465	$ 1,284,507	$ 1,391,549	$ 1,498,591	$ 1,605,634	$ 1,712,676	$ 1,819,718	$ 1,926,760
65	$ 1,084,644	$ 1,193,108	$ 1,301,572	$ 1,410,037	$ 1,518,501	$ 1,626,966	$ 1,735,430	$ 1,843,894	$ 1,952,359
66	$ 1,098,796	$ 1,208,676	$ 1,318,555	$ 1,428,435	$ 1,538,314	$ 1,648,194	$ 1,758,074	$ 1,867,953	$ 1,977,833
67	$ 1,112,879	$ 1,224,167	$ 1,335,455	$ 1,446,743	$ 1,558,031	$ 1,669,319	$ 1,780,607	$ 1,891,895	$ 2,003,183
68	$ 1,126,895	$ 1,239,584	$ 1,352,274	$ 1,464,963	$ 1,577,652	$ 1,690,342	$ 1,803,031	$ 1,915,721	$ 2,028,410
69	$ 1,140,842	$ 1,254,926	$ 1,369,010	$ 1,483,094	$ 1,597,178	$ 1,711,263	$ 1,825,347	$ 1,939,431	$ 2,053,515
70	$ 1,154,721	$ 1,270,193	$ 1,385,665	$ 1,501,137	$ 1,616,610	$ 1,732,082	$ 1,847,554	$ 1,963,026	$ 2,078,498
71	$ 1,168,533	$ 1,285,386	$ 1,402,240	$ 1,519,093	$ 1,635,946	$ 1,752,800	$ 1,869,653	$ 1,986,506	$ 2,103,360
72	$ 1,182,278	$ 1,300,506	$ 1,418,734	$ 1,536,962	$ 1,655,189	$ 1,773,417	$ 1,891,645	$ 2,009,873	$ 2,128,101
73	$ 1,195,956	$ 1,315,552	$ 1,435,148	$ 1,554,743	$ 1,674,339	$ 1,793,935	$ 1,913,530	$ 2,033,126	$ 2,152,722
74	$ 1,209,568	$ 1,330,525	$ 1,451,482	$ 1,572,439	$ 1,693,396	$ 1,814,352	$ 1,935,309	$ 2,056,266	$ 2,177,223
75	$ 1,223,114	$ 1,345,425	$ 1,467,737	$ 1,590,048	$ 1,712,360	$ 1,834,671	$ 1,956,982	$ 2,079,294	$ 2,201,605
76	$ 1,236,594	$ 1,360,253	$ 1,483,913	$ 1,607,572	$ 1,731,232	$ 1,854,891	$ 1,978,551	$ 2,102,210	$ 2,225,869
77	$ 1,250,009	$ 1,375,010	$ 1,500,010	$ 1,625,011	$ 1,750,012	$ 1,875,013	$ 2,000,014	$ 2,125,015	$ 2,250,016
78	$ 1,263,358	$ 1,389,694	$ 1,516,030	$ 1,642,366	$ 1,768,701	$ 1,895,037	$ 2,021,373	$ 2,147,709	$ 2,274,045
79	$ 1,276,643	$ 1,404,307	$ 1,531,971	$ 1,659,636	$ 1,787,300	$ 1,914,964	$ 2,042,629	$ 2,170,293	$ 2,297,957
80	$ 1,289,863	$ 1,418,849	$ 1,547,836	$ 1,676,822	$ 1,805,808	$ 1,934,794	$ 2,063,781	$ 2,192,767	$ 2,321,753
81	$ 1,303,019	$ 1,433,321	$ 1,563,623	$ 1,693,925	$ 1,824,227	$ 1,954,528	$ 2,084,830	$ 2,215,132	$ 2,345,434
82	$ 1,316,111	$ 1,447,722	$ 1,579,333	$ 1,710,944	$ 1,842,556	$ 1,974,167	$ 2,105,778	$ 2,237,389	$ 2,369,000
83	$ 1,329,140	$ 1,462,054	$ 1,594,968	$ 1,727,882	$ 1,860,796	$ 1,993,710	$ 2,126,624	$ 2,259,538	$ 2,392,452
84	$ 1,342,105	$ 1,476,316	$ 1,610,526	$ 1,744,737	$ 1,878,947	$ 2,013,158	$ 2,147,368	$ 2,281,579	$ 2,415,789
85	$ 1,355,007	$ 1,490,508	$ 1,626,009	$ 1,761,510	$ 1,897,010	$ 2,032,511	$ 2,168,012	$ 2,303,513	$ 2,439,013
86	$ 1,367,847	$ 1,504,632	$ 1,641,417	$ 1,778,201	$ 1,914,986	$ 2,051,771	$ 2,188,556	$ 2,325,340	$ 2,462,125
87	$ 1,380,625	$ 1,518,687	$ 1,656,750	$ 1,794,812	$ 1,932,875	$ 2,070,937	$ 2,208,999	$ 2,347,062	$ 2,485,124
88	$ 1,393,340	$ 1,532,674	$ 1,672,008	$ 1,811,342	$ 1,950,676	$ 2,090,010	$ 2,229,344	$ 2,368,678	$ 2,508,012
89	$ 1,405,994	$ 1,546,593	$ 1,687,193	$ 1,827,792	$ 1,968,391	$ 2,108,991	$ 2,249,590	$ 2,390,189	$ 2,530,789
90	$ 1,418,586	$ 1,560,445	$ 1,702,303	$ 1,844,162	$ 1,986,020	$ 2,127,879	$ 2,269,738	$ 2,411,596	$ 2,553,455

CHAPTER 5

Chapter **6**

The Basic Estate Plan:

The Will and the Special Needs Trust

REMEMBER WAY BACK IN THE INTRODUCTION OF THIS BOOK, when we told you that estate planning for families with children who have disabilities is different from other types of estate planning? Well, we've completed the first five chapters of this book and have said almost nothing about wills and trusts, which is where estate planning generally begins.

In this chapter we discuss the basic estate plan, consisting of a will, which you can use to control how your property is to be distributed when you die, and a special needs trust, which will generally be used to receive the property you intend to leave for your child.

The Role of a Will in Your Estate Plan

Nobody likes to think about writing a will because it is an acknowledgment of death. But writing a will is essential if your property is to be distributed the way you intend. If you do not write a will or if you have a legally invalid will, you will lose control over your entire estate plan. In general, a will serves three vital functions.

First, a will permits you to name a guardian for your minor children in the event you and your spouse die before your children reach adulthood. As discussed in Chapter Three, you cannot name a guardian for an adult child in your will even if the child has a disability. The law presumes that adults are competent unless they are found to be incompetent in a guardianship hearing. In most states, however, you can nominate a successor guardian for an adult child if you have previously been appointed guardian in a guardianship hearing. In addition, you can appoint a guardian to act for your minor children, both those who have disabilities and those who do not.

The factors to consider in deciding whom to select have been discussed in Chapter Three. Obviously, you will want someone who cares for your children and can be expected to do a good job in raising them. The guardianship is effective until your children become adults; that is, in most states, until they reach age 18.

Second, a will permits you to select the person who will be responsible for doing the administrative tasks that will need to be performed when you die. This person is known as the *executor* of your estate or, in some states, as your *personal representative*. In general, the executor will be responsible for paying your debts (including burial expenses) and for collecting your assets and distributing them in accordance with the provisions contained in your will. In many cases your executor will be required to submit your will for validation in a court of law in a process known as *probate*, which is the legal process for determining whether your will is valid. The probate system is discussed in Chapter Eight.

In most cases our clients tend to appoint their spouse as executor, with close relatives such as siblings or adult children acting if the spouse cannot. It is expected that the executor will get aid from an attorney if needed.

Third, a will permits you to decide how your property is to be distributed when you die. In general, you can leave your property to whomever you want, except that most states permit your spouse to insist on a fractional share of your estate (typically one-third) if your spouse does not receive a larger share by will. Your spouse can waive this right in a prenuptial or postnuptial agreement. These rights are also forfeited on divorce or, in some states, if you and your spouse are separated.

Most of our clients tend to leave all their property to their spouse, or to their children (in specified shares) if their spouse dies before them. It is also possible to leave certain items of property to a particular individual (perhaps jewelry to your daughter). These are known as specific bequests and are a common way of disposing of personal property. It is best not to go overboard with specific bequests, as things tend to work better if your heirs divide personal property as they choose. However, specific bequests can be a useful way of disposing of property that has sentimental value.

Often our clients write down their wishes about the disposition of their personal property in a separate memorandum that they keep with their other important papers. Although not legally binding in all states, this permits clients to tell their executor who should get which items of property. Because the list is not a part of the will, it can be changed without need of an attorney. Changes to your will typically have to be prepared by your lawyer.

TIP One mistake to avoid: in most cases you will not want to leave money outright to a child who has a disability. It would generally be better to leave money for such a child in trust as described below.

This is true for four reasons. First, leaving money outright to a child who has a disability could result in a loss of eligibility or a reduction in benefits under one or more of the government benefit programs discussed in Chapter Four. These benefits are often relied upon by families to reduce the tremendous costs—often reaching $60,000 annually or more—of providing private care for people with disabilities. As discussed in Chapter Four, some government programs (primarily Medicaid, state cost-of-care residential benefit programs, and the Supplemental Security Income program), have eligibility requirements that could be violated if your child owns more than an insignificant amount of property. Leaving money for your child in the type of trust described below generally

261

avoids this problem because, in most states, property held in such trusts is not considered your child's, even though the property will be used for your child's benefit.

Second, also as described in Chapter Four, some states have laws that permit the state to seize property owned by a person who has a disability to pay for current or past services rendered by the state. This type of law is becoming more common among the states as their economic problems increase. The states seek reimbursements from those recipients who can afford to pay, to lessen the burden on other taxpayers. For example, in Illinois the law provides that a person with a disability who is a recipient of state mental health or developmental disability services must pay the state for all current and past services if the person has the resources to do so. As soon as the person with a disability acquires property (by inheritance or otherwise), the state is entitled to seize the property under its reimbursement right.

Trusts frequently avoid this problem because, in most states, money left for a person who has a disability in the type of trust described below is not considered an asset of the person and therefore is not subject to state reimbursement claims.

The third problem associated with receipt of an inheritance by a person who has a disability is that, depending on the nature and severity of the disability, the person may not be able to manage the money effectively. As a consequence, it is frequently necessary to have a guardian of the estate appointed for this purpose. (If you leave money outright to your child and a guardian of the estate is not appointed, no one will have the legal authority to look out for your child's financial interests.)

As we have discussed in more detail in Chapter Three, the appointment of a guardian of the estate may cause many problems: your child may have to be ruled incompetent, there may be fees, the posting of a bond, restrictive investment rules, and complicated approval procedures for expenditures. Trusts avoid this problem because money management responsibilities are left to trustees whom you select.

Fourth, if you leave money outright to your child, your child will have to plan what happens to the money (if any is left) after his or her own death. This may involve writing a will. If your child does not write a will, or if a court determines that the child lacks sufficient mental capacity to write a valid will, the property would be distributed in accordance with the intestacy laws (discussed below) in the state of residence. This may or may not be what you would prefer. Trusts avoid this problem because a well-drafted trust document will spell out what is to happen to the remaining trust property when the primary beneficiary (your child) dies.

A final point. It is important to understand that not all property passes by will. For example, insurance proceeds pass to the beneficiary designated in the insurance contract. Property that is held in joint tenancy with right of survivorship (often homes and bank accounts) passes to the surviving joint tenant when the first property owner dies. Property in a retirement plan passes under the beneficiary designation contained in the plan.

TIP In preparing your will, it is absolutely critical that you consider what will happen to your property that does not pass by will.

Life insurance is an area where mistakes are possible. Parents will frequently take out insurance policies naming their spouse as primary beneficiary and their children as contingent beneficiaries if their spouse does not survive them. What happens if the insured dies after the spouse? The insurance proceeds go to the children under the terms of the insurance contract which puts money into the hands of a child who has a disability. As an alternative you should consider naming your children without disabilities and the trust established for your child with a disability as contingent beneficiaries. For example, if you have three children, one with a disability, you will likely want to name your children without disabilities and the trust created for the child with a disability, each in one-third shares, as contingent beneficiaries.

Retirement plans are another area where mistakes are common. Parents frequently name their spouse as primary beneficiary and their children as contingent beneficiaries if their spouse dies before them. It is generally better to name the children without disabilities and a trust for a child with a disability as contingent beneficiaries.

 TIP Be careful about naming a trust for a child with a disability as a contingent beneficiary under a retirement plan if a charity is to receive property from the trust when the child dies. This potentially results in disadvantageous income tax consequences for the child.

You will also need to think about grandparents, former spouses, and others who might leave property to your child. You should contact them to make sure the property goes to a properly prepared special needs trust.

Guidelines for Creating a Will

It is important that you consult an attorney when you draft a will. Your attorney will know the legal requirements for a valid will in your particular state. Each state has different requirements. For instance, some states require two witnesses, while others require three. Some states permit handwritten wills, others do not. Never attempt to write a will without an attorney.

Without the aid of an attorney, your will might fail to comply with the state's legal requirements, and the probate court might declare your will invalid. If this happens, you lose control over your estate, and the security of your child may be jeopardized.

Another problem with a self-drafted will is that its validity is more likely to be challenged in probate court. If your executor is forced to pay attorney fees to defend your will, the battle could drain much or all of your estate. Again, if your will loses in court, your wishes will be ignored.

Your will can be revoked or changed at any time. As discussed previously, it is a good idea to have your estate plan reviewed periodically, say every five years, or more frequently if there have been major changes in your life, such as the birth or death of a child or a major change in your financial situation.

Dying Intestate

What happens if you die without a will? (This is known as dying intestate.)

If you die without a will, the state will write one for you. The state will distribute your property according to its probate laws. These laws are designed for the general public and do not consider the special problems faced by families with children who have disabilities.

In most states, the intestacy laws will distribute your property in accordance with rules that are similar to the rules described below:

- If your spouse is living at the time of your death, one-half of your property goes to your spouse and the remaining half goes to your then-living children, with the descendants of a deceased child taking the share the child would have received had the child survived you.

- If your spouse is not living at the time of your death, your property is divided equally among your children (again, with the descendants of any deceased child taking the deceased child's share).

- If your spouse is not living at the time of your death and if you have no descendant then living, your property is distributed to more distant relatives, such as parents or siblings.

- As is the case when you have a will, certain types of property will pass outside the probate system in accordance with contractual arrangements that you have entered into during your life. For example, property held in joint tenancy with right of survivorship will be distributed to the surviving joint tenant, and insurance will be distributed to the beneficiary designated in the insurance contract. Other property, such as benefits under retirement plans, may also be distributed outside the probate system.

Obviously, dying without a will is not a preferred choice. Your property may not be distributed in the manner that you would like. Your children with disabilities are likely to receive outright distributions of property, with all the associated problems discussed above. In addition, you will be unable to select your executor or a guardian for your minor children.

Trust for Beneficiaries with Disabilities

The trust is the most useful estate-planning tool available for providing future financial security for persons with disabilities. The trust can accomplish many estate-planning goals. For example, a trust can

- Avoid the problems of direct inheritance that may render the person with a disability ineligible for government benefits.

- Avoid the problems of direct inheritance that may expose the assets of a person with a disability to cost-of-care reimbursement claims by governmental authorities.

- Through a trustee, manage the money for a person with a disability by investing it properly, conserving the assets of the trust over the entire lifetime of the person, paying bills, and contracting for care. This money management is one of the most beneficial features of a trust, whether or not the family sets up the trust with government benefits in mind.

- Be used by the parents of the child with a disability to control the distribution of their property not only after their deaths, but also after the death of their child.

- Allow the trust property to bypass probate proceedings, which are often lengthy and costly. (This is discussed in detail in Chapter Eight.)

What is a *trust*? In general, a trust is a legal relationship under which property is managed by a person or institution (the *trustee*) for the benefit of those persons or organizations for whom the trust was created (the *beneficiary*). The person who places assets into the trust is commonly referred to as the *creator, settlor, grantor,* or *trustor.* This person establishes the trust through a will, or in a legal document known as a *trust agreement* or a *declaration of trust,* which describes the rights and obligations of the trustee.

In effect, the trust is a legal instrument that separates the responsibility of ownership of specific property from the benefit of ownership. The person who has responsibility of ownership, the trustee, manages the assets according to the instructions written in the trust agreement by the creator of the trust for the benefit of the beneficiary. The trustee derives no benefit from the trust property except compensation received for performing his or her duties.

To consider a typical example, Grandfather Jones gives a bank 10,000 shares of Widget Company stock. The bank agrees to hold the stock in trust for the benefit of his son, Mr. Jones, and for Mr. Jones's two children. The trust agreement states that the bank will give Mr. Jones for life all the dividends accrued from the stock (the stock income). After Mr. Jones's death, the stock will be given to his children and the trust will end.

GRANDFATHER JONES
(Creator or Grantor)

TRUSTEE
(Could be an individual instead of a bank)

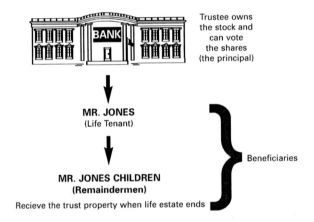

Trustee owns
the stock and
can vote
the shares
(the principal)

MR. JONES
(Life Tenant)

}

Beneficiaries

MR. JONES CHILDREN
(Remaindermen)
Recieve the trust property when life estate ends

Grandfather Jones is the grantor of the trust—that is, the person who established the trust. The bank is the trustee and has legal ownership of the stock which is the trust principal. However, the bank holds the stock for the benefit of Mr. Jones and his two children, the beneficiaries. The bank, as trustee, has the duty of managing the stock or trust property according to the wishes of the creator, Grandfather Jones, as expressed in the trust agreement.

Obviously, the key to any trust is the instructions given to the trustee. These are contained in the document that creates the trust—either your will, a declaration of trust, or a trust agreement. What instructions are appropriate? The answer depends on the purpose for which the trust has been established.

In the case of trusts involving beneficiaries with disabilities, parents generally have four objectives in mind:

✔ They want the trust proceeds to be available to assure a high quality of life for their child;

✔ They do not want the trust to affect their child's eligibility for government benefits;

✔ They want to protect the property in the trust from cost-of-care claims that may be asserted by the government; and

✔ They want the trustee to have sufficient flexibility to use trust funds for their child's primary care if they have difficulty placing their child in government-funded facilities or if such facilities should prove to be inappropriate for their child.

There is more than one way to draft such instructions, and what is appropriate in one state may be inappropriate in another. This is particularly true since applicable law will be partly determined based on the manner in which the state has implemented the joint federal and state Medicaid program, and this will vary by state.

It is therefore critical that you have your child's trust prepared by an attorney knowledgeable about the laws in your own state relating to trusts for beneficiaries with disabilities. The National Academy of Elder Law Attorneys (www.naela.com) is an excellent source for locating knowledgeable attorneys in your state.

The key will be to prepare your child's trust in such a way that the property in the trust is not considered a *resource* of your child under Social Security's rules. The regulations promulgated by the Social Security Administration (Section 416.1201) define resources as follows.

> Resources means cash or other liquid assets or any real or personal property that an individual owns and could convert to cash to be used for his or her support and maintenance. If the individual has the right, authority or power to liquidate the property or his or her share of the property, it is considered a resource. If a property right cannot be liquidated, the property will not be considered a resource of the individual.

This regulation has been interpreted to mean that property in a trust will not be considered the trust beneficiary's property unless the trust beneficiary has the legal right to demand that distributions be made from the trust for support or maintenance purposes. The Department of Health and Human Services Programs Operation Manual System (POMS Section SI 1120.200) states the rule as follows:

> If the individual has legal authority to revoke the trust and then use the funds to meet his food, clothing or shelter needs, or if the individual can direct the use of the trust principal for his/her support and maintenance under the terms of the trust, the trust principal is a resource for SSI purposes. If an individual does not have legal authority to revoke the trust or direct the use of the trust principal for his/her own support and maintenance, the trust principal is not the individual's resource for SSI purposes.

What does this mean for purposes of preparing a trust document for a child with a disability?

First, the trust document should not require the trustee to make distributions for the support and maintenance of a child with a disability or even for purposes that are at all similar to support and maintenance, such as welfare, education or best interests, because your child would have the legal right to go to court and require the trustee to make distributions for these purposes if the trustee did not do so on its own. It does not matter if your child would go to court or even if he or she had the mental capacity to do so. Just having the legal ability to go to court and require the trustee to make distributions would be sufficient to permit the state to seize the trust for past cost of care claims, or to withhold future benefits until the trust was exhausted. As a result, we try to avoid using language requiring the trustee to make distributions for specified purposes.

Second, in many states the trust document should not even expressly state that the trustee has the *discretion* to make distributions for purposes such as support, maintenance, welfare, education or best interests. The reason is that there is a fair amount of case law interpreting trusts that expressly grant the trustee discretion to make distributions for support purposes (these trusts are referred to as *discretionary support trusts*), and the cases are split. Most of the cases hold that the property in a discretionary support trust should not be considered the beneficiary's property for Medicaid purposes because the trustee has absolute discretion to determine whether distributions are to be made. As a result, the cases hold, the beneficiary does not have the legal right to go to court and require the trustee to make distributions.

Other cases hold that by expressly stating that the trustee has discretion to distribute trust property to provide support, the creator of the trust is creating a duty on the part of the trustee to make distributions if needed for the beneficiary's support. As a result, the cases hold that the beneficiary can sue the trustee if support is withheld, and the trusts therefore disqualify the beneficiary from receiving needs based government benefits.

Our view is that the majority of the courts that have addressed the issue are correct and such discretionary support trusts should not prevent the beneficiary from receiving government benefits. This is particularly true if the trust document expressly states that the purpose of the trust is to supplement and not supplant government benefits, and we are unaware of any case in which a discretionary support trust was considered a resource where the trust clarified that the intent was to supplement government benefits. Thus, we believe that a trust providing as follows would probably survive challenge:

The trustee may distribute so much or all of the income and principal of the trust for the benefit of [beneficiary] as the trustee, in the trustee's sole and absolute discretion, determines to be required for [beneficiary's] welfare. In making such determination, the trustee shall consider all other resources available to [beneficiary], including government benefit programs. It is my express intent that the trust be used only to supplement and never to supplant, the government benefits, if any, to which [beneficiary] may be entitled. No part of this trust shall be considered to be owned by [beneficiary] nor shall [beneficiary] have any right to control the amount or frequency of any distributions from this trust.

However, we prefer to avoid mentioning standards such as maintenance, support, welfare, best interests or education. Instead, we prefer trusts that (i) provide the trustee with total discretion, and (ii) clarify the intent regarding government benefits. Language such as the following may be appropriate:

During the life of [beneficiary], who has a certain disability that substantially impairs her ability to provide for her own care or custody, the trustee may pay to [beneficiary], or apply for the benefit of [beneficiary's], such part or all of the income and principal of the trust as the trustee, in the trustee's sole and absolute discretion, deems advisable for [beneficiary], considering all other income and assets known to the trustee to be available for [beneficiary] from any other source (including government benefit programs available to [beneficiary]) and all other circumstances

272

and factors the trustee considers pertinent. In administering the trust, it is my desire that the trustee be guided by my intent that the trust be used to supplement and not supplant government or private benefits, if any, which may be available to [beneficiary]. Notwithstanding the preceding sentence, I intend in no way to restrict the trustee's sole and absolute discretion to use such part or all of the income and principal of this trust (even though exhausting the trust) for anything the trustee, in the trustee's sole and absolute discretion, deems advisable for [beneficiary]. No part of this trust shall be considered to be owned by [beneficiary] nor shall [beneficiary] have any right to control the amount or frequency of any distributions from this trust.

We refer to trusts of this type as *flexible special needs trusts* because they are intended to meet the beneficiary's special needs over and above the needs met through government benefits, but provide sufficient flexibility for the trustee to make greater distributions if the trustee determines that facilities provided by the government are inadequate. We believe that in most states these flexible special needs trusts meet the objectives that parents generally have in mind when preparing trusts for children with disabilities—namely,

- That the trust property is available to assure a high quality of life,

- That the trust does not affect the child's eligibility for government benefits,

- That the property in the trust is protected from state cost-of-care claims, and

- That the property is available for primary care if government funded facilities are unavailable or inadequate.

It is important to note that although the trust language that we provide permits the trustee to make distributions to or for the benefit of the beneficiary, as discussed under Trust Administration *below, distributions directly to the beneficiary are inadvisable if the beneficiary receives needs based government benefits such as SSI or Medicaid. In the interest of flexibility, we generally grant the trustee discretion to make distributions directly to the beneficiary in cases where it is uncertain whether needs based government benefits will be required. It is vitally important, however, that the trustee be aware of the effect that direct distributions to the beneficiary will have on SSI and Medicaid.*

Older special needs trusts were often less flexible because they did not permit use of funds for primary care if government facilities were inadequate. These less flexible trusts are particularly inappropriate for children with disabilities who are higher functioning since parents may not be sure that such children will require government benefits. Such less flexible special needs trusts may, however, be appropriate where they are relatively modest in amount and it is clear that needs based government benefits will be required, or in states that are particularly unfriendly to special needs trusts. In such cases, language like the following may be appropriate:

During the life of [beneficiary], who has a certain disability that substantially impairs her ability to provide for her own care or custody, the trustee may apply for the benefit of [beneficiary], such part or all of the income and principal of the trust as the trustee, in the trustee's sole and absolute discretion, considers advisable for [beneficiary], taking into account [beneficiary's] income and resources known to the trustee (including without limitation any funds available for [beneficiary's] health, maintenance, or education under any federal, state or local government program or under any private agency program). I do not intend that this trust provide for [beneficiary's] basic care, support, or education. Rather, I intend that it supplement funds available for such purposes by providing benefits to [beneficiary] that are not otherwise provided. Under no circumstance shall this trust be considered to be the property of or the "estate" of [beneficiary] or be available to [beneficiary] other than in the absolute discretion of the trustee. This trust shall not be used to provide basic food, clothing, or shelter, nor be available to [beneficiary] for conversion for or to such items or purposes, unless and until all benefits and funds received as the result of [beneficiary's] disability or otherwise from any state, local or federal government or from any private agency, any of which provides services or benefits to persons with disabilities, or from any other sources of which the trustee has knowledge, are expended. The trustee shall not have any discretion to expend trust income or principal to reimburse any government or private agency providing or paying benefits received as the result of [beneficiary's] disability or otherwise from any state, local or federal government or from any private agency, any of which provides services or benefits to persons with disabilities, or from any other sources of which the trustee has knowledge.

There has been some speculation that the Uniform Trust Code, which has been adopted by nine states and the District of Columbia, may make it easier for states to deny government benefits to beneficiaries of special needs trusts. It is our view that the Uniform Trust Code will not have this affect, particularly if the special needs trust has been properly prepared.

A few other provisions should be considered:

Spendthrift Clause

We always insert a spendthrift clause in the trust. This clause protects the trust assets from creditors of the person with a disability. For instance, if someone persuades your child to sign an installment contract to purchase a Rolls Royce automobile, the spendthrift clause will prevent the lender from getting at the trust assets. Language such as the following may be appropriate:

No interest under this instrument shall be assignable or saleable by any beneficiary or be subject to the claims of his or her creditors, including claims for alimony or separate maintenance. Furthermore, because the trust herein for [beneficiary] is to be conserved and maintained for [beneficiary's] special needs throughout [beneficiary's] lifetime, no part of the corpus thereof, neither principal nor undistributed income, shall be construed as part of the [beneficiary's] estate or be subject to the claims of voluntary or involuntary creditors for the provision of goods, care and services, including residential care, by any public entity, office, department or agency of any state, county, municipal, federal or other governmental entity, department or agency. In no event may income or principal of the trust be paid to or for the benefit of or as a requirement of a governmental agency or department and the trust property shall at all times be free of the claims of such governmental bodies.

Trust Terminations

You can include a trust provision that authorizes the trustee to terminate the trust in the event the government attempts to seize the assets of the trust or if the trust imperils your child's eligibility for government benefits. The intent would be to distribute the trust property to people named in the trust document, presumably people who you believe would spend the money on behalf of your child.

There is not sufficient law to determine whether this provision would be enforceable. However, if enforceable, such a provision could prove useful in two circumstances: (i) in states where the status of special needs trusts is uncertain, the provision could be useful if the state were to suddenly start challenging such trusts; and (ii) in states that are currently favorably disposed toward special needs trusts, a trust-termination provision could prove useful if the law were to change in the future. (Given the budgetary pressures faced by all states, this is always a possibility.)

If you include such a trust-termination provision, it is a good idea to premise it on an opinion of counsel that the trust cannot be protected from state action (that is, the trust could not be terminated unless a lawyer told the trustee that the trust imperilled your child's government benefits). You will also need to decide whether the assets should be distributed to the same people who will receive the remaining trust property when your child dies.

For example, on the death of a child with a disability, many of our clients will have the property remaining in the trust go to their surviving children, with grandchildren taking the share of any children who have already died. On termination of the trust due to an attempted government seizure of trust property, clients are frequently less comfortable with grandchildren receiving a share. They know their children and are reasonably confident their children will use the property for the person with the disability, but they are less confident about grandchildren who may be very young—or not yet born. Language such as the following may be appropriate:

> *If a claim is made against trust property by any governmental body, or if any governmental body denies benefits to [beneficiary] as a consequence of the existence of the trust, the trustee may hire legal counsel on behalf of the trust to contest such governmental claim or denial of benefits. If the trustee determines that the governmental claim or denial of benefits is valid, and if the trustee determines that amendment of the trust will not be sufficient to restore such government benefits, and if [trusted relative] is then living, the trustee may terminate the trust, and distribute the trust estate to [trusted relative] free of trust and before paying such governmental claim provided, however, that before terminating the trust pursuant to this paragraph, the trustee shall obtain an opinion from a licensed attorney familiar with trusts involving disabled beneficiaries that the governmental claim or denial of benefits is valid.*

Some clients prefer not to include a trust termination provision because they do not expect their child to require government benefits. They prefer to make sure the trust remains available for their child, regardless of what the future may bring. This tends to be the exception rather than the rule, as government benefits are very important for most people with disabilities. Parents tend not to include a trust termination provision where there are no children without disabilities.

Trust Amendment

This clause is similar to the trust termination provision discussed above. The idea is to permit the trustee to amend the trust if the law changes in such a way that the existence of the trust imperils your child's eligibility for government benefits.

As was the case with the trust termination provision, it is unclear whether this provision would be enforceable. In addition, its use should be premised on receipt of an opinion by the trustee from a lawyer that amendment of the trust is necessary to protect your child's government benefits. Language such as the following may be appropriate:

The basic purpose of this trust is to supplement and not supplant the government and private benefits, if any, which may be available to [beneficiary]. In order to assure that the basic purpose of the trust continues to be fulfilled, as long as such trust is in existence, the trustee is authorized to amend the terms of the trust in such manner as the trustee considers necessary to continue the basic purpose of the trust in light of adjustments or changes in statutes and regulations (or administrative or court interpretations thereof) governing benefits that might be available to [beneficiary] from federal, state and local governmental agencies and departments or private agencies; provided, however, that before amending the trust the trustee shall obtain an opinion from a licensed attorney familiar with trusts involving disabled beneficiaries that the amendment is necessary to assure that the basic purpose of the trust continues to be fulfilled. If necessary, any amendment made under this paragraph shall apply retroactively to the inception of this trust.

No Commingling of Assets

It is important to realize that while the special needs trusts described in this chapter are appropriate for gifts that you or others may wish to make for your child, it is not appropriate to transfer your child's own property to such trusts, even if your child previously received that property by way of gift. Such property can, however, be transferred to other types of trusts, known as *payback trusts*, which are discussed in Chapter Seven.

We generally include language in our special needs trusts to make sure that the child's assets are not added to the special needs trust. Language such as the following may be appropriate:

The trustee shall not commingle with the assets of this trust: (i) [beneficiary's] own assets, including assets held for [beneficiary] in any custodial or similar account, (ii) any government or private benefits that [beneficiary] receives, or (iii) any assets in any trust funded with beneficiary's own assets or any private or government benefits received by [beneficiary].

Trust Protector

Sometimes the power to amend or terminate the trust is given to a person other than the trustee or the person who will receive the property if the trust is terminated. This person, who is appointed in the trust document, is known as the *trust protector.*

The thinking behind this approach is that giving the person who will receive the trust property on termination the ability to terminate the trust creates an incentive to terminate the trust even if termination may not be in the best interest of the person with the disability. In many cases, however, families trust siblings both to make the decision about trust termination with the aid of an attorney, and to use the property for the benefit of the person with a disability in the event the trust is terminated.

Depending on family circumstances, however, a separate trust protector may be advisable. For example, if a bank or other institution is named as trustee, a trust protector may be advisable because the institution may be reluctant to terminate the trust. In rare circumstances, a separate trust protector may also be advisable for estate tax purposes. Estate tax is discussed in Chapter Nine.

Trust protectors can also be given other powers as well, such as the ability to advise the trustee on the needs of the beneficiary, to monitor the performance of the trustee, and to change the trustee if necessary. This function can be particularly important if a corporate trustee is selected. See *Selecting the Trustee—The Corporate Trustee* below.

Trust Remaindermen

In preparing your child's trust, it will also be important to think carefully about who will receive the remaining trust property after your child's death. (These people are known as the *trust remaindermen.*)

In particular, you may need to think about what you want to happen if your child has children. Would you want them to receive the property, or a percentage of it?

For children whose disabilities are very severe, this may not be an issue. For others, it is a possibility that should be considered, and the question becomes more important if you have left a disproportionately large share of your estate to your child's trust.

For example, suppose you have three children, one of whom has a disability. You decide to leave 50 percent of your property to that child's trust and 25 percent to each of your other children. If you decide that the remaining trust property is to go to the children of your child with a disability when that child dies, the effect is to give a disproportionate share to those grandchildren. Some of our clients like this, reasoning that those grandchildren will have greater need of the funds. Others prefer to make an equalizing distribution to their other grandchildren.

Sometimes clients provide that a portion of the property remaining in their child's trust go to charity, perhaps to an organization that helped the child during the child's life. Parents are often very grateful to such organizations and want such organizations to be able to provide others with the services that were provided to their own child. (But see the TIP on page 264.)

Trust Administration

Even if a special needs trust is properly prepared, the trust can affect your child's ability to receive government benefits if the trust is not properly administered. As you may recall from Chapter Four, SSI recipients are entitled to receive $20 of unearned income per month without reduction in SSI benefits. Receipt of unearned income in excess of $20 per month, however, results in a dollar-for-dollar reduction in benefits. Because distributions from trusts are considered unearned income, distributions in excess of $20 per month result in a benefit reduction. In addition, using trust property to provide food, clothing or shelter for your child results in unearned income as well.

How can this limitation on trust distributions be avoided? Have the trust purchase items for your child and retain ownership, permitting your child to use, but not own, the property, and do not use the trust to provide food, clothing, or shelter.

Under the SSI eligibility rules, trust distributions that do not result in your child receiving food, clothing, or shelter, or anything that can be used to obtain these items, do not count as unearned income. Thus, the trustee can use trust assets to pay for items such as vacations, recreation and leisure activities, companion or housekeeping services, special job training, vocational or employment supports, lawn care, laundry services, CD players, airline tickets, television sets, VCRs, computers, medical insurance, improved medical or dental care, telephone bills, or furniture without any reduction in benefits.

If, instead, the trustee were to give your child the money to pay for these items, the distribution to your child would count as unearned income, resulting in a possible reduction in benefits. Similarly, if your child were to actually own, rather than merely have the right to use, the item purchased, the receipt of the item would be considered unearned income because the item could be sold and converted to cash.

Trust distributions can also sometimes be structured to maximize SSI benefits if your child lives with someone who provides food and shelter. As you may recall from Chapter Four, under the one-third reduction rule, your child's SSI benefits are reduced by one-third because the Social Security Administration assumes that the value of the *in kind* benefits received by your child (free room and board) equals one-third of the SSI benefits. If, in fact, the child's share of household expenses is less than that amount, the child can pay his or her share out of the trust and receive a smaller reduction.

For example, suppose your child's share of monthly household expenses is $100 and, but for free room and board, the SSI benefit would be $470. If the $100 were to be paid from the trust, it would be treated as unearned income because the $100 will have been used to pay for food and shelter. The result would be a benefit reduction of $80—$100 of unearned income less the $20 allowance.

If, on the other hand, the one-third reduction rule were applied, benefits would be reduced by $157—one-third of $470. Of course, if your child were to pay his or her fair share from the trust, the trust would also be out of pocket for the $100 expense.

The trustee will also be required to perform various administrative functions related to the trust. The trustee will need to obtain a taxpayer identification number and file annual tax returns. Generally trust income that is used for the beneficiary will be taxed to the beneficiary, and the trustee may need to help the beneficiary with his or her taxes as well. Trust income that is not used for the beneficiary will be taxed directly to the trust.

The trustee will generally have a fair amount of discretion in investing trust assets, but investments should generally be conservative in order to preserve the property in the trust for your child's benefit. Investment in tax-exempt securities may be advisable both to protect the trust property and due to the generally high rate of tax applicable to trust income.

The trustee will need to keep good records of trust income and expenditures both because the trust document is likely to require that accountings be provided to a person specified in the document, and because trust activity may later be questioned by the government to make sure that the trust has not been administered in a way that affects your child's entitlement to government benefits. As mentioned above, the trustee will need to sure to avoid commingling property in the trust with other property owned by the trustee or the beneficiary of the trust. See *No Commingling of Assets* above.

L aws change frequently. It is vitally important that the trustee consult regularly with an attorney familiar with trusts for beneficiaries with disabilities to be sure that trust distributions do not affect eligibility under government benefit programs. Individual trustees should also be willing to consult financial advisors and accountants as appropriate.

Selecting the Trustee

In discussing guardianship and advocacy (Chapter Three), we told you that no matter how carefully thought out your child's life plan might be, much would depend on the skill and commitment of the advocate you select. The same is true of the trustee. Your child's trust is a vital legal document, but it is, after all, a piece of paper. It is the trustee who will manage the money and decide how it should be spent. The key to the plan is to make sure the right person is selected. Several different possibilities are available:

The Corporate Trustee

A corporate trustee is usually a financial institution such as a bank or a trust company that, as part of its business, serves as trustee of a great many trusts. There are three major advantages offered by a corporate trustee:

- Corporate trustees can be relied on to manage and invest the trust property. Usually, banks acting as trustees have several different investment plans. You should inquire about these, because each plan is designed for a different financial objective and each plan invests differently in terms of risk, income generation, and capital appreciation. Corporate trustees are also experienced in handling the paperwork involved in trust administration, such as the filing of tax returns and the preparation of accountings.

- Corporate trustees are independent and impartial and will attempt to treat all the trust beneficiaries fairly.

- Corporate trustees do not die. They will provide continuity of financial management for the entire lifetime of your child.

However, the corporate trustee also has some disadvantages. A major disadvantage is that banks charge an annual fee for their trust services (usually .75 percent to 1.5 percent of the principal per year), often with a minimum annual fee of $1,500 or more. As a result, it may be uneconomical to use a bank trustee if the trust has less than $200,000, and many banks will not accept trust funds below a minimum amount. The minimum amount varies by bank. In addition, though the bank's impartiality was cited as an advantage, it may also be a disadvantage if the bank, as trustee, is not equipped to be a friend and advocate for your child (particularly after your death).

If a bank is used as trustee, it is even more important that you appoint a strong advocate to look out for your child's interests. Advocates are discussed in detail in Chapter Three. Although the advocate will not have any legal authority over the bank trustee, the advocate will have the ability to bring important issues to the attention of the bank trust officer. You might even consider making the advocate a *trust protector* and giving the advocate the ability to switch the trust to a different bank if the advocate feels that the bank you have selected is not performing adequately. See *Trust Protector* above.

Occasionally clients will express concern about bank investment strategies, particularly in light of publicity over recent bank failures. Although mismanagement is possible, banks tend to invest trust funds conservatively and reasonably well. Most publicity about risky investments relates to banks' investments of their own funds and not to investments of funds that they hold in trust for others.

The Individual Trustee

An individual trustee is, as you would expect, an individual who manages the money in a trust. Anyone who cares about the person with a disability and can manage the trust property can be an individual trustee. Often this trustee is a relative, a trusted advisor, or a close friend. There is no minimum trust size, because an individual trustee will manage the trust property regardless of its size and an individual trustee, especially if a relative, might not charge for services.

Here too, however, there is another side to the coin. The individual trustee may not manage money as skillfully as a bank or be familiar with government benefit programs or trust administration requirements. Unlike a bank, the individual trustee may die before the beneficiary with a disability. To safeguard against this problem, you should appoint several trustees, to act one after the other as predecessors die. The last surviving trustee can be given the power to appoint his or her successor. In this way, there will always be a trustee of your choice to care for your child.

Another disadvantage of an individual trustee is the potential for conflict of interest. Often siblings without disabilities are the most natural choice for trustee due to their sincere love for their brother or sister and their knowledge of their brother or sister's wants and desires. However, because siblings often also serve as remaindermen (that is, they are to receive the *remaining* property when the person with the disability dies), a potential conflict of interest is created. It is in the financial interest of the sibling to spend less on the person with the disability in order to receive more when the person with the disability dies.

This is not to say that siblings should not be chosen. Often parents are rightfully confident that their children without disabilities will always act in the interest of the person with the disability out of love and concern for their sibling, despite the potential conflict of interest. In fact, it is often the children without disabilities who cause their parents to begin the estate-planning process out of a concern for their sibling's future. However, potential conflict of interest is a factor to be considered in selecting a trustee. It is often a good idea to select co-trustees (discussed below) to reduce the potential impact of the conflict.

Co-trustees

Co-trustees can often solve the problems associated with both the corporate and individual trustee. In fact, it is possible to combine the strengths of both kinds of trustee by naming a bank and an individual as co-trustees. You select the bank trustee to manage and invest the trust property and handle the paperwork, and name an individual trustee to look after the personal needs of the person with a disability. The bank trustee manages money expertly. The individual trustee understands the needs of the beneficiary. The individual trustee can also act as the personal advocate for the person with a disability. It is even possible to give the individual trustee the power to change the co-trustee to another bank. This power gives leverage to the family member if the bank's services are inadequate.

Appointing co-trustees can also guard against conflicts of interest. If your possible trustee candidates are relatives of your child who have a financial conflict of interest, you can appoint two of them as co-trustees with equal power. For example, suppose you have two sons without disabilities and a daughter with a disability. In the trust document the sons will receive the trust property after the death of your daughter. Both sons love their sister, but you are worried that one of them might be tempted to skimp on goods and services for his sister in order to inherit more money after her death. As a safeguard, you can appoint both sons as co-trustees, so that both of them would have to decide to skimp on goods or become dishonest before your daughter could be harmed. As another option, you could appoint one son and an independent third person as co-trustees.

In this way, you can guard against potential conflicts of interest but still have a loving, concerned relative as a trustee for your daughter. However, this arrangement of co-trustees with equal power does carry the possibility of a stalemate if the trustees disagree about a particular course of action.

Making the Choice: Selecting the Trustee

As in the case of your choice of advocate (see Chapter Three), the proper choice of trustee will depend on your own unique family circumstances. You will probably want people who

- Understand the unique needs and abilities of your child.

- Will carry out your wishes after your death.

- Can manage and invest trust property skillfully.

- Will employ professionals if necessary to help with investments, government benefits, taxes and accounting.

- Most importantly, are people whom you trust.

In most cases, clients will provide a list of trustees to act, one at a time (or two at a time if co-trustees are preferred). That way, if the person with the disability outlives the first trustee, a successor is ready to act. If all the people named by the parents die, a bank takes over. Each person acting as trustee will generally be given the power to revise the list in case a change in circumstances requires a change in plans. In cases where the parents name an individual to act as co-trustee with a bank, the individual is generally given the power to switch banks if the services provided by the named bank are inadequate. Parents who name a bank as sole trustee tend to name a trusted friend or relative as trust protector to advise the bank and make changes as needed.

Sample provision for sole trustee arrangement:

I name the following individuals as are willing and able to act as trustee, one at a time in the order so named: [insert list]. If none of these individuals are willing and able to act [insert bank] shall be trustee. Notwithstanding the foregoing, each individual acting at any time as trustee hereunder (unless limited in the instrument in which the trustee was designated) may, by signed instrument filed with the trust records, (a) designate one or more individuals or qualified corporations to act as successor trustee when such individual is unable or unwilling to act, and (b) revoke any designation previously made by such individual or by any prior trustee, but only before the designated trustee begins to act.

Sample trust provision for co-trustee arrangement involving two individuals:

I name as trustee the following individuals as are willing and able to act, two at a time in the order so named: [insert list]. If just one such individual is willing and able to act, such individual shall act as sole trustee. If no such individuals are able and willing to act as trustee, [insert bank] shall act as sole trustee. Notwithstanding the foregoing, each individual acting at any time as trustee hereunder (unless limited in the instrument in which the trustee was designated) may, by signed instrument filed with the trust records, (a) designate one or more individuals or qualified corporations to act as successor trustee when such individual is unable or unwilling to act, and (b) revoke any designation previously made by such individual or by any prior trustee, but only before the designated trustee begins to act.

Sample trust provision for co-trustee arrangement involving an individual and a bank:

I name as co-trustees hereunder [insert bank], and the following individuals, such individuals acting one at a time in the order so named: [insert list]. If no such individual is willing and able to act, [bank] shall be sole trustee. Any individual acting as co-trustee with a corporation shall have the power to remove the corporation and appoint another qualified corporation to act in its place, or to appoint a different successor co-trustee when such individual shall become unwilling or unable to act. At any time when a corporation is acting as co-trustee with an individual, the corporate trustee shall have custody of the trust property and records, and may perform for the trustees all acts necessary for the acquisition and transfer of personal property and money, including the signing and endorsement of checks, receipts, stock certificates and other instruments, unless all trustees otherwise agree. No person need inquire into the propriety of any such act.

Clients often ask us who is looking over the trustee's shoulder to make sure the trustee is doing a good job. The answer is *no one*. The only recourse against a trustee who is negligent or even dishonest is for one of the beneficiaries under the trust, or an agent representing the person with a disability, to sue the trustee in court. The bottom line, therefore, is that you need to choose trustees whom you sincerely trust.

The Pooled-Income Trust

As previously mentioned, a corporate trustee may not be a viable option for trusts that are not large (for example, trusts that have less than $200,000) because it may be difficult to find corporate trustees willing to act and the trustee fees may be too large in relation to the amount in the trust.

To meet these problems, many states have developed *pooled-income trusts* which, in essence, are smaller trusts that are pooled together to reduce administrative costs. Trustees are typically nonprofit organizations formed specifically to act as trustee of such trusts, and often are professionally managed and familiar with the needs of people who have disabilities.

Although the rules may differ depending on the specific pooled trust involved, generally the property that you contribute to the pooled trust will be used to create a separate account for your child and will be used for your child during his or her life. On the death of the child, a portion of the remaining property from your child's account remains in the trust to help other people with disabilities, and a portion gets distributed pursuant to instructions that you have given to the trustee. Although some parents might object to leaving some money behind with the pooled trust, many parents are pleased to be able to help others with disabilities after their child has died.

You can obtain information about pooled-income trusts in your area from local advocacy organizations or from estate planners knowledgeable about the needs of families with children who have disabilities. Information can also be obtained from organizations such as the Arc of the United States and the National Alliance for the Mentally Ill.

Trusts for Beneficiaries without Disabilities

The plan you develop for your child with a disability will be part of the estate plan you develop for your whole family. This is particularly true if you have children without disabilities who are minors. You will probably want to establish trusts for them as well.

These trusts will generally be similar to trusts for your child with a disability in that distributions will be discretionary in nature. They generally will be a part of your will and not freestanding documents. In essence, the trusts will become effective only if both parents die before your child becomes an adult. Language such as the following is typical:

The trustee may in the trustee's discretion pay to, or use for the benefit of John or any of his descendants such part or all of the income and principal of the trust as the trustee determines to be necessary or desirable for their medical care, support, education (including college and postgraduate), welfare, and best interests.

The trust property would then typically be distributed to John when he reached a specified age—for example, age 23. If the trust was sufficiently large, you could even distribute it in stages—for example, a third at age 25, a third at age 30, and a third at age 35.

Several different methods of structuring these trusts are possible:

- You could leave your property in one trust for all your children, permitting the trustee to *sprinkle* trust property among your children as needed. Property would be used for the child with a disability in accordance with the provisions of a flexible special needs trust, and property would be distributed for other children as needed for medical care, support, education and best interests. The theory behind this *pool approach* is that, if you were living, you would not necessarily spend equal amounts on each of your children because your children may have different needs, and the trustee should have similar flexibility. (For example, one of your children may become very ill, and the entire trust may be necessary to pay the medical bills.) When the youngest of your children (not counting the child with the disability) reaches a specified age (say age 23), the remaining trust property would be split into separate shares for your children. The shares of children without disabilities could either be distributed outright to them, or in stages as described above (depending on your preference). The share of the child with a disability would remain in trust for the child's sole benefit.

- Some parents like the pool approach for their children without disabilities but fear using it for their child with a disability because they want to make sure sufficient funds will be available for that child. In such cases it is possible to carve out the share of the child with the disability, placing it in a separate special needs trust, and to use the pool approach described above for other children.

- Some parents want to make sure that each child receives an equal share. In such cases, the parents' property can be divided equally, with a separate trust being held for each child.

What happens if you leave money outright to a minor child—that is, if you do not provide a trust? The property will be your child's, and a guardian of the estate will be required. As discussed in Chapter Three, the guardian will be subject to restrictions relating to investments, the need to obtain court approval for expenditures, and the obligation to file periodic reports.

As an intermediate step between preparing a trust for minor children and leaving property to them outright, it is possible to provide in your will that property left to minors should be transferred to a *custodian* for your child's benefit under your state's Uniform Transfer To Minor's Act. Under the laws in most states, the custodian holds the property for the benefit of the child, using income and principal as needed, until the child reaches age 21 (18 in some states), at which time the remaining property is distributed outright to the child.

Disinheritance—A Poor Alternative

Some parents disinherit a child with a disability, leaving everything to other children with an informal understanding that the other children will look out for their sibling. This can be a disastrous choice.

The relative who receives the extra money to look after the person with a disability might enter a nursing home and be required by the government to spend the money on his or her own care. The person might go bankrupt and be required to give the money to creditors or get a divorce and be required to split the money with his or her spouse, or die and will the money to others, or simply refuse to spend it on the person with the disability.

As a result, disinheritance tends to be a poor alternative except in states that are hostile to all types of special needs trusts. It is far better to leave the money in trust for the child who has the disability so that a separate fund of guaranteed money is available for the person who really needs it.

Some Sample Estate Plans

Example One

John and Mary have three adult children: Bob, Sam, and Julie. Bob and Julie have good jobs and are financially independent. Sam has a schizoid-affective disorder and has limited employment prospects. Bob and Julie each have small children. Sam does not have children at the current time, but it is possible he will have children in the future.

John and Mary have an estate that is worth approximately $250,000 (including insurance and their home). While they would like to treat all their children equally, the whole family (including Bob and Julie) recognizes that Sam has greater needs. John and Mary decide on the following estate plan:

- On the death of the first of them, all property is to be distributed to the survivor.

- On the death of the second, all property is to be held in a special needs trust for Sam (to be combined with other property which John and Mary may have placed in the trust during their lives). Bob and Julie are to serve as co-trustees, and when either of them becomes unable or unwilling to act, a bank is appointed as successor trustee (or sole trustee when both are unable to act). Bob and Julie are each given the power to name successors to act in lieu of the bank (perhaps their children, should they demonstrate sufficient responsibility and concern for Sam when they grow older). The trust also contains a termination provision, with assets to be distributed to Bob and Julie (or the survivor of them if one of them is deceased) should the law change so that the existence of the trust would imperil Sam's eligibility for government benefits. John and Mary believe that government benefits will be very important for Sam, and they are confident that Bob and Julie would use trust assets for Sam should a trust termination occur.

- On the death of Sam, the trust property is to be distributed to Sam's children if he has any, or if Sam has no children, equally between, Bob (or his children if Sam outlives Bob), Julie (or her children if Sam outlives Julie), and the local chapter of the National Alliance for the Mentally Ill.

Example Two

The facts are the same as described in Example One, except that John and Mary decide they want to treat all their children equally. John and Mary decide on the following estate plan:

- As in Example One, on the death of John or Mary, all property goes to the survivor.

- On the death of the second, their property is divided equally between their children. Bob and Julie receive their shares outright, and Sam's share is held in trust for his life. The trustee arrangement is identical to the arrangement described in Example One, and the trust contains a trust termination provision that is identical to the provision described in Example One.

- On the death of Sam, the property in his trust is distributed to his then-living descendants, or if there are none, to Bob and Julie, or to their children if Sam outlives them.

Example Three

John and Mary have three young children: Bob, Sam, and Julie. Sam has a moderate intellectual disability and is expected to move into a group residential facility when he gets older. Bob has just turned seven and is in the first grade. Julie is age four and attends preschool. John and Mary decide on the following estate plan:

- As in Examples One and Two, on the death of John or Mary, all their property goes to the survivor.

- On the death of the second of them, their property is split into two trusts; one-third of their property is held in a special needs trust for Sam to supplement government benefits that are available to him, and two-thirds of their property goes to a separate trust that is held as a single pool for the benefit of Julie and Bob. When Julie reaches age 23, the property in this separate trust is distributed equally between Bob and Julie. Sam's trust remains unchanged. John and Mary had thought about using a single pool for all their children, but they have rejected that approach because they want to make certain that enough is available for Sam. They have also thought about having separate trusts for Bob and Julie, but they have decided against that because they want extra funds available in case Bob or Julie have extraordinary needs.

- John and Mary name John's sister, Margaret, and Mary's brother, Peter, as trustee of all trusts. If one of them cannot act, a bank becomes co-trustee. Margaret and Peter are each given the power to name a successor, and to change banks if the services provided by the selected bank prove to be inadequate. Margaret is also named guardian for Bob, Sam, and Julie during their minority, with the expectation that Margaret will not pursue a court proceeding to continue the guardianship after Sam reaches age 18, unless she finds it necessary.

- John and Mary have included a provision in Sam's trust that would terminate the trust if the law were to change so that the trust imperilled Sam's eligibility for government benefits. They have thought long and hard about this. On a termination, should the assets go to Margaret and Peter, who they believe would use the assets on Sam's behalf? Or should the assets go to Bob and Julie (or their trust if they have not come of age), so the property will remain in the family? Ultimately they decide that the assets should go to Margaret and Peter, with the understanding that they will revisit the issue as Bob and Julie grow older.

- On Sam's death, the property in his trust is to go to Bob and Julie, or their trust if Julie has not yet reached age 23. John and Mary consider the possibility of Sam having children sufficiently remote that they do not wish to plan for it.

Government Benefits and the Resource Limitation:

Fixing the Problem When a Child Has Excess Assets

P ARENTS AND OTHER RELATIVES OF A CHILD WITH A DISABILITY often make gifts to the child in the hopes of building a nest egg that can be used to help defray the costs that will be incurred when the child grows older. In this chapter we discuss how you can make gifts to a child with a disability without jeopardizing the child's ability to receive government benefits. We also discuss methods of fixing the problem if a child with a disability has received gifts in a manner that would adversely impact the child's eligibility under government benefit programs. Finally, we discuss methods of structuring divorce settlements to maximize your child's government benefits.

SSI and Medicaid—The Basics

As discussed in greater detail in Chapter Four, certain government benefit programs, primarily SSI and Medicaid, are *needs based.* This means that the programs are generally available to people who have limited resources and satisfy certain other requirements.

SSI provides a monthly cash benefit for people who are elderly, blind or disabled and lack sufficient resources to provide for their own needs. The amount of the benefit is reset each year based on inflation. For 2005, the maximum monthly benefit was $579.

To qualify for SSI, a person must satisfy both a resource test and an income test. Under the resource test, the beneficiary generally will not qualify if the beneficiary's countable resources exceed $2,000 ($3,000 in the case of a married couple). Under the income test, the beneficiary generally will not qualify if the beneficiary's monthly countable income exceeds the maximum monthly SSI benefit. As described in detail in Chapter Four, countable income excludes the first $20 in unearned income, the first $65 in earned income, and one-half of all remaining earned income.

Under special *deeming* rules, income and resources of a beneficiary's parents will be considered to be available to the beneficiary if the beneficiary lives with his or her parents and is under age 18. The Social Security Administration Policy Operation Manual (POMS Section SI 1330.200) states the rule with respect to deeming of resources as follows:

> **LEGAL**
>
> In determining SSI eligibility of a child under 18 who lives with his parent(s) or with the spouse of a parent, the resources of the child include the value of the countable resources of the parent(s) or spouse of a parent... The value of parental resources is subject to deeming whether or not those resources are available to the child.

The rule with respect to deeming of income (POMS Section SI 1320.500) is stated as follows:

A child under age 18 who is applying for or receiving SSI and who lives in the same household with his/her parent(s) and/or the spouse of a parent is presumed to share in the parents' income. This presumption continues through the month the child attains age 18 and meets all other requirements of the definition of a child. Under this presumption, and subject to certain exclusions, the parents' income is deemed to be available income to the child.

When the child reaches age 18, the deeming rules generally will not apply, and the child will become eligible for benefits assuming the child satisfies the resource, income and disability tests. However, if the child still lives with his or her parents, the amount of the benefit may be reduced under the one-third reduction rule discussed in Chapter Four.

Example One

Mary has Down syndrome and lives with her parents. Mary's parents have assets and income that substantially exceed the SSI limitations. Mary will not qualify for SSI prior to reaching age 18 because, under the deeming rules, the assets and income of her parents will be considered to be available to her. After Mary turns 18, however, she will be eligible for SSI. Assuming Mary continues to live with her parents and receives free room and board, the amount of the benefit will be reduced under the one-third reduction rule. Thus, for 2005, the benefit will be $386 per month (two thirds of $579).

Medicaid is a medical insurance program designed to provide medical care for people who are elderly, blind or disabled and lack sufficient resources to provide for their own medical care. In the vast majority of states, Medicaid is available to people who are eligible for SSI and for certain other people with limited resources. Certain states, known as Section 209(b) states, have made elections to apply more restrictive financial needs standards. There are currently thirteen Section 209(b) states: Connecticut, Hawaii,

Illinois, Indiana, Minnesota, Missouri, Nebraska, New Hampshire, North Dakota, Ohio, Oklahoma, Utah, and Virginia. Even in Section 209(b) states, however, people with disabilities who are financially needy will generally qualify for Medicaid.

Example Two

Mary has Down syndrome and lives with her parents. Mary's parents have assets and income that substantially exceed the SSI limitations. Mary will not qualify for SSI prior to reaching age 18 because, under the deeming rules, the assets and income of her parents will be considered to be available to her. After Mary turns 18, however, she will be eligible for SSI. Assuming Mary does not live in a Section 209(b) state, Mary will qualify for Medicaid because she qualifies for SSI. Even if Mary lives in a Section 209(b) state, she likely will qualify for Medicaid.

The Problem of Improperly Made Gifts

We strongly encourage parents to apply for SSI for their child when the child turns 18. This is true for several reasons.

First, as discussed above, assuming the child satisfies Social Security's definition of disability, the child will generally become eligible for SSI upon reaching age 18 because the deeming rules no longer apply.

Second, in cases where it is unclear whether a child has a disability under Social Security's definitions, it tends to be easier to establish disability when the child is younger. As discussed in more detail in Chapter Four, a person is considered disabled under Social Security's definition if, by reason of a physical or mental impairment, the person is unable to engage in *substantial gainful activity*. A person is generally considered to be unable to engage in substantial gainful activity if, due to the impairment, the person cannot earn more than $830 per month. The $830 amount is based on 2005 figures and increases each year. In borderline cases, particularly in situations involving a mild intellectual disability, it is probably easier to establish disability when a child is very young and has no earning history.

Third, in most states a person who is eligible for SSI will also be eligible for Medicaid. Although your child may be covered by your health insurance policy, it is good to have Medicaid as a backstop in case your child has medical needs that are not fully covered by private insurance. Also, Medicaid can be used to cover co-payments and deductibles.

Fourth, as discussed in Chapter Four, a child who has a disability before reaching age 22 will be eligible for survivors and dependents benefits under the Social Security system when the parents retire, die or become disabled. Although any Social Security received will reduce the amount of your child's SSI benefit, Social Security benefits are generally substantially larger than SSI benefits. Moreover, once your child begins receiving Social Security, the child will automatically qualify for Medicare within two years. Applying for SSI when the child reaches age 18 establishes that disability occurred before age 22 and therefore avoids possible future dispute with Social Security administrators regarding the date that disability occurred.

TIP Put it on your calendar. When your child turns 18, apply for SSI.

Sometimes, however, a child with a disability will not qualify for SSI even after reaching age 18 because the child will fail the resource test. Typically this occurs because the child has received gifts from well-meaning parents, grandparents or other relatives over the years. Sometimes the gifts are placed in a joint account for the child with the child's parents. More often, the gifts will have been made in special accounts for the child under a Uniform Gift to Minors Act (also known as the Uniform Transfer to Minors Act). Generally speaking, the Uniform Gift to Minors Act creates a form of trust that permits people to make gifts that will be managed by adults for the benefit of minors without going to the expense of creating a trust. Virtually all states have adopted the Uniform Gift to Minors Act in one form or another.

The rule with respect to gifts made directly to a child in a joint bank account is relatively straightforward. Property in a joint account with your child will generally be considered the child's for purposes of SSI eligibility, unless you can establish that the property is really yours. The Policy Operations Manual (POM Section 1150.110) states:

If an eligible individual is a joint-owner of a bank account with an ineligible individual, we assume that the eligible individual owns all of the funds in the account.

Example Three

Mary has an intellectual disability and lives with her parents. Mary's parents have made small deposits in a bank account established jointly with Mary, with the intention of making gifts to Mary. Over time, the account has grown to $5,000. Mary will not qualify for SSI even after reaching age 18 because she will exceed the $2,000 resource limit.

The rule with respect to gifts made under a Uniform Gift to Minors Act (UGMA) is more complex. In general, under the Uniform Gift to Minors Act:

- an individual (donor) makes an irrevocable gift of money or other property to a minor (the donee);

- the gift, plus any earnings it generates, is under the control of a custodian until the donee reaches the age of majority established by State law;

- the custodian has discretion to provide to the minor or spend for the minor's support, maintenance, benefit, or education as much of the assets as he/she deems equitable; and

- the donee automatically receives control of the assets upon attainment of majority.

Because property transferred to an account for a child under the Uniform Gift to Minors Act is under the control of the *custodian*, and not under the control of the child, the property in the account is not considered *income* for the child or a *resource* of the child. However, the child receives legal control of the property upon reaching the age of majority, which is age 18 or 21 depending on the state. Under the Social Security rules, the property is considered income in the month the child reaches the age of majority, and a resource in the following month.

The Policy Operations Manual (POMS Section SI 1120.205) provides:

a. While Donee Remains a Minor

UGMA property, including any additions or earnings, is not income to the minor;

The custodian's UGMA disbursements to the minor are income to the minor;

The custodian's UGMA disbursements on behalf of the minor may be income to the latter if used to make certain third party vendor payments.

b. When Donee Reaches Majority

All UGMA property becomes available to the donee and subject to evaluation as income in the month of attainment of majority.

...

LEGAL
An item received in the current month is income for the current month only. If held by the individual until the following month, that item is subject to resource counting rules.

Example Four

Mary has an intellectual disability and lives with her parents. Mary's parents have made gifts to Mary under the state's Uniform Gift to Minors Act. The state in which Mary lives has an age of majority of 18. Mary will not qualify for SSI even after reaching age 18 because the property in her UGMA account will become available to her, and she will exceed the $2,000 resource limit.

Example Five

Mary has an intellectual disability and lives with her parents. Mary's parents have made gifts to Mary under the state's Uniform Gift to Minors Act. The state in which Mary lives has an age of majority of 21. Mary will qualify for SSI when she reaches age 18 because the deeming rules will not apply and the property in Mary's UGMA account will not be available to her. However, the property in Mary's UGMA account will become available to Mary when she reaches age 21, the age of majority in her state of residence. Accordingly, upon reaching age 21 Mary will exceed the $2,000 resource limit, and she will therefore lose her eligibility under the SSI and Medicaid programs.

Fixing the Problem—Spending Down Excess Resources

There are steps that you can take if you find yourself in a situation where your child has excess resources. The simplest approach is to simply spend the money for your child's benefit. This is probably counter-intuitive. For many years, you have probably been spending large sums of money for your child. Now that government benefits are an issue, you need to get in the habit of spending your child's money to meet your child's needs in order to get your child's assets below $2,000.

How should you spend the money?

You know better than we do. When you take a vacation, have your child pay his or her own way. When you go out to eat, let the child pay for his or her meal. Let the child pay for dental or medical care. You may pay large sums for specialized therapy; this is an excellent opportunity to spend down resources. Remember, though, the property should be spent on your child's expenses, not on your expenses.

If you are concerned about the moral implications of spending your child's money, remember you are doing this so the child can qualify for government benefits. If you want, you can keep track of how much of the child's money you spend, and later make a gift to the child in the proper way, as described below under *Making Lifetime Gifts to a Child With a Disability—The Proper Approach.*

Example Six

Mary has an intellectual disability. Mary's parents have made small deposits in a joint bank account established with Mary and over time the account has grown to $15,000. Mary's parents discover that Mary's bank account will prevent her from qualifying for SSI upon reaching age 18 because the property in the account will cause her to exceed the $2,000 resource limit. Because Mary's parents are co-signatories on the account, they have the authority to spend the money in the account and they begin spending for Mary's food, clothing and other appropriate items. If Mary's resources are reduced to $2,000 before Mary reaches age 18, she will be eligible for SSI.

If your child's property is an UGMA account, the custodian of the account can simply spend the money to satisfy your child's needs. Although the law varies by state, most UGMA statutes provide the custodian with broad powers to spend account assets for the benefit of the minor. Language such as the following is typical:

305

LEGAL

A custodian may deliver or pay to the minor or expend for the minor's benefit so much of the custodial property as the custodian considers advisable for the use and benefit of the minor, without court order and without regard to (i) the duty or ability of the custodian or of any other person to support the minor, or (ii) any other income or property of the minor which may be applicable or available for that purpose.

Example Seven

Mary has an intellectual disability and lives with her parents. Mary's parents have made gifts to Mary under the state's Uniform Gift to Minors Act. The state in which Mary lives has an age of majority of 18. Mary's parents discover that Mary's UGMA account will prevent her from qualifying for SSI upon reaching age 18 because the property in her UGMA account will cause her to exceed the $2,000 resource limit. Accordingly, the custodian under the UGMA account begins spending the money in the account for Mary's benefit. By the time Mary reaches age 18, the UGMA account has been spent down and Mary is eligible for SSI.

If the money is in your child's name alone, and your child has reached the age of majority and has mental capacity, the child can spend the money. Although the definition of mental capacity varies by state, a typical approach is to define mental capacity as *the ability to make responsible decisions*.

Example Eight

Fred has mental illness. With medication, he has the ability to make responsible decisions. Fred has accumulated assets in excess of $2,000 over the years. Fred can spend the money for legitimate purposes and qualify for SSI when his resources fall below $2,000.

If a child has assets in his or her own name and the child does not have sufficient mental capacity to make responsible decisions, the child will not be able to spend the assets down. Instead, the child's parents will need to petition a court to get appointed guardians of the child's estate so they can then begin the spend down process.

Example Nine

Fred has a severe intellectual disability. Fred's parents have made small deposits in a bank account established in Fred's name and over time the account has grown to $15,000. When Fred reaches age 18, Fred's parents discover that Fred's bank account will prevent him from qualifying for SSI because the property in the account will cause him to exceed the $2,000 resource limit. A guardian of Fred's estate will need to be appointed to begin the spend-down process.

 TIP Social Security may investigate how your child's resources were spent. Typically they will look at expenditures made in the three years prior to the SSI application. Keep good records of when money was spent, and what it was spent for. Keep a log of expenditures, along with receipts and cancelled checks.

Fixing the Problem—Placing Excess Resources in Trust

A second method of dealing with the situation where your child has excess resources is to transfer the resources into a trust. It is important to realize, however, that the special needs trust discussed in Chapter Six is not suitable for this purpose. Such a trust works well when either you or a third party transfer their property into trust for your child. However, such a trust is not appropriate when your child's property is used. The Policy Operations Manual (POMS Section SI 1120.201) states:

In the case of a revocable trust established by the individual, the entire corpus of the trust is a resource to the individual.

...

In determining whether an irrevocable trust established by an individual is a resource, we must consider how payments from the trust can be made. If payments from the trust could be made to or for the benefit of the individual or individual's spouse, the portion of the trust from which payment could be made that is attributable to the individual is a resource.

...

An individual is considered to have established a trust if any assets of the individual (or spouse) (regardless of how little) were transferred to a trust other than by a will.

Example Ten

Although Mary has a mild intellectual disability, she has the ability to make responsible decisions. Mary's parents have opened a bank account and have periodically made gifts to Mary over the years. Mary transfers the property into a special needs trust as described in Chapter Six. The special needs trust is considered a resource because the trust was established with Mary's own assets and payments can be made from the trust for Mary's benefit. Accordingly, Mary remains ineligible for SSI.

There are, however, two types of trusts that can be used to deal with a situation where your child has excess resources. These trusts are known as *payback trusts* and *pooled income payback trusts*. The Policy Operations Manual (POMS Section SI 1120.203) describes payback trusts as follows:

308

The resource counting provisions of the new trust statute do not apply to a trust:

- Which contains the assets of an individual under age 65 and who is disabled; and

- Which is established for the benefit of such individual by a parent, grandparent, legal guardian or a court; and

- Which provides that the State will receive all amounts remaining in the trust upon the death of the individual up to an amount equal to the total medical assistance paid on behalf of the individual under a State Medicaid plan.

Pooled income payback trusts are described as follows (POMS Section SI 1120.203):

The provisions of the SSI trust statute do not apply to a trust containing the assets of a disabled individual which meets the following conditions:

- The pooled trust is established and maintained by a nonprofit association;

- Separate accounts are maintained for each beneficiary, but assets are pooled for investing and management purposes;

- Accounts are established solely for the benefit of the disabled individual;

- The account in the trust is established by the individual, a parent, grandparent, legal guardian, or a court; and

- The trust provides that to the extent any amounts remaining in the beneficiary's account upon the death of the beneficiary are not retained by the trust, the trust will pay to the State the amount remaining up to an amount equal to the total amount of medical assistance paid on behalf of the beneficiary under a State Medicaid plan.

Example Eleven

Mary has an intellectual disability. Mary's parents have made small deposits in a bank account established in Mary's name and over time the account has grown to $15,000. If Mary has reached the age of majority and has sufficient mental capacity, she can transfer the property from the account into a payback trust. The trust would need to provide that the State will receive all amounts remaining in the trust upon Mary's death up to an amount equal to the total medical assistance paid on behalf of Mary under the State's Medicaid plan. In addition, the trust would need to be established by Mary's parents, grandparents, legal guardian or by a court, and not by Mary, because the Social Security rules do not allow for the trust to be created by the person with a disability.

Although the trust will be required to payback the government if it has sufficient assets when Mary dies, payback will not be required if the property in the trust is spent for Mary during her life. One strategy would be for Mary's parents to spend the money in Mary's payback trust for Mary's benefit before other family resources are spent for Mary. Mary's parents should keep good records of trust expenditures in case the government has questions.

If your child has assets in his or her own name and does not have sufficient mental capacity to make responsible decisions, you will need to petition a court to get appointed guardians of your child's estate so you can create the trust and transfer the property.

Example Twelve

Mary has an intellectual disability. Mary's parents have made small deposits in a bank account established in Mary's name and over time the account has grown to $15,000. If Mary does not have sufficient mental capacity, her parents will need to petition a court to get appointed guardians of her estate so they can create the trust and transfer the property.

If your child's property is in an UGMA account, an issue arises as to whether the account custodian has the authority to transfer the property into a payback or pooled income payback trust. As stated above, under the law in most states, the UGMA custodian has the power to expend UGMA property for the minor's benefit. The issue is whether transferring UGMA property to a payback or pooled income payback trust for the benefit of the minor is expending UGMA property for the minor's benefit.

Our view is that an UGMA custodian should have the power to transfer property from an UGMA account into a payback or pooled income payback trust. Such a transfer benefits the minor because it allows the minor to receive SSI benefits when the minor turns 18. However, the law in this area is far from settled.

Example Thirteen

Mary has an intellectual disability and lives with her parents. Mary's parents have made gifts to Mary under the state's Uniform Gift to Minors Act. The state in which Mary lives has an age of majority of 18. Mary's parents discover that Mary's UGMA account will prevent her from qualifying for SSI upon reaching age 18 because the property in her UGMA account will cause her to exceed the $2,000 resource limit.

It is unclear whether the UGMA custodian can transfer the UGMA property to a payback or pooled income payback trust for Mary. Upon attaining the age of majority the funds in the UGMA account will be transferred to Mary. Assuming Mary has sufficient mental capacity, she can then transfer the funds to a payback trust as described in Example Twelve. If Mary does not have sufficient mental capacity, Mary's parents will have to petition the court to appoint a guardian of Mary's estate who can create the trust and transfer the property.

Given the uncertainty regarding the ability of an UGMA custodian to transfer UGMA property into a payback or pooled income payback trust, the spend down approach tends to be superior where an UGMA account is involved.

If you decide to transfer property from an UGMA account into a trust for your child, an issue arises as to whether it is necessary to use a payback trust as opposed to a special needs trust. The disadvantage of a payback trust as compared to a special needs trust is that property remaining in the payback trust when your child dies has to be used to payback the state for any amounts paid by the state for your child's medical care.

As discussed above, a payback trust is required if your child's property is used to fund the trust. The issue, therefore, is whether property in an UGMA account is considered your child's property under the self-funded trust rules. The Policy Operations Manual (POMS Section SI 1120.201) states as follows:

> For purposes of this section, an asset is any income or resource of the individual ... including property to which the individual ... is entitled, but does not receive or have access to because of action by ... a person or entity (including a court) with legal authority to act in place of, or on behalf of, the individual ...

We believe that property in an UGMA account is a resource of the minor under this definition and that a payback trust is therefore required. However, the matter is not free from doubt, and it is possible that a special needs trust will suffice. In any event, as discussed above, given the uncertainty regarding the ability of an UGMA custodian to transfer UGMA property into a trust, we believe the spend down approach is superior if an UGMA account is involved.

Transferring Your Child's Property into Your Name

One thing we did not say. We did not tell you to simply transfer your child's property into your name. The reason is that your child's property is not your property, and you do not have the legal authority to transfer your child's property into your name, even if you transfer the property in order to permit your child to qualify for government benefits. Transferring your child's property into your own name is arguably fraud, and you could get into serious trouble. The Policy Operations Manual (POMS Section SI 4070.020) states:

LEGAL If fraud is suspected, we complete all development for the entire period except the determination that fraud exists and refer the case to the Office of Investigation Field Offices.

If your child has reached the age of majority and has sufficient mental capacity, your child can transfer his or her property to you. However, your child would then be ineligible for SSI benefits for a period of time determined by dividing the value of the transferred resources by the federal benefit rate, subject to a maximum ineligibility period of 36 months. The ineligibility period begins running on the date of transfer.

Example Fourteen

Fred has a bank account of $11,580. Although Fred has mental illness, he is on medication and has the capacity to make responsible decisions. Fred determines that it would be beneficial to qualify for SSI and therefore transfers the funds in the bank account to his parents. Using 2005 rates, Fred would be ineligible for SSI for 20 months ($11,580 amount transferred divided by $579 benefit amount), starting with the date Fred transferred the funds to his parents.

If your child's property is in a joint bank account with you, you have the legal authority to transfer the property into your own name. However, the transfer may result in a waiting period if it is made within thirty-six months of the SSI application. The Policy Operations Manual (POMS Section SI 1150.110) states:

> **LEGAL**
>
> In joint bank account situations, it is necessary to develop the ownership of the funds … before determining whether there has been a transfer of resources. If an eligible individual is a joint-owner of a bank account with an ineligible individual, we assume that the eligible individual owns all of the funds in the account. If the eligible individual owns all of the funds, withdrawal of funds by the co-owner would be a transfer of resources for less than FMV … In addition, if the eligible individual takes his/her name off the account, this could also be a transfer of resources unless all the funds belonged to the co-owner.

Example Fifteen

Fred has a bank account with his parents. The account has $11,580. Fred's parents transfer the money from the account into their own names. Using 2005 rates, Fred would be ineligible for SSI for 20 months ($11,580 amount transferred divided by $579 benefit amount), starting with the date Fred's parents transferred the funds from the account. Thus, if Fred was more than 20 months from turning 18 when the account was transferred, Fred would be eligible for SSI upon turning age 18.

Importantly, the SSI ineligibility period does not apply to transfers to payback or pooled income payback trusts. As a result, transfers to such trusts are often superior to outright gifts. The Policy Operations Manual (POMS Section SI 1150.121) states:

The period of ineligibility does not apply to an individual who transfers a resource to a trust established for the sole benefit of an individual including himself or herself who is under age 65 and is blind or disabled. This includes trusts qualifying as *Medicaid trust exceptions* [i.e., payback and pooled income payback trusts].

Example Sixteen

Fred has a bank account of $11,280. Although Fred has mental illness, he is on medication and has the capacity to make responsible decisions. Fred determines that it would be beneficial to qualify for SSI. Fred transfers the funds into a payback or a pooled income payback trust. Fred is immediately eligible for SSI.

Making Lifetime Gifts to a Child With a Disability —The Proper Approach

It is important to realize that gifts can be made to a child with a disability without impacting the child's ability to receive government benefits if the gifts are made to the child in a special needs trust. As discussed in Chapter Six, the Policy Operation Manual (POMS Section SI 1120.200) with respect to trusts that are not created with an individual's own assets states:

If the individual has legal authority to revoke the trust and then use the funds to meet his food, clothing or shelter needs, or if the individual can direct the use of the trust principal for his/her support and maintenance under the terms of the trust, the trust principal is a resource for SSI purposes. If an individual does not have legal authority to revoke the trust or direct the use of the trust principal for his/her own support and maintenance, the trust principal is not the individual's resource for SSI purposes.

Because a special needs trust does not give the beneficiary the ability to revoke the trust or direct the use of the trust principal for his/her own support and maintenance, the trust principal is not the individual's resource for SSI purposes.

Example Seventeen

Mary is born with Down syndrome. Mary's grandma creates a special needs trust for Mary containing the provisions discussed in Chapter Six and makes gifts to the trust for Mary during Mary's childhood. Under the SSI rules, the property in the trust is not considered a resource of Mary's, and the trust does not affect Mary's ability to receive government benefits.

Special considerations apply to gifts made to a child with a disability by people who have taxable estates. These rules will not apply unless the person making the gift has substantial assets—typically over $1 million (or $2 million in the case of a married couple), counting the person's house and the death benefit on any life insurance policies. These considerations are discussed in detail in Chapter Nine.

Correcting the Support Trust

As discussed in Chapter Six, a trust should not require or even expressly permit the trustee to make distributions for the support and maintenance of a child with a disability or even for purposes that are at all similar to support and maintenance, such as welfare, education or best interests. In the case of a trust that requires the trustee to make distributions for the child's support (so-called mandatory support trusts), the child with a disability would have the legal right to go to court and force the trustee to make distributions for support purposes if the trustee did not do so on its own. Such a trust is therefore considered a resource of the child for government benefit purposes. As discussed in Chapter Six, this is even a risk where the trust expressly permits the trustee to make distributions for support purposes (so-called discretionary support trusts).

Example Eighteen

Mary is born with Down Syndrome. Mary's grandma dies and leaves money in a trust for Mary that requires the trustee to make distributions for Mary's maintenance and support. Under the SSI rules, the property in the trust will be considered a resource of Mary's, and the trust will prevent Mary from receiving needs based government benefits.

What can be done in such a case?

Two possibilities exist. First, the parties can go to court and request the judge to convert the trust into a special needs trust. Some states may even have statutes that permit modifications of trusts for beneficiaries with disabilities precisely for this purpose.

Second, if the trust language is sufficiently broad, perhaps permitting the trustee to make distributions for the *benefit of the beneficiary,* the trustee can create a new special needs trust and distribute the assets from the support trust into the special needs trust. The trustee would take the position that a distribution of assets from a support trust into a special needs trust is a distribution for the benefit of the beneficiary with a disability because the distribution permits the beneficiary to qualify for needs based government benefits. It is unclear, however, whether such an approach would succeed, as it is possible that the government would take the position that a distribution from a support trust into a newly created special needs trust is not a distribution for the benefit of the beneficiary.

Special Issues Relating to Divorce

Child support payments made on behalf of an adult child who is receiving SSI are considered unearned income. POMS Section SI 00830.420 states as follows:

Child support payments ... received for an adult child by a parent after an adult child stops meeting the definition of a child are income to the adult child. The support payments are income to the adult child whether or not the adult child lives with the parent or receives any of the child support payment from the parent.

As discussed in Chapter Four, unearned income in excess of $20 a month results in a dollar for dollar reduction in SSI benefits.

Example Nineteen

Fred is twenty-two years old and has Down syndrome. He does not work and receives the maximum SSI benefit of $579 per month. Fred's parents get divorced and the divorce decree requires Fred's father to pay Fred's mother $500 a month in child support for Fred. Fred's SSI benefit is reduced to $99 a month. The first $20 in child support results in no reduction in benefits, but the next $480 in child support reduces Fred's SSI benefits on a dollar for dollar basis.

Several alternatives are available. First, instead of paying child support, Fred's father can be required to make direct payments to providers for items other than food, shelter and clothing. Possibilities include special therapies, tutors, vacations or medical care that is not covered by Medicaid. Such items will not be considered income to Fred for SSI purposes. As discussed in Chapter Four, if Fred's father provides food, shelter or clothing for Fred, the value of such items will be considered unearned income and will result in a reduction in SSI benefits.

Second, instead of paying child support, Fred's father can be required to make payments directly into a payback trust for Fred. As long as the money in the trust is not distributed directly to Fred or used to provide food, shelter or clothing for Fred, money from the trust can be used for Fred's benefit without affecting Fred's ability to receive government benefits. It may even be arguable that Fred's father can use a special needs trust instead of a payback trust, and thereby avoid the requirement that trust property remaining at Fred's death be used to repay the state for Medicaid benefits received by Fred. The law on this issue is unclear.

Third, instead of paying child support, Fred's father can be required to pay increased alimony to Fred's mother.

In the case of child support paid for a child who is a minor, one-third of the payment is excluded from countable income in calculating the SSI payment. This tends not to be important in most cases because minor children are generally not eligible for SSI by reason of the deeming rules discussed above. The exclusion can, however, be important for divorced families if the custodial parent has limited income.

Conclusion—Tying it All Together

If you want to make a gift to a child with a disability, you can do so through a special needs trust without impacting your child's ability to receive government benefits. Similarly, friends or relatives can make gifts to your child through a special needs trust. Outright gifts and gifts through UGMA accounts should not be utilized. If your child has received outright gifts or gifts through an UGMA account, this could affect your child's ability to receive SSI or Medicaid when your child turns 18.

If the child has the property in an UGMA account, you should:

- Attempt to spend the money down before the child reaches the age of majority in your state,

- If you do not think you will be able to spend the money down before the child reaches majority, and if the child has sufficient mental capacity, you should spend down what you can and have the child transfer the remaining property into a payback trust upon reaching majority. As an alternative, the child could transfer the remaining property to you, but this would create an ineligibility period,

- If you do not think you will be able to spend the money down before the child reaches majority, and if the child does not have sufficient mental capacity, you should consider whether the UGMA custodian can transfer the property into a payback trust. As discussed above, we think an UGMA custodian has this authority but the answer is unclear,

- If you are unable to spend the money down before the child reaches majority, the child does not have sufficient mental capacity, and you live in a state where the UGMA custodian does not have authority to transfer the property into a payback trust, you should consider going to go to court to have a guardian appointed to create a payback trust,

- You should not simply transfer the property into your own name.

If the child has property in a joint account with you, you should:

- If the child has not yet reached age 15, simply transfer the property into your own name. Since the transfer will take place more than three years before the child will apply for SSI, there will be no ineligibility period,

- If the child is over age 15, compute whether a transfer will result in an ineligibility period. As illustrated in Example Fifteen, you divide the amount in the account by the maximum SSI benefit. For example, if the amount in the account is $11,580, using 2005 figures, this means the ineligibility period is 20 months ($11,580 divided by $579). If the child is more than 20 months from age 18, you can simply transfer the property into your own name. If the child is not more than 20 months from age 18, or is over the age of 18, you can either try to spend the money down or transfer it into a payback trust.

If the child has property in his or her own name and is beyond the age of majority:

- Assuming the child has sufficient mental capacity, the child should transfer the money into a payback trust. As an alternative, the child could transfer the property to you, but this would create an ineligibility period,

- If the child does not have sufficient mental capacity, you should consider going to go to court to have a guardian appointed to create a payback trust. You should not simply transfer the property into your own name.

If the child is a beneficiary of an improperly drawn trust, you should:

- Consider whether the trust is sufficiently flexible to permit the trustee to transfer the trust property into a special needs trust,

- If it is not, you will need go to court and request the judge to convert the trust into a special needs trust.

In unusual circumstances, it is possible that property will be held directly in the name of a child even though the child is a minor. This is very rare, because banks generally will not open accounts for minors unless a parent is also on the account. If this occurs, however:

- If the child has mental capacity, wait until the child turns 18 and then have the child transfer the property into a payback trust. Alternatively, a guardian can be appointed while the child is a minor to spend the money down or transfer it to a payback trust,

- If the child does not have sufficient mental capacity, you should consider going to go to court to have a guardian appointed to create a payback trust,

- You should not simply transfer the property into your own name.

As is apparent, a lot can be done if your child has excess resources and is therefore unable to qualify for SSI or Medicaid. However, it is clearly best to make sure this does not happen by making sure that those who might make gifts to your child do so through a special needs trust.

 TIP Talk to your parents, adult children, and others who might be inclined to make gifts to your child. Make sure those gifts are made through a special needs trust.

Using Living Trusts to Avoid Probate

T HUS FAR WE HAVE DISCUSSED TRUSTS IN THREE CONTEXTS: special needs trusts for children with disabilities, which can be used to provide funds for your child without jeopardizing eligibility under various government benefit programs; *payback trusts*, which can be used as a receptacle for your child's own money without jeopardizing eligibility for government benefits; and discretionary trusts for children without disabilities, which can be used to provide funds for your other children during the period before they have the judgment and maturity to manage money on their own.

Trusts have a variety of other uses as well, and we will discuss many of these in this and following chapters. For example, in Chapter Nine we will tell you about credit shelter trusts, irrevocable insurance trusts, and generation-skipping trusts, and how these and various other devices can be used to reduce the estate tax owing at your death. (Under current law, you will not have to worry about estate taxes unless the value of your estate at the time of your death, including proceeds payable under life insurance policies which you may own, exceeds $1.5M for people dying in 2005, $2M for people dying in 2006-2008, $3.5M for people dying in 2009, and $1M for people dying in 2011 and thereafter. There is no estate tax for people dying in 2010.)

In this chapter we discuss the living trust, which is a common method of avoiding probate, and the factors you should consider in determining whether a living trust is appropriate for you.

The Probate System

Probate is the legal process that governs how property that you own at the time of your death is to be passed on to your heirs. The essence of the system is to ensure that the right people receive the correct amount of property from your estate. Although the system varies from state to state, it tends to be similar to the following:

- First, the person you name as executor in your will (or more typically, an attorney hired by your executor) files a petition with the probate court to have your will admitted for validation. Notice is sent to interested parties (typically those who would receive your property if your will was considered invalid) to give these people an opportunity to file an objection.

- Your will is then *proved* valid in a court proceeding, typically based on the fact that you signed your will in front of witnesses who signed an *attestation* clause stating that you knew what you were doing when you signed the will, and the person named as executor in your will is appointed by the probate court to administer your estate.

- Your executor then files a notice to creditors that apprises them that you have died and informs them that they have a specified period of time (usually around 6 months) to assert any claims that they may have against your estate. Notice of your death is also published in newspapers to inform the population in general, in case any of them have any claims against you. Claims that are not asserted within the statutory period generally may not be asserted later against your heirs or your estate.

- Depending on the laws in the state where you reside at the time of your death, your executor may also be responsible for filing an inventory of your assets with the probate court and for reporting to the court on distributions to the beneficiaries of your estate.

- In many states, probate is not required for estates that are sufficiently small (typically around $50,000). In such case, property can be passed to heirs through a simplified summary procedure.

Avoiding Probate with a Living Trust

The probate system has been criticized on the grounds that it is excessively burdensome, both in terms of time and cost. The *living trust* represents a private market response to probate. Although we believe that the benefits of a living trust are often overstated, we also believe that a living trust is generally superior to probate in most, but not all, cases. The advantages and disadvantages of a living trust are discussed under *Living Trust Versus Probate—Factors to be Considered* below.

How does a *living trust* avoid the probate system?

The key is to remember that probate is required only if you *own* a significant amount of property at the time of your death. Although the amount varies by state, probate will typically not be required if you own property with a value of less than $50,000.

A living trust operates under the legal fiction that property that is placed in trust is owned by the trust and not by the beneficiaries of the trust. How do you make use of this fiction to avoid the probate system?

You create a trust, naming yourself as beneficiary and trustee, retaining the power to distribute property to whomever you would like and to amend the trust whenever and however you would like. You then transfer your property into the trust during your life. Because the property is owned by the trust and not by you, you own nothing at the time of your death, and probate is therefore avoided.

It sounds complicated, but we assure you that it is not. The existence of the trust will make little, if any, difference during your life. You will be sole trustee and will be able to spend money that you place in the trust however you would like. The only difference is that the name on your bank accounts, your stocks and securities, and your house will read *John Doe, trustee* and not *John Doe*.

In the eyes of all but the probate court, you will own your property as completely as you do currently. There is no obligation that your trust be registered with anyone, or that it file a tax return while you live and are acting as trustee. You simply go to a lawyer, prepare a declaration of trust naming yourself as trustee, and transfer your property to the trust (for example, by signing papers at your bank changing the name on your accounts, contacting financial advisors to make sure the name on your stocks is changed to the trust, and having your attorney prepare a new deed for your home). You then conduct your financial affairs exactly as you do now. Income earned by the trust is reported on your personal tax return with no mention of the trust at all.

When you die, however, the existence of the trust becomes very important. Because your property is owned by your trust at the time of your death, and not by you, there is no need to go through probate. Instead, a successor trustee, whom you select when you prepare your trust document, distributes your property in accordance with the instructions that you have written in the trust document.

TIP Many people create living trusts and then fail to transfer assets into the trust during their lives. This is a mistake. A properly drawn estate plan that makes use of a living trust will include a *pour over will*, that transfers property that you own at your death into the living trust. A pour over will is not a substitute for lifetime transfers. It is a backstop only, designed to make sure your property gets into the trust if you have mistakenly neglected to carry through with property transfers during your life. If your executor is required to use the pour over will to transfer property into your trust at your death, probate will be necessary, and the primary reason for creating a living trust will not be achieved.

Living Trust Versus Probate—Factors to be Considered

There are four legitimate reasons for preferring a living trust to probate in most cases—cost, delay, privacy, and assuring continued management of your property in the event that you become disabled.

Cost. In most cases, settling your estate through probate is more expensive than settling your estate through a living trust. Although it is not possible to accurately quantify the difference, it is generally true that the post-death savings resulting from a living trust will justify the additional cost incurred in setting up a living trust.

Having said that, it is important to realize that the cost saving benefit of a living trust is sometimes overstated. Proponents of the living trust sometimes exaggerate the cost of probate, and ignore the administrative cost involved when probate is avoided. Despite the claims of some that the cost of administering an estate through probate averages 5-10 percent of the value of the estate; in truth, there are no reliable figures. Moreover, even if a living trust is used, some post-death administrative cost will likely be required. Professionals may be needed to interpret trust documents, to see to the distribution of trust assets, and to guide the trustee through the post-death process.

Real savings can be achieved with a living trust, however, primarily due to elimination of the need to make court appearances and to prepare court filings.

Delay. Probate will take no less than six months, which is the period that creditors have to file against the will in most states. In many cases, the probate period will exceed six months, often extending to a year or even eighteen months. In cases where a will is challenged in court, the process can be even longer. By contrast, unless an estate tax return is required (see Chapter Nine below), property that is in a living trust can be distributed to trust beneficiaries much more quickly.

Although beneficiaries under a will admitted to probate can obtain access to probate property if needed during the probate administration process, this can sometimes be difficult, and emotionally people tend to want the process to end.

Privacy. Probate filings are made in court and are matters of public record. By contrast, living trusts are private documents that do not involve court filings. Again, however, the privacy benefits of the living trust can be overstated. In many states, the filings required in probate do not involve a public listing of assets or other information that many consider personal. Moreover, even in states where personal information is included in court filings such filings are rarely inspected by members of the general public.

Disability. A living trust can also be helpful if you become disabled because the trust document will name a successor trustee to act if you are unable to properly manage your affairs. This is particularly useful in the case of families that have a child with a disability because the trust document can also provide that the trust property can be used for your child if you become disabled. Although it is possible to provide similar protection without use of a living trust through a Power of Attorney for Property (see Chapter Ten), a trust tends to be superior because it is easier to tailor the provisions relating to use of property to your particular needs.

The supposed benefit of a living trust *in saving estate tax has become an urban myth. Although a living trust can be used as part of an estate plan to save estate tax, the same estate tax planning objectives that can be achieved with a living trust can be achieved without a living trust. A living trust should never be created because of perceived estate tax savings. Similarly, most living trusts will not be effective in defeating claims that creditors have against you.*

When is a living trust not appropriate?

Although we believe that a living trust tends to be superior to probate in most cases, in certain cases probate is preferred. The primary benefit of the probate system is finality. Notice is given of the decedent's death to creditors and other interested parties, and they are given a certain period of time (typically about six months) to assert any claims against the decedent's estate. Claims that are not asserted within the statutory period are forever lost, and the decedent's heirs will not be forced to give back property that they have received.

Trusts do not afford the same finality. Because there is no formal system for adjudicating the legitimacy of creditors' claims, creditors have a longer period of time to assert them (typically about two years). Although this benefit of the probate system is usually not worth the added time and cost that it engenders, people with complicated debt situations may feel differently.

Moreover, while it is true that a living trust will save money at your death, it does cost more to prepare than a simple will. If you are young and healthy, you are likely to live a long time, and it may be advisable to forego the living trust approach. As time passes you will probably want to revise your estate plan in any case, and you can always prepare a living trust at a later date.

Sample Estate Plans Using Living Trusts

Example One

John and Mary have three adult children: Bob, Sam, and Julie. Bob and Julie have good jobs and are financially independent. Sam has a mild intellectual disability and works as an orderly at the local hospital. John and Mary are proud of Sam's work, but they realize he could lose his job and require government benefits in the future. Bob and Julie each have small children. While Sam does not have children at the current time, it is possible he will have children in the future.

John and Mary have an estate that is worth approximately $250,000 (including insurance and their home). While they would like to treat all their children equally, the whole family (including Bob and Julie) recognizes that Sam has greater needs. John and Mary decide on the following estate plan:

- John and Mary create a living trust, naming themselves as trustees, and transfer all their property to the trust (that is, the trust becomes owner of their home and other property and is named as beneficiary of their insurance). The trust can be amended or revoked at any time, and the trust instrument permits either of them to use trust property for any purpose. On the death of the first of them, the survivor becomes sole trustee and retains the ability to amend or revoke the trust and to use trust property for any purpose. If the survivor feels he or she needs help managing money, Bob or Julie could even be named as co-trustee.

- On the death of the second, the property remains in trust for Sam, converting into a special needs trust that is prepared in accordance with the provisions found in Chapter Six, so Sam will be eligible for government benefits if needed in the future. Bob and Julie are to serve as co-trustees. When they both become unable or unwilling to act, a bank is appointed as successor trustee. Bob and Julie are each given the power to name successors to act in lieu of the bank (perhaps their children, should they demonstrate sufficient responsibility and concern for Sam when they grow older). The trust also contains a termination provision, with assets to be distributed to Bob and Julie (or the survivor of them if one of them is deceased) should the law change in such a way that the existence of the trust imperils Sam's eligibility for government benefits. John and Mary believe that government benefits could be very important for Sam, and they are confident that Bob and Julie would use trust assets for Sam should a trust termination occur.

- On the death of Sam, the trust property is to be distributed equally between Sam's children (if any), Bob (or his children if Sam outlives him), Julie (or her children if Sam outlives her), and the local chapter of The Arc of the United States.

Example Two

The facts are the same as described in Example One, except that John and Mary decide they want to treat all their children equally. John and Mary decide on the following estate plan:

- As in Example One, John and Mary create a living trust, naming themselves as trustees, and transfer all their property to the trust. The provisions of the trust are the same as in Example One. Either of them can amend or revoke the trust at any time or use trust property for any purpose. On the death of the first of them, the survivor becomes sole trustee and retains the ability to amend or revoke the trust and to use trust property for any purpose.

- On the death of the second, the trust property is divided into equal parts—one for each of Bob, Julie, and Sam. Bob and

Julie receive their shares outright. Sam's share remains in trust for his life. As in Example One, the trust is prepared so Sam remains eligible for government benefits. Bob and Julie are named as trustees, and the trust contains a trust termination provision identical to the provision in Example One.

- On the death of Sam, the remaining trust property is to be distributed to Sam's children (if any), or if there are none, in equal shares to Bob (or his children if Sam outlives him) and Julie (or her children if Sam outlives her).

Example Three

John and Mary have three young children: Bob, Sam, and Julie. Sam has Down syndrome and is expected to move into a group home when he gets older. Bob has just turned 7 and is in the first grade. Julie is age 4 and attends preschool. John and Mary decide on the following estate plan:

- As in Examples One and Two, John and Mary create a living trust, naming themselves as trustees, and transfer all their property to the trust. The provisions of the trust are the same as in Examples One and Two. Either of them can amend or revoke the trust at any time or use trust property for any purpose. On the death of the first of them, the survivor becomes sole trustee and retains the ability to amend or revoke the trust and to use trust property for any purpose.

- On the death of the second of them, the trust is split into two parts. One-third of the property is held in a special needs trust for Sam to supplement government benefits that are available to him. Two-thirds of the property is held as a single pool for the benefit of Julie and Bob. When Julie reaches age 23, the remaining property in this separate pool is distributed equally between Bob and Julie. Sam's trust remains unchanged.

- John and Mary name John's sister, Margaret, and Mary's brother, Peter, as successor trustees after their deaths. If one of them cannot act, a bank becomes co-trustee. Margaret and Peter are each given the power to name a successor. Margaret is also named guardian for Bob, Sam, and Julie during their minority, with the expectation that Margaret will not pursue a court proceeding to continue the guardianship after Sam reaches age 18, unless she finds it necessary.

- On Sam's death, the property in his trust is to go to Bob and Julie, or their trust if Julie has not yet reached age 23.

As is apparent, a living trust can be drawn as flexibly as you would like. In fact, as you may have noticed, the examples discussed in this chapter are similar to the examples discussed in Chapter Six. This was done intentionally, to prove a point, that whatever you do with a will, you can do with a living trust as well.

Other Probate Avoidance Techniques

In Chapter Six we told you of certain types of property that pass outside your will. Included were property held in joint tenancy with right of survivorship (often a home or bank account) which passes to the surviving joint tenant by operation of law; and property that passes under a contractual arrangement, such as the proceeds under a life insurance contract or a retirement plan, which pass to the beneficiary designated under the insurance policy or retirement plan.

Because such property does not pass by will, it is not subject to probate. Some estate planners use joint tenancy and beneficiary designations as tools for avoiding the probate system. Unfortunately, while this technique works reasonably well for a married couple to pass property to the surviving spouse, it tends not to work as well for passing property to the next generation. As a result, the surviving spouse generally needs a living trust if probate is to be avoided at his or her death.

Example Four

John and Mary have three children: Bob, Sam, and Julie. Bob and Julie have good jobs and are financially independent. Sam had a serious automobile accident which resulted in severe physical impairments. The value of John and Mary's estate is approximately $450,000, consisting of the following:

- A home that has a value (net of their mortgage) of $100,000
- Stocks with a value of $30,000
- Certificates of deposit with a value of $10,000
- A bank account with a value of $10,000
- John's retirement account with a value of $50,000
- Mary's retirement account with a value of $50,000
- Insurance on John's life with a death benefit of $100,000
- Insurance on Mary's life with a death benefit of $100,000

John and Mary can easily use joint ownership and beneficiary designations to avoid probate on the first of their deaths. All that is necessary is that they hold title to their home, stocks, certificates of deposit, and bank account as joint tenants with right of survivorship and name each other as beneficiaries on their retirement plans and life insurance policies.

If John were to die first, Mary would acquire ownership of the home, stocks, certificates of deposit, and bank account by operation of law without need of probate, because she is the surviving joint tenant. Similarly, she would receive the proceeds from John's retirement account and his life insurance, because she is designated as beneficiary.

However, Mary would need to create an estate plan that would enable her to pass her property to Bob, Sam, and Julie when she dies. What options would she have?

The same options already discussed in this and the previous chapter. She could:

- Create a will and a special needs trust. This is the basic estate plan discussed in Chapter Six. The will would divide Mary's property among her children. The special needs trust would serve as a receptacle for Sam's share of Mary's estate, so that Sam could remain eligible for badly needed government benefits and avoid government claims for cost-of-care reimbursement. For example, Mary's will could leave her property equally between Bob, Julie, and Sam's trust. Mary could also name Bob, Julie, and Sam's trust as beneficiaries of her retirement plan and life insurance policy.

While this approach would enable Mary to divide her property among her children in the manner that she would like and also make sure that Sam remains eligible for government benefits, it would not avoid probate at Mary's death. Alternatively, Mary could:

- Create a living trust (as previously described in this chapter). Mary would transfer all her property to the trust and name the trust as beneficiary under her retirement plan and life insurance policy. During her life, she would be sole trustee and would be entitled to use trust property however she would like. On her death, if Mary wanted to treat her children equally, Bob and Julie would each receive one-third of Mary's property, and Sam's share would remain in trust. This would permit Mary to avoid probate and would also permit Sam to remain eligible for government benefits and avoid cost-of-care reimbursement claims.

If avoiding probate is one of John and Mary's objectives, a living trust will be required. Joint tenancy and beneficiary designations can be used to avoid probate at the first of their deaths, but if they are to avoid probate at the death of the survivor, a living trust is necessary. As long as a living trust will be needed, it makes sense for it to be created while John and Mary are both still living, so that both of them will have input into how their property will be divided. Moreover, if they decided to rely on joint tenancy and beneficiary designations while they were both living with the intention of having the survivor create a living trust after the death of the first of them, they would not avoid probate if they were to die simultaneously.

Why can't John and Mary avoid probate simply by having the survivor create a joint tenancy with his or her children? The answer is that they can, but there are severe drawbacks to doing so.

Example Five

The facts are the same as in Example Four, except that John has died and Mary has received property from John as a joint tenant and as beneficiary under John's retirement plan and life insurance policy. Mary now owns the following:

- A home that has a value (net of their mortgage) of $100,000, which she owned as joint tenant with John and inherited by virtue of being the surviving joint tenant

- Stocks with a value of $30,000, also received as surviving joint tenant

- Certificates of deposit with a value of $10,000, also received as surviving joint tenant

- A bank account with a value of $10,000, also received as surviving joint tenant

- Cash of $150,000, received as beneficiary under John's retirement plan and life insurance policy

- Her own retirement account with a value of $50,000

- Her own insurance with a death benefit of $100,000

Because Mary inherited property from John only as a surviving joint tenant and a beneficiary under John's retirement plan and life insurance policy, probate was not required at John's death.

Mary seeks to avoid probate at her death without creating a living trust so she does the following:

- Places her cash, home, stocks, and certificates of deposit in joint tenancy naming Bob, Julie, and Sam's special needs trust as joint tenants.

- Names Bob, Julie, and Sam's trust as beneficiaries under her retirement plan and life insurance policy.

Like a living trust, this approach has the benefit of avoiding probate at Mary's death and permitting Sam to remain eligible for government benefits. However, the approach also suffers from severe limitations.

First, because Bob and Julie will be joint tenants, they will have ownership rights in Mary's property even while Mary is still living. The law permits a joint tenant to sell his or her interest in the property and to retain a proportionate share of the proceeds. Thus, if Mary and her children were to have a serious disagreement—and this can and does happen—Mary's ability to enjoy her property could be severely restricted.

Mary could guard against this possibility by placing her cash and certificates of deposit in an informal bank-trust account, also known as a *Totten Trust*. Under such an arrangement, Bob, Julie, and Sam's trust would receive the cash at Mary's death only and would have no rights to the property during Mary's life.

However, these informal bank-trust accounts generally cannot be used for other types of assets, such as stocks, bonds, mutual funds, or real estate. Accordingly, if Mary owns assets of these types and wishes to avoid probate at her death, she must place them in joint tenancy and risk losing control of her property during her life. (A few states have special trusts for real estate, known as *land trusts*, which operate much like the Totten trusts described above.)

Second, because Bob and Julie will be joint tenants, any creditors that they may have will have rights against their interests in Mary's property. Thus, if Bob or Julie were to incur significant debts, a creditor could seize their interests in the property, making things extremely uncomfortable for Mary. For example, the creditor could occupy a portion of Mary's house and perhaps even force her to sell it, keeping a pro rata portion of the proceeds.

Finally, a joint tenancy between Mary and her children would restrict Mary's flexibility in deciding how to distribute her property among her children. For example, if Mary were to name Bob, Julie, and Sam's trust as joint tenants, each of them would be entitled to one-third of the joint tenancy property at Mary's death. It would not be possible to give Sam's trust a larger share of the property, say 50 percent, because joint tenancy does not work that way. Each joint tenant receives an equal share by operation of law.

Clearly, a living trust provides far more safety and flexibility than does joint tenancy. As trustee of her own trust, Mary has the absolute right to do whatever she wants with her property and has no need to worry about disputes with family or the possible appearance of her childrens' creditors. She can leave the property to her children in whatever proportions she wants and can freely change her mind whenever she wants.

Moreover, as previously mentioned, a living trust permits Mary to plan for her own disability by giving her the power to name successor trustees. There is no need to endure a guardianship proceeding or to rely on a power of attorney that may not be tailored to Mary's own particular situation.

Conclusion

The probate system has been criticized on the grounds that it is excessively burdensome, both in terms of time and cost. The living trust represents a private market response to probate. Although we believe that the benefits of a living trust are often overstated, we also believe that a living trust is generally superior to probate in most, but not all, cases. In particular, a living trust may not be advisable for young families and for people with complicated debt situations.

Estate planning is not formulaic. What is right for one person may not be right for another. The proper estate plan for a given individual depends on that individual's own particular needs and desires.

For many people, however, the living trust will be an important part of their estate plan. Placing your property in a properly drawn trust will have no effect on your ability to use your property however you would like. A living trust is as flexible as a will. You can change it however you like and leave your property to whomever you would like. For example, some of your property can be distributed to children without disabilities while other property remains in trust for a child with a disability, and the added time and expense of the probate system can be avoided.

TIP If you decide to go with a *living trust*, make sure to transfer your property into the trust during your life. Ask your attorney and financial advisor to help you with the necessary asset transfers and change of beneficiary designations.

CHAPTER 8

Chapter 9

Reducing the Estate Tax Owing at Your Death

IN GENERAL, THE FEDERAL GOVERNMENT PERMITS YOU TO LEAVE any amount of property to your spouse free of federal estate tax (assuming your spouse is a U.S. citizen). In addition, the federal government permits you to leave property with a value equal to the applicable *estate tax exclusion* amount to any person other than your spouse free of such tax. The estate tax exclusion amount is:

- $1.5M for people dying in 2005,
- $2M for people dying in 2006-2008,
- $3.5M for people dying in 2009, and
- $1M for people dying in 2011 and thereafter.
- There is no estate tax for people dying in 2010.

If the value of the property that you own at the time of your death is less than the applicable estate tax exclusion amount, no federal estate tax will be owing, and the planning ideas discussed in the remainder of this chapter (which are designed to reduce the tax owing at your death) will not be relevant to you. There is no need to plan to reduce estate tax if the law already provides that no estate tax is owing.

In determining whether the value of your estate reaches the applicable estate tax exclusion amount, however, there are a few things you should keep in mind:

- First, property that you place in a revocable living trust will be considered your property for purposes of the computation. This may be a little confusing. In Chapter Eight we told you that placing property in a living trust avoids probate because the property is not considered yours by state probate courts. But here we're dealing with the Internal Revenue Service and not the state probate courts, and the Internal Revenue Service applies a different set of rules.

- Second, the proceeds of any life insurance policies payable on account of your death will be considered part of your estate if you have any ownership rights under the policies (for example, the right to change beneficiaries). For example, if you have a term insurance policy with a death benefit of $500,000, the

Internal Revenue Service will count the $500,000 as part of your estate, even though you never owned any of the money during your life. (Life insurance proceeds are generally exempt from income tax, but estate tax is different.)

- Third, if you are married, you need to think about your spouse's assets as well as your own. Remember, estate tax generally will not be owing until the death of the second of you, and you need to consider property that you will receive from your spouse (assuming your spouse dies before you) as well as property you own currently. For example, if you and your spouse own a house with a value (net of debt) of $500,000, stocks and securities worth $250,000, and you each have life insurance of $500,000, your estate is worth $1,750,000.

Why should the estate tax owed be so dependent on the year of death?

- If you die in 2005, you can leave up to $1.5M to any person other than your spouse without any tax,

- If death occurs in 2006-2008 the figure is $2M,

- If death occurs in 2009 the figure is $3.5M,

- If death occurs in 2010 you can leave any amount to anyone without tax effect,

- If death occurs in 2011 or beyond the exclusion is reduced to $1M.

The *system* can be understood only when considered in the context of its creation back in 2001. At that time, a pitched battle took place between those who wanted to repeal the estate tax altogether and those who did not. The current rules represent a compromise, increasing the exclusion through 2009, repealing the estate tax for people dying in 2010, and then bringing back the old rules (a $1M exclusion) in 2011.

> *To quote one of our great former Supreme Court Justices, Learned Hand, "the life of the law is history, not logic," and our current estate tax system is a textbook illustration of that fact.*

Will the exclusion really be reduced to $1M in 2011?

There is a lot of speculation about this, but speculation about future legislation is always uncertain. Many people believe that the $3.5M exclusion will be made permanent. Others believe that the estate tax will be repealed. In truth, no one knows. For now, the rules are what they are, and planning must take place within the context of the current rules.

If you have a taxable estate, the tax is generally figured at a 45 percent rate for people dying prior to 2010, though a 47 percent rate sometimes applies to people dying in 2005 and a 46 percent rate sometimes applies to people dying in 2006. For people who die in 2011 and beyond, the tax rate varies considerably depending on the size of the decedent's estate, beginning at 41 percent and gradually increasing to 60 percent in certain cases. There is no estate tax for people dying in 2010.

Example One

John and Mary have an estate with a value of $2.5 million: a home with a value (net of mortgage) of $500,000; stocks with a value of $500,000; John's retirement account with a value of $500,000; Mary's retirement account with a value of $500,000; insurance on John's life, naming Mary as beneficiary, with a death benefit of $250,000; and life insurance on Mary, also with a death benefit of $250,000, naming John as beneficiary.

This information is summarized below:

Doe Family Balance Sheet

Asset	John	Mary	Joint
Home			$500,000
Stocks			$500,000
Retirement Plan	$500,000	$500,000	
Insurance	$250,000	$250,000	
	$750,000	$750,000	$1,000,000

Assuming John dies first and leaves all his property to Mary, no tax is owing on John's death because federal estate tax does not apply to property left to a surviving spouse, no matter how great the amount. The tax on Mary's death will depend on the size of her estate and the date she dies.

- If Mary dies in 2005, estate tax will be owed if the value of her property exceeds $1.5M. Assuming Mary's estate has a value of $2.5M, the tax will be $450,000 (the first $1.5M will be free of tax and the remaining $1M will be taxed at a 45 percent rate).

- If Mary dies in 2006, 2007 or 2008, estate tax will be owed if the value of her property exceeds $2M. Assuming Mary's estate has a value of $2.5M, the tax will be $225,000 (the first $2M will be free of tax and the remaining $500,000 will be taxed at a 45 percent rate).

- If Mary dies in 2009, estate tax will be owed only if the value of her property exceeds $3.5M.

- If Mary dies in 2010, no estate tax will be owed, regardless of the value of Mary's property.

- If Mary dies in 2011 or thereafter, estate tax will be owed if the value of her property exceeds $1M. Assuming Mary's estate has a value of $2.5M, the tax will be $680,000 (the first $1M will be free of tax and the remaining $1.5M will be taxed at a blended rate equal to 45.33 percent).

The result is unchanged if John and Mary put their property in a living trust to avoid probate as described in Chapter Eight. Fortunately, however, there are steps John and Mary can take to reduce or completely eliminate the tax.

Using the Credit-Shelter Trust to Reduce Estate Tax

The *credit-shelter* trust, also known as the *marital-bypass trust*, is perhaps the best estate-tax planning device available to upper middle-class couples. The trust is used to permit each member of the couple to use their estate tax exclusion.

In Example One above, John and Mary had an estate that was worth $2.5 million. Because their estate plan was designed to leave all their property to the survivor on the death of the first of them, the survivor was left with $2.5 million. That resulted in the survivor having a taxable estate if the survivor died in any year other than 2009 or 2010 (that is, an estate in excess of the applicable estate tax exclusion).

In effect, John wasted his estate tax exclusion. Had John left his $1,250,000 share of their net worth to someone other than Mary (perhaps to his children), no tax would have been owing at his death so long as he died before 2011. The law permits him to leave up to the estate tax exclusion free of tax to people other than Mary, and the estate tax exclusion exceeds $1,250,000 in every year prior to 2011. Similarly, no tax would have been owing at Mary's death so long as she died before 2011, because she would have had less than the estate tax exclusion. It was only because John left his property to Mary that a taxable estate was created. Had he not done so, Mary would have had less than the estate tax exclusion threshold amount.

But John did not want to leave his property to anyone other than Mary. He wanted her to have the use and benefit of his property.

The credit-shelter trust would have offered John a way out of his dilemma. The law permits John to create a trust for Mary, entitling her to the use and benefit of his property. If the trust is properly drawn, the property will not be considered Mary's for purposes of computing the estate tax owing at Mary's death.

In order for this to work, the law requires that certain limitations be placed on Mary's use of the trust property. However, in actual practice, these limitations are more theoretical than real.

For example, Mary can be named sole trustee of the trust after John's death and can be given the right to all the income of the trust, and principal to the extent required for her maintenance in health and reasonable comfort. Mary is not able to use the trust money for whatever purpose she wants because her ability to use trust principal is limited to use for her maintenance in health and reasonable comfort. However, since *reasonable* is interpreted taking into account Mary's prior standard of living, Mary can use the trust principal to continue in her accustomed lifestyle.

Moreover, in the interest of flexibility, Mary will typically be given the ability to direct that the remainder of the trust be distributed among one or more of a selected group of recipients at her death (for example, among such of John and Mary's descendants as are selected by Mary). This ability of Mary's to appoint the remaining trust property away from undeserving children is likely to ensure that Mary's wishes will be respected.

Example Two

John and Mary have three children: Bob, Sam, and Julie. Sam is age 25. He has epilepsy and an intellectual disability. He is expected to move into a group home when John and Mary get older. Bob has just turned 20 and is in college. Julie is age 17 and attends high school.

John and Mary have an estate with a value of approximately $2.5 million: a home with a value (net of mortgage) of $500,000; stocks with a value of $500,000; John's retirement account with a value of $500,000; Mary's retirement account with a value of $500,000; insurance on John's life, naming Mary as beneficiary, with a death benefit of $250,000; and life insurance on Mary, also with a death benefit of $250,000, naming John as beneficiary.

Thus John And Mary's estate is identical to their estate in Example One, the information is summarized below:

Doe Family Balance Sheet

Asset	John	Mary	Joint
Home			$500,000
Stocks			$500,000
Retirement Plan	$500,000	$500,000	
Insurance	$250,000	$250,000	
	$750,000	$750,000	$1,000,000

John and Mary would like all their property to be available for the survivor of them. At the death of the survivor, they want to divide the property equally between their children. They expect that Sam will require group housing and they want to keep their options open by making sure Sam remains eligible for government benefits. They are also fearful of providing too much money for

Bob and Julie at too early an age. They want to make sure Bob and Julie will have the maturity and experience to manage their money properly, and they believe it unhealthy for young adults to inherit significant amounts of money. They don't want to stifle Bob and Julie's initiative.

John and Mary have read Example One and studied it carefully. They realize that if they prepare simple estate plans, leaving all their property to the survivor of them, estate tax will be owing at the death of the second of them unless that person dies in 2009 or 2010. Assuming the survivor dies with an estate of $2.5 million (including insurance), the tax will be either $225,000, $450,000 or $680,000, depending on when that person dies. The calculations are set forth in Example One.

John and Mary decide on the following estate plan:

- John and Mary each create credit-shelter trusts, naming themselves as trustee. That is, John is named trustee of his trust, Mary is named trustee of her trust, and each of them is entitled to use the property in his or her trust however he or she would like. On the death of the first of them, the survivor becomes trustee of the decedent's trust as well, and is entitled to all of the income of the trust and all principal to the extent required for the survivor's maintenance in health and reasonable comfort.

- John and Mary then divide their property between their respective trusts. Each of their trusts receives a one-half interest as tenant in common in their home; each trust receives $250,000 in stock; John's trust is named beneficiary of his retirement plan and the insurance on his life; and Mary's trust is named beneficiary of her retirement plan and the insurance on her life. The new ownership arrangement is summarized below:

Revised Balance Sheet

Asset	John	Mary	Joint
Home	$250,000	$250,000	
Stocks	$250,000	$250,000	
Insurance	$250,000	$250,000	
Retirement Plan	$500,000	$500,000	
	$1,250,000	$1,250,000	$0

John and Mary's estate is identical to their estate in Example One. As in Example One, assume that John dies first (the result is identical without regard to the order of their deaths). Now see what happens on the death of Mary.

- If Mary dies in 2005, estate tax will be owed only if the value of her property exceeds $1.5M. Because John has left his $1.25M to a credit shelter trust for Mary, and not to Mary directly, Mary has just $1.25M and no tax is owed when she dies (assuming as in Example One, no increase in asset values). This represents a savings of $450,000 over the results in Example One.

- If Mary dies in 2006, 2007 or 2008, estate tax will be owed only if the value of her property exceeds $2M. Because John has left his $1.25M to a credit shelter trust for Mary, and not to Mary directly, Mary has just $1.25M and no tax is owed when she dies (assuming as in Example One, no increase in asset values). This represents a savings of $225,000 over the results in Example One.

- If Mary dies in 2009, estate tax will be owed only if the value of her property exceeds $3.5M. This is identical to the results in Example One.

- If Mary dies in 2010, no estate tax will be owed, regardless of the value of Mary's property. This is identical to the results in Example One.

- If Mary dies in 2011 or thereafter, estate tax will be owed only if the value of her property exceeds $1M. Because John has left his $1.25M to a credit shelter trust for Mary, and not to Mary directly, Mary has $1.25M and the tax is approximately $100,000 when she dies (assuming as in Example One, no increase in asset values). This represents a savings of approximately $580,000 over the results in Example One.

- Note that if John also dies in 2011 or thereafter, he can only put $1M in the credit shelter trust for Mary. As a result, Mary's tax is increased to approximately $200,000, which still represents a savings of approximately $480,000 over the results in Example One.

John and Mary have also retained maximum flexibility to decide how their property is to be distributed among their children at the death of the survivor of them. One approach would be to provide that their trusts are split into three shares, one for each of their children. Sam's share would remain in a special needs trust (drafted in accordance with the provisions in Chapter Six), so Sam would remain eligible for government benefits in the future.

Bob and Julie's shares would be distributed among them in stages: a third at age 25, a third at age 30, and a third at age 35. In the meantime, the successor trustee would be directed to use Bob and Julie's shares for their health, education, and general welfare. This would permit John and Mary to make sure the money is available to Bob and Julie but would also restrict their access so that Bob and Julie would not have too much money at too early an age.

John and Mary would also typically retain the flexibility to make needed revisions in case a change in circumstances required a change in plans.

As is apparent, John and Mary have made use of the credit-shelter trust to generate substantial estate-tax savings (more than $580,000, depending on when they die) and have retained maximum flexibility in their estate plan. The key to the estate-tax savings was John and Mary's ability to divide their property between them so that, regardless of who died first, that person would have the ability to fund their credit shelter trust.

In John and Mary's case the property division was very easy. Each of them put $250,000 in life insurance, $250,000 in stocks, $500,000 in retirement plan assets and their interest in their home (also valued at $500,000) in their credit-shelter trust. This left the survivor with $1,250,000 (as well as access to the funds in the credit-shelter trust). The results in Example Two would have been identical if Mary died before John.

Sometimes the property division is not so smooth. For example, in some cases one spouse may own most of the property and may not feel comfortable transferring ownership of significant amounts of property to the other. This is very common in the case of a second marriage or in a first marriage when the couple has not been married for a very long time.

Is a credit-shelter trust helpful when property cannot be divided among spouses? The answer is *maybe*, depending on which of the spouses dies first.

Example Three
John and Mary are in their early sixties and have been married for a long time. John has two children from a previous marriage: Bob, who has a bipolar disorder (also known as manic depression), and Julie, who is married and has a family of her own. Mary's child, Sam, is also married and is a successful businessman.

John has worked for many years and has a sizable estate: a home with a value (net of mortgage) of $500,000; stocks and securities with a value of $500,000; life insurance with a death benefit of $500,000; and a retirement account with a value of $1,000,000. Mary spent most of her life making a home for her family and used what savings she did have to put Sam through school.

The information is summarized below.

Doe Family Balance Sheet

Asset	John	Mary	Joint
Home	$500,000		
Stocks	$500,000		
Insurance	$500,000		
Retirement Plan	$1,000,000		
	$2,500,000		

John and Mary would like most of their property to be available for the survivor of them, though John does want $100,000 to be set aside for Bob, "just in case something should happen." At the death of the survivor, they want to divide the property equally among all of their children. John has read Example Two and understands the value of the credit-shelter trust. However, he does not feel comfortable putting his property in Mary's name. He trusts her implicitly but does not think it appropriate for her to have the ability to disinherit Bob or Julie.

John and Mary decide on the following estate plan:

- John creates a living trust, naming himself as trustee. He transfers ownership of the house and his stock and securities to the trust, and names the trust as beneficiary of his retirement plan. At his death, the trust divides into three parts: $100,000 goes into a special needs trust for Bob; an amount equal to the applicable estate tax exemption goes into a credit-shelter trust so John and Mary can realize the estate tax savings described in Example 2; and the remaining property goes into a special trust, known as a QTIP trust, to be held for Mary. This trust is prepared in accordance with special provisions contained in the Internal Revenue Code that permit John to restrict Mary's use of the money while counting the money as Mary's for estate tax purposes.

- John wants Mary to have the use and benefit of the $2.4 million placed in the QTIP and credit-shelter trusts, but he wants some restriction on her ability to use the money so something will be left for Bob and Julie. John names Mary as trustee and beneficiary of the trusts, but he names a bank, or perhaps Julie, as co-trustee.

- On the death of Mary, the property is divided equally between Bob, Sam, and Julie, except that an equalizing distribution is made to Sam and Julie to account for the fact that Bob received $100,000 when John died. Bob's share remains in a special needs trust, so he remains eligible for government benefits.

Now let's examine the estate-tax consequences of the plan, keeping in mind the general rule that an individual can leave any amount of property to his or her spouse free of tax, and an amount up to the estate tax exemption to any other persons free of tax.

John's estate is identical to John and Mary's joint estate in Examples One and Two—$2.5M. As in Examples One and Two, assume that John dies first, and assume the death occurs in 2005. Now see what happens on the death of Mary.

- If Mary dies in 2005, estate tax will be owed only if the value of her property exceeds $1.5M. John has left his $100,000 to Bob's trust, $1.4M to a credit shelter trust for Mary, and $1M to Mary's QTIP trust. (The $1.4M in the credit shelter trust represents the amount of the 2005 estate tax exemption amount that is left after the $100,000 bequest to Bob's trust.) Because Mary is treated as owning only the property in the QTIP, she has just $1M and no tax is owed when she dies (assuming as in Examples One and Two, no increase in asset values). This is identical to the results in Example Two.

- If Mary dies in 2006, 2007 or 2008, estate tax will be owed only if the value of her property exceeds $2M. Because John has left just $1M to the QTIP, Mary has just $1M and no tax is owed when she dies (assuming as in Examples One and Two, no increase in asset values). Again, this is identical to the results in Example Two.

- If Mary dies in 2009, estate tax will be owed only if the value of her property exceeds $3.5M. If Mary dies in 2010, no estate tax will be owed, regardless of the value of Mary's property. Again, this is identical to the results in Example Two.

- If Mary dies in 2011 or thereafter, estate tax will be owed only if the value of her property exceeds $1M. Because Mary has just $1M, no tax is owed. This is even better than the results in Example Two.

So far so good. The problem arises if Mary dies first. Because John did not make transfers of property to Mary during his life, he is left with $2.5M when Mary dies. Assuming, as in Examples One and Two, that John's estate remains unchanged, the results on John's death will be identical to the results in Example One. That is, John will owe substantial estate tax when he dies, unless he dies in 2009 or 2010. John will owe

- $450,000 if he dies in 2005,

- $225,000 if he dies in 2006, 2007 or 2008, and

- $680,000 if he dies after 2010.

This is not to say that John should make the transfers in his lifetime. He has very good reasons for not doing so. However,

John's failure to make property transfers will cause an increase in estate tax if he dies after Mary.

 TIP The credit shelter trust should be seriously considered if a couple expects their joint assets to exceed the applicable estate tax exemption when they die. It works best from a tax perspective if the couple is able to divide their assets between them. If asset division is not possible, the credit shelter works if the couple dies in the *right* order.

In cases where it is unclear whether a couple's assets will exceed the applicable estate tax exemption, we sometimes use what is referred to as a *disclaimer credit shelter trust*. Under this approach, the couple leaves their property directly to each other but the property goes into a credit shelter trust if the survivor disclaims his or her interest in the property. This gives the couple the ability to avoid the complexity of a credit shelter trust if it is not needed, but obtain the benefit if the credit shelter trust is needed.

 TIP The IRS has very strict rules regarding disclaimers that must be followed if a disclaimer is to serve its intended purpose. Make sure you are familiar with these rules before you use a disclaimer credit shelter trust.

Finally, as a general rule, we advise our clients to avoid using retirement plans to fund credit shelter trusts if they can get sufficient funding from other assets. This is because there are income tax advantages in naming the surviving spouse as beneficiary, though sometimes the credit shelter trust must be named to obtain maximum estate tax savings.

Reducing Estate Tax with the Irrevocable Insurance Trust

As is apparent, the credit-shelter trust can be used by a married couple to shelter a significant amount of assets from estate tax. The *irrevocable insurance trust* can be used to save additional estate tax both by married couples and by individuals.

Properly drafted, the trust permits life-insurance proceeds to escape estate tax altogether. The idea is for the trust to be both owner and beneficiary under the insurance policy. Because the insured has no ownership rights under the policy (for example, the insured is not allowed to change the beneficiary or to borrow against the policy) none of the proceeds are includable for estate-tax purposes.

In order for the plan to succeed, ownership of existing policies must be transferred to the trust at least three years before the insured dies (assuming the insured had ownership rights before the transfer). This three year rule does not apply to polices that are originally issued in the name of the trust.

It is necessary that the trust be irrevocable, and that the insured give up all ownership rights under the policy. For example, the insured cannot retain the right to change beneficiaries or have access to any cash value in the policies or be named trustee of the insurance trust. Thus, the trust is less flexible than the credit-shelter trust, which can be amended or revoked at any time.

Notwithstanding this reduced degree of flexibility, however, the estate-tax savings resulting from the irrevocable insurance trust can be enormous. The trust can therefore be a valuable estate-planning tool for wealthy and upper middle-class individuals and couples. In addition, though the irrevocable insurance trust may not be as flexible as the credit-shelter trust, it remains possible for the insured to retain a considerable degree of flexibility.

For example, the trust can be funded with term insurance. If circumstances change and the insured no longer finds the terms of the trust to be appropriate, the insured can revoke the trust by failing to pay premiums on the policy. Assuming the person remains insurable, a new policy can be issued, perhaps to a new irrevocable insurance trust that is more appropriate to the insured's changed circumstances. Similarly, if the insured is married, the spouse can be given a limited power to alter the disposition of the trust.

Example Four

The facts are identical to the facts in Example Two. Thus, John and Mary's assets are as follows:

Doe Family Balance Sheet

Asset	John	Mary	Joint
Home			$500,000
Stocks			$500,000
Insurance	$250,000	$250,000	
Retirement Plan	$500,000	$500,000	
	$750,000	$750,000	$1,000,000

John and Mary have read Example Two. They are aware that they if they divide their assets equally between them and make use of credit shelter trusts as in Example Two, the survivor will be left with $1,250,000 for estate tax purposes, and estate tax will not be owing if the survivor dies before 2011 because the estate tax exclusion amount exceeds $1,250,000 in each such year. However, if the survivor dies after 2010, approximately $100,000 in estate tax will be owed. If they both die after 2010, the tax will be $200,000.

John and Mary are young, and they both have high paying jobs. They are interested in saving the $200,000 in estate tax that will be owed if they both die after 2010. They are also concerned that the tax may exceed $200,000 because they expect their estate to increase in value over time.

John and Mary decide on the following estate plan:

- First, they each create credit-shelter trusts, naming themselves as trustee. That is, John is named trustee of his trust, Mary is named trustee of her trust, and each of them is entitled to use the property in his or her trust however he or she would like. On the death of the first of them, the survivor becomes trustee of the decedent's trust as well, and is entitled to all of the income of the trust and all principal to the extent required for the survivor's maintenance in health and reasonable comfort.

- Second, they each create irrevocable insurance trusts to serve as owner and beneficiary of the insurance on their lives. That is, John's trust is the owner and beneficiary of the insurance on his life, with Mary named as trustee. Mary's trust is the owner and beneficiary of the insurance on her life, with John named as trustee. The terms of the trusts are substantially similar to the terms of their credit-shelter trusts. On the death of the first of them, the survivor is entitled to all of the income from the trust and principal to the extent required for the survivor's maintenance in health and reasonable comfort.

- Third, they divide their remaining property between their credit-shelter trusts exactly as in Example Two. The new ownership arrangement is summarized below:

Revised Balance Sheet

Asset	John	Mary	Insurance Trust
Home	$250,000	$250,000	
Stocks	$250,000	$250,000	
Insurance	0	0	$500,000
Retirement Plan	$500,000	$500,000	
	_____	_____	_____
	$1,000,000	$1,000,000	$500,00

Now see what happens if John and Mary die after 2010 assuming, as in Example Two, no further appreciation in assets. The survivor has property with a value of $1 million because all their other property is either in a credit shelter trust or an irrevocable insurance trust. This is exactly equal to the estate tax exclusion amount. Accordingly, no estate tax is owed. By contrast, in Example Two where a credit shelter trust was used but an irrevocable insurance trust was not, the tax was $200,000 if John and Mary both died after 2010, and $100,000 if one of them died before 2010 and the other died after 2010.

John and Mary have also retained maximum flexibility to decide how their property is to be distributed among their children at the death of the survivor of them. As in Example Two, one approach would be to provide that their trusts are split into three shares, one for each of their children. Sam's share would remain in a special needs trust (drafted in accordance with the provisions in Chapter Six), so Sam would remain eligible for government benefits in the future.

Bob and Julie's shares would be distributed among them in stages: a third at age 25, a third at age 30, and a third at age 35. In the meantime, the successor trustee would be directed to use Bob and Julie's shares for their health, education, and general welfare. This would permit John and Mary to make sure the money is available to

Bob and Julie but would also restrict their access so Bob and Julie would not have too much money at too early an age.

John and Mary would also typically retain the flexibility to make needed revisions in case a change in circumstances required a change in plans.

As is apparent, John and Mary have used the irrevocable insurance trust to augment the power of the credit-shelter trust without changing their basic estate plan, to make all their property available to the survivor and then to place it in carefully tailored trusts for their children. The only real difference is that the irrevocable insurance trust permits them to shelter a larger share of their property from estate tax.

The irrevocable insurance trust can also be used to save estate tax for those for whom a credit-shelter trust would typically be inappropriate (for example, people who are not married).

Example Five

Mary is a widow with two children: Bob, who is happily married with three children of his own, and Julie, who has schizophrenia and is unable to hold a job. Mary has $1,500,000 in assets: a home with a value of $500,000, insurance with a death benefit of $500,000, and stocks and securities with a market value of $500,000.

Because Mary has more than $1,000,000 in property, without advance planning, estate tax will be owing at Mary's death (if she dies after 2010.). Assuming the value of Mary's estate remains constant, the tax will be approximately $200,000. Because Mary is unmarried, a credit-shelter trust will not be helpful.

Accordingly, Mary decides on the following estate plan:

- First, Mary creates a living trust as described in Chapter Eight, and makes the trust the owner of her home, her stocks, and securities. This will not help with estate tax, but it will enable Mary to avoid probate.

- Second, Mary creates an irrevocable insurance trust, and she names the trust owner and beneficiary under the policy. Because the value of Mary's estate is now reduced to $1,000,000, estate tax will not be owing at her death, even if she dies after 2010 (assuming her estate does not increase in value).

- Third, Mary has the trusts prepared so that, at her death, half the trust property is distributed to Bob, and the remaining half is held in a special needs trust for Julie.

Another use of an irrevocable insurance trust is to reduce estate tax that will be owing if couples who do not want to shift ownership of their assets do not die *in the right order*.

Example Six

The facts are the same as in Example Three. John has an estate with a value of $2.5 million: a home with a value (net of mortgage) of $500,000, stocks and securities with a value of $500,000, life insurance with a death benefit of $500,000, and a retirement account with a value of $1,000,000. He is unwilling (perhaps for very good reasons) to transfer ownership of any of his property to his wife, Mary.

As illustrated in Example Three, John can use a credit-shelter trust to save estate tax if he dies before Mary. However, if Mary dies first, John will be left with the entire $2.5 million, and estate tax will be owing. John can reduce the tax by transferring his $500,000 insurance policy to the irrevocable insurance trust. This reduces his estate to $2,000,000 and thereby reduces the tax substantially.

John can, of course, wait to see if Mary dies first and transfer the policy into trust at that time. This would eliminate a trust-preparation fee that would prove unnecessary if John were to die first. However, as stated above, the irrevocable insurance trust works for existing policies owned by the insured only if the policies are transferred to the trust at least three years before the insured dies. Waiting to see who dies first increases the risk that John will run afoul of this three-year rule.

 TIP In preparing an irrevocable insurance trust, special care has to be taken to reduce any gift tax consequences resulting from payment of premiums or the transfer of policies that have a cash value into the trust. Your attorney will be able to help you with this.

Reducing Estate Tax Through Gifting Programs

Lifetime property transfers, or gifts, represent a common method of reducing estate tax for families that are unable to eliminate the tax through use of the credit-shelter trust and the irrevocable insurance trust. The law imposes a gift tax that is designed to defeat many gifting strategies. However, despite the existence of the gift tax, lifetime gifting can be a very valuable estate planning device for the affluent.

The Gift Tax and the Annual Exclusion Gift

Stripped to its barest essentials, the gift tax serves as a *backstop* to the tax on transfers at death. Without a tax on lifetime transfers, the estate tax would be easy to defeat indeed. A person could simply make lifetime transfers of the bulk of his or her property to family members, perhaps even making such transfers while at death's door.

The gift tax defeats this strategy by imposing a tax on lifetime transfers. In general, the tax works hand in hand with the tax on transfers at death. Lifetime gifts reduce the estate tax exclusion on a dollar for dollar basis and are subject to tax to the extent that they exceed $1 million. Gifts in different years accumulate for purposes of determining whether the $1 million limit is exceeded.

Under an important exception to this rule, however, a person is entitled to give away up to $11,000 *per donee per year* (which increases periodically to account for inflation) without causing a

363

reduction in the estate-tax exclusion or the imposition of any gift tax. This is known as the *annual exclusion gift* and is the most common method of using gifts to reduce transfer taxes. Assuming enough donees and enough years, the amount of estate tax saved can be staggering.

Example Seven

John and Mary have an estate worth approximately $10 million. They have little need for so much money and are interested in making annual exclusion gifts to reduce the tax owing when they die. They have three daughters, each of whom is married with three children of her own.

Assuming John and Mary make annual exclusion gifts to each of their daughters, sons-in-law and grandchildren, they can make a total of $330,000 in gifts each year ($11,000 from each of them to each of nine grandchildren, three daughters, and three sons-in-law) without any reduction in their estate tax exclusions or the imposition of any gift tax. Assuming John and Mary are in the 55 percent gift and estate tax bracket, each year's gifts save a *minimum* of $180,000 in taxes.

In fact, the tax savings attributable to each year's gifts are significantly greater. The property given away will grow through investments, but since John and Mary have given the property away, the appreciation will not be included in their estate. Assuming the property could have been invested at a seven percent annual return, the $330,000 given away each year will double in value every ten years, which means the estate-tax savings attributable to each year's gifts doubles in value as well.

If John and Mary are nervous about the effect that such large gifts might have on family members, the gifts could be made in trust. This would be the typical approach for gifts to young children or grandchildren. The trusts would need to be specially drawn so the gifts would qualify for the annual exclusion.

TIP Annual exclusion gifts probably should not be made to a special needs trust for a child with a disability. The reason is that in order to qualify for the annual exclusion, the beneficiary of the trust has to be given the power to withdraw property from the trust for a specified period. During this withdrawal period, the gift would count as a resource for the beneficiary, which could imperil the beneficiary's entitlement for government benefits. In addition, although the matter is not free from doubt, failure to exercise the withdrawal right could cause the trust to be considered a *self-settled trust*, which also could imperil the beneficiary's eligibility for government benefits. Self-settled trusts are discussed in Chapter Seven.

Gifts Exceeding the Annual Exclusion

A common belief of people who regularly make annual exclusion gifts is that it is unwise to increase such gifts above the annual exclusion amount. This belief could not be further from the truth.

It is true that gifts in excess of the annual exclusion reduce the donor's estate-tax exclusion and result in gift tax to the extent they aggregate over $1 million. However, such excess gifts often result in a net transfer-tax savings. This is true for two reasons.

First, the value of the estate of a wealthy individual tends to increase as time passes because the individual's earnings (including investment earnings) will usually exceed living expenses. By making large gifts, the donor removes both the gifted property and the earnings that the property generates from his or her estate. In effect, then, by using up the estate tax exemption during his or her life, an individual increases the value of that exemption. This principle is demonstrated in Example Eight below.

Second, although the statement seems paradoxical, paying gift tax can actually reduce total transfer taxes. This is because the money used to pay the gift tax is generally not part of the donor's estate. Importantly, however, the gift tax is brought back into the donor's estate if the donor dies within three years of making the gift. This will be illustrated in Example Nine.

Example Eight

John and Mary have a very large estate. In addition to making annual exclusion gifts as described in Example Seven, they each give by $1 million to their children. As described above, this gift reduces each of their estate-tax exclusions by $1 million. However, by accelerating use of the exemption, they have significantly increased its value.

To illustrate, suppose John and Mary had retained the $2 million, invested it at seven percent, and died twenty years later. The $2 million would have been worth $8 million when they died (it would have doubled in value every ten years). In effect, John and Mary have transferred $8 million to their children but have only used up exemptions of $2 million.

Example Nine

John and Mary have a very large estate. In addition to making annual exclusion gifts as described in Example Seven and using up their estate-tax exemptions as described in Example Eight, they make additional gifts giving rise to gift tax of $500,000. Assuming John and Mary live for at least three years after the date of the gift, the gift tax will not be included in their estates and John and Mary will have saved $275,000 in taxes assuming they live past 2010 because, if they did not pay the gift tax and instead kept the $500,000, it would have been taxed at a 55 percent rate. The tax savings potential of the gift will be even greater when we take account of the fact that John and Mary will not be subject to estate tax on the earnings generated by the gifted property.

A final caveat. In making gifts of property other than cash, you will need to give some thought to the income tax that will be owing when the property is ultimately sold. In general, such tax will be based on the gain *realized* when the property is sold. This, in turn, will be measured by the difference between the *sales price* and the property's *tax basis*.

Although tax basis is generally measured by cost, property that is inherited at the owner's death takes a *stepped-up basis* equal to the property's fair market value at the date of death (or sometimes on an alternate valuation date). Because property that is given away during the donor's life retains its cost basis, giving away property that has appreciated in value, or is likely to appreciate in value, will frequently result in increased income tax when the property is eventually sold.

Example Ten

John owns 100 shares of IBM stock, which he bought for $5,000. He gives the stock to Steve, who sells it at John's death when the value of the stock is $15,000. Steve's gain is $10,000, and the tax will be approximately $1,500. Had Steve received the stock as a result of John's death, the stock would have received a stepped-up basis to $15,000 and the tax would have been eliminated.

Of course, by making the gift, John has reduced the value of his estate by $15,000, which could result in a reduction in estate tax of more than $1,500 ($7,500, assuming a 50 percent effective tax rate). In addition, if Steve dies while still owning the stock, it will receive a stepped-up basis at that time.

The loss of a stepped-up basis does not mean gifts of appreciated property should not be made. However, the loss should be considered before any gifting program is begun.

Generation-Skipping Transfers

Thus far we have talked about methods of reducing the amount of estate tax that will be owing at your death. Estate planning can also involve planning to permit the passage of wealth through multiple generations.

To consider an example, suppose you have a taxable estate (that is, an estate with a value in excess of the estate-tax exclusion) and you expect your children to have taxable estates as well. If you leave your property to your children, the property will be subject to estate tax at your death, and also when your children die.

Example Eleven

John and Mary have an estate with a value of $5 million. Their children have good jobs and are expected to amass substantial estates of their own.

Assuming John and Mary live past 2010 and make maximum use of the credit-shelter trust, and assuming the irrevocable insurance trust is not helpful to them (perhaps because they have no life insurance), $3 million of their property will be subject to tax when they die, and the tax will be approximately $1.5 million. Thus, John and Mary's children will receive $3.5 million ($5 million less $1.5 million of tax) at the death of John and Mary.

Assuming the $3.5 million does not increase in value, and assuming John and Mary's children are in the 55 percent estate tax bracket, this $3.5 million will then be subject to a tax of $1.925 million when it is passed on to John and Mary's grandchildren. Thus, John and Mary's grandchildren will receive $1.575 million ($3.5 million less $1.925 million of tax).

Of course, John and Mary can eliminate the tax at the death of their children by giving the money directly to their grandchildren. (Actually they can give their grandchildren only an amount equal to the generation skipping tax exclusion, or they will be subject to a special generation-skipping tax. The generation skipping tax exclusion is equal to the estate tax exclusion, except that it increases each year after 2010 to account for inflation.)

However, it is unlikely that John and Mary will wish to leave a large amount of property to their grandchildren. In most cases, John and Mary will want to leave their money to their children. They want their children to be comfortable, and it may be detrimental to the development of their grandchildren to have access to such a large amount of money.

The *generation-skipping trust*, also known as the *dynasty trust* or *mega-trust*, would enable John and Mary to meet their objective. In general, John and Mary can leave their property in trust for their children, enabling them to have access to trust property if needed. But the trust can be prepared so that the property will not be taxed when John and Mary's children die.

Example Twelve

John and Mary have an estate with a value of $5 million. Their children have good jobs and are expected to amass substantial estates of their own.

As in Example Eleven, assuming John and Mary live past 2010, make maximum use of the credit-shelter trust and divide their property equally between them, $3 million of John and Mary's property will be subject to tax when they die, and the tax will be approximately $1.5 million. However, instead of leaving the remaining $3.5 million (after estate tax is paid) directly to their children, suppose John and Mary place $2 million in generation-skipping trusts and leave $1.5 million directly to their children.

Under the terms of the generation-skipping trusts, John and Mary's children would be entitled to income and principal from the trusts as needed, and the trusts would go to John and Mary's grandchildren on the death of John and Mary's children. John and Mary's children could even be given the power to appoint the trusts away from undeserving grandchildren.

Now look what happens on the death of John and Mary's children. In Example Eleven John and Mary's children received $3.5 million, and the tax when they died was $1.925 million, leaving $1.575 million for the grandchildren. Here, however, John and Mary's children have received $1.5 million though they have access to the entire $3.5 million. The estate tax on the death of John and Mary's children has been reduced to approximately $825,000. Thus, John and Mary's grandchildren end up with $2.675 million ($3.5 million less $825,000). This is $1.1 million more than if a generation skipping trust is not used.

The benefit of the generation-skipping trust appears even greater when we consider the earnings the money could generate. Investing the savings at seven percent results in a doubling of the benefit every ten years.

In fact, the savings can be greater yet, because the trust can be prepared so that the money is not distributed until the death of John and Mary's grandchildren. This means that another generation of tax will be avoided and even more savings will result as a consequence of the accrual of earnings.

Little wonder, then, that the trust is sometimes referred to as a *dynasty* or *mega trust*. (A complicated law known as the *rule against perpetuities* keeps the trust from remaining in existence in perpetuity.)

Conclusion

Planning to reduce the amount of tax owing at your death is complicated, and this chapter is not intended to be a *do it yourself guide* to estate-tax planning. Rather, our intention is to describe some of the more common techniques that are available, to make you aware of the magnitude of savings that is possible, and to enable you to discuss your options intelligently with estate-planning professionals.

- If you expect the value of your estate at the time of your death to be less than the applicable estate tax exemption, no estate tax will be owed at your death, and estate-tax planning will not be necessary.

- If you expect the value of your estate at the time of your death to exceed the applicable estate tax exemption and you are married, a credit shelter trust should be considered.

- If you expect the value of your estate at the time of your death to exceed the applicable estate tax exemption and you are unmarried, or if you are married and the savings generated through a credit shelter trust will not completely eliminate the estate tax owed at your death, an irrevocable life insurance trust should be considered.

- If your estate is sufficiently large, some type of gifting program and generation-skipping strategy should be considered. In fact, a generation-skipping trust can be beneficial even if you are not *rich*, if your children are wealthy.

Some of the more esoteric estate-tax planning strategies have not been discussed, because they are useful only to the very wealthy and only in very limited circumstances. For example, it is possible to make use of limited partnerships, qualified personal residence trusts, grantor retained annuity trusts, private annuities, installments sales to grantor trusts or self-cancelling installment notes to increase potential estate-tax savings.

For those who are charitably inclined, gifts to charities are generally deductible for both income and transfer-tax purposes. It is possible to make such gifts through charitable remainder trusts, so that you will continue to have access to the income generated by the gifted property during your life. Because such trusts are exempt from capital gains tax, they can also be used by those who wish to convert assets that do not produce current income (such as growth stocks or real estate) to income producing property.

One increasingly common technique employed by affluent families that have a child with a disability is to create a charitable remainder trust naming the child's special needs trust as beneficiary. The special needs trust receives income from the charitable remainder trust during the child's life, and a charity that helped the child receives the remaining property when the child dies. This permits the child to receive government benefits and a guaranteed income stream, while the family receives substantial tax benefits in addition to helping a deserving charity.

If it all sounds complicated, that's because it is. If you have a sizable estate, it is very important that you receive assistance from estate planners who are familiar with all the various tax-saving techniques that are potentially available to you. You should be aware that not all estate planners are familiar with the various possibilities. You should look carefully for someone who has the requisite tax expertise.

The Health Care Declaration and the Durable Power of Attorney

W HILE FEW PEOPLE WOULD SERIOUSLY QUESTION THE BENEFITS of the tremendous advances in medical technology over the last fifty years, it is an unfortunate fact that these advances have had a *dark side* as well. Many patients have not made their wishes regarding *end of life care* known to doctors and family members in a legally binding form. This has sometimes resulted in patients who have lost cognitive function either receiving treatment that they would not have desired, or being denied treatment that they would have desired.

Fortunately, documents such as the health care declaration and the durable power of attorney have been developed to enable people to retain some measure of control over the type of medical treatment given to them in the event of catastrophic illness or injury. What can happen if such a document is not prepared for you?

The recent circumstances involving Terri Schiavo represent an obvious case in point. Terri Schiavo collapsed on the morning of February 25, 1990 and suffered severe irreversible brain damage as a result of a lack of oxygen. Most of her cerebral cortex was destroyed, and she had to be fed through a gastric feeding tube. Terri Schiavo never prepared a health care declaration or durable power of attorney, and her family fought bitterly over her treatment from 1993 until her death in 2005.

Michael Schiavo (who is Terri Schiavo's husband), the Schiavos' personal physician, and many other physicians who examined her contended that she was in a *persistent vegetative state*. This means that, in their view, she was wakeful, but not aware, and was unable to respond to external stimuli, except perhaps pain. Michael also maintained that, prior to her accident, Terri had made statements to him indicating that she would not want to live if she were in such a state.

Terri's parents and other doctors claimed that she was in a *minimally conscious state*. They said that she smiles, laughs, cries, moves and attempts speech. Michael and the physicians who care for Terri said that these were reflex or random behaviors that are common to patients who are in a persistent vegetative state. Terri's parents also disputed Michael's claim that Terry indicated a preference for death as compared to her present state. They claimed that Terri was religiously opposed to euthanasia, she had never made such statements to other family members or friends, and that shortly after the injury Michael had told others that he had no idea what Terri's wishes would be.

Michael first sought to remove Terri's feeding tube at the end of 1998. The tube was first removed on April 26, 2001 and was reinserted two days later after Terri's parents objected. In 2004, after protracted litigation, a court ordered that the tube be removed. A few days later the Florida legislature gave the Governor of Florida authority to intervene in the case. Pursuant to the order of the Florida Governor, the tube was reinserted.

In May, 2004, a Florida court declared the action of the Florida legislature unconstitutional. This finding was affirmed by the Florida Supreme Court in September, 2004. The Florida Governor appealed to the U.S. Supreme Court. On January 25, 2005, the U.S. Supreme Court announced that it would not hear the case.

On February 25, 2005 a Florida court ruled that Michael could have the feeding tube removed on March 18. The tube was removed on that day but on March 21 Congress approved a bill transferring the case to federal court. On March 22, 2005 a U.S. District Court Judge refused to order the reinsertion of the tube. Appeals were filed and were denied. Terri Schiavo died on March 31, 2005.

Although Terri Schiavo's case is the most recent high profile case involving the effort to discern a patient's desire in the absence of a health care declaration or durable power of attorney, it is by no means the first such case.

Karen Ann Quinlan was 21 when she lapsed into a coma, apparently after ingesting a mixture of alcohol and barbiturates at a party. She was placed on a respirator and remained in a chronic, persistent vegetative state.

After discussing the matter with his priest, Karen's father requested that the respirator be removed. Viewing this as a violation of medical ethics, the attending physician refused. The local prosecutor and the state attorney general threatened criminal proceedings. A court battle ensued, and Karen remained on a respirator for two years, until the New Jersey Supreme Court finally granted her father's request that the respirator be removed. Karen lived for another nine years, no longer hooked to a respirator, but like Terri Schiavo, fed through a feeding tube.

Perhaps the most famous case, prior to the case of Terri Schiavo, was that of Nancy Cruzan, whose fate was ultimately decided by the United States Supreme Court in 1990.

On January 11, 1983, Nancy Cruzan, then 26, skidded while driving home. Her car overturned and she was thrown more than 20 feet and knocked unconscious. Paramedics arrived approximately 20 minutes later and began resuscitative efforts. On February 3, 1983, with the consent of her (then) husband, a feeding tube was inserted. Ms. Cruzan remained in a persistent vegetative state, and doctors indicated there was no realistic chance of recovery.

Nancy's parents requested that the tube be removed in the fall of 1986, approximately three and a half years after the accident.

The hospital refused, perhaps fearing potential liability under Missouri state law, and a lawsuit was filed. Eventually an order to discontinue feedings was issued, but the State of Missouri appealed.

Like many people, Nancy Cruzan had taken no *formal* steps to indicate the type of medical treatment she would consider appropriate in the event of a tragic accident or incurable illness. Apparently, however, she had told a friend that she would never want to live in an irreversible coma, because she did not consider life worth living under such circumstances.

The Missouri Supreme Court refused to order the hospital to remove the feeding tube, finding Nancy's conversation with her friend to be insufficient proof that she would have wanted the feedings stopped. The United States Supreme Court upheld the decision, finding that the State of Missouri was within its rights to refuse to withhold feedings from a comatose patient who had not clearly expressed her intention. A new case was brought and *new evidence* was presented to indicate Nancy's intent. The tube was removed and Nancy died 12 days later, the day after Christmas, 1990, almost 8 years after the accident.

The cases of Terri Schiavo, Nancy Cruzan, and Karen Ann Quinlan are not the only times bitter battles were fought over the appropriate treatment for patients who had lost nearly all cognitive function.

The cases are many and varied, and it is unwise to generalize too much. However, one point does stand out: if you suffer a tragic accident and are unable to make medical decisions on your own, it is quite possible that decisions will be made regarding your medical treatment that you would not have made if you were capable of making the decisions on your own.

Fortunately, however, techniques are available to insure that you will not suffer the fate endured by Terri Schiavo, Nancy Cruzan, Karen Ann Quinlan, and many others. All states have enacted advance health care declaration and/or durable power of attorney statutes. These permit you to make your feelings known to doctors in a form that will be respected. They also allow you to appoint surrogates to make decisions on your behalf if you are not in condition to do so.

 TIP In most cases, we provide each of our clients with durable powers of attorney for health care and property to provide protection in circumstances of serious illness or injury.

A majority of states have family consent statutes that permit specified family members to make health care decisions for patients who are unable to make decisions for themselves if the patients have failed to prepare powers of attorney or health care directives. Family consent statutes should not be used as substitutes for powers of attorney or health care directives for two reasons.

First, family consent statutes generally specify a priority—the patient's spouse acts first, then adult children, parents, siblings, and maybe even close friends. This may not be the order in which you want people to act. The power of attorney allows you to appoint the people who you prefer, in the order that you prefer.

Second, many states do not have family consent statutes. If you fail to prepare a power of attorney or health care declaration and you become disabled in a state that does not have a family consent statute, decisions about your health care may be made by local doctors and courts who will have no information regarding your wishes.

 TIP While family consent statutes are useful in cases where people fail to exercise powers of attorney or health care directives, they should not be used as substitutes for such documents.

The Power of Attorney for Health Care

The primary purpose of the power of attorney for health care is to enable you to appoint an agent to make medical decisions for you if you are unable to do so. Most people appoint a family member or a close friend as their agent. The document is fully revocable and can be revised at any time. Although the prescribed form varies somewhat by state, the following (which is for use in the State of Illinois) is typical.

TIP Do not allow yourself to suffer the fate of Terri Schiavo, Nancy Cruzan or Karen Ann Quinlan. Make sure you have your attorney prepare a Durable Power of Attorney for Health Care appointing someone who you trust to make medical decisions if you are not able to do so. Although forms are sometimes supplied by hospitals, it is wise to check with an attorney before signing so you can be sure the document is signed with all requisite legal formalities and that it accurately reflects your wishes. Give copies to your doctors, your hospital, your agent, your back-up agent, and other trusted family members. You can even have your power of attorney registered at the US Living Will Registry (www.uslivingwillregistry.com). Make sure to discuss your views with your agent. Review the document periodically to make sure it accurately reflects your wishes. If your agent dies, gets sick, moves away or otherwise becomes an inappropriate choice, direct your attorney to change the document immediately.

ILLINOIS STATUTORY SHORT FORM POWER OF ATTORNEY FOR HEALTH CARE

(Notice: the purpose of this power of attorney is to give the person you designate [your "agent"] broad powers to make health care decisions for you, including power to require, consent to or withdraw any type of personal care or medical treatment for any physical or mental condition and to admit you to or discharge you from any hospital, home, or other institution. This form does not impose a duty on your agent to exercise granted powers; but when powers are exercised, your agent will have to use due care to act for your benefit and in accordance with this form and keep a record of receipts, disbursements, and significant actions taken as agent. A court can take away the powers of your agent if it finds the agent is not acting properly. You may name successor agents under this form but not co-agents, and no health care provider may be named. Unless you expressly limit the duration of this power in the manner provided below, until you revoke this power or a court acting on your behalf terminates it, your agent may exercise the powers given here throughout your lifetime, even after you become disabled. The powers you give your agent, your right to revoke those powers, and the penalties for violating the law are explained more fully in sections 4-5, 4-6, 4-9 and 4-10(b) of the Illinois "Powers of Attorney for Health Care Law" of which this form is a part. That law expressly permits the use of any different form of power of attorney you may desire. If there is anything about this form that you do not understand, you should ask a lawyer to explain it to you.)

POWER OF ATTORNEY made this_____day of

_____, _____

(month) (year)

1. I, _____

(insert name and address of principal)

hereby appoint _____

(insert name and address of agent)

379

as my attorney-in-fact (my "agent") to act for me and in my name (in any way I could act in person) to make any and all decisions for me concerning my personal care, medical treatment, hospitalization, and health care and to require, withhold, or withdraw any type of medical treatment or procedure, even though my death may ensue. My agent shall have the same access to my medical records that I have, including the right to disclose the contents to others. My agent shall also have full power to make a disposition of any part or all of my body for medical purposes, authorize an autopsy, and direct the disposition of my remains.

(The above grant of power is intended to be as broad as possible so that your agent will have authority to make any decision you could make to obtain or terminate any type of health care, including withdrawal of food and water and other life-sustaining measures, if your agent believes such action would be consistent with your intent and desires. If you wish to limit the scope of your agent's powers or prescribe special rules or limit the power to make an anatomical gift, authorize autopsy, or dispose of remains, you may do so in the following paragraphs.)

2. The powers granted above shall not include the following powers or shall be subject to the following rules or limitations (here you may include any specific limitations you deem appropriate, such as: your own definition of when life-sustaining measures should be withheld; a direction to continue food and fluids or life-sustaining treatment in all events; or instructions to refuse any specific types of treatment that are inconsistent with your religious beliefs or unacceptable to you for any other reason, such as blood transfusion, electro-convulsive therapy, amputation, psycho-surgery, voluntary admission to a mental institution, etc.):

_____

_____

_____

(The subject of life-sustaining treatment is of particular importance. For your convenience in dealing with that subject, some general statements concerning the withholding or removal of life-sustaining treatment are set forth below. If you agree with one of these statements, you may initial that statement; but do not initial more than one):

 I do not want my life to be prolonged nor do I want life-sustaining treatment to be provided or continued if my agent believes the burdens of the treatment outweigh the expected benefits. I want my agent to consider the relief of suffering, the expense involved, and the quality as well as the possible extension of my life in making decisions concerning life-sustaining treatment.

I want my life to be prolonged and I want life-sustaining treatment to be provided or continued unless I am in a coma which my attending physician believes to be irreversible, in accordance with reasonable medical standards at the time of reference. If and when I have suffered irreversible coma, I want life-sustaining treatment to be withheld or discontinued.

I want my life to be prolonged to the greatest extent possible without regard to my condition, the chances I have for recovery, or the cost of the procedures.

(This power of attorney may be amended or revoked by you in the manner provided in section 4-6 of the Illinois "Powers of Attorney for Health Care Law." Absent amendment or revocation, the authority granted in this power of attorney will become effective at the time this power is signed and will continue until your death, and beyond if anatomical gift, autopsy, or disposition of remains is authorized, unless a limitation on the beginning date or duration is made by initialing and completing either or both of the following:)

3. (   ) This power of attorney shall become effective on ___

_____

(insert a future date or event during your lifetime, such as a court determination of your disability, when you want this power to first take effect)

4. (   ) This power of attorney shall terminate on _____

_____

(insert a future date or event, such as a court determination of your disability, when you want this power to terminate prior to your death)

(If you wish to name successor agents, insert the names and addresses of such successors in the following paragraph.)

5. If any agent named by me shall die, become incompetent, resign, refuse to accept the office of agent or be unavailable, I name the following (each to act alone and successively, in the order named) as successors to such agent:

_____

_____

_____

_____

For purposes of this paragraph 5, a person shall be considered to be incompetent if and while the person is a minor or an adjudicated incompetent or disabled person or the person is unable to give prompt and intelligent consideration to health care matters, as certified by a licensed physician.

(If you wish to name your agent as guardian of your person, in the event a court decides that one should be appointed, you may, but are not required to, do so by retaining the following paragraph. The court will appoint your agent if the court finds that such appointment will serve your best interests and welfare. Strike out paragraph 6 if you do not want your agent to act as guardian.)

6. If a guardian of my person is to be appointed, I nominate the agent acting under this power of attorney as such guardian, to serve without bond or security.

7. I am fully informed as to all the contents of this form and understand the full import of this grant of powers to my agent.

Signed _____
                               (principal)

The principal has had an opportunity to read the above form and has signed the form or acknowledged his or her signature or mark on the form in my presence.

_____Residing at _____
            (witness)

(YOU MAY, BUT ARE NOT REQUIRED TO, REQUEST YOUR AGENT AND SUCCESSOR AGENTS TO PROVIDE SPECIMEN SIGNATURES BELOW. IF YOU INCLUDE SPECIMEN SIGNATURES IN THIS POWER OF ATTORNEY, YOU MUST COMPLETE THE CERTIFICATION OPPOSITE THE SIGNATURES OF THE AGENTS.)

Specimen signatures of agent (and successors).

I certify that the signatures of my agent (and successors) are correct.

_____   _____
          (agent)   (principal)

(successor agent)	(principal)

(successor agent)	(principal)

As is apparent, you appoint your agent by filling in item 1. Item 2 permits you to place certain limits on your agent's powers. Our clients usually do not fill this in because they are appointing someone whom they trust, and they do not want to restrict their agent's ability to act. Item 2 also permits you to give generalized instructions to your agent by placing your initials by one of three choices. Most people select the top choice, which gives their agent the broadest discretion. Some feel more comfortable with the middle choice.

Items 3 and 4 permit you to state a period during which the document is effective. We usually leave these blank, which makes the power effective from the date the document is signed until the date of revocation.

Item 5 is very important. It permits you to name successor agents in case the person you name in item 1 is unable to act. Remember, there is no guarantee that you won't outlive the person whom you select initially, and it is generally a good idea to have a couple of people named in reserve.

Finally, new rules that became effective in April, 2003 prevent people other than the patient or the patient's personal representative from obtaining access to the patient's medical records. There has been some speculation as to whether this provision could be interpreted to prevent an agent under a person's power of attorney from obtaining access to the person's medical records. The better view is that the agent would have access to such records because the agent should be considered the person's personal representative under this rule. However, to avoid doubt, we generally include the following language in powers of attorney that we prepare:

I hereby authorize my agent hereunder to request, receive and review any information, verbal, or written, regarding my physical or mental health, including but not limited to medical and hospital records, and I hereby consent to the disclosure of such information. I hereby expressly designate my agent hereunder as my Personal Representative under the Health Insurance Portability and Accountability Act of 1996.

As stated above, is a good idea to talk about your feelings respecting appropriate medical care with the person you select as agent. Remember, this person will be attempting to act as you would yourself. There is no better way for them to determine what you would want, than to hear it straight from you.

The Health Care Declaration

A health care declaration, also known as a living will, differs from the health-care power of attorney in that, where a durable power of attorney for health care enables you to appoint and instruct an agent, the health care declaration addresses your doctor directly. In recent years the power of attorney has become the preferred means of protecting a person's right to control medical decisions, and health care declarations have declined in usage. This is true primarily for two reasons.

First, a health care declaration is less flexible than a power of attorney for health care, because the doctor is necessarily confined to the four corners of the document. The doctor can interpret what is said in the document but lacks the flexibility to respond to events that you may not have anticipated when you wrote it. The power of attorney for health care appoints a trusted individual to act for you, and that person will presumably be able to respond to changed circumstances.

Second, a health care declaration is restricted to instructions about life-sustaining treatments. A power of attorney for health care allows your agent to give permission for various types of treatment, as well as to withhold consent for procedures designed merely to artificially extend your life.

Notwithstanding the above, however, some people like to have a health care declaration in addition to a power of attorney for health care. If you fit into this category, you will need to make sure your health care declaration is consistent with the power of attorney for health care. The following is the form of health care declaration prescribed by the state of Illinois.

This declaration is made this_____day of

_____, _____

        (month)   (year)

I,_____ being of sound mind, willfully and voluntarily make known my desires that my moment of death shall not be artificially postponed.

If at any time I should have an incurable and irreversible injury, disease, or illness judged to be a terminal condition by my attending physician who has personally examined me and has determined that my death is imminent except for death-delaying procedures, I direct that such procedures which would only prolong the dying process be withheld or withdrawn, and that I be permitted to die naturally with only the administration of medication, sustenance, or the performance of any medical procedure deemed necessary by my attending physician to provide me with comfort care.

In the absence of my ability to give directions regarding the use of such death-delaying procedures, it is my intention that this declaration shall be honored by my family and physician as the final expression of my legal right to refuse medical or surgical treatment and accept the consequences from such refusal.

Signed_____

City, County and State of Residence _____

The declarant is personally known to me and I believe him or her to be of sound mind. I saw the declarant sign the declaration in my presence, or the declarant acknowledged in my presence that he or she had signed the declaration, and I signed the declaration as a witness in the presence of the declarant. I did not sign the declarant's signature above for or at the direction of the declarant. At the date of this instrument, I am not entitled to any portion of the estate of the declarant according to the laws of intestate succession or to the best of my knowledge and belief, under any will of declarant or other instrument taking effect at declarant's death or directly financially responsible for declarant's medical care.

Witness _____

Witness _____

The Power of Attorney for Property

The power of attorney for property is designed to give someone the power to manage your property if you are unable to do so. As you may recall from Chapter Three, if you become disabled, a guardian of your estate can be appointed to protect your financial interests. However, this entails a court proceeding which can be costly, time consuming, and demeaning. The power of attorney for property is an alternative to guardianship and is designed to protect your financial interests without need of a guardianship proceeding.

For most clients, we recommend that a power of attorney for property be prepared. Clients who prepare living trusts may not need the document because such clients presumably will have transferred their property to their living trusts, which provide for successor trustees in the event of disability (see Chapter Eight). However, the property power of attorney will be useful for property that may, either intentionally or inadvertently, have been left out of the trust. For example, certain assets, such as retirement accounts, cannot be transferred to a living trust, and your spouse may need to be able to make decisions about investments or distributions if you become disabled.

The statutory form of property power of attorney for use in the state of Illinois is shown below.

ILLINOIS STATUTORY SHORT FORM POWER OF ATTORNEY FOR PROPERTY

(Notice: The purpose of this power of attorney is to give the person you designate (your "agent") broad powers to handle your property which may include powers to pledge, sell, or otherwise dispose of any real or personal property without advance notice to you or approval by you. This form does not impose a duty on your agent to exercise granted powers; but when powers are exercised, your agent will have to use due care to act for your benefit and in accordance with this form and keep a record of receipts, disbursements, and significant actions taken as agent. A court can take away the powers of your agent if it finds the agent is not acting properly. You may name successor agents under this form but not co-agents. Unless you expressly limit the duration of this power in the manner provided below, until you revoke this power or a court acting on your behalf terminates it, your agent may exercise the powers given here throughout your lifetime, even after you become disabled. The powers you give your agent are explained more fully in Section 3-4 of the Illinois "Statutory Short Form Power of Attorney for Property Law" of which this form is a part. That law expressly permits the use of any different form of power of attorney you may desire. If there is anything about this form that you do not understand, you should ask a lawyer to explain it to you.)

POWER OF ATTORNEY made this_____day of

_____, _____
         (month)   (year)

1. I, _____
             (insert name and address of principal)

hereby appoint _____
             (insert name and address of agent)

as my attorney-in-fact (my "agent") to act for me and in my name (in any way I could act in person) with respect to the following powers, as defined in Section 3-4 of the "Statutory Short Form Power of Attorney for Property Law" (including all amendments), but subject to any limitations on or additions to the specified powers inserted in paragraph 2 or 3 below:

(YOU MUST STRIKE OUT ANY ONE OR MORE OF THE FOLLOWING CATEGORIES OF POWERS YOU DO NOT WANT YOUR AGENT TO HAVE. FAILURE TO STRIKE THE TITLE OF ANY CATEGORY WILL CAUSE THE POWERS DESCRIBED IN THAT CATEGORY TO BE GRANTED TO THE AGENT. TO STRIKE OUT A CATEGORY YOU MUST DRAW A LINE THROUGH THE TITLE OF THAT CATEGORY.)

(a) Real estate transactions.

(b) Financial institution transactions.

(c) Stock and bond transactions.

(d) Tangible personal property transactions.

(e) Safe deposit box transactions.

(f) Insurance and annuity transactions.

(g) Retirement plan transactions.

(h) Social Security, employment, and military service benefits.

(i) Tax matters.

(j) Claims and litigation.

(k) Commodity and options transactions.

(l) Business operations.

(m) Borrowing transactions.

(n) Estate transactions.

(o) All other property powers and transactions.

(LIMITATIONS ON AND ADDITIONS TO THE AGENT'S POWERS MAY BE INCLUDED IN THIS POWER OF ATTORNEY IF THEY ARE SPECIFICALLY DESCRIBED BELOW.)

2. The powers granted above shall not include the following powers or shall be modified or limited in the following particulars (here you may include any specific limitations you deem appropriate, such as a prohibition or conditions on the sale of particular stock or real estate or special rules on borrowing by the agent):

_____

_____

_____

_____

3. In addition to the powers granted above, I grant my agent the following powers (here you may add any other delegable powers including, without limitation, power to make gifts, exercise powers of appointment, name or change beneficiaries or joint tenants, or revoke or amend any trust specifically referred to below):

_____

_____

_____

_____

(YOUR AGENT WILL HAVE AUTHORITY TO EMPLOY OTHER PERSONS AS NECESSARY TO ENABLE THE AGENT TO PROPERLY EXERCISE THE POWERS GRANTED IN THIS FORM, BUT YOUR AGENT WILL HAVE TO MAKE ALL DISCRETIONARY DECISIONS. IF YOU WANT TO GIVE YOUR AGENT THE RIGHT TO DELEGATE DISCRETIONARY DECISION-MAKING POWERS TO OTHERS, YOU SHOULD KEEP THE NEXT SENTENCE, OTHERWISE IT SHOULD BE STRUCK OUT.)

4. My agent shall have the right by written instrument to delegate any or all of the foregoing powers involving discretionary decision-making to any person or persons whom my agent may select, but such delegation may be amended or revoked by any agent (including any successor) named by me who is acting under this power of attorney at the time of reference.

(YOUR AGENT WILL BE ENTITLED TO REIMBURSEMENT FOR ALL REASONABLE EXPENSES INCURRED IN ACTING UNDER THIS POWER OF ATTORNEY. STRIKE OUT THE NEXT SENTENCE IF YOU DO NOT WANT YOUR AGENT TO ALSO BE ENTITLED TO REASONABLE COMPENSATION FOR SERVICES AS AGENT.)

5. My agent shall be entitled to reasonable compensation for services rendered as agent under this power of attorney.

(THIS POWER OF ATTORNEY MAY BE AMENDED OR REVOKED BY YOU AT ANY TIME AND IN ANY MANNER. ABSENT AMENDMENT OR REVOCATION, THE AUTHORITY GRANTED IN THIS POWER OF ATTORNEY WILL BECOME EFFECTIVE AT THE TIME THIS POWER IS SIGNED AND WILL CONTINUE UNTIL YOUR DEATH UNLESS A LIMITATION ON THE BEGINNING DATE OR DURATION IS MADE BY INITIALING AND COMPLETING EITHER (OR BOTH) OF THE FOLLOWING:)

6. (   ) This power of attorney shall become effective on

_____

_____

(insert a future date or event during your lifetime, such as court determination of your disability when you want this power to first take effect)

7. (   ) This power of attorney shall terminate on _____

_____

(insert a future date or event, such as court determination of your disability, when you want this power to terminate prior to your death)

(IF YOU WISH TO NAME SUCCESSOR AGENTS, INSERT THE NAME(S) AND ADDRESS(ES) OF SUCH SUCCESSOR(S) IN THE FOLLOWING PARAGRAPH.)

8. If any agent named by me shall die, become incompetent, resign or refuse to accept the office of agent, I name the following (each to act alone and successively, in the order named) as successor(s) to such agent:

_____

_____

For purposes of this paragraph 8, a person shall be considered to be incompetent if and while the person is a minor or an adjudicated incompetent or disabled person or the person is unable to give prompt and intelligent consideration to business matters, as certified by a licensed physician.

(IF YOU WISH TO NAME YOUR AGENT AS GUARDIAN OF YOUR ESTATE, IN THE EVENT A COURT DECIDES THAT

ONE SHOULD BE APPOINTED, YOU MAY, BUT ARE NOT REQUIRED TO, DO SO BY RETAINING THE FOLLOWING PARAGRAPH. THE COURT WILL APPOINT YOUR AGENT IF THE COURT FINDS THAT SUCH APPOINTMENT WILL SERVE YOUR BEST INTERESTS AND WELFARE. STRIKE OUT PARAGRAPH 9 IF YOU DO NOT WANT YOUR AGENT TO ACT AS GUARDIAN.)

9. If a guardian of my estate (my property) is to be appointed, I nominate the agent acting under this power of attorney as such guardian, to serve without bond or security.

10. I am fully informed as to all the contents of this form and understand the full import of this grant of powers to my agent.

Signed _____
(principal)

(YOU MAY, BUT ARE NOT REQUIRED TO, REQUEST YOUR AGENT AND SUCCESSOR AGENTS TO PROVIDE SPECI-MEN SIGNATURES BELOW. IF YOU INCLUDE SPECIMEN SIGNATURES IN THE POWER OF ATTORNEY, YOU MUST COMPLETE THE CERTIFICATION OPPOSITE THE SIGNA-TURES OF THE AGENTS.)

Specimen signatures of agent (and successors).

I certify that the signatures of my agent (and successors) are correct.

| _____ | _____ |
| (agent) | (principal) |

| _____ | _____ |
| (successor agent) | (principal) |

| _____ | _____ |
| (successor agent) | (principal) |

(THIS POWER OF ATTORNEY WILL NOT BE EFFECTIVE UNLESS IT IS NOTARIZED, USING THE FORM BELOW.)

State of_____)

County of_____)

The undersigned, a notary public in and for the above county and state, certifies that _____
known to me to be the same person whose name is subscribed as principal to the foregoing power of attorney, appeared before me in person and acknowledged signing and delivering the instrument as the free and voluntary act of the principal, for the uses and purposes therein set forth, and certified to the correctness of the signature(s) of the agent(s).

Dated: _____

(SEAL)_____

Notary Public

My commission expires: _____

(THE NAME AND ADDRESS OF THE PERSON PREPARING THIS FORM SHOULD BE INSERTED IF THE AGENT WILL HAVE POWER TO CONVEY ANY INTEREST IN REAL ESTATE.)

This document was prepared by:

_____

The agent is appointed by filling in item 1. Item 2 permits the person preparing the power to place certain restrictions on their agent's ability to act. Although there are exceptions, our clients usually do not add restrictions. If you want to restrict your agent, you probably should not be preparing the power.

Item 3 gives you the ability to include powers that are not provided to your agent under law. For example, because your agent is required to act for your benefit, your agent may not have the ability to spend money for the benefit of a child with a disability, unless you expressly provide that power. The following are powers that we often include on item 3:

- The power to spend money for the benefit of a child with a disability,

- The power to fund a trust for a child with a disability,

- The power to transfer property to a spouse,

- The power to make gifts to reduce anticipated estate tax.

We tend not to fill in items 6 or 7, which permit you to state when the power becomes effective. It is difficult to know what to say that would be helpful. For example, if you said the power was to be effective upon a court's determination that you were disabled, your agent would need to go to court in order to use the power. But going to court to establish disability is precisely what the power of attorney is designed to avoid. Your loved ones can do that anyway—without the power—to have themselves named as your guardian.

Alternatively, the power could be triggered by some future event, such as a doctor's determination of disability. However, it is questionable how helpful the power would be in this case. People with whom your agent might want to deal might be hesitant to rely on the power.

As a result, we tend to make the power effective upon signing. It then becomes vitally important that steps be taken to make sure it is not misused. Remember, the power gives your agent the right to do virtually anything you could do with your property. You need to make sure that you trust absolutely the person you select as agent. In many cases we hold the document for our clients, with the understanding that we will give it to their agent only after we determine that the client is disabled. Obviously, you must also be able to trust the person you ask to hold the power.

 TIP Although often useful, a power of attorney can be a dangerous document because it gives someone the ability to take action with respect to your property. There are cases where agents misuse a power of attorney and end up costing the principal many thousands of dollars. It is vitally important that you trust absolutely anyone you appoint as your agent. If you have any concern, you should not sign a power of attorney.

Conclusion

The power of attorney for health care offers you the power to appoint an agent to make health-care decisions for you if you are unable to do so. Virtually all of our clients have such documents prepared for them, though some prefer to leave the decision in the hands of their doctor.

The health care declaration gives you the power to give instructions to your doctor. For the reasons discussed earlier, it is less flexible than the power of attorney and is therefore less commonly used.

The power of attorney for property gives you the opportunity to name someone to protect your property in the event you become disabled. Most of our clients have such documents prepared for them, though some do not, preferring the court supervision inherent in a guardianship proceeding.

If you have a power of attorney for property prepared for you, you need to decide whether you want it to become effective immediately, or when triggered by some future event, such as a doctor's determination that you are disabled. For the reasons discussed above, we typically recommend that the document be effective upon signing. Some clients prefer that it not be effective until a doctor's determination of disability, despite the risk that such a provision may make the document less useful in actual practice. It is vitally important that you take steps to make sure the power is not misused—by naming as agent someone whom you trust absolutely and perhaps by asking someone other than the agent to hold the power, with instructions that it not be given to the agent unless you become disabled.

All of these documents—the power of attorney for health care, the living will, and the power of attorney for property—can be amended or revoked at any time.

CHAPTER 10

Developing Your Financial Plan

E STATE PLANNING FOR FAMILIES THAT HAVE A CHILD WITH A disability necessary involves developing financial planning strategies that will enable you to leave enough for your child to meet his or her financial needs.

Assistance is available from many sources. In many areas of the country there are private organizations that specialize in estate planning for families with children who have disabilities. Many of these organizations include financial planning as part of a package that includes counselling the family on the development of a life plan for their child and the drafting of wills and trusts. Often the cost is no more than the cost of a will from a typical estate planner.

It is also possible to obtain advice from financial planners. However, you should be sure to choose an advisor who has experience in dealing with families that have members who have disabilities, so that the planner will be familiar with the special problems that such families encounter. You may be able to get some names from local advocacy organizations or from other organizations that assist people with disabilities and their families.

Whoever you select (assuming you select anyone)—some people have faith in their own investment decisions—you should always feel free to question specific financial advice you are given. If you feel uncomfortable with a pending financial decision, talk to specialists in the field before deciding how you wish to proceed. You might check with several financial planners, comparing their ideas, before accepting any one particular approach. By doing so, you will not only receive a variety of specific financial advice but will also receive general background information likely to help you decide which types of investment are best for you.

Even after hiring an advising firm and learning to work with a particular advisor, you should not lose track of your investments. Watch how each investment opportunity responds to various economic changes. You know your own needs better than any outside advisor and, although you should carefully listen to advice, final decisions about financial matters should always be yours.

One key to a successful financial plan is accurate knowledge of where your money comes from and where it goes. Filling out the forms on the next two pages may help you visualize your current financial status and your future goals. The forms may be reproduced for your convenience.

PERSONAL INCOME STATEMENT

	CURRENT	PROJECTED 1 YEAR	PROJECTED 2 YEAR

ANNUAL INCOME

Salary & Wages

Interest & Dividends

Capital Gains

Other Income

1. Total Annual Income

EXPENSES

Housing

Debt Repayment

Insurance

Transportation

Medical

Education/Training

Food

Repairs/Utilities

Recreation

Furnishings

Gifts/Contributions

Income Taxes

Self-Employment Taxes

Social Security Taxes

Other Expenses

2. Total Annual Expense

FAMILY BALANCE SHEET

Assets

Residence $ _____

Other real estate $ _____

Bank Accounts $ _____

Retirement accounts $ _____

CD's $ _____

Annuities $ _____

Stocks, securities $ _____

Business interests $ _____

Other assets $ _____

Liabilities

Mortgage debt $ _____

Other debt $ _____

Current Net Worth $ _____
(current assets less current liabilities)

Life Insurance

Death Benefit $ _____

Premiums $ _____

Cash Value $ _____
(can be included in net worth)

Potential Inheritances $ _____

The following are some ideas that may help you build an estate large enough to enable you to meet your family's special needs. You should not assume that any of the approaches is necessarily appropriate for you. Each person's financial situation is unique and necessarily involves an investment strategy consistent with individual circumstances.

Using Insurance to Provide Security

There are two basic risks you will want to protect against: (i) the financial insecurity resulting from your death or the death of your spouse (this is typically covered with life insurance), and (ii) the financial insecurity resulting from injury or illness (this can be covered with disability insurance). While it is typical to buy life insurance, disability insurance tends to be overlooked. This is unfortunate, since at most ages your chance of becoming disabled is greater than your chance of dying.

Insurance decisions are complicated because needs are hard to assess (as you know by now) and because insurance policies (i.e., contracts and their options) are extremely complex. It is therefore important that you shop carefully and find experts who you trust and upon whom you can rely. As you are no doubt aware, several different types of life insurance are available.

Term Insurance

Term insurance offers insurance for a set period of time—one year, five years, or longer. It is the least expensive type of policy, with the cost depending on your current age and health.

Term insurance will pay benefits to the beneficiary only if the insured dies during the term of coverage. What if you become seriously ill just as your coverage expires? You would be unlikely to qualify medically for a new policy. To avoid this problem, you can pay extra to include a guaranteed renewable option.

Term insurance is a good option for young parents in good health. However, as your age increases, each new term becomes more expensive. The cost can become prohibitive for people in their 60's. To avoid this problem, you can purchase convertible term insurance, which gives you the choice of converting to a permanent type of insurance up until a stated age (such as 65), without presenting evidence about your health. Term insurance, unlike whole life or universal insurance, does not build up a cash value.

Universal and Whole Life Insurance

Although more expensive than term insurance, universal life insurance and whole life insurance offer certain advantages. Both universal life insurance and whole life insurance, unlike term insurance, cover the insured for an entire lifetime. Premiums are generally paid at a flat rate annually until the death of the insured, or over a limited period, say 10 or 20 years (*limited payment insurance*). Insurance coverage remains in effect as long as the obligations specified in the insurance contract are satisfied.

Because the premium payments made during the early years of the policy exceed the cost of insurance protection, the policy builds a cash value. In the case of universal life insurance, the rate at which the cash value grows depends on the investment returns earned by the insurance company. In the case of whole life insurance, the rate of growth is stated in the insurance contract and is guaranteed so long as the insurance company remains solvent. This cash value can be used in several ways. You can borrow it from the insurance company, often at very low interest rates, and if you fail to pay back the loan, the insurance company will deduct the outstanding amount (including interest) from the proceeds of the policy. It is also possible to use the cash value to pay premiums or to purchase new policies. Most policies even pay dividends that can also be applied to premiums. One of the unique advantages of the cash value is that it grows tax free. When the insured dies, there is generally no income tax due (on either the cash value or the death benefit). However, the death benefit is calculated in for estate-tax purposes if the policy is owned by the insured (see Chapter Nine).

Universal insurance and whole life insurance also assure parents of children who have disabilities that they will always be insured (assuming premiums are paid). Moreover, premiums for such insurance can be set at a flat rate that will not increase as the insured gets older. This is especially important during retirement years, when people are often living on a fixed income.

One method used by some of our clients to pay for a life insurance policy is to set up the premium payments so they will vanish over 8 to 10 years. This type of payment plan is often referred to as a *vanishing premium* plan. Clients who want to pay off their insurance policy before retirement often choose this type of payment plan. This enables Mom and Dad to retire worry free, not always having to worry that every dollar they spend on their retirement will deprive their child of future security.

Some of our clients even place insurance policies into irrevocable special needs trusts for a child with a disability. In essence, the trust is both the owner and the beneficiary of the policy. This enables the parents to guarantee that there will be money in trust for their child, assuming premiums are paid. If Mom or Dad go into a nursing home or get into financial difficulty, the policy is safe from creditors because the trust, and not Mom or Dad, own it. The disadvantage to this approach is that parents lose control over the policy. They can no longer use the cash value or change beneficiaries.

Joint Policies

Another form of life insurance popular among parents who have children with disabilities is commonly referred to as the *second-to-die policy* or a *joint life* policy. This policy pays a death benefit after both of the insureds, usually the mother and father, die. Because this policy pays only after two people die, the premiums are significantly less expensive.

This type of life insurance is used most frequently when there is already enough in the way of assets to provide for the surviving spouse. The joint life policy is generally used to buy less expensive insurance specifically to provide extra support for the child with a disability. The beneficiary of the policy is frequently a special needs trust created for the child with a disability. (See Chapter Six.)

It is also possible to buy joint *first-to-die policies*, which pay at the death of the first of the insureds. Because only one person has to die before the death benefit becomes due, premiums tend to be higher.

Beneficiary Designation

If you purchase life insurance, you will want to make sure that a child with a disability is not a beneficiary or owner. As you may recall, putting assets in the hands of your child could affect eligibility for Medicaid and SSI and could also result in a state claim for cost-of-care liability. You will also want to make sure that the company issuing the policy is on solid financial footing.

Frequently, you will want to make your spouse the primary beneficiary, with your children who do not have disabilities and a trust for your child who has a disability serving as contingent beneficiaries. That is, your children without disabilities and the trust for your child who has a disability would receive the insurance proceeds if your spouse dies before you. If you use a living trust as part of your estate plan, you will usually want the trust to serve as beneficiary. Sometimes you will even want your estate to serve as beneficiary. These matters were all discussed in detail previously in the book.

Medical Insurance

The cost of medical care can be a major item of expense for your child. Therefore, obtaining quality medical insurance can be an important way of providing for your child's supplemental needs. As discussed in Chapter Four, Medicaid and Medicare can help. However, these programs suffer from limitations. Medicare has various copayments and deductibles, and is not helpful for long hospital stays. Medicaid plans differ from state to state. Some states are less generous than others. Finally, some physicians do not accept Medicaid patients.

The Arc of the United States offers a special *hospital dollars* medical insurance program to its members and their dependents. This program can be a good method of supplementing government medical benefits. The program provides up to $200 a day for each day spent in a hospital for a period of up to 365 days. Arc also offers a Medicare group supplement plan to help your child with copayments and deductibles. (If your child receives both Medicaid and Medicare, this help may not be necessary because Medicaid will likely make the copayments.) Medicare supplemental policies are also available from most major insurance carriers.

If your child has a job, medical insurance may be offered as part of the compensation package. During your lifetime, coverage may be provided through your own policy. Many insurance plans cover children who have disabilities even after the children turn 19, so long as the child remains unmarried, lives at home, and is dependent on you, and so long as the insurer is properly notified. However, when your policy lapses (for example, at your death or upon retirement if your insurance is provided through your job), coverage of your child will likely cease as well.

In addition, if you change jobs you will need to make sure your child's disability does not disqualify the child from coverage. Some insurers treat certain types of disabilities as *disqualifying preexisting conditions*. Individual policies differ widely, and you will need to check with your own insurance carrier to determine the extent to which your existing policy covers your child.

It is usually difficult for a person with a disability who is not employed to secure individual coverage. Some states have medical insurance programs for people with disabilities who have been rejected by private companies. The programs provide coverage, underwritten by major insurance companies, to people with disabilities who have been rejected by private insurance companies. Because of the increased risk of coverage, however, premiums can be expensive.

Investments

Choosing a proper investment strategy is important for several reasons. In an inflationary society, the cost of goods increases over time, and an adequate investment return will be necessary to prevent erosion of savings. Moreover, it is often possible to earn investment returns that exceed the rate of inflation. This can result in an increase in your real net worth.

In this section we discuss some of the investment vehicles that are available to you, and we make some general comments to help you choose among them. The section is by no means intended to be a complete guide to investment strategies.

To begin, we limit ourselves to discussing some of the more common types of investments such as stocks, mutual funds, money markets, bonds, treasury bills, and certificates of deposit. We say nothing about more esoteric investments such as real estate, real estate investment trusts, hedge funds, limited partnerships, options, commodities, futures, precious metals, coins, and collectibles. These more esoteric investments tend to be used by experienced investors only, and such investors will have their own financial advisors or will themselves be familiar with these instruments.

Moreover, investment decisions tend to be very personal—what is right for one person is not necessarily right for another. The proper investment strategy for you will depend on such factors as your tolerance for risk, the size of your estate, and your need for liquidity.

Used properly, however, this section can be very useful to you. It can provide you some of the background information you need to talk to your financial advisor and can also give you some of the information you need to develop your own investment strategy.

Much of the information discussed below is very technical, and you may have to read it several times before you understand it. If you do not own a substantial amount of property, much of this will not pertain to your situation and you should feel free to move on to the next chapter.

Stock Investments

Many people associate financial planning primarily with investment in the stock market. This is not the only investment source, but it can be used to advantage if the investor has enough money and time to spend at it. A wise stock investor will *diversify*, spread risk over a variety of stocks. Such a diversified *stock portfolio* lowers the investor's risk because if some stocks decrease in value, others may increase, thereby creating an overall profit, or at least offsetting losses.

A small investor who can buy only a few stocks and who cannot diversify is at a disadvantage. If a particular stock drops in value, the small investor has few other stocks to offset the loss. Small-scale investment in the stock market is rarely profitable enough to justify the long hours that must be spent analyzing stock values.

Mutual Funds

As an alternative to individual stock investments, many firms offer *mutual funds*, which permit people who have similar investment goals to pool their money and, in effect, own shares in a professionally managed, diversified portfolio. The investor purchases shares in the fund (which itself owns shares in other companies) and earns income or incurs losses as the stocks owned by the fund pay dividends or increase or contract in value. Because the funds are managed by professional investors, the fund shareholder receives the benefit of professional investment advice. (The manager is generally compensated by the fund, which reduces the investor's return.)

Shareholders may cash in some or all of their shares at any time. In the case of *closed end funds*, which are actually traded on a stock exchange, such transactions are accomplished on the open market. The seller sells shares of the fund for their market price. In the case of *open end funds*, the fund itself redeems shares for their current *net asset value* (the amount of the original investment plus or minus the amount the shares have earned or lost).

There is a wide variety of mutual funds, and each operates under different investment policies. There are *load funds*, which charge investors a premium to enroll, and *no load funds*, which do not. Although the absence or presence of an enrollment premium is one factor to consider in making your selection, do not automatically assume that no load funds are preferable.

When choosing a mutual fund, you should base your selection on the fund's investment policy (what kinds of stocks or other vehicles does it buy and what criteria are used for selecting securities), the experience of the manager, the turnover rate of the portfolio (excessive trading tends to be bad), the expense ratio of the fund, the absence or presence of a load or of fees on redemption, and other qualitative factors.

You will also want to make sure that the fund manager's investment strategy is consistent with your own approach. Different funds emphasize different types of investments, and you will want to select a fund or funds that fit your own investment style. Two examples of different types of mutual funds are *growth funds* and *income funds*. Investors in a growth fund are generally looking for long-term growth. However, because a growth company's profits will be reinvested to help it expand, the growth fund investor should not expect significant dividends over the short run. On the other hand, investors in income funds seek current income, but generally cannot expect as much long-term increase in their stock prices. In accordance with this goal, managers of income funds buy stocks likely to pay high dividends.

Some funds, known as index funds, take a passive approach. These funds hold portfolios that are designed to achieve returns that match a broad market index, such as the Standard & Poors 500. They attempt to keep expenses down by keeping trading to a minimum.

One common mistake is to place undue reliance on short term performance. Several studies have indicated that past success of a fund is not a reliable indicator of future results. Consistently poor results, however, can indicate that a fund is not well managed.

A mutual-fund investor's profit depends on the value of the stock held by the fund and the dividends paid. Although investment managers study both factors to ensure wise investments, they cannot guarantee their management performance. There is always some risk of loss. Government security mutual funds provide an exception to this risk. Those who invest in a mutual fund that holds U.S. government securities take little risk with regard to repayment of principal because the securities held by the fund are backed by the United States government, though the value of the securities will decline if interest rates increase. In such a case you will suffer a loss if you are forced to sell your interest in the fund on the market or have the fund redeem it.

Information about mutual funds is available from many sources. Many discount brokerage firms will provide you with long-term information about funds that they sell. In addition, in the reference section of most libraries you can find a book called *Investment Companies* (Arthur Wiesenberger Services, New York), that will provide you with some basic information on specific funds. It will also give addresses where you may write for more information, including a prospectus. Using a resource like *Morningstar*, which rates various mutual funds, can also be helpful. *Morningstar* can be found in most public libraries.

Bonds

A bond is a certificate of creditorship that is issued to raise capital. The issuer pledges to pay interest on a bond at specified dates and to redeem it at maturity, repaying principal plus interest due. Bonds also may be sold before maturity at their current market value, which is determined by prevailing interest rates and the company's credit worthiness.

With bonds, as with stocks, it is difficult for a small investor to diversify. Diversification is important in reducing overall risk. With bonds backed by the U.S. government, such diversification is not necessary because there is no risk involved, as long as the government remains solvent. However, the higher yielding corporate bonds are only as good as the issuing corporation's ability to repay.

411

Therefore, for relative safety, a small investor interested in corporate bonds may want to consider a corporate bond mutual fund. Like the stock mutual funds discussed above, these permit the investor to participate in diversified bond portfolios. Make sure you pick the right fund—some funds invest in high yielding corporate bonds (so-called junk bonds). While these funds can be profitable, they can also be risky, and you should be careful before investing in them. Some bond funds specialize in municipal obligations, which yield a relatively safe, partially tax-free return (they're not taxed by the federal government, but often are taxed by the states and localities). Again, as with the stock funds above, you may redeem your shares at any time.

Before investing in corporate or municipal bonds, you should consider checking one or more of the rating systems, such as Moodys or Standard & Poors. These firms rate obligations based on the financial wherewithal of the issuer.

Money Market Funds

Just as mutual fund investors jointly invest in stocks or bonds, money market fund investors pool their dollars to invest in money market instruments such as commercial paper, banker's acceptances, and treasury bills. Because these money market instruments are sold at a high face value, many investors cannot invest in these instruments except through a money market fund.

Most funds require a minimum investment. The shareholder need not wait for individual instruments held by the fund to *mature* before providing investment returns to the fund-holder. Money may be withdrawn at any time. Many funds offer wire redemption services and check writing privileges. When interest rates are high, investment in a money market fund provides high returns. For these reasons, money market instruments can be attractive to investors seeking a reasonable return on liquid investments. When interest rates are low, however, money market funds are less attractive. High bracket investors will want to consider tax-exempt money market funds.

Certificates of Deposit

A certificate of deposit is an interest-bearing bank receipt payable on a specific future date. Certificate of deposit interest rates are set each Tuesday, based on the yield of treasury bills auctioned the day before.

Certificates of deposit that are issued by banks insured by the Federal Deposit Insurance Corporation (FDIC) are insured for up to $100,000 per depositor. However, only the principal is insured, not the interest. The rate of return on a certificate of deposit varies depending on its maturity date, its size, and the creditworthiness of the issuer.

Annuities

Under an annuity plan, an individual contracts to pay the issuer (typically an insurance company) either a lump sum or a series of premium payments in exchange for the company's promise to periodically pay the person a specific amount for life. In most annuity contracts, if the annuitant should die before age 65, the insurance company agrees to pay either the accumulated gross premiums or the cash value of the policy to the annuitant's beneficiary.

A major attraction of annuities is that they grow tax free. The amount invested with the insurance company is not taxed until cash is received by you, and returns can therefore be quite favorable. Annuity contracts are not insured by the government, so you should investigate carefully to make sure that any company you invest with is on solid footing.

The annuity investor or annuitant may choose among several types of contracts, including *fixed-dollar annuities, variable annuities,* and *joint* and *last survivor annuities.* Under fixed-dollar annuity contracts, the company periodically pays the annuitant a fixed sum for a definite length of time agreed to in the contract. Under this plan, the annuitant always knows how much money will be received from the insurance company for a particular period.

Under a variable plan, the annuitant receives payments that will vary. The insurance company combines money from numerous premium payments and invests it, often in common stock. The annuitant's income varies with the success of the investment, increasing and decreasing with the value of the stocks. At some investment risk, an investor in a variable plan has the chance of receiving larger annuity payments.

Under joint and last survivorship annuities, payment is made to the first annuitant at regular intervals for life. After the first annuitant dies, the second receives payment. Contracts for this type of annuity are more expensive than those covering only a single life because the insurance company would probably be making payments for a longer period of time than it would if the contract covered only one person. For those eager to provide greater security for family members who survive the family wage earner, joint and last survivorship annuities, though more expensive, should be considered.

Retirement Plans

Tax-deferred retirement plans are excellent vehicles for increasing investment return. These include 401(k) plans, Keoughs, IRAs, profit sharing plans, defined benefit pension plans, and other defined contribution pension plans. You should check with your employer or your tax advisor regarding your ability to participate.

The major benefit of a retirement plan is that earnings are not taxed until cash is actually withdrawn. Under the current rules, you generally do not have to begin taking distributions until April 1 of the year following the year you reach age seventy and a half. In addition, amounts that you contribute into such plans are generally deductible for income tax purposes. This also has the effect of increasing investment return.

The major disadvantage of a retirement plan is that you can lose liquidity. The plan may not allow you to receive distributions before you terminate employment, and the federal government will generally impose a 10 percent excise tax on distributions which you receive before age 59 and a half, in addition to regular income tax.

Developing an Investment Strategy

No single investment strategy is right for everyone. People differ in earning power, tolerance for risk, and their need for liquidity. All these differences legitimately affect investment decisions.

In deciding how to invest your money, first think about the factors and objectives that affect your finances. Consider your age, present and potential earning power, number and age of dependents, net worth, tax bracket, and other financial data. Think clearly about your family's housing needs, educational goals, and so forth.

Think about your need for liquidity. How often and how urgently would you need to draw on your invested money? A liquid *investment* is one that can be quickly and easily converted to cash. Funds invested in a nonliquid way are inaccessible to the investor for a specified period of time. For example, if you plan to buy a house soon, you should not invest potential down-payment funds in a 30-month savings certificate which cannot, without penalty, be converted to cash for at least 30 months. Instead, you could invest those funds in a highly liquid money market fund, which gives you the option of withdrawing your funds at any time. On the other hand, if you are planning for the future of a child with a disability, you might be willing to tie up your money in a long-term investment if it provides a better return.

Think about risk. How much can you afford to lose? Generally, the higher the potential return, the greater the risk. While everyone desires a large return, clearly not everyone can afford to take large risks. A young couple with a modest income, a mortgage on a new house, and small children should be more cautious with their money than a single person with a higher income and fewer obligations.

To provide some benchmark for what can be expected from various investments, it is helpful to examine historical returns—although, of course, past performance is not a guarantee of future returns. The charts at the end of the chapter may be helpful. Chart 1 depicts year-by-year returns from 1950 through 2004 of common stocks, taxable investment grade bonds, and U.S. treasury bills. As is apparent, stocks have yielded the best average returns, averaging

12 percent annually. This should be compared with a 6.1 percent return for bonds and a 4.9 percent return for treasury bills.

However, stocks have also been riskier. There have been many years in which stocks have gone down in value, sometimes by significant amounts. This suggests that stocks are a good investment for people who can invest their money for long periods of time and can afford to lose money over short-term periods but would not be good as a short-term investment or for people who would have difficulty dealing with losses.

Chart 2 is similar to Chart 1, except that it looks at historical returns over 20-year rolling periods (for example, 1950-1969, 1951-1970, and so on). Chart 2 reveals that over longer periods, there were no periods when bonds outpaced stocks. Going back further, there were four 20-year periods where bonds outpaced stocks, but all such periods included part of the Great Depression. If the future resembles the past, most long term investors would do well to keep a sizable portion of their assets in common stocks, assuming they can deal with short term losses.

As a general rule, depending on a client's earning power, assets, and tolerance for risk, we tend to prefer a diversified approach, with a certain percentage of assets invested in stocks (often through mutual funds to diversify within the market), a certain percentage invested in bonds (also through mutual funds), and a certain percentage in money markets, annuities, and certificates of deposit. We advise against trying to *time the market*—that is, guessing when the market is going up or down, due to the difficulty involved. We also discourage excessive trading to cut down on commissions.

The most important investment decision you will make is the fraction of your wealth you allocate to each of these major asset categories. There is no scientific way to determine this fraction, although historical returns can help you understand the trade-offs. A study by a University of Chicago professor some years ago estimated that 80 percent of a portfolio's return owes to the asset allocation of the portfolio; that is, asset diversification is much more important than security selection within an asset class.

One indispensable way to assess asset class risk is to examine historical results. If a planner or advisor suggests allocating, say 40 percent of your assets to stock mutual funds and 60 percent to bond mutual funds, find out how that allocation would have performed over the past twenty years.

Don't rely on unusual performance. If a particular fund did much better than the average fund or the S&P 500 over a period, don't assume the above average performance will continue. Use the average fund or some index to project performance.

Also, you should not rely exclusively on historical performance. Ask your planner or advisor what your worst case scenario is likely to be. The answer to such questions should provide a good idea of the risks the plan carries. Having said that, every plan, even annuities and CD's, carry some risk. Your job, as an investor, is to make sure the risk is reasonable in light of anticipated returns and alternative investment strategies.

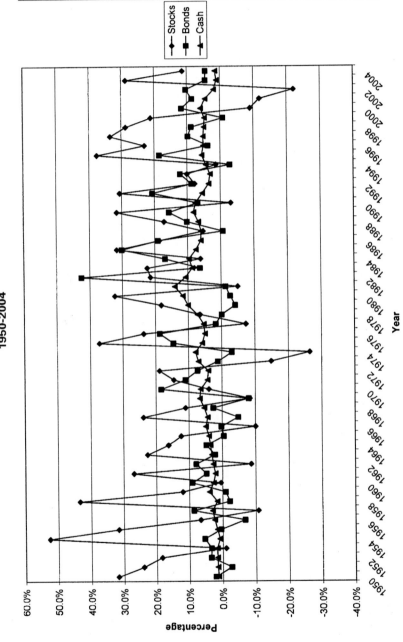

US Capital Market Results: Stocks, Bonds, T-Bills
Annual Returns
1950-2004

US Capital Market Results: Stocks, Bonds, Annualized Rate of Returns Rolling 20 Year Periods: 1950-2004

CHAPTER 11

Personal Injury Awards

O FTEN A DISABILITY RESULTS FROM AN INJURY THAT GIVES RISE to a cause of action under the law. For example, your child may have suffered a head or spinal chord injury in a car accident and the driver of another car may have been at fault, or your child may have been the victim of medical malpractice that resulted in a brain injury.

In such cases, the law gives your child the right to sue the party responsible for his or her injuries. This is accomplished by having an attorney file a lawsuit against the responsible party. The lawsuit will then either be settled by the parties, which will generally result in your child receiving a cash payment or the right to a series of payments over a period of time, or the lawsuit will proceed to trial where the court will determine whether your child is entitled to anything and, if so, how much. In most cases, this determination will be made by a jury.

Personal injury cases are often very complex. The party who is sued (the defendant) often asserts a variety of defenses relating to whether he or she was really at fault and whether the injuries of the party bringing the lawsuit (the plaintiff) are as severe as claimed. Therefore it is very important that you hire an attorney who is expert in handling personal injury cases similar to yours. Such an attorney will likely be able to respond to the defenses raised by the defendant and to present your case in the most favorable light. The attorney will also be able to advise you as to your chances of success and the type of damage award that you can expect, and to represent you in any settlement negotiations.

 TIP It is not advisable to seek to settle a personal injury claim on your own.

Moreover, most personal injury attorneys work on contingency fee arrangements. This means that you pay nothing unless the attorney successfully collects from the party who is sued. The typical arrangement is for the attorney to receive one-third of whatever is collected, in addition to reimbursement for whatever expenses are incurred in bringing the case.

Calculating the Personal Injury Award

The general theory behind the personal injury award is that the award is supposed to *compensate* the injured party for his or her injury. Of course in actual practice this theory is a fiction. No amount of money could ever compensate a quadriplegic for the loss of the use of his or her limbs.

Nevertheless, the theory is compensatory. The injured party receives an amount that the court views as adequate compensation for his or her injury. The greater the extent of the injury, the larger the award.

This is not to say that damage awards are susceptible to precise calculation. They are not, because the award is supposed to compensate the injured party for items such as pain and suffering, or reduced quality of life, which are not objectively determinable.

Moreover, if the defendant's conduct is considered particularly egregious, the jury may award *punitive* damages in addition to *compensatory* damages. Punitive damages are damages awarded to the injured party in excess of the amount a jury determines to be sufficient compensation for the injury. They are awarded to punish the defendant for bad conduct.

Example One

Fred purchases an automobile from a large manufacturer. The manufacturer becomes aware that, due to negligence on the part of an inspector, a possibility exists that a small number of cars that were shipped from a particular plant may have contained a defective bolt that is critical to the braking system. The plant foreman has found three defective bolts out of the thousand that remain on the shop floor and is unsure whether any cars containing defective bolts were actually shipped.

Although the manufacturer is aware of the potential danger, the manufacturer decides not to order a recall of cars shipped from the plant or to take any other remedial action. The manufacturer is unsure whether any defective cars were shipped and, even if some defective cars were shipped, the number is likely to be relatively small— because nine hundred and ninety seven out of the thousand bolts that were inspected had no defect. The manufacturer is also unsure whether any harm will result even if defective cars were shipped because the bolt may never give way. Finally, the manufacturer is concerned about the potential cost and adverse publicity resulting from a recall.

Unfortunately, the automobile that Fred purchases is defective. The bolt gives way while Fred is driving on the highway. The brakes fail, and Fred is severely injured.

The jury determines that Fred is entitled to $1 million as compensation for items such as medical expenses, pain and suffering, and lost wages resulting from a prolonged absence from work. The jury also may decide to award punitive damages, and the amount may be quite substantial, to punish the manufacturer for failing to order a recall when it had evidence of the possibility that defective automobiles were shipped.

As is apparent, the amount that Fred should receive is not susceptible to precise calculation. It is not possible to determine how to adequately compensate Fred for his pain and suffering, or how to punish the manufacturer for its decision to ignore a known risk. Even medical expenses remain an unknown. Fred may have future medical expenses as a result of his injury.

How much should Fred receive? How much should a person with a brain injury be paid as compensation for the reduced quality of life resulting from his or her injury? What is the proper amount to pay someone who has mental retardation as a result of medical malpractice?

In practice, the answer depends on the extent of the injury and the sense of outrage that the jury feels over the defendant's conduct. In cases of severe injury, attorneys will sometimes have a day in the life of the injured party videotaped to enable the jury to experience firsthand the devastating consequences of the injury.

Another factor that is often relevant is the financial wherewithal of the defendant. While a punitive damage award of one hundred thousand dollars might be sufficient to *send a message* to an individual whose conduct is considered particularly venal, such an award might not be adequate to punish a large company.

The following are some of the elements to be considered in determining the adequacy of a settlement offer.

Liability: Is it clear that the defendant was at fault, or is it possible an injury resulted from an accident that was no one's fault? If a jury finds that there was no fault, the injured party will receive nothing.

Bad faith: Was the defendant's conduct merely negligent, or was it something more? Was there an element of intentionality or recklessness that could cause a jury to award punitive damages? The presence of intentionality or recklessness will likely cause a jury to award higher compensatory damages as well, particularly in regard to items such as pain and suffering and diminished life-style which are not objectively determinable.

Pain and suffering: Obviously, the more severe the injury, the higher the award.

Diminished life-style: What was the injured person's life like before the injury? What will it be like afterwards?

Lost wages: How much work was missed as a result of the injury? What was the injured person's salary and what was the salary likely to be in the future? Is work still possible after the injury and at what salary? Is retraining possible? Has there been a loss of fringe benefits such as medical insurance or pension coverage? Note that reduced earnings will generally cause a reduction in pension benefits as well.

Medical expenses: How much was spent on doctors and hospitals? Is the injury likely to result in future medical expenses? If so, what is the expected cost? (Note that the opinion of experts is helpful here.)

Future needs: If the injury is sufficiently severe that substantial lifetime care will be required, what is the projected cost?

The chart in Chapter Five relating to the calculation of supplementary care costs, which is repeated here for your convenience, is helpful to this calculation. You should note, however, that the projected future needs should not serve as a cap on the damages you request because the calculation does not take account of items such as pain and suffering or reduced quality of life. However, information as to the future needs of a person who is injured severely is relevant in determining the adequacy of a settlement offer.

PROJECTED CARE COSTS PER MONTH
(Current Dollars)

$ _____**Housing**

_____Rent/Month

_____Utilities

_____Maintenance

_____Cleaning items

_____Laundry costs

_____Other

$ _____**Care Assistance**

_____Live-in

_____Respite

_____Custodial

_____Guardianship/Advocacy
(approx. $50-$75 per hr.)

_____Other

$ _____**Food**

_____Meals, snacks-home

_____Outside of home

_____Special foods/
gastric tube

_____Other

$ _____**Clothing**

$ _____**Furniture**

$ _____**Medical/Dental Care**

_____General medical/
Dental visits

_____Therapy

_____Nursing services

_____Meals of attendants

_____Evaluations

_____Transportation

_____Medications

_____Other

$ _____**Insurance**

_____Medical/Dental

_____Burial

_____Car

_____Housing/Rental

_____Other

$ _____**Automobile**

_____Payments

_____Gas, oil, maintenance

_____Other

$ _____ **Recreation**

_____Sports

_____Special Olympics

_____Spectator sports

_____Vacations

_____TV/VCR

_____Summer camp

_____Transportation costs

_____Other

$ _____**Education, Training, Etc.**

_____Transportation

_____Fees

_____Books

_____Other

$ _____**Employment**

_____Transportation

_____Workshop fees

_____Attendant

_____Training

_____Other

$ _____**Personal Needs**

_____Haircuts, beauty shop

_____Telephone

_____Cigarettes

_____Church/Temple expenses

_____Hobbies

_____Books, magazines, etc.

_____Allowance

_____Other

$ _____**Special Equipment**

_____Environmental control

_____Elevator

_____Repair of equipment

_____Computer

_____Audio books

_____Ramp

_____Guide dog/other

_____Special animals

_____Technical instruction

_____Wheelchair

_____Other

$ _____**Emergency Reserve**

TOTAL PROJECTED EXPENSES

$_____

After calculating the total required expenses, you are ready to calculate the minimum settlement required to fund those expenses. The calculations are complex, and you may need an accountant, a financial planner, or a specialist in settlement planning to assist you. The considerations are identical to the factors considered in Chapter Five, and the calculations are identical as well. In general, you will need to build in an inflation factor to account for cost increases over time, and a return rate to account for the investment income that the settlement funds will generate. You will then need to account for taxes attributable to the investment income and possibly a fee to compensate a financial planner for investment services. It may also be advisable to build in a reserve for unanticipated emergency expenses.

Example Two
Fred is age 15 when he suffers a brain injury from a car accident. The driver of the other vehicle is clearly at fault. It is determined that Fred will have a normal life expectancy despite his injury. Thus, utilizing Chart 3 from Chapter Five, Fred's life expectancy is estimated at an additional 64 years. With the help of a financial planner, Fred's parents complete the Projected Care Costs chart on the previous pages of this chapter and determine that Fred will need $50,000 per year to fund expenses. If we assume earnings at 4% annually (after investment management fees), a 2.5% inflation rate and a 20% tax rate, Fred will require approximately $2.5 million. This is determined from the chart in Appendix 3, which shows that Fred will need $50,445 to fund $1,000 in annual expenses if we assume 4% annual earnings, 2.5% inflation and a 20% tax rate. Multiplying $50,445 by fifty yields approximately $2.5 million. Note that this figure does not include Fred's initial medical expense, actual damages for pain and suffering and diminished lifestyle, or possible punitive damages if the driver's conduct was particularly reckless.

Settlement Planning and Government Benefits— SSI and Medicaid

As you no doubt recall, certain government benefit programs, principally Medicaid and SSI, have strict income and resource limits. A person who receives a substantial settlement from a personal injury award will fail to qualify because the person will exceed the resource limitation ($2,000 if single, $3,000 if married). Having the settlement paid directly into the type of supplemental needs trust described in Chapter Six does not solve the problem because the trust will be considered a *self-settled trust* and therefore will be considered a resource for SSI and Medicaid purposes. The Policy Operations Manual (POMS Section SI 1120.201) states:

> In the case of a revocable trust established by the individual, the entire corpus of the trust is a resource to the individual.
>
> ...
>
> In determining whether an irrevocable trust established by an individual is a resource, we must consider how payments from the trust can be made. If payments from the trust could be made to or for the benefit of the individual or individual's spouse, the portion of the trust from which payment could be made that is attributable to the individual is a resource.
>
> ...
>
> An individual is considered to have established a trust if any assets of the individual (or spouse) (regardless of how little) were transferred to a trust other than by a will.

Example Three

Fred is severely injured and receives a settlement of $150,000. Assuming all other requirements are satisfied, Fred will qualify for Medicaid and SSI after the $150,000 is spent down to $2,000. Fred cannot accelerate the qualification process by directing that the $150,000 be paid into the type of supplemental needs trust described in Chapter Six.

There are, however, two types of trusts that can receive proceeds from the settlement of a personal injury claim without affecting eligibility for SSI or Medicaid. These trusts, which were discussed in Chapter Seven, are known as payback trusts and pooled income payback trusts. The Policy Operations Manual (POMS Section SI 1120.203) describes payback trusts as follows:

The resource counting provisions of the new trust statute do not apply to a trust:

- Which contains the assets of an individual under age 65 and who is disabled; and

- Which is established for the benefit of such individual by a parent, grandparent, legal guardian or a court; and

- Which provides that the State will receive all amounts remaining in the trust upon the death of the individual up to an amount equal to the total medical assistance paid on behalf of the individual under a State Medicaid plan.

Pooled income payback trusts are described as follows (POMS Section SI 1120.203):

The provisions of the SSI trust statute do not apply to a trust containing the assets of a disabled individual that meets the following conditions:

- The pooled trust is established and maintained by a nonprofit association;

- Separate accounts are maintained for each beneficiary, but assets are pooled for investing and management purposes;

- Accounts are established solely for the benefit of the disabled individual;

- The account in the trust is established by the individual, a parent, grandparent, legal guardian, or a court; and

- The trust provides that to the extent any amounts remaining in the beneficiary's account upon the death of the beneficiary are not retained by the trust, the trust will pay to the State the amount remaining up to an amount equal to the total amount of medical assistance paid on behalf of the beneficiary under a State Medicaid plan.

Example Four

Fred is severely injured and receives a settlement of $150,000. The settlement is paid directly into a payback trust that provides that the trust is to be used for Fred's benefit. The trust provides that the State will receive all amounts remaining in the trust upon Fred's death up to an amount equal to the total medical assistance paid on behalf of Fred under the State's Medicaid plan. The trust would need to be established by Fred's parents, grandparents, legal guardian or by a court, and not by Fred, because the Social Security rules do not allow for the trust to be created by the person with a disability.

The trust does not affect Fred's eligibility for SSI or Medicaid. Although the trust will be required to *payback* the government if it has sufficient assets when Fred dies, payback will not be required if the property in the trust is spent for Fred during his life. One strategy would be for Fred's parents to spend the money in Fred's payback trust for Fred's benefit before other family resources are spent for Fred. It is important that Fred's family keep good records of trust expenditures, in case the government raises questions in the future.

Payback trusts can even be used after a settlement has already been received in order to qualify the recipient for SSI and Medicaid.

Example Five
Fred is severely injured and receives a settlement of $150,000. As described in Example 3, he is not eligible for SSI and Medicaid because he has more than $2,000 in resources. Assuming all other requirements are satisfied, Fred can qualify for Medicaid and SSI by transferring the $150,000 into a payback trust as described in Example 4. If Fred lacks sufficient mental capacity, court approval will likely be needed to effect the transfer. These issues are discussed in Chapter Seven.

One issue that frequently arises in the case of personal injury settlements and payback trusts relates to expenses that are paid by Medicaid prior to the settlement. As discussed in Chapter Four, Federal law requires that states provide for recovery of Medicaid costs if a third party is liable. This is known as the *Medicaid lien*. The issue is whether the Medicaid lien has to be satisfied before a payback trust is funded. In many states, the issue has not yet been addressed.

Example Six
Fred is severely injured and receives a settlement of $150,000, which is to be paid directly into a payback trust. Prior to funding of the trust, Medicaid has paid $50,000 in medical expenses on Fred's

behalf. The issue is whether the entire $150,000 can be paid into the payback trust, or whether $50,000 has to be paid to Medicaid before the payback trust is funded.

 TIP Before accepting a settlement, make sure you are aware of whether Medicaid has a lien on any of the settlement proceeds. If it does, make sure you are aware of how the lien operates in your state. In some states, for example, it is possible to reduce the Medicaid lien as a result of attorney fees.

Example Seven

Fred is injured in an automobile accident and receives a settlement of $150,000. Legal expenses are $60,000. Prior to the settlement, Medicaid has paid $50,000 in medical expenses. Because Medicaid is entitled to one third of the settlement, many states permit Fred to allocate one third of the legal expenses, or $20,000, to Medicaid's share of the settlement. This permits Fred to reduce the Medicaid lien from $50,000 to $30,000, thus increasing the amount of money available for Fred's payback trust.

Medicaid planning for settlement proceeds creates an interesting settlement dynamic. Defense attorneys will sometimes argue for reduced damages on the grounds that the injured person's expenses will not be as great as anticipated due to the ability to structure the settlement so that the injured person qualifies for Medicaid. Sometimes settlement can be reached where not otherwise possible because the *gap* between what the defendant is willing to pay and what the injured person is willing to take can be *bridged* by appropriate Medicaid planning.

Example Eight

Fred is age 15 when he suffers a brain injury from a car accident. The driver of the other vehicle is clearly at fault. It is determined that Fred will have a normal life expectancy despite his injury. Thus, utilizing Chart 3 from Chapter Five, Fred's life expectancy is estimated at an additional 64 years. With the help of a financial planner, Fred's parents complete the Projected Care Costs chart on the previous pages of this chapter and determine that Fred will need $50,000 per year to fund expenses. If we assume earnings at 4% annually (after investment management fees), a 2.5% inflation rate and a 20% tax rate, Fred will require approximately $2.5 million. This is determined from the chart in Appendix 3, which shows that Fred will need $50,445 to fund $1,000 in annual expenses if we assume 4% annual earnings, 2.5% inflation and a 20% tax rate. Multiplying $50,445 by fifty yields approximately $2.5 million.

Taking into account Fred's pain and suffering and his diminished lifestyle, Fred's parents are willing to accept a settlement of $4M. After protracted negotiation, the driver's insurance company will not go above $3 million, arguing that Fred's expenses will be substantially less than $50,000 per year if the settlement is structured so that Fred becomes eligible for Medicaid. Fred's parents may be willing to accept $3 million if Medicaid is available.

 TIP If you accept a settlement based on the availability of Medicaid benefits, try to negotiate for increased payment if Medicaid benefits are reduced or become unavailable in the future.

Settlement Planning and Government Benefits— SSDI and Medicare

Payback trusts are not relevant to SSDI or Medicare because SSDI and Medicare are not needs based. You either qualify or you do not, without regard to available resources. SSDI and Medicare can, however, be impacted by a settlement. The rules differ depending on whether the settlement relates to a worker's compensation claim or a personal injury claim.

Worker's Compensation

In general, the workers compensation system is designed to provide benefits for workers who are injured on the job. If the injured worker is unable to work, he or she is entitled to disability benefits based on the worker's wages; in most states, two-thirds of lost wages. The worker is also entitled to life long medical benefits for costs incurred as a result of the injury. Workers compensation benefits may also be available to a worker's family if the work related injury results in death. Typically benefits are available to the worker's spouse, children up to age 18 (25 if the child is a student), and children with disabilities for life (some states limit the benefit period for children with disabilities to a specified period such as twenty years).

In many cases, people who receive workers compensation benefits also receive SSDI, which also provides benefits for workers with disabilities. Under a special rule known as the *80 percent rule*, combined benefits under SSDI (including family benefits) and state workers compensation programs cannot exceed 80 percent of the person's highest average monthly earnings in the five years preceding the onset of disability. Workers compensation awards that are allocated to medical expenses are not considered for purposes of this rule.

Example Nine

Julie is injured on the job and receives worker's compensation benefits of $1,000 per month in addition to coverage for medical expenses. Based on her work record, Julie is also entitled to SSDI benefits of $800 per month. Julie's highest average earnings in the five years preceding the onset of disability is $2,000 per month. Julie's combined worker's compensation and SSDI benefits cannot exceed $1,600 per month (80% of $2,000). Accordingly, Julie's SSDI benefits will be reduced to $600 per month.

As described in Chapter Four, people who are eligible for SSDI for two years also become eligible for Medicare. Thus, many injured workers are entitled to Medicare benefits. Medicare is not available, however, for medical expenses covered by workers compensation recoveries.

Example Ten

Julie is injured on the job and receives worker's compensation benefits of $1,000 per month. The worker's compensation insurance carrier also retains liability for medical costs incurred as a result of the injury. Medicare need not cover such costs since they are covered by the worker's compensation insurance carrier.

Sometimes a workers compensation case will settle for a fixed dollar amount. In such cases, if the recipient is or may soon become eligible for Medicare, it is important to allocate the settlement amount between medical expenses (including future medical expenses) and lost wages. The portion of the settlement allocated to future medical expenses is referred to as the *Medicare Set Aside*, and is often placed in a trust that is referred to as a *Medicare Set Aside Trust*. Medicare will pay for injury related medical expenses only after the *Medicare Set Aside* amount is spent on such expenses.

The allocation must be reasonable because Medicare will challenge allocations that unreasonably attempt to shift medical expenses over to Medicare. Reasonableness is generally established based on a physician's report or medical history. It is not necessary to allocate an amount equal to all anticipated future medical expenses to the Medicare Set Aside. It is just necessary to be reasonable, and compromise with Medicare is generally possible.

Example Eleven

Fred is injured on the job and receives a lump sum payment of $300,000. If Fred fails to allocate the payment between medical expenses and lost wages, Medicare may allocate the entire settlement to medical expenses. The effect would be to deny Medicare benefits until the entire $300,000 was spent on injury related medical expenses.

If Fred *unreasonably* allocates too little to medical expenses in the hopes that Medicare will begin paying after a minimal amount is paid for medical expenses, Medicare will likely disregard the allocation. For example, if it is clear that future medical expenses are going to exceed $100,000, and Fred allocates just $10,000 to medical expenses in the hope of receiving Medicare reimbursement after spending $10,000 on injury related medical expenses, the allocation likely will not be respected.

If Fred allocates a reasonable amount to medical expenses, perhaps based on past medical bills and a doctor's report, the allocation will likely be respected and Medicare will begin coverage after the portion of the settlement allocated to medical expenses is spent on injury related medical expenses. For example, if Fred allocates $80,000 to future medical expenses based on a realistic assessment, he likely will be entitled to Medicare reimbursement for expenses in excess of $80,000 (assuming he otherwise qualified for Medicare and subject to co-payments and deductibles).

For the purposes of possible SSDI reduction, the 80 percent rule would be applied based on the portion of the settlement allocated to lost wages on a prorated basis. For example, if Fred legitimately allocates $220,000 to lost wages, the 80% rule will be applied by prorating the $220,000, presumably over the period between the date of the injury and normal retirement age.

TIP In many instances, Medicare must approve workers compensation settlements in advance if you are to be sure that allocations will be respected. Advance approval is required where (i) the recipient is already on Medicare, or (ii) the recipient can reasonably be expected to go on Medicare within 30 months and the settlement exceeds $250,000. Settlements are submitted for approval to the Centers for Medicare and Medicaid Services (CMS). Make sure that you comply with the Medicare approval rules.

Personal Injury

A personal injury claim is a lawsuit for damages resulting from an injury other than a lawsuit against an employer as a result of an injury incurred on the job. The effect of a settlement of a personal injury claim on SSDI and Medicare is different than the effect of a settlement of a worker's compensation claim.

First, damages resulting from a personal injury claim do not affect future payments under SSDI. Second, although Medicare is entitled to reimbursement of costs incurred prior to the settlement, it is unclear how settlement will affect Medicare's responsibility in connection with future costs.

Unlike in the case of Workers Compensation settlements, in the case of personal injury settlements, CMS has no formal process for reviewing and approving Medicare set-aside arrangements. However, even though no formal process exists, CMS has stated that there is an obligation to inform CMS when future medical expenses were a consideration in reaching the liability settlement, judgment, or award as well as any instances where a settlement, judgment, or award specifically provides for medical expenses. CMS has also stated that settlement funds that were intended to compensate for future medical expenses should be spent for that purpose before any claims related to the settlement, judgment or award are submitted to Medicare for payment.

In calculating Medicare's reimbursement for costs incurred prior to the injury, there is a reduction based on attorney fees incurred by the injured party.

Example Twelve

Fred is injured in an automobile accident and receives a settlement of $150,000. Attorney fees and costs aggregate $50,000. Prior to the settlement, Medicare has paid $60,000 in medical expenses on Fred's behalf. Medicare is entitled to a reimbursement of $40,000. The calculation is as follows:

- One third of the settlement ($150,000 divided by $50,000) goes to attorney fees and costs

- Medicare's proportionate share of attorney fees and costs is $20,000 (one third of Medicare's $60,000 payout)

- Medicare receives $40,000 ($60,000 minus $20,000)

 TIP Make sure you are aware of any Medicare reimbursement rights before accepting any settlement.

Structured Settlements

The *structured settlement* has become an increasingly popular method of settling personal injury claims in the case of severe injuries where the injured party is expected to require substantial care throughout his or her life.

Talk to any personal injury attorney, and you will be told horror stories of clients who dissipated substantial settlements on luxury items, and were later unable to pay for the basic necessities of life. A structured settlement is designed to deal with this problem by matching damage awards to the injured party's needs. Instead of receiving a single lump sum settlement, the injured party receives a series of payments over his or her lifetime that is carefully structured to meet his or her financial needs.

Example Thirteen

Linda suffers severe injuries when the car she is driving collides with a train. Apparently the gate at the crossing was defective, and Linda's car was struck by an oncoming train. Although Linda has a loving family, her parents are not experienced in dealing with substantial sums of money and they fear that they could make mistakes if they receive a large settlement amount. This is particularly troubling because it is anticipated that Linda will need to live on her settlement for the rest of her life.

Linda's attorney hires a structured settlement specialist who determines that Linda will need $50,000 per year in today's dollars to satisfy ongoing medical and personal needs. Instead of accepting a single lump sum payment, Linda, through her parents and attorney, agrees to release her claim against the driver in exchange for an initial payment of $500,000 to pay Linda's medical expenses and attorney fees, and a series of payments that begin at $50,000 in the year of the settlement and increase by 3 percent each year (to account for inflation) for the rest of Linda's life.

If it is possible to determine that Linda will have extraordinary needs at some point in the future, the settlement can be structured so that Linda receives larger payments in those years. For example, Linda may have a young child who is expected to begin college in five years. In such a case it would be possible to structure the settlement so that Linda receives a larger cash payment at that time. Similarly, Linda may need a special wheelchair or a customized van, and it is possible to structure the settlement so that larger payments can be made when it is anticipated that a new wheelchair or van will be needed, or she may need vocational rehabilitation, and larger payments can be made in those years.

Careful attention to any rehabilitation report that may have been prepared on Linda's behalf can be helpful in anticipating Linda's needs. It can also be helpful to consult medical experts as well as structured settlement specialists to project future medical needs. For example, it may be possible to predict that a young child who is injured will require reconstructive surgery at a definite point in the future.

Structuring the Settlement

A structured settlement is an agreement between the defendant and an injured party, whereby the injured party agrees to accept a series of payments over a period of time, often for life, in lieu of a single settlement amount. Often the structured settlement will include an initial up front payment to cover current bills in addition to the future payments.

In most cases the injured party will not want to rely on the promise of the defendant to make the future payments. The payments may continue for a long period of time, and the defendant may have financial difficulties and become unable to make the payments in the future.

As a result, several methods have been developed to reduce the risk of default. In the typical case, the defendant will pay a structured settlement company to assume the obligation to pay the injured person. The *structured settlement company* then purchases an *annuity* (see Chapter Eleven) from a life insurance company to fund the obligation. In many cases the insurance company will own the structured settlement company. In some cases the defendant will purchase the annuity directly and a structured settlement company will not be involved.

Example Fourteen

Linda suffers severe brain trauma as a result of an automobile accident. A structured settlement is agreed to, the terms of which provide that Linda is to receive an initial payment of $500,000 to fund her medical expenses and attorney fees, and a series of payments that begin at $50,000 in the year of the settlement and increase by 3 percent each year (to account for inflation) for the rest of Linda's life.

Under the terms of the settlement, the defendant pays a structured settlement company to assume its obligation to make future payments to Linda. The structured settlement company purchases an annuity that pays Linda $50,000 in the year of the settlement, with payments increasing by 3 percent each year during Linda's life. The initial $500,000 is paid by the defendant to Linda directly. If it is possible to determine that Linda will have extraordinary needs at some point in the future, the annuity can be structured so that Linda receives larger payments in those years.

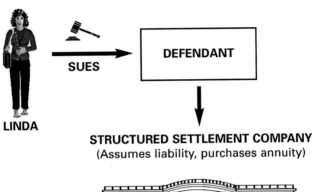

LINDA

STRUCTURED SETTLEMENT COMPANY
(Assumes liability, purchases annuity)

Sometimes United States Treasury Obligations, as opposed to annuities, are used to reduce the default risk. Under such an approach the defendant purchases United States Treasury Obligations which are held by a bank in a custodial account, and the injured party is given a security interest. This means that the injured party gets the right to take possession of the Treasury Obligations if the defendant misses a payment. Alternatively, the Treasury Obligations can be held in trust.

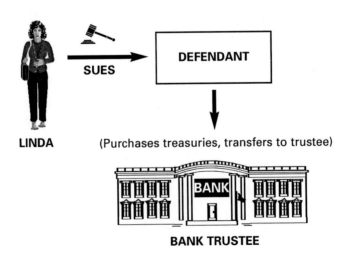

LINDA   (Purchases treasuries, transfers to trustee)

BANK TRUSTEE

Treasury Obligations offer greater security than annuities because it is possible that the insurance company selling the annuity will go bankrupt and will be unable to make the required payments. The United States government is less likely to go bankrupt.

However, Treasury Obligations are less flexible. While it is possible to structure an annuity so that payments are made for the life of the injured party, Treasury Obligations have maximum terms of 30 years.

What are the advantages of a structured settlement approach?

The primary advantage has already been discussed. The structured settlement gives the injured party the right to receive a guaranteed income stream for his or her entire life that cannot be outlived or dissipated prematurely. This is to be contrasted with a single lump sum payment that can be spent unwisely or invested poorly. The value of this benefit depends at least partly on the financial sophistication of the injured person and his or her family.

Example Fifteen

Linda suffers from an intellectual disability as a result of oxygen deprivation during delivery. The hospital and doctors are sued, and settlement discussions commence. Linda's parents are not experienced in financial matters and her attorney suggests a structured settlement, so Linda will have a guaranteed income stream for her life. While it would be possible for Linda's parents to get advice from qualified experts to make up for their lack of expertise, there is a chance that they could hire the wrong person and get poor advice, or they could make unwise expenditures. In addition, substantial management fees could be incurred.

If Linda's parents were sophisticated investors with a great deal of financial discipline, the benefit of a structured settlement would be reduced because Linda's parents would be less likely to dissipate her settlement by purchasing unnecessary luxury items or investing unwisely. However, even in such a case, Linda's parents may not wish to risk her future on their expertise, and they may instead prefer the security of a structured settlement approach.

443

Courts will often appoint a guardian for a person with a disability if the person receives a substantial settlement or judgment as a result of an injury. This is another method of protecting against mismanagement of the person's funds. Guardianship is discussed in Chapter Three.

Structured settlements offer income tax benefits as well. The tax law generally provides that damages received in a personal injury case are not subject to income tax. The same is true of personal injury settlements. However, earnings from investment of personal injury awards are subject to tax, unless the award is invested in tax-exempt vehicles such as municipal bonds.

Example Sixteen

John suffers brain trauma as a result of a motorcycle accident in which the other driver is clearly at fault. He accepts a cash settlement of $500,000 which is invested in an annuity that pays John $40,000 per year for 20 years plus $500,000 at the end of 20 years. The $500,000 that John receives in settlement of his injury is not subject to tax. However, John's earnings as a result of investing in the annuity are subject to tax. If we assume that John is in the 25 percent tax bracket, the $800,000 in earnings ($40,000 per year for 20 years) yield a total tax of $200,000. (For ease of explanation, we ignore the effect of graduated rates and other deductions.)

Suppose that instead of settling for $500,000 and investing the proceeds in an annuity, John agrees to a structured settlement that is identical from an economic perspective. That is, the defendant agrees to pay John $40,000 per year for 20 years and $500,000 at the end of 20 years. The defendant would presumably secure its obligation to John by purchasing the same annuity that John was going to buy.

Although John's situation is unchanged economically, his tax position improves substantially. Instead of receiving $500,000 tax free as a result of his injury and $800,000 in taxable investment earnings, John receives the entire $1,300,000 in compromise of his personal injury claim. As a result, no tax is owing. This results in a savings of $200,000 if John is in the 25 percent tax bracket. In effect, the government pays part of the settlement.

Of course, John could take the $500,000 and receive tax free treatment on the earnings by investing in a municipal bond. However, the return on tax-exempt bonds is generally two to four percent less than the return on an annuity. John could perhaps take the $500,000 and invest in a taxable instrument that would have a higher return than an annuity, maybe even enough to offset the tax advantage of the structured settlement. However, this tends not to occur very often.

One point to keep in mind. The tax benefit of the structured settlement approach depends upon John's tax bracket. If John has substantial medical expenses each year, the benefit of a structured settlement will be reduced because John's medical expenses will be deductible. In addition, as discussed in Chapter Thirteen, the definition of medical expense is quite expansive, and includes items such as nursing care.

Example Seventeen

John suffers brain trauma as a result of a motorcycle accident in which the other driver is clearly at fault. He accepts a cash settlement of $500,000 which is invested in an annuity that pays John $40,000 per year for 20 years plus $500,000 at the end of 20 years. John's medical expenses are $20,000 per year.

The $500,000 that John receives in settlement of his injury is not subject to tax. However, John's earnings as a result of investing in the annuity are subject to tax. If we assume that John is in the 25 percent tax bracket, the $400,000 in earnings ($40,000 in investment income less $20,000 in medical expenses times 20 years) yield a total tax of $100,000.

Thus, the tax benefit of a structured settlement is reduced to $100,000 if John is in the 25 percent bracket. This is because earnings on a lump sum settlement over 20 years result in tax of those amounts while, as discussed in Example Sixteen, the proceeds from a structured settlement are entirely tax free.

If John's annual medical expenses are $40,000 or more, a structured settlement has no tax advantage because the lump sum approach results in no tax. John has $40,000 of gross earnings per year, but no tax is owing after medical expenses and personal exemptions are deducted.

Are there any disadvantages to a structured settlement?

The most obvious is the risk of nonpayment. As stated previously, a structured settlement is an agreement between the defendant and an injured party, whereby the injured party agrees to accept a series of payments over a period of time, often for life, in lieu of a single settlement amount. As such, there is a possibility that the defendant will be unable to pay.

There are, however, a number of methods of reducing the nonpayment risk and several of these methods have already been discussed. In the typical case, the defendant will pay a structured settlement company to assume its payment obligation. The structured settlement company is often owned by an insurance company and has typically been established specifically to act as payer on personal injury claims. The structured settlement company will then purchase an annuity from the insurance company with money provided by the defendant in order to fund its payment obligation. The insurance company will also typically guarantee payment. This means that the insurance company will pay the injured party directly if the structured settlement company does not.

Obviously, it is very important that the injured party and his or her attorney be confident of the insurance company's financial wherewithal. A.M. Best Company publishes periodic reports that rate the financial strength of various insurance companies. Some structured settlement specialists attempt to reduce the risk by using more than one insurance company. In addition, most states have guarantee funds to guarantee payment of annuity contracts in the event that an insurance company becomes insolvent. The funds typically limit their liability to $100,000 in liability per claim. Finally, as discussed previously, the nonpayment risk can be reduced even further by funding the structured settlement with treasury bills.

A second disadvantage to a structured settlement is inflexibility. Once a structured settlement is agreed to, it is set in stone, and there is little flexibility to respond to changed circumstances. For example, if you agree to a structured settlement of $30,000 per year for life, you cannot later change your mind if you decide you need more money shortly after the injury and less later. As discussed in Example Thirteen, it is possible to try and anticipate future needs and structure the settlement so payments match needs. However, it may not be possible to accurately forecast future needs and, once agreed to, a structured settlement cannot be changed.

Example Eighteen

Linda suffers severe brain trauma as a result of an automobile accident. A structured settlement is agreed to, the terms of which provide that Linda is to receive an initial payment of $500,000 to fund her medical expenses and attorney fees, and a series of payments that begin at $50,000 in the year of the settlement and increase by 3 percent each year (to account for inflation) for the rest of Linda's life.

Unfortunately, Linda develops additional medical problems and the $50,000 proves insufficient. Had Linda accepted a cash settlement, she might have had sufficient resources to fund the emergency.

TIP There are companies that are willing to convert structured settlements to cash by purchasing the income stream. Be very leery of such transactions. In general, the transactions are very good for the company buying the income stream, but not as good for the individual selling the income stream. Do not enter into such a transaction without talking to your attorney or a trusted financial advisor.

Finally, if you accept a structured settlement you bear the risk that inflation will increase and the settlement will no longer be sufficient to satisfy your needs. As discussed in Example Thirteen, it is possible to structure the settlement so that payments increase over time. There is no guarantee, however, that inflation will not occur at a higher rate than the payments increase.

Example Nineteen

Linda suffers severe brain trauma as a result of an automobile accident. Careful analysis determines that Linda will require $500,000 initially to pay immediate expenses, and $50,000 per year in today's dollars to meet ongoing needs. A structured settlement is agreed to, the terms of which provide that Linda is to receive an initial payment of $500,000, and a series of payments that begin at $50,000 in the year of the settlement and increase by 3 percent each year (to account for inflation) for the rest of Linda's life. Unfortunately, inflation rises to 5 percent and the settlement proves to be inadequate.

Obviously, the decision as to whether you should accept a structured settlement is complicated, and what is right for one person is not necessarily right for another. If you decide to accept a structured settlement, you will want to be sure that a certain number of minimum payments is guaranteed. This is very important to protect against premature death.

Example Twenty

Linda suffers severe brain trauma as a result of an automobile accident. In lieu of a $1 million cash settlement, her representatives accept an initial payment of $400,000 to fund medical expenses and attorney fees, and a series of payments that begin at $40,000 in the year of the settlement and increase by 3 percent each year (to account for inflation) for the rest of Linda's life.

While this might be a good idea if Linda lives for a long time, it would not be advisable if she lives for only a short time after the accident. Linda's representatives can protect against this risk by insisting that payment be made for a specified period, say ten years, even if Linda dies prematurely. Depending on Linda's age, a ten year guarantee will likely add little to the cost of the annuity used to fund the structured settlement.

It is also advisable that you be aware of the cost of a structured settlement to the defendant before you accept the offer. This is because an offer may sound attractive, but its cost may be significantly less than the amount you would be likely to receive if your case actually went to trial.

Example Twenty One

Linda is injured severely when a drunk driver crashes into her car while pulling out of the parking lot at the local tavern. Although the driver is uninsured and lacks substantial assets of his own, it turns out that the tavern owner continued to serve the man drinks despite the fact that the man was obviously drunk. Under the dram shop laws in the state where the accident occurred, the tavern owner is potentially liable for Linda's injuries. Linda is 40 years old when the injury occurs.

After consultations with her attorney, Linda decides she is willing to accept $500,000 in settlement, but not less. The tavern owner offers Linda a structured settlement of $1,500 per month for the rest of Linda's life, with a ten year guarantee period.

Linda would be ill advised to accept the settlement. This is because, under prevailing interest rates, the cost to the tavern owner of purchasing an annuity for a 40 year old will be approximately

$320,000, which is considerably less than Linda was willing to accept.

In general, the cost of an annuity is based on three factors: the size of the payments to be made, the life expectancy of the injured party and the prevailing interest rate. The importance of interest rates is easily understood if you think about how insurance companies make money from annuity sales— by investing the proceeds. If an annuity costs $100,000 and the insurance company can invest the $100,000 at 8 percent, it can pay a higher monthly annuity than if it earned just 6 percent.

Similarly, if the injured party has a lower life expectancy, an annuity will cost less because the insurance company can expect to be making the payment for a shorter period. For example, if in Example Eighteen Linda was 60 years old, the annuity paying $1,500 per month with a ten year guarantee period would have a cost of $272,000. This dependency on life expectancy can be used by both the injured party and the defendant to lower the annuity cost or increase benefits.

Example Twenty Two

Linda is injured severely when a drunk driver crashes into her car while pulling out of the parking lot at the local tavern. Although the driver is uninsured and lacks substantial assets of his own, it turns out that the tavern owner continued to serve the man drinks despite the fact that the man was obviously drunk. Under the dram shop laws in the state where the accident occurred, the tavern owner is potentially liable for Linda's injuries. Linda is 40 years old when the injury occurs.

After consultations with her attorney, Linda decides she is willing to accept $320,000 in settlement, but not less. The tavern owner offers a Linda a structured settlement of $1,500 per month for the rest of Linda's life, with a ten year guarantee period. Given that Linda is 40 years old, the annuity should have a cost of $320,000.

However, it may be possible for the tavern owner to convince the insurance company issuing the annuity that Linda has a reduced life expectancy as a result of her injuries. If the insurance company decided that Linda had the life expectancy of a 60 year old, this is known as having a rated age of 60, the cost would be $272,000. Similarly, if the tavern owner was willing to spend $320,000, Linda would receive a much better settlement if she could find a financially sound insurance company that gave her a rated age of 60.

Obviously, knowing her rated age is very important for Linda in determining whether a settlement offer is acceptable.

Government Benefits and Structured Settlements

Proceeds from structured settlements can be paid directly into a payback trust to preserve eligibility for SSI and Medicaid.

Example Twenty Three

Linda suffers severe physical injuries from an automobile accident that resulted in complete paralysis. Linda accepts a settlement of $50,000 per year for the rest of her life, with a guaranteed term of twenty years, and directs that the settlement be paid into a payback trust that meets the previously specified requirements. Linda remains eligible for government benefits, and the funds are available to satisfy needs beyond those that the government provides.

An interesting issue arises relating to the choice of beneficiary in a structured settlement designed to maintain eligibility for government benefits. As stated previously, it is generally advisable to have a guaranteed term to protect against premature death. For example, in Example Twenty Three Linda accepted a structured settlement with a guaranteed term of twenty years. If Linda died within the twenty year period, her beneficiary would have the right to receive the payments until the end of the period. The issue in the case of a structured settlement designed to maintain eligibility for government benefits is whether guaranteed payments have to be made available for government reimbursement.

Example Twenty Four

Linda suffers severe physical injuries from an automobile accident which result in complete paralysis. She accepts a settlement of $500,000 and directs that the settlement be paid into a payback trust that meets the previously specified requirements above so as to maintain eligibility for government benefits. Linda incurs medical expenses in excess of $500,000 which are paid by Medicaid, and dies within ten years of the accident. Because the trust has been created to maintain eligibility for government benefits, the remaining funds must be used to reimburse the government for costs incurred under the Medicaid program on Linda's behalf.

Suppose instead that Linda accepts a structured settlement, naming a payback trust as primary beneficiary and a loved one as contingent beneficiary in the event Linda dies within the guarantee period. If we assume that Linda is thirty-five years old, the $500,000 will buy a structured settlement of $36,000 per year with a twenty year guarantee period. If Linda dies five years after the settlement, her beneficiary will be entitled to $36,000 per year for a fifteen year period (the remaining term of the guarantee period). In effect, by naming someone other than the special needs trust as contingent beneficiary, the requirement that the government be repaid from trust moneys has been avoided.

Does the approach work? The answer is unclear. It is possible the government could argue that the law requires that the payback trust be named as contingent beneficiary during the guarantee period. However, our reading of the statute suggests no such requirement.

Conclusion

Handling personal injury claims is complicated, and it is vital that you get attorneys and other advisors who are expert in the area to represent you. In addition to actually bringing the lawsuit, it is important that your advisor be knowledgeable about the benefits and detriments of structured settlements as well as the intricacies of government benefit programs.

If you decide to create a payback trust in connection with a personal injury, it is generally advisable that you contact the Medicaid department in the state where you reside and inform them of your plans so as to avoid unexpected problems. If the state Medicaid agency has provided services prior to the settlement, the agency may seek reimbursement.

If medical payments relating to the injury were paid for by Medicare, Medicare will also have a right to reimbursement. Medicare's rights cannot be deferred through use of a payback trust.

It is vitally important that the injury victim's attorney be aware of all reimbursement claims before funding the trust. This is because the attorney can potentially be liable if reimbursement claims are not satisfied before the trust is funded.

CHAPTER 12

Chapter 13

Income Taxes

ALTHOUGH A DISCUSSION OF INCOME TAX PLANNING MAY NOT strictly belong in a book that is primarily about estate and life planning, our clients frequently have questions about income taxes, and we therefore feel this information may be useful to you. The chapter discusses only the specific deductions and credits that apply to taxpayers who have disabilities and to taxpayers with dependents who have disabilities, and not the various business tax incentives that promote their employment.

The tax laws are tedious, and it is not necessary that you master everything on the first reading. It will be sufficient if you gain a general understanding of the rules relating to the relevant deductions and credits and then use the chapter as a resource if specific questions arise in the future.

Much of the material in this chapter comes from various IRS publications. For further information you should review IRS Publication 907 (Tax Highlights for Persons with Disabilities), IRS Publication 524 (Credit for the Elderly or the Disabled), IRS Publication 502 (Medical and Dental Expenses), IRS Publication 503 (Child and Dependent Care Expenses), IRS Publication 529 (Miscellaneous Deductions), and IRS Publication 596 (Earned Income Credit).

The major points are these:

- Certain types of income received by people with disabilities are not subject to tax. Principal items include SSI benefits, and Social Security benefits unless the recipient has substantial income from other sources.

- You will be entitled to a dependency exemption for your child if your child meets a residency test and an age test. Under the residency test, the child's principal place of abode must be the same as yours for more than half the year. Under the age test, the child has to be under 19 (or in the case of a full-time student, 24). The age test does not apply to a child who is totally and permanently disabled. If a child provides more than half his or her own support, the child is not a qualifying child.

- If you incur medical expenses on your child's behalf you will probably be entitled to a medical expense deduction if your total medical expenses for the year exceed 7.5 percent of your adjusted gross income. Medical expenses are defined broadly to include many types of expenditures that are not typically considered *medical*. A listing of these expenses and a discussion of other general rules and limitations can be found below.

- If your child incurs expenses that are necessary so your child can work, your child may be entitled to a deduction for impairment related work expenses.

- If you incur child-care expenses to enable you to work, you may be entitled to take the child and dependent care credit.

- You may be able to claim the credit for the elderly or disabled if you are 65 or older, or if you are under 65 and you retired on permanent and total disability.

- If you have earned income and your adjusted gross income and investment income are below certain threshold amounts, you may be entitled to take the earned income credit.

Certain Income Items

People with disabilities often have certain items of income that receive favorable tax treatment. The following items are generally not subject to income tax.

- Supplemental Security Income payments,

- Benefit payments from a public welfare fund, such as payments due to blindness,

- Workers' compensation payments for an occupational sickness or injury if paid under a workers' compensation act or similar statute,

- Compensatory (but not punitive) damages for physical injury or physical sickness,

- Disability benefits under a no fault car insurance policy for loss of income or earning capacity as a result of injuries,

- Amounts received under most long-term care insurance policies,

- Compensation for permanent loss or loss of use of a part or function of the body, or for permanent disfigurement,

- Life insurance proceeds,

- Accelerated death benefits received before the death of the insured, including benefits received on the sale of the policy to a viatical settlement provider, if the insured was terminally or chronically ill,

- Certain payments from the Department of Veterans Affairs such as (i) disability benefits, (ii) education, training or subsistence allowances, (iii) grants for homes designed for wheelchair living, (iv) grants for vehicles for veterans who lost their sight or the use of their limbs, and (v) veterans insurance proceeds, including the proceeds of an endowment policy paid before death.

You must report as income any amount that you receive for your disability through an accident or health insurance plan to the extent attributable to premiums paid by your employer. If you paid the premiums, amounts received under the plan are not subject to tax.

Social Security payments, including payments under the SSDI program, are nontaxable unless the recipient receives substantial income from other sources. A portion of a recipient's social security benefits will be taxed if other income plus one-half the social security benefits exceed $25,000 ($32,000 in the case of a married person filing joint returns).

Exemptions for Dependents

You can take an exemption for yourself, and for each person who is your dependent. The exemption amount increases each year to account for inflation. For 2005, the exemption amount was $3,200. Thus, for example, if you had two dependents and you and your spouse file a joint tax return, you would be entitled to a deduction from your taxable income of $12,800. The deduction is reduced by 2 percent for each $2,500 by which a taxpayer's adjusted gross income exceeds a threshold amount (in 2005, $218,950 for married taxpayers filing joint returns and surviving spouses, and $145,950 for single individuals).

A dependent is a child who meets a residency test and an age test. Under the residency test, the child's principal place of abode must be the same as yours for more than half the year. Under the age test, the child has to be under 19 (or in the case of a full-time student, 24). The age test does not apply to a child who is totally and permanently disabled. If a child provides more than half his or her own support, the child is not a qualifying child. You determine whether a child has provided more than half his or her own support by comparing the amount the child contributed to the entire amount of support received from all sources.

Total support includes amounts spent to provide food, shelter, clothing, education, medical and dental care, recreation, allowance, gifts, vacations, and the like. Support is not limited to necessities.

Medical insurance premiums, including premiums you pay for supplementary Medicare coverage, are included in the total support you provide for the dependent. Medical insurance benefits, including basic and supplementary Medicare benefits, are not part of support.

If a dependent receives Social Security benefits and uses them toward his or her own support, the payments are considered as provided by the dependent. State benefit payments based on need are considered as support provided by the state.

Scholarships received by your dependent, if your dependent is a full-time student, are not included in total support. This includes the value of education, room, and board provided for your dependent. This also applies to scholarships for room, board, and tuition provided for a child with a disability attending a special school. It similarly would apply to a scholarship for a child with an intellectual disability to attend an educational institution if the institution certifies that it is making an effort to educate or train the child, even if the payments are made by the state. You can use the following worksheet as an aid in determining whether your child provides more than 50% of his or her support.

WORKSHEET FOR DETERMINING SUPPORT

Income

1) Did the person you support receive any income, such as wages, interest, dividends, pensions, rents, or social security? (If yes, complete lines 2, 3, 4, and 5)   YES   NO

2) Total income received $ _____

3) Amount of income used for support $ _____

4) Amount of income used for other purposes $ _____

5) Amount of income saved $ _____

 (The total of lines 3,4, and 5 should equal line 2)

Expenses for Entire Household (where the person you support lived)

6) Lodging (complete item a or b)

 a) Rent paid $ _____

 b) If not rented, show fair rental value of home.
    If the person you support owns the home, include
    this amount in line 20. $ _____

7) Food $ _____

8) Utilities (heat, light, water, etc., not included in
   line 6a or 6b) $ _____

9) Repairs (not included in line 6a or 6b) $ _____

l0) Other. Do not include expenses of maintaining
    home, such as mortgage interest, real estate taxes,
    and insurance. $ _____

11) Total household expenses (Add lines 6 through 10) $ _____

12) Total number of persons living in household.   _____

Expenses for the Person you Support

13) Each person's part of household expenses
    (line 11 divided by line 12) $ _____

14) Clothing $ _____

15) Education $ _____

16) Medical, dental $ _____

17) Travel, recreation $ _____

18) Other (specify) $ _____

19) Total cost of support for the year
(Add lines 13 through 18) $ _____

20) Amount the person provided for own support
(line 3, plus line 6b if the person you support owns
the home) $ _____

21) 50% of line 19 $ _____

If line 20 is more than line 21, the person has provided more than half his or her own support and may not be claimed as a dependent.

Special rules apply in the case of divorced or separated parents that permit the parents to decide which of them is entitled to claim a dependency exemption. The dependency exemption may also be available in certain cases if you provide support for another relative such as a parent, step-parent, aunt, uncle, niece, or nephew.

Medical Expense Deduction

You are entitled to an income tax deduction for medical expenses for yourself and for your dependents. A dependent must have qualified as such when the medical services were provided or when the bill was actually paid.

A number of hurdles must be passed before medical expenses may be deducted. First, medical expenses are deductible *only* to the extent they exceed 7.5 percent of your adjusted gross income. For example, if your adjusted gross income for a given year is $30,000, only expenses in excess of $2,250 (7.5%) may be deducted.

One potential strategy is to try to time your expenses so a deduction will be possible. For example, if you receive a bill in December, have had little in the way of medical expenses during the year and anticipate large expenses during the next year, you should consider waiting until January to pay your bill since you might then exceed the limitation.

Second, medical expenses may be deducted only if you itemize your deductions. Taxpayers who do not have significant itemized deductions are entitled to take the standard deduction instead. For 2005, the standard deduction is equal to $10,000 for married taxpayers filing joint returns, $7,300 for heads of household and $5,000 for singles. An increased standard deduction is available for taxpayers who are at least 65 years old or blind. You cannot take the medical expense deduction if you use Form 1040A or Form 1040EZ because you must figure the deduction on Schedule A, Form 1040, commonly called the *long form*.

Third, you cannot deduct expenses that are paid by insurance. Only expenses that you pay and that are not reimbursed by your insurance company may be deducted.

Most parents with children who have disabilities deduct larger amounts of medical expenses than other families. As a result, they may draw special notice from the Internal Revenue Service. The IRS computer may single out for review those taxpayers who deduct proportionately higher medical expenses in relation to their income level. To reduce the IRS's suspicions, you can describe your child's disability in a letter written by yourself or your child's doctor and attach it to your tax return. Store your receipts and cancelled checks carefully. One key to good tax planning is good record keeping.

According to the IRS a medical expense includes *any amount paid for the diagnosis, cure, mitigation, treatment, or prevention of disease, or for the purpose of affecting any structure or function of the body, and transportation cost on a trip primarily for and essential to medical care.* Following is a list of items that you should consider in figuring your medical expense deduction. The items are listed in alphabetical order.

Alcoholism

You may include in medical expenses payments to a treatment center for alcohol or drug addiction. This includes meals and lodging provided by the center during medical treatment.

Ambulance

You may include in medical expenses amounts you pay for ambulance service.

462

Artificial limb

You can include the amount you pay for an artificial limb.

Birth control pills

You can include the amount you pay for birth control pills prescribed by your doctor.

Braille books and magazines

You may include the difference in cost of braille books and magazines over regular books and magazines.

Capital expenses

Amounts you pay for special equipment installed in your home or other special improvements that increase the value of the property may be partly deductible as medical expenses, if their main purpose is medical. The amount paid for the improvement is reduced by the increase in the value of the property. The rest is a deductible medical expense.

Example: Your daughter has a heart ailment. On her doctor's advice, you install an elevator in your home so that she will not have to climb stairs. The elevator costs $2,000. An appraisal shows that the elevator increases the value of your home by $1,400.

You figure your medical deduction as follows: The amount you paid for the improvement ($2,000) minus the increase in the value of your home ($1,400) equals your medical expense deduction ($600).

If a capital expense qualifies as a medical expense, amounts you pay for operation and upkeep also qualify as medical expenses, so long as the medical reason for the capital expense exists. This is so even if you are not allowed to deduct any part of the capital expense because the increase in the value of your home is equal to, or more than, the capital expense.

Example: If, in the previous example, the elevator increased the value of your home by $2,000, you would have no medical deduction for the cost of the elevator. However, the cost of electricity to operate the elevator and repairs to maintain it are deductible so long as the medical reason for the elevator exists.

Amounts paid by a person with a disability to buy and install special plumbing fixtures in a rented house, mainly for medical purposes, are medical expenses.

Example: John Smith has cerebral palsy and a heart condition. He cannot climb stairs or get into a bathtub. On his doctor's advice, he installs a bathroom with a shower stall on the first floor of his two-story rented house. The landlord did not pay any of the cost and did not lower the rent. John may include in medical expenses the whole amount paid.

Car

You may include in medical expenses the cost of special hand controls and other special equipment installed in a car for the use of a person with disabilities. If you have a car designed to hold a wheelchair you may include its costs beyond the cost of a regular car. You may not deduct the cost of operating a specially equipped car, except as noted under *Transportation*.

Crutches

Cost of bought or rented crutches is allowable.

Chiropractors

You can include fees you pay to a chiropractor for medical care.

Christian Science practitioners

You can include amounts you pay to Christian Science practitioners.

Cosmetic surgery

Generally, you cannot include in medical expenses the amount you pay for unnecessary cosmetic surgery. This applies to any procedure that is directed at improving the patient's appearance and does not meaningfully promote the proper function of the body or treat illness or disease. Procedures such as face lifts, hair transplants, hair removal (electrolysis), and liposuction generally are not deductible.

You can include in medical expenses the amount you pay for cosmetic surgery if it is necessary to improve a deformity arising from, or directly related to, a congenital abnormality, a personal injury resulting from an accident or trauma, or a disfiguring disease.

Dancing lessons, swimming lessons, etc.

You may not deduct the cost of dancing lessons, swimming lessons, etc., even if they are recommended by your doctor for the general improvement of one's health.

Dental fees

You may include in medical expenses the amounts you pay for dental treatment. This includes fees paid to dentists, X-rays, fillings, braces, extractions, and false teeth.

Diagnostic devices

You can include in medical expenses the cost of devices used in diagnosing and treating illness and disease—for example, a blood sugar kit for diabetes.

Diaper service

Diaper service is usually not deductible. However, if your child will always wear diapers because of a disability, diaper service is probably deductible.

Disabled dependent care expenses

Some disabled dependent care expenses may qualify as either medical expenses or work related expenses for purposes of taking a credit for dependent care. You can apply them either way as long as you do not use the same expenses to claim both a credit and a medical expense deduction.

Drug addiction

You can include in medical expenses amounts you pay for inpatient treatment at a therapeutic center for drug addiction, including meals and lodging at the center during treatment.

Eye surgery

You can include in medical expenses the amount you pay for eye surgery to treat defective vision, such as laser eye surgery.

Eyeglasses

You may include amounts you pay for eyeglasses and contact lenses you need for medical reasons. You may also include fees paid for eye examinations.

Foods, special

You may include in your medicine and drug expenses the cost of special foods or drinks your doctor prescribed to relieve or treat an illness. They must be in addition to your normal diet and not a part of your normal nutritional needs. Do not include the cost of special foods or drinks that replace what you normally eat or drink.

Funeral expenses

Not deductible.

Guide dog or other animal

You may include in medical expenses the cost of a guide dog or other animal for those with visual or hearing impairments. You can also include the cost of a dog or other animal trained to assist persons with other disabilities. Amounts you pay for the care of the dog or other animal are also medical expenses.

Health club dues

You cannot include health club dues, YMCA dues, or amounts paid for steam baths for your general health or to relieve physical or mental discomfort not related to a particular medical condition.

Health Maintenance Organization (HMO)

You may include in medical expenses amounts you pay to entitle you to receive medical care from a health maintenance organization. These amounts are treated as medical insurance premiums.

Hearing aids

You may include in medical expenses the cost of a hearing aid and the batteries you buy to operate it.

Hospital services

You may include in medical expenses amounts you pay for hospital services.This includes amounts paid for meals and lodging.

Household help

You may not deduct the cost of household help, even if your doctor recommends it because you are physically unable to do housework. See *Nursing services.*

Insurance-premiums, policies, and plans

Your medical insurance premiums are amounts paid for medical care, whether the payments under the policy are made directly to the provider of the care (hospital, doctors, dentists, etc.), to the patient, or to you.

You can include in medical expenses premiums you pay for policies that provide payment for: physician fees, hospitalization, surgical fees, X-rays, etc.; prescription drugs; replacement of lost or damaged contact lenses; or membership in an association that gives cooperative or so-called "free-choice" medical service, or group hospitalization and clinical care.

If you have a policy that provides more than one kind of payment, you can include the premiums for the medical care part of the policy if the charge for the medical part is reasonable. The cost of the medical portion must be separately stated in the insurance contract or given to you in a separate statement.

If you are covered under Social Security (or if you are a government employee who paid Medicare tax), you are enrolled in

Medicare A. The tax paid for Medicare A is not a medical expense. If you are not covered under Social Security (or were not a government employee who paid Medicare tax), you may voluntarily enroll in Medicare A. In this situation the premiums paid for Medicare A can be included as a medical expense on your tax return. Medicare B is a supplemental medical insurance. Premiums you pay for Medicare B are a medical expense.

Premiums you pay before you are 65 for insurance for medical care for yourself, your spouse, and your dependents after you reach 65 are medical care expenses. These premiums are included in your medical expenses in the year paid if they are:

1) Payable in equal yearly installments, or more often, and
2) Paid for at least 10 years, or until you reach age 65 (but not for less than 5 years).

You cannot include premiums you pay for: life insurance policies; policies providing payment for loss of earnings; policies for loss of life, limb, sight, etc.; policies that pay you a guaranteed amount each week for a stated number of weeks if you are hospitalized for sickness or injury; or the part of your car insurance premiums that provides medical insurance coverage for all persons injured in or by your care since the portion of the premium for you and your dependents is not stated separately.

Insurance reimbursement

You must reduce your total medical expenses for the year by all reimbursements for medical expenses that you receive from insurance or other sources during the year. This includes payments from Medicare.

If you pay the entire premium for your medical insurance or all the costs of a similar plan and you receive a reimbursement equal to your total medical expenses for the year, you do not have a medical deduction. If insurance payments or other reimbursements are more than your total medical expenses for the year (excess reimbursement), you do not have a medical deduction. Do not include the excess reimbursement in your gross income.

If both you and your employer contribute to your medical insurance plan and your employer's contributions are not included in your gross income, you must include in your gross income the part of your excess reimbursement that is from your employer's contribution.

Example. You are covered by your employer's medical insurance policy. The annual premium is $2,000. Your employer pays $600 of that amount and the balance of $1,400 is taken out of your wages. The part of any excess reimbursement you receive under the policy that is from your employer's contributions is figured like this:

Total annual cost of policy	$2,000
Amount paid by employer	$600
Employer's contribution in relation to the total annual cost of the policy	
($600/$2,000)	30%

You must include in your gross income 30% of the excess reimbursement you received for medical expenses under the policy.

If your employer or your former employer pays the total cost of your medical insurance plan and your employer's contributions are not included in your income, you must report all of your excess reimbursement as income.

Intellectual disability, special homes

You may include in medical expenses the cost of keeping a person with an intellectual disability in a special home, not the home of a relative, on the recommendation of a psychiatrist to help the person adjust from life in a mental hospital to community living.

Laboratory fees

You can include the amount you pay for laboratory fees that are part of your medical care.

Lead-based paint removal

You may include in medical expenses the cost of removing lead-based paints from surfaces in your home to prevent a child who has or had lead poisoning from eating the paint. These surfaces must be in poor repair (peeling or cracking) or within the child's reach. The cost of repainting the scraped area is not a medical expense.

If, instead of removing the paint, you cover the area with wallboard or paneling, you would treat these items as capital expenses. See *Capital Expenses*. Do not include the cost of painting the wallboard as a medical expense.

Learning disability

Tuition or tutoring fees you pay on your doctor's advice for a child who has severe learning disabilities caused by mental or physical impairments may be included in medical expenses. Your doctor must recommend that the child attend the school.

You can also include tutoring fees you pay on your doctor's recommendation for the child's tutoring by a teacher who is specially trained and qualified to work with children who have severe learning disabilities.

Legal fees

You may include legal fees paid to allow treatment for mental illness. If part of the legal fees is not for medical care, you may not include that part in medical expenses.

Lifetime care

You may include in medical expenses a life-care fee or founder's fee you pay monthly or as a lump sum under an agreement with a retirement home. The part of the payment you include is the amount properly allocable to medical care. The agreement must require a lump-sum payment or advance payment as a condition for the home's promise to provide lifetime care that includes medical care.

You may include advance payments to a private institution to provide for the lifetime care, treatment, and training of a dependent with physical or mental disabilities when you die or become unable to provide care. The payments must be a condition for the institution's future acceptance of your dependent and must not be refundable.

Lodging

You can include in medical expenses the cost of meals and lodging at a hospital or similar institution if your main reason for being there is to receive medical care. See *Nursing home*, later.

You can include in medical expenses the cost of lodging (not provided in a hospital or similar institution) while away from home if you meet all of the following requirements.

- The lodging is primarily for and essential to medical care.

- Medical care is provided by a doctor in a licensed hospital or in a medical care facility related to, or the equivalent of, a licensed hospital.

- The lodging is not lavish or extravagant under the circumstances.

- There is no significant element of personal pleasure, recreation, or vacation in the travel away from home.

The amount you include in medical expenses cannot exceed $50 for each night for each person. Lodging is included for a person for whom transportation expenses are a medical expense because that person is traveling with the person receiving the medical care. For example, if a parent is traveling with a sick child, up to $100 per night is included as a medical expense for lodging (meals are not deductible).

Do not include the cost of your meals and lodging while you are away from home for medical treatment that you do not receive at a medical facility, or for the relief of a specific condition, even if the trip is made on the advice of your doctor.

Example. You have a heart condition. You live in an area that has cold winters, which makes your condition worse. Your doctor advises you to spend the winter in a warmer place. You and your family spend the winter in a rented house in Florida. The trip was made for a specific medical reason. You cannot include any of the expenses for food and lodging between your home and Florida or while you are in Florida as a medical expense. However, your share of transportation expenses between your home and Florida is included as a medical expense. Your family's transportation is not deductible. See *Transportation* later.

Medical information plan

You may include in medical expenses amounts paid to a plan that keeps your medical information by computer and that can give you the information when you need it. For example, some organizations can store medical information on your child. This information is accumulated while the parents are alive, and is especially helpful for the guardian of the child after the parents die.

Medical services

You can include amounts you pay for medical services provided by physicians, surgeons, specialists, or other medical practitioners. You cannot include amounts you pay for illegal operations or treatments.

Medicines

You can include in medical expenses amounts you pay for prescribed medicines and drugs. A prescribed drug is one which requires a prescription by a doctor for its use by an individual. You can also include amounts you pay for insulin.

Nursing home

You may include the cost of medical care, including meals and lodging, for yourself, your spouse, or your dependents in a nursing home or home for the aged, if the main reason for being there is to get medical care.

Do not include the cost of meals and lodging if the reason for being in the home is personal. You can, however, include in medical expenses the part of the cost that is for medical or nursing care.

Nursing services

You can include wages and other amounts you pay for nursing services. Services need not be performed by a nurse as long as the services are of a kind generally performed by a nurse. This includes services connected with caring for the patient's condition such as giving medication or changing dressings, as well as bathing and grooming the patient.

Only the amount spent for nursing services is a medical expense. If the attendant also provides personal and household services, these amounts must be divided between the time spent performing household services and the time spent for nursing services.

You can also include part of the amounts you pay for the attendant's meals. Divide the food expenses among the household members to find the cost of the attendant's food, to the extent allocable to nursing services (calculated as described above). If you had to pay additional amounts for household upkeep because of the attendant, you may deduct the extra amounts. This includes extra rent or utilities you pay because you moved to a larger apartment to provide space for the attendant, or the extra cost of utilities for the attendant.

You may deduct any Social Security taxes you pay for a nurse, attendant, or other person who provides medical care.

Operations

You may include in medical expenses amounts you pay for legal operations.

Osteopath

You can include in medical expenses amounts you pay to an osteopath for medical care.

Oxygen

The costs you pay for oxygen or oxygen equipment to relieve breathing problems caused by a medical condition may be included.

Personal use items

You cannot include an item ordinarily used for personal, living, and family purposes unless it is used primarily to prevent or alleviate a physical or mental disability or illness. For example, the full cost of a wig purchased upon the advice of a physician for the mental health of a patient who has lost all of his or her hair from disease can be included with medical expenses.

When an item purchased in a special form primarily to alleviate a physical disability is one that in normal form is ordinarily used for personal purposes, the excess of the cost of the special form over the cost of the normal form is a medical expense (for example, Braille books and magazines).

Psychiatric care

You may include amounts you pay for psychiatric care. This includes the cost of supporting a dependent with mental illness at a specially equipped medical center where the dependent receives medical care.

Psychoanalysis

You may include payments for psychoanalysis. You may not include payments for psychoanalysis that you must get as a part of your training to be a psychoanalyst.

Psychologist

You may include in medical expenses amounts you pay to a psychologist for medical care.

Schools, special

You can include in medical expenses fees you pay on a doctor's recommendation for a child's tutoring by a teacher who is specially trained and qualified to work with children who have learning disabilities caused by mental or physical impairments, including nervous system disorders.

You can include in medical expenses the cost (tuition, meals and lodging) of attending a school that furnishes special education to help a child overcome learning disabilities. A doctor must recommend that the child attend the school. Special education includes

- Teaching Braille to a visually impaired person,

- Teaching lip reading to a hearing impaired person, or

- Giving remedial language training to correct a condition caused by a birth defect.

You cannot include in medical expenses the cost of sending a child to a school where the course of study and disciplinary methods have a beneficial effect on the child's attitude if the availability of medical care in the school is not a principal reason for sending the student there.

Smoking program

You can include the cost of a program to stop smoking. However, you cannot include in medical expenses amounts you pay for nonprescription drugs, such as nicotine gum or patches.

Sterilization

You may include in medical expenses the cost of a legally performed operation to make a person unable to have children.

Telephone

You may include the cost and repair of special telephone equipment that lets a person with a hearing impairment use a regular telephone.

Television

You may include the cost of equipment that displays the audio part of television programs as subtitles for the hearing impaired. This may be the cost of an adapter that attaches to a regular set, or the cost of a specially equipped set to the extent it exceeds the cost of the same model regular television set.

Therapy

You may include in medical expenses amounts you pay for therapy received as medical treatment. For example, payments you make to someone for giving *patterning* exercises are deductible. (These exercises consist mainly of coordinated physical manipulations of the child's arms and legs to imitate crawling and other normal movements.)

Transplants

You may include in medical expenses payments for surgical, hospital, laboratory, and transportation expenses for a donor or a possible donor of a kidney or other transplant.

Transportation

Amounts paid for transportation primarily for, and essential to, medical care qualify as medical expenses.

You can include:

- Bus, taxi, train, or plane fare, or ambulance service,
- Actual car expenses, such as gas and oil (do not include expenses for general repair, maintenance, depreciation, and insurance),
- Parking fees and tolls,
- Transportation expenses of a parent who must go with a child who needs medical care,
- Transportation expenses of a nurse or other person who can give injections, medications, or other treatment required by a patient who is traveling to get medical care and is unable to travel alone, or

- Transportation expenses for regular visits to see a dependent with mental illness, if these visits are recommended as part of treatment.

Instead of deducting actual car expenses, you can take 15 cents a mile for each mile you use your care for medical reasons. Add the cost of tolls and parking to this amount.

Do not include:

- Transportation expenses to and from work, even if your condition requires an unusual means of transportation, or
- Transportation expenses if, for nonmedical reasons only, you choose to travel to another city, such as a resort area, for an operation or other medical care prescribed by your doctor.

Trips

You can include in medical expenses amounts you pay for transportation to another city if the trip is primarily for and essential to receiving medical services. You may be able to include up to $50 per night for lodging. See *Lodging*.

You cannot include in medical expenses a trip or vacation taken for a change in environment, improvement of morale, or general improvement of health, even if you make the trip on the advice of a doctor.

Tuition fees

You may include charges for medical care that are included in the tuition fee of a college or private school if the charges are separately stated in the bill, or given to you by the school.

Weight loss program

You may not deduct the cost of a weight loss program even if a doctor advises the program unless the weight loss program is a treatment for a specific disease diagnosed by a physician such as obesity, hypertension or heart disease. Special diets are deductible only in unusual circumstances.

Wheelchair

You may include in medical expenses amounts you pay for an autoette or a manual or motorized wheelchair used mainly for the relief of sickness or disability, and not just to provide transportation to and from work. The cost of operating and keeping up the autoette or wheelchair is also a deductible medical expense.

X-ray fees

You may include in medical expenses amounts you pay for X-rays.

Calculating Medical Expenses

The following list may help you keep track of your medical expenses.

1. Transportation for taking your child to Special Schools, Institutions, Hospitals, Doctors Office, Special Therapy, Pharmacies, etc.

    a. Mileage (Standard rate .15 cents per mile) or
       actual expenses (gas/oil)   _____

    b. Parking   _____

    c. Toll   _____

    d. Cost of an attendant to go with child   _____

    e. Cost of attendant to ride bus to school   _____

2. Medical Expenses-Standard   _____

3. Hospital Expenses-Standard   _____

4. Medicine, Drugs, Vitamins - prescribed by a doctor only _____

5. Special Education Expenses

    a. Tests and Evaluations at special school   _____

    b. Special instruction in braille, lip-reading speech   _____

    c. Tutoring by a qualified teacher if
       recommended by a doctor   _____

    d. Room, board and tuition at residential facility
       if main reason for attending is to alleviate

medical condition   _____

6. Sheltered Workshop Expenses

  a. If you have to pay the sheltered workshop
for their services   _____

7. Special Equipment

  a. Any special equipment prescribed by a doctor,
i.e. air-conditioning, ramp, elevators, etc.   _____

  b. Repair of equipment including TTD   _____

  c. Closed Caption TV/Adapter   _____

8. Attendant Care

  a. Nursing Services   _____

  b. Meals for Attendants   _____

9. Aids for Persons with Visually Impaired

  a. Audio tapes   _____

  b. Special typewriters   _____

  c. Special lenses, etc.   _____

  d. Cost and care of guide dogs   _____

10. Lifetime Care Payments

  a. If you have to pay non-refundable advance payments
to a private institution for the privilege of having
them care for your child in the future,
those payments are deductible.   _____

11. Transitioning Expenses

  a. The costs involved in helping a person with an
intellectual disability adjust to life in a community
setting   _____

12. Miscellaneous

  a. Expenses involved in providing "patterning exercises"   _____

  b. Disposable diapers for incontinent child or
adult if prescribed by a doctor   _____

  c. Special food and beverage
costs are weighed against costs of "normal" food.   _____

  d. Dental care   _____

  e. Eyeglasses, contacts, eye examinations   _____

f. Hearing aid, batteries, hearing evaluations   _____

g. Wheelchair, braces, other adaptive equipment   _____

h. Birth control pills   _____

i. Legal operation to prevent having children   _____

j. Oxygen equipment and oxygen   _____

k. Medical and Hospital insurance
   premiums (see Formula)   _____

l. Social Security tax for worker providing
   medical services   _____

m. Cost and care of dog or other animals aiding blind,
   deaf and other persons with disabilities   _____

n. Legal abortion   _____

Impairment-Related Work Expenses

The law permits you to deduct, as a business expense, amounts that you incur to enable you to work (impairment-related work expenses). These expenses are not subject to the 2 percent of adjusted gross income limit that applies to other employee business expenses or the 7.5 percent of adjusted gross income limitation that applies to medical expenses. Therefore, it is often better to characterize an expense as an impairment-related work expense, as opposed to a medical expense.

Impairment-related work expenses are deductible only when they are incurred by the person with a disability. Impairment-related work expenses that you incur on behalf of a child with a disability are not deductible by you, though they would be deductible by your child if incurred by your child.

The following examples illustrate whether expenses are medical or business expenses. The expenses in each example are unreimbursed.

Example One

You are blind. You must use a reader to do your work. You use the reader both during your regular working hours at your place of work and outside your regular working hours away from your place of work. The reader's services are only for your work. You can deduct your expenses for the reader as a business expense.

Example Two

You use a wheelchair. Sometimes you must go out of town on business. Your friend or spouse goes with you to help with such things as carrying your luggage or getting up steps. You do not pay your helper a salary, but you do pay for your helper's travel, meals, and lodging while on such trips. In your home town, you do your job without a helper. Because the expenses for travel, meals, and lodging of your helper are directly related to doing your job you can deduct them as business expenses.

Example Three

You use a wheelchair. You must go on overnight out-of-town business trips as a part of your job. Your friend goes with you on these trips to help with your wheelchair, your luggage, and your daily medication. You do not pay a salary to your friend. You do pay for all of your friend's travel, meals, and lodging while on these trips. However, you also need your friend's help regularly during the hours you are not working, while at home and out of town. The expenses for the travel, meals, and lodging of your friend are nursing services. You include them as medical expenses.

If, instead of your friend, your spouse goes with you on the out-of-town business trips, you can include as medical expenses only the out-of-pocket expenses for your spouse's travel. Expenses for your spouse's meals and lodging are not deductible.

Child and Dependent Care Credit

If you pay someone to care for a dependent under age 13, or for a dependent or spouse with a disability, you may be able to take a tax credit for up to 35% of your expenses. Unlike the tax deductions described above, tax credits are subtracted directly from taxes due and are therefore more valuable. To illustrate, if you are in a 30 percent tax bracket a $2,000 deduction will be worth $600 to you. A $2,000 credit, on the other hand, will be worth $2,000.

You can use Form 2441, Credit for Child and Dependent Care Expenses, to figure your credit. To be able to claim the credit, you must meet all the following tests.

1. The care must be for one or more qualifying persons.

   A qualifying person is (i) a dependent of yours who has not attained age 13, or (ii) a dependent or spouse of yours who is physically or mentally incapable of caring for himself or herself and who lives in your principal place of abode for more than one-half of the taxable year.

   Persons who are not able to dress, clean, or feed themselves because of physical or mental disabilities are not able to care for themselves. Also, persons who require constant attention to prevent them from injuring themselves or others are considered not capable of self care.

2. You (and your spouse if you are married) must have income from work during the year.

   Earned income includes wages, salaries, tips, other employee compensation, and net earnings form self employment. Earned income also includes strike benefits and any disability pay you report as wages.

   Earned income does not include pensions or annuities, Social Security payments, workers' compensation, interest, dividends, or unemployment compensation.

   Your spouse is treated as having earned income for any year that he or she is a full time student or physically or mentally not capable of self care. A person is a full time student if the person is enrolled at or attends a school for the number of hours or classes that the school considers full time. The person must have been a student for at least some part of 5 calendar months (not necessarily consecutive) during the year.

The term "school" includes elementary schools, junior and senior high schools, colleges, universities, and technical, trade, and mechanical schools. It does not include on-the-job training courses, correspondence schools, or night schools.

3. You must pay child and dependent care expenses so you (and your spouse if you are married) can work or look for work.

Child and dependent care expenses must be work related to qualify for the credit. Expenses are considered work related only if they allow you (and your spouse if you are married) to work or look for work and they are for a qualifying person's care.

Qualifying expenses include expenses paid for household services (for example, baby-sitters). Expenses incurred for services provided by a day care center qualify only if the center complies with applicable state and local regulations. The cost of overnight camp is not a qualifying expenditure.

4. If you are married at the end of your tax year, you must file a joint return with your spouse to qualify for the credit.

If you are legally separated from your spouse under a decree of divorce or of separate maintenance, you are not considered married. You may claim the credit on a separate return. If you are married and file a separate return, you will not be considered married and will be permitted to take the credit if (i) your home was the home of a qualifying person for more than half the tax year, (ii) you paid more than half the cost of keeping up your home for the tax year, and (iii) your spouse did not live in your home for the last 6 months of the tax year.

5. You must identify the care provider on your tax return.

To identify the care provider, you must give the provider's name, address, and taxpayer identification number. If the care provider is an individual, the taxpayer identification number is often the Social Security number. If the care provider is an organization, then it is the employer identification number (EIN).

The taxpayer identification number is not required if the care provider is one of certain tax-exempt organizations (such as a church or school). In this case, write "Tax-Exempt" in the space where the tax form calls for the number.

If the provider refuses to give you the required information, you should report whatever information you have (such as the name and address) on the form you use to claim the credit. Write "See Page 2" in the columns calling for the information you do not have. On the bottom of page 2, explain that you requested the information from the care provider, but the provider did not give you the information. This statement will show that you used due diligence in trying to furnish the required information.

6. You must pay someone other than a child of yours who is under 19 or a person you can claim as your dependent.

When figuring your credit, you may not use payments you made to your dependent or your child if he or she was under 19 at the end of the year. You may use payments you made to relatives who are not your dependents, even if they lived in your home.

Figuring the Credit: If your adjusted gross income is $15,000 or less, your credit is generally equal to 35% of work-related expenses. The 35% figure is reduced by one percent for each $2,000 or part of $2,000 of adjusted gross income above

$15,000 until the percentage is reduced to 20% for income above $43,000. The limit on work-related expenses is $3,000 for one qualifying person and $6,000 for two or more persons.

Example

A widower pays a housekeeper $5,000 a year to take care of his home and his daughter while he is working. He earns $25,000 during the year. Since there is only one qualifying person, the daughter, the maximum work-related expenses he can claim are $3,000, even though he spent at least $5,000. Therefore, the largest credit he can claim is 30% of $3,000 or $900. The 30% credit is calculated by reducing the 35% credit by one percent for every $2,000 of income above $15,000. Since the widower had income of $25,000, the 35% credit is reduced by 5%.

Earned Income Limit

During any tax year, the amount of work-related expenses that you may use to figure your credit may not be more than

1. Your earned income for the year, if you are single at the end of your tax year, or

2. Your earned income or the earned income of your spouse, whichever is less, for the year, if you are married at the end of your tax year.

If you are married and for any month your spouse is either a full-time student or not able to care for himself or herself, your spouse will be considered to have earned income of $250 a month if there is one qualifying person in your home, or $500 a month if there are two or more qualifying persons in your home. A spouse who cannot care for himself or herself is a qualifying person.

Employer Provided Plans

The amount of any benefit you receive under an employer-provided dependent care assistance plan may be excluded from your income. This means that you do not have to include the amount of the benefit in your income for tax purposes. The plan must meet certain requirements. Your employer can tell you whether the plan qualifies. If it does, you must subtract this excludable amount from the dollar limit ($3,000 or $6,000, whichever applies) to get the reduced limit on the amount of work-related expenses you can use to figure the credit.

Example

You are widower with one child and earn $24,000 a year at work. You pay work-related expenses of $2,900 for your 4-year old child and qualify to claim the credit for child and dependent care expenses. Your employer pays an additional $1,000 under a qualified employer-provided dependent care assistance plan. This $1,000 is excluded from your income. The dollar limit for your work-related expenses is $3,000 (one qualifying person). However, your credit is figured on only $2,000 of the $2,900 work-related expenses you paid because the dollar limit is reduced to $2,000 as a result of the subtraction of the $1,000 excludable benefit from $3,000.

How to Claim Credit

To claim the credit, you must file your return on Form 1040 or Form 1040A. If you file Form 1040, you must complete Form 2441, Credit for Chid and Dependent Care Expenses, and send it in with your Form 1040. If you file Form 1040A, you must complete Schedule 2, Child and Dependent Care Expenses for Form 1040A, and attach it to your Form 1040A. You cannot claim the credit on Form 1040EZ.

Credit for the Elderly and Disabled

You may be able to claim a credit if you are 65 or older or if you are under 65 and you retired on permanent and total disability. Disability is defined by in the same way as for government benefit purposes. Basically, you are considered disabled if you cannot engage in any substantial gainful activity because of your physical or mental condition. A physician must certify that the condition has lasted or can be expected to last for 12 months or more, or can be expected to result in death. You can use the statement set forth in the instructions for Schedule R, Form 1040 or Schedule 3 Form 1040A. You should keep the certification with your tax records. Married taxpayers must file a joint return to take the credit, unless they did not live in the same household at any time during the tax year.

You can use Figures A and B to see if you qualify. Use Figure A to see if you are a qualified individual. Use Figure B to make sure your income is not too high to take the credit.

Figure A. **Are You a Qualified Individual?**

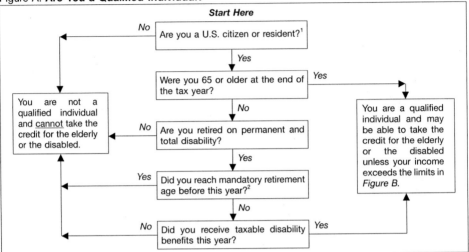

[1] If you were a nonresident alien at any time during the tax year and were married to a U.S. citizen or resident at the end of the tax year, see *U.S. Citizen or Resident* under *Qualified Individual*. If you and your spouse choose to treat you as a U.S. resident, answer "yes" to this question.

[2] Mandatory retirement age is the age set by your employer at which you would have been required to retire, had you not become disabled.

Figure B. **Income Limits**

IF your filing status is . . .	THEN, even if you qualify (see *Figure A*), you CANNOT take the credit if . . .	
	Your adjusted gross income (AGI)* is equal to or more than . . .	OR the total of your nontaxable social security and other nontaxable pension(s) is equal to or more than . . .
single, head of household, or qualifying widow(er) with dependent child	$17,500	$5,000
married filing a joint return **and** both spouses qualify in *Figure A*	$25,000	$7,500
married filing a joint return **and** only one spouse qualifies in *Figure A*	$20,000	$5,000
married filing a separate return **and** you did not live with your spouse at any time during the year	$12,500	$3,750

* AGI is the amount on Form 1040A, line 22, or Form 1040, line 37.

Figuring the Credit. You can figure the credit yourself or IRS will calculate it for you. The credit is figured on Schedule R if you file Form 1040 or Schedule 3 if you file Form 1040A. If you want IRS to calculate the credit and file Form 1040, attach Schedule R to your return, complete Parts I, II and lines 11 and 13 of Part III if they apply to you, and enter CFE on line 48 of Form 1040. If you want IRS to calculate the credit and file Form 1040A, attach Schedule 3 to your return, complete Parts I, II and lines 11 and 13 of Part III if they apply to you, and enter CFE on line 30 of Form 1040A. To calculate the credit yourself, you simply fill in Schedule R if you file Form 1040 or Schedule 3 if you file Form 1040A.

The maximum credit is $750 for single taxpayers and $1,125 for married taxpayers filing joint returns. The credit is reduced for taxpayers who receive certain payments that are excluded from income or for taxpayers whose income exceeds a specified amount.

Earned Income Tax Credit

An earned income tax credit is available for parents of a child who is

- Under age 19 at the end of the year,

- A full time student under age 24 at the end of the year, or

- Permanently and totally disabled, regardless of age.

An earned income credit is also available for certain single taxpayers, though the amount of the credit is reduced and the income limits are more severe.

The earned income credit is not available if your adjusted gross income exceeds a specified amount, or if your investment income exceeds a specified amount. These amounts increase each year and vary depending on the number of qualifying children and filing status. For purposes of this rule, investment income includes capital gain, passive income, interest, dividends tax-exempt interest and non-business rents and royalties.

For 2005, the income limitation figures are as follows:

Earned Income Chart 1

Number of Qualifying Children	Maximum Adjusted Gross Income	Maximum Investment Income
Married Filing Jointly		
No Children	$13,750	$2,700
One Child	$33,030	$2,700
Two or more children	$37,263	$2,700
Other Taxpayers		
No Children	$11,750	$2,700
One Child	$31,030	$2,700
Two Children	$35,263	$2,700

People who are married must file a joint return to take the credit unless they are legally separated. A child will not qualify for purposes of the credit unless you include the child's social security number on your tax return, and the child lives with you for more than one-half of the year.

You must file Form 1040 or Form 1040A to claim the credit if you have a qualifying child, and Schedule EIC must be attached to your return. You can figure the credit yourself, or ask IRS to figure it for you by putting EIC on the dotted line next to line 65a if you file Form 1040 or on the dotted line next to line 41a if you file Form 1040A.

Figuring the Credit. The amount of the credit is based on your earned income, your filing status and the number of qualifying children. The 2005 figures are below. The earned income base-amount represents the maximum amount of earned income eligible for the credit. The amount of earned income up to the earned income base amount is multiplied by the credit percentage to obtain the amount of the credit. Thus, for example, the maximum credit for a taxpayer with earnings of at least $11,000, who is married and has two or more qualifying children, is $4,400 ($11,000 times 40%). The credit is reduced if a taxpayer's adjusted gross income (or earned income, if greater) exceeds the applicable begin phase-out amount.

Earned Income Chart 2

Number of Qualifying Children	Earned Income Base Amount	Credit Percentage	Max Credit	Begin Phase-Out
Married Filing Jointly				
No Children	$5,220	7.65	$399	$8,530
One Child	$7,830	34	$2,662	$16,370
Two or more children	$11,000	40	$4,400	$16,370
Other Taxpayers				
No Children	$5,220	7.65	$399	$6,350
One Child	$7,830	34	$2,662	$14,370
Two Children	$11,000	40	$4,400	$14,370

Example

John and Mary are married with two qualifying children. They have earned income of $10,000, and their adjusted gross income is less than $16,370. John and Mary are entitled to an earned income credit of $4,000 ($10,000 earned income times 40%). Note that if John and Mary had earned income of more than $11,000, only $11,000 of earnings (the amount up to the *earned income base amount*) would be eligible for the credit. If John and Mary's adjusted gross income (or earned income if greater) exceeded $16,370 (the applicable *begin phase-out amount*), the credit would be reduced. If adjusted gross income exceeded $37,263 (the applicable *maximum adjusted gross income amount* per chart 1) no credit would be available. Similarly, if investment income exceeded $2,700 (the applicable *maximum investment income amount* per chart 1) no credit would be available.

Earned income for purposes of this rule is defined to include wages, salaries, tips, earnings from self-employment, and other employee compensation. Earned income does not include items such as interest and dividends, pensions, annuities, and social security benefits.

The earned income tax credit differs from most other types of tax credits because it is a refundable tax credit. This means that if your tax is less than the amount of the credit, you receive a refund. Eligible taxpayers can elect to receive advance payment of the credit through their paychecks by submitting Form W-5 to their employers. The maximum amount that may be received as an advance payment equals 60 percent of the maximum credit available to an individual with one dependent.

You compute the credit by filling out Worksheet A to Schedule EIC (or Worksheet B if you are self-employed). IRS provides tables that can be used to compute the amount of the credit.

Tax Preparers

Now you should realize there are many medical deductions and credits available to families with children who have disabilities. If you are uncertain about whether an expense qualifies as a deduction or about your taxes in general, there are many sources of assistance available. You should look for tax help early in the tax year. Select a tax professional by reference from friends and professionals. Once you find someone to help you with your taxes, agree to a general fee before hiring. Although your tax preparer should sign your tax return, make sure you understand everything that is written on it because you are responsible for any errors.

In addition to tax services, three useful tax guides exist: *Your Federal Income Tax,* available from IRS offices; The Master Tax Guide published by Commerce Clearance House and available at most libraries; and J.K. Lasser's Your Income Tax, available at many book stores.

The following list describes different types of services available that will either prepare your return for you or help you fill it out.

The Internal Revenue Service

The IRS provides many services at no charge. First, you can call the IRS on a toll-free number, available from your local IRS office, to get answers to specific questions. You can also use the TeleTax system, which offers recorded messages of basic tax information. To use the recorded-message system you dial the TeleTax number and then follow instructions. Each tape has a different 3 digit tape number: For example: Dependent: who can be claimed? Tape 155. Medical and Dental Expenses: Tape 302. Child and Dependent Care Credit: Tape 401. For information on how to use TeleTax ask the IRS for publication 910.

Second, you can walk into any IRS office for free tax help. The problem with this free help is that the IRS staff is usually very busy and can spend little time in computing, let alone planning, your taxes. Normally, you will be one of a group being helped by an IRS employee. Only people with disabilities receive one-on-one assistance. In general, seek help at a local IRS office only if your financial situation is not complex. If you seek IRS help, by the way, the IRS cannot ask you to substantiate your deductions. For these visits, they are there to help, not to audit.

Third, the IRS has a program called Outreach in which the Agency will go into communities to offer help, sometimes in cooperation with local organizations.

Telephone help for hearing impaired taxpayers is available for those who have access to TDD equipment. Residents of all states call 1-800-829-4059. Braille materials are made available through the IRS for distribution through the Library of Congress.

Other Free Assistance

Several organizations offer free help in preparing tax returns. One such program is called Tax Counseling for the Elderly, which is run by the American Association of Retired Persons (AARP) and provides help to anyone age 60 or older. Volunteers, many of whom are retired accountants or businessmen, are trained by the IRS and the Association to give one-on-one help to the elderly. For more information, call the IRS after February 1 in any year.

Another free service is called the Volunteer Income Tax Assistance Program, or VITA. Groups from colleges, community associations, and other organizations are trained by the IRS to provide help in their own communities for those with relatively uncomplicated tax returns. For further information, watch for publicity in your area or call the IRS and ask for the Taxpayer Education Coordinator.

Commercial Preparers

These services, such as H&R Block, are convenient, relatively inexpensive, and competent to handle the not-too-complicated tax return. Commercial preparers fill out tax returns, but they do not plan your taxes on an on-going basis.

Enrolled Agents

These tax preparers are not attorneys or certified public accountants, but they have passed an IRS examination and received what is known as a "Treasury Card," which means their background has been checked. Enrolled agents will represent you before the IRS but cannot represent you in court.

Accountants

As your income becomes greater and your tax return more complicated, you should consider hiring an accountant. An accountant deals with taxes regularly and can help you plan your taxes throughout the year. Usually, it is better to hire a certified public accountant (CPA) than a regular accountant, because CPA's have passed a comprehensive accounting exam. CPA's will represent their clients before the IRS but cannot represent clients in court.

Inquire about the type of client the CPA most often handles. From this information, you can determine whether his or her specialty meets your needs—individual tax planning, small business accounting, professional corporations, or whatever.

Tax Attorneys

Generally, tax attorneys deal with the most complicated tax questions. Tax attorneys will often handle tax issues for wealthy individuals, corporate returns, tax forms concerning estates and trusts, or business deals that have tax ramifications. The tax attorney is the only tax preparer who can represent you in court.

The Final Steps:
Putting Your Estate In Order

NOW THAT YOU HAVE COMPLETED OUR BOOK, YOU SHOULD BE aware of the importance of estate planning and have likely developed some general ideas about what your estate plan will look like. You have thought about what your child's life will be like after you are gone: where your child will live, how he or she will continue to enjoy favorite activities, and who will serve as your child's advocate and look out for his or her interests after you are no longer able to do so. Perhaps you have even been made aware of some government programs that might be of benefit to you.

You have probably had some general thoughts about how you want to divide your property, whether you want to establish a trust for your child and, if so, who you will want to act as trustee. You have thought about whether you want a living trust and what type of estate-tax planning, if any, will be required.

All that is left is to begin the process— to take the first steps toward preparation of your estate plan. As we have repeatedly stressed throughout this book, you should not attempt to prepare an estate plan yourself. It is too important, and it is too easy to make mistakes.

In many states there are experts in estate planning for families with children who have disabilities. Referrals can be obtained from local advocacy organizations for people with disabilities, from social workers or agencies you may have worked with in the past, as well as from other parents of children with disabilities who may have been through the estate-planning process themselves. The web site for the National Academy for Elder Law Attorneys (www.naela.com) is an excellent resource for locating knowledgable local attorneys. Shop carefully, and make sure you select advisors who are trustworthy, well informed, and good-hearted.

Completing the form that can be found in Appendix 1 will help you get your thoughts in order before you see your attorney. You may change your mind about certain items after your initial meeting as your attorney may raise issues that you have not considered. You should treat the form as a first attempt to deal with some very difficult questions.

As you work through the planning process, you will want to involve those you intend to rely on to carry out your wishes. Seek out their ideas and make sure you feel confident in their willingness and ability to help.

As a general rule we advise our clients to keep their original documents in a fireproof safe, a safe deposit box, or with their attorney. We also supply our clients with a binder that contains all the information that others will need to carry on after the clients are gone.

The binder should be kept in a place that is readily accessible, so you can update it periodically, and so the people who will act as your child's advocate after you are gone will be able to find it. Many of our clients purchase small fireproof safes for this purpose.

The binder generally contains separate folders in which we place the following:

1. An overview of the estate plan in plain English— that is, without any *legalese*— which we prepare.

2. Important legal papers for any children with disabilities (for example, birth certificates, Social Security cards, and health-insurance cards).

3. A description of the goals and purposes of the Special Needs Trust, which we prepare.

4 A copy of the Letter of Intent, which you should update at least once per year.

5. Unsigned copies of any wills.

6. A letter spelling out any wishes regarding final arrangements (burial, cremation, or religious services or other ceremonies that may be desired).

7. Living wills and/or Power of Attorney for health care that may have been prepared.

8. Extra signed copies of any trusts— special needs trusts, living trusts, or insurance trusts— that may have been prepared. Remember, signed copies will be needed to complete property transfers, and extra signed copies will prove to be useful.

9. A list of major assets and information about where they are kept (for example, a list of insurance policies, stocks, mutual funds, bank accounts, with policy and account numbers and storage locations, and the names of any brokers, insurance agents, and investment advisors).

10. Guardianship papers, if any, and a list of advocacy organizations that may be helpful.

11. The names of government agencies or case workers that the client may have dealt with and the client's thoughts about them.

12. A list of government benefits that the client's child may receive, as well as copies of any filled-out application form. (These application forms will help you the next time you apply for benefits and will be especially helpful to future caregivers who may not understand the complexity of these applications.)

13. Other miscellaneous papers, such as tax returns filed by the child, information about housing options, schooling, photographs of the family, parent's Social Security numbers, parent's birth and marriage certificates, certificates and awards for the person with a disability.

14. Information about where the original documents are kept.

The estate plan organizer, which can be found in Appendix 2, can be a valuable source of information for locating important documents and financial assets. We generally advise our clients to complete the estate plan organizer and place a copy in their binder.

The estate-planning process is long and can often be heart wrenching. But when you are through, you can feel confident that you have done all that you can to assure your child's happiness after you are gone. We wish you the best of luck.

Appendix 1

Preparation For Attorney Meeting

P LANNING FOR YOUR CHILD'S LIFE AFTER YOUR DEATH NECESSARILY involves legal documents— typically wills and trusts. A will is necessary so you can make sure your property goes to the right people, in the proportions that you want. A trust is necessary to receive the property that you want to reserve for your child with a disability, so as to permit proper management and avoid loss of government benefits.

Completing the following form will help you get your thoughts in order before you see your attorney. Feel free to copy it, fill it out and bring it with you when you visit your attorney. You may change your mind about certain items after your initial meeting as your attorney may raise issues you do not consider yourself. You should treat the form as a first attempt to deal with some very difficult questions.

General Information

Most attorney's require information similar to the following before preparing an estate plan. Having this information ready before your initial visit will save both time and money.

APPENDIX 1

Full Name

Father _____

Mother _____

Date of Birth

Father _____

Mother _____

Social Security Number

Father _____

Mother _____

Address

_____

_____

Home Phone

_____

Work Phone

Father _____

Mother _____

Occupation

Father _____

Mother _____

Annual Income

Father _____

Mother _____

Information About Children Without Disabilities

1. Full Name_____Age_____

   Phone # _____

   Address _____

If child is married or has children list name of spouse and names and ages of each child. If the child is an adult and you have concerns about the child's ability to manage money, mention that as well.

_____

_____

2. Full Name_____Age_____

   Phone # _____

   Address_____

If child is married or has children list name of spouse and names and ages of each child. If the child is an adult and you have concerns about the child's ability to manage money, mention that as well.

_____

_____

Information About Child With Disability

1. Full Name_____Age_____

   Phone # _____

   Address_____

   Briefly describe the nature of your child's disability. Include information relating to your child's ability to manage money properly. If child is married or has children, list names of spouse and names and ages of each child.

   _____

   _____

   _____

   _____

   _____

   _____

Former Marriages
   If either of you was formerly married, list names of former spouse and any children from former marriage.

   _____

   _____

   _____

   _____

   _____

Critical People

Executor

The executor will be responsible for paying your debts (including burial expenses) and for collecting your assets and distributing them in accordance with the provisions contained in your will. The executor may also be responsible for filing estate and income tax returns. List in order of preference the people and institutions that you would like to serve as your executor. Include names, the person's relationship to you (for example, spouse, son, brother, friend...), and the person's age, phone number and address.

Mother

1. Full Name_____Age_____

   Relationship _____

   Address _____

   Phone #_____

2. Full Name_____Age_____

   Relationship _____

   Address _____

   Phone #_____

3. Full Name_____Age_____

   Relationship _____

   Address _____

   Phone #_____

Father

1. Full Name_____Age_____

   Relationship _____

   Address _____

   Phone # _____

2 Full Name_____Age_____

   Relationship _____

   Address _____

   Phone #_____

3 Full Name_____Age_____

   Relationship _____

   Address _____

   Phone #_____

Guardians For Minor Children

A guardian is the person appointed to care for your child if you die before your child reaches the age of majority. Guardians do not act until both parents die and are necessary both for children with disabilities and those without disabilities. List in order of preference the people that you would like to serve as guardian for your minor children. Include names, the person's relationship to you (for example: spouse, son, brother, friend...), the person's phone number, and the person's address.

1. Full Name_____Age_____

    Relationship _____

    Address _____

    Phone # _____

2. Full Name_____Age_____

    Relationship _____

    Address _____

    Phone #_____

3. Full Name_____Age_____

    Relationship _____

    Address _____

    Phone #_____

Guardians For Adults With Disabilities

The law presumes that individuals over the age of eighteen (in some states, twenty-one) are competent; that is, that they are able to make their own decisions about what is best for them in their daily lives. This means that, as a legal matter, no matter how severe the disability may be, your child will have the right to make his or her own decisions about the future upon reaching the age of majority. If your child is now over the age of majority and if a guardian has not been appointed, your child already has that right.

This presumption of competence can be overcome only by a court of law in what has come to be known as a *guardianship proceeding*.

1. Has a guardian been appointed by a court for your adult child? If a guardian has been appointed, be sure to bring the court order appointing the guardian with you when you meet with your attorney.

   ❏ yes   ❏ no

2. If a guardian has been appointed for your adult child, list the guardian's name, age, phone number and address. If co-guardians have been appointed, list both names.

(a) Full Name _____Age_____

   Relationship _____

   Address _____

   Phone # _____

(b) Full Name _____Age_____

   Relationship _____

   Address _____

   Phone # _____

(c) Full Name _____Age_____

   Relationship _____

   Address _____

   Phone #_____

3. If a guardian has been appointed for your adult child and successor guardians have been appointed by the court as well, list their names, ages, phone numbers and addresses in the order in which they are to act.

(a) Full Name _____Age_____

Relationship _____

Address _____

Phone # _____

(b) Full Name _____Age_____

Relationship _____

Address _____

Phone # _____

(c) Full Name _____Age_____

Relationship _____

Address _____

Phone #_____

4. If a guardian has not been appointed for your adult child, list in order of preference the people that you would like to serve as guardian should guardianship prove necessary in the future. Include names, the person's relationship to you (for example: spouse, son, brother, friend...), and the person's age, phone number and address.

(a) Full Name _____Age_____

Relationship _____

Address _____

Phone # _____

(b) Full Name _____ Age _____

    Relationship _____

    Address _____

    Phone # _____

(c) Full Name _____ Age _____

    Relationship _____

    Address _____

    Phone # _____

(d) Full Name _____ Age _____

    Relationship _____

    Address _____

    Phone # _____

Trustees

The trustee is the person who will be responsible for managing your child's money. You can use individuals or institutions. Many people appoint co-trustees to increase the chance that their child's interests will be protected. It is even possible to name an individual to act with a bank. The bank takes care of the money management responsibilities, and the individual can look out for your child's personal needs.

List in order of preference the people and institutions that you would like to serve as trustee. Include names, ages, phone numbers, the person's relationship to you, and the person's address. Because the trust will last for your child's entire lifetime, several possibilities should be considered. Be prepared to discuss with your attorney whether you want to have the trustees act by themselves, or whether you would prefer some type of co-trustee arrangement.

Individuals

1. Full Name_____Age_____

   Relationship _____

   Address _____

   Phone # _____

2 Full Name_____Age_____

   Relationship _____

   Address _____

   Phone #_____

3 Full Name_____Age_____

   Relationship _____

   Address _____

   Phone # _____

4. Full Name_____Age_____

   Relationship _____

   Address _____

   Phone # _____

5. Full Name_____Age_____

   Relationship _____

Address _____

Phone #_____

6.Full Name_____Age_____

Relationship _____

Address _____

Phone # _____

Institutions

1. Full Name_____Age_____

Relationship _____

Address _____

Phone # _____

2 Full Name_____Age_____

Relationship _____

Address _____

Phone #_____

Power of Attorney for Healthcare

You can use a power of attorney for healthcare in many states to appoint an agent to make healthcare decisions for you if you are not able to do so. List in order of preference the people you would like to appoint, include complete names and addresses. Most people put their spouse as first choice and friends or other family members thereafter.

1. Full Name_____Age_____

   Relationship _____

   Address _____

   Phone # _____

2. Full Name_____Age_____

   Relationship _____

   Address _____

   Phone #_____

3. Full Name_____Age_____

   Relationship _____

   Address _____

   Phone # _____

4. Full Name_____Age_____

   Relationship _____

   Address _____

   Phone #_____

Disposition of Property

Personal Property

List any specific preferences you have in regard to your personal property (items such as jewelry, pictures, automobiles, crystal....). We generally find that it is best not to go overboard in the list as things tend to work best if your heirs divide personal property as they choose.

If you are married, the personal bequests tend not to take effect until the death of the survivor of you. If you would like particular bequests to take effect before your spouse dies, you should say so specifically.

_____

_____

_____

_____

_____

Residual Property

Your residual property is all property that is not personal. Typically this includes assets such as bank accounts, money markets, stocks, bonds, annuities, mutual funds, retirement accounts and your home, as well as any other items of property which you may own.

1. If you are married and your spouse survives you, would you like all your property to go to your spouse?

   mother ❒ yes ❒ no **father** ❒ yes ❒ no

2. If you are married and the answer to 1 is yes, list how you want your property to be divided when you and your spouse

have both died. If you are not married, you should list how you want your property to be divided when you die. Possibilities include dividing your property between your children in specified percentages, or anything else you consider appropriate.

---

3. If you are married and the answer to question 1 is no, list how you would like your property to be divided, again assuming your spouse survives you.

Trust Remainder

As stated above, in most cases estate plans created by families that have a member with a disability involve the creation of a trust both to manage the inheritance of the person with a disability and to maintain eligibility for government benefits. State how you would like any remaining property to be distributed when your child dies. In particular, you should think about your feelings if your child has children of his or her own. You should also think about whether you want your child to have the ability to say where any remaining property should go. Many families choose to leave a portion of any property that remains in their child's trust to charitable organizations that may have helped the child during his or her life. If you wish to do so, name the charity or charities and the percentage that you would like to leave to each of them. Other possibilities include dividing your property between your other children in specified percentages, or anything else you consider appropriate.

_____

_____

_____

_____

_____

_____

_____

Business Assets

If you own your own business, list your thoughts about how it should be run after your death. Be sure to list the names, phone numbers and addresses of the people who should run it. Also list the names, phone numbers and addresses of people who are critical to business operations.

_____

_____

_____

_____

_____

_____

_____

1. Full Name_____Age_____

    Address _____

    Phone # _____

2 Full Name_____Age_____

    Address _____

    Phone #_____

3 Full Name_____Age_____

    Address _____

    Phone # _____

Financial Assets

To do a thorough estate plan, your attorney will need a general understanding of the size and character of your estate. Exact values are not required. You should complete the following form if you have not already done so. The form is also included in Chapter Five.

Chart Two—Family Balance Sheet

Assets	Joint	Father	Mother
Residence	$ _____	_____	_____
Other real estate	$ _____	_____	_____
Bank accounts	$ _____	_____	_____
Retirement accounts	$ _____	_____	_____
CD's	$ _____	_____	_____
Annuities	$ _____	_____	_____
Stocks, securities	$ _____	_____	_____
Business interests	$ _____	_____	_____
Other assets	$ _____	_____	_____

Liabilities

	Joint	Father	Mother
Mortgage debt	$ _____	_____	_____
Other debt	$ _____	_____	_____

Current Family Net Worth
(current assets less current liabilities) $ _____

Life Insurance	Joint	Father	Mother
Death benefit	$ _____	_____	_____
Premiums	$ _____	_____	_____
Cash value	$ _____	_____	_____
Potential Inheritances	$ _____	_____	_____

Future Expectancies (death benefits plus inheritances) $ _____

Total (current family net worth plus future expectancies) $ _____

519

APPENDIX 1

Estate Plan Organizer

T HE ESTATE PLAN ORGANIZER CAN BE A VALUABLE SOURCE OF information for locating important documents and financial assets. This will ease the burden on your executor, and provide a smooth transition for your child. Feel free to copy the form, complete it and give it to future executors/trustees. You can also keep a copy with your important papers. Make extra copies of pages as needed.

PROFESSIONALS TO CONTACT IN THE EVENT OF DEATH

Information relating to names, addresses and phone numbers of guardians, executors and trustees has presumably been listed in your Letter of Intent. Information relating to names, addresses and phone numbers of friends, relatives and others who can help your child with a disability has also been listed in your Letter of Intent. Obviously these people will need to be contacted in the event of your death. Keep one copy of your Letter of Intent with important records and give additional copies to future executors/trustees. Information relating to financial and legal advisors will be helpful as well.

ATTORNEYS

Name _____Phone # _____

Address _____

Name _____Phone # _____

Address _____

Name _____Phone # _____

Address_____

LIFE INSURANCE AGENTS

Name _____Phone # _____

Address _____

Name _____Phone # _____

Address _____

Name _____Phone # _____

Address_____

TAX ADVISORS

Name _____Phone # _____

Address _____

Name _____ Phone # _____

Address _____

FINANCIAL ADVISORS

Name _____ Phone # _____

Address _____

Name _____ Phone # _____

Address _____

Name _____ Phone # _____

Address _____

COMPANY EMPLOYEE BENEFITS DIRECTORS

Name _____ Phone # _____

Address _____

Name _____ Phone # _____

Address _____

Name _____ Phone # _____

Address _____

OTHER ADVISORS

Name _____ Phone # _____

Address _____

Name _____ Phone # _____

Address _____

Name _____ Phone # _____

Address _____

Name _____ Phone # _____

Address _____

Name _____ Phone # _____

Address _____

Name _____ Phone # _____

Address_____

Final Arrangements

Name of father _____

This is a letter of direction to my executor regarding my own final arrangements.

For my final arrangements I prefer:

_____Burial   ❐ Location _____

                        ❐ Location Unknown

_____Cremation   ❐ Where ashes should be placed _____

                        ❐ Unknown

Regarding a final service:

        Religious   ❐ Yes (if yes, type of religion) _____

                     ❐ No (if no, type of service desired) _____

                     _____

Specific funeral home_____

Specific cemetery _____

Prepaid/insurance _____

Military benefits _____

Other specific details or comments _____

_____

Date _____Signed _____

FINAL ARRANGEMENTS

Name of mother _____

This is a letter of direction to my executor regarding my own final arrangements.

For my final arrangements I prefer:

_____Burial ❐ Location _____

❐ Location Unknown

_____Cremation ❐ Where ashes should be placed _____

❐ Unknown

Regarding a final service:

Religious ❐ Yes (if yes, type of religion) _____

❐ No (if no, type of service desired) ____

_____

Specific funeral home_____

Specific cemetery _____

Prepaid/insurance _____

Military benefits _____

Other specific details or comments _____

_____

Date _____Signed _____

LOCATION OF CRITICAL DOCUMENTS RELATING TO PARENTS

Document	Location
Wills	
Trusts	
Power of attorney for healthcare	
Power of attorney for property	
Living will	
Marriage certificate	
Birth certificate	
Insurance policies	
Home mortgage and ownership	
Automobile title and insurance	
Tax returns	

LOCATION OF CRITICAL DOCUMENTS RELATING TO PERSON WITH DISABILITY

Document	Location
Medical records	
Individual education plan	
Individual program plan	
Individual habilitation pPlan	
Diagnostic testing reports	
Psychological reports	
Information about special equipment	
Residential admission papers	
Residential investigatory papers	
Records related to employment	
Guardianship papers	
Government benefit papers	
Information relating to advocacy organizations	
Certificates and awards	
Recipes for favored foods	

LOCATION OF OTHER IMPORTANT DOCUMENTS

Document	Location

SAFE DEPOSIT BOXES

Bank _____

Address _____

Phone number _____

Location of keys _____

Persons authorized to sign_____

Box number_____

Contents _____

_____

Bank _____

Address _____

Phone number _____

Location of keys _____

Persons authorized to sign_____

Box number_____

Contents _____

_____

Bank Accounts and Certificates of Deposit

Name of bank _____

Account number _____

Address _____

Phone number _____

Names of those authorized to sign _____

Location of checkbook or passbook _____

Name of bank _____

Account number _____

Address _____

Phone number _____

Names of those authorized to sign _____

Location of checkbook or passbook _____

Name of bank _____

Account number _____

Address _____

Phone number _____

Names of those authorized to sign _____

Location of checkbook or passbook _____

MUTUAL FUNDS, BROKERAGE ACCOUNTS AND MONEY MARKET ACCOUNTS

Name of institution _____

Account number_____

Address _____

Phone number _____

Names of those authorized to sign _____

Name, address and phone number of broker_____

_____

Location of records _____

Name of institution _____

Account number_____

Address _____

Phone number _____

Names of those authorized to sign _____

Name, address and phone number of broker_____

_____

Location of records _____

ANNUITIES

Name of institution _____

Account number_____

Address _____

Phone number _____

Name of owner _____

Name of beneficiary _____

Name, address and phone number of broker_____

_____

Location of records _____

Name of institution _____

Account number_____

Address _____

Phone number _____

Name of owner _____

Name of beneficiary _____

Name, address and phone number of broker_____

_____

Location of records_____

INDIVIDUAL RETIREMENT ACCOUNTS, 401(K)'S AND OTHER RETIREMENT ACCOUNTS

Name of institution _____

Account number_____

Address _____

Phone number _____

Names of those authorized to sign _____

Name, address and phone number of broker_____

_____

Location of records _____

Name of institution _____

Account number_____

Address _____

Phone number _____

Names of those authorized to sign _____

Name, address and phone number of broker_____

_____

Location of records _____

LIFE INSURANCE POLICIES

Name of insurance company_____

Policy number _____

Phone number _____

Address _____

Name of owner _____

Name of beneficiary _____

Name, address and phone number of agent _____

_____

_____

Type of policy _____

Date issued _____

Death benefit_____

Loans outstanding _____

Location of policy _____

REAL ESTATE

Description _____

Address _____

Mortgage holder _____

Loan number _____

Location of records _____

Description _____

Address _____

Mortgage holder _____

Loan number _____

Location of records _____

Description _____

Address _____

Mortgage holder _____

Loan number _____

Location of records _____

U.S. Savings Bonds

Face amount _____

Date _____

Maturity date_____

Serial number _____

Series_____

Location of certificate_____

Face amount _____

Date _____

Maturity date_____

Serial number _____

Series_____

Location of certificate_____

Face amount _____

Date _____

Maturity date_____

Serial number _____

Series_____

Location of certificate _____

SECURITIES HELD OUTSIDE BROKERAGE ACCOUNTS

Description _____

Location of certificate_____

How is title held _____

Description _____

Location of certificate_____

How is title held _____

Description _____

Location of certificate_____

How is title held _____

Description _____

Location of certificate_____

How is title held _____

Description _____

Location of certificate_____

How is title held _____

OTHER INSURANCE POLICIES
(DISABILITY, HEALTH, PROPERTY, CASUALTY, LIABILITY)

Type of insurance _____

Name of insurance company_____

Policy number _____

Address _____

Phone number _____

Name, address and phone number of agent _____

_____

_____

Location of policy_____

Type of insurance _____

Name of insurance company_____

Policy number _____

Address _____

Phone number _____

Name, address and phone number of agent _____

_____

_____

Location of policy _____

OTHER ASSETS

Description _____

Contact person (include phone number and address)_____

_____

Location of records _____

Additional information _____

Description _____

Contact person (include phone number and address)_____

_____

Location of records _____

Additional information _____

Description _____

Contact person (include phone number and address)_____

_____

Location of records _____

Additional information_____

LIABILITIES
(CREDIT CARD BALANCES, MORTGAGES, TAXES, OTHER)

Description _____

Person or institution owed_____

Contact person (include phone number and address)_____

_____

Location of records _____

Additional information _____

Description _____

Person or institution owed_____

Contact person (include phone number and address)_____

_____

Location of records _____

Additional information _____

Description _____

Person or institution owed_____

Contact person (include phone number and address)_____

_____

Location of records _____

APPENDIX 2

Supplemental Financial Needs Analysis for Financial Professionals

A S DESCRIBED PREVIOUSLY, THE CALCULATIONS IN CHAPTER FIVE of the main text require assumptions as to rates of return and taxes. While we believe the assumptions to be reasonable for the reasons previously outlined, you may be interested in how the calculations differ if different assumptions are made. The information contained in this appendix is complicated, and is probably unnecessary for most families. We include it only for the sake of completeness, and as a resource for financial professionals and others who are expert in financial matters.

Chart One shows the amount required to fund $1,000 of expenses over varying life expectancies with varying projected rates of return assuming no taxes or trustee fees. Charts Two, Three and Four are the same as Chart One except they assume tax rates of ten percent, twenty percent and thirty percent respectively.

Chart Five shows the amount required to fund $1,000 of expenses over varying life expectancies with varying projected rates of return assuming a one percent trustee fee and no taxes. Charts Six, Seven and Eight are the same as Chart Five except they assume tax rates of ten percent, twenty percent and thirty percent respectively.

The example below illustrates how to use the charts to see how varying assumptions affect the calculation of a child's financial needs. All charts assume a 2.5% inflation rate.

Example

John and Mary complete parts one, two and three of Chart One in Chapter Five and determine that their 39-year-old son, Sam, will need $250 per month to fund his needs. This figure is multiplied by 12 to get Sam's annual needs— $3,000. John and Mary are not concerned about trustee fees because they trust John's sister to handle his finances.

John and Mary then go to Chart Three in Chapter Five and determine that as a 39-year-old male, Sam has a life expectancy of another 41 years, and they add 10 years to be sure the trust fund is sufficient. In the example contained in Chapter Five, we assumed a 5 percent rate of return, a twenty percent tax rate and no trustee fees. Turning to the 5 percent return rate on Chart Three of this appendix (which assumes no trustee fee and a twenty percent tax rate), we see that $34,889 is necessary to provide $1,000 per year for 51 years (multiplying by 3 we get $104,667 to provide $3,000 per year which was the answer derived in Chapter Five). If we assume a 6 percent rate of return, Chart Three tells us we need $29,458 to provide $1,000 per year for 51 years or $88,374 to provide $3,000 per year.

Chart One provides the required information if we assume a zero percent tax rate, Chart Two assumes a ten percent tax rate and Chart Four assumes a thirty percent tax rate. Charts Five, Six, Seven and Eight provide the same information assuming a one percent trustee fee. Chart Five assumes a zero percent tax rate, Chart Six assumes a ten percent rate, Chart Seven assumes a twenty percent tax rate and Chart Eight assumes a thirty percent tax rate.

Starting Portfolio Needed to Fund Various Annual Expenses
Assuming No Trustee Fee and 0% Tax Rate

Assumptions: Initial annual expenses: $ 1,000   inflation: 2.50%   tax rate: 0.00%   TTEE/admin. fee: 0.00%

The following also assumes that needs are paid at end of each year and that TTEE fee is not tax deductible.

Rate of Return (Nominal): Life expectancies	2.50%	3.00%	3.50%	4.00%	4.50%	5.00%	5.50%	6.00%	6.50%	7.00%	7.50%	8.00%	8.50%
1	$ 976	$ 971	$ 966	$ 962	$ 957	$ 952	$ 948	$ 943	$ 939	$ 935	$ 930	$ 926	$ 922
2	$ 1,951	$ 1,937	$ 1,923	$ 1,909	$ 1,896	$ 1,882	$ 1,869	$ 1,856	$ 1,843	$ 1,830	$ 1,817	$ 1,805	$ 1,792
3	$ 2,927	$ 2,899	$ 2,871	$ 2,843	$ 2,816	$ 2,790	$ 2,764	$ 2,738	$ 2,712	$ 2,687	$ 2,663	$ 2,639	$ 2,615
4	$ 3,902	$ 3,855	$ 3,809	$ 3,764	$ 3,719	$ 3,676	$ 3,633	$ 3,591	$ 3,550	$ 3,509	$ 3,469	$ 3,430	$ 3,392
5	$ 4,878	$ 4,807	$ 4,738	$ 4,671	$ 4,605	$ 4,540	$ 4,477	$ 4,416	$ 4,355	$ 4,296	$ 4,238	$ 4,182	$ 4,126
6	$ 5,854	$ 5,755	$ 5,659	$ 5,565	$ 5,474	$ 5,385	$ 5,298	$ 5,213	$ 5,131	$ 5,050	$ 4,971	$ 4,894	$ 4,820
7	$ 6,829	$ 6,698	$ 6,570	$ 6,446	$ 6,326	$ 6,209	$ 6,095	$ 5,984	$ 5,877	$ 5,772	$ 5,670	$ 5,571	$ 5,475
8	$ 7,805	$ 7,636	$ 7,473	$ 7,315	$ 7,162	$ 7,013	$ 6,870	$ 6,730	$ 6,595	$ 6,464	$ 6,337	$ 6,213	$ 6,094
9	$ 8,780	$ 8,570	$ 8,367	$ 8,171	$ 7,982	$ 7,799	$ 7,622	$ 7,451	$ 7,286	$ 7,127	$ 6,972	$ 6,823	$ 6,678
10	$ 9,756	$ 9,499	$ 9,252	$ 9,015	$ 8,786	$ 8,566	$ 8,353	$ 8,149	$ 7,952	$ 7,762	$ 7,578	$ 7,401	$ 7,231
11	$ 10,732	$ 10,424	$ 10,129	$ 9,846	$ 9,575	$ 9,314	$ 9,064	$ 8,823	$ 8,592	$ 8,370	$ 8,156	$ 7,950	$ 7,752
12	$ 11,707	$ 11,344	$ 10,998	$ 10,666	$ 10,348	$ 10,045	$ 9,754	$ 9,475	$ 9,208	$ 8,952	$ 8,707	$ 8,471	$ 8,245
13	$ 12,683	$ 12,260	$ 11,857	$ 11,473	$ 11,107	$ 10,758	$ 10,424	$ 10,106	$ 9,801	$ 9,510	$ 9,232	$ 8,966	$ 8,711
14	$ 13,659	$ 13,172	$ 12,709	$ 12,270	$ 11,852	$ 11,454	$ 11,076	$ 10,715	$ 10,372	$ 10,045	$ 9,733	$ 9,435	$ 9,151
15	$ 14,634	$ 14,079	$ 13,552	$ 13,054	$ 12,582	$ 12,134	$ 11,709	$ 11,305	$ 10,922	$ 10,557	$ 10,210	$ 9,881	$ 9,567
16	$ 15,610	$ 14,981	$ 14,388	$ 13,827	$ 13,298	$ 12,797	$ 12,324	$ 11,875	$ 11,450	$ 11,048	$ 10,666	$ 10,303	$ 9,959
17	$ 16,585	$ 15,879	$ 15,215	$ 14,589	$ 14,000	$ 13,445	$ 12,921	$ 12,426	$ 11,959	$ 11,518	$ 11,100	$ 10,705	$ 10,330
18	$ 17,561	$ 16,773	$ 16,034	$ 15,341	$ 14,689	$ 14,077	$ 13,501	$ 12,960	$ 12,449	$ 11,968	$ 11,514	$ 11,085	$ 10,681
19	$ 18,537	$ 17,662	$ 16,845	$ 16,081	$ 15,365	$ 14,694	$ 14,065	$ 13,475	$ 12,920	$ 12,399	$ 11,909	$ 11,447	$ 11,012
20	$ 19,512	$ 18,548	$ 17,649	$ 16,810	$ 16,028	$ 15,297	$ 14,613	$ 13,973	$ 13,374	$ 12,812	$ 12,285	$ 11,790	$ 11,324
21	$ 20,488	$ 19,428	$ 18,444	$ 17,530	$ 16,678	$ 15,885	$ 15,146	$ 14,455	$ 13,811	$ 13,208	$ 12,644	$ 12,115	$ 11,620
22	$ 21,463	$ 20,305	$ 19,232	$ 18,238	$ 17,316	$ 16,459	$ 15,663	$ 14,922	$ 14,231	$ 13,587	$ 12,986	$ 12,424	$ 11,899
23	$ 22,439	$ 21,177	$ 20,013	$ 18,937	$ 17,941	$ 17,020	$ 16,165	$ 15,372	$ 14,636	$ 13,950	$ 13,312	$ 12,717	$ 12,163

STARTING PORTFOLIO NEEDED TO FUND VARIOUS ANNUAL EXPENSES
ASSUMING NO TRUSTEE FEE AND 0% TAX RATE (CONTINUED)

Assumptions:

Initial annual expenses: $1,000	inflation: 2.50%	tax rate: 0.00%
		TTEE/admin. fee: 0.00%

The following also assumes that needs are paid at end of each year and that TTEE fee is not tax deductible.

Rate of Return (Nominal): Life expectancies	2.50%	3.00%	3.50%	4.00%	4.50%	5.00%	5.50%	6.00%	6.50%	7.00%	7.50%	8.00%	8.50%
24	$ 23,415	$ 22,045	$ 20,786	$ 19,625	$ 18,555	$ 17,567	$ 16,653	$ 15,808	$ 15,025	$ 14,298	$ 13,623	$ 12,996	$ 12,412
25	$ 24,390	$ 22,909	$ 21,551	$ 20,304	$ 19,157	$ 18,101	$ 17,128	$ 16,230	$ 15,399	$ 14,631	$ 13,920	$ 13,260	$ 12,647
26	$ 25,366	$ 23,769	$ 22,309	$ 20,972	$ 19,747	$ 18,622	$ 17,589	$ 16,637	$ 15,760	$ 14,951	$ 14,203	$ 13,510	$ 12,869
27	$ 26,341	$ 24,624	$ 23,060	$ 21,631	$ 20,326	$ 19,131	$ 18,036	$ 17,031	$ 16,107	$ 15,256	$ 14,472	$ 13,748	$ 13,079
28	$ 27,317	$ 25,476	$ 23,803	$ 22,281	$ 20,894	$ 19,628	$ 18,471	$ 17,412	$ 16,441	$ 15,549	$ 14,729	$ 13,974	$ 13,278
29	$ 28,293	$ 26,323	$ 24,539	$ 22,921	$ 21,451	$ 20,113	$ 18,894	$ 17,781	$ 16,763	$ 15,830	$ 14,975	$ 14,188	$ 13,465
30	$ 29,268	$ 27,166	$ 25,268	$ 23,552	$ 21,997	$ 20,587	$ 19,305	$ 18,137	$ 17,072	$ 16,099	$ 15,208	$ 14,392	$ 13,642
31	$ 30,244	$ 28,005	$ 25,990	$ 24,174	$ 22,533	$ 21,049	$ 19,703	$ 18,481	$ 17,370	$ 16,356	$ 15,431	$ 14,585	$ 13,809
32	$ 31,220	$ 28,840	$ 26,705	$ 24,787	$ 23,059	$ 21,500	$ 20,091	$ 18,815	$ 17,656	$ 16,603	$ 15,644	$ 14,768	$ 13,967
33	$ 32,195	$ 29,671	$ 27,413	$ 25,391	$ 23,575	$ 21,941	$ 20,468	$ 19,137	$ 17,932	$ 16,839	$ 15,846	$ 14,942	$ 14,117
34	$ 33,171	$ 30,498	$ 28,115	$ 25,986	$ 24,080	$ 22,371	$ 20,833	$ 19,448	$ 18,198	$ 17,066	$ 16,039	$ 15,107	$ 14,258
35	$ 34,146	$ 31,320	$ 28,809	$ 26,573	$ 24,577	$ 22,790	$ 21,189	$ 19,750	$ 18,453	$ 17,283	$ 16,224	$ 15,263	$ 14,391
36	$ 35,122	$ 32,139	$ 29,497	$ 27,151	$ 25,063	$ 23,200	$ 21,534	$ 20,041	$ 18,699	$ 17,490	$ 16,399	$ 15,412	$ 14,517
37	$ 36,098	$ 32,954	$ 30,178	$ 27,721	$ 25,540	$ 23,600	$ 21,870	$ 20,322	$ 18,936	$ 17,689	$ 16,567	$ 15,553	$ 14,636
38	$ 37,073	$ 33,765	$ 30,853	$ 28,283	$ 26,008	$ 23,991	$ 22,196	$ 20,595	$ 19,163	$ 17,880	$ 16,726	$ 15,687	$ 14,748
39	$ 38,049	$ 34,572	$ 31,521	$ 28,836	$ 26,468	$ 24,372	$ 22,512	$ 20,858	$ 19,383	$ 18,063	$ 16,879	$ 15,814	$ 14,854
40	$ 39,024	$ 35,375	$ 32,183	$ 29,382	$ 26,918	$ 24,744	$ 22,820	$ 21,113	$ 19,594	$ 18,238	$ 17,024	$ 15,935	$ 14,954
41	$ 40,000	$ 36,174	$ 32,838	$ 29,920	$ 27,360	$ 25,107	$ 23,119	$ 21,359	$ 19,797	$ 18,405	$ 17,162	$ 16,049	$ 15,049
42	$ 40,976	$ 36,969	$ 33,487	$ 30,450	$ 27,793	$ 25,462	$ 23,410	$ 21,597	$ 19,992	$ 18,566	$ 17,294	$ 16,158	$ 15,138
43	$ 41,951	$ 37,761	$ 34,129	$ 30,972	$ 28,218	$ 25,808	$ 23,692	$ 21,828	$ 20,180	$ 18,719	$ 17,420	$ 16,261	$ 15,223
44	$ 42,927	$ 38,548	$ 34,766	$ 31,487	$ 28,635	$ 26,146	$ 23,966	$ 22,050	$ 20,361	$ 18,867	$ 17,540	$ 16,359	$ 15,303
45	$ 43,902	$ 39,332	$ 35,396	$ 31,994	$ 29,044	$ 26,476	$ 24,232	$ 22,266	$ 20,535	$ 19,008	$ 17,655	$ 16,451	$ 15,378
46	$ 44,878	$ 40,112	$ 36,020	$ 32,494	$ 29,445	$ 26,798	$ 24,491	$ 22,474	$ 20,703	$ 19,143	$ 17,764	$ 16,540	$ 15,449

TTEE/
admin.

Initial
annual

Assumptions: expenses: $ 1,000   inflation: 2.50%   tax rate: 0.00%   fee: 0.00%

The following also assumes that needs are paid at end of each year and that TTEE fee is not tax deductible.

Rate of Return (Nominal): Life expectancies	2.50%	3.00%	3.50%	4.00%	4.50%	5.00%	5.50%	6.00%	6.50%	7.00%	7.50%	8.00%	8.50%
47	$ 45,854	$ 40,888	$ 36,639	$ 32,987	$ 29,838	$ 27,112	$ 24,743	$ 22,675	$ 20,864	$ 19,273	$ 17,868	$ 16,623	$ 15,517
48	$ 46,829	$ 41,661	$ 37,251	$ 33,473	$ 30,224	$ 27,419	$ 24,987	$ 22,870	$ 21,020	$ 19,397	$ 17,967	$ 16,703	$ 15,580
49	$ 47,805	$ 42,429	$ 37,857	$ 33,952	$ 30,603	$ 27,718	$ 25,224	$ 23,058	$ 21,169	$ 19,515	$ 18,061	$ 16,778	$ 15,640
50	$ 48,780	$ 43,194	$ 38,457	$ 34,424	$ 30,974	$ 28,011	$ 25,455	$ 23,240	$ 21,313	$ 19,629	$ 18,152	$ 16,849	$ 15,697
51	$ 49,756	$ 43,955	$ 39,052	$ 34,889	$ 31,338	$ 28,296	$ 25,679	$ 23,416	$ 21,452	$ 19,738	$ 18,238	$ 16,917	$ 15,751
52	$ 50,732	$ 44,713	$ 39,641	$ 35,347	$ 31,695	$ 28,575	$ 25,896	$ 23,586	$ 21,585	$ 19,843	$ 18,320	$ 16,982	$ 15,801
53	$ 51,707	$ 45,467	$ 40,224	$ 35,799	$ 32,046	$ 28,847	$ 26,108	$ 23,751	$ 21,713	$ 19,943	$ 18,398	$ 17,043	$ 15,849
54	$ 52,683	$ 46,217	$ 40,802	$ 36,244	$ 32,389	$ 29,113	$ 26,313	$ 23,910	$ 21,837	$ 20,039	$ 18,472	$ 17,101	$ 15,894
55	$ 53,659	$ 46,963	$ 41,374	$ 36,683	$ 32,726	$ 29,372	$ 26,513	$ 24,064	$ 21,955	$ 20,131	$ 18,543	$ 17,156	$ 15,937
56	$ 54,634	$ 47,706	$ 41,940	$ 37,115	$ 33,057	$ 29,625	$ 26,707	$ 24,213	$ 22,070	$ 20,219	$ 18,611	$ 17,208	$ 15,978
57	$ 55,610	$ 48,446	$ 42,501	$ 37,541	$ 33,381	$ 29,872	$ 26,895	$ 24,357	$ 22,180	$ 20,303	$ 18,676	$ 17,258	$ 16,016
58	$ 56,585	$ 49,181	$ 43,057	$ 37,962	$ 33,699	$ 30,113	$ 27,078	$ 24,496	$ 22,286	$ 20,384	$ 18,737	$ 17,305	$ 16,052
59	$ 57,561	$ 49,913	$ 43,607	$ 38,376	$ 34,011	$ 30,348	$ 27,256	$ 24,631	$ 22,388	$ 20,461	$ 18,796	$ 17,349	$ 16,086
60	$ 58,537	$ 50,642	$ 44,152	$ 38,784	$ 34,317	$ 30,578	$ 27,429	$ 24,761	$ 22,486	$ 20,535	$ 18,852	$ 17,392	$ 16,118
61	$ 59,512	$ 51,367	$ 44,691	$ 39,186	$ 34,617	$ 30,803	$ 27,597	$ 24,886	$ 22,580	$ 20,606	$ 18,905	$ 17,432	$ 16,148
62	$ 60,488	$ 52,089	$ 45,226	$ 39,582	$ 34,912	$ 31,022	$ 27,760	$ 25,008	$ 22,671	$ 20,674	$ 18,956	$ 17,470	$ 16,177
63	$ 61,463	$ 52,807	$ 45,755	$ 39,973	$ 35,200	$ 31,235	$ 27,919	$ 25,126	$ 22,759	$ 20,739	$ 19,005	$ 17,506	$ 16,204
64	$ 62,439	$ 53,521	$ 46,279	$ 40,358	$ 35,484	$ 31,444	$ 28,073	$ 25,240	$ 22,843	$ 20,801	$ 19,051	$ 17,541	$ 16,229
65	$ 63,415	$ 54,232	$ 46,798	$ 40,737	$ 35,762	$ 31,648	$ 28,222	$ 25,350	$ 22,924	$ 20,861	$ 19,095	$ 17,573	$ 16,254
66	$ 64,390	$ 54,940	$ 47,312	$ 41,111	$ 36,034	$ 31,847	$ 28,368	$ 25,456	$ 23,002	$ 20,918	$ 19,137	$ 17,604	$ 16,276
67	$ 65,366	$ 55,644	$ 47,821	$ 41,480	$ 36,301	$ 32,041	$ 28,509	$ 25,559	$ 23,077	$ 20,973	$ 19,177	$ 17,634	$ 16,298
68	$ 66,341	$ 56,345	$ 48,325	$ 41,843	$ 36,564	$ 32,230	$ 28,646	$ 25,658	$ 23,149	$ 21,026	$ 19,216	$ 17,662	$ 16,318
69	$ 67,317	$ 57,042	$ 48,824	$ 42,201	$ 36,821	$ 32,415	$ 28,779	$ 25,755	$ 23,219	$ 21,076	$ 19,252	$ 17,688	$ 16,338

CHART ONE

STARTING PORTFOLIO NEEDED TO FUND VARIOUS ANNUAL EXPENSES
ASSUMING NO TRUSTEE FEE AND 0% TAX RATE (CONTINUED)

Assumptions: Initial annual expenses: $1,000 inflation: 2.50% tax rate: 0.00% TTEE/admin. fee: 0.00%

The following also assumes that needs are paid at end of each year and that TTEE fee is not tax deductible.

Rate of Return (Nominal): Life expectancies	2.50%	3.00%	3.50%	4.00%	4.50%	5.00%	5.50%	6.00%	6.50%	7.00%	7.50%	8.00%	8.50%
70	$ 68,293	$ 57,736	$ 49,319	$ 42,554	$ 37,073	$ 32,596	$ 28,909	$ 25,848	$ 23,285	$ 21,124	$ 19,287	$ 17,713	$ 16,356
71	$ 69,268	$ 58,427	$ 49,809	$ 42,902	$ 37,320	$ 32,772	$ 29,035	$ 25,937	$ 23,350	$ 21,170	$ 19,320	$ 17,737	$ 16,373
72	$ 70,244	$ 59,114	$ 50,294	$ 43,245	$ 37,563	$ 32,944	$ 29,157	$ 26,024	$ 23,412	$ 21,215	$ 19,352	$ 17,760	$ 16,389
73	$ 71,220	$ 59,798	$ 50,774	$ 43,582	$ 37,801	$ 33,112	$ 29,276	$ 26,109	$ 23,472	$ 21,257	$ 19,382	$ 17,781	$ 16,405
74	$ 72,195	$ 60,478	$ 51,249	$ 43,915	$ 38,035	$ 33,276	$ 29,391	$ 26,190	$ 23,529	$ 21,298	$ 19,411	$ 17,802	$ 16,419
75	$ 73,171	$ 61,156	$ 51,720	$ 44,243	$ 38,264	$ 33,436	$ 29,503	$ 26,268	$ 23,584	$ 21,337	$ 19,438	$ 17,821	$ 16,433
76	$ 74,146	$ 61,830	$ 52,187	$ 44,567	$ 38,488	$ 33,593	$ 29,612	$ 26,345	$ 23,637	$ 21,374	$ 19,464	$ 17,839	$ 16,446
77	$ 75,122	$ 62,500	$ 52,649	$ 44,886	$ 38,708	$ 33,745	$ 29,718	$ 26,418	$ 23,689	$ 21,409	$ 19,489	$ 17,857	$ 16,458
78	$ 76,098	$ 63,168	$ 53,106	$ 45,200	$ 38,925	$ 33,894	$ 29,821	$ 26,489	$ 23,738	$ 21,444	$ 19,513	$ 17,873	$ 16,470
79	$ 77,073	$ 63,832	$ 53,559	$ 45,509	$ 39,137	$ 34,039	$ 29,920	$ 26,558	$ 23,785	$ 21,476	$ 19,536	$ 17,889	$ 16,480
80	$ 78,049	$ 64,493	$ 54,008	$ 45,815	$ 39,344	$ 34,181	$ 30,018	$ 26,624	$ 23,831	$ 21,508	$ 19,557	$ 17,904	$ 16,491
81	$ 79,024	$ 65,151	$ 54,452	$ 46,115	$ 39,548	$ 34,320	$ 30,112	$ 26,689	$ 23,875	$ 21,538	$ 19,578	$ 17,918	$ 16,500
82	$ 80,000	$ 65,806	$ 54,893	$ 46,412	$ 39,748	$ 34,455	$ 30,203	$ 26,751	$ 23,917	$ 21,567	$ 19,597	$ 17,932	$ 16,510
83	$ 80,976	$ 66,457	$ 55,328	$ 46,704	$ 39,945	$ 34,587	$ 30,292	$ 26,811	$ 23,958	$ 21,594	$ 19,616	$ 17,944	$ 16,518
84	$ 81,951	$ 67,105	$ 55,760	$ 46,992	$ 40,137	$ 34,716	$ 30,379	$ 26,869	$ 23,997	$ 21,621	$ 19,634	$ 17,956	$ 16,527
85	$ 82,927	$ 67,750	$ 56,187	$ 47,276	$ 40,326	$ 34,842	$ 30,463	$ 26,925	$ 24,035	$ 21,646	$ 19,651	$ 17,968	$ 16,534
86	$ 83,902	$ 68,392	$ 56,611	$ 47,555	$ 40,511	$ 34,965	$ 30,545	$ 26,980	$ 24,071	$ 21,670	$ 19,667	$ 17,979	$ 16,542
87	$ 84,878	$ 69,031	$ 57,030	$ 47,831	$ 40,693	$ 35,085	$ 30,624	$ 27,032	$ 24,106	$ 21,693	$ 19,683	$ 17,989	$ 16,549
88	$ 85,854	$ 69,667	$ 57,445	$ 48,103	$ 40,871	$ 35,202	$ 30,701	$ 27,083	$ 24,139	$ 21,716	$ 19,697	$ 17,999	$ 16,555
89	$ 86,829	$ 70,300	$ 57,856	$ 48,370	$ 41,045	$ 35,316	$ 30,776	$ 27,132	$ 24,172	$ 21,737	$ 19,712	$ 18,008	$ 16,561
90	$ 87,805	$ 70,929	$ 58,263	$ 48,634	$ 41,217	$ 35,427	$ 30,848	$ 27,180	$ 24,203	$ 21,757	$ 19,725	$ 18,017	$ 16,567

CHART TWO

STARTING PORTFOLIO NEEDED TO FUND VARIOUS ANNUAL EXPENSES
ASSUMING NO TRUSTEE FEE AND 10% TAX RATE

Assumptions:

	Initial annual expenses: $ 1,000	inflation: 2.50%	tax rate: 10.00%	TTEE/admin. fee: 0.00%

The following also assumes that needs are paid at end of each year and that TTEE fee is not tax deductible.

Rate of Return (Nominal): Life expectancies	2.50%	3.00%	3.50%	4.00%	4.50%	5.00%	5.50%	6.00%	6.50%	7.00%	7.50%	8.00%	8.50%
1	$ 978	$ 974	$ 969	$ 965	$ 961	$ 957	$ 953	$ 949	$ 945	$ 941	$ 937	$ 933	$ 929
2	$ 1,958	$ 1,946	$ 1,933	$ 1,920	$ 1,908	$ 1,896	$ 1,883	$ 1,871	$ 1,860	$ 1,848	$ 1,836	$ 1,825	$ 1,813
3	$ 2,941	$ 2,915	$ 2,890	$ 2,865	$ 2,840	$ 2,816	$ 2,792	$ 2,769	$ 2,745	$ 2,723	$ 2,700	$ 2,678	$ 2,656
4	$ 3,926	$ 3,883	$ 3,841	$ 3,800	$ 3,759	$ 3,719	$ 3,680	$ 3,641	$ 3,603	$ 3,566	$ 3,529	$ 3,493	$ 3,458
5	$ 4,914	$ 4,850	$ 4,787	$ 4,725	$ 4,664	$ 4,605	$ 4,547	$ 4,490	$ 4,434	$ 4,379	$ 4,325	$ 4,273	$ 4,221
6	$ 5,904	$ 5,814	$ 5,726	$ 5,640	$ 5,556	$ 5,474	$ 5,394	$ 5,315	$ 5,238	$ 5,163	$ 5,090	$ 5,018	$ 4,948
7	$ 6,896	$ 6,776	$ 6,659	$ 6,545	$ 6,434	$ 6,326	$ 6,220	$ 6,118	$ 6,017	$ 5,920	$ 5,824	$ 5,731	$ 5,640
8	$ 7,891	$ 7,737	$ 7,587	$ 7,441	$ 7,299	$ 7,162	$ 7,028	$ 6,898	$ 6,772	$ 6,649	$ 6,529	$ 6,413	$ 6,299
9	$ 8,889	$ 8,695	$ 8,508	$ 8,327	$ 8,152	$ 7,982	$ 7,817	$ 7,657	$ 7,502	$ 7,352	$ 7,206	$ 7,064	$ 6,927
10	$ 9,888	$ 9,652	$ 9,424	$ 9,204	$ 8,991	$ 8,786	$ 8,587	$ 8,395	$ 8,209	$ 8,030	$ 7,856	$ 7,687	$ 7,524
11	$ 10,890	$ 10,607	$ 10,334	$ 10,072	$ 9,819	$ 9,575	$ 9,340	$ 9,113	$ 8,894	$ 8,683	$ 8,480	$ 8,283	$ 8,093
12	$ 11,895	$ 11,560	$ 11,239	$ 10,930	$ 10,633	$ 10,348	$ 10,074	$ 9,811	$ 9,558	$ 9,314	$ 9,079	$ 8,853	$ 8,635
13	$ 12,902	$ 12,511	$ 12,137	$ 11,779	$ 11,436	$ 11,107	$ 10,792	$ 10,490	$ 10,200	$ 9,921	$ 9,654	$ 9,398	$ 9,151
14	$ 13,912	$ 13,461	$ 13,030	$ 12,619	$ 12,227	$ 11,852	$ 11,493	$ 11,150	$ 10,822	$ 10,508	$ 10,207	$ 9,918	$ 9,642
15	$ 14,924	$ 14,408	$ 13,918	$ 13,451	$ 13,006	$ 12,582	$ 12,177	$ 11,792	$ 11,424	$ 11,073	$ 10,737	$ 10,416	$ 10,110
16	$ 15,938	$ 15,354	$ 14,799	$ 14,273	$ 13,773	$ 13,298	$ 12,846	$ 12,416	$ 12,007	$ 11,618	$ 11,246	$ 10,893	$ 10,555
17	$ 16,955	$ 16,298	$ 15,676	$ 15,087	$ 14,529	$ 14,000	$ 13,499	$ 13,023	$ 12,572	$ 12,143	$ 11,735	$ 11,348	$ 10,979
18	$ 17,975	$ 17,240	$ 16,546	$ 15,892	$ 15,274	$ 14,689	$ 14,137	$ 13,614	$ 13,119	$ 12,650	$ 12,205	$ 11,783	$ 11,383
19	$ 18,997	$ 18,180	$ 17,412	$ 16,688	$ 16,007	$ 15,365	$ 14,760	$ 14,188	$ 13,648	$ 13,138	$ 12,656	$ 12,199	$ 11,767
20	$ 20,021	$ 19,118	$ 18,271	$ 17,476	$ 16,730	$ 16,028	$ 15,368	$ 14,746	$ 14,161	$ 13,609	$ 13,089	$ 12,597	$ 12,133
21	$ 21,048	$ 20,055	$ 19,126	$ 18,256	$ 17,442	$ 16,678	$ 15,962	$ 15,289	$ 14,658	$ 14,063	$ 13,504	$ 12,978	$ 12,482
22	$ 22,077	$ 20,989	$ 19,975	$ 19,027	$ 18,143	$ 17,316	$ 16,542	$ 15,818	$ 15,138	$ 14,501	$ 13,903	$ 13,342	$ 12,813
23	$ 23,109	$ 21,922	$ 20,818	$ 19,791	$ 18,834	$ 17,941	$ 17,109	$ 16,331	$ 15,604	$ 14,924	$ 14,287	$ 13,690	$ 13,129

CHART TWO

STARTING PORTFOLIO NEEDED TO FUND VARIOUS ANNUAL EXPENSES ASSUMING NO TRUSTEE FEE AND 10% TAX RATE (CONTINUED)

Assumptions: Initial annual expenses: $ 1,000   inflation: 2.50%   tax rate: 10.00%   TTEE/admin. fee: 0.00%

The following also assumes that needs are paid at end of each year and that TTEE fee is not tax deductible.

Rate of Return (Nominal): Life expectancies	2.50%	3.00%	3.50%	4.00%	4.50%	5.00%	5.50%	6.00%	6.50%	7.00%	7.50%	8.00%	8.50%
24	$ 24,144	$ 22,853	$ 21,656	$ 20,546	$ 19,514	$ 18,555	$ 17,662	$ 16,831	$ 16,055	$ 15,331	$ 14,655	$ 14,022	$ 13,430
25	$ 25,181	$ 23,782	$ 22,489	$ 21,293	$ 20,185	$ 19,157	$ 18,203	$ 17,316	$ 16,492	$ 15,724	$ 15,008	$ 14,340	$ 13,717
26	$ 26,220	$ 24,710	$ 23,317	$ 22,032	$ 20,845	$ 19,747	$ 18,731	$ 17,789	$ 16,914	$ 16,102	$ 15,347	$ 14,644	$ 13,989
27	$ 27,263	$ 25,635	$ 24,140	$ 22,763	$ 21,496	$ 20,326	$ 19,246	$ 18,248	$ 17,324	$ 16,467	$ 15,673	$ 14,935	$ 14,249
28	$ 28,307	$ 26,559	$ 24,957	$ 23,487	$ 22,136	$ 20,894	$ 19,750	$ 18,695	$ 17,720	$ 16,820	$ 15,986	$ 15,213	$ 14,496
29	$ 29,354	$ 27,481	$ 25,769	$ 24,203	$ 22,768	$ 21,451	$ 20,242	$ 19,129	$ 18,104	$ 17,159	$ 16,286	$ 15,479	$ 14,732
30	$ 30,404	$ 28,401	$ 26,576	$ 24,911	$ 23,390	$ 21,997	$ 20,722	$ 19,551	$ 18,476	$ 17,486	$ 16,575	$ 15,733	$ 14,956
31	$ 31,456	$ 29,320	$ 27,378	$ 25,612	$ 24,002	$ 22,533	$ 21,191	$ 19,962	$ 18,836	$ 17,802	$ 16,851	$ 15,976	$ 15,169
32	$ 32,511	$ 30,236	$ 28,175	$ 26,305	$ 24,606	$ 23,059	$ 21,649	$ 20,362	$ 19,185	$ 18,106	$ 17,117	$ 16,209	$ 15,373
33	$ 33,569	$ 31,151	$ 28,967	$ 26,991	$ 25,200	$ 23,575	$ 22,097	$ 20,750	$ 19,522	$ 18,400	$ 17,373	$ 16,431	$ 15,566
34	$ 34,629	$ 32,064	$ 29,754	$ 27,670	$ 25,786	$ 24,080	$ 22,534	$ 21,128	$ 19,849	$ 18,683	$ 17,618	$ 16,643	$ 15,750
35	$ 35,692	$ 32,975	$ 30,536	$ 28,341	$ 26,363	$ 24,577	$ 22,960	$ 21,496	$ 20,166	$ 18,956	$ 17,853	$ 16,846	$ 15,926
36	$ 36,757	$ 33,885	$ 31,313	$ 29,006	$ 26,931	$ 25,063	$ 23,377	$ 21,853	$ 20,472	$ 19,219	$ 18,079	$ 17,041	$ 16,093
37	$ 37,825	$ 34,793	$ 32,085	$ 29,663	$ 27,491	$ 25,540	$ 23,784	$ 22,200	$ 20,769	$ 19,472	$ 18,296	$ 17,226	$ 16,252
38	$ 38,895	$ 35,699	$ 32,852	$ 30,313	$ 28,043	$ 26,008	$ 24,182	$ 22,538	$ 21,056	$ 19,717	$ 18,504	$ 17,404	$ 16,403
39	$ 39,968	$ 36,603	$ 33,615	$ 30,957	$ 28,586	$ 26,468	$ 24,570	$ 22,867	$ 21,335	$ 19,953	$ 18,704	$ 17,574	$ 16,548
40	$ 41,044	$ 37,505	$ 34,373	$ 31,593	$ 29,121	$ 26,918	$ 24,949	$ 23,187	$ 21,604	$ 20,180	$ 18,897	$ 17,736	$ 16,685
41	$ 42,122	$ 38,406	$ 35,125	$ 32,223	$ 29,649	$ 27,360	$ 25,320	$ 23,497	$ 21,865	$ 20,400	$ 19,081	$ 17,891	$ 16,816
42	$ 43,203	$ 39,305	$ 35,874	$ 32,846	$ 30,168	$ 27,793	$ 25,682	$ 23,800	$ 22,118	$ 20,611	$ 19,258	$ 18,040	$ 16,940
43	$ 44,287	$ 40,202	$ 36,617	$ 33,463	$ 30,680	$ 28,218	$ 26,035	$ 24,094	$ 22,363	$ 20,815	$ 19,428	$ 18,182	$ 17,059
44	$ 45,373	$ 41,097	$ 37,356	$ 34,072	$ 31,184	$ 28,635	$ 26,380	$ 24,379	$ 22,600	$ 21,012	$ 19,591	$ 18,317	$ 17,171
45	$ 46,462	$ 41,991	$ 38,090	$ 34,676	$ 31,680	$ 29,044	$ 26,717	$ 24,657	$ 22,829	$ 21,201	$ 19,748	$ 18,447	$ 17,279
46	$ 47,554	$ 42,883	$ 38,819	$ 35,273	$ 32,169	$ 29,445	$ 27,046	$ 24,928	$ 23,051	$ 21,384	$ 19,899	$ 18,571	$ 17,381

Assumptions:

| Initial annual expenses: | $1,000 | inflation: 2.50% | tax rate: 10.00% | TTEE/admin. fee: 0.00% |

The following also assumes that needs are paid at end of each year and that TTEE fee is not tax deductible.

Rate of Return (Nominal): Life expectancies	2.50%	3.00%	3.50%	4.00%	4.50%	5.00%	5.50%	6.00%	6.50%	7.00%	7.50%	8.00%	8.50%
47	$ 48,648	$ 43,773	$ 39,544	$ 35,864	$ 32,651	$ 29,838	$ 27,368	$ 25,191	$ 23,266	$ 21,561	$ 20,043	$ 18,690	$ 17,479
48	$ 49,745	$ 44,662	$ 40,264	$ 36,448	$ 33,126	$ 30,224	$ 27,682	$ 25,446	$ 23,475	$ 21,731	$ 20,182	$ 18,803	$ 17,571
49	$ 50,845	$ 45,548	$ 40,980	$ 37,026	$ 33,594	$ 30,603	$ 27,988	$ 25,695	$ 23,677	$ 21,894	$ 20,315	$ 18,912	$ 17,660
50	$ 51,947	$ 46,433	$ 41,691	$ 37,599	$ 34,054	$ 30,974	$ 28,288	$ 25,937	$ 23,872	$ 22,052	$ 20,443	$ 19,015	$ 17,744
51	$ 53,052	$ 47,317	$ 42,398	$ 38,165	$ 34,508	$ 31,338	$ 28,580	$ 26,172	$ 24,061	$ 22,205	$ 20,566	$ 19,114	$ 17,824
52	$ 54,160	$ 48,198	$ 43,100	$ 38,725	$ 34,955	$ 31,695	$ 28,866	$ 26,401	$ 24,245	$ 22,352	$ 20,684	$ 19,209	$ 17,900
53	$ 55,270	$ 49,078	$ 43,798	$ 39,279	$ 35,395	$ 32,046	$ 29,145	$ 26,623	$ 24,422	$ 22,494	$ 20,797	$ 19,300	$ 17,973
54	$ 56,383	$ 49,956	$ 44,492	$ 39,827	$ 35,829	$ 32,389	$ 29,417	$ 26,839	$ 24,594	$ 22,630	$ 20,906	$ 19,387	$ 18,042
55	$ 57,499	$ 50,833	$ 45,181	$ 40,369	$ 36,257	$ 32,726	$ 29,683	$ 27,049	$ 24,760	$ 22,762	$ 21,011	$ 19,469	$ 18,108
56	$ 58,618	$ 51,707	$ 45,865	$ 40,906	$ 36,677	$ 33,057	$ 29,943	$ 27,254	$ 24,921	$ 22,889	$ 21,111	$ 19,549	$ 18,170
57	$ 59,739	$ 52,580	$ 46,546	$ 41,437	$ 37,092	$ 33,381	$ 30,197	$ 27,453	$ 25,077	$ 23,011	$ 21,207	$ 19,624	$ 18,230
58	$ 60,863	$ 53,452	$ 47,222	$ 41,962	$ 37,501	$ 33,699	$ 30,445	$ 27,646	$ 25,228	$ 23,130	$ 21,300	$ 19,697	$ 18,287
59	$ 61,990	$ 54,321	$ 47,894	$ 42,482	$ 37,903	$ 34,011	$ 30,687	$ 27,834	$ 25,375	$ 23,244	$ 21,388	$ 19,766	$ 18,341
60	$ 63,119	$ 55,189	$ 48,562	$ 42,996	$ 38,300	$ 34,317	$ 30,924	$ 28,017	$ 25,516	$ 23,353	$ 21,474	$ 19,832	$ 18,392
61	$ 64,252	$ 56,055	$ 49,225	$ 43,505	$ 38,690	$ 34,617	$ 31,154	$ 28,195	$ 25,653	$ 23,459	$ 21,556	$ 19,896	$ 18,441
62	$ 65,387	$ 56,920	$ 49,884	$ 44,008	$ 39,075	$ 34,912	$ 31,380	$ 28,368	$ 25,786	$ 23,561	$ 21,634	$ 19,956	$ 18,488
63	$ 66,525	$ 57,783	$ 50,539	$ 44,506	$ 39,454	$ 35,200	$ 31,600	$ 28,536	$ 25,915	$ 23,660	$ 21,710	$ 20,014	$ 18,533
64	$ 67,665	$ 58,644	$ 51,190	$ 44,999	$ 39,827	$ 35,484	$ 31,815	$ 28,700	$ 26,039	$ 23,755	$ 21,782	$ 20,069	$ 18,575
65	$ 68,809	$ 59,504	$ 51,837	$ 45,486	$ 40,195	$ 35,762	$ 32,026	$ 28,859	$ 26,160	$ 23,846	$ 21,852	$ 20,122	$ 18,615
66	$ 69,955	$ 60,361	$ 52,480	$ 45,969	$ 40,557	$ 36,034	$ 32,231	$ 29,014	$ 26,277	$ 23,935	$ 21,918	$ 20,173	$ 18,654
67	$ 71,104	$ 61,218	$ 53,119	$ 46,446	$ 40,914	$ 36,301	$ 32,431	$ 29,164	$ 26,390	$ 24,020	$ 21,983	$ 20,221	$ 18,690
68	$ 72,256	$ 62,072	$ 53,754	$ 46,918	$ 41,266	$ 36,564	$ 32,627	$ 29,311	$ 26,500	$ 24,102	$ 22,044	$ 20,268	$ 18,725
69	$ 73,410	$ 62,925	$ 54,384	$ 47,385	$ 41,612	$ 36,821	$ 32,818	$ 29,453	$ 26,606	$ 24,181	$ 22,103	$ 20,312	$ 18,758

CHART TWO

STARTING PORTFOLIO NEEDED TO FUND VARIOUS ANNUAL EXPENSES ASSUMING NO TRUSTEE FEE AND 10% TAX RATE (CONTINUED)

Assumptions:

Initial annual expenses:	inflation:	tax rate:	TTEE/admin. fee:
$ 1,000	2.50%	10.00%	0.00%

The following also assumes that needs are paid at end of each year and that TTEE fee is not tax deductible.

Rate of Return (Nominal): Life expectancies	2.50%	3.00%	3.50%	4.00%	4.50%	5.00%	5.50%	6.00%	6.50%	7.00%	7.50%	8.00%	8.50%
70	$ 74,568	$ 63,776	$ 55,011	$ 47,847	$ 41,953	$ 37,073	$ 33,005	$ 29,591	$ 26,708	$ 24,257	$ 22,160	$ 20,354	$ 18,790
71	$ 75,728	$ 64,626	$ 55,634	$ 48,304	$ 42,289	$ 37,320	$ 33,187	$ 29,726	$ 26,808	$ 24,331	$ 22,215	$ 20,395	$ 18,820
72	$ 76,891	$ 65,473	$ 56,253	$ 48,757	$ 42,621	$ 37,563	$ 33,365	$ 29,857	$ 26,904	$ 24,402	$ 22,267	$ 20,433	$ 18,848
73	$ 78,057	$ 66,320	$ 56,868	$ 49,204	$ 42,947	$ 37,801	$ 33,539	$ 29,984	$ 26,997	$ 24,470	$ 22,317	$ 20,470	$ 18,875
74	$ 79,226	$ 67,164	$ 57,479	$ 49,647	$ 43,268	$ 38,035	$ 33,709	$ 30,108	$ 27,088	$ 24,536	$ 22,365	$ 20,506	$ 18,901
75	$ 80,398	$ 68,007	$ 58,086	$ 50,085	$ 43,585	$ 38,264	$ 33,875	$ 30,228	$ 27,175	$ 24,600	$ 22,412	$ 20,539	$ 18,926
76	$ 81,573	$ 68,848	$ 58,690	$ 50,519	$ 43,896	$ 38,488	$ 34,037	$ 30,345	$ 27,260	$ 24,661	$ 22,456	$ 20,572	$ 18,950
77	$ 82,750	$ 69,688	$ 59,289	$ 50,947	$ 44,204	$ 38,708	$ 34,195	$ 30,459	$ 27,342	$ 24,720	$ 22,499	$ 20,603	$ 18,972
78	$ 83,930	$ 70,526	$ 59,885	$ 51,372	$ 44,506	$ 38,925	$ 34,350	$ 30,570	$ 27,421	$ 24,777	$ 22,540	$ 20,632	$ 18,993
79	$ 85,113	$ 71,362	$ 60,477	$ 51,792	$ 44,804	$ 39,137	$ 34,501	$ 30,678	$ 27,498	$ 24,832	$ 22,579	$ 20,660	$ 19,014
80	$ 86,300	$ 72,197	$ 61,066	$ 52,207	$ 45,098	$ 39,344	$ 34,648	$ 30,782	$ 27,573	$ 24,885	$ 22,617	$ 20,687	$ 19,033
81	$ 87,489	$ 73,030	$ 61,650	$ 52,618	$ 45,387	$ 39,548	$ 34,792	$ 30,884	$ 27,645	$ 24,937	$ 22,654	$ 20,713	$ 19,051
82	$ 88,680	$ 73,862	$ 62,231	$ 53,024	$ 45,672	$ 39,748	$ 34,933	$ 30,983	$ 27,714	$ 24,986	$ 22,688	$ 20,738	$ 19,069
83	$ 89,875	$ 74,692	$ 62,808	$ 53,427	$ 45,953	$ 39,945	$ 35,070	$ 31,079	$ 27,782	$ 25,033	$ 22,722	$ 20,762	$ 19,085
84	$ 91,073	$ 75,520	$ 63,382	$ 53,825	$ 46,229	$ 40,137	$ 35,204	$ 31,173	$ 27,848	$ 25,079	$ 22,754	$ 20,784	$ 19,101
85	$ 92,274	$ 76,346	$ 63,952	$ 54,218	$ 46,502	$ 40,326	$ 35,335	$ 31,264	$ 27,911	$ 25,123	$ 22,785	$ 20,806	$ 19,117
86	$ 93,477	$ 77,171	$ 64,519	$ 54,608	$ 46,770	$ 40,511	$ 35,463	$ 31,353	$ 27,972	$ 25,166	$ 22,815	$ 20,826	$ 19,131
87	$ 94,684	$ 77,995	$ 65,082	$ 54,993	$ 47,034	$ 40,693	$ 35,588	$ 31,439	$ 28,032	$ 25,207	$ 22,843	$ 20,846	$ 19,145
88	$ 95,893	$ 78,817	$ 65,641	$ 55,375	$ 47,295	$ 40,871	$ 35,710	$ 31,523	$ 28,089	$ 25,247	$ 22,870	$ 20,865	$ 19,158
89	$ 97,106	$ 79,637	$ 66,197	$ 55,752	$ 47,551	$ 41,045	$ 35,830	$ 31,604	$ 28,145	$ 25,285	$ 22,897	$ 20,883	$ 19,170
90	$ 98,321	$ 80,456	$ 66,749	$ 56,125	$ 47,804	$ 41,217	$ 35,946	$ 31,683	$ 28,199	$ 25,322	$ 22,922	$ 20,900	$ 19,182

CHART THREE

STARTING PORTFOLIO NEEDED TO FUND VARIOUS ANNUAL EXPENSES
ASSUMING NO TRUSTEE FEE AND 20% TAX RATE

Assumptions:
Initial annual expenses: $ 1,000   inflation: 2.50%   tax rate: 20.00%   TTEE/admin. fee: 0.00%

The following also assumes that needs are paid at end of each year and that TTEE fee is not tax deductible.

Rate of Return (Nominal): Life expectancies	2.50%	3.00%	3.50%	4.00%	4.50%	5.00%	5.50%	6.00%	6.50%	7.00%	7.50%	8.00%	8.50%
1	$ 980	$ 977	$ 973	$ 969	$ 965	$ 962	$ 958	$ 954	$ 951	$ 947	$ 943	$ 940	$ 936
2	$ 1,966	$ 1,954	$ 1,943	$ 1,931	$ 1,920	$ 1,909	$ 1,898	$ 1,887	$ 1,877	$ 1,866	$ 1,856	$ 1,845	$ 1,835
3	$ 2,956	$ 2,933	$ 2,910	$ 2,887	$ 2,865	$ 2,843	$ 2,822	$ 2,800	$ 2,779	$ 2,758	$ 2,738	$ 2,717	$ 2,697
4	$ 3,950	$ 3,912	$ 3,874	$ 3,837	$ 3,800	$ 3,764	$ 3,728	$ 3,693	$ 3,658	$ 3,624	$ 3,591	$ 3,558	$ 3,525
5	$ 4,950	$ 4,892	$ 4,836	$ 4,780	$ 4,725	$ 4,671	$ 4,618	$ 4,566	$ 4,515	$ 4,465	$ 4,416	$ 4,367	$ 4,320
6	$ 5,955	$ 5,874	$ 5,794	$ 5,716	$ 5,640	$ 5,565	$ 5,492	$ 5,420	$ 5,350	$ 5,281	$ 5,213	$ 5,147	$ 5,082
7	$ 6,964	$ 6,856	$ 6,750	$ 6,646	$ 6,545	$ 6,446	$ 6,350	$ 6,255	$ 6,163	$ 6,073	$ 5,984	$ 5,898	$ 5,814
8	$ 7,979	$ 7,839	$ 7,703	$ 7,570	$ 7,441	$ 7,315	$ 7,192	$ 7,072	$ 6,955	$ 6,841	$ 6,730	$ 6,622	$ 6,516
9	$ 8,999	$ 8,823	$ 8,653	$ 8,488	$ 8,327	$ 8,171	$ 8,019	$ 7,871	$ 7,727	$ 7,588	$ 7,451	$ 7,319	$ 7,190
10	$ 10,023	$ 9,809	$ 9,601	$ 9,399	$ 9,204	$ 9,015	$ 8,831	$ 8,653	$ 8,480	$ 8,312	$ 8,149	$ 7,990	$ 7,837
11	$ 11,053	$ 10,795	$ 10,546	$ 10,305	$ 10,072	$ 9,846	$ 9,628	$ 9,417	$ 9,213	$ 9,015	$ 8,823	$ 8,637	$ 8,458
12	$ 12,087	$ 11,782	$ 11,488	$ 11,204	$ 10,930	$ 10,666	$ 10,411	$ 10,165	$ 9,927	$ 9,697	$ 9,475	$ 9,261	$ 9,053
13	$ 13,127	$ 12,770	$ 12,427	$ 12,097	$ 11,779	$ 11,473	$ 11,179	$ 10,896	$ 10,623	$ 10,359	$ 10,106	$ 9,861	$ 9,625
14	$ 14,172	$ 13,759	$ 13,363	$ 12,984	$ 12,619	$ 12,270	$ 11,934	$ 11,611	$ 11,301	$ 11,002	$ 10,715	$ 10,440	$ 10,174
15	$ 15,221	$ 14,749	$ 14,297	$ 13,865	$ 13,451	$ 13,054	$ 12,674	$ 12,310	$ 11,961	$ 11,626	$ 11,305	$ 10,997	$ 10,701
16	$ 16,276	$ 15,740	$ 15,228	$ 14,740	$ 14,273	$ 13,827	$ 13,401	$ 12,994	$ 12,605	$ 12,232	$ 11,875	$ 11,533	$ 11,206
17	$ 17,337	$ 16,732	$ 16,156	$ 15,609	$ 15,087	$ 14,589	$ 14,115	$ 13,663	$ 13,232	$ 12,820	$ 12,426	$ 12,051	$ 11,691
18	$ 18,402	$ 17,725	$ 17,082	$ 16,472	$ 15,892	$ 15,341	$ 14,816	$ 14,318	$ 13,843	$ 13,390	$ 12,960	$ 12,549	$ 12,157
19	$ 19,473	$ 18,719	$ 18,005	$ 17,329	$ 16,688	$ 16,081	$ 15,505	$ 14,957	$ 14,438	$ 13,944	$ 13,475	$ 13,029	$ 12,604
20	$ 20,548	$ 19,714	$ 18,925	$ 18,180	$ 17,476	$ 16,810	$ 16,180	$ 15,583	$ 15,018	$ 14,482	$ 13,973	$ 13,491	$ 13,033
21	$ 21,629	$ 20,709	$ 19,843	$ 19,026	$ 18,256	$ 17,530	$ 16,844	$ 16,196	$ 15,583	$ 15,004	$ 14,455	$ 13,936	$ 13,444
22	$ 22,716	$ 21,706	$ 20,758	$ 19,866	$ 19,027	$ 18,238	$ 17,495	$ 16,794	$ 16,134	$ 15,510	$ 14,922	$ 14,365	$ 13,839
23	$ 23,808	$ 22,704	$ 21,670	$ 20,700	$ 19,791	$ 18,937	$ 18,134	$ 17,380	$ 16,670	$ 16,002	$ 15,372	$ 14,779	$ 14,218

STARTING PORTFOLIO NEEDED TO FUND VARIOUS ANNUAL EXPENSES
ASSUMING NO TRUSTEE FEE AND 20% TAX RATE (CONTINUED)

Assumptions: Initial annual expenses: $ 1,000 inflation: 2.50% tax rate: 20.00% TTEE/admin. fee: 0.00%

The following also assumes that needs are paid at end of each year and that TTEE fee is not tax deductible.

Rate of Return (Nominal): Life expectancies	2.50%	3.00%	3.50%	4.00%	4.50%	5.00%	5.50%	6.00%	6.50%	7.00%	7.50%	8.00%	8.50%
24	$ 24,905	$ 23,703	$ 22,579	$ 21,529	$ 20,546	$ 19,625	$ 18,762	$ 17,953	$ 17,193	$ 16,479	$ 15,808	$ 15,177	$ 14,582
25	$ 26,007	$ 24,702	$ 23,486	$ 22,352	$ 21,293	$ 20,304	$ 19,379	$ 18,513	$ 17,702	$ 16,942	$ 16,230	$ 15,560	$ 14,932
26	$ 27,115	$ 25,703	$ 24,390	$ 23,169	$ 22,032	$ 20,972	$ 19,984	$ 19,061	$ 18,198	$ 17,392	$ 16,637	$ 15,930	$ 15,267
27	$ 28,228	$ 26,705	$ 25,292	$ 23,981	$ 22,763	$ 21,631	$ 20,578	$ 19,597	$ 18,682	$ 17,828	$ 17,031	$ 16,286	$ 15,588
28	$ 29,347	$ 27,707	$ 26,191	$ 24,787	$ 23,487	$ 22,281	$ 21,161	$ 20,121	$ 19,153	$ 18,252	$ 17,412	$ 16,629	$ 15,897
29	$ 30,471	$ 28,711	$ 27,087	$ 25,588	$ 24,203	$ 22,921	$ 21,734	$ 20,633	$ 19,612	$ 18,663	$ 17,781	$ 16,959	$ 16,193
30	$ 31,601	$ 29,716	$ 27,981	$ 26,384	$ 24,911	$ 23,552	$ 22,296	$ 21,135	$ 20,059	$ 19,062	$ 18,137	$ 17,277	$ 16,478
31	$ 32,736	$ 30,721	$ 28,872	$ 27,174	$ 25,612	$ 24,174	$ 22,848	$ 21,625	$ 20,495	$ 19,450	$ 18,481	$ 17,584	$ 16,751
32	$ 33,877	$ 31,728	$ 29,761	$ 27,958	$ 26,305	$ 24,787	$ 23,390	$ 22,105	$ 20,920	$ 19,826	$ 18,815	$ 17,879	$ 17,013
33	$ 35,024	$ 32,735	$ 30,647	$ 28,738	$ 26,991	$ 25,391	$ 23,923	$ 22,574	$ 21,333	$ 20,191	$ 19,137	$ 18,164	$ 17,264
34	$ 36,176	$ 33,744	$ 31,530	$ 29,512	$ 27,670	$ 25,986	$ 24,445	$ 23,033	$ 21,736	$ 20,545	$ 19,448	$ 18,438	$ 17,505
35	$ 37,334	$ 34,753	$ 32,411	$ 30,281	$ 28,341	$ 26,573	$ 24,958	$ 23,481	$ 22,129	$ 20,889	$ 19,750	$ 18,702	$ 17,737
36	$ 38,497	$ 35,764	$ 33,289	$ 31,044	$ 29,006	$ 27,151	$ 25,462	$ 23,920	$ 22,512	$ 21,222	$ 20,041	$ 18,956	$ 17,959
37	$ 39,666	$ 36,775	$ 34,164	$ 31,803	$ 29,663	$ 27,721	$ 25,956	$ 24,349	$ 22,884	$ 21,546	$ 20,322	$ 19,201	$ 18,172
38	$ 40,841	$ 37,788	$ 35,037	$ 32,556	$ 30,313	$ 28,283	$ 26,442	$ 24,769	$ 23,248	$ 21,861	$ 20,595	$ 19,437	$ 18,377
39	$ 42,022	$ 38,801	$ 35,908	$ 33,304	$ 30,957	$ 28,836	$ 26,918	$ 25,180	$ 23,602	$ 22,166	$ 20,858	$ 19,665	$ 18,573
40	$ 43,208	$ 39,816	$ 36,776	$ 34,047	$ 31,593	$ 29,382	$ 27,386	$ 25,581	$ 23,946	$ 22,462	$ 21,113	$ 19,884	$ 18,762
41	$ 44,400	$ 40,831	$ 37,641	$ 34,785	$ 32,223	$ 29,920	$ 27,846	$ 25,974	$ 24,282	$ 22,750	$ 21,359	$ 20,095	$ 18,943
42	$ 45,598	$ 41,848	$ 38,504	$ 35,518	$ 32,846	$ 30,450	$ 28,297	$ 26,358	$ 24,610	$ 23,029	$ 21,597	$ 20,298	$ 19,116
43	$ 46,802	$ 42,865	$ 39,365	$ 36,246	$ 33,463	$ 30,972	$ 28,740	$ 26,734	$ 24,929	$ 23,300	$ 21,828	$ 20,494	$ 19,283
44	$ 48,012	$ 43,883	$ 40,223	$ 36,969	$ 34,072	$ 31,487	$ 29,174	$ 27,102	$ 25,239	$ 23,563	$ 22,050	$ 20,682	$ 19,443
45	$ 49,228	$ 44,903	$ 41,078	$ 37,688	$ 34,676	$ 31,994	$ 29,601	$ 27,461	$ 25,542	$ 23,818	$ 22,266	$ 20,864	$ 19,597
46	$ 50,449	$ 45,923	$ 41,931	$ 38,401	$ 35,273	$ 32,494	$ 30,021	$ 27,813	$ 25,837	$ 24,066	$ 22,474	$ 21,039	$ 19,744

Initial
annual

Assumptions: expenses: $ 1,000   inflation: 2.50%   tax rate: 20.00%   TTEE/admin. fee: 0.00%

The following also assumes that needs are paid at end of each year and that TTEE fee is not tax deductible.

Rate of Return (Nominal): Life expectancies	2.50%	3.00%	3.50%	4.00%	4.50%	5.00%	5.50%	6.00%	6.50%	7.00%	7.50%	8.00%	8.50%
47	$ 51,677	$ 46,945	$ 42,781	$ 39,110	$ 35,864	$ 32,987	$ 30,432	$ 28,156	$ 26,125	$ 24,306	$ 22,675	$ 21,208	$ 19,885
48	$ 52,911	$ 47,967	$ 43,629	$ 39,813	$ 36,448	$ 33,473	$ 30,836	$ 28,493	$ 26,405	$ 24,540	$ 22,870	$ 21,370	$ 20,021
49	$ 54,151	$ 48,990	$ 44,475	$ 40,512	$ 37,026	$ 33,952	$ 31,233	$ 28,821	$ 26,678	$ 24,766	$ 23,058	$ 21,527	$ 20,151
50	$ 55,396	$ 50,015	$ 45,318	$ 41,206	$ 37,599	$ 34,424	$ 31,622	$ 29,143	$ 26,944	$ 24,986	$ 23,240	$ 21,678	$ 20,276
51	$ 56,648	$ 51,040	$ 46,158	$ 41,896	$ 38,165	$ 34,889	$ 32,004	$ 29,458	$ 27,203	$ 25,200	$ 23,416	$ 21,823	$ 20,396
52	$ 57,906	$ 52,067	$ 46,996	$ 42,581	$ 38,725	$ 35,347	$ 32,380	$ 29,765	$ 27,455	$ 25,407	$ 23,586	$ 21,963	$ 20,511
53	$ 59,171	$ 53,094	$ 47,832	$ 43,261	$ 39,279	$ 35,799	$ 32,748	$ 30,066	$ 27,701	$ 25,608	$ 23,751	$ 22,098	$ 20,622
54	$ 60,441	$ 54,122	$ 48,665	$ 43,936	$ 39,827	$ 36,244	$ 33,110	$ 30,361	$ 27,941	$ 25,803	$ 23,910	$ 22,228	$ 20,728
55	$ 61,718	$ 55,152	$ 49,496	$ 44,607	$ 40,369	$ 36,683	$ 33,466	$ 30,649	$ 28,174	$ 25,993	$ 24,064	$ 22,353	$ 20,830
56	$ 63,001	$ 56,182	$ 50,324	$ 45,274	$ 40,906	$ 37,115	$ 33,814	$ 30,930	$ 28,401	$ 26,177	$ 24,213	$ 22,473	$ 20,927
57	$ 64,290	$ 57,214	$ 51,150	$ 45,936	$ 41,437	$ 37,541	$ 34,157	$ 31,206	$ 28,623	$ 26,355	$ 24,357	$ 22,589	$ 21,021
58	$ 65,585	$ 58,246	$ 51,973	$ 46,593	$ 41,962	$ 37,962	$ 34,493	$ 31,475	$ 28,839	$ 26,529	$ 24,496	$ 22,701	$ 21,111
59	$ 66,887	$ 59,280	$ 52,794	$ 47,246	$ 42,482	$ 38,376	$ 34,823	$ 31,738	$ 29,049	$ 26,697	$ 24,631	$ 22,809	$ 21,197
60	$ 68,196	$ 60,314	$ 53,613	$ 47,895	$ 42,996	$ 38,784	$ 35,147	$ 31,996	$ 29,254	$ 26,860	$ 24,761	$ 22,913	$ 21,280
61	$ 69,510	$ 61,350	$ 54,429	$ 48,539	$ 43,505	$ 39,186	$ 35,465	$ 32,248	$ 29,454	$ 27,019	$ 24,886	$ 23,013	$ 21,360
62	$ 70,831	$ 62,386	$ 55,243	$ 49,179	$ 44,008	$ 39,582	$ 35,778	$ 32,494	$ 29,649	$ 27,172	$ 25,008	$ 23,109	$ 21,436
63	$ 72,159	$ 63,423	$ 56,055	$ 49,814	$ 44,506	$ 39,973	$ 36,085	$ 32,736	$ 29,838	$ 27,322	$ 25,126	$ 23,202	$ 21,509
64	$ 73,493	$ 64,462	$ 56,864	$ 50,445	$ 44,999	$ 40,358	$ 36,386	$ 32,971	$ 30,023	$ 27,467	$ 25,240	$ 23,291	$ 21,580
65	$ 74,834	$ 65,502	$ 57,671	$ 51,072	$ 45,486	$ 40,737	$ 36,681	$ 33,202	$ 30,203	$ 27,607	$ 25,350	$ 23,378	$ 21,647
66	$ 76,181	$ 66,542	$ 58,475	$ 51,694	$ 45,969	$ 41,111	$ 36,972	$ 33,427	$ 30,379	$ 27,744	$ 25,456	$ 23,460	$ 21,712
67	$ 77,535	$ 67,584	$ 59,278	$ 52,313	$ 46,446	$ 41,480	$ 37,257	$ 33,648	$ 30,549	$ 27,876	$ 25,559	$ 23,540	$ 21,774
68	$ 78,895	$ 68,626	$ 60,077	$ 52,927	$ 46,918	$ 41,843	$ 37,537	$ 33,864	$ 30,716	$ 28,005	$ 25,658	$ 23,617	$ 21,834
69	$ 80,262	$ 69,670	$ 60,875	$ 53,537	$ 47,385	$ 42,201	$ 37,811	$ 34,075	$ 30,878	$ 28,130	$ 25,755	$ 23,692	$ 21,891

CHART THREE

STARTING PORTFOLIO NEEDED TO FUND VARIOUS ANNUAL EXPENSES
ASSUMING NO TRUSTEE FEE AND 20% TAX RATE (CONTINUED)

Assumptions:
Initial annual expenses: $ 1,000   inflation: 2.50%   tax rate: 20.00%   TTEE/admin. fee: 0.00%

The following also assumes that needs are paid at end of each year and that TTEE fee is not tax deductible.

Rate of Return (Nominal): Life expectancies	2.50%	3.00%	3.50%	4.00%	4.50%	5.00%	5.50%	6.00%	6.50%	7.00%	7.50%	8.00%	8.50%
70	81,636	70,714	61,670	54,143	47,847	42,554	38,081	34,281	31,036	28,251	25,848	23,763	21,946
71	83,017	71,760	62,463	54,745	48,304	42,902	38,346	34,483	31,190	28,369	25,937	23,832	21,999
72	84,404	72,807	63,253	55,342	48,757	43,245	38,606	34,680	31,340	28,483	26,024	23,898	22,049
73	85,798	73,854	64,041	55,936	49,204	43,582	38,861	34,873	31,487	28,594	26,109	23,962	22,098
74	87,199	74,903	64,827	56,525	49,647	43,915	39,112	35,062	31,629	28,701	26,190	24,024	22,145
75	88,607	75,953	65,611	57,111	50,085	44,243	39,358	35,247	31,768	28,806	26,268	24,083	22,189
76	90,022	77,003	66,392	57,693	50,519	44,567	39,599	35,428	31,903	28,907	26,345	24,140	22,232
77	91,444	78,055	67,171	58,270	50,947	44,886	39,836	35,604	32,035	29,005	26,418	24,195	22,273
78	92,872	79,108	67,948	58,844	51,372	45,200	40,069	35,777	32,163	29,101	26,489	24,248	22,313
79	94,308	80,162	68,722	59,414	51,792	45,509	40,298	35,946	32,288	29,193	26,558	24,299	22,351
80	95,750	81,217	69,494	59,980	52,207	45,815	40,522	36,111	32,410	29,283	26,624	24,348	22,387
81	97,200	82,272	70,264	60,542	52,618	46,115	40,743	36,273	32,529	29,371	26,689	24,396	22,422
82	98,657	83,329	71,032	61,100	53,024	46,412	40,959	36,431	32,645	29,456	26,751	24,441	22,456
83	100,121	84,387	71,798	61,655	53,427	46,704	41,172	36,586	32,757	29,538	26,811	24,485	22,488
84	101,592	85,446	72,561	62,206	53,825	46,992	41,380	36,737	32,867	29,618	26,869	24,528	22,519
85	103,071	86,506	73,322	62,753	54,218	47,276	41,585	36,885	32,974	29,695	26,925	24,568	22,549
86	104,556	87,567	74,081	63,296	54,608	47,555	41,786	37,030	33,078	29,770	26,980	24,608	22,577
87	106,049	88,629	74,837	63,836	54,993	47,831	41,983	37,171	33,180	29,843	27,032	24,646	22,604
88	107,550	89,693	75,592	64,372	55,375	48,103	42,177	37,310	33,279	29,914	27,083	24,682	22,631
89	109,057	90,757	76,344	64,904	55,752	48,370	42,367	37,445	33,376	29,983	27,132	24,717	22,656
90	110,572	91,822	77,094	65,433	56,125	48,634	42,554	37,578	33,470	30,050	27,180	24,751	22,680

CHART FOUR

STARTING PORTFOLIO NEEDED TO FUND VARIOUS ANNUAL EXPENSES
ASSUMING NO TRUSTEE FEE AND 30% TAX RATE

Assumptions: Initial annual expenses: $ 1,000 inflation: 2.50% tax rate: 30.00% TTEE/admin. fee: 0.00%

The following also assumes that needs are paid at end of each year and that TTEE fee is not tax deductible.

Rate of Return (Nominal): Life expectancies	2.50%	3.00%	3.50%	4.00%	4.50%	5.00%	5.50%	6.00%	6.50%	7.00%	7.50%	8.00%	8.50%
1	$ 983	$ 979	$ 976	$ 973	$ 969	$ 966	$ 963	$ 960	$ 956	$ 953	$ 950	$ 947	$ 944
2	$ 1,973	$ 1,963	$ 1,953	$ 1,943	$ 1,933	$ 1,923	$ 1,913	$ 1,904	$ 1,894	$ 1,885	$ 1,875	$ 1,866	$ 1,857
3	$ 2,970	$ 2,950	$ 2,930	$ 2,910	$ 2,890	$ 2,871	$ 2,851	$ 2,832	$ 2,814	$ 2,795	$ 2,777	$ 2,758	$ 2,740
4	$ 3,975	$ 3,941	$ 3,907	$ 3,874	$ 3,841	$ 3,809	$ 3,777	$ 3,746	$ 3,715	$ 3,684	$ 3,654	$ 3,624	$ 3,595
5	$ 4,987	$ 4,936	$ 4,885	$ 4,836	$ 4,787	$ 4,738	$ 4,691	$ 4,644	$ 4,598	$ 4,553	$ 4,509	$ 4,465	$ 4,422
6	$ 6,007	$ 5,934	$ 5,864	$ 5,794	$ 5,726	$ 5,659	$ 5,593	$ 5,528	$ 5,465	$ 5,402	$ 5,341	$ 5,281	$ 5,222
7	$ 7,034	$ 6,937	$ 6,843	$ 6,750	$ 6,659	$ 6,570	$ 6,483	$ 6,398	$ 6,314	$ 6,232	$ 6,152	$ 6,073	$ 5,995
8	$ 8,068	$ 7,944	$ 7,822	$ 7,703	$ 7,587	$ 7,473	$ 7,362	$ 7,253	$ 7,147	$ 7,043	$ 6,941	$ 6,841	$ 6,744
9	$ 9,111	$ 8,954	$ 8,802	$ 8,653	$ 8,508	$ 8,367	$ 8,229	$ 8,095	$ 7,963	$ 7,835	$ 7,710	$ 7,588	$ 7,468
10	$ 10,160	$ 9,969	$ 9,782	$ 9,601	$ 9,424	$ 9,252	$ 9,085	$ 8,922	$ 8,763	$ 8,609	$ 8,458	$ 8,312	$ 8,169
11	$ 11,218	$ 10,987	$ 10,763	$ 10,546	$ 10,334	$ 10,129	$ 9,930	$ 9,736	$ 9,548	$ 9,365	$ 9,188	$ 9,015	$ 8,847
12	$ 12,284	$ 12,010	$ 11,745	$ 11,488	$ 11,239	$ 10,998	$ 10,764	$ 10,537	$ 10,317	$ 10,104	$ 9,898	$ 9,697	$ 9,503
13	$ 13,357	$ 13,036	$ 12,726	$ 12,427	$ 12,137	$ 11,857	$ 11,587	$ 11,325	$ 11,072	$ 10,826	$ 10,589	$ 10,359	$ 10,137
14	$ 14,438	$ 14,067	$ 13,709	$ 13,363	$ 13,030	$ 12,709	$ 12,399	$ 12,100	$ 11,811	$ 11,532	$ 11,263	$ 11,002	$ 10,751
15	$ 15,528	$ 15,101	$ 14,691	$ 14,297	$ 13,918	$ 13,552	$ 13,201	$ 12,862	$ 12,536	$ 12,221	$ 11,918	$ 11,626	$ 11,344
16	$ 16,625	$ 16,140	$ 15,675	$ 15,228	$ 14,799	$ 14,388	$ 13,992	$ 13,612	$ 13,247	$ 12,895	$ 12,557	$ 12,232	$ 11,919
17	$ 17,730	$ 17,183	$ 16,658	$ 16,156	$ 15,676	$ 15,215	$ 14,773	$ 14,350	$ 13,943	$ 13,553	$ 13,179	$ 12,820	$ 12,475
18	$ 18,844	$ 18,229	$ 17,643	$ 17,082	$ 16,546	$ 16,034	$ 15,544	$ 15,075	$ 14,626	$ 14,197	$ 13,785	$ 13,390	$ 13,012
19	$ 19,965	$ 19,280	$ 18,627	$ 18,005	$ 17,412	$ 16,845	$ 16,305	$ 15,789	$ 15,296	$ 14,825	$ 14,375	$ 13,944	$ 13,532
20	$ 21,095	$ 20,335	$ 19,612	$ 18,925	$ 18,271	$ 17,649	$ 17,056	$ 16,491	$ 15,953	$ 15,439	$ 14,949	$ 14,482	$ 14,036
21	$ 22,234	$ 21,394	$ 20,598	$ 19,843	$ 19,126	$ 18,444	$ 17,797	$ 17,182	$ 16,596	$ 16,039	$ 15,509	$ 15,004	$ 14,522
22	$ 23,380	$ 22,457	$ 21,584	$ 20,758	$ 19,975	$ 19,232	$ 18,529	$ 17,861	$ 17,227	$ 16,626	$ 16,054	$ 15,510	$ 14,993
23	$ 24,535	$ 23,525	$ 22,571	$ 21,670	$ 20,818	$ 20,013	$ 19,251	$ 18,529	$ 17,846	$ 17,198	$ 16,584	$ 16,002	$ 15,449

CHART FOUR

STARTING PORTFOLIO NEEDED TO FUND VARIOUS ANNUAL EXPENSES ASSUMING NO TRUSTEE FEE AND 30% TAX RATE (CONTINUED)

Assumptions:

					TTEE/admin.	
Initial annual expenses:	$ 1,000	inflation: 2.50%	tax rate: 30.00%		fee: 0.00%	

The following also assumes that needs are paid at end of each year and that TTEE fee is not tax deductible.

Rate of Return (Nominal): Life expectancies	2.50%	3.00%	3.50%	4.00%	4.50%	5.00%	5.50%	6.00%	6.50%	7.00%	7.50%	8.00%	8.50%
24	$ 25,699	$ 24,596	$ 23,558	$ 22,579	$ 21,656	$ 20,786	$ 19,963	$ 19,187	$ 18,453	$ 17,758	$ 17,101	$ 16,479	$ 15,890
25	$ 26,871	$ 25,672	$ 24,546	$ 23,486	$ 22,489	$ 21,551	$ 20,667	$ 19,833	$ 19,047	$ 18,305	$ 17,605	$ 16,942	$ 16,316
26	$ 28,052	$ 26,752	$ 25,534	$ 24,390	$ 23,317	$ 22,309	$ 21,361	$ 20,470	$ 19,630	$ 18,840	$ 18,095	$ 17,392	$ 16,729
27	$ 29,242	$ 27,837	$ 26,522	$ 25,292	$ 24,140	$ 23,060	$ 22,046	$ 21,095	$ 20,202	$ 19,362	$ 18,572	$ 17,828	$ 17,128
28	$ 30,440	$ 28,925	$ 27,511	$ 26,191	$ 24,957	$ 23,803	$ 22,723	$ 21,711	$ 20,762	$ 19,872	$ 19,037	$ 18,252	$ 17,514
29	$ 31,647	$ 30,018	$ 28,501	$ 27,087	$ 25,769	$ 24,539	$ 23,390	$ 22,316	$ 21,312	$ 20,371	$ 19,490	$ 18,663	$ 17,887
30	$ 32,863	$ 31,115	$ 29,491	$ 27,981	$ 26,576	$ 25,268	$ 24,049	$ 22,912	$ 21,850	$ 20,858	$ 19,931	$ 19,062	$ 18,249
31	$ 34,088	$ 32,216	$ 30,481	$ 28,872	$ 27,378	$ 25,990	$ 24,699	$ 23,498	$ 22,378	$ 21,334	$ 20,360	$ 19,450	$ 18,598
32	$ 35,322	$ 33,322	$ 31,472	$ 29,761	$ 28,175	$ 26,705	$ 25,341	$ 24,074	$ 22,896	$ 21,799	$ 20,778	$ 19,826	$ 18,937
33	$ 36,566	$ 34,432	$ 32,464	$ 30,647	$ 28,967	$ 27,413	$ 25,975	$ 24,641	$ 23,403	$ 22,254	$ 21,185	$ 20,191	$ 19,264
34	$ 37,818	$ 35,546	$ 33,456	$ 31,530	$ 29,754	$ 28,115	$ 26,600	$ 25,199	$ 23,901	$ 22,698	$ 21,582	$ 20,545	$ 19,580
35	$ 39,079	$ 36,665	$ 34,448	$ 32,411	$ 30,536	$ 28,809	$ 27,217	$ 25,747	$ 24,389	$ 23,132	$ 21,968	$ 20,889	$ 19,887
36	$ 40,350	$ 37,788	$ 35,441	$ 33,289	$ 31,313	$ 29,497	$ 27,826	$ 26,287	$ 24,867	$ 23,556	$ 22,344	$ 21,222	$ 20,183
37	$ 41,631	$ 38,915	$ 36,434	$ 34,164	$ 32,085	$ 30,178	$ 28,427	$ 26,818	$ 25,336	$ 23,971	$ 22,710	$ 21,546	$ 20,470
38	$ 42,920	$ 40,047	$ 37,428	$ 35,037	$ 32,852	$ 30,853	$ 29,021	$ 27,340	$ 25,796	$ 24,375	$ 23,067	$ 21,861	$ 20,747
39	$ 44,219	$ 41,184	$ 38,422	$ 35,908	$ 33,615	$ 31,521	$ 29,606	$ 27,854	$ 26,246	$ 24,771	$ 23,415	$ 22,166	$ 21,015
40	$ 45,528	$ 42,324	$ 39,417	$ 36,776	$ 34,373	$ 32,183	$ 30,185	$ 28,359	$ 26,688	$ 25,158	$ 23,753	$ 22,462	$ 21,275
41	$ 46,846	$ 43,470	$ 40,413	$ 37,641	$ 35,125	$ 32,838	$ 30,755	$ 28,856	$ 27,121	$ 25,535	$ 24,082	$ 22,750	$ 21,526
42	$ 48,175	$ 44,619	$ 41,408	$ 38,504	$ 35,874	$ 33,487	$ 31,318	$ 29,345	$ 27,546	$ 25,904	$ 24,403	$ 23,029	$ 21,769
43	$ 49,512	$ 45,774	$ 42,405	$ 39,365	$ 36,617	$ 34,129	$ 31,874	$ 29,826	$ 27,962	$ 26,265	$ 24,716	$ 23,300	$ 22,004
44	$ 50,860	$ 46,932	$ 43,402	$ 40,223	$ 37,356	$ 34,766	$ 32,423	$ 30,299	$ 28,371	$ 26,617	$ 25,020	$ 23,563	$ 22,231
45	$ 52,218	$ 48,096	$ 44,399	$ 41,078	$ 38,090	$ 35,396	$ 32,964	$ 30,764	$ 28,771	$ 26,962	$ 25,317	$ 23,818	$ 22,451
46	$ 53,586	$ 49,263	$ 45,397	$ 41,931	$ 38,819	$ 36,020	$ 33,498	$ 31,222	$ 29,163	$ 27,298	$ 25,605	$ 24,066	$ 22,664

Initial
annual

Assumptions: expenses: $ 1,000   inflation: 2.50%   tax rate: 30.00%

TTEE/
admin.
fee: 0.00%

The following also assumes that needs are paid at end of each year and that TTEE fee is not tax deductible.

Rate of Return (Nominal):	2.50%	3.00%	3.50%	4.00%	4.50%	5.00%	5.50%	6.00%	6.50%	7.00%	7.50%	8.00%	8.50%
Life expectancies													
47	$ 54,963	$ 50,436	$ 46,395	$ 42,781	$ 39,544	$ 36,639	$ 34,026	$ 31,672	$ 29,548	$ 27,627	$ 25,886	$ 24,306	$ 22,870
48	$ 56,351	$ 51,613	$ 47,394	$ 43,629	$ 40,264	$ 37,251	$ 34,547	$ 32,115	$ 29,925	$ 27,948	$ 26,160	$ 24,540	$ 23,069
49	$ 57,749	$ 52,795	$ 48,393	$ 44,475	$ 40,980	$ 37,857	$ 35,060	$ 32,551	$ 30,295	$ 28,262	$ 26,427	$ 24,766	$ 23,261
50	$ 59,158	$ 53,981	$ 49,392	$ 45,318	$ 41,691	$ 38,457	$ 35,568	$ 32,980	$ 30,657	$ 28,569	$ 26,686	$ 24,986	$ 23,448
51	$ 60,577	$ 55,172	$ 50,393	$ 46,158	$ 42,398	$ 39,052	$ 36,068	$ 33,401	$ 31,013	$ 28,868	$ 26,939	$ 25,200	$ 23,628
52	$ 62,006	$ 56,367	$ 51,393	$ 46,996	$ 43,100	$ 39,641	$ 36,562	$ 33,816	$ 31,361	$ 29,161	$ 27,185	$ 25,407	$ 23,803
53	$ 63,446	$ 57,568	$ 52,394	$ 47,832	$ 43,798	$ 40,224	$ 37,050	$ 34,224	$ 31,702	$ 29,447	$ 27,425	$ 25,608	$ 23,971
54	$ 64,896	$ 58,773	$ 53,396	$ 48,665	$ 44,492	$ 40,802	$ 37,531	$ 34,625	$ 32,037	$ 29,727	$ 27,659	$ 25,803	$ 24,135
55	$ 66,358	$ 59,982	$ 54,398	$ 49,496	$ 45,181	$ 41,374	$ 38,006	$ 35,020	$ 32,366	$ 30,000	$ 27,886	$ 25,993	$ 24,293
56	$ 67,830	$ 61,197	$ 55,401	$ 50,324	$ 45,865	$ 41,940	$ 38,475	$ 35,408	$ 32,688	$ 30,267	$ 28,108	$ 26,177	$ 24,445
57	$ 69,312	$ 62,416	$ 56,404	$ 51,150	$ 46,546	$ 42,501	$ 38,938	$ 35,790	$ 33,003	$ 30,528	$ 28,323	$ 26,355	$ 24,593
58	$ 70,806	$ 63,640	$ 57,408	$ 51,973	$ 47,222	$ 43,057	$ 39,395	$ 36,166	$ 33,312	$ 30,783	$ 28,533	$ 26,529	$ 24,736
59	$ 72,311	$ 64,869	$ 58,412	$ 52,794	$ 47,894	$ 43,607	$ 39,845	$ 36,536	$ 33,616	$ 31,032	$ 28,738	$ 26,697	$ 24,875
60	$ 73,827	$ 66,102	$ 59,416	$ 53,613	$ 48,562	$ 44,152	$ 40,290	$ 36,900	$ 33,913	$ 31,275	$ 28,937	$ 26,860	$ 25,009
61	$ 75,353	$ 67,341	$ 60,421	$ 54,429	$ 49,225	$ 44,691	$ 40,729	$ 37,257	$ 34,205	$ 31,513	$ 29,131	$ 27,019	$ 25,138
62	$ 76,892	$ 68,584	$ 61,427	$ 55,243	$ 49,884	$ 45,226	$ 41,163	$ 37,609	$ 34,490	$ 31,745	$ 29,320	$ 27,172	$ 25,263
63	$ 78,441	$ 69,832	$ 62,433	$ 56,055	$ 50,539	$ 45,755	$ 41,591	$ 37,955	$ 34,771	$ 31,972	$ 29,504	$ 27,322	$ 25,385
64	$ 80,002	$ 71,085	$ 63,440	$ 56,864	$ 51,190	$ 46,279	$ 42,013	$ 38,296	$ 35,045	$ 32,194	$ 29,684	$ 27,467	$ 25,502
65	$ 81,575	$ 72,343	$ 64,447	$ 57,671	$ 51,837	$ 46,798	$ 42,430	$ 38,631	$ 35,315	$ 32,410	$ 29,858	$ 27,607	$ 25,615
66	$ 83,159	$ 73,606	$ 65,454	$ 58,475	$ 52,480	$ 47,312	$ 42,841	$ 38,960	$ 35,579	$ 32,622	$ 30,028	$ 27,744	$ 25,725
67	$ 84,755	$ 74,873	$ 66,462	$ 59,278	$ 53,119	$ 47,821	$ 43,247	$ 39,284	$ 35,837	$ 32,829	$ 30,194	$ 27,876	$ 25,831
68	$ 86,362	$ 76,146	$ 67,471	$ 60,077	$ 53,754	$ 48,325	$ 43,648	$ 39,603	$ 36,091	$ 33,031	$ 30,355	$ 28,005	$ 25,934
69	$ 87,982	$ 77,424	$ 68,480	$ 60,875	$ 54,384	$ 48,824	$ 44,043	$ 39,916	$ 36,340	$ 33,229	$ 30,512	$ 28,130	$ 26,033

CHART FOUR

STARTING PORTFOLIO NEEDED TO FUND VARIOUS ANNUAL EXPENSES ASSUMING NO TRUSTEE FEE AND 30% TAX RATE (CONTINUED)

Assumptions:

Initial annual expenses:	inflation:	tax rate:	TTEE/ admin. fee:
$ 1,000	2.50%	30.00%	0.00%

The following also assumes that needs are paid at end of each year and that TTEE fee is not tax deductible.

Rate of Return (Nominal): Life expectancies	2.50%	3.00%	3.50%	4.00%	4.50%	5.00%	5.50%	6.00%	6.50%	7.00%	7.50%	8.00%	8.50%
70	$ 89,613	$ 78,707	$ 69,489	$ 61,670	$ 55,011	$ 49,319	$ 44,434	$ 40,225	$ 36,584	$ 33,422	$ 30,665	$ 28,251	$ 26,129
71	$ 91,256	$ 79,995	$ 70,499	$ 62,463	$ 55,634	$ 49,809	$ 44,819	$ 40,528	$ 36,823	$ 33,611	$ 30,814	$ 28,369	$ 26,222
72	$ 92,912	$ 81,287	$ 71,510	$ 63,253	$ 56,253	$ 50,294	$ 45,199	$ 40,827	$ 37,058	$ 33,795	$ 30,959	$ 28,483	$ 26,312
73	$ 94,579	$ 82,585	$ 72,521	$ 64,041	$ 56,868	$ 50,774	$ 45,575	$ 41,120	$ 37,287	$ 33,975	$ 31,100	$ 28,594	$ 26,399
74	$ 96,259	$ 83,888	$ 73,532	$ 64,827	$ 57,479	$ 51,249	$ 45,945	$ 41,409	$ 37,513	$ 34,151	$ 31,237	$ 28,701	$ 26,484
75	$ 97,952	$ 85,196	$ 74,544	$ 65,611	$ 58,086	$ 51,720	$ 46,311	$ 41,693	$ 37,734	$ 34,323	$ 31,371	$ 28,806	$ 26,565
76	$ 99,656	$ 86,510	$ 75,557	$ 66,392	$ 58,690	$ 52,187	$ 46,672	$ 41,973	$ 37,950	$ 34,491	$ 31,502	$ 28,907	$ 26,644
77	$ 101,374	$ 87,828	$ 76,570	$ 67,171	$ 59,289	$ 52,649	$ 47,028	$ 42,248	$ 38,163	$ 34,655	$ 31,629	$ 29,005	$ 26,720
78	$ 103,104	$ 89,151	$ 77,583	$ 67,948	$ 59,885	$ 53,106	$ 47,380	$ 42,518	$ 38,371	$ 34,816	$ 31,753	$ 29,101	$ 26,794
79	$ 104,847	$ 90,480	$ 78,597	$ 68,722	$ 60,477	$ 53,559	$ 47,727	$ 42,784	$ 38,575	$ 34,972	$ 31,873	$ 29,193	$ 26,865
80	$ 106,602	$ 91,814	$ 79,611	$ 69,494	$ 61,066	$ 54,008	$ 48,069	$ 43,046	$ 38,775	$ 35,125	$ 31,990	$ 29,283	$ 26,934
81	$ 108,371	$ 93,153	$ 80,626	$ 70,264	$ 61,650	$ 54,452	$ 48,407	$ 43,303	$ 38,971	$ 35,275	$ 32,105	$ 29,371	$ 27,001
82	$ 110,152	$ 94,498	$ 81,642	$ 71,032	$ 62,231	$ 54,893	$ 48,741	$ 43,556	$ 39,164	$ 35,421	$ 32,216	$ 29,456	$ 27,066
83	$ 111,947	$ 95,847	$ 82,658	$ 71,798	$ 62,808	$ 55,328	$ 49,070	$ 43,806	$ 39,352	$ 35,564	$ 32,324	$ 29,538	$ 27,128
84	$ 113,755	$ 97,202	$ 83,674	$ 72,561	$ 63,382	$ 55,760	$ 49,395	$ 44,051	$ 39,537	$ 35,704	$ 32,430	$ 29,618	$ 27,189
85	$ 115,576	$ 98,562	$ 84,691	$ 73,322	$ 63,952	$ 56,187	$ 49,716	$ 44,292	$ 39,718	$ 35,840	$ 32,533	$ 29,695	$ 27,247
86	$ 117,411	$ 99,928	$ 85,709	$ 74,081	$ 64,519	$ 56,611	$ 50,033	$ 44,529	$ 39,896	$ 35,974	$ 32,633	$ 29,770	$ 27,304
87	$ 119,259	$ 101,299	$ 86,726	$ 74,837	$ 65,082	$ 57,030	$ 50,345	$ 44,762	$ 40,070	$ 36,104	$ 32,730	$ 29,843	$ 27,359
88	$ 121,121	$ 102,675	$ 87,745	$ 75,592	$ 65,641	$ 57,445	$ 50,654	$ 44,991	$ 40,241	$ 36,231	$ 32,825	$ 29,914	$ 27,412
89	$ 122,997	$ 104,057	$ 88,764	$ 76,344	$ 66,197	$ 57,856	$ 50,958	$ 45,217	$ 40,408	$ 36,355	$ 32,918	$ 29,983	$ 27,463
90	$ 124,886	$ 105,444	$ 89,783	$ 77,094	$ 66,749	$ 58,263	$ 51,259	$ 45,439	$ 40,573	$ 36,477	$ 33,008	$ 30,050	$ 27,512

Starting Portfolio Needed to Fund Various Annual Expenses Assuming 1% Trustee Fee and 0% Tax Rate

Assumptions:	Initial annual expenses: $ 1,000	inflation: 2.50%	tax rate: 0.00%	TTEE/ admin. fee: 1.00%

The following also assumes that needs are paid at end of each year and that TTEE fee is not tax deductible.

Rate of Return (Nominal): Life expectancies	2.50%	3.00%	3.50%	4.00%	4.50%	5.00%	5.50%	6.00%	6.50%	7.00%	7.50%	8.00%	8.50%
1	$ 985	$ 980	$ 976	$ 971	$ 966	$ 962	$ 957	$ 952	$ 948	$ 943	$ 939	$ 935	$ 930
2	$ 1,980	$ 1,966	$ 1,951	$ 1,937	$ 1,923	$ 1,909	$ 1,896	$ 1,882	$ 1,869	$ 1,856	$ 1,843	$ 1,830	$ 1,817
3	$ 2,985	$ 2,956	$ 2,927	$ 2,899	$ 2,871	$ 2,843	$ 2,816	$ 2,790	$ 2,764	$ 2,738	$ 2,712	$ 2,687	$ 2,663
4	$ 4,000	$ 3,950	$ 3,902	$ 3,855	$ 3,809	$ 3,764	$ 3,719	$ 3,676	$ 3,633	$ 3,591	$ 3,550	$ 3,509	$ 3,469
5	$ 5,024	$ 4,950	$ 4,878	$ 4,807	$ 4,738	$ 4,671	$ 4,605	$ 4,540	$ 4,477	$ 4,416	$ 4,355	$ 4,296	$ 4,238
6	$ 6,059	$ 5,955	$ 5,854	$ 5,755	$ 5,659	$ 5,565	$ 5,474	$ 5,385	$ 5,298	$ 5,213	$ 5,131	$ 5,050	$ 4,971
7	$ 7,104	$ 6,964	$ 6,829	$ 6,698	$ 6,570	$ 6,446	$ 6,326	$ 6,209	$ 6,095	$ 5,984	$ 5,877	$ 5,772	$ 5,670
8	$ 8,159	$ 7,979	$ 7,805	$ 7,636	$ 7,473	$ 7,315	$ 7,162	$ 7,013	$ 6,870	$ 6,730	$ 6,595	$ 6,464	$ 6,337
9	$ 9,225	$ 8,999	$ 8,780	$ 8,570	$ 8,367	$ 8,171	$ 7,982	$ 7,799	$ 7,622	$ 7,451	$ 7,286	$ 7,127	$ 6,972
10	$ 10,301	$ 10,023	$ 9,756	$ 9,499	$ 9,252	$ 9,015	$ 8,786	$ 8,566	$ 8,353	$ 8,149	$ 7,952	$ 7,762	$ 7,578
11	$ 11,387	$ 11,053	$ 10,732	$ 10,424	$ 10,129	$ 9,846	$ 9,575	$ 9,314	$ 9,064	$ 8,823	$ 8,592	$ 8,370	$ 8,156
12	$ 12,485	$ 12,087	$ 11,707	$ 11,344	$ 10,998	$ 10,666	$ 10,348	$ 10,045	$ 9,754	$ 9,475	$ 9,208	$ 8,952	$ 8,707
13	$ 13,593	$ 13,127	$ 12,683	$ 12,260	$ 11,857	$ 11,473	$ 11,107	$ 10,758	$ 10,424	$ 10,106	$ 9,801	$ 9,510	$ 9,232
14	$ 14,712	$ 14,172	$ 13,659	$ 13,172	$ 12,709	$ 12,270	$ 11,852	$ 11,454	$ 11,076	$ 10,715	$ 10,372	$ 10,045	$ 9,733
15	$ 15,842	$ 15,221	$ 14,634	$ 14,079	$ 13,552	$ 13,054	$ 12,582	$ 12,134	$ 11,709	$ 11,305	$ 10,922	$ 10,557	$ 10,210
16	$ 16,984	$ 16,276	$ 15,610	$ 14,981	$ 14,388	$ 13,827	$ 13,298	$ 12,797	$ 12,324	$ 11,875	$ 11,450	$ 11,048	$ 10,666
17	$ 18,136	$ 17,337	$ 16,585	$ 15,879	$ 15,215	$ 14,589	$ 14,000	$ 13,445	$ 12,921	$ 12,426	$ 11,959	$ 11,518	$ 11,100
18	$ 19,300	$ 18,402	$ 17,561	$ 16,773	$ 16,034	$ 15,341	$ 14,689	$ 14,077	$ 13,501	$ 12,960	$ 12,449	$ 11,968	$ 11,514
19	$ 20,475	$ 19,473	$ 18,537	$ 17,662	$ 16,845	$ 16,081	$ 15,365	$ 14,694	$ 14,065	$ 13,475	$ 12,920	$ 12,399	$ 11,909
20	$ 21,662	$ 20,548	$ 19,512	$ 18,548	$ 17,649	$ 16,810	$ 16,028	$ 15,297	$ 14,613	$ 13,973	$ 13,374	$ 12,812	$ 12,285
21	$ 22,861	$ 21,629	$ 20,488	$ 19,428	$ 18,444	$ 17,530	$ 16,678	$ 15,885	$ 15,146	$ 14,455	$ 13,811	$ 13,208	$ 12,644
22	$ 24,072	$ 22,716	$ 21,463	$ 20,305	$ 19,232	$ 18,238	$ 17,316	$ 16,459	$ 15,663	$ 14,922	$ 14,231	$ 13,587	$ 12,986
23	$ 25,294	$ 23,808	$ 22,439	$ 21,177	$ 20,013	$ 18,937	$ 17,941	$ 17,020	$ 16,165	$ 15,372	$ 14,636	$ 13,950	$ 13,312

CHART FIVE

STARTING PORTFOLIO NEEDED TO FUND VARIOUS ANNUAL EXPENSES
ASSUMING 1% TRUSTEE FEE AND 0% TAX RATE (CONTINUED)

Assumptions: Initial annual expenses: $ 1,000   inflation: 2.50%   tax rate: 0.00%   TTEE/admin. fee: 1.00%

The following also assumes that needs are paid at end of each year and that TTEE fee is not tax deductible.

Rate of Return (Nominal): Life expectancies	2.50%	3.00%	3.50%	4.00%	4.50%	5.00%	5.50%	6.00%	6.50%	7.00%	7.50%	8.00%	8.50%
24	$ 26,528	$ 24,905	$ 23,415	$ 22,045	$ 20,786	$ 19,625	$ 18,555	17,567	16,653	15,808	$ 15,025	$ 14,298	$ 13,623
25	$ 27,775	$ 26,007	$ 24,390	$ 22,909	$ 21,551	$ 20,304	$ 19,157	18,101	17,128	16,230	$ 15,399	$ 14,631	$ 13,920
26	$ 29,034	$ 27,115	$ 25,366	$ 23,769	$ 22,309	$ 20,972	$ 19,747	18,622	17,589	16,637	$ 15,760	$ 14,951	$ 14,203
27	$ 30,305	$ 28,228	$ 26,341	$ 24,624	$ 23,060	$ 21,631	$ 20,326	19,131	18,036	17,031	$ 16,107	$ 15,256	$ 14,472
28	$ 31,589	$ 29,347	$ 27,317	$ 25,476	$ 23,803	$ 22,281	$ 20,894	19,628	18,471	17,412	$ 16,441	$ 15,549	$ 14,729
29	$ 32,885	$ 30,471	$ 28,293	$ 26,323	$ 24,539	$ 22,921	$ 21,451	20,113	18,894	17,781	$ 16,763	$ 15,830	$ 14,975
30	$ 34,194	$ 31,601	$ 29,268	$ 27,166	$ 25,268	$ 23,552	$ 21,997	20,587	19,305	18,137	$ 17,072	$ 16,099	$ 15,208
31	$ 35,517	$ 32,736	$ 30,244	$ 28,005	$ 25,990	$ 24,174	$ 22,533	21,049	19,703	18,481	$ 17,370	$ 16,356	$ 15,431
32	$ 36,852	$ 33,877	$ 31,220	$ 28,840	$ 26,705	$ 24,787	$ 23,059	21,500	20,091	18,815	$ 17,656	$ 16,603	$ 15,644
33	$ 38,200	$ 35,024	$ 32,195	$ 29,671	$ 27,413	$ 25,391	$ 23,575	21,941	20,468	19,137	$ 17,932	$ 16,839	$ 15,846
34	$ 39,562	$ 36,176	$ 33,171	$ 30,498	$ 28,115	$ 25,986	$ 24,080	22,371	20,833	19,448	$ 18,198	$ 17,066	$ 16,039
35	$ 40,937	$ 37,334	$ 34,146	$ 31,320	$ 28,809	$ 26,573	$ 24,577	22,790	21,189	19,750	$ 18,453	$ 17,283	$ 16,224
36	$ 42,325	$ 38,497	$ 35,122	$ 32,139	$ 29,497	$ 27,151	$ 25,063	23,200	21,534	20,041	$ 18,699	$ 17,490	$ 16,399
37	$ 43,727	$ 39,666	$ 36,098	$ 32,954	$ 30,178	$ 27,721	$ 25,540	23,600	21,870	20,322	$ 18,936	$ 17,689	$ 16,567
38	$ 45,143	$ 40,841	$ 37,073	$ 33,765	$ 30,853	$ 28,283	$ 26,008	23,991	22,196	20,595	$ 19,163	$ 17,880	$ 16,726
39	$ 46,573	$ 42,022	$ 38,049	$ 34,572	$ 31,521	$ 28,836	$ 26,468	24,372	22,512	20,858	$ 19,383	$ 18,063	$ 16,879
40	$ 48,017	$ 43,208	$ 39,024	$ 35,375	$ 32,183	$ 29,382	$ 26,918	24,744	22,820	21,113	$ 19,594	$ 18,238	$ 17,024
41	$ 49,476	$ 44,400	$ 40,000	$ 36,174	$ 32,838	$ 29,920	$ 27,360	25,107	23,119	21,359	$ 19,797	$ 18,405	$ 17,162
42	$ 50,948	$ 45,598	$ 40,976	$ 36,969	$ 33,487	$ 30,450	$ 27,793	25,462	23,410	21,597	$ 19,992	$ 18,566	$ 17,294
43	$ 52,436	$ 46,802	$ 41,951	$ 37,761	$ 34,129	$ 30,972	$ 28,218	25,808	23,692	21,828	$ 20,180	$ 18,719	$ 17,420
44	$ 53,937	$ 48,012	$ 42,927	$ 38,548	$ 34,766	$ 31,487	$ 28,635	26,146	23,966	22,050	$ 20,361	$ 18,867	$ 17,540
45	$ 55,454	$ 49,228	$ 43,902	$ 39,332	$ 35,396	$ 31,994	$ 29,044	26,476	24,232	22,266	$ 20,535	$ 19,008	$ 17,655
46	$ 56,986	$ 50,449	$ 44,878	$ 40,112	$ 36,020	$ 32,494	$ 29,445	26,798	24,491	22,474	$ 20,703	$ 19,143	$ 17,764

Assumptions:

Initial annual expenses: $ 1,000	inflation: 2.50%	tax rate: 0.00%	fee: 1.00%

The following also assumes that needs are paid at end of each year and that TTEE fee is not tax deductible.

Rate of Return (Nominal): Life expectancies	2.50%	3.00%	3.50%	4.00%	4.50%	5.00%	5.50%	6.00%	6.50%	7.00%	7.50%	8.00%	8.50%
47	$ 58,532	$ 51,677	$ 45,854	$ 40,888	$ 36,639	$ 32,987	$ 29,838	$ 27,112	$ 24,743	$ 22,675	$ 20,864	$ 19,273	$ 17,868
48	$ 60,094	$ 52,911	$ 46,829	$ 41,661	$ 37,251	$ 33,473	$ 30,224	$ 27,419	$ 24,987	$ 22,870	$ 21,020	$ 19,397	$ 17,967
49	$ 61,671	$ 54,151	$ 47,805	$ 42,429	$ 37,857	$ 33,952	$ 30,603	$ 27,718	$ 25,224	$ 23,058	$ 21,169	$ 19,515	$ 18,061
50	$ 63,264	$ 55,396	$ 48,780	$ 43,194	$ 38,457	$ 34,424	$ 30,974	$ 28,011	$ 25,455	$ 23,240	$ 21,313	$ 19,629	$ 18,152
51	$ 64,873	$ 56,648	$ 49,756	$ 43,955	$ 39,052	$ 34,889	$ 31,338	$ 28,296	$ 25,679	$ 23,416	$ 21,452	$ 19,738	$ 18,238
52	$ 66,497	$ 57,906	$ 50,732	$ 44,713	$ 39,641	$ 35,347	$ 31,695	$ 28,575	$ 25,896	$ 23,586	$ 21,585	$ 19,843	$ 18,320
53	$ 68,138	$ 59,171	$ 51,707	$ 45,467	$ 40,224	$ 35,799	$ 32,046	$ 28,847	$ 26,108	$ 23,751	$ 21,713	$ 19,943	$ 18,398
54	$ 69,794	$ 60,441	$ 52,683	$ 46,217	$ 40,802	$ 36,244	$ 32,389	$ 29,113	$ 26,313	$ 23,910	$ 21,837	$ 20,039	$ 18,472
55	$ 71,467	$ 61,718	$ 53,659	$ 46,963	$ 41,374	$ 36,683	$ 32,726	$ 29,372	$ 26,513	$ 24,064	$ 21,955	$ 20,131	$ 18,543
56	$ 73,156	$ 63,001	$ 54,634	$ 47,706	$ 41,940	$ 37,115	$ 33,057	$ 29,625	$ 26,707	$ 24,213	$ 22,070	$ 20,219	$ 18,611
57	$ 74,862	$ 64,290	$ 55,610	$ 48,446	$ 42,501	$ 37,541	$ 33,381	$ 29,872	$ 26,895	$ 24,357	$ 22,180	$ 20,303	$ 18,676
58	$ 76,585	$ 65,585	$ 56,585	$ 49,181	$ 43,057	$ 37,962	$ 33,699	$ 30,113	$ 27,078	$ 24,496	$ 22,286	$ 20,384	$ 18,737
59	$ 78,325	$ 66,887	$ 57,561	$ 49,913	$ 43,607	$ 38,376	$ 34,011	$ 30,348	$ 27,256	$ 24,631	$ 22,388	$ 20,461	$ 18,796
60	$ 80,082	$ 68,196	$ 58,537	$ 50,642	$ 44,152	$ 38,784	$ 34,317	$ 30,578	$ 27,429	$ 24,761	$ 22,486	$ 20,535	$ 18,852
61	$ 81,856	$ 69,510	$ 59,512	$ 51,367	$ 44,691	$ 39,186	$ 34,617	$ 30,803	$ 27,597	$ 24,886	$ 22,580	$ 20,606	$ 18,905
62	$ 83,648	$ 70,831	$ 60,488	$ 52,089	$ 45,226	$ 39,582	$ 34,912	$ 31,022	$ 27,760	$ 25,008	$ 22,671	$ 20,674	$ 18,956
63	$ 85,457	$ 72,159	$ 61,463	$ 52,807	$ 45,755	$ 39,973	$ 35,200	$ 31,235	$ 27,919	$ 25,126	$ 22,759	$ 20,739	$ 19,005
64	$ 87,284	$ 73,493	$ 62,439	$ 53,521	$ 46,279	$ 40,358	$ 35,484	$ 31,444	$ 28,073	$ 25,240	$ 22,843	$ 20,801	$ 19,051
65	$ 89,129	$ 74,834	$ 63,415	$ 54,232	$ 46,798	$ 40,737	$ 35,762	$ 31,648	$ 28,222	$ 25,350	$ 22,924	$ 20,861	$ 19,095
66	$ 90,993	$ 76,181	$ 64,390	$ 54,940	$ 47,312	$ 41,111	$ 36,034	$ 31,847	$ 28,368	$ 25,456	$ 23,002	$ 20,918	$ 19,137
67	$ 92,874	$ 77,535	$ 65,366	$ 55,644	$ 47,821	$ 41,480	$ 36,301	$ 32,041	$ 28,509	$ 25,559	$ 23,077	$ 20,973	$ 19,177
68	$ 94,774	$ 78,895	$ 66,341	$ 56,345	$ 48,325	$ 41,843	$ 36,564	$ 32,230	$ 28,646	$ 25,658	$ 23,149	$ 21,026	$ 19,216
69	$ 96,693	$ 80,262	$ 67,317	$ 57,042	$ 48,824	$ 42,201	$ 36,821	$ 32,415	$ 28,779	$ 25,755	$ 23,219	$ 21,076	$ 19,252

CHART FIVE

STARTING PORTFOLIO NEEDED TO FUND VARIOUS ANNUAL EXPENSES
ASSUMING 1% TRUSTEE FEE AND 0% TAX RATE (CONTINUED)

Assumptions: Initial annual expenses: $ 1,000   inflation: 2.50%   tax rate: 0.00%   TTEE/admin. fee: 1.00%

The following also assumes that needs are paid at end of each year and that TTEE fee is not tax deductible.

Rate of Return (Nominal): Life expectancies	2.50%	3.00%	3.50%	4.00%	4.50%	5.00%	5.50%	6.00%	6.50%	7.00%	7.50%	8.00%	8.50%
70	$ 98,631	$ 81,636	$ 68,293	$ 57,736	$ 49,319	$ 42,554	$ 37,073	$ 32,596	$ 28,909	$ 25,848	$ 23,285	$ 21,124	$ 19,287
71	$ 100,588	$ 83,017	$ 69,268	$ 58,427	$ 49,809	$ 42,902	$ 37,320	$ 32,772	$ 29,035	$ 25,937	$ 23,350	$ 21,170	$ 19,320
72	$ 102,564	$ 84,404	$ 70,244	$ 59,114	$ 50,294	$ 43,245	$ 37,563	$ 32,944	$ 29,157	$ 26,024	$ 23,412	$ 21,215	$ 19,352
73	$ 104,560	$ 85,798	$ 71,220	$ 59,798	$ 50,774	$ 43,582	$ 37,801	$ 33,112	$ 29,276	$ 26,109	$ 23,472	$ 21,257	$ 19,382
74	$ 106,576	$ 87,199	$ 72,195	$ 60,478	$ 51,249	$ 43,915	$ 38,035	$ 33,276	$ 29,391	$ 26,190	$ 23,529	$ 21,298	$ 19,411
75	$ 108,611	$ 88,607	$ 73,171	$ 61,156	$ 51,720	$ 44,243	$ 38,264	$ 33,436	$ 29,503	$ 26,268	$ 23,584	$ 21,337	$ 19,438
76	$ 110,666	$ 90,022	$ 74,146	$ 61,830	$ 52,187	$ 44,567	$ 38,488	$ 33,593	$ 29,612	$ 26,345	$ 23,637	$ 21,374	$ 19,464
77	$ 112,742	$ 91,444	$ 75,122	$ 62,500	$ 52,649	$ 44,886	$ 38,708	$ 33,745	$ 29,718	$ 26,418	$ 23,689	$ 21,409	$ 19,489
78	$ 114,838	$ 92,872	$ 76,098	$ 63,168	$ 53,106	$ 45,200	$ 38,925	$ 33,894	$ 29,821	$ 26,489	$ 23,738	$ 21,444	$ 19,513
79	$ 116,954	$ 94,308	$ 77,073	$ 63,832	$ 53,559	$ 45,509	$ 39,137	$ 34,039	$ 29,920	$ 26,558	$ 23,785	$ 21,476	$ 19,536
80	$ 119,092	$ 95,750	$ 78,049	$ 64,493	$ 54,008	$ 45,815	$ 39,344	$ 34,181	$ 30,018	$ 26,624	$ 23,831	$ 21,508	$ 19,557
81	$ 121,250	$ 97,200	$ 79,024	$ 65,151	$ 54,452	$ 46,115	$ 39,548	$ 34,320	$ 30,112	$ 26,689	$ 23,875	$ 21,538	$ 19,578
82	$ 123,430	$ 98,657	$ 80,000	$ 65,806	$ 54,893	$ 46,412	$ 39,748	$ 34,455	$ 30,203	$ 26,751	$ 23,917	$ 21,567	$ 19,597
83	$ 125,631	$ 100,121	$ 80,976	$ 66,457	$ 55,328	$ 46,704	$ 39,945	$ 34,587	$ 30,292	$ 26,811	$ 23,958	$ 21,594	$ 19,616
84	$ 127,854	$ 101,592	$ 81,951	$ 67,105	$ 55,760	$ 46,992	$ 40,137	$ 34,716	$ 30,379	$ 26,869	$ 23,997	$ 21,621	$ 19,634
85	$ 130,099	$ 103,071	$ 82,927	$ 67,750	$ 56,187	$ 47,276	$ 40,326	$ 34,842	$ 30,463	$ 26,925	$ 24,035	$ 21,646	$ 19,651
86	$ 132,366	$ 104,556	$ 83,902	$ 68,392	$ 56,611	$ 47,555	$ 40,511	$ 34,965	$ 30,545	$ 26,980	$ 24,071	$ 21,670	$ 19,667
87	$ 134,655	$ 106,049	$ 84,878	$ 69,031	$ 57,030	$ 47,831	$ 40,693	$ 35,085	$ 30,624	$ 27,032	$ 24,106	$ 21,693	$ 19,683
88	$ 136,967	$ 107,550	$ 85,854	$ 69,667	$ 57,445	$ 48,103	$ 40,871	$ 35,202	$ 30,701	$ 27,083	$ 24,139	$ 21,716	$ 19,697
89	$ 139,302	$ 109,057	$ 86,829	$ 70,300	$ 57,856	$ 48,370	$ 41,045	$ 35,316	$ 30,776	$ 27,132	$ 24,172	$ 21,737	$ 19,712
90	$ 141,660	$ 110,572	$ 87,805	$ 70,929	$ 58,263	$ 48,634	$ 41,217	$ 35,427	$ 30,848	$ 27,180	$ 24,203	$ 21,757	$ 19,725

Chart Six

Starting Portfolio Needed to Fund Various Annual Expenses
Assuming 1% Trustee Fee and 10% Tax Rate

Assumptions:
annual expenses: $ 1,000 inflation: 2.50% tax rate: 10.00% admin. fee: 1.00%

The following also assumes that needs are paid at end of each year and that TTEE fee is not tax deductible.

Rate of Return (Nominal): Life expectancies	2.50%	3.00%	3.50%	4.00%	4.50%	5.00%	5.50%	6.00%	6.50%	7.00%	7.50%	8.00%	8.50%
1	$ 988	$ 983	$ 979	$ 975	$ 970	$ 966	$ 962	$ 958	$ 954	$ 950	$ 946	$ 942	$ 938
2	$ 1,988	$ 1,974	$ 1,961	$ 1,948	$ 1,936	$ 1,923	$ 1,911	$ 1,898	$ 1,886	$ 1,874	$ 1,862	$ 1,850	$ 1,839
3	$ 3,000	$ 2,973	$ 2,947	$ 2,921	$ 2,896	$ 2,871	$ 2,846	$ 2,822	$ 2,798	$ 2,774	$ 2,751	$ 2,728	$ 2,705
4	$ 4,024	$ 3,980	$ 3,936	$ 3,893	$ 3,851	$ 3,809	$ 3,768	$ 3,728	$ 3,689	$ 3,650	$ 3,612	$ 3,574	$ 3,537
5	$ 5,062	$ 4,994	$ 4,928	$ 4,864	$ 4,800	$ 4,738	$ 4,678	$ 4,618	$ 4,560	$ 4,502	$ 4,446	$ 4,391	$ 4,337
6	$ 6,112	$ 6,017	$ 5,924	$ 5,834	$ 5,745	$ 5,659	$ 5,574	$ 5,492	$ 5,411	$ 5,332	$ 5,255	$ 5,180	$ 5,106
7	$ 7,175	$ 7,048	$ 6,924	$ 6,803	$ 6,685	$ 6,570	$ 6,459	$ 6,350	$ 6,244	$ 6,140	$ 6,039	$ 5,941	$ 5,845
8	$ 8,251	$ 8,086	$ 7,926	$ 7,771	$ 7,620	$ 7,473	$ 7,331	$ 7,192	$ 7,058	$ 6,927	$ 6,799	$ 6,676	$ 6,555
9	$ 9,341	$ 9,133	$ 8,932	$ 8,738	$ 8,549	$ 8,367	$ 8,190	$ 8,019	$ 7,853	$ 7,692	$ 7,536	$ 7,385	$ 7,238
10	$ 10,444	$ 10,188	$ 9,942	$ 9,704	$ 9,474	$ 9,252	$ 9,038	$ 8,831	$ 8,631	$ 8,437	$ 8,250	$ 8,069	$ 7,894
11	$ 11,560	$ 11,252	$ 10,955	$ 10,669	$ 10,394	$ 10,129	$ 9,874	$ 9,628	$ 9,391	$ 9,163	$ 8,942	$ 8,730	$ 8,524
12	$ 12,691	$ 12,324	$ 11,971	$ 11,633	$ 11,309	$ 10,998	$ 10,698	$ 10,411	$ 10,134	$ 9,869	$ 9,613	$ 9,367	$ 9,130
13	$ 13,835	$ 13,404	$ 12,991	$ 12,597	$ 12,219	$ 11,857	$ 11,511	$ 11,179	$ 10,861	$ 10,556	$ 10,263	$ 9,982	$ 9,713
14	$ 14,993	$ 14,492	$ 14,015	$ 13,559	$ 13,124	$ 12,709	$ 12,312	$ 11,934	$ 11,571	$ 11,225	$ 10,893	$ 10,576	$ 10,272
15	$ 16,166	$ 15,590	$ 15,042	$ 14,521	$ 14,025	$ 13,552	$ 13,103	$ 12,674	$ 12,266	$ 11,876	$ 11,504	$ 11,149	$ 10,810
16	$ 17,353	$ 16,696	$ 16,072	$ 15,481	$ 14,920	$ 14,388	$ 13,882	$ 13,401	$ 12,945	$ 12,510	$ 12,096	$ 11,702	$ 11,327
17	$ 18,555	$ 17,810	$ 17,106	$ 16,441	$ 15,811	$ 15,215	$ 14,650	$ 14,115	$ 13,608	$ 13,127	$ 12,670	$ 12,236	$ 11,824
18	$ 19,772	$ 18,934	$ 18,144	$ 17,399	$ 16,697	$ 16,034	$ 15,408	$ 14,816	$ 14,257	$ 13,728	$ 13,226	$ 12,752	$ 12,302
19	$ 21,004	$ 20,066	$ 19,185	$ 18,357	$ 17,578	$ 16,845	$ 16,155	$ 15,505	$ 14,891	$ 14,312	$ 13,766	$ 13,249	$ 12,761
20	$ 22,251	$ 21,207	$ 20,230	$ 19,314	$ 18,455	$ 17,649	$ 16,892	$ 16,180	$ 15,511	$ 14,881	$ 14,288	$ 13,729	$ 13,202
21	$ 23,513	$ 22,357	$ 21,278	$ 20,270	$ 19,327	$ 18,444	$ 17,618	$ 16,844	$ 16,117	$ 15,435	$ 14,795	$ 14,192	$ 13,626
22	$ 24,791	$ 23,516	$ 22,330	$ 21,224	$ 20,194	$ 19,232	$ 18,334	$ 17,495	$ 16,710	$ 15,974	$ 15,286	$ 14,640	$ 14,033
23	$ 26,085	$ 24,685	$ 23,385	$ 22,178	$ 21,057	$ 20,013	$ 19,041	$ 18,134	$ 17,289	$ 16,499	$ 15,761	$ 15,071	$ 14,425

Chart Six

Starting Portfolio Needed to Fund Various Annual Expenses Assuming 1% Trustee Fee and 10% Tax Rate (Continued)

Assumptions:

	Initial annual expenses:	$1,000	inflation: 2.50%	tax rate: 10.00%	TTEE/ admin. fee: 1.00%

The following also assumes that needs are paid at end of each year and that TTEE fee is not tax deductible.

Rate of Return (Nominal): Life expectancies	2.50%	3.00%	3.50%	4.00%	4.50%	5.00%	5.50%	6.00%	6.50%	7.00%	7.50%	8.00%	8.50%
24	$ 27,394	$ 25,862	$ 24,444	$ 23,131	$ 21,915	$ 20,786	$ 19,737	$ 18,762	$ 17,855	$ 17,010	$ 16,223	$ 15,488	$ 14,801
25	$ 28,720	$ 27,049	$ 25,507	$ 24,084	$ 22,768	$ 21,551	$ 20,424	$ 19,379	$ 18,409	$ 17,508	$ 16,670	$ 15,890	$ 15,163
26	$ 30,063	$ 28,245	$ 26,573	$ 25,035	$ 23,617	$ 22,309	$ 21,101	$ 19,984	$ 18,950	$ 17,992	$ 17,103	$ 16,278	$ 15,510
27	$ 31,421	$ 29,450	$ 27,643	$ 25,985	$ 24,461	$ 23,060	$ 21,768	$ 20,578	$ 19,479	$ 18,463	$ 17,523	$ 16,652	$ 15,845
28	$ 32,797	$ 30,665	$ 28,717	$ 26,934	$ 25,301	$ 23,803	$ 22,427	$ 21,161	$ 19,996	$ 18,922	$ 17,930	$ 17,014	$ 16,166
29	$ 34,189	$ 31,890	$ 29,794	$ 27,883	$ 26,136	$ 24,539	$ 23,076	$ 21,734	$ 20,502	$ 19,368	$ 18,325	$ 17,363	$ 16,474
30	$ 35,599	$ 33,124	$ 30,875	$ 28,830	$ 26,967	$ 25,268	$ 23,716	$ 22,296	$ 20,996	$ 19,803	$ 18,707	$ 17,699	$ 16,771
31	$ 37,026	$ 34,368	$ 31,960	$ 29,777	$ 27,794	$ 25,990	$ 24,347	$ 22,848	$ 21,479	$ 20,226	$ 19,078	$ 18,024	$ 17,056
32	$ 38,471	$ 35,621	$ 33,049	$ 30,722	$ 28,616	$ 26,705	$ 24,970	$ 23,390	$ 21,951	$ 20,638	$ 19,437	$ 18,338	$ 17,330
33	$ 39,934	$ 36,885	$ 34,141	$ 31,667	$ 29,434	$ 27,413	$ 25,583	$ 23,923	$ 22,413	$ 21,039	$ 19,785	$ 18,641	$ 17,593
34	$ 41,414	$ 38,158	$ 35,237	$ 32,611	$ 30,247	$ 28,115	$ 26,188	$ 24,445	$ 22,865	$ 21,429	$ 20,123	$ 18,933	$ 17,846
35	$ 42,913	$ 39,442	$ 36,336	$ 33,554	$ 31,056	$ 28,809	$ 26,785	$ 24,958	$ 23,306	$ 21,809	$ 20,450	$ 19,215	$ 18,089
36	$ 44,431	$ 40,735	$ 37,440	$ 34,496	$ 31,861	$ 29,497	$ 27,374	$ 25,462	$ 23,737	$ 22,179	$ 20,767	$ 19,487	$ 18,323
37	$ 45,967	$ 42,039	$ 38,547	$ 35,437	$ 32,661	$ 30,178	$ 27,954	$ 25,956	$ 24,159	$ 22,539	$ 21,075	$ 19,750	$ 18,548
38	$ 47,522	$ 43,353	$ 39,658	$ 36,377	$ 33,457	$ 30,853	$ 28,526	$ 26,442	$ 24,571	$ 22,889	$ 21,373	$ 20,003	$ 18,764
39	$ 49,097	$ 44,677	$ 40,773	$ 37,316	$ 34,249	$ 31,521	$ 29,090	$ 26,918	$ 24,974	$ 23,230	$ 21,661	$ 20,248	$ 18,971
40	$ 50,690	$ 46,012	$ 41,892	$ 38,254	$ 35,036	$ 32,183	$ 29,646	$ 27,386	$ 25,368	$ 23,562	$ 21,941	$ 20,484	$ 19,171
41	$ 52,304	$ 47,357	$ 43,014	$ 39,192	$ 35,820	$ 32,838	$ 30,195	$ 27,846	$ 25,753	$ 23,885	$ 22,213	$ 20,712	$ 19,362
42	$ 53,937	$ 48,713	$ 44,140	$ 40,128	$ 36,599	$ 33,487	$ 30,735	$ 28,297	$ 26,130	$ 24,200	$ 22,476	$ 20,932	$ 19,547
43	$ 55,591	$ 50,079	$ 45,271	$ 41,064	$ 37,374	$ 34,129	$ 31,269	$ 28,740	$ 26,498	$ 24,506	$ 22,731	$ 21,144	$ 19,724
44	$ 57,265	$ 51,457	$ 46,405	$ 41,998	$ 38,145	$ 34,766	$ 31,795	$ 29,174	$ 26,858	$ 24,804	$ 22,978	$ 21,349	$ 19,894
45	$ 58,959	$ 52,845	$ 47,543	$ 42,932	$ 38,912	$ 35,396	$ 32,313	$ 29,601	$ 27,210	$ 25,094	$ 23,217	$ 21,547	$ 20,057
46	$ 60,675	$ 54,244	$ 48,685	$ 43,865	$ 39,675	$ 36,020	$ 32,824	$ 30,021	$ 27,554	$ 25,376	$ 23,449	$ 21,738	$ 20,214

Assumptions:

Initial annual expenses: $1,000	inflation: 2.50%	tax rate: 10.00%	TTEE/admin. fee: 1.00%	

The following also assumes that needs are paid at end of each year and that TTEE fee is not tax deductible.

Life expectancies	Rate of Return (Nominal):												
	2.50%	3.00%	3.50%	4.00%	4.50%	5.00%	5.50%	6.00%	6.50%	7.00%	7.50%	8.00%	8.50%
47	$ 62,412	$ 55,654	$ 49,830	$ 44,797	$ 40,433	36,639	33,328	30,432	27,890	25,651	$ 23,674	$ 21,922	$ 20,365
48	$ 64,170	$ 57,075	$ 50,980	$ 45,728	$ 41,188	37,251	33,826	30,836	28,218	25,919	$ 23,892	$ 22,100	$ 20,511
49	$ 65,950	$ 58,507	$ 52,134	$ 46,658	$ 41,938	37,857	34,316	31,233	28,540	26,179	$ 24,104	$ 22,272	$ 20,650
50	$ 67,751	$ 59,951	$ 53,291	$ 47,587	$ 42,685	38,457	34,799	31,622	28,854	26,433	$ 24,308	$ 22,438	$ 20,784
51	$ 69,576	$ 61,405	$ 54,453	$ 48,515	$ 43,428	39,052	35,276	32,004	29,161	26,680	$ 24,507	$ 22,597	$ 20,913
52	$ 71,422	$ 62,872	$ 55,618	$ 49,443	$ 44,166	39,641	35,746	32,380	29,461	26,920	$ 24,699	$ 22,752	$ 21,037
53	$ 73,292	$ 64,350	$ 56,788	$ 50,369	$ 44,901	40,224	36,209	32,748	29,754	27,154	$ 24,886	$ 22,901	$ 21,156
54	$ 75,184	$ 65,839	$ 57,961	$ 51,295	$ 45,632	40,802	36,666	33,110	30,041	27,381	$ 25,067	$ 23,044	$ 21,271
55	$ 77,100	$ 67,340	$ 59,139	$ 52,220	$ 46,358	41,374	37,116	33,466	30,322	27,603	$ 25,242	$ 23,183	$ 21,380
56	$ 79,039	$ 68,853	$ 60,320	$ 53,143	$ 47,081	41,940	37,561	33,814	30,596	27,819	$ 25,412	$ 23,317	$ 21,486
57	$ 81,003	$ 70,378	$ 61,506	$ 54,066	$ 47,801	42,501	37,999	34,157	30,864	28,029	$ 25,577	$ 23,446	$ 21,588
58	$ 82,991	$ 71,915	$ 62,696	$ 54,988	$ 48,516	43,057	38,431	34,493	31,126	28,233	$ 25,736	$ 23,571	$ 21,685
59	$ 85,003	$ 73,464	$ 63,889	$ 55,909	$ 49,227	43,607	38,857	34,823	31,382	28,432	$ 25,891	$ 23,692	$ 21,779
60	$ 87,040	$ 75,025	$ 65,087	$ 56,829	$ 49,935	44,152	39,277	35,147	31,632	28,626	$ 26,041	$ 23,808	$ 21,869
61	$ 89,102	$ 76,599	$ 66,289	$ 57,749	$ 50,639	44,691	39,691	35,465	31,877	28,814	$ 26,186	$ 23,920	$ 21,956
62	$ 91,190	$ 78,185	$ 67,495	$ 58,667	$ 51,339	45,226	40,099	35,778	32,116	28,997	$ 26,327	$ 24,028	$ 22,039
63	$ 93,303	$ 79,783	$ 68,706	$ 59,584	$ 52,035	45,755	40,502	36,085	32,350	29,176	$ 26,463	$ 24,133	$ 22,119
64	$ 95,443	$ 81,394	$ 69,920	$ 60,501	$ 52,728	46,279	40,899	36,386	32,579	29,350	$ 26,596	$ 24,233	$ 22,196
65	$ 97,609	$ 83,017	$ 71,139	$ 61,417	$ 53,417	46,798	41,290	36,681	32,803	29,519	$ 26,724	$ 24,331	$ 22,270
66	$ 99,801	$ 84,654	$ 72,361	$ 62,332	$ 54,102	47,312	41,676	36,972	33,021	29,684	$ 26,848	$ 24,425	$ 22,341
67	$ 102,021	$ 86,303	$ 73,588	$ 63,245	$ 54,784	47,821	42,057	37,257	33,235	29,844	$ 26,969	$ 24,515	$ 22,410
68	$ 104,268	$ 87,965	$ 74,819	$ 64,158	$ 55,462	48,325	42,432	37,537	33,444	30,000	$ 27,086	$ 24,603	$ 22,475
69	$ 106,543	$ 89,640	$ 76,054	$ 65,071	$ 56,136	48,824	42,802	37,811	33,648	30,152	$ 27,199	$ 24,687	$ 22,538

Starting Portfolio Needed to Fund Various Annual Expenses
Assuming 1% Trustee Fee and 10% Tax Rate (Continued)

Assumptions: Initial annual expenses: $1,000   inflation: 2.50%   tax rate: 10.00%   TTEE/admin. fee: 1.00%

The following also assumes that needs are paid at end of each year and that TTEE fee is not tax deductible.

Rate of Return (Nominal): Life expectancies	2.50%	3.00%	3.50%	4.00%	4.50%	5.00%	5.50%	6.00%	6.50%	7.00%	7.50%	8.00%	8.50%
70	$108,846	$91,329	$77,294	$65,982	$56,807	$49,319	$43,167	$38,081	$33,847	$30,300	$27,309	$24,769	$22,599
71	$111,178	$93,030	$78,538	$66,892	$57,474	$49,809	$43,527	$38,346	$34,042	$30,444	$27,415	$24,848	$22,657
72	$113,538	$94,745	$79,786	$67,802	$58,138	$50,294	$43,882	$38,606	$34,233	$30,584	$27,518	$24,923	$22,713
73	$115,927	$96,474	$81,038	$68,710	$58,798	$50,774	$44,232	$38,861	$34,420	$30,721	$27,618	$24,997	$22,767
74	$118,346	$98,216	$82,295	$69,618	$59,455	$51,249	$44,577	$39,112	$34,602	$30,853	$27,715	$25,068	$22,819
75	$120,795	$99,972	$83,556	$70,525	$60,108	$51,720	$44,917	$39,358	$34,780	$30,983	$27,809	$25,136	$22,868
76	$123,274	$101,742	$84,821	$71,431	$60,757	$52,187	$45,253	$39,599	$34,954	$31,109	$27,900	$25,202	$22,916
77	$125,783	$103,525	$86,091	$72,336	$61,404	$52,649	$45,583	$39,836	$35,125	$31,231	$27,988	$25,265	$22,962
78	$128,324	$105,323	$87,364	$73,240	$62,046	$53,106	$45,910	$40,069	$35,291	$31,350	$28,073	$25,327	$23,006
79	$130,896	$107,135	$88,643	$74,143	$62,685	$53,559	$46,231	$40,298	$35,454	$31,466	$28,156	$25,386	$23,049
80	$133,499	$108,961	$89,925	$75,046	$63,321	$54,008	$46,548	$40,522	$35,613	$31,579	$28,236	$25,443	$23,089
81	$136,135	$110,801	$91,213	$75,947	$63,954	$54,452	$46,861	$40,743	$35,769	$31,689	$28,314	$25,498	$23,129
82	$138,804	$112,656	$92,504	$76,848	$64,583	$54,893	$47,169	$40,959	$35,921	$31,796	$28,390	$25,552	$23,166
83	$141,505	$114,525	$93,800	$77,747	$65,209	$55,328	$47,473	$41,172	$36,069	$31,900	$28,463	$25,603	$23,203
84	$144,239	$116,410	$95,100	$78,646	$65,831	$55,760	$47,773	$41,380	$36,215	$32,002	$28,534	$25,653	$23,237
85	$147,008	$118,309	$96,405	$79,544	$66,450	$56,187	$48,069	$41,585	$36,357	$32,101	$28,602	$25,700	$23,271
86	$149,810	$120,223	$97,714	$80,441	$67,066	$56,611	$48,360	$41,786	$36,496	$32,197	$28,669	$25,747	$23,303
87	$152,648	$122,152	$99,028	$81,338	$67,678	$57,030	$48,648	$41,983	$36,631	$32,290	$28,734	$25,791	$23,334
88	$155,520	$124,096	$100,346	$82,233	$68,287	$57,445	$48,931	$42,177	$36,764	$32,381	$28,796	$25,834	$23,363
89	$158,427	$126,055	$101,669	$83,128	$68,893	$57,856	$49,211	$42,367	$36,894	$32,470	$28,857	$25,876	$23,392
90	$161,371	$128,030	$102,996	$84,021	$69,496	$58,263	$49,486	$42,554	$37,021	$32,556	$28,916	$25,916	$23,419

CHART SEVEN

STARTING PORTFOLIO NEEDED TO FUND VARIOUS ANNUAL EXPENSES
ASSUMING 1% TRUSTEE FEE AND 20% TAX RATE

Assumptions: Initial annual expenses: $ 1,000   inflation: 2.50%   tax rate: 20.00%   TTEE/admin. fee: 1.00%

The following also assumes that needs are paid at end of each year and that TTEE fee is not tax deductible.

Rate of Return (Nominal): Life expectancies	2.50%	3.00%	3.50%	4.00%	4.50%	5.00%	5.50%	6.00%	6.50%	7.00%	7.50%	8.00%	8.50%
1	$ 990	$ 986	$ 982	$ 978	$ 975	$ 971	$ 967	$ 963	$ 960	$ 956	$ 952	$ 949	$ 945
2	$ 1,995	$ 1,983	$ 1,971	$ 1,960	$ 1,948	$ 1,937	$ 1,926	$ 1,915	$ 1,904	$ 1,893	$ 1,882	$ 1,871	$ 1,861
3	$ 3,015	$ 2,991	$ 2,967	$ 2,944	$ 2,921	$ 2,899	$ 2,876	$ 2,854	$ 2,832	$ 2,811	$ 2,790	$ 2,769	$ 2,748
4	$ 4,049	$ 4,009	$ 3,970	$ 3,931	$ 3,893	$ 3,855	$ 3,818	$ 3,782	$ 3,746	$ 3,710	$ 3,676	$ 3,641	$ 3,607
5	$ 5,100	$ 5,039	$ 4,980	$ 4,921	$ 4,864	$ 4,807	$ 4,752	$ 4,698	$ 4,644	$ 4,592	$ 4,540	$ 4,490	$ 4,440
6	$ 6,166	$ 6,080	$ 5,996	$ 5,914	$ 5,834	$ 5,755	$ 5,678	$ 5,602	$ 5,528	$ 5,456	$ 5,385	$ 5,315	$ 5,247
7	$ 7,247	$ 7,132	$ 7,020	$ 6,910	$ 6,803	$ 6,698	$ 6,596	$ 6,496	$ 6,398	$ 6,302	$ 6,209	$ 6,118	$ 6,028
8	$ 8,345	$ 8,196	$ 8,050	$ 7,909	$ 7,771	$ 7,636	$ 7,505	$ 7,378	$ 7,253	$ 7,132	$ 7,013	$ 6,898	$ 6,786
9	$ 9,459	$ 9,271	$ 9,088	$ 8,910	$ 8,738	$ 8,570	$ 8,407	$ 8,249	$ 8,095	$ 7,945	$ 7,799	$ 7,657	$ 7,519
10	$ 10,590	$ 10,358	$ 10,133	$ 9,915	$ 9,704	$ 9,499	$ 9,301	$ 9,109	$ 8,922	$ 8,741	$ 8,566	$ 8,395	$ 8,230
11	$ 11,737	$ 11,456	$ 11,185	$ 10,923	$ 10,669	$ 10,424	$ 10,187	$ 9,958	$ 9,736	$ 9,522	$ 9,314	$ 9,113	$ 8,918
12	$ 12,901	$ 12,567	$ 12,244	$ 11,933	$ 11,633	$ 11,344	$ 11,066	$ 10,797	$ 10,537	$ 10,287	$ 10,045	$ 9,811	$ 9,585
13	$ 14,083	$ 13,689	$ 13,311	$ 12,947	$ 12,597	$ 12,260	$ 11,936	$ 11,625	$ 11,325	$ 11,036	$ 10,758	$ 10,490	$ 10,231
14	$ 15,282	$ 14,824	$ 14,384	$ 13,963	$ 13,559	$ 13,172	$ 12,800	$ 12,443	$ 12,100	$ 11,771	$ 11,454	$ 11,150	$ 10,857
15	$ 16,499	$ 15,971	$ 15,466	$ 14,983	$ 14,521	$ 14,079	$ 13,655	$ 13,250	$ 12,862	$ 12,490	$ 12,134	$ 11,792	$ 11,464
16	$ 17,735	$ 17,130	$ 16,554	$ 16,005	$ 15,481	$ 14,981	$ 14,504	$ 14,048	$ 13,612	$ 13,196	$ 12,797	$ 12,416	$ 12,052
17	$ 18,988	$ 18,302	$ 17,650	$ 17,030	$ 16,441	$ 15,879	$ 15,345	$ 14,835	$ 14,350	$ 13,887	$ 13,445	$ 13,023	$ 12,621
18	$ 20,260	$ 19,487	$ 18,754	$ 18,059	$ 17,399	$ 16,773	$ 16,178	$ 15,613	$ 15,075	$ 14,564	$ 14,077	$ 13,614	$ 13,172
19	$ 21,551	$ 20,685	$ 19,865	$ 19,090	$ 18,357	$ 17,662	$ 17,004	$ 16,381	$ 15,789	$ 15,227	$ 14,694	$ 14,188	$ 13,707
20	$ 22,861	$ 21,895	$ 20,984	$ 20,125	$ 19,314	$ 18,548	$ 17,823	$ 17,139	$ 16,491	$ 15,878	$ 15,297	$ 14,746	$ 14,224
21	$ 24,191	$ 23,119	$ 22,111	$ 21,162	$ 20,270	$ 19,428	$ 18,635	$ 17,888	$ 17,182	$ 16,515	$ 15,885	$ 15,289	$ 14,726
22	$ 25,540	$ 24,356	$ 23,245	$ 22,203	$ 21,224	$ 20,305	$ 19,440	$ 18,627	$ 17,861	$ 17,139	$ 16,459	$ 15,818	$ 15,212
23	$ 26,910	$ 25,606	$ 24,387	$ 23,247	$ 22,178	$ 21,177	$ 20,238	$ 19,357	$ 18,529	$ 17,751	$ 17,020	$ 16,331	$ 15,682

STARTING PORTFOLIO NEEDED TO FUND VARIOUS ANNUAL EXPENSES
ASSUMING 1% TRUSTEE FEE AND 20% TAX RATE (CONTINUED)

Assumptions: Initial annual expenses: $ 1,000 inflation: 2.50% tax rate: 20.00% TTEE/admin. fee: 1.00%

The following also assumes that needs are paid at end of each year and that TTEE fee is not tax deductible.

Rate of Return (Nominal): Life expectancies	2.50%	3.00%	3.50%	4.00%	4.50%	5.00%	5.50%	6.00%	6.50%	7.00%	7.50%	8.00%	8.50%
24	$ 28,299	$ 26,870	$ 25,537	$ 24,293	$ 23,131	$ 22,045	$ 21,029	$ 20,078	$ 19,187	$ 18,351	$ 17,567	$ 16,831	$ 16,138
25	29,710	28,148	26,695	25,343	24,084	22,909	21,813	20,790	19,833	18,939	18,101	17,316	16,580
26	31,141	29,439	27,861	26,396	25,035	23,769	22,591	21,493	20,470	19,514	18,622	17,789	17,008
27	32,594	30,745	29,035	27,452	25,985	24,624	23,361	22,187	21,095	20,079	19,131	18,248	17,423
28	34,068	32,065	30,217	28,511	26,934	25,476	24,125	22,873	21,711	20,632	19,628	18,695	17,825
29	35,564	33,399	31,407	29,573	27,883	26,323	24,882	23,550	22,316	21,173	20,113	19,129	18,214
30	37,082	34,747	32,605	30,639	28,830	27,166	25,633	24,218	22,912	21,704	20,587	19,551	18,591
31	38,623	36,110	33,812	31,707	29,777	28,005	26,377	24,878	23,498	22,225	21,049	19,962	18,956
32	40,187	37,488	35,027	32,779	30,722	28,840	27,114	25,530	24,074	22,734	21,500	20,362	19,310
33	41,774	38,881	36,250	33,853	31,667	29,671	27,845	26,174	24,641	23,234	21,941	20,750	19,653
34	43,384	40,289	37,482	34,931	32,611	30,498	28,570	26,809	25,199	23,724	22,371	21,128	19,985
35	45,019	41,712	38,722	36,012	33,554	31,320	29,288	27,437	25,747	24,203	22,790	21,496	20,307
36	46,677	43,151	39,970	37,096	34,496	32,139	30,001	28,057	26,287	24,673	23,200	21,853	20,619
37	48,361	44,605	41,227	38,184	35,437	32,954	30,707	28,669	26,818	25,134	23,600	22,200	20,921
38	50,069	46,076	42,493	39,274	36,377	33,765	31,406	29,273	27,340	25,586	23,991	22,538	21,214
39	51,803	47,562	43,768	40,368	37,316	34,572	32,100	29,870	27,854	26,028	24,372	22,867	21,497
40	53,562	49,064	45,051	41,465	38,254	35,375	32,788	30,459	28,359	26,461	24,744	23,187	21,772
41	55,348	50,582	46,343	42,565	39,192	36,174	33,470	31,041	28,856	26,886	25,107	23,497	22,038
42	57,160	52,117	47,644	43,669	40,128	36,969	34,145	31,616	29,345	27,302	25,462	23,800	22,296
43	58,999	53,669	48,954	44,775	41,064	37,761	34,815	32,183	29,826	27,710	25,808	24,094	22,545
44	60,865	55,237	50,273	45,885	41,998	38,548	35,479	32,743	30,299	28,110	26,146	24,379	22,787
45	62,759	56,822	51,601	46,998	42,932	39,332	36,138	33,297	30,764	28,502	26,476	24,657	23,022
46	64,681	58,425	52,938	48,115	43,865	40,112	36,790	33,843	31,222	28,885	26,798	24,928	23,249

	Initial annual						TTEE/ admin.					

Assumptions: expenses: $ 1,000   inflation: 2.50%   tax rate: 20.00%   fee: 1.00%

The following also assumes that needs are paid at end of each year and that TTEE fee is not tax deductible.

Rate of Return (Nominal): Life expectancies	2.50%	3.00%	3.50%	4.00%	4.50%	5.00%	5.50%	6.00%	6.50%	7.00%	7.50%	8.00%	8.50%
47	$ 66,632	$ 60,045	$ 54,284	$ 49,234	$ 44,797	$ 40,888	$ 37,437	$ 34,383	$ 31,672	$ 29,262	$ 27,112	$ 25,191	$ 23,469
48	$ 68,612	$ 61,683	$ 55,640	$ 50,357	$ 45,728	$ 41,661	$ 38,078	$ 34,915	$ 32,115	$ 29,630	$ 27,419	$ 25,446	$ 23,682
49	$ 70,621	$ 63,338	$ 57,005	$ 51,484	$ 46,658	$ 42,429	$ 38,714	$ 35,441	$ 32,551	$ 29,991	$ 27,718	$ 25,695	$ 23,889
50	$ 72,660	$ 65,011	$ 58,379	$ 52,613	$ 47,587	$ 43,194	$ 39,344	$ 35,961	$ 32,980	$ 30,345	$ 28,011	$ 25,937	$ 24,089
51	$ 74,729	$ 66,703	$ 59,763	$ 53,746	$ 48,515	$ 43,955	$ 39,969	$ 36,474	$ 33,401	$ 30,692	$ 28,296	$ 26,172	$ 24,283
52	$ 76,829	$ 68,413	$ 61,156	$ 54,882	$ 49,443	$ 44,713	$ 40,588	$ 36,981	$ 33,816	$ 31,032	$ 28,575	$ 26,401	$ 24,470
53	$ 78,960	$ 70,141	$ 62,559	$ 56,022	$ 50,369	$ 45,467	$ 41,202	$ 37,481	$ 34,224	$ 31,365	$ 28,847	$ 26,623	$ 24,652
54	$ 81,123	$ 71,888	$ 63,971	$ 57,165	$ 51,295	$ 46,217	$ 41,810	$ 37,975	$ 34,625	$ 31,691	$ 29,113	$ 26,839	$ 24,828
55	$ 83,318	$ 73,654	$ 65,394	$ 58,311	$ 52,220	$ 46,963	$ 42,414	$ 38,463	$ 35,020	$ 32,011	$ 29,372	$ 27,049	$ 24,999
56	$ 85,545	$ 75,439	$ 66,826	$ 59,461	$ 53,143	$ 47,706	$ 43,012	$ 38,944	$ 35,408	$ 32,324	$ 29,625	$ 27,254	$ 25,165
57	$ 87,806	$ 77,244	$ 68,268	$ 60,614	$ 54,066	$ 48,446	$ 43,604	$ 39,420	$ 35,790	$ 32,631	$ 29,872	$ 27,453	$ 25,325
58	$ 90,100	$ 79,068	$ 69,719	$ 61,770	$ 54,988	$ 49,181	$ 44,192	$ 39,890	$ 36,166	$ 32,932	$ 30,113	$ 27,646	$ 25,480
59	$ 92,428	$ 80,912	$ 71,181	$ 62,930	$ 55,909	$ 49,913	$ 44,774	$ 40,353	$ 36,536	$ 33,227	$ 30,348	$ 27,834	$ 25,631
60	$ 94,791	$ 82,776	$ 72,653	$ 64,093	$ 56,829	$ 50,642	$ 45,352	$ 40,811	$ 36,900	$ 33,516	$ 30,578	$ 28,017	$ 25,776
61	$ 97,189	$ 84,660	$ 74,135	$ 65,260	$ 57,749	$ 51,367	$ 45,924	$ 41,264	$ 37,257	$ 33,799	$ 30,803	$ 28,195	$ 25,918
62	$ 99,622	$ 86,565	$ 75,627	$ 66,430	$ 58,667	$ 52,089	$ 46,492	$ 41,710	$ 37,609	$ 34,077	$ 31,022	$ 28,368	$ 26,054
63	$ 102,092	$ 88,490	$ 77,129	$ 67,603	$ 59,584	$ 52,807	$ 47,054	$ 42,151	$ 37,955	$ 34,349	$ 31,235	$ 28,536	$ 26,187
64	$ 104,598	$ 90,436	$ 78,642	$ 68,780	$ 60,501	$ 53,521	$ 47,612	$ 42,587	$ 38,296	$ 34,615	$ 31,444	$ 28,700	$ 26,315
65	$ 107,142	$ 92,403	$ 80,165	$ 69,961	$ 61,417	$ 54,232	$ 48,164	$ 43,017	$ 38,631	$ 34,876	$ 31,648	$ 28,859	$ 26,440
66	$ 109,723	$ 94,392	$ 81,698	$ 71,145	$ 62,332	$ 54,940	$ 48,712	$ 43,441	$ 38,960	$ 35,132	$ 31,847	$ 29,014	$ 26,560
67	$ 112,343	$ 96,402	$ 83,242	$ 72,332	$ 63,245	$ 55,644	$ 49,255	$ 43,861	$ 39,284	$ 35,383	$ 32,041	$ 29,164	$ 26,677
68	$ 115,001	$ 98,434	$ 84,797	$ 73,523	$ 64,158	$ 56,345	$ 49,794	$ 44,275	$ 39,603	$ 35,628	$ 32,230	$ 29,311	$ 26,790
69	$ 117,699	$ 100,488	$ 86,363	$ 74,717	$ 65,071	$ 57,042	$ 50,327	$ 44,684	$ 39,916	$ 35,869	$ 32,415	$ 29,453	$ 26,900

CHART SEVEN

STARTING PORTFOLIO NEEDED TO FUND VARIOUS ANNUAL EXPENSES
ASSUMING 1% TRUSTEE FEE AND 20% TAX RATE (CONTINUED)

Assumptions: Initial annual expenses: $ 1,000 inflation: 2.50% tax rate: 20.00% TTEE/admin. fee: 1.00%

The following also assumes that needs are paid at end of each year and that TTEE fee is not tax deductible.

Rate of Return (Nominal): Life expectancies	2.50%	3.00%	3.50%	4.00%	4.50%	5.00%	5.50%	6.00%	6.50%	7.00%	7.50%	8.00%	8.50%
70	$ 120,437	$ 102,564	$ 87,939	$ 75,915	$ 65,982	$ 57,736	$ 50,856	$ 45,088	$ 40,225	$ 36,105	$ 32,596	$ 29,591	$ 27,006
71	$ 123,216	$ 104,663	$ 89,526	$ 77,116	$ 66,892	$ 58,427	$ 51,381	$ 45,486	$ 40,528	$ 36,336	$ 32,772	$ 29,726	$ 27,109
72	$ 126,036	$ 106,785	$ 91,124	$ 78,321	$ 67,802	$ 59,114	$ 51,901	$ 45,880	$ 40,827	$ 36,563	$ 32,944	$ 29,857	$ 27,208
73	$ 128,898	$ 108,929	$ 92,733	$ 79,529	$ 68,710	$ 59,798	$ 52,416	$ 46,269	$ 41,120	$ 36,785	$ 33,112	$ 29,984	$ 27,305
74	$ 131,803	$ 111,097	$ 94,353	$ 80,741	$ 69,618	$ 60,478	$ 52,927	$ 46,653	$ 41,409	$ 37,002	$ 33,276	$ 30,108	$ 27,398
75	$ 134,750	$ 113,288	$ 95,984	$ 81,957	$ 70,525	$ 61,156	$ 53,434	$ 47,032	$ 41,693	$ 37,215	$ 33,436	$ 30,228	$ 27,489
76	$ 137,741	$ 115,504	$ 97,626	$ 83,176	$ 71,431	$ 61,830	$ 53,936	$ 47,406	$ 41,973	$ 37,424	$ 33,593	$ 30,345	$ 27,577
77	$ 140,777	$ 117,743	$ 99,280	$ 84,398	$ 72,336	$ 62,500	$ 54,433	$ 47,776	$ 42,248	$ 37,629	$ 33,745	$ 30,459	$ 27,662
78	$ 143,858	$ 120,006	$ 100,945	$ 85,625	$ 73,240	$ 63,168	$ 54,927	$ 48,141	$ 42,518	$ 37,829	$ 33,894	$ 30,570	$ 27,744
79	$ 146,985	$ 122,294	$ 102,621	$ 86,854	$ 74,143	$ 63,832	$ 55,416	$ 48,501	$ 42,784	$ 38,026	$ 34,039	$ 30,678	$ 27,824
80	$ 150,158	$ 124,607	$ 104,309	$ 88,088	$ 75,046	$ 64,493	$ 55,900	$ 48,857	$ 43,046	$ 38,218	$ 34,181	$ 30,782	$ 27,901
81	$ 153,378	$ 126,945	$ 106,009	$ 89,325	$ 75,947	$ 65,151	$ 56,381	$ 49,209	$ 43,303	$ 38,407	$ 34,320	$ 30,884	$ 27,976
82	$ 156,646	$ 129,308	$ 107,720	$ 90,566	$ 76,848	$ 65,806	$ 56,857	$ 49,556	$ 43,556	$ 38,592	$ 34,455	$ 30,983	$ 28,049
83	$ 159,962	$ 131,697	$ 109,443	$ 91,810	$ 77,747	$ 66,457	$ 57,330	$ 49,899	$ 43,806	$ 38,773	$ 34,587	$ 31,079	$ 28,119
84	$ 163,328	$ 134,112	$ 111,178	$ 93,058	$ 78,646	$ 67,105	$ 57,798	$ 50,237	$ 44,051	$ 38,951	$ 34,716	$ 31,173	$ 28,187
85	$ 166,744	$ 136,553	$ 112,925	$ 94,309	$ 79,544	$ 67,750	$ 58,262	$ 50,571	$ 44,292	$ 39,125	$ 34,842	$ 31,264	$ 28,253
86	$ 170,210	$ 139,021	$ 114,683	$ 95,565	$ 80,441	$ 68,392	$ 58,722	$ 50,901	$ 44,529	$ 39,296	$ 34,965	$ 31,353	$ 28,317
87	$ 173,728	$ 141,515	$ 116,454	$ 96,824	$ 81,338	$ 69,031	$ 59,178	$ 51,227	$ 44,762	$ 39,463	$ 35,085	$ 31,439	$ 28,379
88	$ 177,299	$ 144,037	$ 118,237	$ 98,086	$ 82,233	$ 69,667	$ 59,630	$ 51,549	$ 44,991	$ 39,626	$ 35,202	$ 31,523	$ 28,439
89	$ 180,922	$ 146,585	$ 120,033	$ 99,353	$ 83,128	$ 70,300	$ 60,078	$ 51,867	$ 45,217	$ 39,787	$ 35,316	$ 31,604	$ 28,497
90	$ 184,599	$ 149,162	$ 121,840	$ 100,623	$ 84,021	$ 70,929	$ 60,522	$ 52,181	$ 45,439	$ 39,944	$ 35,427	$ 31,683	$ 28,553

STARTING PORTFOLIO NEEDED TO FUND VARIOUS ANNUAL EXPENSES
ASSUMING 1% TRUSTEE FEE AND 30% TAX RATE

Assumptions:
Initial annual expenses: $ 1,000   inflation: 2.50%   tax rate: 30.00%   TTEE/admin. fee: 1.00%

The following also assumes that needs are paid at end of each year and that TTEE fee is not tax deductible.

Rate of Return (Nominal): Life expectancies	2.50%	3.00%	3.50%	4.00%	4.50%	5.00%	5.50%	6.00%	6.50%	7.00%	7.50%	8.00%	8.50%
1	$ 993	$ 989	$ 986	$ 982	$ 979	$ 976	$ 972	$ 969	$ 966	$ 962	$ 959	$ 956	$ 953
2	$ 2,002	$ 1,992	$ 1,982	$ 1,971	$ 1,961	$ 1,951	$ 1,941	$ 1,931	$ 1,922	$ 1,912	$ 1,902	$ 1,893	$ 1,883
3	$ 3,030	$ 3,009	$ 2,988	$ 2,967	$ 2,947	$ 2,927	$ 2,907	$ 2,887	$ 2,868	$ 2,849	$ 2,830	$ 2,811	$ 2,792
4	$ 4,075	$ 4,039	$ 4,004	$ 3,970	$ 3,936	$ 3,902	$ 3,869	$ 3,837	$ 3,805	$ 3,773	$ 3,741	$ 3,710	$ 3,680
5	$ 5,138	$ 5,084	$ 5,032	$ 4,980	$ 4,928	$ 4,878	$ 4,828	$ 4,780	$ 4,732	$ 4,684	$ 4,638	$ 4,592	$ 4,547
6	$ 6,220	$ 6,144	$ 6,069	$ 5,996	$ 5,924	$ 5,854	$ 5,784	$ 5,716	$ 5,649	$ 5,584	$ 5,519	$ 5,456	$ 5,394
7	$ 7,321	$ 7,218	$ 7,118	$ 7,020	$ 6,924	$ 6,829	$ 6,737	$ 6,646	$ 6,558	$ 6,471	$ 6,386	$ 6,302	$ 6,220
8	$ 8,440	$ 8,307	$ 8,177	$ 8,050	$ 7,926	$ 7,805	$ 7,686	$ 7,570	$ 7,457	$ 7,346	$ 7,238	$ 7,132	$ 7,028
9	$ 9,579	$ 9,411	$ 9,248	$ 9,088	$ 8,932	$ 8,780	$ 8,632	$ 8,488	$ 8,347	$ 8,210	$ 8,076	$ 7,945	$ 7,817
10	$ 10,738	$ 10,531	$ 10,329	$ 10,133	$ 9,942	$ 9,756	$ 9,575	$ 9,399	$ 9,228	$ 9,062	$ 8,899	$ 8,741	$ 8,587
11	$ 11,918	$ 11,666	$ 11,422	$ 11,185	$ 10,955	$ 10,732	$ 10,515	$ 10,305	$ 10,100	$ 9,902	$ 9,709	$ 9,522	$ 9,340
12	$ 13,117	$ 12,816	$ 12,526	$ 12,244	$ 11,971	$ 11,707	$ 11,452	$ 11,204	$ 10,964	$ 10,731	$ 10,505	$ 10,287	$ 10,074
13	$ 14,337	$ 13,983	$ 13,641	$ 13,311	$ 12,991	$ 12,683	$ 12,385	$ 12,097	$ 11,818	$ 11,549	$ 11,288	$ 11,036	$ 10,792
14	$ 15,579	$ 15,166	$ 14,768	$ 14,384	$ 14,015	$ 13,659	$ 13,315	$ 12,984	$ 12,664	$ 12,356	$ 12,058	$ 11,771	$ 11,493
15	$ 16,842	$ 16,365	$ 15,906	$ 15,466	$ 15,042	$ 14,634	$ 14,242	$ 13,865	$ 13,501	$ 13,152	$ 12,815	$ 12,490	$ 12,177
16	$ 18,127	$ 17,581	$ 17,057	$ 16,554	$ 16,072	$ 15,610	$ 15,166	$ 14,740	$ 14,330	$ 13,937	$ 13,559	$ 13,196	$ 12,846
17	$ 19,435	$ 18,813	$ 18,219	$ 17,650	$ 17,106	$ 16,585	$ 16,087	$ 15,609	$ 15,151	$ 14,712	$ 14,291	$ 13,887	$ 13,499
18	$ 20,765	$ 20,063	$ 19,393	$ 18,754	$ 18,144	$ 17,561	$ 17,004	$ 16,472	$ 15,963	$ 15,476	$ 15,010	$ 14,564	$ 14,137
19	$ 22,118	$ 21,330	$ 20,580	$ 19,865	$ 19,185	$ 18,537	$ 17,918	$ 17,329	$ 16,767	$ 16,230	$ 15,717	$ 15,227	$ 14,760
20	$ 23,495	$ 22,614	$ 21,778	$ 20,984	$ 20,230	$ 19,512	$ 18,830	$ 18,180	$ 17,562	$ 16,974	$ 16,413	$ 15,878	$ 15,368
21	$ 24,896	$ 23,917	$ 22,989	$ 22,111	$ 21,278	$ 20,488	$ 19,738	$ 19,026	$ 18,350	$ 17,707	$ 17,096	$ 16,515	$ 15,962
22	$ 26,320	$ 25,237	$ 24,213	$ 23,245	$ 22,330	$ 21,463	$ 20,643	$ 19,866	$ 19,130	$ 18,431	$ 17,768	$ 17,139	$ 16,542
23	$ 27,770	$ 26,576	$ 25,449	$ 24,387	$ 23,385	$ 22,439	$ 21,545	$ 20,700	$ 19,901	$ 19,145	$ 18,429	$ 17,751	$ 17,109

CHART EIGHT

STARTING PORTFOLIO NEEDED TO FUND VARIOUS ANNUAL EXPENSES
ASSUMING 1% TRUSTEE FEE AND 30% TAX RATE (CONTINUED)

Assumptions: Initial annual expenses: $ 1,000   inflation: 2.50%   tax rate: 30.00%   TTEE/admin. fee: 1.00%

The following also assumes that needs are paid at end of each year and that TTEE fee is not tax deductible.

Rate of Return (Nominal): Life expectancies	2.50%	3.00%	3.50%	4.00%	4.50%	5.00%	5.50%	6.00%	6.50%	7.00%	7.50%	8.00%	8.50%
24	$ 29,245	$ 27,933	$ 26,699	$ 25,537	$ 24,444	$ 23,415	$ 22,444	$ 21,529	$ 20,665	$ 19,850	$ 19,079	$ 18,351	$ 17,662
25	$ 30,746	$ 29,309	$ 27,961	$ 26,695	$ 25,507	$ 24,390	$ 23,340	$ 22,352	$ 21,421	$ 20,545	$ 19,718	$ 18,939	$ 18,203
26	$ 32,272	$ 30,704	$ 29,236	$ 27,861	$ 26,573	$ 25,366	$ 24,233	$ 23,169	$ 22,170	$ 21,230	$ 20,347	$ 19,514	$ 18,731
27	$ 33,825	$ 32,118	$ 30,524	$ 29,035	$ 27,643	$ 26,341	$ 25,123	$ 23,981	$ 22,911	$ 21,907	$ 20,964	$ 20,079	$ 19,246
28	$ 35,405	$ 33,552	$ 31,826	$ 30,217	$ 28,717	$ 27,317	$ 26,010	$ 24,787	$ 23,644	$ 22,574	$ 21,572	$ 20,632	$ 19,750
29	$ 37,013	$ 35,005	$ 33,141	$ 31,407	$ 29,794	$ 28,293	$ 26,893	$ 25,588	$ 24,370	$ 23,232	$ 22,169	$ 21,173	$ 20,242
30	$ 38,648	$ 36,479	$ 34,469	$ 32,605	$ 30,875	$ 29,268	$ 27,774	$ 26,384	$ 25,089	$ 23,882	$ 22,756	$ 21,704	$ 20,722
31	$ 40,312	$ 37,974	$ 35,812	$ 33,812	$ 31,960	$ 30,244	$ 28,652	$ 27,174	$ 25,800	$ 24,522	$ 23,333	$ 22,225	$ 21,191
32	$ 42,005	$ 39,489	$ 37,168	$ 35,027	$ 33,049	$ 31,220	$ 29,527	$ 27,958	$ 26,504	$ 25,154	$ 23,901	$ 22,734	$ 21,649
33	$ 43,727	$ 41,025	$ 38,539	$ 36,250	$ 34,141	$ 32,195	$ 30,398	$ 28,738	$ 27,201	$ 25,778	$ 24,459	$ 23,234	$ 22,097
34	$ 45,479	$ 42,582	$ 39,923	$ 37,482	$ 35,237	$ 33,171	$ 31,267	$ 29,512	$ 27,891	$ 26,393	$ 25,007	$ 23,724	$ 22,534
35	$ 47,262	$ 44,161	$ 41,322	$ 38,722	$ 36,336	$ 34,146	$ 32,133	$ 30,281	$ 28,574	$ 27,000	$ 25,547	$ 24,203	$ 22,960
36	$ 49,075	$ 45,761	$ 42,736	$ 39,970	$ 37,440	$ 35,122	$ 32,996	$ 31,044	$ 29,250	$ 27,599	$ 26,077	$ 24,673	$ 23,377
37	$ 50,920	$ 47,384	$ 44,164	$ 41,227	$ 38,547	$ 36,098	$ 33,856	$ 31,803	$ 29,919	$ 28,189	$ 26,599	$ 25,134	$ 23,784
38	$ 52,797	$ 49,029	$ 45,606	$ 42,493	$ 39,658	$ 37,073	$ 34,713	$ 32,556	$ 30,581	$ 28,772	$ 27,111	$ 25,586	$ 24,182
39	$ 54,707	$ 50,697	$ 47,064	$ 43,768	$ 40,773	$ 38,049	$ 35,567	$ 33,304	$ 31,237	$ 29,347	$ 27,615	$ 26,028	$ 24,570
40	$ 56,650	$ 52,388	$ 48,537	$ 45,051	$ 41,892	$ 39,024	$ 36,419	$ 34,047	$ 31,886	$ 29,914	$ 28,111	$ 26,461	$ 24,949
41	$ 58,626	$ 54,103	$ 50,025	$ 46,343	$ 43,014	$ 40,000	$ 37,267	$ 34,785	$ 32,528	$ 30,473	$ 28,598	$ 26,886	$ 25,320
42	$ 60,637	$ 55,841	$ 51,528	$ 47,644	$ 44,140	$ 40,976	$ 38,112	$ 35,518	$ 33,164	$ 31,025	$ 29,078	$ 27,302	$ 25,682
43	$ 62,683	$ 57,604	$ 53,047	$ 48,954	$ 45,271	$ 41,951	$ 38,955	$ 36,246	$ 33,794	$ 31,569	$ 29,549	$ 27,710	$ 26,035
44	$ 64,764	$ 59,391	$ 54,582	$ 50,273	$ 46,405	$ 42,927	$ 39,795	$ 36,969	$ 34,417	$ 32,106	$ 30,012	$ 28,110	$ 26,380
45	$ 66,882	$ 61,202	$ 56,133	$ 51,601	$ 47,543	$ 43,902	$ 40,632	$ 37,688	$ 35,033	$ 32,636	$ 30,467	$ 28,502	$ 26,717
46	$ 69,036	$ 63,039	$ 57,699	$ 52,938	$ 48,685	$ 44,878	$ 41,466	$ 38,401	$ 35,644	$ 33,159	$ 30,915	$ 28,885	$ 27,046

Initial
annual

Assumptions: expenses: $ 1,000   inflation: 2.50%   tax rate: 30.00%   TTEE/admin. fee: 1.00%

The following also assumes that needs are paid at end of each year and that TTEE fee is not tax deductible.

Rate of Return (Nominal): Life expectancies	2.50%	3.00%	3.50%	4.00%	4.50%	5.00%	5.50%	6.00%	6.50%	7.00%	7.50%	8.00%	8.50%
47	$ 71,228	$ 64,901	$ 59,282	$ 54,284	$ 49,830	$ 45,854	$ 42,297	$ 39,110	$ 36,248	$ 33,675	$ 31,355	$ 29,262	$ 27,368
48	$ 73,458	$ 66,789	$ 60,882	$ 55,640	$ 50,980	$ 46,829	$ 43,125	$ 39,813	$ 36,846	$ 34,183	$ 31,788	$ 29,630	$ 27,682
49	$ 75,726	$ 68,703	$ 62,497	$ 57,005	$ 52,134	$ 47,805	$ 43,951	$ 40,512	$ 37,438	$ 34,685	$ 32,214	$ 29,991	$ 27,988
50	$ 78,034	$ 70,643	$ 64,130	$ 58,379	$ 53,291	$ 48,780	$ 44,773	$ 41,206	$ 38,025	$ 35,180	$ 32,632	$ 30,345	$ 28,288
51	$ 80,382	$ 72,610	$ 65,779	$ 59,763	$ 54,453	$ 49,756	$ 45,593	$ 41,896	$ 38,605	$ 35,669	$ 33,044	$ 30,692	$ 28,580
52	$ 82,771	$ 74,605	$ 67,446	$ 61,156	$ 55,618	$ 50,732	$ 46,411	$ 42,581	$ 39,179	$ 36,151	$ 33,448	$ 31,032	$ 28,866
53	$ 85,201	$ 76,627	$ 69,130	$ 62,559	$ 56,788	$ 51,707	$ 47,225	$ 43,261	$ 39,747	$ 36,626	$ 33,846	$ 31,365	$ 29,145
54	$ 87,674	$ 78,678	$ 70,831	$ 63,971	$ 57,961	$ 52,683	$ 48,036	$ 43,936	$ 40,310	$ 37,095	$ 34,237	$ 31,691	$ 29,417
55	$ 90,189	$ 80,756	$ 72,550	$ 65,394	$ 59,139	$ 53,659	$ 48,845	$ 44,607	$ 40,867	$ 37,557	$ 34,622	$ 32,011	$ 29,683
56	$ 92,748	$ 82,864	$ 74,286	$ 66,826	$ 60,320	$ 54,634	$ 49,651	$ 45,274	$ 41,418	$ 38,014	$ 35,000	$ 32,324	$ 29,943
57	$ 95,352	$ 85,000	$ 76,041	$ 68,268	$ 61,506	$ 55,610	$ 50,455	$ 45,936	$ 41,964	$ 38,464	$ 35,371	$ 32,631	$ 30,197
58	$ 98,000	$ 87,166	$ 77,814	$ 69,719	$ 62,696	$ 56,585	$ 51,255	$ 46,593	$ 42,504	$ 38,908	$ 35,737	$ 32,932	$ 30,445
59	$ 100,695	$ 89,362	$ 79,605	$ 71,181	$ 63,889	$ 57,561	$ 52,053	$ 47,246	$ 43,039	$ 39,346	$ 36,096	$ 33,227	$ 30,687
60	$ 103,437	$ 91,589	$ 81,414	$ 72,653	$ 65,087	$ 58,537	$ 52,848	$ 47,895	$ 43,568	$ 39,779	$ 36,450	$ 33,516	$ 30,924
61	$ 106,226	$ 93,846	$ 83,243	$ 74,135	$ 66,289	$ 59,512	$ 53,641	$ 48,539	$ 44,092	$ 40,205	$ 36,797	$ 33,799	$ 31,154
62	$ 109,064	$ 96,135	$ 85,090	$ 75,627	$ 67,495	$ 60,488	$ 54,430	$ 49,179	$ 44,611	$ 40,626	$ 37,138	$ 34,077	$ 31,380
63	$ 111,951	$ 98,456	$ 86,956	$ 77,129	$ 68,706	$ 61,463	$ 55,218	$ 49,814	$ 45,124	$ 41,041	$ 37,474	$ 34,349	$ 31,600
64	$ 114,888	$ 100,808	$ 88,842	$ 78,642	$ 69,920	$ 62,439	$ 56,002	$ 50,445	$ 45,632	$ 41,450	$ 37,804	$ 34,615	$ 31,815
65	$ 117,876	$ 103,193	$ 90,747	$ 80,165	$ 71,139	$ 63,415	$ 56,784	$ 51,072	$ 46,135	$ 41,854	$ 38,129	$ 34,876	$ 32,026
66	$ 120,916	$ 105,611	$ 92,672	$ 81,698	$ 72,361	$ 64,390	$ 57,563	$ 51,694	$ 46,633	$ 42,253	$ 38,448	$ 35,132	$ 32,231
67	$ 124,009	$ 108,063	$ 94,617	$ 83,242	$ 73,588	$ 65,366	$ 58,339	$ 52,313	$ 47,126	$ 42,646	$ 38,762	$ 35,383	$ 32,431
68	$ 127,155	$ 110,548	$ 96,582	$ 84,797	$ 74,819	$ 66,341	$ 59,113	$ 52,927	$ 47,614	$ 43,034	$ 39,071	$ 35,628	$ 32,627
69	$ 130,357	$ 113,068	$ 98,567	$ 86,363	$ 76,054	$ 67,317	$ 59,884	$ 53,537	$ 48,097	$ 43,416	$ 39,374	$ 35,869	$ 32,818

CHART EIGHT

STARTING PORTFOLIO NEEDED TO FUND VARIOUS ANNUAL EXPENSES
ASSUMING 1% TRUSTEE FEE AND 30% TAX RATE (CONTINUED)

Assumptions:

Initial annual expenses: $ 1,000	inflation: 2.50%	tax rate: 30.00%	TTEE/admin. fee: 1.00%

The following also assumes that needs are paid at end of each year and that TTEE fee is not tax deductible.

Rate of Return (Nominal): Life expectancies	2.50%	3.00%	3.50%	4.00%	4.50%	5.00%	5.50%	6.00%	6.50%	7.00%	7.50%	8.00%	8.50%
70	$133,613	$115,623	$100,573	$87,939	$77,294	$68,293	$60,652	$54,143	$48,575	$43,794	$39,672	$36,105	$33,005
71	$136,927	$118,213	$102,600	$89,526	$78,538	$69,268	$61,418	$54,745	$49,048	$44,166	$39,966	$36,336	$33,187
72	$140,298	$120,839	$104,647	$91,124	$79,786	$70,244	$62,182	$55,342	$49,516	$44,534	$40,254	$36,563	$33,365
73	$143,727	$123,502	$106,716	$92,733	$81,038	$71,220	$62,942	$55,936	$49,980	$44,896	$40,537	$36,785	$33,539
74	$147,216	$126,201	$108,806	$94,353	$82,295	$72,195	$63,700	$56,525	$50,439	$45,254	$40,816	$37,002	$33,709
75	$150,766	$128,938	$110,918	$95,984	$83,556	$73,171	$64,456	$57,111	$50,893	$45,606	$41,090	$37,215	$33,875
76	$154,377	$131,713	$113,052	$97,626	$84,821	$74,146	$65,209	$57,693	$51,343	$45,954	$41,360	$37,424	$34,037
77	$158,051	$134,526	$115,208	$99,280	$86,091	$75,122	$65,959	$58,270	$51,788	$46,297	$41,625	$37,629	$34,195
78	$161,789	$137,378	$117,386	$100,945	$87,364	$76,098	$66,707	$58,844	$52,229	$46,636	$41,885	$37,829	$34,350
79	$165,592	$140,269	$119,587	$102,621	$88,643	$77,073	$67,452	$59,414	$52,665	$46,970	$42,141	$38,026	$34,501
80	$169,461	$143,201	$121,810	$104,309	$89,925	$78,049	$68,195	$59,980	$53,096	$47,300	$42,393	$38,218	$34,648
81	$173,397	$146,173	$124,056	$106,009	$91,213	$79,024	$68,935	$60,542	$53,524	$47,625	$42,641	$38,407	$34,792
82	$177,401	$149,186	$126,326	$107,720	$92,504	$80,000	$69,673	$61,100	$53,947	$47,946	$42,884	$38,592	$34,933
83	$181,475	$152,241	$128,619	$109,443	$93,800	$80,976	$70,408	$61,655	$54,365	$48,262	$43,123	$38,773	$35,070
84	$185,620	$155,338	$130,936	$111,178	$95,100	$81,951	$71,141	$62,206	$54,780	$48,574	$43,359	$38,951	$35,204
85	$189,837	$158,478	$133,277	$112,925	$96,405	$82,927	$71,871	$62,753	$55,190	$48,882	$43,590	$39,125	$35,335
86	$194,127	$161,662	$135,642	$114,683	$97,714	$83,902	$72,599	$63,296	$55,596	$49,186	$43,818	$39,296	$35,463
87	$198,491	$164,890	$138,032	$116,454	$99,028	$84,878	$73,324	$63,836	$55,998	$49,486	$44,041	$39,463	$35,588
88	$202,931	$168,162	$140,446	$118,237	$100,346	$85,854	$74,047	$64,372	$56,396	$49,781	$44,261	$39,626	$35,710
89	$207,449	$171,480	$142,885	$120,033	$101,669	$86,829	$74,767	$64,904	$56,790	$50,073	$44,478	$39,787	$35,830
90	$212,045	$174,844	$145,350	$121,840	$102,996	$87,805	$75,485	$65,433	$57,180	$50,361	$44,690	$39,944	$35,946

576

Appendix 4

Glossary

A

Accountings: Report of expenditures and receipts filed by guardian of the estate in probate court.

Administrator\Administratrix: Person appointed by probate court to administer a decedent's estate if an executor or personal representative is not properly appointed by will.

Adult Foster Care: A family-type living arrangement whereby a person with a disability lives with an unrelated foster caregiver.

Adult Service Agencies: Agencies formed and operated to provide services to adults with disabilities. Services may include employment support, independent living support or day programs.

Advocate: An advocate is a friend, family member, or institution that looks out for the interests of a person with a disability. Advocates lack the legal standing of guardians.

Age of Majority: At the age of majority a person is entitled by law to manage his or her own affairs. The age of majority in most states is 18.

Annual Exclusion Gift: A gift of property worth $11,000 or less, often intended to reduce the estate tax owing at the donor's death.

Attestation Clause: A clause often found in wills and other legal documents wherein witnesses attest to the signature of the person preparing the document.

B

Beneficiary: In general, a beneficiary is a person or institution named to receive property. For example, the beneficiary named in a life insurance policy will receive the insurance proceeds at the death of the insured. The beneficiary of a trust receives income and/or principal from the trust. The beneficiary under a will receives property from the decedent's estate.

Blind Work Expenses: SSI recipients with blindness are allowed to deduct the cost of blind work expenses both for purposes of determining eligibility for SSI and for computing the SSI benefit. A blind work expense is any reasonable expense that helps the beneficiary earn income.

C

Codicil: A codicil is a formally executed addition to or change in the terms of a will, not requiring the complete rewriting of the will.

Community Residential Settings: See *Integrated Living*.

Credit Shelter Trust: Trust created by married individuals for estate tax purposes. Typically used to allow married couple to fully utilize estate tax exclusion amount.

Crummey Powers: Powers included in certain trusts to permit contributions to the trust to qualify as an annual exclusion gift.

Custodian: Person responsible for making investment and expenditure decisions in respect of account created for minor under Uniform Transfer to Minor's Act or Uniform Gift to Minor's Act.

D

Decedent: A decedent is a person who has died. The term is used frequently in the course of estate settlement.

Deeming: Refers to the process of considering a parent's resources and income available to a child for purposes of determining eligibility under the SSI program.

Disability: For government benefit purposes, a person is considered to have a disability if the person is unable to do any substantial gainful activity by reason of any medically determinable physical or mental impairment which can be expected to result in death or which has lasted or can be expected to last for a continuous period of not less than 12 months.

Discretionary Support Trust: A trust that expressly grants the trustee the discretion to use trust property for the support of the beneficiary.

Discretionary Trust: A trust in which the trustee has the discretion to determine whether or not to make distributions to the beneficiary.

Donor/Donee: A donor is a person who gifts property to another. A donee is the person who receives the gift.

E

Earned Income Exclusion: For purposes of calculating SSI benefits, the earned income exclusion permits an SSI recipient to exclude the first $65 in earnings ($85 if the SSI recipient does not have any unearned income) plus one-half of any remaining earnings.

Employment Network: An organization that has agreed with Social Security to provide employment and vocational rehabilitation services under the ticket to work program.

Employment Support: Employment support is used in two ways. First, it is used to refer to supports, such as job coaches, provided to people with disabilities in the workplace. Second, it is used to refer to provisions of government benefit programs that are designed to encourage work.

Estate Planning: Estate planning is the process of arranging for the transfer of one's property and the care for one's children at death.

Estate Tax: Tax due on death of decedent.

Estate Tax Exclusion Amount: The amount that the federal government permits a decedent to leave to any person other than the decedent's spouse free of estate tax. Under current law, the estate tax exclusion amount is: $1.5M for people dying in 2005, $2M for people dying in 2006-2008, $3.5M for people dying in 2009, and $1M for people dying in 2011 and thereafter. There is no estate tax for people dying in 2010.

Estate, Probate Estate, Taxable Estate: A person's estate is all the money and all the real and personal property owned by that person or treated as owned by the person under the Internal Revenue Code.

A decedent's probate estate is that part of an estate that passes through the probate system.

A decedent's gross estate is the total property for estate-tax purposes, and his or her adjusted gross estate or taxable estate is the gross estate less certain deductions. The estate pays an estate tax based on the taxable estate. Thus, a decedent's estate is itself a taxpayer, managed as such by an administrator or executor.

Executor/Executrix: An executor is a person or institution named in a will to carry out the terms of the will. Executrix is the female version of executor.

Extended Period of Eligibility: After the expiration of the trial work period, SSDI beneficiaries are entitled to a 36 month extended period of eligibility. During this extended period of eligibility, the beneficiary is entitled to full benefits during any month in which income falls below the substantial gainful activity level (for 2005, $830 a month).

F

Family-Type Living Arrangement: Arrangement whereby a person with a disability lives in the private home of friends or family.

Federal Benefit Rate: Maximum federal benefit provided under SSI program. Increased each January to account for inflation. Some states provide supplemental benefits.

Fiduciary: A fiduciary is a person or institution that takes the responsibility of acting on behalf of another person. In reference to wills, estates, and trusts, the following act in a fiduciary capacity for the maker of the will, for the estate, and for the beneficiaries: the attorney(s), executor(s), trustee(s), and guardian(s). All are bound by the standard of good faith and trust.

G

Generation Skipping Trust: Tax potentially applicable on transfers of property to grandchildren and more remote descendants.

Gift, Gift Tax: A gift is a voluntary transfer of money and/or property from one person to another who accepts it without giving something of equal value in return. If the gift is to an individual or an organization not qualifying as nonprofit, it may be subject to a gift tax. If such a tax is due, it is computed on the amount of money given or on the fair market value of the property given.

Grace Period: A three-month period during which SSDI benefits continue after Social Security decides that an SSDI beneficiary can work at the substantial gainful activity level.

Grantor: The grantor of a trust, also known as the settlor, is the person who creates a trust.

Group Home: A residential facility designed for several people with disabilities.

Guardian: A guardian is a person appointed by the court to control and manage another person's affairs and/or property. Most typically, a guardian is appointed to manage the affairs of a minor or of an adult who is considered incapable of looking after his or her own affairs.

A guardian is limited in power by the court making the appointment. The guardian must submit regular accountings to the court and must follow the direction of the court at all times. Guardians can also be appointed by will to look after the affairs of minor children.

Guardian Ad Litem: A guardian ad litem is a guardian appointed by the court for the purpose and duration of a lawsuit or similar action. Typically guardians ad litem are appointed for people determined by a court to need assistance in protecting their interests in the lawsuit.

Guardian-Limited: A guardian appointed to exercise care and custody of the ward and/or management of the ward's estate in a restricted sense. This restriction takes the form of a determination by the court that the ward is unable to act only in specific areas.

Guardian-Natural: The parent who is lawfully in control of a minor child; natural guardianship ceases when the child attains the age of majority.

Guardian of the Estate: A person appointed by the court to handle the care, management, and investment of the estate (real and personal property) of another person, with the duty to protect and preserve such property.

Guardian of the Person: An individual appointed by the court to see that the person with a disability has proper care and protective supervision in keeping with personal needs.

Guardian-Plenary: A person appointed by the court to exercise total legal control and management of the person, estate, or both.

Guardian-Public: A public official empowered to accept court appointment as a legal guardian.

Guardian-Successor: A legal guardian appointed by a court when an already functioning guardian dies, is removed by the court, or resigns.

Guardian-Temporary: A legal guardian appointed by a court for a temporary period of time when the court is given notice that a person is in immediate need of guardianship, generally for an emergency situation. A temporary guardian may be of the person, of the estate, or both.

Guardian-Testamentary: A testamentary guardian is a person designated by the last will and testament of a natural guardian.

Guardianship Proceeding: Legal proceeding whereby need for guardianship is established in court.

H

Health Care Declaration: See *Living Will*.

I

Impairment Related Work Expense (IRWE): An expense incurred by a person with a disability to enable the person to work. IRWEs can be used under both the Social Security Disability Insurance Program (SSDI) and the Supplemental Security Income (SSI) program. Under SSDI, they are deducted for purposes of determining whether a person is able to engage in substantial gainful activity. Under SSI, they are deducted both for purposes of the substantial gainful activity test and for purposes of computing benefit levels.

Income Cap States: States that do not permit a person with excess income to qualify for Medicaid even if the person's income is reduced below the state's income cap after deducting medical expenses.

Income Limitation: Under the rules of the SSI program, a person who has a disability is denied benefits for any month in which the person's income exceeds the allowable SSI limitation. The limitation is reset each year and is generally equal to the maximum federal benefit under the SSI program. Importantly, certain items of income, including significant amounts of earned income, are excluded.

Independent Living: A residential situation in which people with disabilities live by themselves with limited assistance from others.

Inherit: To inherit property is to receive it by will or by applicable state statutes (laws of descent or distribution) at the death of the owner of that property.

Individualized Education Plan (IEP): An individualized plan that covers education services to be offered to a child with a disability. IEPs are mandated by IDEA.

Individualized Family Service Plan (IFSP): A plan developed for children with disabilities covering from birth to age 3. The plan addresses required services and outcomes to be achieved. IFSPs are mandated by IDEA.

Individualized Transition Plan: Under IDEA, beginning when a child is age 16 (or younger, if appropriate), the child's IEP must include a listing of transition services needed to help the child prepare for leaving school.

Individuals With Disabilities Act (IDEA): A federal law governing required education services for individuals with disabilities.

Individualized Written Rehabilitation Plan: A plan developed as part of a vocational education program that covers employment services to be offered to a person with a disability.

In-Kind Income: For SSI purposes, support provided to SSI recipient in form of food, clothing or shelter, and noncash items that can be used by SSI recipient to obtain food, clothing or shelter.

Institutional Care: Care provided in large institutions, typically provided to people with severe disabilities.

Intermediate Care Facilities (ICFs): Group residential facilities, often funded by Medicaid and other government benefit programs.

Integrated Employment: A type of employment whereby people who have disabilities work alongside those who do not.

Integrated Living: A type of living arrangement in which people who have disabilities live alongside those who do not.

Inter Vivos: Made during one's lifetime (literally, between living persons). An inter vivos trust becomes effective during the creator's lifetime.

Intestate: To die intestate is to die without having a will. If a person dies intestate, the person's property passes to the person's heirs as required by the applicable state statute (the laws of descent and distribution), regardless of how the person who died may have intended the property to pass.

Involuntary Commitment: Legal process whereby person with a disability is committed to a treatment facility, typically on the grounds that the person is a danger to himself, herself or to others.

Irrevocable Insurance: **Trust**: Trust created for estate tax purposes. Typically used to avoid estate tax on proceeds of life insurance policies.

Irrevocable Trust: A trust that cannot be changed.

J

Job Coach: A person who assists people with disabilities in integrated employment situations.

Joint Tenancy With Right of Survivorship: Two or more persons owning property with each having the legal right of survivorship, which means that the ownership on the death of any joint tenant remains with the survivors. See *Tenancy In Common*.

L

Least-Restrictive Alternative: A policy based on the belief that persons should be free to live as they please and that when government must interfere with a person's liberty, the services should be designed to maximize the developmental potential of the person and should be provided in the setting that is least restrictive of personal liberty.

Legacy, Legatee: A legacy (also known as a bequest) is a gift of personal property by will. The recipient of such a gift is the legatee.

Letter of Intent: A nonbinding document that passes vital information about a person with a disability to future caregivers.

Letters of Office: Document issued by probate court granting guardian power over ward. Also issued to executor to evidence authority to dispose of decedent's estate.

Life Estate: A person with a life estate (or life interest) in property has a right to use the property during his or her own or another designated person's lifetime.

Life Plan: A plan developed for a person with a disability that covers all the major areas of life: Residential, Education, Employment and Social/Recreational.

Life Tenant: A life tenant is the person who has the use of property during his or her lifetime.

Limited Payment Insurance: Limited payment insurance is a type of life insurance for which premiums are payable for a definite period of time, after which the policy is fully paid. Also known as vanishing premium insurance.

Listing of Impairments: List maintained by Social Security that describes impairments for each major body system that are considered severe enough to prevent a person from doing any gainful activity.

Living Trust: Trust created by beneficiary to avoid probate.

Living Will: A living will is a document prepared for health care providers expressing the creator's desire not to be kept alive by artificial means. Also known as a *Health Care Declaration*.

M

Mandatory Support Trust: A trust that expressly requires the trustee to use trust property for the support of the beneficiary.

Marital Bypass Trust: See *Credit Shelter Trust.*

Marital Deduction: Mechanism by which transfers of property to spouse, whether during life or at death, is exempted from gift and estate tax. Each person has an unlimited marital deduction, which means that any amount of property can be transferred to a spouse without imposition of gift or estate tax.

Medicaid: A federally sponsored program administered by the states to pay medical expenses of certain low-income individuals, principally those who are blind, disabled, elderly, or in families with dependent children.

Medicaid Lien: Lien imposed by Medicaid on assets of Medicaid recipient that permits Medicaid to obtain reimbursement if Medicaid recipient receives or sells property.

Medicaid Transfer Lookback Period: Period Medicaid authorities will consider for purposes of determining whether a transfer of assets will affect eligibility under Medicaid program.

Medicare: A federal health insurance program run by the Social Security Administration. It is designed to pay the cost of health care for people over the age of 65 and for people with disabilities under the age of 65 who have been eligible to receive Social Security benefits for at least two years, or who need kidney dialysis treatments or a kidney transplant.

Medicare Set Aside: Portion of worker's compensation benefit that must be spent on injury related medical expenses before Medicare becomes available.

Mental Capacity: Although the definition of mental capacity varies by state, a typical approach is to define mental capacity as the ability to make responsible decisions.

Mental Health Treatment Declaration: A legal document signed by a person with mental illness governing the type of treatment that such person desires if the person becomes incapable of making rational treatment decisions.

Miller Trust: A trust designed to permit qualification for Medicaid by an elderly person living in an income cap state where the person needs nursing home assistance but has income in excess of the state's income cap. The trust must (i) be composed only of pension, Social Security, and other income to the individual (and accumulated income in the trust), (ii) provide that the State will receive all amounts remaining in the trust upon the death of the individual up to an amount equal to the total medical assistance paid on behalf of the individual under the State's Medicaid plan; and (iii) be established for a beneficiary in an income cap state.

Minor: A person who has not reached the age of majority (18 years old in most states).

N

Nonprobate Estate: Property of a deceased person which passes to beneficiaries or persons sharing ownership in the property without being subject to the probate process.

Nursing Home: A home designed to provide medical or custodial care to its residents. Typically the residents are aged or ill.

O

One-Third Reduction Rule: Reduction in SSI benefits resulting when an SSI recipient lives in the home of another and receives free room and board.

P

Payback Trust: A trust funded with the beneficiary's own assets that permits the beneficiary to qualify for needs-based government benefits such as Medicaid or SSI. The trust must (i) contain the assets of an individual under age 65 and who is disabled; (ii) be established for the benefit of such individual by a parent, grandparent, legal guardian or a court; and (iii) provide that the State will receive all amounts remaining in the trust upon the death of the individual up to an amount equal to the total medical assistance paid on behalf of the individual under a State Medicaid plan.

Per Capita: Used in wills and trusts to refer to distributions without representation. For example, leaving property to your descendants, per capita, means that each of your descendants receives an equal share.

Performance Bond: Amount of money pledged by guardian to secure performance. Bond is forfeited if guardian does not properly perform obligations.

Personal Property: All property owned by a person or institution except real estate.

Personal Representative: Same as executor. Some states use the term *personal representative* instead.

Per Stirpes: Used in wills and trusts to refer to distributions with representation. For example, leaving property to your descendants, per stirpes, means that your property is divided equally among your children, with grandchildren dividing the shares of children who have died.

Petitioner: A person who asks the court (a) for action or relief, or (b) to exercise its authority in some way. In guardianship proceedings, the petitioner is generally the person asking that a guardian be appointed for a person with a disability.

Plan For Achieving Self-Support (PASS): A plan for achieving self-support allows an SSI beneficiary to set aside income and/or resources for a specified time for a work goal, such as for education, vocational training, or starting a business. Income and resources set aside under a PASS is not counted in calculating the SSI payment amount or in determining initial and continuing eligibility for SSI.

Pooled Income Payback Trust: A trust funded with the beneficiary's own assets that permits the beneficiary to qualify for needs-based government benefits such as Medicaid or SSI. The trust must (i) be established and maintained by a nonprofit association; (ii) provide for separate accounts maintained for each beneficiary, with assets pooled for investing and management purposes; (iii) provide an account established solely for the benefit of a person with a disability, which account is established by the individual, a parent, grandparent, legal guardian, or a court; and (iv) provide that to the extent any amounts remaining in the beneficiary's account upon the death of the beneficiary are not retained by the trust, the trust will pay to the State the amount remaining up to an amount equal to the total amount of medical assistance paid on behalf of the beneficiary under a State Medicaid plan.

Pour-Over Will: A will that directs that all, or a portion of, a testator's estate flow into an already-existing or independently established trust.

Power of Attorney/Health Care: A power of attorney for health care is a legal document used to appoint someone to make health care decisions for a person who is not able to do so.

Power of Attorney/Property: A power of attorney for property is a legal document used to appoint someone to make property decisions for a person who is not able to do so.

Preschool Grants Program: Program provided under IDEA for children with disabilities from ages 3 to 5.

Principal: In a trust, the principal amount is all the capital, the property that produces income.

Private Guardianship Agencies: Private agencies that act as guardian for people with disabilities.

Probate, Probate Court: The court process of probate specifically involves the validation of a will as the genuine and legally acceptable last directions of the maker of the will (the testator) and the carrying out of those directions. Most commonly, a state will have a special court that handles estates and probate proceedings. This court is called probate court in most states.

Program Operations Manual (POMs): Administrative rules applied by Social Security.

Prudent Person Rule: Trustees (as fiduciaries) must manage trust property in accordance with the prudent person rule. This requires the trustee to handle the trust property with the same care that a prudent, honest, intelligent, and diligent person would use to handle the property under the same circumstances. If a trustee is accused of mismanaging the assets, the court will often judge the trustee's conduct by applying the prudent person rule.

Q

QTIP: Stands for Qualified Terminal Interest Property. Property left in a QTIP trust for a person's spouse is considered the spouse's for estate-tax purposes, and therefore qualifies for the marital deduction, even though the spouse's ability to use property can be restricted.

R

Real Property: Real property (also known as real estate or realty) is land and the buildings or other fixed improvements on that land.

Remainderman: The remainderman of a trust receives the remaining principal of the trust when the income beneficiary or life tenant dies.

Representative Payee: A person or organization that is authorized to cash and manage public assistance checks (Social Security, Supplemental Security Income) for a person deemed incapable of doing so.

Residue, Residual (or Residuary) Clause, Residual Estate: The residue is what remains, what is left over. A residual estate is what remains of an estate after all claims and taxes have been paid and all specific distributions have been made. A residual (residuary) clause in a will arranges for the distribution of this residual property of the estate.

Resource Limitation: A limitation on available resources that must be satisfied if a person is to qualify for benefits under the SSI program.

Resources: Cash, liquid assets such as stocks and bonds, and any other items of property that an individual can convert to cash to use for food, clothing, or shelter.

Revocable Trust: A revocable trust is a trust that can be revised or revoked at any time during the grantor's life.

S

Sheltered Workshop: A separate employment entity, all of whose workers have some type of disability. The workshop contracts with private businesses to perform certain tasks for the business at negotiated rates.

Social Security Disability Insurance (SSDI): A cash benefit program for people with disabilities. People with disabilities can qualify for SSDI in either of two ways. First, SSDI is generally available for workers who become disabled prior to attaining age 65, assuming the worker's work history satisfies Social Security's requirements. Second, SSDI is also available to children (even adult children) of retired, disabled or deceased social security participants if the child has a disability that developed before the child reached 22 years of age.

Special Needs Trust: A trust created for a beneficiary with a disability that is designed to provide for the needs of the beneficiary while permitting the beneficiary to qualify for needs-based government benefits such as SSI and Medicaid. Also referred to as a Supplemental Needs Trust.

Spend Down States: States that permit a person with excess income to qualify for Medicaid if the person's income is reduced below the state's eligibility threshold after deducting medical expenses.

Spendthrift Clause: A spendthrift clause in a trust agreement provides that the named beneficiary has a right to trust distributions only and thus cannot voluntarily dispose of the assets of the trust or the income before it is earned and paid. As a result the trust principal and unpaid income are protected from creditors of the beneficiary.

Sprinkling, Sprinkle and Spray Trust: A provision for "sprinkling" in a trust agreement allows the trustee to use personal judgment in distributing income from the trust fund. He or she controls the timing and the amount of the distributions and decides which beneficiaries will receive those distributions. A trust with such a provision is sometimes referred to as a "sprinkle and spray" trust.

Spousal Income Allowance: Special rule for married couples that permits the stay at home spouse to retain a larger share of the couple's income when one of the spouses enters a nursing home.

Spousal Resource Allowance: Special rule for married couples that permits the stay at home spouse to retain a larger share of the couple's joint assets when one of the spouses enters a nursing home.

Student Earned Income Exclusion: For purposes of calculating SSI benefits, the student earned income exclusion permits unmarried students under age 22 who are regularly attending school to exclude a specified amount of earned income per month, subject to an annual limitation. For 2005, students were permitted to exclude up to $1,410 of earned income per month, subject to a maximum yearly exclusion of $5,670. These amounts are adjusted each year based on the cost-of-living.

Subsidy and Special Work Conditions: The value of additional support a person receives in order to work. The value of such support can be subtracted from wages for purposes of determining eligibility under both the Social Security Disability Insurance Program (SSDI) and the Supplemental Security Income (SSI) program. Subsidy and Special Work Conditions cannot be deducted for purposes of computing benefit levels under SSI.

Substantial Gainful Activity: For government benefit purposes, a person is considered to have a disability if the person is unable to do any substantial gainful activity by reason of any medically determinable physical or mental impairment which can be expected to result in death or which has lasted or can be expected to last for a continuous period of not less than 12 months. Although substantial gainful activity is determined based on a variety of factors, the cornerstone of the analysis is a determination as to whether or not a person is capable of earning more than a threshold amount, which increases each year to account for inflation. For 2005, the critical issue is whether Social Security believes that the person is capable of earning $830 a month after deducting impairment related work expenses and employer subsidies. If the person is visually impaired, the threshold for 2005 is $1,390 per month.

Successor: A successor is one who follows another in a particular office. For example, a successor guardian is a person named to follow the originally named guardian if the originally named individual or institution can no longer hold office. A successor trustee is a person who takes over management of a trust after the initial trustee ceases to act.

Supplemental Needs Trust: See *Special Needs Trust.*

Supplemental Security Income Program (SSI): A needs based cash benefit program designed to supplement the income of people who are elderly, blind, or disabled and lack sufficient resources to provide for their own needs.

Supported Employment: An employment option for people with disabilities that is integrated into the community at large. The person with a disability generally receives assistance from a job coach, who may be a fellow employee or an employee of an adult service agency.

Surety: Surety is a financial guarantee that an act will be carried out or that a debt will be paid by another person. To post bond is to provide such surety.

Surety Bond: See *Performance Bond.*

T

Tenancy In Common: Form of joint ownership in which tenants do not have right of survivorship. For example, if two individuals each own a one-half interest in a house as tenants in common, each of them can dispose of his or her interest by will. See *Joint Tenancy With Right Of Survivorship.*

Term Insurance: Term insurance is a form of pure life insurance having no cash surrender value and generally furnishing insurance protection for only a specified or limited period of time, though term insurance is usually renewable from term to term.

Testament, Testamentary Capacity: A person's testament is the final disposition of his or her property. Anything that is testamentary relates to a will. Testamentary capacity is the legal competence to make a will.

Testamentary Trust: A trust set up by will.

Testator/Testatrix: A testator is a person who is making a will. Testatrix is the female version of testator.

Ticket to Work Program: The Ticket To Work And Self-Sufficiency Program (the Ticket Program) is for people who receive benefits under SSDI or SSI because of disability or blindness. The program is strictly voluntary and offers greater choices in getting recipients services needed to go to work. The goal of the program is to help SSDI and SSI recipients earn enough money so they will not need Social Security cash benefits.

Trial Work Period: The trial work period allows an SSDI recipient to test work ability without loss of benefits even if earnings during the trial work period exceed the substantial gainful activity level. An SSDI recipient is generally permitted nine months of trial work during any rolling sixty-month period. A month counts against the trial work period only if the beneficiary's earnings for the month exceed a specified amount (for 2005, $590).

Trust: Property in trust is held and managed by a person or institution (the trustee) for the benefit of those persons or institutions for whom the trust was created (the beneficiaries). The creator of a trust is commonly referred to as the settlor, grantor, or trustor.

Trust Instrument: Document creating a trust. Often referred to as a trust agreement or a declaration of trust.

Trust Property: Trust property is the principal amount (the corpus or body) of a trust. It is the income-producing property of a trust.

Trustee: Person responsible for operating a trust. Makes decisions about investments and expenditures in accordance with provisions of trust instrument.

U

Unearned Income Exclusion: For purposes of computing SSI benefit level, exclusion for first $20 of unearned income. Also referred to as General Exclusion.

Uniform Gift to Minor's Act (UGMA): An act creating a form of trust that permits people to make gifts that will be managed by adults for the benefit of minors without going to the expense of creating a trust. Same as *Uniform Transfer to Minor's Act*.

Uniform Transfer to Minor's Act (UTMA): An act creating a form of trust that permits people to make gifts that will be managed by adults for the benefit of minors without going to the expense of creating a trust. Same as *Uniform Gift to Minor's Act.*

Universal Life Insurance: Like whole life insurance except the growth of the policy's cash value depends on investment performance. See *Whole Life Insurance.*

Unsuccessful Work Attempt: An unsuccessful work attempt is an effort to do substantial work that is stopped or reduced to below the substantial gainful activity level after a short time (6 months or less) because of an impairment or removal of subsidies or special work conditions related to an impairment and essential to the further performance of work. Earnings during an unsuccessful work attempt are not considered for purposes of making a substantial gainful activity determination.

V

Vanishing Payment Insurance: See *Limited Payment Insurance.*

Vocational Rehabilitation: Vocational rehabilitation is a federally funded state-operated program designed to increase or develop employment skills.

W

Ward: A person, either a minor or an individual with a disability, under the care of a guardian.

Whole Life Insurance: With whole life insurance, the insured can fix a premium which remains constant for the insured's life. It is also possible to arrange premiums so the policy is paid off after a specified period. Because premiums exceed the insurance cost, the policy builds a cash value that the insured can borrow. The cash value grows at a rate specified in the insurance contract.

Will: A will is a legal document that controls the passage of an individual's property at death.

Workstation/Enclave: A type of employment wherein a group of people with disabilities work in a group in an integrated employment environment, typically for a particular job.

Notes...

Notes...

Notes...

Order Form
Save your Book. Photocopy this form.

PLANNING FOR THE FUTURE
PROVIDING A MEANINGFUL LIFE FOR A CHILD
WITH A DISABILITY AFTER YOUR DEATH

Fax order: 1-419-281-6883
Web orders: www.specialneedslegal.com or orders@bookmasters.com
Telephone orders: Call Toll Free: 1-800-247-6553. Have your AMEX, Discover, VISA or Master Card ready.
Mail orders: Send your check payable to "BookMasters" to:
BookMasters, Inc.
30 Amberwood Parkway
Ashland, OH 44805

Please send me _____copies of Planning For The Future:
Providing a Meaningful Life for a Child with a Disability
After Your Death (6th Edition) at $89.95. $_____

Shipping and handling: $7.00 (per book) $_____

IL address, add $5.50 (per book) sales tax $_____

OH address, add $6.50 (per book) sales tax $_____

TOTAL: ($96.95, unless multiple copies or sales tax applies) $_____

Name: _____

Company Name: _____

Address: _____

City: _____State:_____ Zip: _____

Payment (please check one box):
❑ Check payable to "BookMasters"

Credit card: ❑ Visa ❑ MasterCard ❑ AMEX ❑ Discover

Card Number: _____Exp.Date: _____

Name on card:_____

Signature (required for credit card orders)

_____

Call 1-800-247-6553 toll free and order now!